College Admissions Counseling

β β β β β

A Handbook for the Profession

William R. Lowery and Associates

College Admissions Counseling

Jossey-Bass Publishers

San Francisco • Washington • London • 1982

COLLEGE ADMISSIONS COUNSELING
A Handbook for the Profession
by William R. Lowery and Associates

Copyright © 1982 by: Jossey-Bass Inc., Publishers
433 California Street
San Francisco, California 94104
&
Jossey-Bass Limited
28 Banner Street
London EC1Y 8QE

Library of Congress Cataloging in Publication Data

Lowery, William R.
        College admissions counseling.

        Bibliography: p. 573
        Includes index.
        1. Personnel service in higher education.
2. Universities and colleges—Admission. I. Title.
LB2343.L58   1982   378'.105'0973   82-48086
ISBN 0-87589-549-2

Manufactured in the United States of America

The paper in this book meets the guidelines for
permanence and durability of the Committee on
Production Guidelines for Book Longevity of the
Council on Library Resources.

JACKET DESIGN BY WILLI BAUM

FIRST EDITION

Code 8241

The Jossey-Bass
Series in Higher Education

Foreword

✍ ✍ ✍ ✍ ✍

✍   Challenging times demand intelligence, understanding, and accountability to deal with tough issues and new problems. A body of knowledge, awareness of the environment, and adherence to standards of conduct are the resources we use to meet the challenges, to solve the problems.

In recent years, society has come to expect the federal government to provide a strong shoulder. When Congress enacted the National Defense Education Act in 1958—at President Dwight D. Eisenhower's request—it said: "the security of the nation requires the fullest development of the mental resources and technical skills of its young men and women. . . . We must increase our efforts to identify and educate more of the talent of this nation. This requires programs that will give assurance that no student of ability will be denied an opportunity for higher education because of financial need. . . ."

With the presidency of Ronald Reagan, we have seen a change in this philosophy. The federal government is abdicating its "father" image to education. The thrust is to the individual to bear responsibility for his or her education. The challenge to students and their parents is to find ways to realize their dreams, their expectations. The challenge to their high school and college counselors is to help them find the way.

The transition process is really one of making the step into another phase of life—never an easy process. The process is not easy for the student because very often 'independence' and 'adult' status are frightening as well as desired. The decision-making process is a personal one, and the influences brought to bear on the student are complex and confusing. . . . The difficulties of parental expectations and child's reconciliation come into focus.

This is where the professional counselor comes to the forefront. That individual has the professional expertise to bring expectation to reconciliation—while meeting the needs of both student and parent and always taking into account the numerous factors that play a part in that process.*

High school and college counselors are the most qualified to alert students to the bumps and gaps they will face during their transition from high school to college. These persons have access to information that, when shared in an appropriate manner, can help difficult decisions become informed ones.

Focusing on the needs of the students during this critical period in their lives; being informed about issues that are outside their control but that could, nevertheless, affect the transition process; availing themselves of opportunities to increase their professional proficiency—these are the highest goals of members of the National Association of College Admissions Counselors (NACAC).

The primary mission of this association is to serve students' needs by enhancing the professionalism of the counselors who guide and influence their lives. Through counseling, our members reach out and touch the lives of many thousands of students. Results-oriented societies such as ours measure achievement by tangible evidence. How do counselors measure

*Lois C. Mazzuca, president, National Association of College Admissions Counselors, from testimony for the U.S. Department of Education at the National Commission on Excellence in Education, May 1982.

their achievement, their success? They may never see the results, but to the young people they help send off into the
world, their influence and the informed guidance they provide
can make the difference between success or failure, happiness or
frustration, achievement or just getting along.

From its inception, NACAC has been an innovator in providing assistance to the college-bound student. One of the first
actions taken by the founding fathers was to create a Code of
Ethics. After many years of review, updating, and rewriting, the
code became today's "Statement of Principles of Good Practice," a crucial first step in developing a body of knowledge to
help guide the admissions process.

As the association that represents counselors on both
sides of the transition process, NACAC has taken a leadership
role in meeting the need for a body of knowledge. To help
achieve this goal, the association has developed a curriculum
outline for training counselors and will use it to design future
training programs. The main objective of these training programs is to ensure that secondary school and college counselors
are prepared and competent to serve the interests of their students and to improve the admissions process. It is our intention
to use the present handbook as a basic text in all NACAC-
designed training programs.

Counselors look to their colleagues for professional enhancement, guidance, exchange of ideas, and help with problem
solving. This handbook, written by forty counselors who are involved in the transition process, provides an important resource
—a support to the body of knowledge this association is committed to create for the professional counselor.

In our society we use education as a substantial measuring device of a person's worth, potential, achievement, social
progress, and self-esteem. At that point when high school students are preparing themselves for a higher education, the
zenith in this measuring process is gaining admission to the institution of choice; the student who has done well in high
school is ready to meet the challenge. The counselor, in turn,
plays a critical role in helping students achieve their desired
goals and make a successful transition from secondary to higher

education. The smoothness of that process puts pressure on counselors to maintain high standards of professional competence, to acquire a vast amount of knowledge, and to be sensitive to the needs of the students they serve. These standards help counseling professionals in the accountability process with school principals, school boards, and the local community—or, on the college side, presidents, boards of trustees, and faculties.

Currently there is no program of higher education leading toward a degree or certification in college admissions. Therefore, to ensure that a certain level of competence is being met by counselors at all institutions, it is important to the students and to the credibility of the profession that the counseling community ultimately establishes a common foundation of information.

In the true spirit of NACAC—the spirit of helping and reaching out—William R. Lowery of Pomona College deserves our grateful appreciation for shepherding this book from inception to completion. His devotion, patience, and hard work deserve a special commendation.

Charles A. Marshall, D.S.Ed.
Executive Director, National Association
of College Admissions Counselors

Preface

❧ ❧ ❧ ❧ ❧

❧ The decisions high school graduates make about their futures—whether to obtain further education and, if so, where and in what fields—have significant consequences, not only for the students themselves but also for their families, the entire educational system, and society in general. The "right" choices vary widely, depending on individual needs, goals, and personal circumstances; selecting the best option means knowing what the possibilities are and being able to evaluate benefits as well as drawbacks. The process of going on for advanced training or education—selecting, applying to, and being accepted by a postsecondary school—is complex, constituting one of the most critical transitions in students' lives. If the process is not fully understood, if information or guidance is lacking, "wrong" choices result.

College admissions counselors serve as advocates for students making the transition from high school to postsecondary institution. With direct responsibility for guiding and advising young people, these professionals work to ensure that students and everyone else involved in the college decision make wise choices, based on accurate information and sound advice. Unfortunately, given the range of possibilities and the variety of options for each student, in addition to the numbers of students

needing guidance, counselors in secondary schools may not realize they lack information or—if they do—may consider it a
Herculean task to be fully informed. Others, working under
pressure, may push for expedient decisions on college choice,
such as a nearby state institution with relatively low tuition,
whether or not the institution is truly appropriate for the individual at hand. Admissions counselors in colleges and universities, facing pressures to meet enrollment quotas, may also fail to
assess adequately whether prospective student and institution
are a good "match." In attempting to serve their schools and
help them fulfill their educational missions, they may end up
performing a disservice through not knowing enough about potential enrollees or not communicating enough about the school
and its goals to students and their high school counselors.

This handbook is designed to help overcome the problems and pitfalls inherent in college admissions counseling. Written by seasoned admissions counselors from a variety of settings
—public high schools, private academies, postsecondary institutions, independent consulting firms—it is intended for all professionals who participate in the transition process. It stresses the
need for liaison between secondary school and college, shows
that counselors in both settings perform complementary functions, and demonstrates that exchanging information and ideas
is critical to successful admissions counseling. In so doing, the
volume reaffirms the principles of the National Association of
College Admissions Counselors (NACAC), which is unique
among professional associations in providing a forum for discussion among professionals from both secondary schools and colleges and universities.

Until now, no one book has covered the admissions process from the perspectives of those involved at various stages
and in a variety of settings. Past volumes focused heavily on
what should happen in the schools and were written primarily
for practitioners in private or public schools with well-to-do students; an unstated but apparent goal was to enable counselors
to place students in prestigious colleges. More recent books are
mainly concerned with the college side of the process, with emphasis on marketing approaches to admissions. A comprehensive

and current view of the profession and the ways in which all college admissions counselors can perform most effectively has long been needed—and this volume seeks to fill that need.

Sponsored by NACAC, the handbook is a teaching tool that reflects what the profession has learned and how members can help each other in best serving students and other constituencies affected by the admissions process. It is a forum for communicating the accumulated body of knowledge about admissions counseling to those with varying degrees of responsibility and varying levels of experience. The handbook thus speaks to professionals who work full-time as admissions counselors as well as to those who spend only a portion of their time in that area; it is a ready reference for seasoned professionals who wish to learn about successful techniques or practices in other settings as well as newcomers who want detailed information on all aspects of the process; and it is a guide for graduate students planning to become admissions counselors as well as teachers or counselors considering, or recently appointed to, guidance responsibilities. Further, it serves as an informational resource for college admissions officers and other administrators who oversee admissions counseling or whose policy decisions affect the admissions process. For everyone interested in understanding the overall process, what happens when and how, and ways to meet the challenges as successfully as possible, this volume will prove invaluable.

The contributions, commissioned expressly for the handbook, address specific aspects of college admissions counseling. Because this is a service profession, the chapters are organized into six parts that consider how the profession can best serve various groups. Readers may proceed sequentially through the book for an overview of the entire process and the issues involved or may turn to individual chapters for information or advice on special areas. Since the chapters in each part are written from a particular perspective, each provides fresh insights to common problems or phenomena.

Part One, "Scope of the Service," considers the multifaceted nature of postsecondary education in America, which is unlike any other educational system in the world, and examines why the potential for service is so broad. The authors underscore that able college admissions counselors need to be acquainted with the goals and history of higher education, as well as its current status and how demographic changes are affecting it.

Part Two, "Service to the Student," emphasizes that admissions counselors are unique in that they are concerned only with the needs of students in transition; in order to be successful advisers, they must know how their counsel can affect students' lives. Chapters present information on the educational opportunities that can be shaped through careful evaluation of institutions and student "fit," how individual work with students provides special rewards, and the value of advising students about curriculum as well as college choice.

Part Three, "Service to Society," demonstrates that counselors have to be attuned to the needs and demands of society as well as to the aspirations of students. The goals of equal opportunity require that counselors work to increase the educational possibilities of minority populations; to do so, they need to understand the cultural underpinnings of these subgroups and implement strategies that will help overcome barriers to college acceptance and student adaptation. Serving the larger society also means helping such nontraditional students as adults seeking higher education, those returning to college after several years of work, and those who are transferring from two-year to four-year institutions. The authors in this part thus examine the need for an educated society and how best to serve black, Mexican American, adult, and transfer students; since financial assistance may influence the educational choices of students in these groups, the concluding chapter outlines the basics of financial aid and directs counselors to sources for further information.

Part Four, "Service to School and Community," discusses the responsibilities of college admissions counselors to the schools and communities that sustain them. The authors, from both private and public schools, show how to work effectively with various constituencies—parents, teachers, administrators, school board members, and community members—in advising and preparing students for college. They describe developmental and group approaches to admissions counseling, including a detailed four-year program, and underline the need to involve families in college choice as well as the need to inform community members about the school's admissions program. The last chapter looks at the contributions of independent educational counselors to the admissions process.

Part Five, "Service to the College or University," explores how college admissions professionals can most effectively help their institutions during periods of enrollment declines and increased competition for students. Chapters consider marketing in higher education; provide guidelines for conducting marketing research and using the results in enrollment planning; and offer strategies for reaching those students that the institution can best service. Authors also discuss recruiting students from abroad; the activities, operations, and problems of college admissions offices; and ways of training and organizing regular and volunteer staff.

Part Six, "Service to Members of the Profession," makes it clear that college admissions counselors are the primary sources of information and instruction for each other. Authors address several topics that professionals need solid grounding in—such as ways in which school visitations can be handled most effectively, how to cope with pressures brought about by special interest groups, methods to make reference letters serve both students and colleges well, the process of recruitment and selection at highly selective colleges, the nature and appropriate use of standardized admissions testing, and techniques that will enable professionals to benefit from what their colleagues have learned.

The two resources that conclude the book—statement of principles of good practice and statement of students' responsibilities and rights—are reprinted from NACAC's Governance Directory; they are included to round out the picture of the professional and ethical responsibilities of college admissions counselors.

Acknowledgments

To all the authors represented in this handbook, I express my deep gratitude. They have worked with me to produce an integrated volume; their willingness to expand, contract, recast, and even rewrite their contributions is greatly appreciated. Members of the NACAC publications committee provided judicious assessments of the essays at a crucial stage in the editorial process. In addition, I thank all the old and new friends in the profession who have educated me through their suggestions and their nudges; they are so numerous as to exceed the capacity of a faulty memory. But even as I extend a general expression of thanks to all I have known and worked with over the years, I mention specifically three colleagues in Claremont, California, who first welcomed me to the profession: Marilyn J. Blum, then director of admissions at Scripps College and now college counselor at the Webb School of California; John E. Quinlan, then dean of admissions and financial aid at Pomona College and now associate professor of chemistry there; and Emery E. Walker, Jr., then dean of admission and financial aid at Claremont Men's College (now Claremont McKenna College) and Harvey Mudd College and now retired. Without them this book could not exist.

And beyond words, love and gratitude to my wife Elizabeth.

Claremont, California   William R. Lowery
October 1982

Contents

❦ ❦ ❦ ❦ ❦

Foreword   ix
Charles A. Marshall

Preface   xiii

The Authors   xxvii

Part One: Scope of the Service   1

1. Function of Postsecondary Education
   for Individuals and Society   4
   John T. Casteen III

Examines the complex forces shaping the varieties of American higher education and challenges the educational community to recognize that its decisions can have irrevocable consequences.

2. Impact of Demographic Changes on Students,
   Counselors, and Institutions   17
   Michael F. Cundiff

Overview of available demographic data and projections; considers the effects of changes on students and the choices they make, along with concomitant changes in the responsibilities of admissions counselors.

Part Two: Service to the Student   37

3.   Effects of Types of College on Students   42
   Jack H. Schuster, Ann Coil

   Summarizes and analyzes the literature that shows how different kinds of colleges affect different students along different lines of development, thus emphasizing the significance of college choice; concludes with a comprehensive bibliography of studies on the outcomes of higher education, comments on their methodologies, and caveats for interpreting them.

4.   Placing Students for Stability and Success   86
   Paul Painter, Nancy Painter

   Offers practical advice for counselors on how to place students where they will study happily for four years; stresses that students' needs—both personal and intellectual—must be evaluated carefully.

5.   Working Individually with College Applicants   111
   Stanley Bosworth

   Demonstrates that the process of selecting and applying to college can be an important stage in a student's education —and one that challenges the counselor to be the best sort of teacher and leader.

6.   Advising Students on Integrating Academic
   Learning and Career Preparation   126
   Julie C. Monson

   Indicates how college choice *and* choices within college affect career goals and job satisfaction—and, hence, what advice counselors should give students.

Part Three: Service to Society   147

7.   Need for an Educated Society   154
   Clifford J. Caine

   Encourages professional admission counselors to reaffirm that the rationale for education in American society is, or should be, more than simply fulfilling pragmatic and self-seeking goals.

8. Admissions Counseling for Black Students   161
       Jewelle Taylor Gibbs

       Analyzes the effects of affirmative action programs for black
       students; describes trends in enrollment and recruitment,
       student adaptation, counseling needs and strategies, and im-
       plications for the future.

9. Recruiting, Advising, and Retaining
     Mexican American Students   191
       Raymond Buriel, Sally Rivera

       A historical and demographic profile of the growing popula-
       tion of Mexican American college students; examines ad-
       missions testing issues and research and importance of ethnic
       values to recruitment; suggests ways to increase recruitment
       and admissions of these students.

10. Providing Special Services for
      Adult Students   220
       Eileen M. Rose, Irene Kovala Campanaro

       Advises admissions counselors of the unique needs of older
       students for such special services as educational brokering,
       sensitive counseling, and informed admission processes.

11. Advising Students About Two-Year Colleges
      and Transfers   231
       Karl L. Wolf

       Identifies ways high school and college counselors can help
       decrease the problems faced by students who transfer from
       two-year to four-year colleges.

12. Introduction to Components of the
      Financial Aid System   240
       Leonard M. Wenc

       Outlines the basic components of the financial aid system
       and the functions of the college admission counselor in ap-
       prising students of what is available.

Part Four: Service to School and Community   251

13. Discerning the Basis for College Counseling
    in the Eighties   257
    Steven C. Munger, R. Fred Zuker

    Highlights professional principles underlying successful
    counseling—honesty, consistency, sensitivity to individuals
    —and implications for advising students, particularly con-
    cerning institutions that have retrenched.

14. Developing Links Among Constituencies   269
    Philip Martin

    Presents a pattern for thorough counseling of students and
    parents within a framework of professional concern, along
    with suggestions for using and improving interchanges
    among constituent groups.

15. Viewing College Counseling as Part of General
    Student Counseling: A Developmental Approach   290
    Margaret Elizabeth Tracy

    Pragmatic approach to college counseling for generalist
    counselors; discusses theoretical framework, developmental
    tasks, and goals that parallel choosing a college; shows ways
    of involving volunteers in the guidance process.

16. Building Support for Specific Student
    Populations   307
    Jack L. Wright

    Illustrates how a well-designed counseling program can pro-
    duce excellent postsecondary results; draws specifically on
    experiences with minority/disadvantaged populations yet
    pertains to all secondary schools.

17. Utilizing a Group Approach to Help Students
    Plan for College or Career   321
    Betty Schneider

    Describes group meeting approaches to student counseling,
    starting in the junior year; provides samples of question-
    naires useful in admissions counseling.

18. Involving Families in College Selection   332
     Helene Reynolds

     Examines the importance of the family context to a stu-
     dent's choice of college and the need for counselors to in-
     clude family members in planning and decision making.

19. Educating the Community About Student
     Options   346
     Barbara B. Reinhold

     An expanded view of the college counseling program's con-
     stituency as comprising parents and community members
     as well as students; shows how a carefully constructed and
     implemented system of public outreach and information
     can be crucial to a program's success.

20. Contributions of Independent Educational
     Counselors   361
     Marilyn J. Blum, Phyllis S. Steinbrecher

     Explains the function of the independent counselor, in-
     cluding professional qualifications and services rendered;
     offers advice on choosing educational counselors wisely.

     Part Five: Service to the College or University   373

21. Marketing Higher Education: Research,
     Planning, and Promotion   377
     James C. Walters

     Outlines a thorough-going marketing approach to the ad-
     missions process; suggests ways to tackle various inherent
     problems; stresses ethical implications of program market-
     ing.

22. Sharing the Market: Implications of Increased
     Competition for Students   385
     Theodore D. Kelly

     Considers how marketing strategies can affect admissions;
     presents scenarios of what will happen as colleges' market-
     ing techniques become more sophisticated.

23.   Using Marketing Research to Develop
      an Admissions Plan   395
          Jan Krukowski, Herman W. Kane

      Details the importance of careful marketing research in any
      admissions plan for the future; tells what should be included
      in a research program; includes guidelines for proceeding,
      especially with an outside consultant.

24.   Recruiting and Enrolling Students from Abroad   407
          Karen Lowe Raftus

      Elaborates the perils and professional responsibilities of re-
      cruiting foreign nationals and Americans living abroad, with
      full discussions of necessary practices and lists of resources
      and addresses.

25.   Staff Development and Training in the
      Admissions Office   430
          B. Barbara Boerner

      Reveals how to make an admissions office effective in its
      marketing, recruiting, counseling, and other professional re-
      sponsibilities through well-timed staff development strate-
      gies.

      Part Six: Service to Members of the Profession   439

26.   Preparing for Visits from College Personnel   444
          Mary Anne Schwalbe

      Informative discussion of how schools and professional
      counseling staffs can take advantage of the information, as
      well as the possibilities for professional growth, that col-
      leges and universities provide through visits, publications,
      and professional contacts.

27.   Job-Related Pressures Affecting Secondary
      School Counselors   457
          Ina Miller

      Looks at the special pressures exerted on secondary school
      counselors and recommends ways to deal with them to fos-
      ter professional growth and effective student guidance.

28. Communicating Individuality When Writing
Reference Letters   473
Pamela K. Fay

Emphasizes the importance of reference letters in the admissions process; describes their most effective forms, their
legal ramifications in light of the Buckley Amendments, and
their usefulness in counseling subsequently matriculated
students.

29. Understanding Admissions Procedures at
Highly Selective Colleges   491
Douglas C. Thompson

Illuminates admissions counseling and selection in colleges
that admit fewer than half their applicants; states what a
counselor should know in advising students about such institutions.

30. Standardized Testing in Admissions
Counseling   509
Stephen Lovette

Summarizes the psychometric significance of standardized
admissions testing, the legitimate function of tests in counseling, and the controversy over such testing; makes recommendations for future use of testing and test scores.

31. Evaluating the Validity and Equity of
Standardized Tests   528
Jane W. Loeb

Depicts ways of measuring the validity of tests and other
statistical evidence; discusses how absence of tests changes
the nature of admissions decisions; and offers valuable insights regarding objective testing as an admissions criterion.

32. Learning from Members of the Profession   549
Marilyn Kimball, James E. Cavalier

Delineates ways counselors can learn from other professionals, specifically those whose experiences shed light on both
standard and unusual aspects of college admissions counseling.

Resource A: Statement of Principles of Good
            Practice for Members of the
            National Association of College
            Admissions Counselors   560

Resource B: Statement of Students'
            Rights and Responsibilities in the
            College Admissions Process   570

Bibliography   573

Index   597

The Authors

ᒬ ᒬ ᒬ ᒬ ᒬ

ᒬ　　　William R. Lowery is director of annual giving at Pomona College in Claremont, California. He received his B.A. degree in English from Wabash College (Crawfordsville, Indiana) in 1963 and his M.A. and Ph.D. degrees in English from Northwestern University (Evanston, Illinois) in 1964 and 1970, respectively. Prior to his present position, Lowery served as dean of admission and associate professor of English at Pitzer College in Claremont and earlier as assistant professor of English at Pomona College. He was president of the Western Association of College Admissions Counselors (1979-80) and served on the faculty of workshops in admissions counseling sponsored by the Rocky Mountain Association of College Admissions Counselors.

Marilyn J. Blum, formerly an independent educational counselor, is now college counselor at the Webb School of California, Claremont, California.

B. Barbara Boerner, formerly director of admissions at Goucher College, Towson, Maryland, is now headmistress of The Lincoln School, Providence, Rhode Island.

Stanley Bosworth is headmaster of Saint Ann's Episcopal School, Brooklyn Heights, New York.

Raymond Buriel is assistant professor of psychology at Pomona College and chair, Chicano Studies Center of the Claremont Colleges, Claremont, California.

Clifford J. Caine is assistant headmaster at Saint Paul Academy and Summit School, Saint Paul, Minnesota.

Irene Kovala Campanaro, formerly counselor and admissions coordinator at Itasca Community College in Grand Rapids, Minnesota, is now registrar at Anoka Ramsey Community College in Minneapolis.

John T. Casteen III, formerly dean of admissions at the University of Virginia, is now secretary of education of the Commonwealth of Virginia.

James E. Cavalier is head of the Senior School at Sewickley Academy, Sewickley, Pennsylvania.

Ann Coil is a founder of Coil, Ballback, and Slater Associates, a career management firm based in Santa Ana, California.

Michael F. Cundiff is college consultant at Parkway West Senior High School, Ballwin, Missouri.

Pamela K. Fay is college counselor at St. Catherine's School, Richmond, Virginia.

Jewelle Taylor Gibbs, formerly staff psychiatric social worker at Cowell Student Health Center, Stanford University, is now assistant professor, School of Social Welfare, University of California, Berkeley.

Herman W. Kane is president of Kane, Parsons & Associates, a New York-based firm specializing in consulting and market research for the nonprofit and public sectors.

Theodore D. Kelly is president of Consultants for Educational Resources and Research, Inc., Washington, D.C.

Marilyn Kimball, formerly director of admissions at Chatham College, Pittsburgh, Pennsylvania, and associate director of admissions, Wellesley College, Wellesley, Massachusetts, is now enrolled in law school at Northwestern University, Boston, Massachusetts.

Jan Krukowski is president of Jan Krukowski Associates Inc., a New York firm specializing in institutional promotion and market research.

Jane W. Loeb, formerly director of admissions, is now associate vice-chancellor for academic affairs and professor of educational psychology at the University of Illinois, Urbana-Champaign.

Stephen Lovette is academic dean at Saint Ignatius College Preparatory School, San Francisco, California.

Philip Martin is college counselor at St. Louis Priory School, St. Louis, Missouri.

Ina Miller is guidance director at St. Pius X High School, Albuquerque, New Mexico.

Julie C. Monson is director, Career Planning and Placement at the University of Chicago, Illinois.

Steven C. Munger is assistant to the headmaster and director of college counseling at Worcester Academy, Worcester, Massachusetts.

Nancy Painter is college counselor for Family Guidance, Inc., St. Louis, Missouri.

Paul Painter is a child psychiatrist and director of Family Guidance, Inc., St. Louis, Missouri.

Karen Lowe Raftus is associate director of admissions and director of international admissions at the College of Wooster, Wooster, Ohio.

Barbara B. Reinhold is director of guidance at Brookline High School, Brookline, Massachusetts.

Helene Reynolds is director of Helene Reynolds and Associates, Educational Consultants (Miami, Florida, and Princeton, New Jersey), and consultant for Miami Country Day School.

Sally Rivera, formerly director of the Office of Admissions for Chicano Students, is now associate dean of students at the Chicano Studies Center of the Claremont Colleges, Claremont, California.

Eileen M. Rose is director of admissions at Portland State University, Portland, Oregon.

Betty Schneider is college counselor at the Laboratory Schools of the University of Chicago, Illinois.

Jack H. Schuster is associate professor of education and public policy, Claremont Graduate School, Claremont, California.

Mary Anne Schwalbe, formerly associate dean of admissions and financial aid, Harvard and Radcliffe Colleges, is currently director of college counseling at the Dalton School, New York, New York.

Phyllis S. Steinbrecher is director of Phyllis S. Steinbrecher Associates, Educational Consultants, Westport, Connecticut.

Douglas C. Thompson, formerly associate dean of admission at Brown University, Providence, Rhode Island, is now dean of admission at Hamilton College, Clinton, New York.

Margaret Elizabeth Tracy is guidance counselor at Clayton High School, Clayton, Missouri.

James C. Walters is director of admissions at Ohio University, Athens, Ohio.

Leonard M. Wenc is director of financial aid at Carleton College, Northfield, Minnesota.

Karl L. Wolf is assistant professor of business administration and director of admissions at Shepherd College, Shepherdstown, West Virginia.

Jack L. Wright is college counselor at Benjamin Franklin High School, Los Angeles, California.

R. Fred Zuker, formerly director of admission at Tulane University of Louisiana, New Orleans, is now dean of admissions and financial aid at Pomona College, Claremont, California.

College Admissions Counseling

✒ ✒ ✒ ✒ ✒

A Handbook for the Profession

Part One

Scope of the Service

In most countries, students do not decide their educations or their futures; the decisions are made for them, based on examinations administered by agencies over which they and their parents have no control. The pattern in the United States is different. At almost every stage of education, parents and children make choices limited only by aspiration and sometimes by finances; in many cases, students try to achieve educational and social goals that have never been entertained by other members of their families. They may not attain their goals, but they can aim for them. And if students have not followed a certain pattern by eleven or twelve, they can begin—at eighteen, twenty-eight, or fifty—a new path leading to a goal. There are myriad openings into the American educational system.

But the openings are mystifying. Hardly any parent or student knows all the routes to educational success or brilliant careers, so schools and colleges have gradually developed the profession of college admissions counseling. Although not seeking to direct students into narrow channels, members of the profession try to make students recognize the variety of choices available to them and the consequences of making different decisions.

In this section, John T. Casteen III and Michael F. Cundiff supply members of the profession with useful background information. In Chapter One, Casteen traces some of the forces that created the complexity within the American educational system, and Cundiff (Chapter Two) discusses possible and likely consequences of the demographic shifts that affect institutions of higher education and therefore the students who use them.

Casteen concludes that we cannot allow major decisions regarding institutions of higher learning to be made by default. He describes how a combination of practical and ideal goals has always shaped American education. The development of basic liberal arts curricula preceded the widespread general education curricula of this century, with general education being based on the unstated and perhaps unnoticed assumption that the skills developed by liberal arts programs had become universal and thus need not be formally addressed. The failure of these assumptions led to the social and educational upheavals of the 1960s, to a lack of public credibility as a result of educational weakness and slackness.

Casteen points out that American colleges' roots were different from the European ones, which were created by communities of scholars to pursue and transmit learning. American schools were inspired by compacts within communities. These agreements were planned by nonscholars, who hired scholars to teach other nonscholars. The educated nonscholars then left campus and went out into the world to work. Thus, in America social constraints and desires preceded the development of scholarly ideals, and different social patterns and desires in different parts of the country dictated different patterns of higher education.

Casteen maintains that students do not always know what they need, so educational facilities are inherently responsible for informing students of what they need to know if they are to succeed in the working world. Concomitantly with this obligation, Casteen insists that institutions must be accountable through due process.

Today's world is complex and often unpleasant, but Casteen warns against the simplification of back-to-the-basics. He feels that both the schools and those who must counsel today's students about their educational futures must properly educate the students to be skilled, wise, critical, and capable of governing themselves.

Noting the impossibility of accurately predicting population changes and the vast differences in predictions regarding the effect of the current decline in the eighteen-year-old population, Cundiff discusses various possible patterns of enrollment decline and the accompanying impact on the economy and work force deployment. There will be special impact in large cities, in community colleges, and in some individual public and private institutions, both with and without continued tax support through scholarship aid.

Among the possible ramifications of enrollment declines, Cundiff discusses changes in faculty and program strength and the resulting diminution of available choices for students. As a result, both counselors and students will need to be more cautious; admissions officers will become more important in their institutions and perhaps more biased in the advice they give as counselors. Employment patterns—and the educational needs for job seekers—may change because of shrunken college programs. According to some experts, there will be greater need than ever for liberal arts education in difficult times, but others argue that technical and specialized schools perhaps better prepare students for difficult or challenging futures. According to Cundiff, bachelor's degrees may be devalued and society may lower its expectations that graduates be familiar with history and the patterns of civilization, or even that they have a wide range of developed skills, in which case society will become more mechanistic and individuals less self-reliant. Institutions will be facing difficult decisions and may have to reduce their number of employees, yet there will still be a need for counseling offices, especially to meet the needs of older students.

Casteen and Cundiff do not advise admissions counselors how to work with their clients or prescribe significant changes in the kind of advice the professional finds valuable. Each is convinced, however, that wise advice can come only from those who understand the social and historical pressures that have created our educational system, because those forces, always continuing and changing, affect our schools and determine the nature of the world in which students will carry out the careers for which their chosen educations prepare them.

1

Function of Postsecondary Education for Individuals and Society

John T. Casteen III

A description of American education includes several common distinctions: to train is not necessarily to educate; what may be good for one student may be bad for another; private schools may legitimately differ from public schools in various ways; not all students learn successfully in all schools. These and similar dichotomies are as old as education itself in this country and grew from opposing notions about the purposes of education in a free society.

The founders of America's early colleges and universities acted out of contrary motives, and these motives often dealt less with governance or education itself than with social purposes. The very first colleges tried to accomplish practical ends. They trained young men to be preachers; later they trained students to be teachers, lawyers, and practitioners of other useful professions. Harvard College and other schools operated under charters that proclaimed lofty educational and religious ideals, but their daily business was preparing men to do certain jobs.

Sometimes, practicality rode roughshod over idealism: The College of William and Mary quickly forgot that its mission was to teach American Indians to read and write and instead began to educate the sons of Virginia's gentry in "proper English fashion." Elsewhere, idealism accommodated practicality with few signs of distress: For example, in 1866 the trustees and faculty of Union College in Schenectady, New York, had no trouble fitting the study of engineering into what had been a liberal arts curriculum.

The colleges formed at the time of the Revolution or because of it pursued goals more idealistic than practical. With certain notable exceptions and a fair amount of local eccentricity, they tried to educate citizens capable of governing themselves rather than vocational specialists. Each college adhered to its own odd vision of democratic man and tried to spread literacy (variously defined) and perhaps political savvy. The schools addressed vocational competence only within the context of this larger goal.

The extreme instance was Jefferson's design for the University of Virginia: He deliberately made education the business of the state, in the hope that self-government would succeed as a consequence of the spread of literacy. Dumas Malone observed that Jefferson's faith in education was all but religious, that he saw salvation in education—the judgment makes sense. Jefferson's university intended to do for the common man almost everything except make him employable. (For a discussion of the political bases of Jefferson's educational experiment, see Peterson, 1970, pp. 961-988.)

Subsequent educational foundations hover between these extremes, trying to reconcile the extremes of practicality and idealism. The original land-grant colleges attempted to graduate farmers, mechanics, engineers, and other specialists with both practical skills and the general knowledge necessary for participatory citizenship. Women's colleges, technical colleges (a development not originally our own—we imitated England), and other schools bespeak the diverse purposes now pursued by higher education in this country. The American liberal arts college has no counterpart elsewhere; only we of all nations support colleges devoted solely to the cultivation of the human mind and spirit.

Thus, as a nation, we have never really found a comfortable middle ground between the extremes of practicality and idealism. Our inability in recent years to decide how formal education ought to relate to daily life is one clue to this confusion. Another clue is the differences between today's land-grant colleges, many of them now great national universities in the European sense rather than technical colleges, and their predecessors.

Our shifting educational needs, repeated imports from Europe, and evolving notions of educational prestige have collaborated with our basic indecision as to what college is really for (to elevate the human spirit? to perfect mankind? to provide refuge from a hostile world? to produce leaders or followers or scholars or ladies and gentlemen?) and shaped a national educational system neither national nor systematic. We have let a massive educational establishment develop without ever defining our ultimate purposes, goals, or methods. Consequently, no other nation has such a diverse and complex array of postsecondary schools. As the century draws toward an end, we have and believe in hundreds of independent institutions with divergent purposes, populations, standards of quality, and governing boards.

Yet there are certain norms we can agree to and use to discuss the individual learner's place in our educational scheme. By 1825 or so, American education developed a remarkably practical curriculum (writing, literature, sometimes theology, history, mathematics, foreign languages, natural science) yet called it "the liberal arts," hence claiming the respectability of European elitist education while actually teaching the core competencies that made for success in the American environment. In the early years, Harvard, Yale, and others tried to teach the medieval trivium (grammar, rhetoric, and logic) and quadrivium (arithmetic, music, geometry, and astronomy). Few American colleges continued after Jefferson's time to build their curricula on the classical model; they decided what education ought to do for a democracy's citizens, or they borrowed someone else's scheme and carefully called the new curricula by their old names.

Even now we resist the urge toward the wholly practical, which may mean antihumanistic to some people. We reject the cold efficiency of Europe's early selection systems, retributive grading systems, and do-or-die national entrance examinations and assert that less constraint is better than more, that students who cannot succeed in traditional programs deserve access to nontraditional ones. We have chosen to believe that the system's very inefficiency protects the educational rights of individual students.

However, we should acknowledge that what we rejected in the European way of doing things *can* work. Well-designed examinations can in fact identify most kinds of academic talent when students are twelve to fifteen years old. Grades that punish probably accomplish efficiently what encouragement or benign neglect accomplishes inefficiently. For example, based on their net societal or economic outcomes, Sweden, Russia, and Germany do not surpass us in cultivating critical minds, teaching basic skills, or guaranteeing that adequate numbers of thoughtful leaders will graduate from schools. The differences may have to do with the way in which human loss occurs. We may lose inefficiently—by failing to demand enough of ourselves or our students, by discriminating, by failing to provide adequate financial support for schools and students—what other nations lose efficiently—by tracking students into or out of their systems.

American education has changed more in the generation since World War II than most of us realize. We now have an establishment far larger than anyone before 1945 or even 1960 imagined, with far more diverse kinds of institutions and proclaimed purposes and promises and far more able when willing to accommodate students from segments of society not traditionally included in the ranks of our more educated, hence privileged, citizens.

These changes occurred so quickly that we could not name them properly. Struggling to explain what was happening to the university, we talked briefly about the multiversity and even the megaversity. Believing that we were satisfying society's infinitely expandable hunger for education, we added programs, faculty, and buildings and talked in ever grander terms about new markets, new demands for learning, and larger opportunities for growth for postsecondary education.

This generation of growth had its price. An example is today's overbuilt, poorly built, and ineptly maintained buildings on many campuses as we face a long generation of contraction, less demand for our services, and lower budgets. (*High School Graduates: Projections for the Fifty States,* published in 1979 by the Western Interstate Commission for Higher Education, documents just how sharply our student-age population will decline by 1995. The book is a suitable traveling companion for admissions officers.) A more complex example, one that directly touches the individual student, was the occurrence between 1945 and 1975 of a process of homogenization, especially in curricula. As a result, ironically, students in 1985 may face fewer real choices than did students in 1945 or even 1960.

These curricular changes affect the counseling and admissions processes. Between 1875 or so and 1965 or so, the American liberal arts curriculum changed relatively little. We built professional programs on top of the liberal arts lower division, and we adjusted, usually downward, our specific requirements. But the typical student continued to take writing, literature, a social science, a foreign language, mathematics, and a natural science as required introductory courses. Even as one or another requirement disappeared from many lists, the broad concept endured.

This relatively rigid structure collapsed because of two new forces that emerged in the late 1950s and throughout the 1960s. One force was the development in our national private colleges and universities, whose prestige gave the old curriculum its authority, of the concept of general education, the notion that experience in generally defined cultural areas matters more than mastery of prescribed skills. Now itself the target of Henry Rosovsky and others who promote the so-called core curriculum, at its beginning general education was proclaimed as a step toward freedom from the old rigidity.

The other force for change was more social than educational. Beginning in the mid-1960s at Berkeley, Antioch, Stony Brook, and a dozen other campuses where faltering national policy on war and the Vietnam conflict, poverty, racism, and other ills were debated and often the target of violence; the old basic education and the new general education were both attacked as elitist, irrelevant, and reactionary. Thus, society forced curricula to change, sometimes directly, but more often indirectly. (For a general discussion of curriculum change in recent years, see the several essays contained in *Change Magazine* editors' *The Great Core Curriculum Debate: Education as a Mirror of Culture,* 1979.)

As a result of these and other changes, foreign language, mathematics, and natural science requirements were substantially reduced in most American colleges by about 1970, to be replaced, if at all, by more general requirements. In a sense, in this period we tried to define the social relevance of our disciplines rather than to spread measurable skills. Vagueness set in. We began to claim that we were unable to assess competence or to teach students how to write, and we eliminated the idea that every student should master the "hard" subjects. The diminution of foreign language and mathematics requirements tells much of the story. At the beginning of a decade that brought us into closer dependence on other nations than ever before in our history and into daily contact with computers, in higher education we stopped asserting that competence in life's basic skills matters.

Analogously, our educational purposes have shifted in recent years. Responding to demand, the land-grant colleges and other technical schools have drifted into liberal education. The number of single-sex schools has decreased, although not always because of well-drawn plans. Racial desegregation finally seems to have begun in earnest, and the courts have at last put teeth into the Fourteenth Amendment. Because of these and other developments, faculties that hardly came to grips with the 1960s entered the 1970s with greater obligations but less readiness to meet them.

Poorly rationalized curricula, changed conditions of existence, and the sudden arrival of larger-than-expected student bodies combined to guarantee two outcomes: First, the 1970s would be a disastrous decade for education, more in implications for the future than in immediate fact. Second, we would enter the century's final quarter without a national plan for survival; without the security offered by our pious charters, rich endowments, and ever more generous financial supporters; and without responses to the new problems of shrinking demand for our services, aging physical plants, and insecure faculties. That the 1970s were disastrous is clear now to most observers. We lost public credibility as our students proved progressively less competent in reading, writing, and doing mathematics, and we took on the guilts of a nation whose leaders seemed unable to formulate military policy, define the goals of foreign policy, find cures for our cities' ills, or make responsible moral choices. In the 1970s, America came to demand too much of education, and education faltered beneath the burden.

When we move from consideration of our system to consideration of the individual within the system, yet another view of our origins may clarify the issues. We planned and built our colleges from the outside in. They did not develop, as Oxford and Cambridge did, from communities of scholars, who pursued studies of mutual interest and (eventually) taught students to become scholars like themselves, but from community compacts, agreements forged by nonscholars, who gathered scholars to teach other nonscholars, who would then leave the campus and go to work. Colonial villages needed preachers, teachers, and magistrates. With the industrial revolution and the advent of modern agriculture, society needed engineers, scientific farmers, and other specialists. Even the fledgling nation met its practical needs by designing colleges to produce citizen-leaders. Jefferson's letters on education say much about the perfection of society but essentially assume the perfection of man as an individual. To paraphrase Malone (1953, pp. 17-29), the salvation seen in education by Jefferson and others was more societal or general than personal.

Many of today's challenges touch more closely on questions about the future of our educational system than on questions about the individual within the system. But we need to rethink our attitudes toward individual students and their right to pursue postsecondary education that works. The end of an era of rapid growth, the appearance of new demands for vocational training, emerging student populations, and declining resources all mean that from now until the end of the century students will require of education something different from what earlier generations required.

Here I must make a distinction and acknowledge an assumption. What students demand is not always what they need, and faculties have an inherent obligation to tell students what they need to know if they are to succeed in later life. (This assumption sits atop another assumption: that faculties must in fact know what students need to know.) Both the distinction and the assumption seem to have suffered in the last two decades; yet both matter vitally in a democratic society. Students ought to express their desires or demands, and faculties ought to respond openly and thoughtfully to them. However, by the same token, faculties must spell out their core beliefs, especially those about education. Students who choose not to pursue rigorous educations should be able to exercise that choice; and faculties who choose not to take meaningful stands about the relationship between curricula and society should face certain consequences.

We can reverse these deliberately negative formulations. Despite back-to-the-basics, core curricula, reassertions of general education, and the dozens of other dogmas and quasi-dogmas currently bandied about in our discussion of what to do next, certain individual rights should be basic. Students have the right to study in schools that define the terms of the offered contract, follow curricula that work in a world where change may be the only constant, and teach how to choose among options that make sense by offering advanced work of sufficient complexity to challenge leaders, not followers. Students have the right to be trained in usable skills, such as finance, agriculture, and law, and simultaneously educated in the areas of knowledge that support self-government. They also have the right to enjoy the protections guaranteed to all citizens under constitutional law, especially the Fourteenth Amendment (equal protection and due process). This list of rights is not exhaustive, but it is relevant to the question of what we must accomplish in higher education for the next generation. The final right especially matters because it underlies Congress's and the Court's determination to force higher education to cease discriminating by sex, race, handicap, and other arbitrary classifications and to open higher education's benefits to all citizens.

How far have we come? In the area of curriculum, we have begun to move. No matter where one stands on the core curriculum, Henry Rosovsky and the Harvard faculty have defined a new direction by asserting that on graduation, students should be able to do certain things that are discrete, measurable, and susceptible of concise statement. Formal education involves an implicit contract as to what a student will be and will be able to do at the end of four years. Whether a faculty seeks the "basics" and the good old days, joins Harvard in trying to define educational relevance in today's terms, clings to general education as the last bastion of bookish learning, or strikes off in another direction, in this age it must stand accountable for its product. A school's catalogue, admissions presentations, and profile all must say what it promises, and a school must disclose how well it accomplishes its goals and what standard of judgment it is following. We lost credibility by failing to meet these obligations. Despite the obvious triviality of our early efforts to regain credibility ("full-disclosure" catalogues and the like), we must now find ways to accomplish what we promise and to persuade a properly skeptical public of our success.

In the area now called student services, we have progressed a certain amount—especially when Congress ordered us to, after being pressured by students and other concerned people. Yet our colleges and universities are now only marginally better able to meet the needs of nontraditional, nonmainstream students than they were in 1945 or 1960. The community college was originally formed to prepare such students for transfer to more prestigious colleges and universities. But annually the community colleges move more into terminal occupational programs, adult education, and other fields that deserve coverage and draw students but fail to provide the necessary entree into the mainstream.

Many colleges and universities now have support centers for dyslexic students, women's programs, black studies programs, and other services. These programs make sense, but we cannot afford to believe that their mere existence gives our students the right to learn. Genuinely effective support for women or nonwhite students who want to cross uncharted territory, succeed in professions not historically open to them, and lead our society must be more than window dressing, random moments of group solidarity, and tutorial services. In the end, the measure of success must be our ability to graduate men and women whose lives prove that what we did for them worked. Sooner or later, the black lawyer or female surgeon succeeds on personal terms, or fails. Analogously, our services for physically handicapped or dyslexic students must stand tests of effect. Building ramps and providing reading support are fine gestures, but they approach only the surface of vast problems. We must now make these first gestures, but we are foolish indeed if these gestures are our only effort.

Finally, we come to the issue called "accessibility." The relevant section of the Fourteenth Amendment simply states that "No State shall make or enforce any law which shall abridge the privileges or immunities of citizens of the United States; nor shall any State deprive any person of life, liberty, or property, without due process of law; nor deny to any person within its jurisdiction the equal protection of the laws." The legal language disguises a point that Congress and the Court have made repeatedly in recent years with regard to education: It is contrary to this country's law for government or government's money to support discrimination by arbitrary classifications of persons. Due process, with its implication that persons have the right to know how business is done and to deal on an equal basis with institutions and other persons, and equal protection, with its implication that all persons have the right to enjoy the full benefits of the law, should be as basic to our educational philosophies as they are to American law. *A Critical Examination of the Adams Case: A Source Book* (Haynes, 1978) discusses the exposition of this principle and its implications in terms that make sense to the layperson.

Take away these two concepts or deny their validity, and the concept that education is in fact the route of access to the good things of life, to Jeffersonian salvation, crumbles. The painful process by which Congress and the Court have persuaded

us that women, members of racial or ethnic minorities, handicapped students, and others *belong* is perhaps the best single
clue to our entrenched attitudes.

Whether higher education is more open now than in 1945 is
largely a matter of how one measures. More women, more nonwhite students, more nonsuburban students, more older students: These convenient indexes mean little if we cannot also
document the laterlife successes promised by education. In this
era of affirmative action, goals, and timetables, we have been
too eager to sing our success in recruiting and too hesitant to
affirm that access works two ways: Successful students ought to
graduate; having graduated, they should be able to build success
after college. These two notions about the proper outcomes of
access imply vast new areas of concern for higher education. If
we prove our social responsibility by recruiting and enrolling
new groups of minority students, we should be at least as eager
to advertise our success in graduating these students, in accelerating their progress toward the financial and personal independence that education promises. And having graduated these students, we should use every weapon at our command to guarantee
them a chance of success in later life at least equal to what our
more traditional students have enjoyed. In other words, we have
specific obligations to end discriminatory admissions patterns
based on race, sex, handicap, and other categorical labels. If we
ignore these obligations, we have no way of proving that we de-
liver what we promise.

Every teacher and every parent knows that higher education faces remarkable threats during the next two decades. Declining student populations, aging faculties, deteriorating facilities, shrinking resources, loss of public credibility, incoherent
curricula—each item in the long list has its own validity; together, the threats amount to the gravest crisis since the Great Depression. We have all heard the warnings: Colleges will close;
faculties will retrench; competition among colleges for enrollees will soon grow feverish. Concern for the individual's
place in the larger scheme must command more of our attention
as this era progresses, if for no other reason than colleges that
deal effectively with their students may survive, whereas those

that fail to do what they should with their students must face the consequences of becoming society's surplus property.

Because of educational, societal, and economic changes since 1945, higher education today has greater potential worth than ever before to the individual student, but the worth is tempered by processes still in motion. From now until the end of the century, our students will be those wise or lucky enough to seek superior credentials in an era of declining personal and institutional resources. Thoughtful men and women know that life's rewards—money, influence, personal happiness, even good health—belong to those who pursue advanced educations. For institutions that want to face their proper responsibilities toward individuals and to thrive in the next two decades, the Carnegie Council on Policy Studies in Higher Education (1979), in its report on fair practices in higher education, gives excellent advice. Colleges and universities that succeed in discovering and teaching how to master our increasingly hostile environment and simultaneously attract broad constituencies will meet the council's challenge and dominate education. Those that do not will falter and fail.

Which way to go? Accelerating technological growth, our changing position in world affairs, and the knowledge explosion itself all say that back-to-the-basics is the wrong direction. The good old days were not all that good; they were merely simpler. Woefully underpaid teachers, who were often women trapped in jobs without futures, taught students who knew from birth that the rules of the game dictated one way of life for white males and other ways of life and opportunities for other people. A myth whose truth cannot be tested claims that these students read, wrote, and did arithmetic well. If so, nothing proves that they did well because their teachers were exploited and their own horizons were confined within narrower bounds than the Constitution supports.

Yet these narrowed horizons often seem to be the essential "basic" for those preaching back-to-the basics. In defense of Harvard's core curriculum, Jencks (1972) asserts that back to complexity should properly be the rallying cry. To my mind, he is right. Basics are not good enough for men and women who must live in a world where power has shifted, where calculus stands behind even the simplest machine calculation, where natural resources promise to run out within our own lifetimes if we fail to develop new ways of deploying them. Basics may be good enough for followers, for workers content to take life as it comes and to let others think for them. But basics are too simple for young adults who are to build careers by thinking for themselves and out of their thoughts to lead a free society. Our mission in higher education in this country is properly to educate men and women who will govern skillfully, wisely, subtly, and critically govern themselves and society.

Concern for the future of American higher education is in the end concern for the future of life as we have wanted it to be and for the futures of all the people who pass through our classrooms year after year. Our founders knew just how vital education would come to be in our society, so they made education their chief concern after the law itself. In recent years, we in education have suffered because we have underestimated our influence. More than once, we failed to see just how important our choices were when we voted on curricular changes, acted or failed to act in response to student needs, made or missed the chance to change the world into which our students went. For the remainder of this century, the issues are too important for us to ignore by default. We can retreat into our specialties, deny responsibility for what happens to the students who come to us to prepare for their own moments in history, worry about defending what we have while refusing to learn what can be; or we can see crises as challenges to be met, as guides to tell us how to do better what we do, as stars to show us which way to go. Those of us who make the latter choices, and make them well, will mold American life as no previous generation of educators has.

2

Impact of Demographic Changes on Students, Counselors, and Institutions

Michael F. Cundiff

Many authors address population trends with alarmed concern, particularly as the trends relate to population growth in the United States, where the goal of zero population growth (ZPG) has not been attained. After being barraged with relentless propaganda espousing the desirability of ZPG and with ominous projections depicting people stacked on top of people, we have become inured to the entire concept.

For colleges, the intricacies of population demographics affect their programs and even their very survival. Declining enrollments, a serious problem affecting institutions of higher education, are inevitably accompanied by the need to reassess philosophies, plans, curricula, and budgets. As colleges struggle to survive in the grip of economic hardships, and as they attempt to adjust programs designed for larger enrollments to the expectations projected from a declining pool of college-age students, their existing programs cannot be offered intact. Scheduling, staffing, and financial constraints necessitate establishment of a minimum essential program, an austerity measure to permit planned reduction of courses and programs. An essential program ideally should be based on the school's philosophy and reflect the needs of its student body. Just how the numbers of students will affect schools is not exactly known, and uncertainty prevails in the offices of demographers and educational institutions.

Here I address these uncertainties, and I do so with much of the same conflicting information that continues to confuse planners.

Impact on the Institutions

According to the *Population Bulletin* (1975, p. 4), "The radical and frequent fluctuations in the birthrate in the 1940s caused embarrassment to those demographers who had not forecast any increase in fertility; and their projections, once accepted without hesitation, began to be seriously questioned. . . . Population forecasting is not a simple matter. Available techniques do not permit reliable predictions to be made for five, ten, twenty, or fifty years ahead. The best may be far wrong." On the one hand, some experts predict no significant decline in college attendance for the foreseeable future. "With an increase in the proportion of persons in the eighteen to twenty-one age group in college (from 40.3 percent to 51.3 percent), enrollments should hover around 10 million from the late 1970s to 1990, and the projected enrollment for 2000 should be about 12.5 million—or about three million more than are presently registered" (p. 5). But a sizable number of authors disagree, predicting dire consequences to college enrollments. *College Recruiting in the Next Ten Years* (Chapman and others, 1979, p. 1) notes: "The next ten years pose a serious challenge for those in college admissions. The simultaneous pressures of increasing costs, declining enrollments and compliance with new state and federal regulations make recruiting students more difficult," and (p. 2) "High school counselors (62 percent) tend to see recruiting students as more difficult for colleges now than it was ten years ago. Admissions officers from many private colleges (45 percent) tend to agree. Those from public institutions, however, overwhelmingly disagree. Over 70 percent do *not* believe attracting students has become more difficult, a view that reflects the dramatic growth of public higher education in the last decade. Still, it is surprising to note that the high school counselors hold a more grim picture of the recent past than do admissions officers themselves. One can only speculate on how that affects the advice they give to students seeking admission to college."

The private sector, once synonymous with quality higher education, now competes against a seemingly endless resource of public funds for faculty and for physical plants and resources to attract a shrinking pool of students. Hence, the work of population experts holds the studied interest of educators. The uncertainty of college-going patterns adds to the difficulty predictors will face in accurately forecasting enrollment in the next decade and beyond. In many instances, increasing enrollment in adult education and lifelong education have changed traditional student bodies. With fewer eighteen- to twenty-two-year-old college men and women, schools will inevitably turn their attention to nontraditional students.

> The outlook for college enrollments during the next decade is at best uncertain. The number of eighteen year olds in the total population has begun and will continue to decline until the early 1990s. What is far less certain, and poses difficulties for those attempting to predict college enrollment, is the extent to which college-going patterns will alter during those same years. Historically, college enrollments have been more affected by increases in the percentages of students attending college than by actual population increases. Yet, when one also considers the potential impact of major public policy decisions, shifting societal attitudes about learning as a lifelong activity, the increased availability of student financial assistance, and possible new interpretations of the relationship between work and education, enrollment predictions become even more risky [Chapman and others, 1979, pp. 1-2].

The impact of these trends on the educational system is uncertain. The peculiarly American notion of Manifest Destiny, of the biggest and the best, of solving problems through expansion occupies as prominent a part of our culture and national thinking as baseball, apple pie, and the backyard barbeque. Military expansion and corporate growth careened through the decades of the 1960s and 1970s with a rage for bigness and proliferation of programs at boom proportions. Almost every aspect of American life—including education—felt the growth surge during this era.

But today, the "bigger is better" notion receives closer scrutiny, being seriously questioned by a cautious and conservative public. In an economy of shrinking resources, unemployment, fuel shortages, inflation, high taxes, and public discontent, the public and the institutions of higher learning are responding to the harsh prospects of the 1980s and the unfavorable realities already upon them. As Abramowitz and Rosenfeld (1978, p. 16) say: "The prospects for higher education are particularly gloomy. The number of people in the traditional college-age group will decline 25 percent between 1980 and 1994, causing enrollment to drop by 1.8 million. In order to accommodate this smaller number of anticipated students, total faculty size could be reduced by as much as 100,000. If this is the case, total academic demand, in fact, will only be one third the supply." Thus, the consequences of declining enrollment may be grim.

The problem of maintaining a program on reduced revenues is not merely one of reducing costs proportionately to the reduced enrollment. "Decline thus means less money with which to operate while, at the same time, many of the fixed and semifixed expenses cannot be reduced proportionately" (Abramowitz and Rosenfeld, p. 8). Due to inflation alone, it is becoming increasingly difficult to maintain a program without a decrease in quality. During periods of expansion, utilization of staff and facilities was maximized and administrators proudly accounted for their plants' service load. "Two full decades after 1957 conditions are quite different. New problems are facing educators for which the experiences and lessons of the past leave them inadequately prepared. They now confront underutilization—situations traditionally associated with inefficiency" (Abramowitz and Rosenfeld, p. 6).

Traditional students (between eighteen and twenty-four years old) increased until the mid-1970s both in number and percentage of attendance, but today's schools can only hope that the *rate* of attendance will continue to grow if adequate numbers of postsecondary students are to be available to fill the void created by the decreasing fertility in the 1960s. Consequences of a static or decreasing rate of attendance clearly spell the demise of many institutions, most significantly the private ones. With demographic data revealing a precipitous decline in the number of traditional students, colleges may have to reduce programs and staff; many schools will not be able to survive at all.

Urban areas are especially hard hit, vulnerable not only to enrollment decline—caused by the reduced number of available students and the "white flight" to the suburbs—but also to the national economic recession that plagues the present administration. Typically, urban institutions are further beset by old, outdated, energy-inefficient buildings; lacking the funds to replace them, they resort to stopgap measures or near-total abandonment of maintenance procedures.

"The problem of enrollment decline for urban areas is not just a matter of fewer students. The cities are becoming increasingly populated by lower income, minority families whose children usually are more difficult to educate because of their disadvantaged backgrounds" (Abramowitz and Rosenfeld, p. 12). Abramowitz and Rosenfeld cite other urban problems affecting institutions of higher learning: a dwindling tax base, unemployment, business failure and disinvestment, and emigration of high- and middle-income population groups.

Fishlow also discusses the likely impact of population trends on postsecondary institutions, whose enrollments depend heavily on both the size of the eighteen- to twenty-four-year-old population and their rate of enrollment. Over the past years, we have witnessed nearly continual growth in both the college-age population and rate of enrollment; both were especially high in the 1960s. However, future trends suggest that postsecondary enrollment growth will cease and be replaced by decline in the 1980s because of the falling birthrate, whose decline began in the early 1960s.

Citing a Carnegie Council study, Fishlow suggests that not all types of institutions of higher learning will endure through this decline. The institutions best able to survive the declining enrollments will be those that are now well managed and whose administrators are willing and able to plan for flexibility in their academic programs and the use of their resources. Those institutions will then experience rapid (but short-lived) growth in demand as the 1980s "echo" of baby-boom births reaches college age around the year 2000 (Abramowitz and Rosenfeld, p. 10).

As institutions struggle to adapt to the demands attending smaller size, they may overreact to the extent that recovery of some lost students may occur, and the institution may not be equipped to accommodate them. In their haste to reduce staffs, trim budgets, and gear down to changed circumstances, schools could find themselves sacrificing students to competitors who had not so quickly forfeited their ability to recover. Enrollment projections indicate that growth may reoccur sporadically or steadily because the factors affecting birthrate may change, including abortion and divorce rates, the family roles of women, employment generally, and the aspiration of women to remain in the work force. Furthermore, even though national demographic data project a declining enrollment trend throughout the decade, many influences could affect this projection. "Postsecondary enrollments may begin to decline in 1982 and continue through the forecast period. However, increased participation rates of those beyond compulsory attendance age could change this, as could designing programs to serve the increasing numbers in the twenty-five to thirty-four age group who are normally in the work force" (Davis and Lewis, 1978, p. 42).

The creation of programs designed for nontraditional students has long been the forte of the community college, which must be carefully tuned to the needs of the community it serves and which may reach a student body whose mean age is nearly thirty. Career training and evening programs may provide sufficient revenues to supplement the traditional studies. However, such programs will not permit the survival of some institutions because at least a temporary decline appears inevitable in spite of forecasts projecting increased numbers of traditional students. "It is the difficult task of educators to prepare not only for the substantial and inevitable decline of the next few years, but also to plan for a reasonably certain upturn thereafter. There are very likely to be as many children in elementary school in 1995 as there were in the peak years of 1970, before the current decline" (Fishlow, 1978, p. 61).

Adaptation will certainly be the key for survival in the coming decade, if survival means retaining near-present enrollment levels. It appears that many colleges and universities (how many is the question) will not be able to continue as institutions of higher learning, so it is best to confront this probability realistically. Perpetuation for the sake of perpetuation holds far less appeal than perpetuation for the sake of filling definite needs and providing society with a valuable contribution.

Various authors have approached the problem from conflicting points of view. Some, namely the Carnegie Commission and the United States Bureau of Census, take a relatively optimistic stand; others, the preponderance of current writers, have a gloomy outlook.

Given recent government willingness to fund financially strapped students, the prospect for improving or at least maintaining present attendance proportions is realistic. The argument that everyone may not benefit from postsecondary training is counter to the arguments of those seeking to expand rates of attendance. In any case, the federal and state grant programs have greatly helped private education by enabling lower-income students to select their schools with little regard for expense. The private sector, without this massive infusion of tax monies, would be hard put to compete with its less expensive, publicly supported counterparts. If present levels of funding continue, private education may be able to attract sufficient students to permit the continued richness and diversity that the private sector has long added to the American educational system. But federal direction and example are at this point uncertain, even unlikely.

State schools will, in all probability, survive the impact of

enrollment competition since they will, because of their funding
and comparatively lower costs, continue to attract students
from all income ranges. Some state institutions may even experience growth.

As Fishlow (1978, p. 73) says, "The effects of this probable decline, however, will not be felt equally by all institutions
of higher education. The differential effect by type of institution is the subject of the Carnegie volume *More Than Survival.*
Carnegie does not predict much, if any, decline in overall enrollments because they assume a rising enrollment rate."

Those well-managed and flexible institutions have already
undertaken steps to solve enrollment problems by defining first
minimum essential programs and then priority programs to be
offered only if sufficient enrollment permits. New attention to
retaining students and an emphasis on preserving the strongest
programs may help many institutions endure the present decline
in enrollments.

Impact on the Student

Students may have to shop very discriminately to select
the institution that best provides quality education while meeting their needs. They will have to look beyond the colorful brochures and attractive admissions gimmicks and closely scrutinize
schools. Roark (1980) cautions that federal support of research
in higher education has declined sharply, thereby affecting the
quality of some programs. "Another decade of low investment
will result in laboratories that are inadequate and equipment
that is obsolete, according to the report." Roark further states
that one fourth of United States institutions share their equipment and that many more plan to do so, but she sees problems
with this arrangement: "Although the trend is logical . . . there
would be serious losses if medical schools were divested of their
interest in fundamental science, and reverted to being trade
schools limited to applied research."

Fiscal requirements in this time of decline appear certain
to eliminate programs not contributing their fair share to the institutions' budgets. The danger here lies in the possibility of

many good and valuable options being lost. Students may have to settle for the next best thing, or even for a completely unacceptable substitute. And the question of quality arises again as financial constraints dictate program survival, expenditures for equipment, and hiring policies. Everywhere institutions search for answers to the difficulties brought on by finances and declining enrollments.

Magarrell (1980) cites the approach several prestigious institutions have pursued. "At Wesleyan University, which has had an ample supply of applicants for admission, a plan for the 1980s calls for teaching a larger number of students with a smaller number of faculty members. Enrollment would rise 6 percent, the size of the faculty would be cut by 10 percent, and the student-faculty ratio would rise to 12 to 1 from the present 10 to 1." The foremost priority of administrators should be programs and departments for which the institution has the resources and the faculty that attract students and produce a quality product. Magarrell continues, "Columbia University's Commission on Academic Priorities in the Arts and Sciences, after two years of study, has called for a program of 'selective excellence' in which the university will 'do only what it can do superlatively.' " Ideally, this priority will continue to dominate administrators' thinking as they chart their schools' directions through the next decade. Education has suffered charges of poor quality in better times, and it can certainly do without the additional burden of having to rebuild the quality of programs and the public's confidence in them should it be allowed to slip to an inferior status.

Quality education ranks at the top of important issues to the student in the long run because institutions whose programs suffer low public esteem produce graduates unable to compete for jobs. Conversely, graduates of more highly respected colleges and universities enjoy better prospects of employment at higher starting salaries. However, the enrollment crunch is accompanied, according to much of the current literature, by a probable decline in quality of programs and a compromise of standards. Fiske (1979, p. 93) addresses this issue: "As enrollments dwindle and competition for tuition paying students intensifies, more and more colleges and universities are resorting to hard-sell strategies which in some cases impinge upon the traditional standards and canons of higher education." Yet the answer must lie in institutions doing well what they can do well and abandoning weaker programs. For example, as Jacobson (1980, p. 10) notes, "At Carnegie-Mellon University, the principles of strategic planning have led officials to place greater emphasis on research—especially in fields where the institution has already made a mark, such as computer science and polymer chemistry. Enrollments are then expected to take care of themselves without the need to recruit 'nontraditional' students."

Although the concern for maintaining quality remains the primary charge to our institutions of higher learning, recruiting continues to dominate administrators' attention. Jacobson continues, "More aggressive recruiting efforts simply will not be enough, the managers have concluded. Instead, they say, many colleges will have to eliminate relatively weak or unpopular programs so that they can reinforce areas of greater promise" (p. 9).

The changing emphasis in college recruiting has implications for the colleges and for prospective entering students, since both will have to rely on printed materials to a much greater extent than they have in the past. In a recent study by the University of Michigan, a majority of responding colleges expected to pursue more aggressive recruiting strategies, but they also indicated an increased reliance on printed materials. "A substantial number of colleges, around half, expect to spend more time on campus and make more use of mailing lists to attract prospective students" (Chapman and others, 1979, p. 4). Inflation and energy costs have influenced the going-off-to-college tradition. For the student, the pinch of inflationary prices often causes a reevaluation of extensive travel, so the in-state public institution with its lower comparative costs has much appeal. For the institution, inflation has been equally devastating, necessitating a reduction in travel budgets, according to the Chapman report. The study also recommended that colleges carefully examine the adequacy of their publications and found colleges willing to develop a staff to publish their admissions material rather than use consultants.

The relationships between the high school counselor and the admissions officer certainly involve cooperation, but the counselor's influence is recognized as very important, according to the University of Michigan study: "Both the high school and college respondents overwhelmingly agreed that the high school counselors are influential in helping students choose a college. Nearly all recognize that working with the high school is an important admissions strategy for most colleges. In particular, students will be receiving materials from increased numbers of colleges as those colleges engage in more aggressive recruiting. Indeed a majority of high school counselors believe an important role will be to protect students from aggressive college recruiting practices" (Chapman and others, pp. 9-10). The Michigan study concludes that the 1980s will bring significant changes in the college admissions process.

The *NACACtion News,* in a May 4, 1980, article titled "Demographics and Economics Force Educators to Detour," summarizes a Carnegie Council report forecasting the consequences of declining enrollments on institutions of higher education:

> Enrollments will decline as much as 40 to 50 percent because a glut of former college students in the labor market is driving down the salaries of college graduates.
>
> As a result, colleges and universities will compete for students in destructive and unethical ways—including false advertising, easy academic credits, soft courses, and grade inflation. Public confidence in higher education erodes and controls increase.
>
> Public authorities will penetrate even further into the internal life of institutions increasingly determining what shall and shall not be done. They will undertake to manage the decline of enrollment by direct intervention both quantitatively and qualitatively.
>
> The future of institutions is only marginally in their own hands.
>
> The private sector of higher education will

be decimated because of its inability to compete
due to higher tuition; meanwhile, public controls
and public financial support make it only quasi-
private—reducing its rationale for continuation
[p. 4].

The article recommends that colleges and universities develop professional standards and codes to maintain integrity in
recruiting practices and inspire confidence in higher education.
For themselves, schools need to focus on their strengths and develop them to their fullest extent, thereby making the most of
the problems confronting educators as they approach the end of
the twentieth century.

A buyer's market, which has developed in admissions,
promises to promote the admissions officer to a new role of
greater importance. No longer will admissions staffs be mere
clerical order-takers, a role sometimes relegated to them during
the years of rapid growth in college enrollments; they will become key figures in college and university governance. The director may be a powerful administrator who influences many
of the institution's decisions and determines its directions. Institutional policy will necessarily involve heavy input from admissions experts, from whose domain decisions about programs,
buildings, staffing, costs, and budgets will emanate.

Moll (1978, p. 3) makes the following observation of the
role of the admissions office: "Whitney Griswold, the late president of Yale, once said, 'The admissions office is the umbilical
cord of the university.' If the undergraduate college has many
purposes (as a place for training the mind, as a national instrument for social access and change, and as an internal vehicle for
self-survival, et cetera), the admissions office must make certain that the human material is there, so that the institution
may go about its variety of chores and reach its manifold goals.
Diversity—by design—is essential to each incoming and outgoing
class."

Many observers of educational trends call for more creative recruiting measures, including accelerating efforts to attract nontraditional students to fill enrollment quotas. In light of

this suggestion, it is interesting to note the identity of all college enrollees. Geiger (1978-79, p. 64) claims, "In the last academic year American higher education passed a milestone of sorts: For the first time women outnumbered men among college-age matriculants." Geiger states that this event is not entirely caused by increased female enrollment but by a decline in the percentage of males attending college for reasons ranging from inflation to peer values. Further noting the impact of this phenomenon on education, Geiger says, "Affirmative action pressures have aggravated the market conditions for white males by reserving many of the already scarce graduate entry-level positions for minorities and women" (p. 64). But what of the males who have chosen not to go to college? With unemployment rates rising, the prospect for stable employment is dim for unskilled and undereducated job seekers. The "union card" alternative can only absorb so many applicants. Our society has long held that the degree was the surest route to the "good life" and a successful career. "But a college education has always offered more than just an economic payoff. There is ample justification for a student to attend college for reasons of personal fulfillment, even if it looks like a low-grade economic investment. And, while the degree can no longer guarantee either a good job or a good income, the absence of a degree quite definitely precludes the possibility of the best professional or managerial careers" (Geiger, pp. 64-65). So why do these youngsters look elsewhere?

In predicting employment trends through the 1980s, the United States Department of Labor's publication *Occupational Outlook Quarterly* optimistically forecasts the following: "White-collar occupations include professional, managerial, sales, and clerical jobs. They already account for over half the work force. The rising demand for people to work in environmental protection, energy development, and medicine will increase the need for many types of professional workers" (Nardone, 1980, p. 3).

If these assumptions hold true, the prospect for college graduates is expected to increase, so our young people's disenchantment with the value of college is not easily understood. In its "Grab Bag" section (p. 31), the spring 1980 *Occupational*

Outlook Quarterly observes: "The employment market for college graduates is expected to continue to improve in 1980. But the demand will still be for graduates who studied technical subjects, such as engineering, accounting, and computer programming. That's the word from the College Placement Council, Inc., in Bethlehem, Penn., which conducts surveys of major employers each year."

In an effort to comply with federal funding guidelines and attract students, many schools have adopted career and technically oriented programs. Some of these programs, although excellent, have been highly touted as the replacement for the outdated liberal arts degree. Considerable inroads have already been made into the domain of liberal studies, and what a loss it would be if these opportunities to pursue liberal education were significantly further reduced.

John Sawhill, in a 1978 address to the College Board National Forum in New York City, argued eloquently for the preservation of the liberal arts in higher education. He stressed that the federal government along with corporate influences had "bought" the universities' present preoccupation with the specialized and technical. It is most important to preserve a wide range of options from which educational choices can be made. These choices are not luxuries; they represent some of the finest opportunities in our country. There is a need to ensure continued quality and diversity in our educational system lest we sacrifice the very programs upon which our system was built and from which its greatness emanates.

The adaptability built into the liberal arts studies, along with the broad-based fund of knowledge that Western civilization has prized throughout recorded history, combine to speak for the continued necessity of liberally educated men and women. Cranford (1979, p. 8) argues that "Forcing everyone into particular molds during academic preparation and during the entry years of liberal arts graduates into the job market accomplishes little more than a dilution of the general creativity and resourcefulness of the individual involved." Cranford further argues for the diversity of talent fostered in liberal arts programs, stating, "Moreover, woe be unto higher education and also to society itself if the liberal arts as a conglomerate discipline becomes completely unmarketable and thus undesirable as preparation for a career."

Thus, the liberal arts institutions are under fire, but the probable demise of many of these institutions receives impetus from their not dealing successfully with the changes in society in the last twenty years, succumbing to the success of the more salable business and technological degrees. The "better mousetrap," built by the engineering and business schools and financed by the federal government's patronage of the specialized, has largely displaced the liberal arts degree. The technical and business schools' emphasis on job placement has further enhanced this appeal. The public's expectations of a college degree have narrowed to a single question: What kind of job will it command? These factors account for declining enrollment in the colleges of arts and sciences, and they threaten to fulfill the prophecy of Robert Maynard Hutchins, who in earlier days of higher education's development cautioned that technical degrees might cause the university to become the "filling station of society."

Dunn (1979, p. 385) believes that higher education, especially liberal education, as we know it today will be significantly changed. "Many institutions won't be able to survive the transition. By the year 2000, 25 percent of the currently existing residential liberal arts colleges will be gone. Many other colleges will find themselves in dire straits and will be searching hard for ways to survive." Not only will the thrust of education continue to be toward the technical and the specialized, but public expectation will, if it continues its present course, place less emphasis on the benefits of a broad-based education.

According to Dunn (p. 388), "Public expectations for the college graduate will be lowered in the future. The B.S. degree holder will not be expected to have great familiarity with the past, with civilization or with the arts. The typical graduate of the future will not be expected to have sharp analytic abilities, nor be able to philosophize in depth about himself and his environment."

Should this prophecy be fulfilled, the path of humanity

envisioned by seers, predicting a highly mechanistic society, will become reality. Such a reality places much more emphasis and reliance on the ability and capabilities of an all-need-providing society than it does on the individual. Emerson's self-reliance will have passed the way of countless anachronisms in people's search for a culture and life-style that eases their place in the world.

Conclusions

Careful planning is the single most important directive to institutions trying to endure the test of the 1980s. Providing high-quality education while attempting to meet student needs will continue as a success strategy, as it has been in the past. The institutions that survive the next decade will undoubtedly find reduced competition as the turn of the century approaches. Fishlow (1978, p. 47) expresses concern for our immediate future, noting: "Principal suggestions are to increase flexibility both in physical plant and staffing and to protect the interests of those likely to be affected by change. Planning for flexibility ten to fifteen years from now is perhaps not too difficult; preparing for more immediate changes, mostly decline, requires greater effort." As anxiety levels are heightened by the prospect of lost jobs and reduced budgets, objective perspective is also affected. Although no magical steps ever solved education's problems, the involvement of faculty, students, and community broadens the base of support. "Careful preparation may not avoid all strife and controversy, but it should ameliorate the situation. Lack of preparation for decline will also surely contribute to a great waste of resources, particularly human resources" (Fishlow, 1978, p. 47).

Staff reductions can be very destructive to an institution already in the throes of reducing programs and budgets. Staff reductions ideally should be tied to attrition as much as possible. In situations where attrition does not account for sufficient numbers and layoffs are necessary, there should be a seniority system to determine which faculty should be retained. The last-in, first-out approach to layoffs, appears fairest, but it is not

always in the institution's best interests, particularly with tenure laws protecting teachers whose performances may lag in
comparison with those of their untenured colleagues. Here suggestions from faculty may be indicated. Staff morale suffers
during periods of decline, and institutions owe it to themselves
and their staffs to keep people informed of trends and help
them locate suitable alternative employment. Such measures
make the best of somewhat adverse circumstances. "Opportunities for retraining and placement in other jobs might encourage those tired of teaching to leave the field, opening positions
for the more enthusiastic" (Fishlow, 1978, p. 79). Salaries in
business and industry may be an added impetus to seek employment outside academe.

Inducements to faculty for early retirement and sabbatical
programs also may ease reduction-in-force problems. "At the university level, the sabbatical system helps refresh teachers and
also brings in new faces as their replacements" (Fishlow, 1978,
p. 79). The consortium arrangement is promising for sustaining
institutional vigor, permitting several cooperating schools to
share teachers and programs. Certainly, the arrangement nets an
economy of facilities, particularly such ones as library services,
laboratory facilities, and building utilization.

Mergers between institutions and consolidations instead
of closing will spell survival for many schools now faced with
reduced student populations. The opportunity for colleges to
divest themselves of outmoded buildings can logically occur
during periods of reduced enrollment. Finding alternative uses
for buildings (if not outright dispatching of them) is one solution to the problem.

Strategies for dealing with the years ahead require planning to adjust to circumstances based on the likely enrollment a
school might encounter. Scheduling programs to meet the special needs of different constituencies may be one approach. For
example, providing for the special needs of other groups like the
handicapped may ensure an institution some continued support.

Attracting the nontraditional student may, like the spe-
cial-needs group, offer some relief to a dwindling population of
students. In any case, the "over twenty-two" students hold

promise not only for a better-educated society but also for a
viable solution to dwindling enrollments of traditional students.
These nontraditional collegians were largely overlooked in an
earlier time in favor of a more easily cultivated high school student. But in 1980, we have come to view adult or lifelong education as a survival tactic for institutions beset by the trends of
ZPG.

> The adult population (twenty-five years or
> over) of the year 2000 will be much better edu-
> cated than its counterpart of 1975. Assuming that
> present age-specific educational attainment rates
> (for example, the proportion of persons twenty-
> five to twenty-nine years with a high school diplo-
> ma) will increase slightly, it becomes relatively easy
> to project the educational attainment levels in
> 2000. (Remember that these persons are already
> born.) Over three fourths of the adult population
> of all ages will have completed at least a secondary
> school education. Among those twenty-five to
> twenty-nine years old, over 90 percent will have
> high school diplomas. Close to 25 percent of the
> adult population will have at least a college degree,
> and one third of those twenty-five to twenty-nine
> years old will have such an education. Presently,
> the median number of school years completed by
> adult Americans is 12.1; this should increase slight-
> ly to about 12.8 by the turn of the century.
> But perhaps even more important than
> knowing future educational attainment is having
> some idea of the future size of the school popula-
> tion. Such informaton could be useful whether one
> is concerned with taxes for more school buildings
> or investigating entering the teaching profession.
> Poor estimates can have serious consequences.
> [*Population Bulletin*, 1975, pp. 4-5.]

Hence, the high school counseling office may become a
secondary source of information about colleges and universities,
with libraries, post offices, and social service agencies encroach-

ing on the once sole information service. With the increased competition for the projected fewer students, colleges may lower admissions standards to meet enrollment quotas. This tendency is a threat to the preservation of quality higher education, placing institutions in the dilemma of relaxing standards or losing students. Institutions, as they try to cope, will continue to change their recruiting strategies and pay greater attention to student retention. With the trend away from travel by college recruiters, the college, the counselor, and the students will inevitably rely more on printed information. Counselors and students face reduced contact with college admissions personnel, so they must give greater attention to printed materials.

For the students, opportunities in higher education will continue to diminish as programs are reduced and schools are closed. Such prospects threaten the variety of choices available to students and represent a serious loss to our educational system. Another loss is the present disenchantment with the liberal arts degree and the resulting fewer students who choose them. These trends carry forward the struggle higher education has encountered in its lengthy journey with Western civilization.

Part Two

✍ ✍ ✍ ✍ ✍

Service to the Student

✍   The function of college admissions counselors is different from that of any other persons in the educational community. As a teacher, the counselor has no subject; as a counselor, no agreed-on basis for measuring success; and as an administrator, many masters, often conflicting. Yet all professional college admissions counselors believe that their first allegiance is to the students they serve. Admissions counselors know that the advice they give has important impact on their clients.

But is there proof that professional admissions counseling really makes a difference? Does it make any difference what kind of college or university a student chooses after finishing secondary school? The admissions counseling profession has been predicated on the assumption that there is indeed a difference, one of great consequence in the lives of individuals; but until recent years the assumption has been grounded principally in faith, not research. Even those who have had the greatest experience in working with young people moving from one state of education to another have had to base their descriptions of the nature of the change upon impressions, anecdotes, and bias.

Now a significant body of research material has accumulated, most of it published in the last fifteen years. In Chapter Three, Jack H. Schuster and Ann Coil have for the first time summarized the findings of that research and present it for admissions counselors, many of whom—especially on the college side—come from backgrounds in which the material assessed is unfamiliar.

Schuster and Coil, on the basis of the best available evidence, identify the characteristics of the college experience that most affect growth among students. Discussed are institutional characteristics; areas of student change as they relate to institutions; involvement, congruency, and persistence; and the implications of the authors' discoveries. A much-needed overview of the literature and a bibliography of works that should be consulted lead the professional through the morass of research problems.

The institutional characteristics considered include entering students' own characteristics, selectivity, type of control, residential nature, size, single-sex or coeducational, and religious affiliation. Student changes include academic achievement; intellectual, cultural, and esthetic orientation; attitudes, beliefs, and values; personal development in self-esteem and self-understanding; career orientation and implementation; and general satisfaction with college.

Schuster and Coil next point out that involvement with an institution is closely related to satisfaction with college and is therefore important in assessing different kinds of colleges. Congruency is "the match . . . between a prospective student's needs and the campus's ability to meet those needs and to respond to those interests." No simple correlation between achievement and congruency has been discovered. And for colleges facing difficult enrollment declines, persistence is of crucial importance.

In their final section, Schuster and Coil state that contemporary research demonstrates that institutional type has less influence on cognitive than on noncognitive development; noncognitive development occurs most measurably in relatively small, predominantly residential, and relatively selective institutions. The authors suggest ways that larger institutions and commuter institutions can increase involvement and thereby decrease attrition; by implication, they show counselors what to look for if they want to provide optimum experiences for their clients who wish to or must attend large institutions.

Paul Painter, a psychiatrist, and Nancy Painter have counseled college-bound students for many years and have monitored their progress and happiness after they have arrived on campus. They judge the success of their counseling by the degree to which the colleges they recommend produce few complaints from students and their parents. In Chapter Four, they carefully assess the effects of inappropriate college choice—effects that they have seen often in their clinical practice and that their counseling practice was designed to avoid.

The authors suggest ways to reduce dissonance between the student and the institution and thereby diminish the number—normally more than 50 percent—of entering freshmen who will leave their colleges before graduating. The Painters discuss complaints that occur when "college adjustment is failing" and that reflect both superficial and deeper reasons for student unhappiness; reactions to failure in college by students who do not fit; and matching procedures that counselors can use to avoid the results of wrong choice. The Painters' own practice has resulted in more than twice as high a percentage of students going to recommended colleges than to nonrecommended colleges. Because they are pleased with that result, they recommend simple personal counseling techniques that any counselor can use, even those without access to the Painters' sophisticated survey and computer analysis.

The Painters' work is pragmatic, whereas the advice of most counselors is based on some ideal conception of the function of higher education and its impact on the individual who embraces it. The Painters' viewpoint is relatively unusual among professional counselors but needs careful consideration and adaptation by members of the profession who seriously care about the nature of the lives they help create.

In Chapter Five, Stanley Bosworth describes a highly personal approach to the process of helping students apply to college. Because he sees college guidance and college choice as part of the process of secondary education, Bosworth thinks it important for counselors to find out as much as possible about

each individual student. Learning enough to write a good essay
or recommendation demands many correlated techniques. Self-
revealing essays written by students can teach the counselor if
the students are honest and candid enough; Bosworth gives
examples of essays that fulfill that function.

Because choosing a college is part of a student's education, Bosworth—taking a different point of view from the
Painters'—counsels students to be realistic and yet to aim high.
"I question," he says, "those advisers who boast of a high percentage of students admitted to 'first-choice' colleges. The implication . . . is that . . . the choices have to be limited to 'safe'
institutions."

Bosworth gives pertinent advice for students (and counselors) preparing for interviews; writing the reference letter,
with examples, is a final topic for the counselor. The ultimate
justification in advising is educating the students: "Their discovery of the sacredness and importance within them is the ultimate justification for advisement at its best."

In Chapter Six, Julie C. Monson approaches the question
of the effect of college from another point of view, as the person who watches graduates go forth to build careers. She points
out the importance of college for many professional careers, a
direct benefit; but she also emphasizes that work done in college
may be greatly beneficial even in areas seemingly unconnected
to careers ultimately chosen, because the work helps teach critical thinking and encourages various patterns of personal development.

Clearly, a liberal arts program or a general curriculum will
have different impact on career preparation than a technical or
vocational major; technical education can lead directly to a job,
but most liberal arts programs develop skills and strengths necessary in the practice of administration, regardless of the area.
Monson discusses opportunities for career education for undergraduates, stressing that students are likely to be exposed to
more indicators of desirable career choices than they think. For
example, extracurricular activities and jobs on and off campus
will tell them something about what they like to do and what
they are good at.

Monson also discusses undergraduate preparation for graduate and professional training. Covering the relationship between sex, college choice, and career patterns, she advises women what to look for in colleges they choose. For the high school counselor, she describes typical undergraduate career planning and placement centers available on most campuses and by implication suggests what students and their parents should look for. Finally, Monson points out that on many campuses there is increasing awareness that a prime function of a college is to provide students with training and "space" with which to make intelligent, informed, self-confident decisions regarding careers.

3

Effects of Type of College on Students

Jack H. Schuster

Ann Coil

At a conference for high school guidance counselors hosted by Tulane University in the mid-1960s, one of the authors witnessed this exchange: A counselor from a well-known Chicago North Shore high school, whose top graduates were courted by colleges everywhere, was commenting on the escalating costs of education. He observed that his township was now spending a thousand dollars per high school student. A heretofore quiet participant, a counselor from a rural southern school, spoke up: "Why we spend every bit that much in our little ol' district." But the suburban counselor was talking about costs per annum, his rural counterpart about costs for four years of high school. The difference in resources, or "inputs," was substantial.

The different inputs in postsecondary education are also substantial, however they are measured: library holdings and faculty salaries, endowments and physical plant, availability of health care services and student affairs staff. Some institutions can often spend much more per student than other institutions. But does this make a difference? Do different kinds of postsecondary institutions yield different educational outcomes? If so, just how much difference is there?

Relating outcomes to kinds of postsecondary institutions is confounded by the critical input of the students themselves. Different colleges attract different clientele; entering students, whether considered individually or totally as an entering class, have quite different characteristics—differences, for example, in status, in personal qualities, and in accomplishments (Wing and Wallach, 1971). Some institutions are much more "selective" than others, so their students enter better prepared for the college experience and graduate better prepared for more advanced schooling or professional careers. But to what extent do such highly selective schools make a difference? After all, how poorly *could* students able to enter Harvard fare if, en masse, they enrolled instead at Impecunious A & M?

We are left, therefore, with a large and very important question: Are the differences in "outcomes" (the effects on students attributable to college) proportionate to the substantial difference in inputs (the differences among entering classes of students and the various arrays of resources available to these students once they matriculate)? Within that weighty question is the narrower issue we discuss here: Are there significant differences in ways that students develop, and are these differences attributable to the *type* of postsecondary institution they attend? Does the type of college really make a difference? Which type of institution provides a bigger education (outcome) for the money (input)?

The questions cannot be easily answered because the innumerable factors affecting the interaction between college and student are not easy to analyze. During the past fifteen or twenty years, many researchers have tackled aspects of these questions, resulting in a literature that deserves the attention of educators in secondary schools and postsecondary institutions. But because of the extraordinarily complex relationship between institutions of higher education and their students, the research findings preclude crisp summaries and clean cause-and-effect links. To make this discussion as useful as possible, we drew from the literature whatever generalizations we could, choosing to err on the side of more aggressive interpretation rather than overcaution.

We present the material in four segments. Segment one deals with institutional characteristics (inputs) associated with student change; segment two covers areas of student change (outcomes) as they relate to type of institution. By necessity, the material in those two segments is somewhat overlapping. The third segment identifies three factors—involvement, congruency, and persistence—that do not easily fit into the first two sections but that merit special attention. The fourth segment discusses some implications of our interpretation of the research. We end with an overview of the literature on the impact of college and a concise bibliography of the major original studies and works.

Inputs of Institutional Characteristics

The pluralism characteristic of American society is reflected in its system of higher education. Institutions differ considerably in their size, setting, facilities, traditions, curricula, procedures, and standards. Likewise, student profiles—their demographic characteristics, aptitudes and achievements, interests, and personalities—vary widely. The limited evidence indicates that certain institutional characteristics contribute to different impacts on students.

American colleges and universities are typically classified according to (1) degree of exposure: two-year versus four-year; (2) control: public or private, sectarian or secular; (3) sex: co-educational or single-sex; (4) emphasis of curricula and general emphasis: liberal arts, teacher training, vocational-technical, and so forth. These classifications have endured attempts to discover alternative dimensions along which to categorize institutions of higher learning. Although these nominal categories are useful, particularly as a starting point in research, they are not inclusive descriptions; caution must be exercised in attempting to assess their respective influence as change agents. To illustrate: "If public and private institutions are found to have differential impacts on students, the 'publicness' or 'privateness' of the school offers little in the way of explanation. More than this, it is possible that colleges *within* these familiar classifications are diverse with respect to impact factors. If so, these classifications might conceal the environmental differences that are causing differential impacts" (Feldman and Newcomb, 1969, p. 122).

Other features researchers utilize include size of institution, residential arrangements, and selectivity. Among these categories, selectivity is the most ambiguous term; we think of it "as the average academic ability of the entering freshman, and two closely related measures—prestige and affluence" (Astin, 1977, p. 277). Yet another important factor involved in the impact of college is the extent of student participation in campus life. Interaction among these factors creates complex forces that confuse attempts to isolate differences in environmental influences. "Colleges do not differ along just one or even a few measurable dimensions. Thus, any attempt to describe college in terms of only one or two factors, such as size or prestige, represents a drastic and perhaps destructive oversimplification" (Astin, 1968, p. 139).

Salience of Entering Students' Characteristics. As noted, institutions differ according to the characteristics of their students. Furthermore, studies consistently find that a substantial degree of the documented changes in student achievement and personality are a function of the initial skills and attributes students bring with them at the time of matriculation (Feldman and Newcomb, 1969; Clark and others, 1972; Chickering, 1974; Bowen, 1977). Bowen (1977) summarizes the situation: "The differences [in graduates] . . . may be explained only partly by differences in institutional characteristics. To a larger degree, they are due to differences among institutions in the characteristics of the students they attract, recruit, and retain" (p. 237). Clark and his associates (1972, p. 9) also acknowledge the influence of students' entering characteristics on distinguishing change: "It is increasingly clear that what the individual is when he leaves is relative to what the individual was when he entered. If the effect of college experience is to be assessed, it is essential to know the characteristics of both the product and the original material." Feldman and Newcomb (1969, p. 144) note further that "certain types of colleges are in fact predominantly peopled by certain kinds of students. Academic capacity and family background . . . in particular, have a great deal to do with what goes on where." Student characteristics vary greatly, not only among institutions but *within* institutions. Feldman and Newcomb state that students from similar-status backgrounds within one college may not be alike in all other characteristics. "It can be expected therefore that different subgroups of students within a status group will react differently to the same overall college environment, and will change differentially" (p. 284).

Family background, particularly educational climate, appears to be a significant entering attribute that distinguishes various college populations (Clark and others, 1972; Chickering, 1974; Bowen, 1977). Clark found that students from families of high cultural sophistication (measured by the father and grandfather's educational level, number of books in the home, and family's stress on the importance of being educated) are more motivated and self-assured about college, more ready for a college education, have higher aspirations, and little interest in the popular culture. They are more apt to believe that a liberal education is more important than job preparation and aspire to the highest professions. Also, they are not as deeply religious and are politically liberal and independent.

Chickering found interesting differences between family backgrounds of students who commute to college and those who live in campus residences. Residential students live in the suburbs, come from families with high incomes, and tend to have parents who are professionals and have higher levels of education. Students who commute tend to live in the city, come from families of lower-income levels, and have parents who are skilled or semiskilled workers and have little or no higher education.

Besides family background, Clark and others (1972) found meaningful differences in the characteristics of entering students at the eight institutions they studied. At the three selective, private institutions, entering students tended to score higher in the following areas than did the freshmen at the other five less prestigious institutions: (1) academic achievement (SAT or other comparable test scores); (2) intellectual disposition (greater interest in ideas, theories, esthetics; greater familiarity with books; better developed taste for poetry); (3) beliefs and attitudes (more nonauthoritarian and liberal attitudes on political and social issues); (4) personal development (greater autonomy and social maturity); and (5) career and professional life (greater value on the intrinsic rewards of a job and opportunities to use abilities). Given these differences among entering freshman classes, it is not surprising to discover that these same students, as seniors, tended to score higher in these areas than did their counterparts at the other five institutions.

Selectivity of Institution. Attending a selective institution tends to yield pronounced changes in attitudes, beliefs, and values. Social and political views tend to become more liberal and tolerant; conversely, religiousness declines. Students from such schools are more likely to value a broad, general education, and job satisfaction is more likely associated with intrinsic rewards.

In the area of intellectual, cultural, and esthetic orientation, students at selective institutions—both at entrance and on graduation—show a higher level of cultural sophistication than do students at other institutions. Alumni of selective liberal arts schools responded most positively to the esthetic and humanistic benefits of college and engaged in more cultural activities than students at most other institutions (Pace, 1974). In the area of personal development, selective institutions appear to foster in students a spontaneity and flexibility for coping with the demands of a given situation. On the other hand, these students showed less-than-average decreases on an anxiety and alienation scale; this finding is consistent with other evidence that selective schools place greater demands on students (Astin, 1977, p. 179).

Students at selective institutions tend to score higher on items measuring intellectual disposition to change (Clark and others, 1972, p. 232). Although students who attend selective institutions tend to be more self-critical, their experience appears to have no negative effect on intellectual self-esteem. This finding is particularly interesting in view of another finding: Attending a selective institution substantially reduces the prospect

of attaining two traditional indicators of academic achievement: high grade point average and participation in honors programs.

Selectivity positively affects the formulation, implementation, and success of career and professional plans. Association
with a prestigious college or university enhances long-range
earning potential and increases the prospect of attending graduate school and entering the older professions (medicine, nursing,
and college teaching, but curiously, not law). Finally, and perhaps most significantly, overall satisfaction with the college experience is likely to be greatest if the student attends a selective,
prestigious, affluent college or university.

Type of Control. Generalizations about the public-private
dichotomy are hazardous because public and private institutions
have many overlapping features that influence changes in students. Also, some influential characteristics—for example, small
size and single-sex enrollments—are associated predominantly
with private institutions (Astin, 1977, p. 231). It is nevertheless
instructive to analyze the differences.

Astin (1977, p. 231) found that private institutions have
a substantial effect on students: "Practically all the effects associated with college attendance are more pronounced among students at private institutions." Private institutions appear to
facilitate involvement with the campus, as indicated by the following findings: Attendance at a private school increases the
students' chances of interacting with the faculty, becoming involved in campus government, and becoming familiar with instructors from their major field. On the whole, students at private institutions view their campus more positively. They are
more satisfied with instruction, faculty-student contacts, closeness to faculty, their institution's reputation, administrative
structure, curricula, and social life (Astin, 1977, p. 231). In the
realm of attitudes and personal development, increases are
greater at private than public institutions for political liberalism
and religious apostasy, intellectual and interpersonal self-esteem,
and artistic interests. Thus, even when controlling for the complex interaction of other variables, the "privateness" of a college appears to exert potent independent effects.

Residential Nature of Institution. Among the most influential dimensions of the college experience is whether a student attends a predominantly residential or commuter campus. Chickering's large-scale study (1974) found substantial differences in the relative influence attributable to those two types of institutions. Furthermore, the same differences were found for all types of schools, independent of students' entering characteristics or institutional size and selectivity.

The overriding variable among residential and commuter campuses seems to be participation in campus life. Students who live at home or off campus are considerably less involved in the institution's social life, and they are much less engaged in all types of academic activity (Chickering, 1974). They fail more courses, arrive later to class, and fail to complete assignments more frequently than residential students. They are less likely to study, to do extra reading, to discuss schoolwork with peers, to have contact with faculty, and to plan to return to full-time study (p. 61). They are less inclined to read unassigned poetry, and they less often visit art galleries (p. 63). In all, the evidence suggests that they are less interested and less involved in the intellectual, cultural, and esthetic aspects of campus life.

In the area of attitudes, beliefs, and values, commuting students tend to be more conservative than their in-residence counterparts, for example, holding more steadfastly to traditional beliefs in the role of women. They are more oriented toward law and order, censorship, and clear control by an authority. The same conservatism is seen in their attitudes toward the political process, domestic priorities, legal issues, international relationships, civil rights, and racial integration (Chickering, 1974, p. 76).

In the two-year colleges, which almost always are predominantly commuter institutions, students tend to value the monetary benefits of a college education rather than the intrinsic rewards that come from a broad preparation for life (Astin, 1977, p. 233). Commuters report lower opinions of themselves on abilities and personal characteristics and rate themselves lower on self-confidence and popularity in general. They are less inclined to enter educationally and developmentally useful experiences. They report fewer areas of competence and seem less committed to long-range goals. Commuter students are less involved in a college's social aspects and have fewer close college friends.

A larger proportion of those students living at home plan to get only an associate degree or aspire to no degree at all. They more frequently expect careers in engineering and science and place greater value on being successful in their own business and being well-off financially (Chickering, 1974, p. 74). Attendance at a two-year college substantially reduces the chances of implementing career or professional plans (Astin, 1977, p. 234). This may partly be a function of low persistence in college for these students. Commuter and two-year college students demonstrate less overall satisfaction with the college experience (p. 221). However, the commuting students are satisfied with curricula, and two-year college students are relatively satisfied with campus social life (pp. 234, 235).

Occupying somewhat of a middle ground are those "hybrid" students who share characteristics with both the "pure" commuter residing at home and the on-campus resident: Commuting students who live in private, off-campus housing. They differ markedly from students who live at home, but they more closely resemble students living at home than they do those domiciled on campus. These off-campus residents participate more in almost every extracurricular activity than do those living at home. The hybrids fall between the other two groups in interaction with teachers. Perhaps their mixed status takes a toll; for, on the whole, students in private off-campus housing tend to be less satisfied with their college experience than either the dormitory residents or students living at home (Astin, 1977, p. 55).

Size of Institution. The impact of institutional size is a complicated matter (Feldman and Newcomb, 1969; Clark and others, 1972; Bowen, 1977). It is difficult to isolate distinctive variables related to size because so many small colleges are liberal arts and sectarian institutions. One effect of size is certainly clear: All types of participation in various aspects of campus life are enhanced at small institutions. Thus, large institutions decrease a student's chances of achievement in campus leadership, athletics, journalism, and theater (Astin, 1977, p. 230). Attending a large university does increase the chances of student involvement in demonstrations; but, perhaps paradoxically, attending a university appears to affect altruism negatively. Large institutions, particularly those that are selective or private, facilitate graduation with honors. Pursuing a career in business is enhanced by attending a large university (p. 230).

Student satisfaction with the college environment, when viewed through the lens of institutional size, is mixed. Students at large universities are considerably less satisfied with the quality of classroom instruction and relationships with faculty; on the other hand, they tend to be more satisfied with their social life, the school's academic reputation, and the variety of curricula.

Because involvement in campus life—facilitated at smaller institutions—has a pervasive, salubrious effect on almost every aspect of the student's experience, Bowen's summary statement is not surprising: "Many researchers have found evidence that smallness is associated with educational advantage" (1977, p. 248).

Single-Sex or Coeducational. Astin (1977, p. 232) concludes that some of the most dramatic effects of institutional characteristics occur as a result of attending an all-male or all-female college. Single-sex colleges enhance overall satisfaction with all aspects of the undergraduate experience, except social life, and encourage student involvement in academic areas and interaction with faculty.

Women who attend women's colleges are less likely to get good grades; in other words, they do worse academically (as measured by grades) if they compete only with women. However, they develop higher aspirations and tend to persist to graduation if they attend all-women colleges. A study by Oates and Williamson (1978) on women's colleges and women achievers questions the claim that attendance at a women's college encourages women to enter nontraditional occupational fields. They found that achievers from women's colleges were distributed among five basic occupational groups in proportions similar to coeducational institutions. The differences they found in occupational distribution between single-sex and coeducational colleges were related to the types of skills required; coed colleges seemed to prepare women for occupations that require specific skills, such as government officials, deans of professional schools, and librarians. The authors conclude that "American higher education has produced women leaders, but the pattern of their occupational choices seems to conform to society's expectations of women at work" (p. 805).

Women's colleges foster more politically liberal attitudes and strengthen artistic interests. Women become more involved in campus activities such as student government and more readily assume positions of leadership at all women's colleges. They are less likely to pursue careers in business or nursing, but they are more likely to pursue plans to become teachers. Similarly, a Douglass College Women's College Study Committee (1974) concludes that women's colleges offer women more opportunities for extracurricular leadership and give young women more positive role models for success and achievement than do coeducational institutions. Overall, the conclusion appears warranted that women students tend to be less involved and less assertive in the presence of men (Astin, 1977, p. 233).

Men who attend all-male colleges tend to get higher grades and participate in honors programs. The most pronounced effect of men's colleges is to increase a student's likelihood of entering law school. Men's colleges also are conducive to pursuit of business and college teaching careers.

Religious Affiliation of Institution. Although there are observable differences between Protestant and Catholic institutions, and between selective and nonselective religious institutions, on the whole, these institutions have a limited effect on changes in students' attitudes, beliefs, and values. Generally, students' traditional attitudes, values, and religious beliefs are sustained in these colleges (Feldman and Newcomb, 1969, p. 25). In some cases, religious beliefs are accentuated. However, religious apostasy tends to increase more at selective Protestant institutions than at less selective ones. Church-linked institutions are more likely to have a positive effect on altruism. Artistic and esthetic interests are positively affected at selective Protestant universities; the same is true for hedonism.

A positive impact on academic achievement is somewhat more characteristic of selective Protestant schools (Astin, 1977, p. 235), which have a more positive influence on enrolling in graduate school; by comparison, at nonselective Protestant colleges, students' aspirations for graduate degrees decrease. In career and professional areas, sectarian colleges generally increase the chances of being a college professor (p. 236). Enrolling in law school is enhanced at nonselective Protestant institutions but not at selective institutions (p. 236).

Satisfaction with college for students enrolled at religious institutions is greatest in the area of closeness and student friendships, particularly for white Protestant women (p. 236). Religious institutions tend to accentuate and maintain student attitudes and values. Their press on students is not strong, nor does their influence run contrary to their students' initial predispositions.

Outcomes of Student Change

We now examine the phenomenon of student change by looking "backward" at types of institutions most closely linked with six student outcomes. Research on the impact of college reveals areas of student development seemingly affected consistently by the college experience. The two broad dimensions—cognitive and noncognitive development—together reflect the total person. For decades, scholars have exhorted higher education to recognize that ideally the development of the educated person extends beyond the intellectual realm to encompass cultural, social, emotional, and moral development (Dewey, 1916; Broudy, 1961; Sanford, 1967; Katz and Associates, 1968; Feldman and Newcomb, 1969; Pace, 1974; Cross, 1976). Their argument is that the accommodation of knowledge, or "filling the bin," as a solitary goal of education is woefully inadequate, given the diversity of needs and interests in America's pluralistic society. This interest in the student's total development is reflected in the studies of differential impact. A review of seminal studies

(Feldman and Newcomb, 1969; Clark and others, 1972; Chick-ering, 1974; Astin, 1977) reveals broad concern with the multi-faceted dimensions of personal development attributable to the college experience. In addition to (1) academic achievement, college students show changes in (2) intellectual, cultural, and esthetic orientation; (3) attitudes, beliefs, and values concerning such issues as politics, religion, the role of women, and minority groups; (4) personal development in areas such as self-esteem and self-understanding; (5) career orientation and implementa-tion; and (6) general satisfaction with college.

Academic Achievement. Whatever impact different col-leges may have, none is more central to higher education than academic achievement. Actually, academic achievement is only one facet of the cognitive development that researchers have tried to measure during the college years. Here we group various aspects of cognitive growth, as reported in the literature, into three categories:

1. *Acquisition of knowledge or academic achievement.* This category views cognitive development in terms of increases in substantive knowledge. To establish the magnitude of learning, researchers typically rely on such quantitative measures as GPA, SAT, and GRE scores and on such binary indicators as enrollment in honors programs. This can be considered a *product*-oriented approach.
2. *Intellectual skills.* This *process*-oriented view includes di-mensions such as critical and analytical thinking, creative expression, problem definition and solution. These skills typically are believed to develop gradually in learners and in sequenced stages of development.
3. *Intellectual disposition.* This term describes one's inclina-tion and preference for intellectual pursuits; it is essentially *attitude* oriented. Intellectual disposition encompasses commitment to learning, intellectual and cultural orienta-tion (curiosity), intellectual tolerance, and so forth.

First we address academic achievement/acquisition of knowledge. Next we briefly discuss intellectual disposition; the acquisition of intellectual skills is minimally covered in the literature and so is not examined here.

Pace (1979) conducted a national survey of students' scores on such achievement tests as the Test of General Education, the Graduate Record Examination (GRE), the College Level Examination Program, and the Undergraduate Assessment Program. He consistently found that seniors scored higher than freshmen and students who had taken more classes in an academic subject scored higher on the test in that area than did students who had not taken as many courses. Not surprisingly, Pace concludes, "Students learn what they study, and the more they study, the more they learn" (p. 18). Thus far, logic prevails; colleges and universities would be hard put to account for results which failed to show that cognitive growth in a given area was related to formal course work in that area. But the question then arises: Does type of institution make a difference? Does one type of college appear to give a bigger boost to cognitive development? The findings fail to establish consistent different impacts on academic achievement by type of college.

Researchers have used various measures to assess achievement: GRE (Nichols, 1964; Astin and Panos, 1969; Rock, Centra, and Linn, 1969); Scholastic Aptitude Test (SAT) (Rock, Centra, and Linn, 1969); GPA (Astin, 1977). Similarly, researchers have investigated various environmental factors that might positively affect cognitive growth: level of competitiveness and financial resources (Astin and Panos, 1969); number of library books, institutional revenue per student, faculty-student ratio, faculty with doctorates, type of control (Rock, Centra, and Linn, 1969); and differences in teaching methodology (Dubin and Taveggia, 1968). Despite such a variety of approaches, the relationships between academic achievement and institutional "quality" appear negligible. Any gains found in cognitive growth tend to be closely related to initial ability and/or socioeconomic status (Astin and Panos, 1969). Studies comparing initial ability, as measured by National Merit Scholarship Qualifying Test and SAT scores, with achievement, measured by GRE scores (Nichols, 1964; Rock, Centra, and Linn, 1969), support other research that links achievement more closely to initial ability than to institutional characteristics.

Heist and others (1961, p. 367) found, however, that highly able students attending a quality institution, as measured by the relative number of students who pursue a doctoral degree, were more likely to exhibit intellectual and scholarly traits. Centra and Rock (1971) found that student achievement was higher in institutions which prominently featured instructors' personal interest in students, student latitude in choosing courses, and cultural facilities and programs.

Astin (1977, p. 228) found that the most important institutional characteristic influencing academic achievement, at least as measured by GPA, is the institution's selectivity. Students tend to earn lower grades in a highly selective institution than in a less selective one. Highly selective public and private colleges seem to have equally stringent grading policies. The least selective grading standards are in nonselective, Protestant, and Roman Catholic colleges. The chances of participating in honors programs also decrease for those attending selective public and private colleges, although they increase at men's colleges and predominantly black colleges. Women tend to receive higher grades in college than do men, even when their higher high school GPAs are accounted for. Men tend to earn higher grades if they attend a men's college.

Thus, the level of academic achievement varies greatly across institutions. Only one consistent finding emerges from the multidimensional research on differential impact: Differences in gains are closely related to the student's initial ability level. Bowen (1977, p. 243) concludes, "This in no sense implies that college education in general makes little or no contribution to cognitive learning. Nor does it imply necessarily that many colleges do not uniquely affect the cognitive development of particular individuals. It only suggests that colleges produce similar results in their average contribution to cognitive learning." Whatever the reasons for attending affluent, selective colleges and universities, the evidence shows that a student should not expect to receive an extra cognitive boost from doing so.

Intellectual, Cultural, and Esthetic Orientation. College

attendance does have a decided positive effect on students' intellectual, cultural, and esthetic orientation. Generally, however, the type of college attended appears to make more difference in the cultural-esthetic realm than in intellectual growth.

Feldman and Newcomb (1969, p. 28) found that seniors, as compared to freshmen, generally show more interest in reflective thought and independent thinking and are more critical and creative. Not all increases in this intellectual variable were large. Clark and others (1972, p. 157) discovered a positive change in intellectual commitment for students at the eight varied institutions they studied; however, there was little evidence to suggest that the eight institutions had a differential impact on their students.

Gains in general cultural knowledge seem to be facilitated by small institutions, predominantly black colleges, and public four-year colleges. In contrast, nonselective religious colleges, public two-year colleges, and large institutions tend to have a negative effect on the acquisition of general knowledge (Astin, 1977, p. 131). On the other hand, Clark and others (1972, p. 214) found that students in less selective institutions increased their cultural sophistication over four years of college, although they still remained substantially below the cultural sophistication of seniors at selective institutions. Chickering (1974, p. 63) found that commuting students participated less in cultural activities than students who lived on campus. Artistic interests are positively influenced by women's colleges, private institutions, and living on campus (Astin, 1977, pp. 50, 70). Feldman and Newcomb's synthesis of research led to the conclusion that one of the strongest and most consistent freshman-to-senior changes occurred on the esthetic scale. Positive changes in esthetic appreciation tend to be higher for women than for men, although this may simply reflect the fact that women take more courses in the arts (Clark and others, 1972, p. 174; Bowen, 1977, p. 83).

When Pace (1974) analyzed the responses of alumni and upper-division students to a questionnaire on the benefits of college, he found distinct differences in alumni scores on a scale of humanistic-esthetic benefits and activities. Selective liberal arts colleges, general liberal arts colleges, and teachers' colleges

yielded higher scores than did other types of institutions, with
the selective liberal arts colleges scoring highest. Marked differences in esthetics existed between these three types of institutions compared to the other types (pp. 29, 91). On a measure of
involvement in cultural activities, alumni and upperclassmen
from the selective liberal arts schools scored higher than students from the other types of institutions (pp. 68, 69).

College seems to have a decidedly positive effect on intellectual, cultural, and esthetic orientation. Intellectual growth is
pervasive, indicating that all students seem positively affected
in this area, although slight differences among institutions were
found. Growth in cultural and esthetic interests and involvement are more clearly visible within the class of those small,
select institutions.

Attitudes, Beliefs, and Values. Here, attitudes, beliefs,
and values include religious orientation, liberal or conservative
social and political views, values attached to education, and altruism. Once again, matriculation at a selective, prestigious institution seems to accelerate already liberal leanings (Astin, 1977,
p. 227). Students at selective institutions show increased liberal
views toward women and the disadvantaged, evidence more autonomy and power, and exhibit a decrease in religiousness
(Astin, 1977, p. 38).

Political liberalism tends to increase more among students
at private rather than public institutions. Women's colleges also
seem to encourage more liberal views (Astin, 1977, p. 233). Students attending selective colleges place more value on a general
or liberal education than on professional or vocational preparation (Clark and others, 1972, p. 213). Altruism appears to decrease among students at larger institutions, whereas religious
institutions have a positive effect on altruism. Students at religious colleges seem less inclined to change traditional beliefs
and score lower on measures of liberalism (Astin, 1977, p. 235).
This trend is more dramatic at Roman Catholic colleges, where
peer groups are more homogeneous, behavior controls are imposed more directly, and faculty wield a great influence (Astin,
1977, p. 235).

Interest in purely monetary benefits of a college education declines in selective institutions. At two-year colleges, how-

ever, students consistently value the prospective monetary rewards of an education. Two-year and commuting students also have more conservative political and social attitudes and tend to cling to traditional beliefs about the role of women (Chickering, 1974, p. 66). Schools in the South show smaller-than-average decreases in religiousness and traditional views toward roles of women; less movement toward liberalism is evident.

Personal Development. Personal development—which here encompasses such areas as authoritarianism, autonomy, social maturity, intellectual disposition to change, and self-esteem —tends to be enhanced particularly by attendance at private, more highly selective institutions. Bowen (1977) cites a study by Trent and Medsker which found that, for most types of institutions, changes in nonauthoritarianism and social maturity were similar, although there were relatively smaller gains for men and women attending church-affiliated institutions. Likewise, Clark and others (1972, p. 183) found comparable changes in autonomy for students at all the diverse institutions in his sample, except for men attending religious, less selective institutions. The dearth of significant changes in these areas may be due to differences in students' initial scores.

To assess personal development, Clark and his colleagues used two scales from the Omnibus Personality Inventory (OPI) that purport to measure (1) spontaneity and flexibility and (2) alienation and anxiety in coming to terms with the demands of a situation. The changed scores of students at the three selective institutions studied suggest that the students' college experience may have fostered spontaneity and flexibility in coping with immediate situations, but their scores decreased less than average on the anxiety and alienation scales, suggesting that honed coping skills are paid for, to some degree, with less peace of mind. On the other hand, scores on the anxiety and alienation scales decreased more than average for students at the three church-related institutions, indicating that the friendly, supportive atmosphere of these three institutions encourages greater self-acceptance and ease in being oneself. The students' spontaneity and flexibility scores, however, changed less than the average experience (Clark and others, 1972, p. 196).

Clark and others (1972) attempted to measure students'

intellectual disposition to change. They used the Thinking In-
troversion (TI) scale of the OPI because it seeks to measure the
intellectual spirit and state of mind higher education strives to
create in students. These intellectual qualities encompass an
interest in ideas, philosophical thought, independent thinking,
and value placed on individualism. The study found that students who had high TI scores made positive changes in the other
areas. Furthermore, those whose TI scores increased were more
likely to change in other areas. Thus, individuals with high or increasing TI scores tended to place more value on the intrinsic rewards of education, to enroll in graduate schools, to express a
preference for the intrinsic values of their jobs, and to increase
their level of cultural sophistication. TI scores at the three elite
institutions started higher and changed more over the undergraduate years than did the TI scores of students at the other
five institutions.

In Pace's (1974) study on the diversity of institutions,
personal development was defined to include understanding
one's abilities, limitations, and interests as well as standards of
behavior (p. 51). Alumni of selective liberal arts colleges, de-
nominational liberal arts colleges, and teachers' colleges showed
more growth in this realm than alumni from other types of institutions, such as the selective university, the general university,
and engineering and science schools, whose alumni score much
lower. Engineering and science schools scored the lowest (p.
83). The upperclassmen's responses found selective liberal arts
colleges associated with distinctively greater growth in "personal development," but there was considerable growth as well
among upperclassmen at general liberal arts institutions. Upperclassmen at state colleges and universities, teachers' colleges,
general universities, and engineering and science schools scored
considerably lower in this area (p. 100).

Only one institutional variable appears to influence interpersonal self-esteem positively: the private college or university.
Two types of private institutions are associated with greater-
than-expected increases in intellectual self-esteem: colleges for
women and Roman Catholic colleges. Although students tend
to receive lower grades at selective institutions, attendance at a

selective school does not negatively affect intellectual self-esteem; in fact, the more highly competitive setting appears to have no effect on the high-ability students' self-concept one way or the other (Astin, 1977, p. 228).

The less intensive experience of students at commuter and two-year colleges yields a less positive impact on personal development. Chickering (1974, pp. 67, 69, 74) states that students at commuter institutions have a lower opinion of themselves on abilities and personal characteristics, are less disposed to enter into educationally and developmentally facilitative experiences, report fewer areas of competence, and evidence less commitment to long-range goals. Astin (1977, p. 233) reports that students at two-year colleges manifest less interpersonal self-esteem.

Overall, growth in personal development tends to be enhanced by attendance at private, more highly selective institutions.

Career Orientation and Implementation. The extent of a college's selectivity influences patterns by which students formulate and implement career plans. Although there is no consistent effect on starting salaries, the quality of an institution, as measured by selectivity, is positively related to lifetime earnings (Astin, 1977, p. 229; Bowen, 1977, p. 255). Interestingly, this effect is true for both dropouts and those attaining a degree (Bowen, 1977). Solmon and Taubman speculate that an institution's selectivity may entail greater self-confidence and higher aspirations, a grading-and-labeling effect which facilitates access to better job and career opportunities, or a superior education which leads to more productive economic endeavors (Bowen, 1977, p. 255). Although education generally tends to increase students' desire for postgraduate education, the effect is most pronounced for selective institutions (Clark and others, 1972, p. 131). Attending a selective institution also tends to increase the possibility of entering the professions and medical school (Astin, 1977, p. 229). According to Clark and others (1972, p. 131), a higher proportion of students entering selective colleges aspire to enroll in graduate school and to enter one of the older professions. These students also place more value on the intrinsic rewards of their prospective jobs or careers. Clark found that, by their senior year, students at less selective institutions tended to change their views about the rewards of a career; they placed more value on a liberal education and were more inclined to look for the intrinsic rewards in their career.

Women's colleges enhance implementation of plans to become schoolteachers but are less likely to encourage women to enter the nursing or business professions (Astin, 1977, p. 233). Heavy emphasis on the humanities may partly account for these findings. Men's colleges tend to facilitate business and law careers. Astin maintains that the most significant impact of attending a community college may be the negative effect on persistence and its concomitant deleterious effect on entering careers. He found that these students' "chances of implementing career plans are reduced in almost all fields: business, engineering, school teaching, nursing, and social work" (p. 234).

Astin (1977, pp. 145-154) summarizes the effect of college type on students' career plans for nine different careers:

1. *Business.* Attending a prestigious institution, a private institution, or a university increases the chances of successfully pursuing a career in business; four-year public or private two-year schools decrease the chances considerably.
2. *Engineering.* Attending a technological institution tends to increase engineering majors' chances of maintaining career plans. Students who associate with peers and faculty in the humanities are less likely to embark on engineering careers.
3. *Law.* Students who attend selective institutions are less likely to become lawyers. The lower grades awarded at selective institutions or some students' determination to enter only a select few law schools or none at all may account for this phenomenon. Attending a men's college substantially increases chances of a legal career.
4. *Medicine.* Chances for entering medicine are increased by enrollment in a selective, private university and are decreased by attendance at a public four-year college.
5. *Nursing.* A career in nursing is facilitated by attending a

selective Protestant college. Chances are substantially reduced for students enrolling in two-year public colleges.

6. *School teaching.* Attending a women's college or public four-year institution enhances a woman's chance of entering the teaching profession. Teachers' colleges likewise have a positive impact.

7. *College teaching.* Pursuing a career in college teaching is enhanced by attending a selective or prestigious college.

8. *Science research.* A science research career is facilitated for those students attending a private college, particularly a private, nonsectarian, four-year college.

9. *Social work.* College characteristics have only a minimal, rather inconsequential effect on plans to enter social work.

10. *Homemaking.* A career choice in homemaking occurs most readily for students who attend small, nonselective institutions, particularly Roman Catholic ones.

General Satisfaction with College. College type affects satisfaction. One of the most significant conclusions from the research is that students' overall degree of satisfaction with college appears to depend less than other outcomes on the entering students' attributes and more on the institution's characteristics (Astin, 1977, p. 168). In his longitudinal study, Astin (1977, p. 167) found that overall student satisfaction with the undergraduate experience remained rather consistent throughout the ten-year period he examined; however, students' positive ratings of the college environment tended to decrease from the freshman to senior year; freshmen presumably bring more enthusiasm to their new adventures. The most important institutional characteristic positively related to satisfaction appears to be small size. Likewise, student satisfaction seems strongly related to participation in social and academic campus life, an issue examined in more detail below (Astin, 1977, p. 169). The tandem variables —small size and degree of participation—appear to go hand in hand and reinforce one another; the findings make clear that smaller campuses enhance opportunities for participation. Another clue to general satisfaction is the finding that both institutional size and participation in campus life appear related to the degree and quality of student-faculty interaction. Dissatisfaction with student-faculty relationships at large institutions is most likely caused by the perceived neglect of undergraduate teaching and the impersonality that frequently results from large bureaucratic structures.

Generally, student satisfaction is likely to be greatest at prestigious, selective, affluent colleges and universities (Astin, 1977, p. 168). Students who attend single-sex colleges rather than coeducational institutions evidence more satisfaction in the areas of student-faculty relationships, quality of instruction, curriculum variety, student and peer relationships, and quality of the science curriculum. Not surprisingly, these students are less satisfied with social life.

Student satisfaction with academic reputation and intellectual environment is strongly linked to attendance at selective, affluent, private high-cost institutions and to men's colleges (pp. 170, 171). Curiously, satisfaction with the administration is most positively related to two quite different types of institutions: selective, high-cost institutions and two-year colleges (p. 174). Students attending two-year colleges are relatively satisfied with their social life but are the least satisfied with college in general. Because involvement in campus life is such a potent factor underpinning satisfaction with college, the typical commuting aspects of the two-year college tend to limit involvement and thus significantly reduce overall satisfaction.

In summary, satisfaction with college appears closely linked to three related factors: institutional selectivity, smallness of institutional size, and a preponderance of students living on campus. The presence of a small student body mainly in residence appears to contribute heavily to a fourth factor closely associated with general satisfaction: student involvement in campus life. Table 1 summarizes the kinds of outcomes associated with different college characteristics.

Involvement, Congruency, and Persistence

Three other dimensions of the college experience deserve special attention. Involvement and congruency reflect aspects of students' interaction with the institutional environment; persistence is an issue of escalating importance when enrollments are dear.

Involvement. From the sea of research data, "involvement" emerges as especially noticeable. Indisputably, one's satisfaction with college is closely related to one's degree of involvement with the institution. The literature consistently attests to the strong association between student involvement in the campus's academic and social life and positive changes in the expected outcomes of college (Feldman and Newcomb, 1969; Clark and others, 1972; Chickering, 1974; Bowen, 1977). Indeed, Astin (1977, p. 168) found that, for some outcomes, student involvement is more strongly related to positive change than either students' entering characteristics or institutional features.

According to Astin, institutional type does account for some differences. Although college characteristics had a weak relationship with degree of *academic involvement,* students attending women's or two-year colleges were more likely to become involved in academic life beyond the classroom. Findings for the two-year college may be a function of the limited peer interaction associated with this type of school. Four-year institutions and single-sex colleges facilitate *student-faculty interaction.* As mentioned, the salubrious effect of smallness is not a matter of reduced student-faculty ratios but of reduced bureaucratic impediments and less faculty preoccupation with research. Again, dormitory living is instrumental in fostering participation in *student government,* as is attendance at a Protestant or Roman Catholic institution. *Athletic involvement* is negatively related to large size but positively related to all-male colleges, Protestant colleges, and southern colleges.

Astin (1977, p. 91) found that for four areas—academic involvement, student-faculty interaction, familiarity with major field, and involvement in student government—interpersonal self-esteem is the best predictor of involvement; the greater the self-esteem, the more actively a student is likely to become involved—probably because participation in the campus's social and academic life requires a respectable degree of self-confidence and assertiveness. Similarly, Feldman and Newcomb (1969, p. 197) found that sociability and gregariousness were

Table 1. Type of Institution.

Dimension	General Comments	Selectivity (highly selective to open access)	Religious Affiliation (religious vs. nonsectarian)
Academic achievement	Inconclusive: related to initial ability	(−) Effect on gpa	
Intellectual, cultural, and esthetic orientation	General increase in intellectual commitment shown for most institutions (CL)	(+) Humanistic-esthetic benefits (P) (+) Cultural activities (P) (+) Cultural sophistication	(+) Protestant: (select) artistic and esthetic interests (A) (−) Religious: (nonselect) general cultural knowledge
Attitudes, beliefs, and values		(+) *Liberal leanings*: re. political and social, women, disadvantaged, power (+) Value liberal education and intrinsic benefit of education (CL)	(+) Altruism (+) Some accentuation of religious beliefs (−) Liberalness (FN, CL, A)
Personal development	Change in nonauthoritarianism and social maturity similar for most institutions (B); changes strongly related to initial students (CL)	Flexibility and spontaneity (CL) (+) Intellectual disposition to change (CL) (+) *Generally seems to enhance personal development*	(+) Self-acceptance (CL) (+) Religious (liberal arts): self-understanding (P) (+) Private Roman Catholic: intellectual self-esteem (A)
Career orientation and implementation		(+) Lifetime earnings (A) (+) Desire for postgraduate education (CL) (+) Careers in: business, medicine, teaching (A) (+) Entering professions (+) Value intrinsic rewards of career	(+) Protestant: (select) chances of entering nursing (+) Sectarian chances of being a college professor (A)
General satisfaction with college	Satisfaction with academic reputation and intellectual environment; depends less on entering students' attributes and more on institution's characteristics; strongly related to involvement	(+) *Overall greatest satisfaction with college* (A) (+) Satisfaction with academic reputation and intellectual environment (A) (+) Satisfaction with administration (A)	(+) Religious: closeness and student friendships
Involvement	For some outcomes, involvement is more related to positive change than either entering student characteristics or institutional features		(+) Protestant and Roman Catholic: involvement in student government

Key to effects: + = positive effect or increase in effect over time; − = negative effect or decrease in effect over time; A = Austin, 1977; B = Bowen, 1977; CH = Chickering, 1974; CL = Clark and others, 1972; FN = Feldman and Newcomb, 1969; P = Pace, 1974.

Control (public vs. independent)	Domicile (res. vs. commuter)	Two-Year vs. Four-Year	Size	Sex (single-sex vs. both sexes)
	(−) Commuter: involvement in academic activity		(+) Small: interaction with faculty (A)	(+) Men's inst.: high grades (−) Women's inst.: high grades
(+) Pub. four-year: gains in cultural knowledge (A) (+) Pvt.: artistic interests (A) (−) Pub. two-year: acquisition of general cultural knowledge (A)	(+) Residential: artistic interests (A) (−) Commuter: participation in cultural activities	(−) Pub. two-year: negative acquisition of general knowledge	(+) Small: gains in cultural knowledge (A) (−) Large: gains in cultural knowledge (A)	(+) Women's inst.: artistic interests (A)
(+) Pvt.: political liberalism and religious apostasy	(−) Commuter: liberal attitudes (CH) (+) Conservative attitudes (CH)	(+) Two-year: conservative, political, and social attitudes	(−) Large: altruism	(+) Women's inst.: liberal political views (A)
(+) Pvt.: *personal self-esteem* (+) Pvt.: intellectual and interpersonal self-esteem	(−) Commuter: personal development and opinion of selves and abilities (CH) (−) Social involvement with campus	(−) Two-year: personal development (−) Two-year: interpersonal self-esteem		(+) Women's Pvt.: intellectual self-esteem (A)
	(+) Commuter: value of having own business, being well off financially (A)	(−) Two-year: implementing career for all fields (−) Two year: intrinsic value of education		(+) Men's inst.: chances of pursuing career in business and college teaching (A) (+) Men's inst.: chances of entering law prof. (A) (−) Women's inst.: business and nursing careers
(+) Pvt.: satisfaction with academic reputation (+) Pvt.: view campus more positively		(+) Two year: satisfaction with administration (−) Two-year: satisfaction with college in general	(+) Small: interaction (CL, A, B) (−) Large: satisfaction with student-faculty relationships (A)	(+) Single-sex: satisfaction with student-faculty relationships, quality of instruction, curriculum variety, student-peer relationships. (−) Social life (+) Men's inst.: academic reputation and intellectual environment
(+) Pvt.: campus involvement: faculty, government, major field instructors	(+) Dormitory: involvement in student government and campus life		(+) Small: involvement in campus life (FN, CL) (−) Large: involvement in campus life	(+) Women's inst.: involvement: academics, government, leadership (+) Single-sex: faculty-student (+) Men's inst.: athletic involvement

important factors related to involvement in fraternities and
sororities, taking precedence even over socioeconomic status.

Feldman and Newcomb, emphasizing the importance of
living on campus and participating in campus life, were particularly impressed with the salience of those factors regardless of
the type of institution. This consistency in the face of diverse
institutional types is not surprising if one accepts Feldman and
Newcomb's view that residence groups, particularly social fraternities and sororities, facilitate the process of socialization
into academe. Regardless of differing institutional features, the
on-campus living groups initiate the neophyte to the campus's
resources, processes, and traditions. They encourage involvement, show the way, and provide practical and moral support.
Thus, residence itself may be the most noteworthy variable
among the interwoven factors: involvement, satisfaction, persistence. Hence, residence emerges as a potent force for positive
student development and change.

Congruency. A key consideration in both recruiting and
student selection of a campus is the issue of congruency—the
match or mismatch between a prospective student's needs and
the campus's ability to meet those needs and respond to those
interests.

Many researchers, both within and outside the field of
education, view the person-environment interaction in terms of
a "needs-press" or congruency model (Pervin, 1968; Stern,
1970; Nahemow and Lawton, 1973; Carp, 1976; Wohlwill and
Altman, 1976; Lawton, 1977). Generally, this approach maintains that "behavior varies as a result of an interaction between
an individual's personal needs and the capability of environmental press in fostering the gratification of such needs. Thus,
the optimal environment is person-specific, and its characteristics are defined by the degree of congruence it offers with the
needs of the individual" (Lawton, 1977, p. 295). The needs-
press/congruency model is appealing in light of prevalent developmental theories applied to college students (for example,
Inhelder and Piaget, 1958; Kohlberg and Kramer, 1969; Perry,
1970), which emphasize the important influence of the environment in facilitating or inhibiting human growth. An "opti-

mum match," in this view, does not depend on absolute congruence; rather, students should select a college with characteristics —or presses—sufficiently different from their own to provide a challenge and thereby instigate change. On the other hand, the environment should not be so deviant that it threatens or overwhelms the student.

The research findings are mixed. Needs-press studies conducted by Stern (1970; reported also in Walsh, 1973) hypothesized that success in college and satisfaction with the environment is more likely to occur if the relationships between individuals and their environments are congruent. But that research failed to show a correlation between achievement and congruency. Conversely, one study revealed positive correlations between low congruency and attrition (Walsh, 1973). It seems reasonable to assume that low achievers will be highly sensitive to what they perceive as negative environmental influences; therefore, low achievers may be "pressed out" (drop out or transfer) at an early stage. Those students who persist apparently develop coping strategies to deal with those perceived inhospitable aspects of the environment and/or simply ignore or endure unpleasant pressures. Hence, they achieve despite their perceived incongruency with the environment.

Another study (Wohlwill and Altman, 1976) makes a case *for* incongruency by suggesting that, if incongruency stimulates interest and exploratory behavior, college students who perceive a discrepancy between their needs and the campus's response to their needs may be stimulated to search and work more aggressively. Students may become more active participants in the educational experience, despite negative satisfaction or a lack of affective response to the college environment.

Another explanation for the surprising finding that low congruency is correlated with achievement can be drawn from Tinto (1975). In his view, persistence in college is a function of an individual's social *and* academic integration into the college. A student could be integrated into the academic sphere but not the social sphere. We conclude that some students may have low congruency yet achieve well because the discrepancy is on the social but not the academic level.

Perhaps the lesson is analogous to a "rule" in invest-ments: High potential yields (greater personal growth) are likely a function of assuming greater risks (a campus setting not whol-ly congruent with the student's prematriculation values and competencies). The lesser the risk, the less likely that growth will be substantial.

Persistence. Persistence in college is a variable closely re-lated both to student satisfaction with college and involvement in campus life. It is reasonable to assume that there is a relation-ship among students' positive attitudes toward their college en-vironment, the degree to which they take advantage of the insti-tution's activities and opportunities, and their tenaciousness in earning a degree. Astin (1977, p. 109) reports that every in-volvement factor found in his 1966-1970 sample is positively re-lated to persistence. As might be expected, dormitory living is a key factor related to persistence; it is of course closely related to involvement. Astin found that high grades, which are related to academic involvement, likewise strongly correlate with per-sistence.

The chances of persisting are reduced for students attend-ing public or private two-year colleges; this is not surprising, since two-year colleges tend to be commuter campuses with relatively low degrees of student involvement (Chickering, 1974, p. 68; Astin, 1977, p. 109). When residence is controlled, the negative effect disappears for women attending two-year colleges.

Is size related to persistence? The findings are incon-sistent. Astin's study (1977, p. 110) found negligible negative effects of size on persistence. Selectivity was associated with persistence, but only when the nonselective two-year colleges were included in the data. It appears, then, that selectivity is not a factor in persistence across other types of four-year insti-tutions. By the same token, Astin found that selectivity does not negatively affect persistence even though students at selec-tive institutions receive lower grades than students attending less selective institutions. Astin concludes that size per se has little effect on persistence. However, he warns that data con-cerning persistence must be viewed cautiously, since student traits associated with persistence may have been present before the student entered college.

The issues of congruency, persistence, involvement, and satisfaction seem inextricably related; research to date has not successfully isolated the factors in detailing the sequence of their cause and effect. Do satisfaction and involvement foster persistence? Or does persistence facilitate satisfaction and involvement? What is the cause-and-effect relationship between involvement and satisfaction with college? In what areas and to what degree is congruency a factor in student satisfaction, involvement, and persistence? Perhaps it is futile to attempt to describe such complex phenomena in a linear cause-and-effect fashion. The interaction of these factors might better be described as a dialectic process. Whatever the nature and relationship of these phenomena, clearly they are important variables affecting the impact of college on students, and it is imperative that the higher education community rigorously and assiduously pursue these issues and their implications for both students and institutions.

Implications

Type of institution appears to have relatively little effect on growth in cognitive areas. That fact may be unsettling to proponents of institutions which invest relatively larger resources to stimulate greater academic achievement; nevertheless, the sobering fact remains that academic achievement is very closely bound to students' academic quality at the time they enter college. (There is no evidence that entering students *lose* any initial advantage they bring with them to the more highly selective colleges and universities; on the whole, the intellectual gifts with which they enter seem to be adequately nurtured.)

In contrast, different impacts are more readily discernible in noncognitive areas, where it appears that three institutional characteristics are closely associated with accentuated changes in students: relative smallness, predominantly residential, and relative selectiveness in admissions policies. These characteristics, taken together, are most commonly associated with the better-quality liberal arts colleges and appear to reinforce one another to magnify positive development in a number of non-cognitive areas.

It appears, therefore, that the environment associated with the quality liberal arts colleges does yield a larger payoff, not so much in cognitive growth as in the broader sense of holistic student development.

As to "overall satisfaction" with college, we must ask how much weight should be accorded to student satisfaction. After all, students who only infrequently find it necessary to venture forth from the rathskeller may be the most "satisfied" with their "education"—although most educators would not regard such phenomena as indicators of institutional effectiveness. Making allowances for the vulnerability of satisfaction as a criterion of success, the evidence again points to small size, residential nature, and relative selectiveness as being most closely associated with overall satisfaction. Again, the higher-quality liberal arts colleges appear to have an edge.

One factor—namely, student involvement and participation—threads its way through the research and points toward some "do-able" tasks that may have special relevance for colleges and universities looking toward ten to fifteen years of anticipated enrollment shortfalls. Generally, where students are involved in the campus life—whether in academic or cocurricular or extracurricular activities—a higher degree of satisfaction and, more to the point, a higher rate of persistence are found. The implications, we believe, are rather obvious because the degree of student involvement-participation is inversely related to that loathsome *bête noir*, attrition. If we are correct, in some measure large institutions' task is to carve subcommunities, with greater opportunities for participation, out of amorphous, sprawling educational environments. This process can be attacked on many fronts. For example, on the academic side, freshman seminars and faculty working with small clusters of academic advisees as a group are two strategies. In the nonacademic realm, expanded institutional support to make cocurricular and extracurricular activities more attractive and more accessible seem to be in order. True, budgets are tight, tough decisions about priorities must be made, and there almost surely will be short-run diseconomies linked to establishing small-unit activities. But the evidence must be considered when developing an overall institutional strategy. Efforts to enhance student involvement are an effective strategy for combating attrition and helping, over the longer haul, to create an attractive institutional reputation for the quality of undergraduate life.

For the larger institutions, one major step toward a "solution" is the idea of "subcolleges," theme colleges, cluster colleges, or what have you. In theory, these should really help provide a sense of community, partly through intensified student participation-involvement. In practice, the subcollege approach, which seemed to hold such promise in the mid-1960s and early 1970s, has all but vanished, apparently a victim of the student stampede toward vocationally linked programs and a lack of interest among the faculty at large. Nevertheless, we believe that for larger institutions the time is ripe to reexamine the feasibility of establishing or reestablishing such subcommunities.

Commuter campuses present their own special problems. Because commuting students tend to have minimal contact with the environment, they are less influenced by traditional campus agencies—such as student services and academic advisement— that help ease the neophyte into the campus milieu and foster active social and academic involvement. For numerous reasons, most commuting students are not touched by these support services, despite sometimes vigorous efforts to engage the students. The obstacles are manifold. Students are unaware that services exist, misunderstand the nature and value of the services, or lack support and encouragement and hence are too timid to seek assistance. Who, then, has most influence on the commuting student? The answer is the *faculty*, who must be drawn into the process if programs to provide for commuting students' well-being are to be effective. Admittedly, faculty are burdened by existing responsibilities, but creative planning by student services and other personnel can heighten faculty awareness about the link between support services and student persistence.

In summary, the question of which students "fit" which

colleges and universities has taken on a new importance as American higher education moves deeper into a decade of anticipated hard times. The number of college and university students soared throughout the 1950s and 1960s and continued to increase, less dramatically, throughout the 1970s, but the issue of fit had a different significance. In the seller's market, colleges by the hundreds were able to be moderately to highly selective; they could make admissions choices partly by looking for student characteristics that would best fit a given institution. This is not to suggest that highly sophisticated uses of the research literature were made in the matchmaking process. But it is our impression that a number of colleges were keenly aware of their student body characteristics and took these into account when recruiting new students—whether striving for greater diversity or more homogeneity.

Paradoxically, probably less and less use of evidence about student development is being made today in formulating institutional policies for recruiting students. This is hardly surprising, given the diminishing number of students in the age cohort that traditionally has attended college and the corresponding mounting pressures on colleges to enroll qualified students. In the prevailing buyer's market, pressures on college admissions staffs to produce are intensifying. As the task of recruiting qualified students grows more difficult, the importance of adequate numbers overshadows finer issues of fit. Accordingly, as a practical matter, what we know about the interaction between students and college environments may recede to lesser importance. We are reminded of Maslow's hierarchy: The first priority is to survive.

To confront the challenges upon us, we should give the literature far more serious attention than it has received. Studies on colleges' effects on students have explored virtually every aspect of the college experience. Researchers have examined the impact of college on cognitive development; they have probed many dimensions of noncognitive development: shifts in student attitudes, beliefs, values, self-perception, career orientation, and so on. Yet this literature is considerably underappreciated. To the best of our knowledge, administrators and college faculty are virtually illiterate when it comes to understanding the multidimensional effects of their colleges on students. This is a degree of negligence all the more regrettable because they undeniably have a substantial stake in the quality of the interaction between institution and student. To illustrate, in a recent survey, prominent higher education scholars and administrators were asked what reading would be most important for recently selected college presidents (Drew and Schuster, 1980). Very few of the respondents named studies identifying the effects of college.

Admittedly, existing studies are not flawless, a point not lost on Harvard's President Derek Bok. Making a plea for "sustained research" at Harvard "to enlighten the faculty and administrators" committed to improving undergraduate education there, he comes directly to the point: "The available studies are scattered and most of them focus on issues of emotional and psychological development that fascinate the psychologists who carry them out but do precious little to help the faculty committee or administrator make decisions about the course of undergraduate education" (Bok, 1978, p. 10).

In fairness, the situation is not so grim as that, nor is the research as esoteric as Bok suggests. In fact, the higher education community has access to much more evidence than ever before about the effects of the college experience on students. Such studies surely do not—and cannot—establish the indispensable components of an undergraduate curriculum or lead to overall excellence in teaching, but neither is the existing research without significance. It *is* important to educators seeking to match students with an "appropriate" undergraduate setting; and it *should be* important to administrators and faculty members determined to understand better the many facets of student development—a prerequisite for optimizing the overall college experience for students and, accordingly, for reducing student attrition.

Different types of institutions do have different impacts on their clientele. The différences are not dramatic, but they are identifiable. Especially in the difficult times ahead, educators at all types of colleges and universities must familiarize themselves with the evidence—both general and specific to their own campus—and vigorously seek ways to make their campus environments function more effectively toward producing the kinds of student outcomes they seek.

Overview of the Literature

The feature of American higher education that most rivets the attention of foreign observers is its rampant diversity. There are so many different *types* of postsecondary institutions. Not surprisingly, the impact of the undergraduate experience on students has fascinated researchers throughout much of this century, especially since the 1950s as higher education rose in prominence on the nation's agenda. Some of these studies focus on the extent to which different types of postsecondary institutions variously affect students.

Now we present an overview of the literature on student development, with emphasis on its strengths and weaknesses, its evolution, and its current directions. We place the studies discussed in the preceding sections in the broader perspective of research on student development. First we describe and classify the kinds of research that have been accomplished; next we comment on the limitations that constrain research of this type. We end with a comprehensive bibliography.

Categories of Research. Astin and Panos (1966, p. 5) note the paucity of useful research in higher education: "Until recently, comprehensive empirical studies of our higher educational system were virtually nonexistent." Prior to the age of "postsecondary" education, the existing research was largely an assortment of unrelated, local studies conducted by individual investigators using diverse methodological approaches. Thus, the data were rarely interchangeable, and the findings and conclusions were seldom transferable.

As Chickering (1969) points out, several early studies were beacons for guiding contemporary forays into the area of student development and change. The classic study by Learned and Wood (1938) examined differences in college student achievement and aptitude; it is significant because it was one of the first large-scale investigations of differences among students and institutions. Other benchmarks for contemporary research are the Bennington study (Newcomb, 1943) and the Vassar study (Sanford, 1956, 1962; Sanford, Webster, and Freedman, 1957). Jacob's (1957) survey, which found that college had a negligible impact on values, was a major impetus to the field. The studies that emerged in the late 1960s and 1970s can be grouped into four categories: comprehensive empirical studies, studies centered around the development of an assessment instrument, integrative studies, and research that focuses on the different impacts of different types of colleges on students.

Large-scale, empirical studies of students attending various institutions include Katz and Associates' (1968) *No Time for Youth.* Interviews were conducted with about 200 students and data collected on several thousand more over a four-year period. On a smaller scale, Heath (1968) studied the relationship between environmental features and student development at Haverford College. Brawer (1973) looked at 1,876 freshmen entering three diverse California community colleges: urban, suburban, and rural. Her purpose was to begin answering questions about student differences resulting from the increasing diversity of American higher education and the type of "new" students seeking admission to postsecondary institutions. One of the most recent and massive longitudinal studies of college impact is Astin's (1977) *Four Critical Years,* a report on ten years of research covering approximately 200,000 students in 300 postsecondary institutions.

Studies that center on the development of instruments to measure reliably the college environment and its many effects on students include Astin (1963), whose research at ten colleges used the Environmental Assessment Technique (EAT) to measure ways that aspects of the environment are related to changes in goals and self-ratings. Stern (1966) used his Activities Index (AI) and the College Characteristics Index (Pace and Stern, 1958) to assess the degree of needs-press/congruency between students and their environment. Pace (1969) reports on the College and University Environment Scales (CUES), one of the most widely used instruments for measuring student change and institutional characteristics. Using factor analysis, Pace was able to reduce his 160-item inventory to a few salient clusters that reflect major differences among colleges. Baird (1980) presents a useful directory of the key instruments for assessing campus environments, including a summary of the research projects in which each instrument was used.

A third category of research on college impact is integrative studies. One of the earliest compilations of research findings concerning the structure, function, and policies of institutions of higher learning that affect students is in *The American College* (Sanford, 1962). This monumental volume contains a useful section on the effects of a college education, focusing particularly on personality changes. *The Impact of College on Students* (Feldman and Newcomb, 1969), another important milestone, synthesizes four decades of empirical studies on the influence of college. One chapter, "The Diverse American College," addresses the differential impact of various types of institutions on students. A more recent integrative work is *Investment in Learning* (Bowen, 1977). An economist, Bowen breaks new ground by assessing the impact of college in terms of cost effectiveness; that is, the ratio between inputs and outcomes. More than an economist, Bowen identifies the less tangible, ubiquitous, and noble outcomes of education that nurture the human spirit and enhance society. His sweeping synthesis includes a comprehensive discussion of the impact of different types of institutions.

In the late 1960s and 1970s, higher education benefited from a number of key studies specifically directed at investigating the differences among colleges and universities. Astin (1968) surveyed approximately 30,000 students at the end of their freshman year in an effort to account for differences among 246 institutions. This study focuses on observed behavior—rather than student perceptions—as influenced by four environmental settings: peer, classroom, administrative, and physical. *The Distinctive College* (Clark, 1970) analyzes from a historical perspective the character of the private, liberal arts college. Seeking to discover what gives a distinctive quality to this type of institution, which once dominated higher education in America,

Clark examines Antioch, Reed, and Swarthmore, exploring their basic orientations, organizational structures, and the critical changes each institution experienced that contributed to their distinctive character and influence. In *Students and Colleges: Interaction and Change* (Clark and others, 1972), the authors used the OPI to assess the impact of eight different institutions over approximately four years—Clark's original three highly selective, private colleges and three small religiously oriented colleges and two large public universities.

In *The Demise of Diversity,* Pace (1974) attempted to determine in what respect and to what degree institutions of higher learning are distinct and diverse. He surveyed upperclassmen and alumni of the class of 1950 from eight institutions whose historical development, programs, and students have given each a distinctive profile. The questionnaires tapped student and alumni views and activities related to the college experience and both their professional and educational progress and performance. A seminal work in the field of differential impact is *Commuting Versus Resident Students: Overcoming Educational Inequities of Living Off Campus* by Chickering (1974). He used sophisticated methods to examine, in exhaustive detail, the nature and effects of living on campus versus commuting to college.

Limiting Factors. The studies discussed provide numerous insights, but they fall far short of yielding conclusive evidence of differential impact by type of college. The obstacles are formidable: The environment being studied is complex, the process being examined is elusive, and current research methods are limited.

Colleges are complicated and multidimensional, and each inhabitant is as complex as the college. The impact of the institution, its people, and its processes is therefore hard to measure. Dressel (1976, p. 166) depicts a tangle of dimensions: "campus mores, traditions, rules; acceptable standards of behavior and achievement; innovative-conservative balance; issues and controversies; grounds, architecture, facilities; values, orientations, and priorities; organization structure."

Study is further confounded by heterogeneity and change

within American higher education. Accustomed in the past to dealing primarily with the most able students, institutions are now confronted by a great influx of socially, economically, ethnically, and educationally diverse students. These changing enrollment patterns dilute the college experience, interspersing it with noncollege activity, deflecting efforts to measure the impact of college. Thus, many students, enamored of the "real world of work," tend to take fewer courses, are more likely to drop out for a period of time, and are more disposed to transfer to other institutions. As Dressel (1976, p. 165) says, "The day of the four-year stay on a small campus is gone. Many students now attend class and use facilities between classes but are otherwise not involved." The reduced intensity of the higher education experience is reflected in such phenomena as the increasing number of graduate and professional students whose campus contact is limited, off-campus work and service programs, the rash of external degree programs, the granting of credit for informal learning and work experience, and study-abroad programs. In light of these various trends in higher education, Dressel (p. 166) voices concern over current efforts to assess environmental influences from outdated perspectives: "In some sense environment does play a vital role in all these alternatives, but not quite in the manner envisaged in the efforts at environmental assessment to date; in approach and substance, these efforts hark back to an earlier concept of a unified total campus experience."

Further Obstacles. Like all social science research, the study of differential impact is impeded by weaknesses in methodology. Differential impact eludes easy identification and measurement because it is multifaceted, covert, unplanned, and unsystematic. The changes that are documented during the college years cannot be accurately accounted for. Indeed, changes probably occur as readily, if not more readily, in informal situations —such as the dormitory—as in the formal classroom setting (Sanford, 1967; Feldman and Newcomb, 1969; Cross, 1976; Bowen, 1977). Differential effects that are discovered must not be confused with simple maturation. Weak assessment measures have limited ability to detect subtle but important differences between variables.

Bowen (1977) points to another methodological pitfall. Much of the literature reports *average*—and often mild—changes in individuals, based on shifts in an array of cognitive and affect variables. But this approach may well obscure substantial changes in students, changes that would be more evident if they were viewed holistically, as being part of total personalities. Dressel (1976) agrees, pointing out that supposedly limited findings on the impact of college are in no small part due to the use of average or mean scores for groups of students—thereby obscuring significant changes in individual students.

In the multifaceted world, methodological pitfalls abound. Even so, the studies reported, especially those during the past fifteen years, provide extraordinary insights into the effects of college and, more to the point, the varying consequences associated with attending different types of undergraduate institutions. An awareness of that literature enables us more effectively to match students with the undergraduate setting most likely to respond to their individual needs.

Bibliography

Astin, A. W. "Further Validation of the Environmental Assessment Technique." *Journal of Educational Psychology*, 1963, *54*, 64-71.

Astin, A. W. *The College Environment*. Washington, D.C.: American Council on Education, 1968.

Astin, A. W. *Four Critical Years: Effects of College on Beliefs, Attitudes, and Knowledge*. San Francisco: Jossey-Bass, 1977.

Astin, A. W., and Panos, R. "A National Research Data Bank for Higher Education." *Educational Record*, 1966, *47*, 5-17.

Astin, A. W., and Panos, R. *The Educational and Vocational Development of College Students*. Washington, D.C.: American Council on Education, 1969.

Baird, L. L., Hartnett, R. T., and Associates. *Understanding Student and Faculty Life: Using Campus Surveys to Improve Academic Decision Making*. San Francisco: Jossey-Bass, 1980.

Bok, D. *President's Report, 1976-1977*. Cambridge, Mass.: Harvard University, 1978.

Bowen, H. R. *Investment in Learning: The Individual and Social Value of American Higher Education.* San Francisco: Jossey-Bass, 1977.

Brawer, F. B. *New Perspectives on Personality Development in College Students.* San Francisco: Jossey-Bass, 1973.

Broudy, H. S. *Building a Philosophy of Education.* Englewood Cliffs, N.J.: Prentice-Hall, 1961.

Carp, F. M. "Housing and Living Environments of Older People." In R. H. Binstock and E. Shanas (Eds.), *Handbook of Aging and the Social Sciences.* New York: Van Nostrand Reinhold, 1976, pp. 244-271.

Centra, J. A., and Rock, D. A. "College Environments and Student Academic Achievement." *American Educational Research Journal,* 1971, *8,* 623-634.

Chickering, A. W. *Education and Identity.* San Francisco: Jossey-Bass, 1969.

Chickering, A. W. *Commuting Versus Resident Students: Overcoming Educational Inequities of Living Off Campus.* San Francisco: Jossey-Bass, 1974.

Clark, B. R. *The Distinctive College: Antioch, Reed, and Swarthmore.* Hawthorne, N.Y.: Aldine, 1970.

Clark, B. R., and others. *Students and Colleges: Interaction and Change.* Berkeley: Center for Research and Development in Higher Education, University of California, 1972.

Cross, K. P. *Accent on Learning: Improving Instruction and Reshaping the Curriculum.* San Francisco: Jossey-Bass, 1976.

Dewey, J. *Democracy and Education.* New York: Macmillan, 1916.

Douglass College Women's College Study Committee. *Summary of Research Literature and Working Bibliography.* New Brunswick, N.J.: Douglass College, Rutgers University, 1974.

Dressel, P. L. *Handbook of Academic Evaluation: Assessing Institutional Effectiveness, Student Progress, and Professional Performance for Decision Making in Higher Education.* San Francisco: Jossey-Bass, 1976.

Drew, D. E., and Schuster, J. H. "Recommended Reading for College Presidents." *Change,* July-August 1980, pp. 33-38.

Dubin, R., and Taveggia, T. C. *The Teaching-Learning Paradox.*

Eugene: Center for Advanced Study of Educational Administration, University of Oregon, 1968.

Feldman, K. S., and Newcomb, T. M. *The Impact of College on Students.* San Francisco: Jossey-Bass, 1969.

Heath, D. H. *Growing Up in College.* San Francisco: Jossey-Bass, 1968.

Heist, P., and others. "Personality and Scholarship." *Science,* Feb. 10, 1961, pp. 362-367.

Inhelder, B., and Piaget, J. *The Growth of Logical Thinking from Childhood to Adolescence.* New York: Basic Books, 1958.

Jacob, P. E. *Changing Values in College.* New York: Harper & Row, 1957.

Katz, J., and Associates. *No Time for Youth: Growth and Constraint in College Students.* San Francisco: Jossey-Bass, 1968.

Kohlberg, L., and Kramer, R. "Continuities and Discontinuities in Childhood and Adult Moral Development." *Human Development,* 1969, *12,* 93-120.

Lawton, M. P. "The Impact of Environment on Aging." In J. E. Birren and K. W. Schaie (Eds.), *Handbook on the Psychology of Aging.* New York: Van Nostrand Reinhold, 1977, pp. 276-301.

Learned, W. S., and Wood, B. D. *The Student and His Knowledge.* Bulletin 29. New York: Carnegie Foundation for the Advancement of Teaching, 1938.

Nahemow, L., and Lawton, M. P. "Toward an Ecological Theory of Adaptation and Aging." In W. R. E. Preiser (Ed.), *Environmental Design Research.* Vol. 1. Stroudsberg, Pa.: Dowden, Hutchinson, and Ross, 1973, pp. 24-32.

Newcomb, T. M. *Personality and Social Change: Attitude Formation in a Student Community.* New York: Holt, Rinehart and Winston, 1943.

Nichols, R. C. "Effect of Various College Characteristics on Student Aptitude Test Scores." *Journal of Educational Psychology,* 1964, *55*(1), 45-54.

Oates, M. J., and Williamson, S. "Women's Colleges and Women Achievers." *Signs,* Summer 1978, *3*(4), 795-806.

Pace, C. R. *College and University Environment Scales: Techni-*

cal Manual. (2nd ed.) Princeton, N.J.: Educational Testing Service, 1969.

Pace, C. R. *The Demise of Diversity?* Berkeley, Calif.: Carnegie Commission on Higher Education, 1974.

Pace, C. R. *Measuring Outcomes of College: Fifty Years of Findings and Recommendations for the Future.* San Francisco: Jossey-Bass, 1979.

Pace, C. R., and Stern, G. G. "An Approach to the Measurement of Psychological Characteristics of College Environments." *Journal of Educational Psychology,* 1958, *49,* 269-277.

Perry, W. G. *Forms of Intellectual and Ethical Development in the College Years.* New York: Holt, Rinehart and Winston, 1970.

Pervin, L. A. "Performance and Satisfaction as a Function of Individual-Environment Fit." *Psychological Bulletin,* 1968, *69,* 56-58.

Rock, D. A., Centra, J. A., and Linn, R. L. *The Identification and Evaluation of College Effects on Student Achievement.* Princeton, N.J.: Educational Testing Service, 1969.

Sanford, N. (Ed.). "Personality Development During the College Years." *Journal of Social Issues,* 1956, *12*(4), entire issue.

Sanford, N. "The Developmental Status of the Entering Freshman." In N. Sanford (Ed.), *The American College.* New York: Wiley, 1962.

Sanford, N. *Where Colleges Fail: A Study of the Student as a Person.* San Francisco: Jossey-Bass, 1967.

Sanford, N., Webster, H., and Freedman, M. "Impulse Expression as a Variable of Personality." *Psychological Monographs,* 1957, *71*(11), entire issue.

Stern, G. G. *Studies of College Environments.* Syracuse, N.Y.: Syracuse University Press, 1966.

Stern, G. G. *People in Context: Measuring Person/Environment Context in Education and Industry.* New York: Wiley, 1970.

Tinto, V. "Dropout from Higher Education: A Theoretical Synthesis of Recent Research." *Review of Educational Research,* Winter 1975, *45*(1), 89-125.

Walsh, W. B. *Theories of Person-Environment Interaction: Im-*

plications for the College Student. Princeton, N.J.: American College Testing Program, 1973.

Wing, C. W., Jr., and Wallach, A. *College Admissions and the Psychology of Talent.* New York: Holt, Rinehart and Winston, 1971.

Wohlwill, J. F., and Altman, I. *Human Behavior and Environment.* New York: Plenum, 1976.

4

Placing Students for Stability and Success

Paul Painter
Nancy Painter

Thousands of students go off to hundreds of colleges each year, and we tend to think of them as "college students" in one hunk. But that "big-block" thinking causes problems in successfully placing college students. We know each high school graduate as an individual, as a friend, a classroom student, a neighbor. Similarly, we know college reputations. The right choice will match the student with a college that fits personal abilities and personality, with understandable consequences of feelings of gratification. The wrong choice will cause frustration and angry blame-fixing by the student and the college.

The best advice regarding college placement is to know the student and the college precisely, for they will interact with each other as soon as the student enters a college. As a distinctive and singular part, that student indeed becomes the college. As a group, the students become the college and are the key determinant of the college's nature and quality. As examples, books in the library are bought on group demand; professors come and go on group demand; courses of study are instituted and dropped based on their popularity. There is much beard-stroking and intellectualization, but we need look no further than the profound changes in college quality brought about by students in the late 1960s to know that the student group truly holds the power.

If our students are to be happy, the group they propose to become a part of on entering college must be plausible for them to join. It is possible to send a poet to M.I.T., an artist to Colorado School of Mines, a loner to DePauw, or a dullard with good grades to Pomona. But the likely results are obvious and predictable.

More than half of these entering freshmen will leave their colleges. Misplacement is a major reason and should be a major challenge to the college counselor. Other varied reasons reflect dissonance between students and institutions. One review (Panos and Astin, 1967) found that about half the students were dissatisfied with the institution; the rest felt that their experiences were not helping their future career plans and personal development. Naturally, each student conceptualized the final decision to leave according to personal conscious thought; yet each clearly registered discomfort, a feeling of being in the wrong place. As professionals, we have many reasons for agreeing.

The consequences of poor college choice are serious, chiefly because the college is the first experience of the world away from home. If that experience is successful, it is most supportive to the student's ego and imparts self-confidence for future ventures. If it is a failing experience, it is discouraging and causes a regression.

We begin by examining those painful complaints that arise when college adjustment is failing and some of the superficial and deeper reasons for the unhappiness. (This is really why the right choice matters: The happy students do not complain but sing the praises of alma mater.) We then review reactions to failure and, finally, discuss matching procedures that might eliminate such results of the wrong choice.

Scope of the Problem

For students beginning to dislike the colleges they chose, blame is easy to place. The students have either negative feelings toward the colleges or positive feelings toward themselves. They feel that the college disappointed them with deficiencies or that they have grown, improved, and matured enough

so that they no longer fit in the college. In one study of malad-
justed students (Kuehn and Kuehn, 1975), only 19 percent saw
academic or career problems in their college careers as their own
doing; the rest developed emotional complaints and had complaints about the college. In another study (Panos and Astin,
1967), 27 percent of the students commonly gave their reason
for dropping out as unhappiness with aspects of the school environment. Twenty-three percent did not think they could afford the costs, and 11 percent were tired of being students.
Twenty-two percent changed goals, and 26 percent wanted time
to rethink careers. Fifteen percent saw their academic progress
as poor. But overall, the students could see problems only when
they experienced discomfort.

Thus, students are most likely to complain about the
proximate, or immediate, cause of their discomfort. It hurts, so
their wounded snarl is turned in that direction.

Proximate Causes of Feeling Misplaced

1. *Living arrangements.* High on any list in the literature
is students' immediate physical environment. A look at individual rooms (as well as unique houses, neighborhoods, or towns)
reveals diversity. Students bring that diversity to the college environment as they try to change their dorm rooms to please
their senses. Decorations can help, but there are other needs
that run deeper. A fraternity offers a more cohesive group than
a residence hall. A residence hall provides more privacy than a
fraternity. Clearly, the students' social comfort requires a fit between the students and living arrangements that cannot be met
by thoughtlessly plugging them into any room. Moos (1979) extensively studied student social environments and believes that
there are two basic living situations: one sociable and interactive; the other private, intimate, and individualistic. Generally,
the more outgoing students prefer the parties, the competitive
social life, and the practical environment of the single-sex dorm
or the fraternity house. The intellectual, private, and perhaps
shy student prefers a coeducational dorm or individual housing
with much supportive organization (clubs, social planned activi-

ties, discussion groups). If the student feels at home, such things as the mess in the hallways or a faulty heating system will not be blamed for unhappiness; they will be mere conversation pieces.

2. *Lack of warm friendships.* We all have known the power of friends in times of need. To have those friends, there must be a group available, one large enough to permit or make likely chance meetings. A student who belongs to such a larger group can avoid a minority group's defensive psychology. Social psychology has well demonstrated that we most easily identify with those who have personality characteristics similar to our own: Birds of a feather flock together. Fewer adjustments and exceptions need to be made to love the other person if that person is like us.

Friendship groups are complex, but there are basically three groups that begin at age fifteen (in the sophomore year of high school) and continue into college: the athletic group (jocks, leaders), the big sociable group (popular, socies, squares), and the intellectual group (rebels, nonconformists, freaks). Various colleges have varying proportions of these groups, and there should be enough students in the appropriate group to fit the individual we are trying to advise.

Of these three groups, clearly the intellectual most risks misplacement. Members of this group are not as adept at making friends and dealing with the administration. The professors themselves typically derive from this group, but they prefer more conforming young students. Thus, the intellectual is easily isolated. Lacking friends, the intellectual student feels the school is snobbish or uncaring. This situation is illustrated by Hood's (1968) observations about Minnesota colleges. He found that the nonconformist student did best in a large metropolitan college. In turn, these colleges attracted a mixture of less sociable students with whom the rebel could feel more comfortable. On the other hand, an outgoing, sociable student misplaced into an intellectual school, such as a Minnesota technical or agricultural college, fared badly. He would be critical of the college, probably seeing it as excessively sober and boring.

These basic qualities of sociability versus nonconformity

run in families, are recognizable in high school and early childhood as unchanging attributes of the child, and can reasonably
be considered inborn attributes of the personality.

3. *Lack of friends of similar background.* Values associated with socioeconomic group are taught within the family,
and as learned concepts they slowly become a part of the person. Political pollsters can ask a person the political party of his
parents and know which way he will vote. So also with grammar, accent, dress, manners, dealing with authority and money,
and many other learned values: The ways of the family are
clearly imprinted. If the college has a great majority of students
from local and conservative religious backgrounds, the college
will have an associated ambience of the locale, say, the Ozarks,
the Deep South, or the Northern Plains wheat belt. Although
many studies have shown that all socioeconomic groups are
found in any college, socioeconomic matching is truly valuable
when placing a student (Astin, 1975). It is simplistic to say that
the college is balanced and gray because the five social classes of
Hollingshead and Redlich (1958) may be found somewhere
among the students. Some colleges simply cost a lot, others are
local and almost free. The culture shock experienced when students from affluent and culturally sophisticated backgrounds go
to a college in which great numbers of students come from different and simpler backgrounds is real and a matter of personal
dismay.

4. *Low grades.* There is a high correlation between failure and a student's being handed low grades by a particular college's faculty. As shown by Astin (1971) in his analysis of college grades and high school function, grades can be estimated,
given the college, with dreadful accuracy. And those students,
especially boys, on academic probation tend to drop out (Astin,
1975). Furthermore, of the low students in a class, only 8 percent can be thought of as true underachievers; the rest are low
in aptitude. There is plenty of room for working with this situation. For example, Hood's (1968) survey of Minnesota colleges
showed that the grade averages at small liberal arts and Catholic
women's colleges were much higher than at technical schools.
Also, professors tend to hand out grades in the same pattern they

are used to in their particular college, even when higher- or lower-quality students begin to flow into the class. Courses in which there is much subjective and personal interaction with the professor, such as art and music, tend to result in high grades and few failures; yet most students look down on such workable stunts as enrolling in those courses to improve their grades. They prefer to see themselves as "normal," taking standard courses without thinking about the importance of a good grade to the school and themselves. As a result, those students will get low marks and feel dumb. We have to expect that the student will want to feel normal; we cannot hope the student will learn to manipulate the system. The professors will not change. Thus, the student must fit with the grade expectations in the college chosen, not be overplaced into a college that has a grade-giving pattern the student will fail to match.

5. *Contempt from the professor.* Sensitive students may feel rejected if they cannot perform at a profesor's minimal level of expectations. After years of high school fantasy about, say, making the college newspaper staff, criticism in English class may be too depressing. Professors like students to be "prepared"—that is, to match their concept of a college student. They complain bitterly about working at what they feel are demeaning levels of teaching, as with "remedial" courses. This anger is unloaded in the form of contempt on the confused students. Especially when this experience occurs in the freshman year, the students may later avoid the very area of study in which they would be most competent.

6. *Confusing material.* Students have individual learning styles, and sometimes they have learning disabilities demonstrated by spotty high school grades and lopsided ACTs or SATs. For example, we advised a student recently who had a math SAT of 580 and verbal of 430. His history suggested a mild reading disability, and we aimed him toward a list of possible colleges with modest verbal function but still a wide choice of liberal arts courses. Such a student in an abstract English course—for example, poetry analysis—would feel confused and lost, unaware that his and the professors' minds had very different abilities and comprehension.

7. *Unavailable courses.* Students constrained by ability, pattern of thinking, and family background are likely to have some ideas about what they would like to do or be after college. These ideas are highly significant, even though pastel colored at first, and they become more set as the years in college progress (Astin and Panos, 1969). A lack of course work available for the student's goals is a serious defect; it shows that the college is not really prepared to educate that student, who is likely to be shunted into ill-fitting courses that need more seats occupied.

8. *Lack of support services.* Advisers and counselors are very valuable to students, especially the shy ones. Not being able to deal with friends for advice, the shy student needs specialists and support groups as technical "friends." Without such folks around, shy students feel that the college is competitive and cold and that people do not care about them. Outreach services are less necessary at small, highly sociable, and closely knit colleges, such as those with a sense of mission or a strong religious orientation. The student group is more apt to support the shy ones in such places and make them feel included.

9. *Poor recreational facilities.* This complaint reflects a need to escape and an inner feeling of pressure. There is always opportunity for taking a break, be it social or private, indoors or out, at any college. The happy student rarely leaves campus, and all counselors raise their eyebrows if a college under consideration by a student is known to empty out on weekends.

Several underlying problems motivate the outspoken complaints of the student who drops out; these problems are not in the student's awareness and consciousness because they involve a degree of self-criticism and admission of personal failure. Yet they are important for the counselor to understand and recognize, so that the student can be helped to avoid those very failures.

Underlying Causes of Misplacement

1. *A student's low ability for the particular college attended.* Although the optimist feels that on a given day any student could go to any college and make it, the facts simply prove

otherwise. Actually, there is a college somewhere that any of us, if so misplaced, would flunk out of.

When we counselors recommend colleges, we should be fully aware of this problem. The colleges' admissions goals are different from the counselors'. Admissions officers want a group of students without problems. They rate grades heavily—2:1 up to 12:1 over SATs, according to Hood (1968)—because a student willing to work for grades in high school will continue to do so in college. If at the same time an institution can get some Merit Scholars, that is fine. But basically it is even more important to attract problem-free grade-getters. If a college, in its eagerness to accept students with good grades, overlooks poor SAT scores and admits low-ability students and those students enroll, they may be asking for trouble, both for the college and themselves. Those low scores may mean, for example, that a student of only average intelligence has worked hard at a school only moderately competitive and been able to earn good grades. If most of the students at the individual's college are more able, the student runs a high risk of emotional damage and failure, no matter how hard the student works. A student in the bottom 15 percent of the ability and test range of the college is likely to be so overly challenged. Someone has to struggle in the bottom, but do not let it be someone we as counselors are responsible for.

2. *Learning disabilities.* In the grade school years, a child two years behind intellectual expectations in a given learning area may be called learning disabled. These disabilities are not well understood and go by recondite Greek names (such as dysgraphia and dyslexia), which cover our ignorance. Learning disabled students usually go underground at high school; a child with reading deficiency may well show only phonetic misspellings in high school. Clues to the college counselor of the existence of old learning disabilities are 100 or more points difference on SATs, either direction; unusually low grades in a single subject, with a history of the weakness going back to grade school; or the student's intense dislike of certain kinds of courses. Thus, a child slow in numeration in third grade, failing to grasp algebra in ninth grade, and stopping math after tenth-grade geometry, is likely to want to avoid math in college. The

student's wish is to be respected. "Shape up and try harder" is a motto that belongs in grade school teaching while the young mind is developing. By tenth grade, one should counsel the students to concentrate on their strengths, not on weaknesses and makeup work. So also should the college be selected; that is, with an eye to an institution that does not emphasize math. Misplacement means an unhappy student.

3. *Wrong peer group.* The group inhabiting the college colors the whole college, its enthusiasms, values, and goals. The guests make the party, and the students make the school. Indeed, it is very hard to demonstrate just what difference the college and faculty do make (Astin and Panos, 1969) because student qualities seem to change so little between entrance and graduation. Certainly, counselor awareness of the kind of social group that uses the particular college cannot be too detailed. The college a student attends should be one in which the dominant group matches on many factors—for example, socioeconomic group, educational goals, personal values and goals, religious surroundings, and career interests. The degree of the students' sociability versus independence is another important quality to consider. If at least three important characteristics are similar, a student's chances of success are good. We are aware that admissions officers want diversity for their colleges, but as college counselors we should aim for similarity for the students we advise. There are plenty of other accidentally arriving students who can give the college its modest diversity. For example, even Merit Scholars, who should know better, sometimes pick colleges haphazardly (Hood, 1968). They may add intellectual diversity to an intellectually average college, but should they? The more adjustments our students have to make, the harder it is for them; thus, those students most different feel uncomfortable, deny the problem in themselves, and put down the college. However, the root of their complaint may not be the college at all but a poor choice of a particular peer group which happens to use that college. If the college wants diversity, let others than our advised students be the sacrificial lambs.

4. *Wrong college for student's intellectual and occupa-*

tional preparation. Almost all the colleges (except a handful of technical institutions) call themselves liberal arts institutions. They feel they can, under this umbrella, prepare a student for anything. We doubt that premise. Premedical, foreign language, engineering, psychology, sociology, administration, and coaching, to name a few studies, require involvement in a large body of knowledge. If the college does not have courses, professors, and money to back up an area of knowledge sought by a student, it is the wrong place for that student. If the student's interests are extremely specialized, perhaps he will have to await graduate school, but his interests are based on years of personal experience with his abilities, and they must be respected if he is to be happily placed in college.

5. *Grading system too stringent.* Technical schools and newly popular, growing colleges should be approached with trepidation. The technical schools grade hard. For example, in a study of Minnesota colleges (Hood, 1968), technical colleges had a freshman average GPA of 1.45, even though technical colleges attract the brightest students. But the freshman GPA at Catholic women's colleges was 2.25. If a college has a newly academically improved student body, one would think that the professors would happily give out more A's; but the proportion of the various grades stays the same (Hood, 1968). Since it is well established that poor grades relate to dropping out of college, the college counselor should be aware of this underlying problem, especially for borderline cases and low-ability students.

6. *Individual student is repugnant to college.* The nonconformist rates high in all colleges as persona non grata. Such a student must be placed where the rules are flexible and the faculty members have egalitarian relationships with the students. Because the college is a group structure, it should surprise none of us that rebels to group control are problems to the college and its administration. Panos and Astin (1969) compared successful seniors to dropouts and found that a college's quality often correlated in different directions for these two groups. Qualities were items such as independence, career orientation, and administrator toughness. The dropout was affected oppo-

sitely from the senior. Thus, as is always the case in group function, those who did not fit were systematically weeded out. The
rules are made by the dominant members. A very sociable student suffers in a technical school, being seen as a bubblehead.
An effeminate boy is threatening and unsettling to an athletical-
ly oriented college. An intellectual is obnoxious to a fraternity-
sorority, sociable college.

Naturally, some artful counseling is required to avoid
such misplacements because there is no printed number or a
trustworthy college statement that can alert the college counselor to these traps. Common sense, backed up by clues, will
help. So will a preacceptance college campus visit by the student.

7. *Expectation of self-discipline by the college is too
high.* In the unusually liberal, nonstructured college, much has
to be expected of the individual student, who has to plan study,
time, and goals rather thoroughly. At Hampshire College, the
student may even prepare his own examinations. Self-discipline
becomes critical, and regrettably, it is less likely to be found in
the nonconformist than in the more average student. The small,
and often religious, college tends to have more required courses,
more parental-type follow-up from faculty. Such a direction is
appropriate for mildly (and nonrebellious) low-social students,
the introverted intellectuals. Poorly disciplined students do better at low-selectivity colleges, where they can often get by by
using their intellects as crutches. Overall, each college develops
a set of expectations of its student body. Although they differ
from college to college, these expectations are set in stone within each institution. If students cannot meet them, they should
move or, better, avoid the institution in the first place.

8. *Family values.* Some families seem to train children
from early childhood to be good college students. They praise
their sons and daughters for a gold star in first-grade reading,
and then are pleased in due time by a collegiate A. However,
other families may have values and reward expectations that
the college cannot satisfy: money, power, travel, for example.
In such cases, the rewards of grades or professional praise may
not seem worth all the work to students. It is too bad to lose

students because they find grades not even as meaningful as a scout merit badge. For such students, friendly reinforcement of the concrete relevance of their work is important and vocational goals recommendable. Unless necessary student behavior, such as studies and library work, appears useful to the person, it turns into distasteful work and begins to be ignored. Failure then follows.

9. *Economic pressures.* The need to pay for an expensive college education and for the non-income-productive years is so difficult that much has been written about payment for college. A few hours' work at a paying job may help solidify the student's commitment to education, but too many hours cause a breakdown. For example, according to one study (Astin, 1975), if a student works more than twenty-five hours per week, failures begin to pile up. Borrowing money or leaving school to accumulate funds is to be recommended instead of combining work and study. The college counselor can respect students' money limitations with only minor risk to their happy placement. Naturally, there are more offspring of rich and powerful families at the few extremely expensive institutions. But to claim that an education from an expensive institution is better than one at a similar but cheaper place is not true. If incoming freshmen characteristics are controlled—that is, if the student is similar at colleges A and B (Astin and Panos, 1969)—there is no evidence that the college education at an expensive institution is any better than at the less costly one. There may be some fine points of social prestige at the very expensive institutions, and certainly an effort at socioeconomic matching is good, but a need to work too many hours a week outweighs it. Our students can be placed with an eye toward cost and should not have to work at outside jobs too much. There is much in college missed by those who work their way through. It is an American myth that much time spent in simple jobs is a good thing; it may cause dropping out.

10. *Preexisting problems.* Sometimes the best efforts of the college counselor come to naught because of a preexisting problem in the student or even in the college. For example, the student may be homosexual but still in the closet and not able

to share this sexual conflict with the counselor. Or a parent may offer money for education, only to have the savings wiped out by an illness. And in the college there could be a collapsing department, a rebellion of part of the faculty against the administration, or even very serious financial deficiencies that will result in major change or closing of the college. One must accept some powerlessness in this work of college placement.

Practical Reactions to Misplacement

Although conventional advice from both college staff and professional advisers usually emphasizes prevention of dropout, it is usually best for the student and the college if the student drops out when the college experience is not going well. Unhappy freshmen become more unhappy by senior year (Vacher, 1974) if they have not solved their problems by leaving. As in second marriages, students may do better if they change schools. Roughly two thirds of the dropouts go to other colleges eventually (Panos and Astin, 1967), and about 15 percent go to two or more colleges. Studies of dropouts at Penn State (Ford and Urban, 1966) showed the more changes the better. Of 2,500 freshmen studied, 60 percent earned a degree from the Pennsylvania State college system. There were ten colleges in the system graduating those students. Of those who stayed in their freshmen choice of college, an expected 62 percent graduated; changing twice, 78 percent; three or more changes, 91 percent. Clearly, the searchers found what they needed, although those with only a single change included searchers who should have made more than one change of direction in their education. Of those who dropped out, 50 percent went on to complete their education elsewhere. Because the searchers never know what they may find, but know what they want to leave, personal maladjustment is the motivation for escape. This escape reduces anxiety, so the dropouts typically feel a sense of relief. Their panic at being worthless or failing persons can now subside. If it is indeed the college environment, together with individual psychology, that causes the problem, then leaving can be wise and is one of several forms of adjustment effort.

Quitting a college is drastic surgery, but if students' perceptions are correct about the etiology of their discomfort, it is a quick solution. Not everyone belongs in college, and not everyone feels happy on a given college campus. Most students who leave college take a little time off for readjustment and then make new plans. Most ultimately go on to graduate, so a transfer to another college is most usually the final step in this adjustment response.

Transferring should not have the bad name it does. Probably a great many of the failures come from poorly advised junior college students. A review of outcomes (Cope, 1975) showed that only 10 to 20 percent of the students who withdraw from junior college earn bachelor's degrees eventually, while 85 to 90 percent of the dropouts from good private institutions and 50 to 60 percent of the dropouts from average state universities later receive their bachelor's degrees. The trick to successfully transferring is learning from experience and choosing a college that fits the student's personality better the second time around. Most especially, it should not be too academically difficult. Good grades are easier to obtain in a junior college than in most four-year colleges.

Changing colleges within a university is a convenient way of handling this escape problem. To be successful, it has to be done with the same thought as transferring or choosing a college in the first place. But most of all, the student must really like fellow students and the academic atmosphere. The problem causing a change should be in the area of grades or course content. If the problems are social or emotional, a change within a university will be a disappointment. We think this is why a single impulsive change of college within a university is so often a failure.

One of the most useful practical steps for the failing student to take is *working* for one year. This is especially useful for the most common pattern of failure: a creative, nonconforming, and underachieving student who does not see the value of college from the beginning. Taking a simple entry-level job in the home community provides a real-life experience. During the working year, the relevance of education usually becomes clear.

Those students who believe that a college can help in later life are heavily inclined to stay to completion of their degree (Reed, 1974).

A brief *return home* for emotional refueling can be valuable for those students with separation and loneliness problems. They can, in a few days in their childhood rooms and relationships, remind themselves of their resolve to leave home, finish their education, and move into independent life.

Because some—perhaps 30 percent—of the potential dropouts are having more personal than academic problems, *on-site counseling* may help. This includes talking with friends or seeking more formal counseling from psychological or psychiatric services affiliated with the school. These services should work with milder problems in cases when the student is quite well placed academically. Regrettably, psychological-psychiatric services are often clogged with serious and pressing problems presented by students who later drop out, so that the services neglect the very students who could most benefit from their help. The student with moderate personal problems but no serious academic problems can receive much from problem-oriented counseling. More serious psychiatric illness should be referred to medical facilities.

Unsuccessful Responses to Misplacement

When a student complains of tension or suicidal thoughts, those feelings are given credit for causing academic and social problems. Most frequently, however, they are emotional reactions secondary to college stress and exist as long as the conflict remains unsolved. When the counseling cases at one university were studied (Kuehn and Kuehn, 1975), 90 percent of the students complained of emotional problems. Yet half of those emotionally troubled students had ACT scores judged less than "college potential," and 40 percent had unsatisfactory academic standing. Only 8 percent were thought true emotionally determined underachievers. When considering emotional states, one must understand the student as indeed suffering and in need of help. But the counselor placing a student should realize that overplacement is one of the major stresses contributing to the maladjustments found in college.

The most common emotional state is *depression.* In clinical services, mood complaints are common. Indeed, approximately 70 percent of adolescents have had feelings of substantial depression at some time. Suicide is rare, even with the increase over the past fifteen years taken into account. The mortality rate in the college-age population in 1975 was about 3,000 per year (Holinger, 1979), less than murder (3,500) and auto accidents (7,500 deaths) that year. Suicide is no higher in the elite colleges than the more ordinary ones (Eisenberg, 1980). The reaction of the misplaced student is not often the tragedy of suicide but the gloom of pervasive unhappiness, which usually manifests itself by a rather long-term feeling of frustration and failure without the relief of success. Of about 1,500 men studied who dropped out of Harvard, 39 percent had emotional problems and sought help, especially for depression (Nicholi, 1974). This is indeed a quiet desperation to be avoided through the best placement.

Another common sign of student maladjustment is an *anxiety state.* The student feels tense and apprehensive, as if some fearful incident were about to happen. The state of fear is meaningless only on the surface, for in personal emotions the student is torn with conflict. There are many causes of conflict, but the most common is a failure to perform in the college at the level of self-expectation. A typical example is poor grades for certain academic efforts that in similar previous situations had been successful for the student. In the extremity of panic, a student's anxiety is frightening, both personally and to others. Such extreme anxiety has a negative effect on test scores and function, especially with middle-ability students (Spielberger, 1974). Bright students are helped by anxiety, and a little anxiety is necessary to motivate most students.

Students usually come from comfortable homes and successful high school adjustments. New college friends are hard to develop for the average student, and some have real difficulties achieving friends and a group position. Such students can feel lonely, powerless, and angry. Shy students appear withdrawn on the surface but emotionally angry that they find themselves in this position. That anger translates itself into anger at the college, the food, the dormitories—usually before anger at self.

Preoccupied and confusional states are signs of acute failure to cope. These symptoms are found in those with a need to dramatize their plight—hence, in manipulatory or socially scheming students. The situations are found in clear circumstances—for example, amnesia, or wandering across the campus at odd times or in odd clothes, so that attention follows. Conscious, purposeful components are present; these states occur more often around exam time.

Young adults are painfully aware of *sexual expectations,* from their own ideals as well as from their boyfriends' or girl friends'. When a student feels worried, the fragile complex of sexual behavior and responses can break down. That is the cart; the horse is the maladjustment, even though the student may say "I can't study because I'm worried I might be a homosexual." Many stresses, including academic, can show up as sexual complaints.

A student's *angry outbursts,* which let off steam, can destroy the calm of a college campus, yet they are seldom dangerous. Successful students exhibit mild aggression in the form of pranks, but too much aggressive behavior, vandalism, or tantrums can signal strong underlying frustrations. Usually found in students with a long history of temper outbursts, overaggressive behavior is an individual's way of crying out.

Personality disorders are the most basic problem, but in psychological treatment these disorders interest the psychiatrist more than the college counselor. We review them briefly. The most common is the passive-aggressive student who characteristically copes with stress by procrastination. All persons show some foot-dragging at times, but when the student has such a pattern and is routinely uncooperative as well as being late with assignments, there will be a clash with the college. At the point and time of the clash, the presenting symptoms will be neurotic and anxiety ridden, and it takes some therapy to get down to and to outline the underlying pattern. Other personality disorders include hostile dependency (blaming others), passive dependency (clinging, childlike), aggressiveness (overassertive), and antisocial behavior (delinquency).

Maladaptation in the college, caused by a personality disorder and poor ability for the particular college, is the most likely basis for such emotional problems as anxiety or depression.

Drug and alcohol use are pervasive American problems. The student with personality disorder or other chronic maladjustment commonly turns to drugs. This solution to problems provides only temporary relief. The drug changes the structure of the mind and its capacity to look critically at itself. The user is awarded a temporary chemical vacation. The student needs that vacation because of the high tension experienced at college. Rather than giving puritanical warnings, the wise counselor attempts to minimize the many college-adjustment problems by superior placement. We think the common collegiate existence by drinking and drug use reflects the great internal tension experienced at college and the blithe professional acceptance of that state of tension. The popular image of happy days on the campus should not be believed by any professional in the face of the stunning 50 percent attrition rate. Drinking and drug use (which diminish after college) are signs of maladjustment and show that the student is willing to pay the dollar and hangover costs for the moments of escape.

Major *psychiatric illness,* chiefly manic-depressive disease and schizophrenia, are not set off by added collegiate stress, but they are complicated by the usual pressures of college adjustment. Most psychiatrists agree with the theory of primary biochemical causes of these major psychoses. Regrettably, students suffering from them are the least likely to return to campus (Nicholi, 1974), and if they do return, they are most likely to drop out a second time. These are not common diseases. Schizophrenia occurs in only .85 percent of the population, and the typical onset is later, at twenty-five to thirty-five years of age, than at the high school and college ages.

The anxieties, depressions, and sex problems are usually and wrongly seen as emotional, as causes of college attrition. Except in a few cases, it is better to see these problems as symptoms of doing less well than expected in the college's academic and social competition.

Professional Planning to Avoid College Failure

There is great value in doing the legwork necessary to prevent college failure. First, students have four years they will always remember, and in which we hope they have success. Usually, students' fantasies can be met with reality and they can receive a meaningful education with good feelings and adequate preparation for the next phase of their lives. Their new friends should be solid and their extracurricular activities satisfying.

When all goes well, the college receives a student who fits, who adds to the college, and who does not complain or overuse support facilities. We believe colleges should spend more time understanding themselves and picking appropriate students rather than overstudying dropouts. It is human nature to focus on failure and discomfort, but in this case the dropout is gone, and such focus is of dubious value. It is painfully clear from the literature that the colleges have learned little about student choice over the past fifty years. The dropout rate has stayed essentially the same since early studies, through war and progress, to the present (Cope, 1975). If as a college counselor you can guide students to appropriate colleges, you have helped them and, in spite of itself, the institution also.

Finally, an appropriate college choice prevents moves. The public is aware that moves, or transfers to other colleges, are not all bad; students today talk casually about transferring. As stated earlier, a move is usually helpful and may increase the student's happiness and collegiate success. However, it is a very crude way to bring about change, usually involves lost time and much anxiety, and still may not be successful. Those students who moved just once in the Pennsylvania study (Ford and Urban, 1966) had the lowest rate of graduation. Only for brave souls who kept trying did success rates go up.

Our own private college counseling service is based on a structured interview with the student to elicit a rating on eighteen points. These arbitrary points are chosen because they are scorable in the colleges; they include such factors as SAT scores; interest in social sciences, humanities, and other study areas; socioeconomic group; athletic commitment; and college size. After the student scores are determined, they are run through an involved computer program that prints between forty and seventy colleges which roughly fit in the characteristics judged important for each student. These colleges are hand-scored and evaluated with thoughtful judgment, our personal knowledge of the student, and some degree of unscored knowledge of the colleges. A student's final list has twenty to thirty colleges ranked high to low, according to overall fit. A report is written and discussed with the student and family. Our results have been gratifying. In 1978 we followed up on 107 students to see how they liked their colleges after they had spent at least one year there. We found:

- Of those who went to recommended colleges, 92 percent were happy, 8 percent were not.
- Of those who went to unrecommended colleges, 39 percent were happy, 61 percent were not.

We believe that those who went to unrecommended colleges had such a dismal showing partly because the whole group was made up of students who felt a special need for college counseling. Many of the students we saw represented quite challenging placement problems. Thus, the usual 50 percent dropout rate might have been increased. In addition, the group of students who went their own way may have been more rebellious, or perhaps they were holding on to an unreasonable fantasy of college life.

Although the time involved in our process might be too much for an average college counselor, there are concrete steps that can be taken immediately to improve the success rate of students. One should decide that students are persons already well set in their ways, with certain personal and intellectual qualities. The colleges are variables. Basically, you try to understand the student's needs and search for a proper college with these needs in mind.

1. Match for SATs or ACTs. Estimate; the student should not be in the bottom or top 15 percent; the middle 50 percent is best.

2. Match for GPA the same way, remembering to adjust with knowledge of one's own school. For example, if yours is an average suburban public high school and your student is considering a selective college where many students come from private schools, you might want to drop your student's GPA a half or a whole point—and vice versa for less competitive colleges with fewer freshman from private schools.

3. The colleges should have departmental strength in the areas of interest to the student. We have found that this list of areas is not unending. Students have to be asked which subjects they liked and which they got their best grades in. They are usually the same, but liking the subject (if with an unpretentious and unassuming attitude) should take precedence over grades. Occupational thoughts should be explored. Ask students to discuss the following areas, with an aim of rating their strengths. These groupings are partly developed from college departmental structure and partly empirically. For example, we found that students who scored well in social studies quite often had business in their minds as a likely career, and the less selective colleges on their lists often had business departmental strength.

- *Social studies.* Presented as history in high school, but includes political science, economics, administration, and business. These areas reflect an interest in friends, power, and groups.
- *Sciences.* Given as biology and chemistry in high school, but includes higher math, geology, astronomy, physics, chemistry, biology, and engineering. Strength in this area reflects an interest in the real world, usually low involvement in verbal skills.
- *Humanities.* Taught as English in high school, but includes literature, writing, philosophy, communication, and education. Strength here reflects high verbal and abstractive ability and a desire to communicate.

- *Behavioral sciences.* Psychology in high school (perhaps an interest in mysticism or controlling others if psychology is not offered), but includes sociology, anthropology, mythology, and marketing. These strengths indicate finding meaning in intellectually controlling the social environment.
- *Art, music, foreign language, and skilled sports.* These stand alone, as separate qualities. The student may be good or poor, bright or average, academically disciplined or not, and still be gifted in one of these areas or hopeless in them. Probably they require special abilities in the brain cells and need only be explored in high school for the answer concerning whether to look for such a department as a strong field in the final choice of college.

Next, locate possible colleges with departmental strength and interest pattern similar to the students'. To find departmental strengths in given colleges, look at the percent of students graduating with that major (*Barrons'*, 1978; Cass and Birnbaum, 1979). You can go further, as we have for our computer data base, by counting the professors in the crucial department when you need a special question answered about a specific college. For example, the number of Russian language teachers could be crucial for a student gifted in language. But usually the pattern of the three or four most common majors will suffice.

Specialized programs are offered by universities as exciting and attractive intellectual adventures, or, in some cases, even serve as a flagship of the institution. Examples include journalism at Missouri University, the engineering program at the University of California at Berkeley, aeronautical engineering at Purdue University, and early admission to medical school for selected undergraduate freshmen at Washington University. Since many more students are attracted than can be taken into these and similar programs, most students are rejected and sometimes stranded without alternate plans. With good precollege counseling, those lost and frustrated students could have been helped.

Students interested in special programs should be guided to apply to a range of institutions appropriate to their grades, testing, interests, and proven abilities. In addition to Purdue University, for example, thirty-eight other institutions have a wide variety of locations and selectivity levels and also offer substantial courses of study in aeronautical engineering. Application to five institutions, including a likely safety, is recommended.

Students who select a highly specialized program to enter directly after high school lose by narrowing their options but gain enormously by putting themselves on a golden road to their goal. In addition, they will be highly motivated to do the work along that academic road, since their studies are personally relevant. Special programs are similar to early decision plans for graduate schools, and they should be judged as such. The counselor should interview carefully, to bring out the students' occupational goals, and offer guidance on their direction as well as selectivity level. For example, is medical school a reasonable goal, and in what colleges could the student achieve good grades in a premed program? As with all graduate programs, it is advisable to recommend those institutions with large departments in the area considered and having highly qualified staff and proven academic track records. Worth avoiding are newer programs with trendy, recently popular courses. One should take an especially hard look at schools with colorful recreational overtones, such as forestry, oceanography, and ecological studies.

Specialized programs are no different from the traditional ones of business, education, or agriculture. Indeed, many small colleges are quite specialized, with a high percentage of men entering business and a similar percentage of women traditionally entering education. These fields represent similar guidance problems, but ones a bit easier to conceptualize in that they are common occupations and offer more diverse work placements after graduation, compared to the more glamorous elite programs. Thus, a college counselor should advise applicants for any specialized program to be sure they want to limit their options so early. If they do, the counselor should guide them toward a range of specialized programs varying in selectivity level, location, rigor of grading practices, and relative success of the graduates in reaching their goals.

We believe the counselor should not be dazzled by the fame of the university, the glamour of the program, or the expected status of the potential graduate. Those are visions. Just as many successful physicians come from unsophisticated medical schools as from the famous schools when the entering students' abilities are matched. Findings in other fields, where matched samples are used for study, yield the same results. As Astin (1971) points out, if entering freshmen at several universities are matched and then compared on later Graduate Record Examinations, there arc no differences attributable to the famous university. Prestige comes from individual achievement; entry into an elite institution is only one way to begin a lifetime of prestige.

4. Match social quality if possible. A quick way to estimate high sociability is by the percentage of students in fraternities or single-sex dorms, or those belonging to the dominant religion of the college. On the other hand, independent students like to live in coeducational dorms, or in their junior and senior years they like to live off campus.

5. There are some negatives:

- Do not make a "challenge" placement. College is already difficult to handle. Aim for realism.
- Do not use the "old boy" network in serious college placement. It is tempting to call a friend in the admissions office of a neighboring college to ask for help in placement. But admissions officers want to fill the college, whereas you as a counselor want a solid placement: They are different things.
- Do not worry too much about climate, physical surroundings, books in the library, faculty with doctorates. It is the students in the college and their qualities that are important. There are largely similar schools east and west, in warm and cold climates. And if the students at a certain college need doctorate-quality professors, they will laugh the incompetent professors out of office.
- Do not try to remake the students. If a student is poor in, say, English, accept it and find an engineering- or business-oriented college. Roll along with students' strengths; do not rub their noses in their weaknesses.

We believe that the college counselor working in a school setting can contribute to students' success in college in two other ways:

1. Give a few lectures and handouts on the differences between high school and college. Tell the precollege students, for example, that they will have to plan to study more of the time, that grades will be harder to come by, that the freedom they feel as freshmen is only partly real.
2. Encourage teachers on the college track to explain a little about how their course works in college and how it differs from the high school course being offered.

We believe that the college counselors in high school and the admissions officers in college are in very crucial positions to affect the welfare of the college-bound student. Recall those fifty-fifty odds on dropouts in college. Because the admissions officer does not really know the counselor's student and because the officer is loyal to the institution, the importance of the help offered by the high school college counselor doubles.

5

Working Individually with College Applicants

Stanley Bosworth

> *... but when I became*
> *a man I put away childish*
> *things.*
> > 1 Corinthians 13:11

The uninitiated are often surprised to discover that colleges—certainly any of worth—have distinct and different personalities. So do children. This latter fact seems to astonish counselors.

Yet the primary role of college counselors is to determine with whom they are dealing. It is indeed a sacred professional duty to know the young person who is presented, all coltish and vulnerable, to be guided into an uncertain future. Furthermore, it is a process that must be a form of giving: If I am to know you, I must, in a sense, accept you, your values, your major concerns, your limits, your inviolate center.

Four years of pleasure or pain are at stake. A lifetime of friends, lovers, and spouses may be a part of that decision. Potency and options of a pervasive nature are presented to someone so young as to be barely able to conceive of the consequences of choice. Indeed, the applicant-supplicant is essentially concerned with "getting in"—wherever and whatever that may imply. The counselor's truly sacred duty is to help determine *who* is getting in and into *what*.

So major an inquiry, so portentous a decision deserves a proportional effort and involvement. The counselor should be

111

that most calibrated person in a staff. The time allotted to working with the student should be greater than the sum of all other kinds of administrative involvement that have been part of the high school experience. The counselor must have the verve, empathy, worldliness, and dedication necessary to so important an undertaking. A young person's values and purposes are about to be evaluated; a child is about to confront the irrevocable. The insight and commitment required for the task are consummate. The following discussion proposes a best-case scenario for providing these values.

Beginning the Itinerary: Counselor as Travel Agent

> Mon enfant, ma soeur,
> Songe a la douceur
> D'aller la bas vivre ensemble!
> Aimer a loisir
> Aimer et mourir
> Au pays qui te ressemble!
> —Charles Baudelaire

You begin with a blank piece of paper and a somewhat anxious applicant. "What are your interests?" you ask. The applicant often wheels about—anxious, threatened, confused. "You mean academic?" "I mean anything you care about," you reply. "I mean intellectual interests, spiritual interests, hobbies, athletics, politics—anything in any order."

The order of commitment is important. This free association elicits a kind of rank order of importance or, at the very least, a self-image that determines the ordering of the information. Each area described has a reality component. The student must be allowed to understand that we care as much about the examples as we do about the activity. "Oh, I like reading" should be followed by "What's your favorite book, author, kind of book?" "I sail!" should be checked for class of boat, conditions, races (if any), and so forth. "I backpack." "Where? When? How often?" A difference between whimsical intent and operationally real activities is thereby distinguished. The student is being held to specificity and thus gradually being prepared for the college interview lurking in the future.

The priorities and itemization of achievements begin to appear on your paper. It becomes clear to both student and adviser that whatever college is sought must have a first-rate music department (the kind of music and the accent on musicology versus performance is carefully noted). Or perhaps a fairly clear math-science profile emerges, with even a hint of a possible premed future. In the course of eliciting interests and supporting activities, other valuable glimpses have emerged: This person has or has not survived alone in summer experiences, trips abroad, and so on. Summer and after-school work have been part of the student's routine, or have been eschewed. The person we are dealing with is fairly diffident and withdrawn or is a gregarious extrovert.

The blank page is filling up with desires, accomplishments, points of reference, and attitudes. It is at once biography, résumé, reference, and game plan. Scores are carefully noted, to confine or expand possibilities. On one side colleges are proffered—perhaps as many as fifteen—for a first inspection. They are discussed with the student, who is reminded, "Every college has a major drawback." Tufts has Holiday Inn architecture; Harvard has large classes, inacessible teachers, and walls of arrogance. Yale is in New Haven—a kind of desperate fortress staving off the barbarian hordes. It also demands more of majors than it should. Middlebury is so isolated that, on a winter's day, a trip to California takes less time. Bennington suffers from a certain number of flaky, entropic princes and princesses. Brown does not have sufficient funds, range, and organization to allow an urban studies major who is also a brilliant artist to be both.

It has seldom dawned on the student that there must be a choice between imperfections. Now is the time to draw from the counselor's hundreds of thousands of miles of travel those qualities—good and bad—that will realistically acquaint the student with options. Tufts has a wide range of programs, superb art and drama, and is set in the beautiful city of Boston. Harvard is the alpha and omega of the power elite, home of many of each generation's finest minds, and a summa of competitive struggle. Yale has its best teachers on the firing line, has incomparable humanities and music, and has a single-minded dedication to real learning. Middlebury, surrounded by a crown of mountains, is in the most idyllic location for pursuing serious studies while worshiping nature. Bennington has more writers, artists, and performers in both student and teaching populations per capita than any college in the country. Brown, with its Ivy power and irreverent energy, is not only wildly popular with bright independent students but adds to its high morale a superb range of studies, from media to science.

The tourist agent's work has only begun. The fit is now a matter of further research, travel, interviews, essays, and competition. But for the job to be done properly, the agent must never lose sight of the client. The purpose is never to push an institution; it is to find a best fit based on two kinds of knowledge: first about the student and then about the facilities that appear to conform best to the student's needs.

Priorities: The College Essay as an Ontological Investigation

Eke Plato seith, who so that can him rede
The wordes mote be cousin to the dede.
Geoffrey Chaucer

The best knowledge about the student must come from the student, who needs help in revealing this information. A sense of priorities must be developed. Style must be a product of sincerity rather than its mask. A perception of *who* is writing must flow from how it is said and what the saying says about the speaker. The counselor is really involved in something far more important than editing: the unfathoming of the sense of a human being. The final writing should almost be automatic. The processes that lead to it should involve the most uncompromising introspection. If this is done, and when it is done, not only will the counselor truly know the advisee, the advisee will have achieved self-knowledge.

In a sense, this kind of discovery involves a student's coming to grips with existential truths and being able to present them in the terms of an adult world. A confessional is not wanted. A series of platitudes about intentions is guaranteed failure. A list of chronological events is boring. How, then, can the student solve the problem of expository writing of the most demanding nature? For many adolescents, this is a personal kind of exposure of the most painful sort.

I have found, working with hundreds of students, that it helps them to reconsider both what we (adults) expect and what they truly consider important. "Don't begin with the beginning!" I remind them, when the soppy first line of a projected college essay reads, "I was born . . ." "They know that you were born!" I insist. After one such feeble effort, I exhorted a particularly brilliant young person to give me phenomenological rather than chronological time. The next day the student presented me with an essay of a totally different character. Instead of reading "I was born," it began with "My father is an actor." Not a word had to be changed. Priorities had been reassessed, and levels of importances had replaced chronological detail.

A superbly gifted young woman wrote a carefully crafted essay detailing her many accomplishments. I read it and suggested that it would do. She heard the deadness in my voice, tore it up, and in a fury wrote the following:

I could tell you all about my wonderful achievements, slightly exaggerated of course, but I'd rather tell you what affects me, what I remember. The things like the way six shadows of my tennis racket converged on the ball as it sat clearly marked in its yellow on the huge green court. And how the same ball was caught in the net by the back wall, like a fish. The way the herring plane in Maine swoops down on me all little on the long field. And the piece of hay stuck between my toes that stayed with me even as I went in to talk to my old aunt. How I promised to remember that and the time I was walking down the marble stairs of St. Ann's in my green knit skirt so I would know I existed then, that my past was not something simply planted in my brain. The way I've felt myself growing, almost physically, and listened to my growth settling into me, and welcomed it because it meant I was becoming more realistic about myself, so that not living in a world of illusions I could exist more in this world and feel all its happinesses and wonders which are greater than anything imagined because they are real —the most amazing thing of all.

The things that I love to feel and discover are the subtleties happening between people and events. How one person helplessly tries to make himself known to others, the way the others might ignore him, and the way he will stay with the others as friends because he's been saved from something he doesn't want to acknowledge anyway. The way masses of a nation of people will ignore some huge, very true situation, and then slowly discover it in a way that's as useless as if they'd never found it. The way I myself fit into everyone's patterns and the way my actions affect me, why they make me feel good or bad, and whether they really do. The things that are observed and given: trees, animals, ourselves, snow and winds. Using my body to certain ends and to an end in itself: sexual, transportation, exploration, and to an immersion into an environment and discovering the physical realities of the world, as skiing does. Traveling, the feeling of "wanderlust" raging satisfied, going wherever I wish to, encountering, dealing with, and enjoying new people, situations, and places.

And somewhere within this huge scheme of myself, learning fits in as a major part. Education brings all these parts of the world to me, and me to them, and I can work with them and myself, as I use my own mind to deal with them, to cast light on them, and encompass them. And so now I wish to present myself at one of the "great educational institutions" to gather, process, and give more.

She majored in English at Harvard.

Another brilliant girl bemoaned her "typical" upper-middle-class background. Her parents were professionals. They were also interracial, and, when challenged to confront the atypical in her life, she wrote this essay:

Family legends passed down through generations grow more incredible each time they are told. Sitting at my grandmother's feet listening to her tell of my great great grandmother, Kate Travis, I knew *that* story would never change. The ideal of it was too important to be stretched and exaggerated, too important to be tampered with for the sake of a happy tale.

My great great grandmother was born an enslaved person in about 1845. She lived in a small, rural community—Horse Pasture, Virginia. She was allowed to keep part of her wages and when she was freed she had money saved to buy a restaurant in nearby Martinsville. With freedom a great desire to succeed came to Kate Travis. Money was not the important part of her dream. She wanted to raise her children with pride. She wanted them to be educated and have a chance to become what they wanted to be.

The restaurant was a success. Two of Kate's children died of smallpox. Her remaining son, Raleigh, went to school and grew up into an ambitious young man. But the dream of Reconstruction was dying. Martinsville was changing: Kate was constantly being hounded to sell her restaurant. There was no place for Raleigh there. With high hopes Kate traveled North with her son to help him establish a business in Chicago. She returned to Martinsville to find that the Jim Crow laws had become more oppressive. A sturdy partition was constructed down the center of the restaurant and she was forced to run a segregated business.

Kate learned to live within the new laws, but that was not enough. Close by the court house, her land was desirable property. A victim of legal manipulations and her own illiteracy, she finally lost her restaurant, and was forced to accept, as compensation, land on the outskirts of town. Raleigh returned to Virginia, his ambition crushed. Chicago was not what he had dreamt it to be. He died, leaving a baby daughter for Kate to raise. She earned a living working as a cook.

I wish I could have known my great great grandmother in her later years, her bitter years. I would tell her that her dreams were not lost, they lived on in her granddaughter, my grandmother, who grew up into a woman with the same strong convictions as Kate Travis.

I would tell her that the proud tradition she started the day she was freed in Horse Pasture lives on in her great and great great grandchildren. I would tell her that her strong desire to succeed lives on in me.

She too had a brilliant career at Harvard.

One may reply that few students have the insight, the verve, the fundamental skills to write so stirringly and originally.

That is true, but it is also true that students have some part of their life which is, to them, of enormous importance. They must learn that our true beginnings are never chronological but always concerned with those events and experiences which somehow act as a formative part of our lives.

The foregoing procedures take time and involve many short advisement sessions rather than preestablished hours. In other words, they require dedication from a person who has the literacy, the time, and the empathy to make this follow-through a major commitment. Since that same person will be representing the student at the colleges of the student's choice, the greater the investment in these aspects of advisement, the fuller the presentation. Subsequent to the birth of the essay, the adviser is truly advised; the student's inner strivings have been unfolded.

The result can be valuable for all concerned. For the student, insight has been developed, and, no doubt, writing quality has been vastly improved. The adviser has a profoundly greater sense of the kind of person who is being represented. The colleges can only gain from a better fit and a possible diminution of dropouts. Thus, the search for self is both a process and an outcome. In what better form of education can a school invest?

Finding the College: The Art of the Possible

> Suddenly she came upon a
> little three-legged table
> made of solid glass; there
> was nothing on it but a tiny
> golden key, and Alice's first
> idea was that this might
> belong to one of the doors
> of the hall; but alas! either
> the locks were too large, or
> the key was too small, but at
> any rate it would not open
> any of them.
>
> —Lewis Carroll

Almost any dean of admissions or admissions manual will inform the counselor that College Board scores "don't matter," "mean very little," or are "but one of many factors." This is about as loose a generalization as the one which states that personal income is unrelated to "happiness." Both are true. Both are untrue beyond measurable thresholds.

The scores don't matter when the college is hanging on for dear life and wants nothing more than tuition and a live body. They mean very little when the college is—often legitimately—seeking a very special personality and a set of talents. Institutions such as Sarah Lawrence, Bennington, and Oberlin seek (and often get) high-scoring students but are quite capable of judging alternatives, such as a set of poems and short stories, real proficiency at the cello, musical compositions, superior dance and/or dramatic skills, and so on. "Wimps," whatever their scores, had best beware of such institutions.

Of course, the score factor is one of many, but here is where thresholds count. A standard is implicit at Yale. An athletic, intelligent, proletarian black candidate might squeak through with scores in the 500s, but his black bourgeois counterpart needs another 100 points. The white middle-class candidate had better have notable concerns or Olympic-level athletics behind the application for it to be seriously considered with less than 1,300 combined SATs. For certain rather more conventional schools (such as Dartmouth, Williams, Princeton) and to some extent for all schools, the "legacy" is also an important ingredient in the mix.

The thresholds remain, and the adviser should calculate them when planning with the advisee. The range should be inclusive of those schools that meet the counselor cum "travel agent's" prerequisites from least to most likely. Such ambition means of course that disappointment is likely at some point along the line—the student should be so informed. I question those advisers who boast of a high percentage of students admitted to "first choice" colleges. The implication is that to avoid trouble with both admissions people and parents, the choices have to limited to "safe" institutions.

The danger in reaching high, however, is that the student will fixate on the most competitive rather than the most (for the student) desirable college. This tendency should be confronted as often as it appears. "But you said you wanted a small country college," I remonstrate, "and the University of Penn-sylvania, while excellent, is both large and very urban." "I guess I really want a good premed school," they may admit. If so, it is my job to restructure the choices. On the other hand, if the pur-suit is prestige per se, the student's purposes need restructuring. For such a student does not know what is desired, will not stand up to an interview, and will, above all, be totally unpre-pared for the environment of the ultimate choice of college.

The list should be geared to the developing self-realiza-tion of the advisee, which inevitably will take some turns before final applications are made. A candid appraisal of possibilities should accompany this list, along with a constant emphasis on intrinsics peculiar to individual institutions. This way the elu-siveness of a given college will be "one of many factors," just as scores are. A handful of keys will thus be distributed that will open many, if not all, the doors desired.

Interviews: Nothing But the Truth, But Not All of It

> Prepare a face to meet the faces that
> you meet.
>
> —T. S. Eliot

One prepares not for an interview but for an interviewer. The most unscientific kind of predictor, the interview is none-theless a significant factor in the college's decision-making pro-cess, especially at the most competitive colleges (a fact they frequently deny). Whatever the official policy, I can—as one who for years has been closeted with admissions personnel dur-ing the March endgame—confirm that almost all schools rely heavily on the interview.

One reason for this is obvious. If scores and factored and quantified records are the ultimate criteria, then the human ele-ment is nullified. Because admissions people would therefore be redundant, they are apt to rely on their own and their coprofes-sionals' percipience. A less venal reason is that many serious purposes of a college—for instance, the desire for creative stu-dents or the search for a kind of social and spiritual fit—are not quantifiable. However inaccurate interviews may be for predict-ing "success," they do seemingly collect under one institutional roof a fairly coherent kind of person. Clearly, they enjoy golf, the stock market, and short haircuts at Williams. The student at Oberlin is very apt to be "into" all manner of causes, mystiques, and arcane arts. They seem to grow students tall, kinetic, and ebullient at Pomona. Somewhere in all this the interview played a role.

It follows that there are two kinds of attitudes students need to be best prepared for the interview. One is a sense of the kind of institution interviewing them (since institutional personalities extend to personnel). The other is an ability to vary the interview approach according to the interviewer's characteristics. This bit of gamesmanship often quite surprises students, who feel their very real integrity should be a plus in the admissions decision! It is hard to change the world but less difficult to inform an advisee about how the world is made.

A well-placed professional woman will probably not enjoy a male student's allusions to conquests or other manifestations of his prurience. A black interviewer will have some difficulty with a student's experiences in a parent's overseas corporation, the more so if patronizing remarks are made about the indigenous population. An athletic-looking interviewer will be disappointed by a student's persistent intellectual disdain for sports. Almost any interviewer will frown at the capital sin of disrespect for the institution, for the student's high school, or for the student's family. Personal problems are best left to confidants or therapists.

It is neither dishonest nor fatuous to omit those aspects of one's personality calculated to antagonize a person in authority. Learning that alone is worth the trouble this advisement entails. We disadvantage the student when we court the bias of the interviewer. We also disadvantage an institution when we give it cause to reject for such prejudicial reasons.

The Reference: Portrait by an Artist

> For one man loved the Pilgrim soul
> in you.
>
> —William Butler Yeats

The reference written by the key person in a student's

career (principal, adviser, high school head, or ideally all three) is the critical outcome of the entire advisement process. If the student has been led to greater insight and becomingness, if the essay has revealed this insight, and the interviews have sharpened it, the reference should confirm it.

This requires that the author has taken the trouble to *notice* the person being written about. That seems self-evident, but it does not always happen. The student has struggled to determine priorities, to manifest special interests and abilities, and to present them with charm and urgency. No lesser effort is acceptable on the part of the writer.

Yet the reference must reconfirm priorities and talents while doing much more. It must, with whimsy, humor, deference, love—even anger—create a vignette that makes the student real. This is not a matter of painstakingly learning an art. The art is there: behind anyone worthy of being in education. It is manifest when among friends the teacher or adviser discusses students amid laughter and tears. It is there in every frank anecdote reported to colleagues. The author of the reference needs only the courage of conviction, the humor of native irreverence, and the enthusiasm of one who loves the young.

It follows that the writer must either know the student personally, *be* the counselor, or consult at length with others. Something else follows—something more difficult to obtain. If the reference is being written for a very superior student aiming at a highly competitive college, the writer must be no less exceptional. We have been really talking all along about the kind of student, adviser, and advisement appropriate to those few institutions. There is a voice, a way of communication, a frame of references common to the truly educated in our land. They are very few in number, but that is true in every country. It is only in our country, however, that by equating the name "higher learning" with myriad vocational schools we have confused the issue. Our advisees deserve better than confusion if they are persons of exceptional talent and promise.

To some extent, this is always the case. Any student deserves the best, the most consistent, engaging, and coherent reference possible.· Following are two headmaster references, to suggest the candor and vividness desired.

Deborah's non sequiturs are the most coherent footnotes to her generational malaise. They (she) make sense because she is a survivor. Her staggeringly brilliant mind (almost unique among the giants in her class!) has transmuted *tsouris* into gold. She has survived the vicissitudes of owning a fine house in a desperately dangerous neighborhood. She has transcended the screeching drivenness of two fabulously successful parents. She is unique.

Her wisdom flows from a kind of comedic verve. It varies between the highest kind of sentience and the most devastating satire. It impresses by its self-deprecating literacy and wit. It disarms the mighty and the pompous. It hypnotizes her friends (both peers and adults) by its unremitting truths—truths inconvenient, wondrous, and undiscovered.

She will write brilliant books, will Deborah, if she ever fully masters prepositions and the use of the comma. She will dominate the stage and media by her acting, her voice, and, above all, her gentle, loving jibes at the stuffiness of the world around her. Indeed, her masterful, ongoing, outrageous *reductio* make Deborah, in my opinion, the most fascinating and intellectually exciting young person I know.

Deborah's College Board scores are all but an assault on the propriety of psychometrics. As someone who has built an elitist school around measuring systems, I am delighted to see them so guilelessly dismantled by this young woman's perversity.

Not, in fact, entirely. Her Binet (over 160) eluded Deborah's *bel dedain.* Her catholic reading, her musicality, her impeccable memory and performing skills, her superb (if offbeat) writing give her away. But most of all Deborah herself—a small, pert, vibrant giant—tells it all. She brings health and insight and wonderment to those who know and love her. I have no better candidate for Vassar. If they are very wise, they will discover her and crown their literature and performing arts department with a wonder. If they are not wise, Deborah will migrate to another great institution, hop along behind it, and wrinkle its fastidious train.

One student and only one of the scores who have read a lesson in the "Festival of Lessons and Carols" does so with conviction and insight. His absolutely magnificent voice intones and interprets at the same time. It would never occur to Cyril that words—least of all sacred words—can be without meaning.

It is a voice we shall hear from. Cyril—a fierce, powerful, beautiful, intense, fuguelike young man—is a leader, an author, an actor, an athlete, and angry. He has seen the price his race has paid for failure and the almost equally painful price of middle-class respectability. He has grappled with all the paradoxes of both sides of the human and most specifically the black condition and has emerged with more understanding than is meted to men twice his age.

Cyril attains respectable Board scores more easily than classroom *punctilio*. He is impatient with the dross of scholarship, though passionate with its conceptual and literary implications. I remember Cyril enacting an old man in a prize-winning play written by a fellow student—beaten, fragile, proud, and foolish—and I marveled at the dignity and grace inherent in both the projected character and the actor himself.

He understands better than he records. He needs the best, the very best, of colleges so that his deep voice can resonate and test his anger and rhetoric against the finest minds in our country. For Cyril has just such a mind.

I offer Cyril to Brown as a profoundly talented, uniquely intelligent, agonizingly reflective young man. I offer him as a black man, aware of the odyssey of his becomingness as few men of any race have been. I offer him with a sense of the difficulties and frustrations he and Brown may encounter in each other, and the certainty that there is more worth and reality in his eventual transcendence than will be found in a gross of the mindless, diligent, ambitious young people who turn out to college to be discovered. Cyril will be a discoverer.

Both students were admitted to the colleges of their choice.

Why Bother? A Justification of Concern

> I learned how to walk: since
> then I have let myself go. I learned
> how to fly: since then I do not wish
> to be pushed in order to get away.
>   Now I am light; now I fly; now I
> see myself; now a god dances through me.
>   —Friedrich Nietzsche

When we say it matters, when we make it matter by giving unstintingly of hours and concern, when the entire process of choice is made into a kind of major liturgical event—then the student understands that it really matters! Behind the selection is, after all, a student's perception of self-image, of importance, of the future. A college choice serves in the same primitive way as a large church wedding: Through the extravagance of ceremony, it reminds the participant that a significant troth is taking place.

One wonders which of all the many factors in a life make for the mystery of outcomes. Events concatenate in a seemingly arbitrary way, yet there is forever the temptation to imagine how, with the slightest change, push, accent, they might have led somewhere else. The college dropout is a majority of freshmen. Might not the precision of choice, the marshaling of purpose, the endorsement of authorities, and the sheer ceremony of selection preclude many of those dropouts?

If so, the several hours of counseling time are worth far more than any possible cost entailed. If thirty hours of intelligent and patient guidance clarify purpose and facilitate future, then thousands of human hours have been salvaged from the rubbish pile of ignorance and disappointment.

In sum, the counselor should be an educator. The advisee should be learning how to inventory abilities, structure goals, and struggle to prevail. Seventeen-year-olds really begin this process with very little self-knowledge. Even more confusing is their lack of knowledge of how other neophytes take their first steps toward their adult life. Thus do they learn to see themselves beneath themselves. Their discovery of the sacredness and importance within them is the ultimate justification for advisement at its best.

✍ 6

Advising Students on Integrating Academic Learning and Career Preparation

Julie C. Monson

✍   One prevailing myth about the value of a college education is that the bachelor's degree is a ticket to a job. It is not. A college education is the beginning of a career. In tomorrow's world, new careers will be created in areas that we can now only dimly perceive. Graduates are likely to change careers several times in their working life and change jobs every three or four years. Technology and its application, levels of government spending, demographic movements, peace and war all dictate unpredictable changes in the economy. We can prepare for tomorrow's career most effectively by acquiring the basic building blocks of cognitive skill and elusive but nonetheless crucial abilities in interpersonal relations, the exercise of judgment, and tolerance for new ideas and different people. Most important of all these assets are the interest and willingness to keep learning.

A sound college education is a stepping-stone on the way to adulthood and satisfying employment. Today's students will have to keep learning for the rest of their lives, if for no other reason than to keep up in their fields.

The prevailing assumption that a college education is beneficial to the future employment of college graduates is statistically correct. Graduates have higher incomes, lower rates of unemployment, higher-status positions as administrators and professionals, and greater job satisfaction than people without college degrees (Pace, 1979). Many professional careers are open only to persons who have a college degree, and other occupations require the knowledge and talents taught and developed during four years in college. A college degree, then, if not a guarantee of success or a job, is an admission ticket to a wide spectrum of professional careers—in medicine, law, college teaching, the ministry, public administration, scientific research, and many other fields—many of which also require two or more years of graduate study.

Less obvious to the student entering college is the relationship of non-career-related curricula to future work. Courses in literature, botany, classic drama, or anthropology have no apparent connection to any future work except research or teaching in these areas. The evidence is slim that an undergraduate exposure to these and other noncareer subjects helps one's future success on the job. We accept on faith that a breadth of knowledge of many subjects is good and that the skills acquired through learning unfamiliar information will help when we need to acquire future new knowledge. In fact, surveys of college graduates indicate that "they themselves believe that they have made progress toward such ends as critical thinking, acquiring a body of facts and knowledge of a special field, personal and social development, tolerance, broadened literary acquaintance, and so on" (Pace, 1979, p. 5). It is our assumption, bolstered by observation, that these ends indeed contribute to future career success.

Of the many career choices students can consider when selecting a college, this chapter discusses only a few. Perhaps the most important choice is selecting between a general (liberal arts) curriculum and a technical or vocational major. These are not exclusive choices because students can include technical courses in a basically liberal arts education, and even the most vocational degree requires a few courses in English or history. But the emphasis on one approach or the other leads to quite different sequences of courses and career paths.

Opportunities for career exploration in undergraduate education is the second topic this chapter addresses. Institutions vary considerably in their emphasis on out-of-classroom work and extracurricular opportunities. Students who anticipate using their college years for personal, intellectual, and career exploration will want to assess opportunities for activities as diverse as study-abroad programs, participation in the arts, internships in off-campus organizations, or athletics. The third topic is undergraduate preparation for graduate or professional training, followed by a discussion of sex, college choice, and career patterns. The chapter concludes with a brief review of typical undergraduate career planning and placement services.

Liberal Arts or Vocational-Technical Training

Two of the undergraduate curriculum approaches are not necessarily exclusive but require different curriculum tracks leading to different career options. One approach, the liberal arts undergraduate curriculum, is frequently described as including a breadth of intellectual inquiry combined with specialized concentration in a more narrowly defined academic discipline. For instance, Stanford University's catalogue uses the following language to define its mission:

> Like all distinguished universities and most undergraduate colleges, Stanford provides the means for its undergraduates to acquire a liberal education: an education which broadens the student's knowledge and awareness in each of the major areas of human knowledge: significantly deepens it in one or two; and prepares him or her for a lifetime of continual learning in the varied and changing application of knowledge to career and personal life [p. 8].

The second approach to undergraduate education includes majors or concentrations in engineering, computer science, business, applied technology, or health care fields, which require far more precisely defined sequences of courses than typical liberal arts majors. By the time students schedule the prerequisites, there is not much room left for classes outside their major. The future consequences of keeping options open involve both benefits and costs. Upon graduation, the technical major has skills in immediate demand by employers and can shift later into professions such as law and business. The drawback is that professions such as law or business frequently utilize functional skills with language, human interactions, and broad problem solving, which the technically trained person may not have had the opportunity to exercise and develop in college.

Graduates with technical, engineering, or business degrees will find that the content of undergraduate courses is directly related to the actual work of their first (and perhaps second and third) jobs; they will also generally find employers willing to hire them for the specific skills and knowledge they acquired in college. The process is fairly direct and uncomplicated. After four years, the student graduates with a degree in engineering and seeks a job in engineering as an engineer. The neatness of this process is enhanced by the language used for describing and labeling academic disciplines and occupations. One studies engineering and becomes an engineer. One studies accounting and becomes an accountant. But one can study the liberal arts and become almost anything. The only way to make history, political science, English, or philosophy a career is to teach or write it. At this point, the undecided and unsure become confused; the links between education and work seem to dissolve.

This brings us to the rationale for the liberal arts major, the other approach to a college education. What good is the major to a future career? What does one do with a major in French, art history, religion, or sociology? The answer is that the degree opens up an awesome occupational choice because most likely the liberal arts graduate has the talent and knowledge to be successful in a host of occupations. The problem is one of choosing. The liberal arts degree is also a standard prerequisite for graduate and professional schools in business, law, public administration and public policy, theology, social service, education, and other fields.

Our educational system emphasizes career-specific, *technical* knowledge in technical and business curricula at the undergraduate level and career-specific *professional* training at the graduate level. A person successful in any occupation often

has a combination of career-specific knowledge and the administrative ability to get things done. The managers and administrators in any occupational area in our society are not only trained
college graduates and advanced degree holders but persons who
have strongly developed administrative abilities. The basic components of administrative competency—verbal and written communications, interpersonal skills, and facility in analyzing problems—are the very talents likely to be highly developed in
undergraduate liberal studies. The importance of these skills,
transferable to any job in any occupation, is highlighted by a
recent survey of college graduates in administrative positions.
Nine years after graduation, the surveyed graduates recommended undergraduate courses in English, psychology, mathematics, and administration as preparation for their professions
(Bisconti and Solmon, 1976). The graduates knew from their
experience that competence with language, human relations,
and logical problem solving, subjects taught in courses in
English, psychology, and mathematics, were essential to success in their work as administrators.

The strength of the relationship of an undergraduate
major to a future career seems to depend on the major, the profession, and to some extent, when you ask the question. Pace
(1979), in his review of surveys of college graduates, found that
two thirds to three fourths of college graduates held jobs in
fields similar to their major field of study in college. The percent tends to decline during a depression and declines, in some
surveys, the longer the graduate is in the work force. The results
of a 1976 survey conducted by the Associated Colleges of the
Midwest are particularly interesting because the graduates surveyed were from eleven midwestern liberal arts colleges that
offer little vocational or technical training. All graduates of the
class of 1975 were surveyed, along with a sample of graduates
from the classes of 1970, 1965, and 1960. Of the 1975 graduates who completed the questionnaire only months after receiving their degrees, 85 percent had majored in traditional liberal arts subjects. The remaining 15 percent had majored in such
fields as education, business, or nursing. Of those working, 58
percent of the men and 68 percent of the women indicated that

their jobs were closely or somewhat related to their major field of study. Of the graduates five, ten, and fifteen years out of college, 75 percent of the men and women were in related fields.

Results from this survey and other surveys reviewed by Pace also show that the relationship of undergraduate major to work does not significantly affect job satisfaction. Persons in careers unrelated to their major field of undergraduate study tend to find their jobs satisfying. In another survey of college graduates, conducted by the Higher Education Research Institute, also reviewed by Pace, 74 percent of those surveyed responded that their job was closely or somewhat related to their undergraduate major field. Jobs highly related were in health service, education, accounting, and engineering. Of the 26 percent whose jobs were unrelated to undergraduate major, only 6 percent were not at all satisfied with their current jobs. These results strongly indicate that once in the work force, most college graduates perceive that their college education is related to their jobs. For the approximate 25 percent whose jobs are unrelated to undergraduate studies, job satisfaction is positive for all but a few.

Another approach to the relationship of college education to future work is to chart the incidence of change in career plans during the four years of college. In a series of nationwide surveys conducted by the Cooperative Institutional Research Program (CIRP) (Astin, 1977), freshmen were asked to specify their intended career choice and then asked in a follow-up survey four years later about their current career plans. Postgraduate career activity included graduate school and employment. A substantial number of students had changed career plans during the four years of college. In the CIRP surveys of four different classes (1966-70, 1967-71, 1968-72, and 1969-74), students switched from school teaching, engineering, scientific research, medicine, social work, and nursing to the fields of business, homemaking, college teaching, and law. Two fields, college teaching and homemaking, attracted the largest number of students from other fields. Only 10 percent of the students who on graduation chose these fields had indicated in their freshman year that these were their preferred choices. One can speculate about the socialization process during college in the late 1960s, which directly or indirectly encouraged men to become college professors and women to become wives and mothers. As we move into the decade of the 1980s, career changing of this magnitude in these fields seems unlikely, partly because of the absolute decline in employment for college teachers and partly because of the seriousness with which college women plan professional careers. In the CIRP study, business attracted students who as freshmen had planned to enter other careers and also held 56 percent of the freshmen who had indicated this as their first choice. Only 19 percent of the freshmen who selected law entered law school four years later.

A look at the changes in career plans that occur during four years of college does not imply that such changes are either positive or negative. Certainly, many young people today are familiar with only a few professional careers. Many college students have had limited work experience on which to base intelligent career choices. They tend to select obvious or well-known occupations, such as law, business, and medicine, choices which may become less interesting or reasonable over time: Premeds flunk organic chemistry; a geology major discovers music; the would-be lawyer does poorly on bar examinations; the engineering major becomes excited about medicine. College years should encourage opportunities for career exploration and thoughtful evaluation of interests and aptitudes appropriate for different occupations.

In fact, many students postpone specific career decisions until after graduation. In one typical, contemporary pattern, college graduates work for two or more years after receiving their degrees and then attend graduate school for the professional training required for their chosen fields. This pattern relieves undergraduates of making career commitments too early and gives them the exploration and intellectual adventure a non-career-specific major permits. The choice of graduate program follows a work experience during which graduates test assumptions and values about professional work and develop certainty about the importance of continued education.

Opportunities for Career Exploration
in Undergraduate Education

From course selection to intramural sports, there are many varied opportunities for undergraduates to explore career options during their college years. But most students are unaware of these activities' value for future career decisions or as entries on a résumé. However, for students anxious about their future employment possibilities, these opportunities for career exploration in and out of the classroom balance the nonoccupational nature of classes and add a touch of "practicality" to the seemingly "impractical" quality of academic learning. By combining a varied curriculum with nonclassroom activities, on and off campus, and by making some effort to evaluate these experiences as they relate to personal values, abilities, and interests, students gradually discover new career potential in themselves. This is indeed valuable, because career selection is a matter of having preferences, some intuitive and some rational. Students need to develop their ability to make choices and to increase their knowledge of the realities of work.

A simple model for this process divides the undergraduate years into two parts. In the first part, students set aside career decisions and instead make a concerted effort to be intensely curious about all aspects of their undergraduate life. They cast a net as wide as possible, not discriminating about what is caught in it. In the second part, students examine the pieces caught in the net, discard some, set others aside for another time, and select a few as important and worth pursuing. Actually, the processes of net casting and examining the contents continue simultaneously throughout one's life. It is helpful, however, to distinguish between indiscriminate collecting and judicious selecting. "Keeping options open" implies initial consideration of multiple options followed by a narrowing down to a select few.

Course Selection. Students in the liberal arts are often unaware of the indifference with which employers view their undergraduate majors. Typically, recruiters and other employers interviewing college graduates for positions in management training programs, for example, are more concerned about students' experience, attitudes, and abilities to get along with others. They look for a quality of being well rounded and an interest in the company's services or products, but they also look for signs that students have had more than a passing interest in business over the past four years. Given this fact, students will find it advantageous to take a core of classes that many employers perceive as basic preparation for a career in business, government, or the nonprofit sector: basic accounting, economics, psychology, computer science, mathematics through calculus, and English composition or its equivalent. With this core, students can major in Spanish, religion, anthropology, biology, or any other field and still qualify for entry-level positions in many professions or for entry into graduate professional schools.

With exceptions, such as scientific and technical majors, students have considerable freedom to experiment with and taste a variety of academic subjects. The potential exists for the art major to try mathematics and for the geology major to try music. In career exploration, not being afraid to learn about the unfamiliar is an asset that presents understanding and increases the ability to face an unpredictable and uncertain future.

Experiential Learning. Increasingly, off-campus work experiences are an accepted part of undergraduate education. Opportunities available vary widely from institution to institution. Many are for academic credit; others are not. Some are full-time opportunities within a Cooperative Education program or a leave of absence; others are part-time, designed to supplement a regular schedule of classes. Although almost all undergraduate institutions have some type of experiential learning program, in some colleges this component is emphasized very strongly as an integral part of one's undergraduate education, as at Antioch University, Yellow Springs, Ohio. In other institutions, it is peripheral, barely complementary to the academic quality of undergraduate learning. The rationale for these programs, however, is similar no matter at what school the learning occurs and includes some or all of the following factors:

1. To relate liberal learning to the nonacademic world; to see the importance and application of one's education to professional work.
2. To explore career opportunities in a professional setting.
3. To acquire practical, work-related skills, including interpersonal skills necessary in working closely with others.
4. To gain practical experience helpful or necessary for successful application for graduate schools or professional employment.
5. To earn money.
6. To gain self-confidence. College life is frequently highly competitive, intense, and intellectually rigorous; rewards go to the highest academic achievers. Even students who do well in this environment boost their self-confidence by discovering that they are competent outside the classroom and that their supervisors highly praise their performance. Students who are marginally successful in academe are delighted to make the same discovery and end up with greater appreciation and understanding of their own talents.
7. For diversity. Many students discover, midway through college, that they have scarcely left school since they were five; they feel on a treadmill of papers, exams, and lectures, and they need to find a temporary, acceptable way to escape. An off-campus work experience, in a new environment with people of different ages and life-styles, is a way to refresh the spirit and regain a perspective on the role of college learning in one's life.

College catalogues typically describe internships and off-campus field experience programs. Like study-abroad programs, some internship programs are administered by the home institution, some by consortia of colleges and universities, and others by organizations whose only function is coordinating internship experiences. The variety of ingenious arrangements is staggering. For example, the University of California at Davis has long administered a program of part-time internships for students in and around the university and full-time, semester-long internships as far away as San Francisco and Los Angeles. With the approval of an academic department, students may receive academic credit for completing their internships. Frequently, an academic component of the internship, such as a reading list or a paper, is a requirement for obtaining credit.

Another example is a smaller program administered at Pomona College. The Liberal Arts Field Experience Program offers part-time, ten-week, preprofessional internships, most of which are in schools, businesses, agencies, and government offices convenient to the college. Academic credit is not awarded for these internships, but students may receive a small stipend for completing the full eighty hours. Antioch University is recognized for its alternating semesters of study combined with semesters away from campus in a variety of work settings. Students receive academic credit for their work semesters. An example of a consortium of institutions is the College Venture Program administered at Brown University for students from Colgate, Cornell, Bates, Wesleyan, William and Mary, Brown, Skidmore, and the University of Chicago. College Venture sets up full-time temporary jobs for undergraduates who want a leave of absence from their undergraduate studies. Job placements are located in government agencies, museums, newspapers, social service agencies, schools, and other organizations. This too is a noncredit program, except where credit is granted by an academic department of a member college.

The federal Cooperative Education Program is established on many college and university campuses and offers two work patterns: part-time work for enrolled students or alternating semesters of full-time work and study. Cooperative Education has been particularly successful in occupational areas where experience is an important ingredient for developing occupational expertise—for instance, in accounting and engineering. Also successful is the Federal Summer Intern Program, which offers full-time summer jobs to undergraduate and graduate students with federal agencies.

For entry-level employment in a host of professions, an internship, summer job, or temporary placement is more than helpful: It is essential. In such fields as journalism, museum work, publishing, municipal administration, architecture and landscape architecture, urban planning, and graphic arts and in administrative positions in Washington, D.C., or state capitals, a high value is placed on experience, not unlike the craft apprenticeships of an earlier era. Students interested in these fields will find it advantageous to seek these experiences and attend institutions that sponsor such programs or, at a minimum, easily tolerate leaves of absence for work experience.

Part-Time and Summer Jobs. Students can often find interesting work on their own campus. In addition to the plethora of student jobs washing dishes or taking tickets, colleges and universities have a wide array of skilled jobs in laboratories, libraries, and offices, with responsibilities ranging from research in physics to cataloguing botanic specimens to bibliographic research for a faculty member. Many premed students, for instance, discover from their part-time college jobs whether they enjoy, just tolerate, or dislike medical research. In some institutions, on-campus part-time jobs are linked to financial aid and are available first to qualified students with financial need. The federal College Work-Study Program funds on- and off-campus part-time and summer jobs for college students with financial need. Because the program pays for 80 percent of the student's wages and the employer pays only 20 percent, students eligible for this program are frequently able to work for employers who could otherwise not afford to hire them. This opens up job opportunities with nonprofit organizations such as schools, museums, government agencies, and community social service agencies.

Extracurricular Experiences. Student participation in extracurricular activities is another aspect of career exploration in undergraduate education. Students involved with a campus newspaper, theater production, university orchestra, competitive sports, or student government have ample opportunity to test their administrative talents, develop organizational skills, and gain leadership experience. Employers know this and look for such experiences on résumés. They know that the graduate who has interests outside the classroom and experience in working closely with others to accomplish common goals is likely to be a better employee than the straight-A student who seldom veers from the path between library and classroom.

Admissions officers of graduate professional programs, particularly MBA programs, also look at admissions applications for evidence of campus leadership. In most instances, students engage in these activities not because doing so has a future practical application but because they want to. But campus leadership activities also give students an opportunity for low-risk exploration. A student can try writing theater criticism for the campus paper or acting in a theater production or designing a set, all at low risk. Although it may not feel like low risk to the student, in the scheme of a lifetime the costs of nonsuccess are very low, whereas the rewards of success are satisfying and revealing.

Setting of the Institution. We tend to have ambivalent attitudes toward the quality of isolation in higher education. The ivory tower is as much a positive as a negative image because we cling to the notion that intellectual inquiry and study are best conducted away from the bustle of people's everyday affairs. At the same time, we have a nagging fear of too much isolation, of intellectual inquiry more cerebral than practical, of learning too far removed from the necessities of making a living.

Academic isolation occurs as easily in the middle of big cities as it does in rural, small towns. The responsibility for escaping isolation, if only occasionally, lies with the student. Field experiences and internships, part-time and summer jobs, volunteer opportunities, or a semester spent in an urban institution will compensate for an undergraduate education in idyllic, rural isolation. The point is that students should acquire some experience and facility in coping with city living, not only because college graduates may eventually live in cities but because cities are still the centers of cultural and economic life and it is important to know what this means experientially. For career exploration, undergraduates will find in large urban centers an infinitely greater variety of occupational and professional opportunities than can be sustained economically in less populated areas.

Preparation for Graduate or Professional Training

Somewhere between 30 and 60 percent of the graduates of selective colleges will go directly to graduate study. Another 20 percent or so will obtain a graduate degree at some time in the future. These percentages vary by institution, are not always easy to come by, and seem to be shifting toward a larger percentage postponing graduate study for a year or two.

What is clear is that graduates from the top-selective undergraduate institutions are accepted into top graduate programs in greater numbers than students from less selective colleges. In graduate programs where admission is highly competitive, such as schools of medicine, veterinary medicine, law, top business schools, and programs in clinical psychology, the undergraduate institution is a significant ingredient in students' successful applications. In part, students receive more rigorous undergraduate preparation and therefore perform better on such entrance examinations as the LSAT, GRE, MCAT, and GMAT. In part, these colleges guide and counsel students regarding successful undergraduate academic preparation and application procedures. Many colleges have prelaw and premed advisers or faculty in selected departments who are available to advise students. Finally, the selection process tends to reward those who are already successfully selected. Not all college graduates need or want to enter the country's top graduate schools, however, and for this group their choice of undergraduate institution is not as crucial. These students have greater flexibility in selecting other variables on which to base choice of college.

Curriculum requirements for entry into graduate programs are fairly precisely prescribed in fields such as medicine and the physical sciences. Although it does not frequently occur, physics and mathematics majors can enter graduate programs in engineering. Law schools look favorably on all majors but suggest courses in philosophy, logic, and history and any course that requires a sophisticated manipulation of language. Graduate academic departments look for a broad undergraduate background of courses in their own academic disciplines.

Many colleges have rather complete statistics on their alumni's postgraduate plans. High school seniors who have a keen interest in knowing the acceptance rates of graduates into schools of law or medicine can obtain this information fairly easily from college admissions officers or by talking with prelaw or premed advisers. They may also want to know which graduate schools have admitted a particular college's graduates. Admissions officers for professional schools and graduate departments keep such statistics and can provide some information. The very ambitious student may want to carry this process one step further and essentially start backward by, for instance, asking the officers of prestigious law firms at which law schools they prefer to recruit and then asking these law schools at which undergraduate institutions they prefer to recruit. The answers will produce the names of a small group of colleges and universities that have successfully placed their graduates in top graduate programs and professional schools.

Sex, College Choice, and Career Patterns

Women today are entering college in greater numbers than their male counterparts. They are considering and selecting traditionally male-dominated professions when making their career choices. In the academic year 1979-80, for the first time in this country's history, women constituted more than 50 percent of all persons enrolled in higher education. The percentage of women attending coeducational institutions has grown dramatically over the past eighty years. In 1900, about half of the 4,500 women graduating from college attended women's colleges. By the mid 1970s, only 9 percent of the 400,000 women receiving college degrees had attended women's colleges.

What, if any, is the effect of attendance at a single-sex or a coeducational institution? Does attending college in the presence or absence of men make a significant difference to women's future career plans? Do women, for example, who attend women's colleges tend to become more successful in their professional careers than women who attend coeducational institutions? Does it make any difference if women attend a small liberal arts college or a large state university?

The literature on this subject is tantalizing but inconclusive. There is evidence that women who attend small women's colleges are more likely to have successful, professional careers than women attending other institutions. However, the issue is a complicated one. Studies that trace the undergraduate backgrounds of currently successful women who attended college during the 1930s to 1950s shed insight on the important influences of college in the lives of these women. But college environments and female work patterns have shifted during the 1960s and 1970s toward greater acceptance of women as full-fledged members of the professional work force. Enrollment in small women's colleges today may prove not as significant to future success as it once was (Brown, 1979).

In a study of the relationship of college choice to future career, Tidball (1973) traced the undergraduate experience of women listed in *Who's Who in American Women*. Tidball calculated a rate of achievement for graduates of women's colleges and coeducational institutions by decades from 1910 to 1960. In each of the six decades, the rate of achiever production was greater for women's colleges. In the two decades of the 1940s and 1950s, it was more than twice the rate of coeducational institutions. Tidball also found that as the women faculty–women student ratio increased, so did the output of achievers. Similarly, the higher the percent of enrolled male students, the lower the rate of women achievers.

In a later study of women listed in the 1974-1975 *Who's Who in America* (Oates and Williamson, 1978), 61 percent were graduates of coeducational colleges and 39 percent graduated from women's colleges. (The sample includes the 1,735 women whose entries indicated they had received a college degree from an accredited institution in this country. Over 3,000 women were listed.) This statistic is misleading because during the decade 1930 to 1939, the period during which almost a third of all women achievers received their degrees, the "rate of achiever production" (per 10,000 women graduates) of small, selective

women's colleges was higher than the rate of achiever production at other institutions. The seven sisters (Barnard, Bryn
Mawr, Mount Holyoke, Radcliffe, Smith, Vassar, and Wellesley)
accounted for 61 per 10,000 women as compared with 18 per
10,000 produced by small (under 500) coeducational institutions and 12 per 10,000 produced by larger (over 500) coeducational institutions. Overall, 20.8 percent of the achievers identified in the 1974-75 *Who's Who in America* had graduated from
one of the seven sister colleges. In a less formal study of high-
ranking women in management (Hennig and Jardim, 1976),
only one of the twenty-five women who formed the core of the
study had attended a woman's college.

    If, as the evidence suggests, women who aspire to high ca-
reer achievement may gain an advantage by attending a small
women's college, especially one of the seven sisters, it is important to evaluate the possible reasons for this tentative but documented advantage. The authors of these studies and others have
conjectured that (1) leadership opportunities for women students are greater in women's colleges; (2) some colleges, like the
seven sisters, are very selective and tend to admit women who
by birth, wealth, talent, or ambition are likely to become high-
achieving adults; (3) women develop behavior patterns in wom-
en's colleges that carry over outside that environment to professional career settings; (4) women in women's colleges receive
greater encouragement from faculty and peers than women in
coeducational institutions; (5) women in coeducational settings
tend to have a role conflict between femininity and career aspiration. The presence of men reinforces this conflict. In wom-
en's colleges, femininity and career aspirations are not perceived
as opposites but are integrated, thus giving women "permission"
to be both feminine and ambitious. Hennig and Jardim, on the
basis of their quite different study, conjecture that a coeducational setting permits women students to engage competitively
with men and from that experience to gain interpersonal skills
that will enable them to succeed in male-dominated professions
such as business management.

    What seems important from all this is that young women
who aspire to future distinction and professional advancement

must, during the critical college years, obtain experience in asserting themselves, running things, being taken seriously, exercising leadership and being competitive, and learning not to be afraid to be ambitious. These characteristics may be encouraged to a greater extent at women's colleges. They may be only benignly tolerated or even discouraged at some coeducational institutions and at some religious colleges. Women keenly interested in this issue may want to review some common indexes of campus life on a coeducational campus:

1. The percentage of women on the faculty. Astin's (1977) hypothesis of "progressive conformity" indicates that campuses have prevailing expectations and attitudes concerning appropriate career fields. These attitudes may strongly affect the acceptability of certain majors and career plans for women students. A clue to prevailing attitudes is the number of high-ranking women professors in all academic disciplines.
2. The percentage of women holding elected and appointed student body offices.
3. The campus newspaper. A look at several issues of the student newspaper will reveal the gender of those who make the news on a particular campus.
4. The percentage of men and women receiving academic and other prizes and awards.
5. The postgraduate plans of men and women.

Typical Undergraduate Career Planning and Placement Services

Assistance for students seeking part-time, summer, and full-time employment, career counseling, and guidance is now a standard service in virtually all undergraduate institutions. The titles of offices providing these services vary, and in many institutions placement is in a different office and location from career guidance and counseling. The front sections of college catalogues describe available student services and where they are located. For entering freshmen, the most frequently sought service is assistance in finding a part-time job. Listings of on- and off-campus positions are posted in placement or student employment offices. Special part-time job programs, such as the federal College Work-Study Program, may be administered along with other student employment, or because this program is basically a component of financial aid, it is found in the financial aid office. Large institutions may have separate offices to administer and coordinate internships and cooperative education programs. Students concerned about opportunities for part-time and summer work should be encouraged to talk with a student employment counselor or administrator. These staff members are very familiar with the range of jobs available and the prevailing hourly wage rates. Placement offices also accumulate listings of summer jobs and summer internships and may have two or three of the excellent directories of undergraduate internships now published annually.

For students seeking assistance with career decisions, professional staffs are ready to help with career counseling, directing the students to numerous useful books and references. Most career planning offices have small libraries that contain these guides and directories and shelves of information about employers. Institutions with a large contingent of seniors going to graduate and professional schools also have a good collection of graduate program catalogues and graduate program directories such as the *Peterson's Guides.* A few institutions also have files of alumni who can help with career information.

A large and busy career planning and placement office may be intimidating to freshmen. In the fall and spring, these offices are bustling with seniors and graduate students who are interviewing on campus with employers for jobs. Many of these offices' services are designed for underclassmen, however. The bustle should not interfere with scheduling appointments with a counselor, reviewing references in the library, or even spending an hour or two with videotapes or computer career guidance programs, if they are available. Typically, placement workshops, career seminars, and career planning courses are also scheduled throughout the year, and in some institutions a variety of vocational tests are given regularly.

The Context of Career Planning

This chapter has focused on a few of the less obvious—perhaps less traditional—bonds between college and career. I have deliberately slighted the strength of academic preparation for professions and occupations. I have also ignored the typical homage paid to theories of career development and choice. The business of making career choices is far more complicated than selecting a major, choosing electives, talking with a career counselor, or following the advice of a parent or professor. Students, counselors, and advisers tend to simplify this process and prescribe partial answers to very complex questions. For better or worse, there is no simple connection between a college education and a future lifetime of work or a simple answer to how one lives a good and productive life.

Fortunately, career planning and placement offices have moved from their basic recruiting and placement functions of a decade ago toward a varied program of services that emphasize students' responsibility for decisions affecting their futures. Placement staff no longer "find" students jobs. They help students find their own jobs and, in the process, hope to teach students something about the diversity of work options, how to select appropriate employment opportunities, and how to get hired.

Career planners are increasingly aware of the importance of a varied background of work experience, breadth of academic background, and diversity of interests as contributions to mature and confident career decision making. Students with little work experience are placed in the uncomfortable position of having to make career-related decisions, such as choosing a major, when they can make only naive and unrealistic decisions. It is not unlike asking a seven-year-old what she wants to be when she grows up and being told "A fireman." College freshmen, however, tend to answer the same question with respectable professions such as law, business, or medicine. The four undergraduate years can provide the breathing space for personal as well as intellectual growth, for exploration of self and society, and the development of interests, values, and talents re-

lated to future career plans. The challenge is to make the complexity of career decision making manageable and comprehen-
sible, to place career planning in the broad context of all of
life's learning, and to perceive the links between past accomplishment, present challenge, and expectations for the future. This
cannot be done solely in the classroom.

Part Three

✍ ✍ ✍ ✍ ✍

Service to Society

✍   To cure the perceived ills of society is often the charge of the nation's educational institutions. New modes of education are supposed to prevent the most recently discovered forms of antisocial behavior. If any sector of society has been identified as receiving less than its share of the world's goods, educational institutions are often asked to prepare the next generation to be more competitive. From time to time, colleges and universities are asked to produce more farmers, more engineers, more students aiming for medicine or teaching, more caretakers for the nation's economy.

     Colleges and universities are not always actually able to do all they are asked by the society that creates and supports them, but they do try. The women and men who carry the message of education's important social function to the citizens, to the future students and their parents, are admissions counselors, who therefore must know not only the usual data concerning the institutions they serve or interpret but also special information regarding the institution's ability to perform socially beneficial functions.

     Over the next decade, the special concerns of postsecondary education will grow and change; even today, the list could be expanded beyond the issues addressed in this book. On any list of social concerns with which college admissions coun-

147

selors are asked to familiarize themselves, however, several items would appear: the admission of minority students, especially blacks and Mexican Americans; the recruiting and admission of older students; the unusual needs of two-year-college transfer students; and explaining the American financial aid system to parents and their children and helping them make full use of it.

To introduce the idea of the social function of the college admissions counseling profession, Clifford J. Caine (in Chapter Seven) discusses his vision of the proper function of higher education. His vision is less pluralistic than Casteen's; and, because it is more normative, it should provoke discussion among those who must interpret the function of colleges and universities to students and parents. Caine argues simply that the ultimate function of higher education is to keep American democratic society operating. He is concerned about the nature of American culture and the educational process that preserves and creates it. Since moral action comes through choosing, American educational programs, at their best, foster moral development. Admissions counselors should remember that moral development must be one goal of educational processes; choosing a college or university is one of those processes. Caine's approach is holistic and ideal, not pragmatic.

Many minorities have been excluded from American higher education at different times; different degrees of special action have been necessary to include them. Generally, most white Christian minorities have made their way into mainstream educational institutions with relatively little trouble; prestigious private institutions were mostly slow to admit Jews and, in many cases, women or men. Individually, people of color often gained admission to private institutions as long as they demanded no special attention or understanding; but many public institutions remained segregated until the last quarter of this century. Within that period, blacks and later Mexican Americans and others of Spanish descent pressed the case that because of their different cultures and backgrounds, they received less than a fair shake in the educational sorting process. In many different ways, both public and private institutions have responded to pressures from minority groups and the majority public, easing access to higher education for these people.

But for no minority group is it the *same* as it is for the majority. (Some groups, including many Asian Americans and Asian immigrants, find access easier or at least as easy as for the majority of Americans, so such groups need little special understanding from admissions counselors. Thus, no chapter here is addressed to these groups, but from the point of view of educational sociology, their situation is still different and of interest and should be studied by properly trained analysts.) For blacks, the largest minority group, and Mexican Americans, soon to be the largest minority group, differences in culture have often prevented the usual admissions counseling patterns from being effective. Chapters Eight and Nine address the situations of those groups so that admissions counselors in both secondary schools and colleges will be able to serve minority clients more effectively.

In Chapter Eight, Jewelle Taylor Gibbs notes that for black students to maintain or increase present enrollment levels at integrated institutions, both the schools and the students must develop a mutual understanding and accommodation of the institutions' priority goals, the societal forces shaping those goals, and the students' educational aspirations and career goals. Recent affirmative action programs were well intentioned and broadly based, but because they were hastily conceived and promulgated, they contained the beginnings of their own destruction. As a result, the movement in the late 1960s to make postsecondary schools more responsive to black students' needs and goals has gradually diminished to a ripple.

Gibbs points out that the characteristics of black college students vary widely, but in general they differ from majority students in average family background, academic preparation, previous academic achievement, test scores, and career aspirations—and all these facts must be understood by those who counsel black students. She discusses trends in black student enrollment, various issues concerning the recruitment and selection of black students, and problems of black student adaptation and retention.

As she covers counseling needs and strategies for black students, Gibbs establishes standards for institutional behavior against which admissions officers should judge their own institutions as they recruit black students and explain their institutions to counselors who work with black students. She also discusses the implications of current developments for the future of black students in integrated institutions.

Gibbs makes five recommendations aimed at increasing and maintaining the enrollment of black students at predominantly white colleges and universities. These institutions must, she says, first reassess and reaffirm their commitment to black enrollment; second, they should evaluate their current programs and compare them with successful patterns elsewhere; third, they should monitor the internal climate to foster an environment that encourages interracial communication and contact at all levels; fourth, they should strengthen ties with secondary schools, to develop large pools of able black students; and fifth, they should increase the "fit between black student backgrounds and goals and institutional resources and priorities."

Admissions counselors cannot by themselves ensure that either colleges or secondary schools fulfill the ambitious goals Gibbs prescribes, but they need to be aware that, as the principal outreach persons for their institutions, they have a duty to interpret the developments of the world outside to the institution within. Gibbs's useful information is a foundation for such a program.

Mexican Americans will be the largest minority in the United States by the end of the century. In Chapter Nine, Raymond Buriel and Sally Rivera present the historical and demographic profile of the Mexican American population. Not only is the Mexican American percentage of the United States population growing, it is growing in different ways from the rest of the population. Thirteen percent of the group is under five years old and 47 percent is under eighteen, as opposed to 7 percent and 13 percent for the population as a whole. This fact has enormous implications for college admissions, especially in states which contain large numbers of Mexican Americans.

Even as the number of Mexican American students increases, some public institutions—like the University of California, in the state with the largest percentage of the Mexican American population—have increased their reliance on standardized tests. But some scholars argue that tests are less reliable predictors of college success for Mexican Americans than for the population as a whole. (The authors' thoughtful discussion of admissions tests and Mexican American students is controversial and should be read in conjunction with Chapters Thirty and Thirty-One, which consider aspects of standardized tests.)

More than for other minority groups, dominant cultural and religious patterns inhibit the inclination of young Mexican Americans to choose college paths, especially aside from community colleges. Some of the factors discussed by Buriel and Rivera may not be shared by majority students: (1) identification with family, community, and ethnic group; (2) personalization of interpersonal relationships; (3) status and role definitions in family and community; (4) Mexican Catholic ideology.

Because of these idiosyncratic cultural patterns, successful recruiters will have to utilize unusual routes to students, recognize the important role of other family members in the decision process, and provide support throughout the application process. Special cultural factors also must be taken into account in evaluating applications. Mexican American students may feel it a violation of family values to attempt to distinguish themselves in a descriptive essay. An astute admissions officer will also attend to the roles of the sexes within the traditional Mexican American family. The success of Mexican American students in college, once they are on campus, depends on institutional sensitivity to their cultural expectations.

Another group that has made its presence felt within American colleges and universities is called "nontraditional," or "older," or "returning." This group consists of the thousands of women and men (mostly women) who have discovered a need to begin or continue postsecondary education at ages well beyond those formerly thought appropriate for students. Now we know that at any point in the middle years, adults may find new need to improve the fit between the self and either occupation or avocation. In Chapter Ten, Eileen M. Rose and Irene Kovala Campanaro point out that such need often involves formal education and new demands of both counselors and institutions—demands that must be understood by those asked to provide services.

Rose and Campanaro discuss how to deal with the demands of this group. The authors describe the nature of the group and its reasons for entering college and discuss the necessity of finding ways of acquainting these students with systems of information, including "educational brokering." They prescribe ways to make the process as simple as possible and point out limitations admissions counselors must accept; they must recognize that as admissions officers they cannot solve all the problems that bring these new clients to their doors. But they must know what on- and off-campus services are available for referral, and they should comprehend and be aware of institutional offerings and limitations when dealing with adult students.

In the world of admissions counseling, the two-year college is often misunderstood by both high school counselors and admissions officers at four-year institutions. Karl L. Wolf avoids a synoptic view, instead focusing in Chapter Eleven on the difficulties that admissions officers at four-year colleges and universities have in dealing with students who have attended two-year colleges and want to transfer to four-year schools. Wolf also advises secondary school counselors how to provide appropriate advice to high school students who want to begin their tertiary education at a two-year school.

Wolf describes the problems faced by community and junior college students planning to transfer: the failure of courses to transfer; incorrect or improper advising at the two-year college; changing a major after transferring or not having chosen a major by the time of transfer; and waiting too long to begin the transfer process. Wolf provides solutions to these problems and also describes the process by which standing articulation agreements can be constructed.

Because the many intricacies of the relationships Wolf writes about are beyond the scope of this book, readers may want to consult *The American Community College* (Cohen and Brawer, 1982), especially chapter 7, "Student Services: Providing Adequate Assistance," and chapter 11, "Collegiate Function:

New Directions for the Liberal Arts." Cohen and Brawer also provide an extensive annotated bibliography.

In Chapter Twelve, Leonard M. Wenc's introduction to the intricacies of the financial aid process is an informed and knowledgeable sketch for those entering the profession; it is not meant to instruct counselors on day-to-day financial aid administration. All professionals have access to workshops and timely instructions provided by, among others, the College Scholarship Service and the American College Testing program. Those who need detailed information—which necessarily varies from state to state—should seek such information from those sources.

Wenc delineates the history and growth of the concept of financial aid and describes principal sources and types of financial aid funds. When discussing what financial aid is designed to do, he points out the impact of financial aid on a student's choice of college. He considers the concepts of demonstrated financial need and net cost, likely to be mystifying to parents sending children to college for the first time, and provides caveats for students who are offered awards that may not be in their best interests. Finally, Wenc points out that there may be special counseling needs as a result of current changes in federal and state programs.

When dealing with all these discrete populations—minorities, adult students, transfer students, and students with financial need—college admissions counselors act as extensions of their employers, helping American educational institutions perform currently recognized social functions. But even as they perform these functions at the behest of their constituencies, counselors should be aware that in the future they will be called on to redress other social problems. If they see problems and possible solutions before other segments of society do, they may also help maintain the vitality and function of the American educational system.

$\mathscr{A\!S}$ 7

Need for an Educated Society

Clifford J. Caine

$\mathscr{A\!S}$ *"We may as well make up our minds to it. If our hopes of democracy are to be realized, every citizen of this country is going to have to be educated to the limit of his capacity"* (Robert Maynard Hutchins, former chancellor of the University of Chicago, 1959, p. 17).

From the inception of the Republic, Americans have given more than nodding assent to ideas present in Hutchins's strong statement. Indeed, Massachusetts Bay, deeming education crucial, passed a law in 1647 requiring each town of fifty families to support a school. As the Republic grew, and its peoples became more diverse and democratic, the old Puritan emphasis on education, which had been based largely on religious grounds, gave way to a new rationale. Leaders such as Franklin and Jefferson saw that unless a republic had an educated citizenry capable of making critical, intelligent decisions, a democracy could not work. Jefferson asserted that "no other sure foundation than the diffusion of knowledge among the people can be devised for the preservation of freedom and happiness."

And we know that while our democracy has grown and flourished, our strong, diverse educational system has been an integral part of this development—indeed, in many ways the envy of the world, for the old idea, the need for an educated society, has renewed itself and remained alive to this day.

At the same time that we affirm the viability of the old

idea, we sense a great disparity between the educational ideals of Franklin, Jefferson, Hutchins, and others and today's educational practices. And many of us, looking at modern education, would suggest that there is even a more frightening difference— the difference between the educational practices of even several decades ago and those of today.

The problem runs deeper than the practice of education in our schools, colleges, and universities. If the several leaders I have cited were alive, perhaps their lamentation to us would begin something like this: "What does it profit a nation to gain the material world and lose its soul, its integrity in the process?" Clearly, they would recognize that, despite our general material well-being, we are also a nation with millions of illiterate and semiliterate citizens and that we spend more on amusements and luxuries than on education. Furthermore, we sometimes seem to be a people more concerned about the intricacy of our machinery and the grandness of our buildings and bridges than about the quality of our culture and the ideals of genuine individualism and freedom upon which our democratic society is based.

What can be done?

Initially, those of us who profess to be educators, whether we serve as guidance professionals, teachers, or administrators, must step aside from the demands of our daily tasks and reappraise the high calling in our profession. The words of Woodrow Wilson remind us of our responsibility; in the great tradition of Franklin, Jefferson, and other leaders, Wilson proclaimed, shortly after the turn of the century, that education should be "in the nation's service."

It was Wilson's view—and it is mine—that only if education serves the nation can responsible citizens for a democratic society be assured. I point out some ways in which education can more truly fulfill this important role.

If education is in any significant way to serve the nation, it must first have goals that the nation sees as important. Clearly, education not only serves the nation of the moment, but it also allows the nation to reproduce itself, to continue; if the nation does not hand down its knowledge, its values, its "being," how can it long be perpetuated? This is particularly true of a democracy, which depends on the transmutation of its ideas and principles not from one elite coterie of leaders to another but as common heritage from one generation of its citizenry to another.

When examining some of education's problems and goals, we should avoid the mistake of believing that education—making facts, ideas, and attitudes a part of oneself—leads necessarily to morality. History tells us of "educated" men who have been responsible for major errors of moral judgment or even for seriously inhumane acts to their fellow man. William Sloan Coffin, Jr., a leading clergyman and former college chaplain, commenting on Watergate, expressed his wish that he had instructed Jeb Magruder, his former ethics students and one of the convicted Nixon aides, that it is not the mass mind but the great individual consciences that "best represent the universal conscience of mankind." Coffin saw the lesson of Watergate to be that a person who does evil need not be an evil person, "only a nice guy who is not yet a good man" (1973, p. 39).

Looking further at history, we are confronted by unspeakable crimes that "educated" men under Hitler committed. A prime example is Albert Speer, an architect by profession and the person in charge of Nazi war production. He alone among the leaders took full responsibility for the actions of the regime he served. Speer was the most highly educated Nazi leader and was widely regarded as the most intelligent, liberal, and humane among them. Speer was asked in an interview, "How could a man of your intelligence and sensibility allow himself to remain part of so evil a system, however gradually it enveloped you?" Speer replied: "There is, unfortunately, no necessary correlation between intelligence and decency; the genius and the moron are equally susceptible to corruption." Speer went on to state in his memoirs: "My moral failure is not a matter of this item and that; it resides in my active association with the whole course of events" (1970, p. 523). Such testimony should further convince us of the need to inculcate the idea that we must strive to produce the educated *moral* person.

One of the greatest paradoxes we face as a nation is that

although we have freedom of choice in most areas of our lives, we often do not choose; we let the leaders of our government and our industrial complex make our choices for us. Our actions are often akin to those of a robot: predetermined by forces beyond its control and responsive only to the unfeeling touches of its masters. This is a dangerous situation because although we do not have to struggle for our sustenance, there are conflicts going on that affect us directly, whether or not we choose to recognize them. In the educational arena, it is the fight for ascendancy of technical training per se versus liberal thought; between, on the one hand, the pragmatic, immediate problem solving necessary to our national defense and industry and, on the other, the philosophical ideas that made us the nation we are. Many observers say that how we solve this intramural struggle will greatly affect our survival individually and collectively. Some people argue that rockets and bombs are all-important, whereas others say that what we believe and strive for intellectually and spiritually are basic. I feel strongly predisposed toward the latter view as being a necessary part of the development of the educated, moral person. Toward what tangible goals must our educational system direct itself to achieve this end?

One goal that education must continue to strive for is a wide variety of educational choices for everyone. Certainly, one of our American goals from the beginning has been equality of opportunity for all. Universal education has become a fact of life in America—but is it always truly education? Too often a student is kept in a school program in which he has no interest or for which he has no talent, only to be turned out in middle adolescence and told to go to work at a job for which he is not prepared. We in the guidance profession must be vigilant in our counseling—so that this waste of human resources, this injustice to our citizenry, seldom occurs. We also have the heavy responsibility at both the secondary and higher education levels for placing students in programs that are right for them. Thus, we should allow a young person who is interested in college and equipped mentally for college work the privilege of following her interest in gaining a good educational background for this, and we should also equally provide the child who desires a job in a trade not only a basic background in the humanities and sciences but a good vocational background.

If education is to be in the nation's service, it must be relevant to the integral parts of the nation: its individual citizens. To punctuate this thought, consider again the words of Robert Hutchins when he suggests that the realization of "our hopes of democracy" depends on educating each American citizen "to the limit of his capacity." To the limit of the individual's capacity—we must never forget this; unless individuality is taken into consideration, we are not only unrealistic but unwise. Furthermore, by diversifying our educational curriculum, we will enhance the atmosphere for individual learning in the classroom by having a higher proportion of naturally motivated students. In this milieu, teaching can be far more creative, intellectual discipline generally more rigorous, and the cultivation of the talents and capacities of our students more fully assured.

For education to be truly in the nation's service, the schools must water and nurture the roots of the past. We are rapidly becoming a "cut-flower" nation; a nation that looks to the future as primary and to the past as dead. We are a culture that often seems more interested in the transitory than the permanent. Our democracy, our culture, does not automatically perpetuate itself. Indeed, there is no way that our society can be perpetuated unless education helps students emphasize the continuity that underpins our culture and finally informs our lives. Kenneth Clark succinctly speaks to this point in his book *Civilization*: "I believe that in spite of the recent triumphs of science, men haven't changed much in the last two thousand years; and in consequence we could still try to learn from history. History is ourselves" (pp. 346-347). Thus, until we emphasize strongly that our schools deal more thoroughly with the past *as related to the present,* we cannot expect the students of today and tomorrow to have the understanding and enlightenment required of responsible citizens in a democracy as they attempt to understand the demanding present and judge what the future will bring.

One basic goal of education should be the repair and, in

many cases, the restoration of the rapport found in close relations between individuals, an orientation away from a person as a well-dressed slave to the machine and back to a reexamination of what brotherhood is operationally. One of the chief ways of achieving this is to look on the school—grammar or high school, college or university—as a learning community of teachers and pupils. Thus, rather than setting up the teacher as an authoritarian attempting to bend the pupil's spirit to the teacher's will, one should try to engender a communal spirit in which the freedom to exchange ideas can be of great benefit in developing the students' respect for learning and for the teacher as not only a purveyor of knowledge but also a fellow inquirer. The guidance profession has a major responsibility to convey this attitude of concern. As a consequence of this approach, perhaps organized learning can measure up more fully to Silberman's (1970, p. 114) high standard: "Education should prepare people not just to earn a living but to live a life—a creative, humane, and sensitive life." Such a stance within an empathetic educational system would be regenerative, not just in regard to the spirit of inquiry but also in attitudes toward all interpersonal relations.

Very fundamentally, and along with the above, the school must be made a place where process as well as product is emphasized. Schools have a high and holy responsibility to the nation to rejuvenate the concept that ideas themselves are important; that tangible material results and mere words have no lasting importance unless their meanings are examined and understood. Our nation is buttressed by such concepts as equality, freedom, compromise—ideas that had meaning beyond the printed page; ideas that people in the throes of creating this land talked about, fought for, and often died for; ideas that, unfortunately, have become meaningless jargon for many Americans. By training the individual student to examine these and other ideas through the processes of critical thinking, whereby the student approaches each learning situation under the influence of careful, analytical, nonprejudging thought, education not only serves the student but also meets a need of the nation.

Under the influence of and with the implementation of this critical method, the student should be encouraged to question the very framework of our nation. Only in this way will we ever be assured that there is true understanding of what it means to be a citizen. Thus, I propose that education must bring its techniques and skills to bear on a reexamination of the nation's basic values, indeed, on the concept of nation. Archibald MacLeish, in his essay "Mr. Wilson and the Nation's Needs" (1960), points out that when Wilson made his speech suggesting that a basic purpose of education should be to serve the nation, the nation was conceived of as a society of men and women and not, as it often is today, as a social machine with a life of its own. MacLeish indicates that Wilson was talking about the duty of colleges and universities to turn out people who would take their places in "the society of men that the nation was" by leading it. Today, he states, the emphasis is more on the turning out of people with specialized skills "which the nation as Nation finds it needs; not to lead it but to work for it" (p. 3).

Thus, there seems to be a direct correlation between how we regard education and how we regard the nation; if we look critically at the basic values that have sustained our society for most of its existence and the important techniques and insights of true interpersonal relations, we will tend to regard the nation as a body of fellow men with life and breath and not as some fearsome, impersonal power to be served and worshiped only by the offering up of our specialized skills. The former view—and, I suggest, the correct one—is vivified by the remarks that W. G. Todd made over a century ago when addressing the graduating class of Derby Academy in Hingham, Massachusetts: "It is not the men whom we send to the state house and to Washington who made our laws, but we who have made them before the men were sent" (see Cucio, 1963, p. 49). If those of us who educate would concentrate on imbuing our students with the spirit of learning, if we would test the imaginations of our charges so that they connect the search for knowledge with a sense of joie de vivre, then I believe we would more often see the ideal product of educational endeavors: individuals living near the fullness of their powers and a nation whose foundations are ensured.

8

Admissions Counseling for Black Students

Jewelle Taylor Gibbs

The year 1968 was a watershed in the awakening of American institutions of higher learning to the unmet needs and thwarted educational aspirations of black youth. In response to the assassination of the Reverend Martin Luther King, Jr., black youth protested, demonstrated, and exhorted college and university administrators to translate the King dream of equal opportunity into a social reality by eliminating barriers and increasing access to higher education for minority youth in predominantly white public and private colleges and universities.

Now that more than a decade has passed since those initial protests were launched, it is possible to view the nature and content of the response of these institutions of higher education to the legitimate concerns of these students, particularly in the context of black student recruitment, enrollment, adaptation, and retention in predominantly white colleges and universities. With the wisdom of hindsight, it is possible to evaluate objectively the positive and negative aspects of the characteristic response of higher education to black student "demands"—specifically, its ideological framework, structural features, and program content, as well as the effects on black students and the impact on the academic environment of implementing special programs.

This chapter evaluates these factors within the context of the current status of black students at integrated institutions. It focuses on a brief historical review of affirmative action programs for black students in integrated colleges and universities, characteristics of black college students, trends in black student enrollment statistics, evaluation of the problems involved in recruiting and selecting black students, problems of black student retention and adaptation to integrated university environments, counseling strategies and techniques relevant to these issues, and implications of current educational and political developments for the future of black students in higher education.

An evaluation is particularly relevant at a time when the national political climate is becoming increasingly conservative, when programs of affirmative action are increasingly being eroded by legislative and judicial actions, and when financial resources for higher education are shrinking because of an inflationary economy and revised federal and state budget priorities. As funds for higher education shrink rather than expand in the decade of the 1980s, administrators and governing boards will be faced with difficult budgetary decisions that may be increasingly determined by the criteria of cost effectiveness and fiscal accountability rather than the criteria of equal opportunity and societal benefit, as the affirmative action programs of the 1960s and 1970s were frequently judged.

Finally, changes taking place within the wider society have had an impact on educational administrators' perspectives of the mission of the university and on the students' view of their educational objectives. Although these views are not necessarily always congruent or even compatible, it seems clear that many colleges and universities are strengthening their curricula in science and technology at the expense of the social sciences and humanities while students are focusing earlier and more intensively on those undergraduate majors that will prepare them for immediate jobs or entry to professional schools. As fewer job opportunities are available for those with doctorates in humanities and social sciences, enrollment in these graduate programs will continue to decline, with a concomitant increase in the professional, scientific, and technological programs. Both of these developments have significant implications for black students in predominantly white institutions, particularly in view of their traditional concentration in the nonscientific and technological fields and their long-established preference for a relatively narrow range of professions, such as law, medicine, and social services. If black students are going to maintain or increase their present levels of enrollment at integrated colleges and universities, it is imperative that the institutions and the students develop a mutual understanding and accommodation of the institutions' priority goals, the societal forces shaping these goals, and the students' educational aspirations and career goals.

Review of Affirmative Action Programs

The concept of "affirmative action" to increase minority student enrollment in predominantly white colleges and universities was developed in the late 1960s as educational institutions responded to external pressures to provide access and increase educational opportunities for youth from socioeconomically disadvantaged groups. These programs were initially aimed at black youth, but they were soon expanded to encompass other major ethnic groups, such as the Hispanics and Native Americans (Boyd, 1974; Peterson and others, 1978; Sedlacek and Webster, 1977; Epps, 1972).

Initially established at major public and private institutions, with the more selective colleges generally shaping the structure and content of the programs, the basic concept swiftly spread to all segments of higher education so that, by the mid-1970s, affirmative action had become a principle accepted in philosophy if not in substance.

The more comprehensive programs were organized to offer special services to minority students in the following major areas: admissions recruitment, financial aid, remedial tutoring services, academic advising, and personal counseling. Later, on campuses where black student organizations were especially effective, special facilities for housing, recreation, and cultural activities were provided. Accompanying special student services for black and other minority students were two other major developments related to the affirmative action philosophy: the recruitment of minority faculty and staff and the establishment of ethnic studies programs.

Even though these programs were initiated with good intentions and the mutual optimism of both administrators and students, in the very nucleus of their beginnings were the seeds of their eventual emasculation. As many critical observers have pointed out, these programs began with a number of fundamental weaknesses inherent in their conceptualization, structure, financing, and administration (Boyd, 1974; Peterson and others, 1978; Astin and others, 1972; Willie and McCord, 1972).

First, the programs were hastily conceived and established as university administrators suspended their usual caution, rational analysis, and long-range planning strategies in an effort to respond to the "demands" and "ultimatums" of small groups of protesting students. On a number of campuses, the protests were accompanied by violent demonstrations and vandalism, hostile confrontations between administrators and students, and disruptions to academic and extracurricular activities. Faced with this unprecedented attack on the traditionally tranquil halls of academe, it is possible to understand, if not condone, the nearly universal tendency of college administrators in the late 1960s to suspend their critical judgment and set up new programs without a careful formulation of policies, an orderly development of procedures, an effective monitoring of implementation, and a reasonable anticipation of educational implications and consequences.

For example, administrators usually accepted the demands of the black student organizations at face value rather than making a concerted effort to consult with others—namely, the broad spectrum of black students, black leaders in education and the professions, administrators of black colleges, and leaders of established black organizations such as the NAACP and National Urban League—about methods of recruiting and selecting black students, development of "alternative" admissions criteria, financial aid issues, need for remedial services, and sociocultural issues involved in the adaptation and retention of these students. If university administrators had followed their usual procedures of establishing new programs and made greater efforts to anticipate the impact of increased black student enrollment on both the students and the academic environment, they might have avoided many of the pitfalls that resulted from ill-conceived and prematurely established programs.

Second, the programs were frequently set up on the periphery of existing academic services within the university, funded out of special accounts or "soft money." For example, in many institutions, a separate office, usually staffed by an assistant dean, was set up to deal with black student problems of advising, counseling, financial aid, remedial services, and other special services. An alternative arrangement was the hiring of black staff members to work solely with black students in each functional office. However, in both cases, the "special office" or the "special assistants" were viewed as separate from the regular services offered to the majority students. Both as a result of special funding arrangements and services to a small segment of the student population, these programs were vulnerable to cutbacks, incorporation into existing structures, and complete elimination. Recent trends suggest that many institutions have radically modified their programs for minority students in one of these directions (Peterson and others, 1978; Garcia and Seligsohn, 1978; Spurlock, 1976).

The administration of these special programs and services has also been subjected to harsh criticism. Again, in their haste to implement a variety of services for black students, university administrators frequently hired staff members valued more for their ability to "relate" to their constituency rather than for their professional experience and ability to administer the programs effectively. Administration of these programs, with notable exceptions, was characterized by inexperienced staff members, informal rules and procedures, budgetary problems, and poor channels of communication with other offices and staff members serving the general student population. Claims of lack of fiscal accountability and/or fiscal mismanagement were leveled against some of the program administrators. Moreover, these programs experienced a high rate of staff turnover, internal dissension as to priorities and goals, and declining staff morale as they evolved during the 1970s (Peterson and others, 1978; Spurlock, 1976; Washington, 1977).

Along with the structural problems and the funding constraints, the weaknesses in the administration of these programs have provided top administrators with ample justification for substantially modifying and reducing these special services. Whether these programs have undergone major reductions because of financial constraints, lack of commitment, or an evaluation that they are no longer either appropriate or effective, the fact remains that the significant wave of the late 1960s to make institutions of higher education more responsive to the needs and aspirations of black students has gradually diminished in the early 1980s to a ripple on the surface of academe.

Characteristics of Black College Students

One major question never adequately framed or answered in the initial efforts to increase the enrollment of black students at integrated institutions was: Who comprise the potential pool of black students and what are their characteristics? Because the question was not posed so that it could be answered with empirical data at the crucial stage when these special admissions programs were instituted, many myths quickly emerged and became entrenched as dogma about the black students who aspired to attend college.

These myths were examined by Boyd (1974, 1979) in his nationwide survey of more than 800 black college students in forty integrated colleges and universities in 1973, with a followup in 1975. Although Boyd found that the majority of these students came from families where the parents were not college educated and where financial need was a major concern, 72 percent of the students still expected to complete their college education.

As a group, 90 percent were graduates of public high schools and 91 percent were single. Over half of the group rated their academic preparation for college as "fair" or "poor," while 71 percent felt that they had some type of academic deficiencies.

Regarding their attitudes about integration, these students reported more positive experiences in 1975 than in 1973. Just over one fourth (27 percent) cited "race" as a major factor in their choice of friends and activities, but only 8 percent said they preferred all-black housing facilities. Although over one fourth of the students were admitted under special admissions criteria, over two thirds obtained GPAs of B or better. Finally, students from private preparatory schools adjusted better academically and socially to highly selective colleges than did students from public schools.

These results contradict a number of widely held assumptions about black students: that they prefer to have segregated social relationships, that they prefer segregated housing facilities, that lowered admissions standards will result in lowered academic achievement, and that all black students have problems of academic and social adjustment to an integrated academic environment.

Other studies of black students have emphasized the diversity rather than the homogeneity of the group, noting that they are from all socioeconomic levels; live in all regions of the United States; attend public, private, and parochial high schools; have varying levels of academic ability and potential; engage in a wide variety of athletic and extracurricular activities; and express a wide range of educational and occupational aspirations (Peterson and others, 1978; Jones, 1979; Burlew, 1980; Smith, 1979.) On the other hand, higher proportions of black than white students come from economically disadvantaged families, with parents who did not attend college, and are probably the first generation in their family to attend college (Erikson, 1979; Reed, 1978; Boyd, 1974). In addition, as compared to white students, blacks are more likely to have deficient academic backgrounds, lower GPAs, and lower scores on standardized achievement tests.

However, in spite of these educational handicaps, several studies have found that the educational aspirations and career goals of black students are equal to or higher than those of whites (Thomas, 1979; Peng and Fetters, 1978). In a large-scale follow-up study of 7,249 black and white high school graduates from the class of 1972, Thomas (1979) found that, when family status and test performance are controlled, a higher proportion of blacks than whites attend four-year as compared to two-year colleges.

Data from this same study indicated that, contrary to expected findings, white students were more likely than blacks to withdraw from college when the variables of socioeconomic status, achievement, and aspirations were controlled (Peng and Fetters, 1978). Another study of dropout rates at Oberlin College found that a higher proportion of white students in groups from both regular and special academic programs dropped out than black students in the same programs (Brown and Ervin, 1979).

Finally, the educational aspirations and career goals of black students tend to cluster around a more narrow range of options than do those among white students. For example, as noted, blacks are more likely to select undergraduate majors in the social sciences, humanities, and preprofessional fields. Their career aspirations tend to be geared to professions traditionally valued as sources of high income, high status, and low risk within the black community—professions such as law, medicine, and dentistry and, for women, social work and teaching (Reed, 1978). In recent years, there has been some increase in the number of blacks entering graduate programs of engineering and business administration, but there has not been a comparable increase in their enrollment in the expanding fields of science and technology (Johnson, 1977; Boyd, 1974).

Thus, although black students constitute a heterogeneous group with diverse backgrounds, abilities, and interests, they can fairly be characterized, in general terms, as different from the modal group of white students in their "average" family background, academic preparation, academic achievement grades and test scores, and career aspirations.

Trends in Black Student Enrollment

Since 1975, when black student enrollment at integrated colleges peaked at 7 percent for all two- and four-year accredited colleges and universities, the trend has leveled off, and since then there have been no dramatic changes. However, even though it is difficult to obtain accurate statistics on this phenomenon because of an array of different statistical baselines, there were spurts in black enrollment in predominantly white colleges after World War II, after the Supreme Court school desegregation decision in 1954, and after the first compliance survey of the federal office of civil rights in 1967 (Peterson and others, 1978). Most analysts attribute the dramatic increase from 4 percent in 1967 to 7 percent in 1975 to two major factors: (1) federal legislative, judicial, and bureaucratic actions, including large increases in financial aid to minority students; and (2) political and civil rights activities of blacks and liberal whites.

The largest black enrollments are in community colleges, but it is not surprising that public colleges and universities have larger enrollments than private institutions. However, while there was an overall 2.1 percent increase in black student enrollment in all institutions of higher education (including black colleges) from 1976 to 1978, their rate of increase in private institutions was six times greater than it was in public institutions (National Center for Education Statistics, 1978).

Between 1970 and 1976, black enrollment in a comprehensive survey of more than 2,000 United States institutions of higher education (including black colleges) increased from 6.9 to 10.2 percent. In the fall of 1979, there was an increase of 1.1 percent in the enrollment of black college freshmen in a group of 383 institutions sampled by the American Council on Education, but four-year colleges in the sample recorded an increase of 2 percent over 1978 figures (American Council on Education, 1979).

The shift in black college enrollment indicates that more than half of the nation's black college students are now enrolled in integrated institutions, a trend that has major implications for higher education in general and for the survival of the black colleges in particular. That the majority of black students are currently matriculating at predominantly white institutions increases the pressure on these institutions to provide these students with educational experiences both academically enriching and personally growth-enhancing.

Recruitment and Selection of Black Students

Recruiting and selecting black students for admission to predominantly white colleges and universities are complex and problematical issues, particularly in view of a decade of experience during which much rhetoric has been advanced but much less research has been conducted to evaluate the results of current admissions policies and procedures.

This chapter does not argue the merits of integrated versus segregated education for black students, nor does it examine the philosophical rationale underlying the movement of integrated institutions to provide increased access and opportunities to black and other minority students. Given the social realities that many black students prefer to attend integrated colleges and the well-launched efforts of these colleges to recruit them, there are a number of issues that must be addressed to maximize the "fit" between student needs and institutional goals. The focus here is on four-year college and university admissions.

These issues can be framed as a series of questions:

1. What are the best sources for a pool of potential black college students?
2. How can this pool be reached and tapped most effectively?
3. How important is financial aid as a factor in recruitment?
4. What perceptions of the university are likely to influence a black applicant's decision?
5. How much significance should be attached to "traditional criteria" as compared to "nontraditional criteria" and noncognitive characteristics—such as strong motivation, community involvement, and family factors—in evaluating black students?
6. What input, if any, should be sought from current black students, faculty, and staff in the admissions process?
7. What characteristics of the university academic program and support services should be relevant to the selection of black students?
8. What characteristics of the university environment and community milieu should be relevant to the selection of black students?
9. What can admissions officers do to *increase* the pool of qualified black students?

To answer these questions, it is necessary to utilize a wide variety of sources, including demographic data, social science findings, educational studies, and empirical data from relevant recent research on black students.

First, after more than a decade of experience, most college admissions officers are aware of the demographic and educational factors influencing the pool of potential black college students. Demographically, the largest pool of students can be found in the South and the urban areas of the Northeast and Middle West, with far smaller groups in the states west of the Mississippi River. However, population size is not a sufficient indicator of black student availability, since this pool is also influenced by the interaction of family socioeconomic status, high school educational facilities, and previous interracial experiences. In their initial recruitment efforts, many institutions used the scatter-shot approach and did not evaluate the contribution of these factors to the potential adjustment of black students to integrated campuses, thus resulting in widespread lack of fit between black students and institutions. As admissions officers have gained experience in recruiting black students, they have refined their strategies and identified particular pools of applicants that are appropriate targets for their institutions. For example, the more selective institutions, who wish to attract students with demonstrated intellectual ability, focus their recruitment efforts on students recognized by the National Merit Scholarship and the National Achievement Scholarship Competition for Black Students for their outstanding performance on College Board achievement tests. Initially, many colleges recruited black students from inner-city and segregated southern high schools, but in recent years they have concentrated on identifying capable black students in private and parochial schools as well as suburban and small town high schools.

Second, trial and error in recruitment has also yielded some approaches for reaching the pool of black students and tapping it most effectively. Colleges have begun to define and differentiate subgroups within the pool of black students, to match student abilities, interests, and needs with institutional programs, goals, and resources.

Competition among the more selective colleges for the most able students has been very intense, but less selective colleges have used similar approaches and have also developed some innovative strategies for identifying and recruiting the middle range of black students through contacts with high school administrators and counselors, mass media campaigns, contacts with black community leaders, contacts with alumni groups, career days in target high schools, and inviting groups of students for visits to the campus. In addition, some colleges have sponsored summer enrichment programs, such as Upward Bound, for local students. Community colleges, in particular, have successfully attracted minority students through more informal community organizations and networks such as black churches, fraternal organizations, political groups, and even beauty and barber shops. In the black community, these formal institutions and informal networks are significant instruments of social influence and social control and thus should not be underestimated as legitimate sources of student recruitment.

Third, the issue of financial aid as a factor in black student recruitment has been a major point of controversy. In the initial phase of recruitment, when efforts were focused on economically disadvantaged first-generation college blacks, extensive financial aid was not only an incentive but a necessity for enrollment. However, as colleges have broadened their recruiting efforts to include more blacks from middle-income and professional families, it has become increasingly clear that financial aid formulas should be worked out according to a needs criterion. Moreover, several studies have shown that, although financial aid may be a significant factor in the black student's decision to enroll in college, it does not appear to be an important determinant of the student's decision to remain in college (Peng and Fetters, 1978). However, Astin's (1975) data suggest that various forms of financial aid are related to black student persistence rates, so more research is needed in this area.

With the prospect of continued financial constraints and declining enrollments in these institutions, it is imperative for financial aid decisions to be based on criteria universally applied to all students regarding their family and personal economic resources.

Fourth, very few data are available on how the perceptions of the institution may influence a black student's decision to enroll. However, if we extrapolate from attitudes and perceptions expressed in several studies of black student adjustment to these institutions, we have some clues in this area (see Boyd, 1974; Epps, 1972; Peterson and others, 1978; Willie and McCord, 1972). Blacks, like other students, are often initially impressed, positively or negatively, by a recruiter who visits their high school. The friendliness, warmth, and openness of this recruiter is especially important to the black student, whose impression may be shaped more by the nature of the interpersonal transaction than by the content of the information about the institution (Gibbs, 1980). Next, the printed information about the school makes an impact on black students according to its emphasis on cultural diversity, the composition of the student body, the special programs available to black and other minority students, and the social and recreational opportunities available.

Another factor influencing perceptions, if the institution is located nearby, is the attitude of the black community toward the institution. Is it viewed as supportive, benign, or antagonistic toward the black community's efforts to obtain equal educational and employment opportunities?

Finally, if they have an opportunity to visit the campus, the students are affected by the contacts with the admissions office staff, classroom atmosphere, student living arrangements, and the campus's interracial climate. Whether black students choose to enroll in a particular institution is thus determined by an interaction of these several factors—that is, whether they perceive that there is a climate of tolerance, acceptance, and support from their initial contacts with a recruiter to their visit to the campus.

Fifth, the issue of employing traditional criteria in evaluating black students for admission is still the subject of continued debate, the parameters of which extend well beyond the scope of this chapter. However, there are at least three findings that help admissions officers determine which set of criteria to apply to black students: (1) achievement test scores are a good predictor of college achievement for black and white students;

(2) high school grades tend to be stronger predictors of college achievement for white than black students; and (3) black college freshman perform slightly below their expected achievement as predicted by their high school grades and aptitude test scores (Astin, 1972). Since traditional criteria are not as reliable predictors of achievement for black as they are for white students, admissions officers need to weigh other factors when evaluating the majority of black students.

In view of these findings, admissions officers must decide if and when it is appropriate to use nontraditional criteria and noncognitive characteristics, such as evidence of strong motivation, community involvement, and family background. There is ample evidence that noncognitive characteristics may be significant predictors of black retention and academic success in college, thus making them legitimate criteria in admissions decisions when cognitive characteristics do not satisfy traditional criteria. Because a large number of black students are both educationally and economically handicapped, it is important to develop alternative ways of evaluating their *potential* ability and achievement rather than focusing on *past* measures of their academic success. A number of other groups have been historically treated with special consideration in the admissions process— for example, outstanding athletes, alumni children (called legacies in some colleges), faculty children, children of large contributors (recommended by the development/fund-raising office), and students with highly prized special talents in music and the arts. These subcategories are identified, labeled, and have their own lobbying group in most major private colleges and universities. Thus, the concept of noncognitive criteria is not alien to institutions of higher education, but two questions should be raised: Which groups of students will be the beneficiaries of such a policy, and what goals of the institutions are served by pursuing such a policy?

Sixth, another thorny issue is the degree and nature of input that should be sought from black students, faculty, and staff in the admissions process. When the affirmative action programs were begun, admissions officers frequently enlisted the aid of currently enrolled black students in planning recruitment programs and making admissions decisions. This process became increasingly politicized in the early 1970s, when separate black admissions committees were set up and criteria were applied that favored the most disadvantaged applicants to the detriment of the more advantaged and academically more qualified black students. As Boyd (1974) has pointed out, this group of multiply disadvantaged students had the most difficult problems of adjustment to the academic environment and the highest attrition rates. In the late 1970s, most institutions eliminated separate admissions committees and returned to a uniform admissions process, although they often had black admissions officers who were advocates for black applicants. As black students have become a more integral segment of the university community, and admissions offices have had more than a decade to evaluate their performance, it has become increasingly important to view them relative to the total group of applicants. The goal of diversity among black students and their ability to succeed in a competitive academic environment, as measured by a set of cognitive and noncognitive characteristics carefully developed through rational discussion and analysis, should supersede the goal of conformity and potential community commitment as imposed by a special-interest group with a set of ideological beliefs and preconceived behavioral norms.

Seventh, if colleges and universities are going to maintain or increase their current levels of black enrollment, they should evaluate their experiences with and response to the institutions' academic programs and support services. Selective institutions should particularly examine the performance and retention rates of black students to be sure that they are enrolling only those students who have a very high potential for success, for failure or withdrawal at these high-status institutions can be particularly damaging to the black student's self-esteem and career aspirations.

Institutions that emphasize scientific and technological fields must be especially concerned about black students' preparation in math and science and their educational goals, for major deficiencies in these areas place the students at a severe competitive disadvantage and result in the self-fulfilling prophecy of academic failure.

If altered admissions criteria continue to be used for

some black students, institutions should carefully assess their support services to ensure adequate programs in academic advising, tutoring and remedial services, counseling and housing facilities. Experience has demonstrated that black students admitted under special programs can survive and succeed in predominantly white institutions if adequate support services are made available to them (Brown and Ervin, 1979; Boyd, 1974; Pfeifer, 1976).

Eighth, factors such as the total university environment and community milieu should be considered when making decisions to admit black students. As stated, if students perceive the university as a hospitable environment, the possibility of friction and conflict between students and administrators is lessened. Characteristics contributing to a hospitable environment are: options in housing facilities, a wide range of extracurricular activities, opportunities for social and recreational activities, ease of access to faculty and administrators, and flexibility in bureaucratic policies and procedures (Peterson and others, 1978). In addition, the community surrounding the university is an important element, particularly for students from communities with a large black population. These students may be interested in establishing social, cultural, and civic ties with a black community. If an institution is located in a rural or suburban area that is not near a black community, the chances increase that some black students will feel lonely, culturally isolated, and socially deprived. There have been instances where black athletes have been recruited to rural and suburban campuses, only to experience overt discrimination in the nearby communities and social rejection and isolation on the campuses. These factors should be considered at both the recruitment and selection stage, for the same college may be a hospitable environment for some black students but a hostile environment for others because of the balance of institution-community characteristics.

Ninth, there are strategies that admissions officers can adopt to *increase* the pool of qualified black and other minority students. These strategies include:

1.   Closer cooperation with administrators and counselors in inner-city high schools, to foster early identification of aca-

demically capable students, who can then be tracked into appropriate college-preparatory programs.

2. Development of a liaison with formal institutions and informal networks in the black community, to raise the level of consciousness and interest in higher education for black youth.

3. Sponsorship of summer enrichment programs, such as Upward Bound, for high school sophomores and juniors, to strengthen the students' academic skills and to familiarize the students with a college campus environment.

4. Collaboration with industry to sponsor year-long programs of academic enrichment and summer employment, such as the Mathematics, English and Science Achievement Program (MESA) in California, initiated by scientists at the University of California at Berkeley and funded by a coalition of major corporations. This program is intended to increase the pool of black students in engineering and scientific fields and involves several other major universities.

5. Establishment of work-study programs that pay black college students to tutor and provide other educational services in inner-city elementary, junior high, and high schools; these efforts provide not only much-needed remedial services to educationally disadvantaged youth at all levels but also role models of successful and competent black college students to younger blacks for whom college may become a possible goal.

To summarize, it is essential for academic institutions to apply the same process of rational analysis and evaluation to the issues involved in maintaining or increasing black student enrollment as they apply to other educational issues. The application of this process is especially crucial if admissions officers are going to maximize the fit between a new generation of black applicants and the changing institutions they represent.

Problems of Black Student Adaptation and Retention

In their comprehensive study of thirteen fairly diverse colleges and universities, Peterson and his colleagues (1978) identified a period of "transitional trauma" and a period of "active accommodation" as two phases in the institutional response to increased black student enrollment. In the period of transitional trauma, black students made unanticipated demands, displayed uncharacteristic behaviors, and created high levels of conflict within these institutions. The next phase—active accommodation between the university administrators and the black students—was shaped by two major factors: the interracial attitudes of both groups and the structure of organized programs for blacks. The authors point out that an overarching factor influencing both of these phases was the lack of congruency between black students' expectations of college life and the institutional expectations that blacks would fit into the mold of the traditional middle-class college student.

The specific dimensions of these incongruent expectations have been outlined by Gibbs (1973). She points out that college administrators shared a series of implicit and explicit expectations about black students: (1) that they would be absorbed in the university community without any substantial modification of existing structure or programs; (2) that they would be able to compete effectively with white students whose academic preparation, achievement test scores, and study skills were generally superior; (3) that they would be assimilated into the campus's social, cultural, and recreational activities without any consideration of sociocultural differences; and (4) that they should be grateful for the opportunity to obtain an integrated education as passive recipients rather than active participants.

On the other hand, the black students' expectations were less clearly definable, partly because they were primarily first-generation collegians and partly because their cultural experiences had not prepared them to negotiate with large, impersonal bureaucracies. However, they also shared certain expectations: (1) that the institutions would be very flexible in responding to their individual and group needs; (2) that college academic work and standards of evaluation would be a continuation of high school courses and grading standards rather than qualitatively and quantitatively more demanding and competitive; (3) that there would be a greater diversity of and tolerance for a broad range of activities, interests, and life-styles, including those that reflected their own Afro-American cultural heritage and ethnic identity; (4) that they would have greater contact and involvement with the black community near their institutions; and (5) that there would be a mutual process of adjustment and accommodation between black students' interests and needs and institutional responses. These disparate expectations were the source of much of the tension and conflict generated in the period of transitional trauma and of the chronic problems of poor communication and lack of mutual trust in the period of active accommodation as described by Peterson and his colleagues (1978).

A number of authors have documented the problems of accommodation and adaptation of black students during the 1970s in all areas of student life: academic, social, and personal (Lyons, 1973; Gibbs, 1977; Coles, 1970; Mackey, 1972; Harper, 1975). In her three-year study of black student utilization of mental health services at Stanford University, Gibbs (1975) found that they expressed multiple complaints, most frequently concerning problems in heterosexual relations (48 percent); problems in interpersonal relationships with other students, staff, and faculty members (40 percent); ethnic-identity conflicts (46 percent); academic problems (35 percent); problems with parents and families (24 percent); feelings of depression, anger, or anxiety (74 percent); psychosomatic symptoms (25 percent); and career concerns (10 percent). Although many of these problems are commonly associated with late adolescent development, black students more frequently experienced severe identity conflicts, which were exacerbated by membership in a minority group; interpersonal difficulties, which were often related to their perceptions of discriminatory treatment; and academic anxiety, which was linked to their feelings of insecurity about their ability to survive successfully in a very competitive academic environment.

Studies of the psychological problems of black students at a wide range of other integrated institutions reinforce these findings that their sociocultural marginality is a major factor in their ability to adapt to these institutions in a growth-enhancing manner. In an analysis of how black students cope with their marginal status in integrated college settings, Gibbs (1974) identified four patterns of adaptation: separation, withdrawal, assimilation, and affirmation. The separation mode is characterized by anger, hostility, interpersonal conflicts expressed as rejection of whites, and contempt for middle-class white values and norms, together with active protests against white-dominated institutions and activities. Withdrawal is characterized by feelings of depression, apathy, hopelessness, alienation, and depersonalization, culminating in extreme forms of psychological withdrawal and/or suicide attempts. The assimilation mode is characterized by desire for acceptance and approval, conformist behavior, high social anxiety in interracial situations, compensatory overachievement, and heightened racial sensitivity, resulting in efforts to avoid other blacks and to minimize or deny their ethnicity. Affirmation is characterized by self-acceptance, hyperactivity, high achievement motivation, and positive ethnic identity, resulting in self-actualizing behavior and efforts to promote cultural pluralism.

The problems black students experience and the coping mechanisms they develop to handle their marginality in integrated institutions provide some clues to reasons for their retention or attrition. In studies where black students were asked to identify the major causes of their discontent, maladjustment, or failure at integrated campuses, the following factors were mentioned: feelings of loneliness and alienation, financial problems, lack of adequate support services, problems of cultural differences, academic competition, hostility and prejudice of white students and faculty, racial discrimination, inadequate number of black faculty and staff as role models (Smith, 1979; Willie and McCord, 1972; Boyd, 1974; Jones, 1979; Sedlacek and Webster, 1977).

One consistent finding in all these surveys is the black students' perception that white faculty are indifferent, ambivalent, or prejudiced toward them. Faculty responses to black students were characterized as condescending, demeaning, or depersonalizing. Many students felt that they were stereotyped by the faculty as poorly prepared, culturally disadvantaged low achievers who were not worthy of their interest or time. Recent news reports from a number of highly selective colleges, including several prestigious Ivy League schools, indicate that even the most academically capable black students perceive faculty members as remote, uncaring, and unwilling to treat them as individuals. Conversely, faculty members have confirmed these perceptions in a survey of their responses to black students (Peterson and others, 1978).

Empirical studies of factors correlated to retention of black students from integrated institutions suggest that these factors vary according to the type of institution and the type of student enrolled. In their study of 103 large universities, Sedlacek and Webster (1977) point out that, along with a leveling off of black freshmen since 1969, the number of special minority programs has decreased in public universities while remaining stable in private universities. They also note that the number of schools using different admissions criteria for minorities has decreased back to 1969 levels. They conclude from their data that private universities are doing a more effective job of enrolling and retaining minority students than public institutions. In his survey of 800 black undergraduates in 40 four-year colleges, Boyd (1979) reaches a similar conclusion.

Copeland (1976), in a study of the causes of black student attrition at integrated colleges, found that dropouts entered college for nonspecific reasons significantly more often than the "stayers." In the group of dropouts, the decision to leave was related to experiences of racial discrimination but not to the level of financial aid.

In their study of dropout rates of black and white students at Oberlin, Brown and Ervin (1979) showed that blacks participating in special programs had significantly lower dropout rates than nonparticipating blacks. Moreover, fewer black students in both regular and special programs dropped out as compared to white students in both programs.

Results from the longitudinal study of the high school class of 1972 showed that black students had higher educational aspirations than whites, in spite of lower class rank and test scores, and that they were less likely than whites to withdraw during the first two years of college when the variables of socioeconomic status, achievement, and aspirations were accounted for (Peng and Fetters, 1978).

Finally, there appears to be a relationship between black student retention and their perception of institutional racism. In a study at the University of Maryland, black students expressed more serious problems as victims of racism and discrimination than whites, Asians, or Hispanics (Webster, Sedlacek, and Miyares, 1979). In an earlier study at the same school, those blacks who perceived the university climate negatively and reported experiencing more personal racism received higher grades and felt they had a greater chance of obtaining a college degree than other blacks (Pfeifer, 1976). One could interpret the findings of these two studies as support for the hypothesis that blacks who can attribute their problems to external sources are able to avoid self-attribution of failure and, consequently, can overcome external barriers to their achievement.

The results of these empirical studies indicate a complex relationship between black student retention and institutional variables. More recent studies suggest that black retention rates are as high as or higher than white rates; earlier claims of high attrition rates among black students probably reflected inappropriate recruitment strategies and admissions decisions of students who were ill prepared and poorly motivated for college. If current trends continue, black retention rates will probably be more influenced by financial aid factors and adequate support services than by any other institutional variables.

Counseling Needs and Strategies for Black Students

It is important to view the problems of black students on three levels: problems experienced because they are in a transitional developmental stage from late adolescence to young adulthood; problems experienced because they are marginal ethnically and socioeconomically in a predominantly white middle-class society; and problems experienced because they are black students in predominantly white institutions. The latter perspective is most relevant to our current discussion because it combines all three elements: the developmental, the sociocultural, and the institutional.

To counsel black students, counselors must consider all three factors. Without the developmental perspective, counselors tend to misinterpret the symptoms and behaviors characteristic of this age group in its quest for identity, autonomy, and vocational commitment. Without the sociocultural perspective, they tend to minimize the attitudes and behaviors shaped by the experience of ethnic marginality in American society (Derbyshire and Brody, 1964; Pierce, 1968). Without the institutional perspective, counselors tend to underestimate the impact of institutional structures and policies on black students' attitudes and behaviors. This section focuses on what can be done to make institutions more responsive to black students.

When evaluating black students' special problems and needs, admissions officers and counselors must address three dimensions of their institutions: structural, attitudinal, and professional. First, they should evaluate the effectiveness of current structural arrangements in dealing with the problems of black students. In view of increasing financial constraints and decreasing levels of commitment from within and without higher education, it may be necessary to incorporate the special programs for black and other minority students into the regular administrative structures. If this should be necessary, an important factor in the success of the consolidation process will be the degree to which flexibility can be maintained in these programs, so that black students can continue to perceive options which take into account their sociocultural background and experiences.

Four examples of this type of flexibility are (1) "drop-in" counseling services, whereby appointments do not have to be made weeks in advance; (2) peer counseling services, where students who have experienced similar problems are available for informal discussions; (3) tutoring and remedial services, which permit the students to participate in regular academic programs without the stigma of special tracks; and (4) financial aid officers who are responsive to short-term financial crises, which black students are more likely to experience than white students. If these offices are organized along functional lines, it will continue to be relevant to have integrated staffs—so that black students will perceive that there are understanding and sympathetic persons to whom they can turn, even if these staff members do not have a specific responsibility for serving their needs.

Second, the attitudes of administrators, faculty, and professional student services staff are significant elements in the successful adjustment of black students to integrated campuses. As noted, faculty and staff attitudes have not only been perceived by black students as negative, but surveys have reported self-admitted ambivalent, negative, or hostile attitudes in this group (Peterson and others, 1978). Very few reports in the literature indicate that any organized efforts have been made to alter the negative attitudes of these groups. However, because this is a major source of black student discontent, institutions must begin to take the initiative in promoting changed attitudes. It is not enough for presidents and deans to make clichéd commencement addresses or to issue annual reports that reaffirm administrative support for equal opportunity programs. These efforts are primarily directed to the various external constituencies of educational institutions; the internal groups largely ignore or discount these pronouncements as propaganda and public relations. If black students are ever to become an integral part of the academic world, all faculty and staff must become more sensitive to their historical, social, and cultural background; to their patterns of behavior and communication; and to their values, goals, and aspirations. The shared experience of over 350 years of racial prejudice, discrimination, and economic disadvantage has inevitably shaped the social and psychological development of black students. Without any understanding of the dimensions of these experiences, white faculty and staff will continue to behave toward black students in demeaning, condescending, and overtly discriminative ways.

It is obvious that administrators cannot issue edicts to compel faculty and staff to change their attitudes and behaviors toward black students, but there should be mechanisms established to foster such changes, such as human relations workshops, departmental seminars and retreats, and incentive awards for extraordinary service to minority students. Additionally, increased informal and social contacts between black students and faculty/staff may reduce tensions and improve relationships. Finally, if there are substantiated reports of faculty-staff discrimination against black students, there should be channels for processing complaints, such as an ombudsman's office, where students can be assured of obtaining a fair and impartial hearing to redress their grievances.

The use of counseling strategies and techniques for black students is a more difficult area to assess because of the diversity among black students in academic preparation, prior experience with integration, and level of social and psychological awareness. Students from integrated, middle-class backgrounds may be relatively comfortable at predominantly white institutions, may cope successfully with college pressures, and may not require any special counseling approaches. However, the majority of black students are not from these backgrounds and may not be responsive to the traditional counseling approaches used with white students.

For these students, counselors may need to launch aggressive outreach programs through student residences and student organizations to familiarize black students with their services. The outreach programs might include satellite "minicounseling" offices in dormitories and cultural and recreational facilities where black students congregate, thus providing convenient and informal access to such services. Staff members from the counseling center and the mental health clinic could rotate daily in these satellite offices for those students who do not wish to label themselves "problems" or "disturbed" by seeking appointments at the regular offices.

Another strategy is establishing training programs for student residential staff members and peer counselors in the residential units, with particular focus on human relations issues, early identification of interracial tension, and referral procedures for emotionally troubled students.

In conjunction with training residential staff, some institutions have established informal liaisons between counselors and dormitory staff, faculty, and other administrative staff for the purposes of preventive mental health education and crisis intervention. These counselors may visit dormitories for rap sessions around a number of sensitive topics, meet informally with black student leaders, respond to concerns of faculty and staff about individual black students, and generally monitor the climate of race relations on the campus.

Finally, there are legitimate differences of opinion over whether counseling techniques need to be modified for black students. Again, the answer probably depends on what subset of black students are under consideration. For those black students who do not fit the mold of the "ideal client," for whom counseling techniques have been developed, there is some empirical evidence that modifications are both necessary and appropriate.

Initially, the counselor should spend some time describing the counseling process to the black student, who may be very confused, anxious, and defensive about seeking help. An understanding of the counseling process, techniques, and goals should minimize the student's anxiety and decrease defensiveness.

Black students respond more positively to directive rather than nondirective techniques, which they apparently experience as lack of interest in their problems. They are much more likely than white students to compare counseling to medical treatment; thus, they expect a diagnosis, a treatment, and a cure. Active engagement, advice, and guidance are preferred to passive listening, reflecting back, and neutrality (Haettenschwiller, 1971; Gibbs, 1975; Hammond, 1970).

These students may prefer shorter and more frequent appointments rather than the standard fifty-minute hour. If they are unused to self-exploration, shorter sessions help allay their anxiety and simultaneously build up mutual trust with the counselor.

Specific techniques that may be useful in building a counseling relationship with black students are role playing, behavior modification, and reality-oriented techniques. Those techniques address themselves to identifiable problems in the students' lives and allow the students to rehearse or practice immediate ways to alleviate these problems. The methods are probably viewed as more beneficial by many black students than those techniques that emphasize the development of insight and self-actualization.

In summary, if institutions are strongly committed to continued enrollment of significant numbers of black students, they must be willing to reassess their responsiveness to the problems and needs of these students and to institute modifications in structural, attitudinal, and professional areas.

Implications of Current Developments for the
Future of Black Students in Integrated Institutions

This discussion of black students has focused primarily on the interaction between the problems and needs of the students and the response of integrated institutions to these problems and needs. This final section examines the interface between these institutional interactions and the broader context of educational and sociopolitical developments that impinge on colleges and universities.

A number of trends in higher education will have a significant impact on enrollment of black students at predominantly white institutions. First, sources of funding that were expanding during the 1960s will probably continue to contract during the 1980s at federal, state, and county levels. Reduced revenues, combined with anticipated high rates of inflation, will decrease levels of financial aid, decrease funds for special programs, and decrease funds for new initiatives in academic and nonacademic areas. Additionally, community colleges, which have traditionally enrolled a high proportion of black students and which are typically funded from local property tax assessments, have been forced to retrench because of taxpayer revolts, such as California's Proposition 13, which radically reduced property taxes and resulted in immediate loss of major revenues to the community college system.

Second, with the last crop of the baby boom of 1946 to 1964 due to graduate from high school in 1982, college enrollments are expected to decline, further reducing income and particularly threatening small, private colleges. These two developments have made all institutions more concerned about cost effectiveness and fiscal accountability. Those programs that have been most vulnerable—because of their lack of integration into the institutional organization, their external funding, or their controversial status—are often the easiest targets to eliminate from the budget.

Third, the growing emphasis on scientific and technological fields has led many institutions to allocate a greater proportion of their faculty, courses, and equipment to these fields at the expense of the social sciences and humanities. Although this trend may reflect the general direction of the society toward high technology, it is not congruent with the educational background or career aspirations of the majority of black students.

Related to this trend is a fourth factor, an increasing oversupply of the fields that black students traditionally prefer, such as law, public school teaching, social work, and college teaching. Thus, these latter two trends suggest a need to diversify the academic majors and to extend the range of career options for black students.

Three major political and social developments will influence the response of integrated institutions to future levels of black student enrollment. First, judicial decisions in the area of civil rights and affirmative action have become increasingly more cautious and circumscribed, reflecting a conservative tenor in the higher courts. It is too early to make a definitive analysis, but it seems likely that the *Bakke* case has inhibited black graduate enrollments.

Second, legislative and executive actions in this area will be increasingly responsive to the backlash of the white majority against affirmative action programs, which many now view as "reverse discrimination" against whites. Politicians now find themselves on the defensive against conservative political action committees and members of the Moral Majority, who measure a politician's effectiveness by his position on issues such as affirmative action. Thus, the 1980s will presumably witness a steady retreat from the civil rights gains of the 1960s in judicial, legislative, and executive actions. This retreat in turn will undermine the waning level of public support for affirmative action programs in education and employment.

Third, in the late 1970s the focus on affirmative action programs began to shift away from blacks and other minorities and toward other historically disadvantaged groups, such as women and the handicapped. Moreover, many white liberals who had given personal and financial support to the civil rights movement have redirected their energies to issues concerning women's rights, the environment, and alternative sources of energy. These trends have further eroded the level of public support and commitment for affirmative action programs for minority students.

In spite of these educational and sociopolitical trends, the prospects for black students at integrated colleges may be far from grim. Even when the baby boom subsides, the higher black birthrate will continue to produce a potential pool of college students. Thus, it is essential that institutions improve their recruitment strategies, clarify their admissions criteria, and provide adequate levels of support for black students.

In summary, I propose five recommendations aimed at increasing and maintaining the enrollment of black students at predominantly white colleges and universities. First, institutions must reassess their commitment to provide equal access to higher education for black students. This reassessment must include decisions about institutional long-range priorities and goals, allocation of resources, and programmatic structure. If black students are going to succeed in integrated institutions, past experience dictates that there must be strong and committed leadership at the highest administrative levels, official endorsement and legitimation within the institution, well-developed strategies of programming and resource support, and built-in procedures of evaluation and assessment (see Peterson and others, 1978).

Second, institutions must evaluate their specific programs for black students—specifically, the organizational structure of these programs, their staffing patterns, their level of financing, and their overall effectiveness. Programs that generally have been more effective have been characterized by their high level of institutional integration, their competent and cooperative staffs, the incorporation of their financing into the regular budget process, and their professional management and implementation (Peterson and others, 1978).

Third, institutions must monitor their internal climate to foster an environment that encourages interracial communication and contact at all levels. Racial prejudice is extremely pervasive in our society, but any evidence of prejudice or discrimination among white faculty, administrators, and students should be firmly and consistently discouraged and penalized. On the other hand, black separatism should neither be encouraged nor reinforced because that stance will not prepare blacks to deal with the complexities of a multiracial society or to compete successfully in their future careers. At institutions where there was a climate of mutual acceptance and trust, black student programs tended to be either fully integrated into the community or to emphasize cultural pluralism (Peterson and others, 1978).

Fourth, institutions should make greater efforts to strengthen ties with secondary schools, to develop a larger pool of academically capable black students. These efforts could include making counselors more aware of the need for math and science courses, providing college tutors for interested students, and sponsoring summer and four-year enrichment programs.

Finally, institutions should make greater efforts to increase the fit between black students' backgrounds and goals and institutional resources and priorities. Since the pool of black students is highly diverse, subgroups with similar aptitudes, interests, and career goals can be identified. Such matching of students with institutions would enhance the educational experiences for the students, increase the rates of retention, and allow institutions to direct their energies away from a crisis-management model and toward a growth-enhancing model of dealing with black students.

The challenge before higher education has never been clearer, nor have the potential rewards ever been greater. If integrated institutions can meet this challenge in the decades ahead, they will not only establish a more stimulating and diverse academic environment, but they will also make a lasting contribution to increased economic opportunities for blacks, resulting in greater benefits to the society as a whole.

✒ 9

Recruiting, Advising, and Retaining Mexican American Students

Raymond Buriel
Sally Rivera

✒ Census Bureau projections indicate that, within the next decade, Mexican Americans will become this nation's largest ethnic minority. But despite their rapidly increasing numbers in the population, there is a paucity of accurate information concerning them and their problems in the area of higher education, particularly in regard to recruitment and admissions. This chapter sheds light on these neglected issues, to help college recruiters and admissions officers increase the number of Mexican American students at their particular institutions. The chapter is divided into four sections. First is a brief historical and demographic profile of the Mexican American population, with particular emphasis on the postsecondary educational situation of this group. The second section reviews admissions testing issues and research relating to Mexican Americans. The third section briefly describes the traditional Mexican American value system and is the context for understanding the material presented in the final section. The fourth section is a pragmatically oriented discussion of culturally relevant recruitment and admissions procedures based on the information presented in the previous sections, primarily section three. The conclusion notes our concerns about the proper interpretation of the information and suggestions presented and discusses the role of the

Mexican American experience in the total recruitment and admissions procedure as a reflection of "equal opportunity."

Before proceeding, we should note our reasons for using the term "Mexican American" to identify those who are the subject of this chapter. There is no universally accepted ethnic term to describe persons of the Mexican-descent population living in the United States. The terms "Mexican American," "Chicano," "Spanish American," "Latin American," "Latino," and "Hispanic" have all been used; however, the usage of these terms, and even more importantly their acceptance, is primarily a function of both a person's age and the region of the country in which he or she lives. Generally, the term "Chicano" is most popular and widely accepted by younger members of this group. However, this term is usually not accepted, and in some cases is considered offensive, by older persons. Different ethnic terms are also more popular in different regions of the Southwest because of the unique histories of these areas. In general, the term "Spanish American" is most often used and preferred in New Mexico and parts of southern Colorado; "Latino" and "Latin American" are heard most often in Texas; and "Mexican American" is most widely used in California, Arizona, and other parts of the Southwest. The term "Hispanic" is used throughout the Southwest and the entire United States to refer to anyone of Indo-Hispanic ancestry, including Mexican Americans.

Our own preference is to use the term "Chicano." However, realizing that many readers may not be familiar with this term or consider it offensive, we defer to the term "Mexican American," which is probably the most widely recognized and accepted term used to refer to persons of Mexican descent living in the United States. However, we use the term "Hispanic" when referring to everyone of Indo-Hispanic ancestry. Recruiters and admissions officers should familiarize themselves with the preferred ethnic term of the individuals with whom they work.

Historical and Demographical Profile of the Mexican-American People

In 1848 the Treaty of Guadalupe Hidalgo formally ended the Mexican American War and forced Mexico to cede to the

United States territories that included the present-day states of Arizona, California, Colorado, Nevada, New Mexico, Texas, and Utah. As a consequence, the Mexican residents of these territories became, through default, this nation's first Mexican American minority. Thus, unlike European, Asian, and black minorities—whose ancestors made transoceanic voyages to arrive on this continent—Mexican Americans, like Native American Indians, became a minority in their own land through conquest and annexation. This fact, and other historical facts, remind us that, although Mexican Americans share some similarities with other ethnic minorities, attempts to describe their experience as being "just like" that of blacks, Asian Americans, or various other minority groups overlook important differences which distinguish the Mexican American population (Cortes, 1977).

In the half century following the Mexican War, there was only a slow trickle of Mexican immigration to the United States. However, beginning in the early twentieth century, the first of several great waves of Mexican immigrants began their northward movement to the United States. The influx was (and still is) so heavy that today the overwhelming majority of Mexican Americans can trace their ancestry back to Mexico within only the past sixty years.

The Spanish-surnamed population, which is made up primarily of Mexican Americans, is fast becoming this nation's largest ethnic minority. Of the estimated 11 to 19 million Spanish-surnamed persons living in the United States, approximately 60 percent are of Mexican ancestry (U.S. Bureau of the Census, 1977). The majority of Mexican Americans (87 percent) live in five southwestern states: California (41 percent), Texas (36 percent), Arizona (5 percent), New Mexico (3 percent), and Colorado (2 percent). In addition, although Mexican Americans are commonly stereotyped as being farm workers, relatively more of them are concentrated in cities than the rest of the nation's population. Today, 85 percent of all Mexican Americans are urban dwellers. Nearly half (46 percent) live in central cities, 32 percent in suburban areas surrounding these cities, 11 percent in smaller urban areas, and only 15 percent in rural areas (U.S. Department of Health, Education and Welfare, 1974).

There are interesting and important variations in the age compositions between Mexican Americans and the rest of the United States population. For example, 13 percent of all Mexican Americans are under the age of five, and 47 percent are under eighteen. In contrast, only 7 percent of the rest of the nation's population is below the age of five, and only 13 percent is under eighteen. Not surprisingly, the median age for Mexican Americans is nineteen years, compared to twenty-eight years for the rest of the population. This difference in age trends has important implications for college enrollments, as discussed in section four.

Other demographic characteristics of the Mexican American population include a relatively high unemployment rate (6.2 percent for Anglo Americans and 10.8 percent for Mexican Americans in 1977) and lower family incomes. In 1975 the median family income of all families in the United States was $13,700, compared to $9,600 for Mexican American families (U.S. Bureau of the Census, 1977). Partially because Mexican Americans have larger families, the per capita income of Mexican American families is $1,176 versus $4,139 for the total United States population (U.S. Department of Health, Education and Welfare, 1974). The disparity in incomes between Anglo and Mexican Americans has important implications for college attendance, as discussed in the final section.

With the exception of Native American Indians, no other group receives fewer years of schooling than Mexican Americans. For example, by the senior year in high school, about 60 percent of Mexican Americans are still in school, compared to about 67 percent of blacks and 85 percent of Anglo Americans (U.S. Commission on Civil Rights, 1971).

In general, there is scant information on Mexican Americans in institutions of higher education, but the few data available present a disheartening picture. The college enrollments of Mexican Americans lag far behind that of Anglo Americans. Figure 1 (U.S. Commission on Civil Rights, 1971) shows the "school-holding power" for Anglo Americans, Mexican Americans, and blacks in five southwestern states. The data in Figure 1 indicate that, of a hypothetical 100 Anglo Americans who enter

Figure 1. School-Holding Power Rates for Each Ethnic Group
in Five Southwestern States.

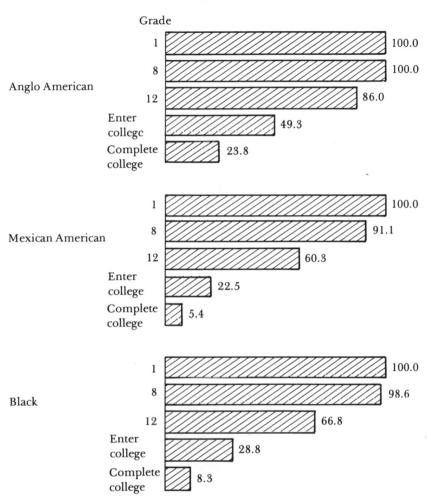

the first grade, 24 will eventually graduate from college. For
every 100 Mexican Americans entering the first grade, only 5
will complete four years of college. And for every 100 blacks
entering the first grade, 8 will complete a B.A. degree. Paren-
thetically, this same civil rights study found that although Mexican Americans and blacks were underrepresented in college,

they were overrepresented—and Anglo Americans underrepresented—in the military services and in technical and vocational schools.

There are substantial variations in the proportion of Mexican American students attending different kinds of institutions of higher education. Comprehensive data from California, the only state for which such information is available, indicate that, by percentage, Mexican Americans are primarily enrolled in two-year community colleges, followed by the state college system, private institutions, and the University of California system, in that order. Table 1 presents a breakdown of Anglo

Table 1. California Undergraduate Enrollments, Fall 1974,
by Ethnicity and Type of Institution.

Ethnicity	Community Colleges, %	California State University and Colleges System, %	University of California, %	Private Institutions, %
Anglo American	79.0	79.5	79.7	78.9
Mexican American	8.9	6.8	5.0	5.6
Black	8.4	6.3	4.5	5.8
Other	3.7	7.4	10.8	9.7

Note: Adapted from Carter and Segura, 1979.

American, Mexican American, and black college enrollments in California in 1974. An earlier study by the College Entrance Examination Board (1972) suggests a similar trend throughout the Southwest. Based on information from 153 institutions, the College Board found that the number of Mexican Americans attending community colleges was more than double the number attending state colleges and universities. Community colleges are popular because they are close to home, relatively inexpensive, and have flexible admissions requirements.

As recently as 1978, there were still substantially more Hispanic undergraduates enrolled in two-year than in four-year colleges. Enrollment figures for 1978 are presented in Table 2, which includes information on all Hispanic groups in the United States, including Mexican Americans.

Table 2. Hispanic Participation in Postsecondary Education
by Type of Enrollment: 1978.

Type of Enrollment	Number of Hispanics Enrolled	Hispanics as a Percent of Total Enrollment
Colleges and universities		
Undergraduates	345,403	4.0
Two-year	198,091	5.9
Four-year	147,312	2.8

Note: Adapted from Brown and others, 1980.

A breakdown of Hispanic college enrollments by state is presented in Table 3. In addition to information about undergraduate enrollments, Table 3 includes data on the number of Hispanics attending graduate and professional schools in the fall of 1978.

The information in Table 3 may be useful for developing effective strategies for recruiting Hispanics. Because Mexican Americans and other Hispanics attend college in their own state, Table 3 should give recruiters some idea of the geographical areas in the country where recruitment efforts are likely to be most successful. Inspection of Table 3 also reveals that New Mexico has the highest percentage of Hispanic enrollment, partially because Spanish Americans make up most of the population in that state.

Barriers to Higher Education: Admissions Testing and Mexican Americans

In 1978 the University of California Board of Regents adopted a new admissions policy that increased reliance on SAT scores over high school grade point average (HSGPA) for admissions to the university. The regents' action was motivated by a concern over growing inflation in high school grades, which they felt weakened the validity of HSGPA as a source of admissions.

The university's increased reliance on test scores had its most adverse effect on Mexican American enrollments and came at a time when access to the university seemed increasingly in reach for members of this group. Table 4 gives Anglo American

Table 3. Hispanic College Enrollment in Each State by Level of Enrollment: Fall 1978.

State or Other Area	Total		Undergraduate		Graduate		Professional	
	Number	%	Number	%	Number	%	Number	%
Alabama	525	0.3	448	0.3	59	0.4	6	0.2
Alaska	337	1.3	217	1.3	13	1.1	—	—
Arizona	15,465	8.8	13,811	9.6	346	2.5	25	2.1
Arkansas	267	0.4	227	0.4	20	0.3	5	0.3
California	147,629	8.9	123,430	9.8	4,659	4.1	1,458	4.7
Colorado	8,981	5.9	6,455	5.7	431	3.2	120	4.1
Connecticut	2,640	1.7	2,013	1.8	325	1.4	89	3.0
Delaware	181	0.6	147	0.6	4	0.3	—	—
District of Columbia	1,329	1.6	698	1.6	279	1.4	205	2.3
Florida	27,015	7.2	22,641	7.5	989	3.7	305	5.1
Georgia	906	0.5	738	0.5	59	0.3	37	0.7
Hawaii	1,436	3.0	1,237	3.2	55	1.4	3	0.6
Idaho	341	0.9	282	0.9	27	0.9	—	—
Illinois	13,909	2.3	11,147	2.4	689	1.2	203	1.2
Indiana	2,061	0.9	1,664	1.0	190	0.7	73	1.2
Iowa	650	0.5	536	0.5	56	0.4	48	0.8
Kansas	1,718	1.3	1,425	1.5	150	0.9	35	1.6
Kentucky	391	0.3	279	0.3	57	0.3	19	0.4
Louisiana	2,038	1.3	1,674	1.3	235	1.4	52	1.3
Maine	82	0.2	71	0.2	6	0.3	1	0.3
Maryland	2,020	0.9	1,657	1.0	161	0.8	27	0.8
Massachusetts	5,032	1.3	3,642	1.4	569	1.2	183	1.6
Michigan	6,621	1.4	5,394	1.3	450	0.9	170	1.6
Minnesota	834	0.4	605	0.4	97	0.6	70	1.1
Mississippi	131	0.1	112	0.1	11	0.1	4	0.2
Missouri	1,664	0.8	1,257	0.8	155	0.6	49	0.5

Montana	133	0.4	98	0.4	5	0.2	—	—
Nebraska	775	0.9	654	1.0	54	0.8	38	1.3
Nevada	821	2.4	524	2.2	27	1.7	—	—
New Hampshire	269	0.6	239	0.7	10	0.4	11	2.5
New Jersey	11,317	3.7	8,837	4.2	623	2.0	165	3.1
New Mexico	13,277	23.8	10,501	26.1	939	15.3	149	23.9
New York	46,925	4.9	38,789	5.8	3,287	2.7	441	2.0
North Carolina	1,022	0.4	815	0.4	74	0.4	16	0.4
North Dakota	54	0.2	48	0.2	4	0.3	—	—
Ohio	2,639	0.6	2,144	0.6	306	0.6	77	0.6
Oklahoma	1,185	0.8	1,034	0.8	69	0.5	25	0.7
Oregon	1,589	1.1	1,273	1.2	66	0.7	32	0.9
Pennsylvania	3,475	0.7	2,624	0.7	337	0.7	135	0.9
Rhode Island	351	0.6	272	0.6	31	0.5	5	2.0
South Carolina	332	0.3	273	0.3	37	0.3	4	0.2
South Dakota	293	0.9	283	1.1	2	0.1	1	0.2
Tennessee	663	0.3	553	0.3	49	0.3	26	0.5
Texas	78,954	12.0	68,451	12.7	4,521	6.8	874	6.4
Utah	1,169	1.3	1,047	1.3	68	0.9	25	2.0
Vermont	147	0.5	125	0.5	19	0.8	—	—
Virginia	1,441	1.3	763	0.5	71	0.4	13	0.3
Washington	3,641	1.3	1,813	1.3	138	1.0	52	1.5
West Virginia	167	0.2	123	0.2	22	0.2	3	0.2
Wisconsin	2,029	0.8	1,570	0.8	196	1.0	72	2.1
Wyoming	349	1.8	297	2.0	8	0.8	2	0.9

Note: Adapted from Brown and others, 1980.

Table 4. Anglo American and Mexican American Undergraduate
Enrollment at the University of California.

Group	1972-73, %	1973-74, %	1974-75, %	1975-76, %	1976-77, %
Anglo American	86.5	85.9	72.8	80.9	73.9
Mexican American	3.9	4.1	4.9	6.0	6.6
Other	9.6	10.0	22.3	13.1	19.5

Note: Adapted from Educational Opportunity Program, University of California, Irvine, 1977-78.

and Mexican American enrollment figures for the University of California system between 1972 and 1977.

Mexican American enrollments showed a steady increase between 1972 and 1977. A minority impact study examined the effect that the new admissions criteria would have had on students who enrolled in the university in the fall of 1976. Under the new formula, 16.2 percent of the Mexican American students, 8.8 percent of the black students, and 2 percent of the Anglo American students would not have been admitted (Martinez, 1978).

Criticisms of aptitude tests as criteria for admission to colleges and universities should not be construed as a call for lower admissions standards for Mexican Americans. Criticisms of these tests arise from the tests' failure to predict academic success for Mexican American students with the same accuracy as for Anglo American students.

Unfortunately, the tendency to treat Mexican Americans "just like" other minorities has led to the false conclusion that admissions tests are valid for this group, since most studies of test bias have involved blacks and Anglo Americans and generally have found no evidence of bias against the minority group (Olmedo, 1977). However a review of those few studies that have used Mexican American subjects reveals a pattern of test bias against members of this group. In the earliest of these studies, Borup (1971) found that although the American College Test (ACT) scores of Mexican Americans were lower than those of Anglo Americans, there was no difference in the first-semester college grade point averages between these two groups.

Goldman and Richards (1974) also found that SAT scores were more valid for Anglo American students than for Mexican American students.

Subsequently, Lowman and Spuck (1975) found that, for Mexican American students in a transition-year program at selective private colleges, nontraditional predictors accounted for more variance in first-year college success than SAT scores and HSGPA. These findings prompted Lowman and Spuck (1975, pp. 46-47) to conclude that "Mexican American students who are capable of succeeding in highly selective colleges and universities are likely to be passed over for admission if only the traditional predictors of success are used."

Other studies with Mexican Americans cast greater doubts on the wisdom of placing increased reliance on test scores over HSGPA in determining college admissions for members of this group. Thus, Goldman and Hewitt (1975) found that, for Mexican American students, SAT scores predicted less than an additional 1 percent of college GPA variance *beyond* that already predicted by HSGPA. In contrast, for Anglo American students, SAT scores accounted for a sizable increment in prediction of college GPA beyond that already predicted by HSGPA. These authors also note that there is a greater difference between the mean test scores of Anglo Americans and Mexican Americans than between their mean criterion (college GPA) scores. This situation leads to test bias against Mexican Americans, according to Thorndike's (1971) definition of the term. Thus, if success is defined by a given level of college GPA, more Mexican American students will achieve that level of success than would be accepted to college if acceptance depended solely on test scores.

A study by Warren (1976) obtained results that parallel the findings of Goldman and Hewitt: HSGPA almost always showed a stronger relationship with college GPA than either SAT or ACT scores. He also found that, in a small number of cases, SAT and ACT scores were more accurate predictors of college GPA for non-Mexican American students.

Why should HSGPA predict college success differently for Anglo American and Mexican American students? One possibility is that grade inflation—the original impetus for increased reliance on test scores in college admissions—is more prevalent in predominantly Anglo American high schools than in predominantly Mexican American high schools. Haro (1978) argues that grade inflation is greater at segregated majority high schools because such schools want to continue to ensure that a large number of their graduates will proceed to the university. In contrast, the press for grade inflation in segregated minority high schools is not as great because the common expectation is that only 2 to 4 percent of the graduates of these schools will go on to prestigious universities (Haro, 1978).

Perhaps the clearest, "no nonsense" presentation of the issue of testing and Mexican Americans is reflected in a study by Goldman and Widawski (1976). These researchers note that the use of tests in the selection of Mexican American college applicants inevitably involves a value judgment by colleges and universities. These institutions of higher education must often decide either to accept or reject a Mexican American applicant on the basis of test scores. Either choice carries certain potential liabilities for both the institution and the student, depending on the student's ultimate likelihood of success or failure. On the one hand, if the institution decides to "admit" and the student fails, a "false-positive" selection error occurs. The outcome for the institution is an unsuccessful commitment of its resources to a student who was unable to profit from them. The outcome for the student is a possible loss of self-esteem for having tried and failed. On the other hand, if the institution decides to "reject" and the student possesses the potential to succeed, a "false-negative" selection error occurs. The institutional cost is the loss of a potential college graduate of that particular school. The individual cost, however, is shared by society and amounts to the loss of a college-educated individual in the community.

Using an imaginative research design that utilized students already in college, Goldman and Widawski (1976) determined the frequency of false-positive and false-negative selection errors based on SAT scores for Mexican American students. Their findings reveal that any slight increase in correct selection accompanying the use of SAT scores is offset by decreased admissability of potentially successful Mexican American applicants.

As long as institutions of higher education exist in society and draw on societal resources (people and money) for their continued existence, and as long as such institutions continue to affect the quality of life in society through the educational and professional preparation they give society's members, then the question of testing and college admissions will continue to be a value-laden issue. Despite claims by some colleges and universities that the small number of minorities in these institutions is a reflection of inequalities in society and, therefore, not the fault of these institutions, such institutions nevertheless have an obligation to help tear down the barriers that maintain and perpetuate invidious social, economic, and political distinctions between minority and majority members of society. Since there are far fewer Mexican American college graduates than Anglo Americans, the loss of a Mexican American college graduate due to false-negative selection errors is a bigger burden for the Mexican American community, which has a greater need of such persons.

Mexican American Value System: Prelude to Recruitment and Admissions Strategies

The following brief description of the dominant value system of Mexican Americans is a frame of reference for understanding the culturally based recruitment and admissions recommendations made in the next section. Obviously, any attempt to describe the Mexican American value system runs the risk of stereotyping because not all Mexican Americans are alike. Still, we believe that there is a common core of values at the center of Mexican American culture and that these values, to a greater or lesser degree, influence the lives of most Mexican Americans. However, by discussing Mexican American values, we do not mean to imply that such values are categorically different from those held by most Anglo Americans. Differences in Anglo American and Mexican American values are more often a matter of degree rather than absolute.

Our description of Mexican American values is based on the research of Ramirez and Castañeda (1974) and focuses on four major conceptual areas: (1) identification with family, community, and ethnic group; (2) personalization of interpersonal relationships; (3) status and role definitions in family and community; (4) Mexican Catholic ideology. We focus only on those Mexican Americans who are strongly identified with this core set of values. Note, however, that not all Mexican Americans are equally identified with this value system. See Ramirez and Castañeda (1974) for a discussion of those factors influencing Mexican Americans' degree of identification with the values of their culture.

Identification with Family, Community, and Ethnic Group. Mexican American childrearing practices encourage the development of a self-identity embedded firmly within the context of the *familia* (family). One's individual identity is therefore part of a larger identity with the family. As a result, Mexican Americans seldom think of their feelings, needs, and interests as being separate from the feelings, needs, and interests of the family. Not only do individuals consider themselves extensions of the family, but so does the rest of the Mexican American community. Consequently, both the family and the community view one's actions and accomplishments as the actions and accomplishments of the family.

The desire to be close to the family usually results in many members of the same family living in the same community. The family network extends further into the community through kinships formed by intermarriage between families and *el compadrazco,* the practice of having special friends become godparents for one's children in baptism, confirmation, first communion, or marriage. Adults united through *el compadrazco,* called *compadres* or *comadres,* have mutual obligations to one another similar to those of brothers and sisters. Extended family ties in the community give rise to a sense of identity with the community.

The world view of most Mexican Americans includes a sense of affiliation with *la raza* (the race), a term referring to the cultural and spiritual bonds that unite all people of Indo-

Hispanic descent, not just Mexican Americans. Individuals see themselves as members of an international community throughout the Americas—a community that shares a common history of Spanish conquest and miscegenation with indigenous Indian groups, giving rise to a "new race" of *mestizo* people. Among some Mexican Americans, the term *la raza* carries with it the belief that the destiny of this "new race" is yet to be fulfilled.

Personalization of Interpersonal Relationships. Mexican American culture heavily emphasizes sensitivity to the social domain. Individuals are socialized to be sensitive to the feelings and needs of others and to personalize interpersonal relationships (*personalismo*). For Mexican Americans, the expectation is that interpersonal relationships should be characterized by openness, warmth, and a commitment to mutual help. This expectation often leads to cooperative group effort as a desired means of achieving some goal, rather than individual competitive effort. The paramount importance of the social domain is reflected in the term *bien educado,* which means "well educated" in either a social or academic sense. *Bien educado,* therefore, refers not only to someone with a good formal education but to a person who can function successfully in any interpersonal situation without being either disrespectful or rude. A *persona educada* is expected to maintain proper relationships with others through actions that strictly adhere to the society's "respect" and "responsibility" rules.

Status and Role Definitions in Family and Community. Mexican American culture has clearly defined norms of behavior that govern an individual's action within both the family and the community. Age and sex are important determinants of status and respect. Children are expected to be obedient and respectful toward their parents, even after they are grown and have children of their own. Grandparents, and old persons in general, have considerable status and respect in the family. Exceptions to the age norm are physicians, clergy, and teachers, who, because of their unique status in the culture, are treated with much deference and respect regardless of age.

A person's sex also influences his or her role in the family and community. Males are expected to have more knowledge about business and politics, while women are expected to know more about childrearing, health care, and education. Although decision making is often shared between husbands and wives, the father is usually the final authority in the family. Children are also expected to consult with parents about important decisions, even if for no other reason than to show respect. Girls are given less freedom than boys and are expected to remain closer to home and the family.

Mexican Catholic Ideology. Religion strongly influences the lives of most Mexican Americans inasmuch as Mexican Catholicism reinforces and supports their value system. Identity with the family and community is facilitated through religious practices such as weddings and *el compadrazco,* which help extend the family network. Identity with the ethnic group is reinforced by the common knowledge that almost all members of *la raza* are Catholic. In addition, the image of the Virgin of Guadalupe, the *mestizo* equivalent of the Virgin Mary, is both a religious and an unofficial national symbol of *la raza.* The cultural emphasis on respect, harmony, and cooperation in interpersonal relations is consistent with religious themes of peace, community, and self-denial. Honor and respect for parents, adults, and other authority figures are also common themes in Mexican Catholicism. The history of the Mexican people is also influenced by Catholicism, beginning with the Mexican War of Independence, which was led by a priest (Miguel Hidalgo), up to the present-day struggle of Cesar Chavez's farm workers' union, which relies heavily on support from the Catholic Church. The church is also the center of activity, religious as well as social, in many Mexican American communities.

The value system of Mexican Americans influences many aspects of their behavior and has important implications for successfully recruiting and retaining members of this group in institutions of higher education. Now we discuss how knowledge and sensitivity to the Mexican American value system can be used to develop innovative recruitment and admissions procedures that are culturally relevant for Mexican Americans.

Recruitment and Admissions Strategies: Sociocultural Factors

Sociocultural factors influence students' decisions not only about applying to college but also about which college they will eventually attend. After enrollment, sociocultural factors continue to influence students' decisions about social relationships, academic courses, and whether they will matriculate through the institution.

Since the recruitment and retention of Mexican American students are influenced by sociocultural factors, there is much for admissions counselors to know and consider in order to be successful in recruiting members of this group. In addition, admissions officers must work hand in hand with the college's support services staff to implement an effective retention plan.

We have had numerous firsthand experiences with the sociocultural factors affecting Mexican Americans in a variety of admissions situations, in relation to both high school counselors and Mexican American students and their families; and we have often required the use of creative methods that might be considered unorthodox by traditional or mainstream admissions counselors.

For example, admissions counselors (recruiters) typically spend a great deal of time cultivating rapport with high school counselors whose function is to advise students about colleges and their admissions criteria. This rapport often involves placing full responsibility in the hands of a high school counselor. That is, the counselor is trusted to refer students who not only meet the qualifications of the college but who will fit into the social environment of the particular college. When recruiting at schools with a high proportion of Mexican American students, recruiters may want to try another approach that we have found successful. In addition to the counselor, the recruiter can establish lines of communication with the faculty sponsor of MECHA (Movimiento Estudiantil Chicano de Aztlan, a Mexican American student organization on high school and college campuses, whose purpose is to motivate and assist students in academic endeavors) or with a teacher who the recruiter knows has good rapport with Mexican American students and is thus able to identify potential college applicants. This strategy is especially helpful at schools with large concentrations of Mexican Americans, where counselors repeatedly seem unable to identify potential college applicants during the recruiter's visit.

This type of unconventional recruitment strategy is often needed because high school counselors tend to rely on students to communicate to them their intentions or interest in college. And since many Mexican Americans tend to display modesty when discussing their college or career goals, counselors may assume that these students are uninterested in higher education. However, such a perception by counselors probably reflects an ignorance of status and role relationships in Mexican American culture. Because of their age and educational status, counselors are viewed with considerable *respeto* by Mexican American students—and *respeto* requires that they be unassuming in their relationship with these people. Consequently, the students will discuss business matters, or seek information about careers or colleges, only after they perceive that they have "permission" to approach the counselors. A counselor bestows this permission by establishing a personal relationship prior to beginning a business encounter. Following a basic protocol, the counselor asks students about their social well-being (which implies concern for their individuality) and inquires about their family (which implies an understanding that all subsequent decisions will affect the *familia*).

Recruitment of Mexican American students also necessitates unorthodox methods in the recruiter-student context. For example, mainstream admissions counselors prefer to interview a student alone, with the understanding that the parent may ask any questions of the counselor at another time. The philosophy behind this method is that this is a personal matter. However, unless a Mexican American student states otherwise, it is usually understood that a parent or relative arriving with a prospective student expects to be included in the interview. The decision to attend college and the choice of an institution are family matters. Because of this cultural consideration, deliberate exclusion of the third party may insult the student and the relative. Observance of the custom indicates that the counselor is a *persona educada,* thus gaining the family's approval. For this reason, it is very helpful if the admissions counselor is able to speak the language of the parents and has some understanding of their values and attitudes. Some knowledge of Spanish seems especially desirable because 84 percent of all Mexican American college students report coming from homes where Spanish is spoken (Brown and others, 1980).

Some practices in Mexican American recruitment are considered unorthodox, not so much because they are counter to mainstream philosophy but mainly because "it has not been the practice." Some things are not practiced because of time constraints. For example, admissions recruiters seldom offer to help prospective students throughout the application and decision process—fill out forms, speak to parents, and answer questions about career and education planning. Normally, students would be asked to see their high school counselor about these matters. However, it is necessary to make such an offer to Mexican American students, because minority students usually do not have the same support services in their schools as schools that are predominantly Anglo American (U.S. Commission on Civil Rights, 1974) and also because Mexican American students may be the first members of their family planning to attend college; consequently, although they may have strong parental support for their action, their parents may not be familiar with the forms and processes required to formally apply to colleges. In addition to the pragmatic function, stating one's desire to be of assistance also adds an element of *personalismo* to the relationship between the recruiter and the prospective student, thus enhancing the desirability of the institution the recruiter represents.

Having made the decision to advise a prospective student during the application process, the admissions counselor must continue to keep aspects of the culture in mind while describing the information needed by an admissions committee. This is so because of the necessarily subjective nature of the admissions procedures followed by most institutions. In this process, a committee notes all accomplishments, honors, and unusual endeavors that distinguish a prospective student from others applying to the same institution. This is usually done through an autobiography in which students describe their special talents and achievements to an admissions committee. Writing such an autobiography, however, may create personal conflicts for Mexican Americans, since elaborating on one's distinguishing attributes is a violation of one's *educación*. Mexican American socialization stresses modesty and humility regardless of one's physical attributes, degree of accomplishments, or accumulation of wealth. To brag or to point out one's strong assets is to bring attention to others who have less and therefore violates the cultural philosophy that all are equal before God and that each person is unique and deserves respect as an individual. Because of this training, Mexican American students often write sketchy essays that gloss over or totally omit reference to some of their distinguishing accomplishments. This is also why Mexican American students often publicly state lower educational aspirations and goals than those they privately hold. An adviser must understand this cultural attitude and stress very strongly to a student the importance of giving as much information as possible to readers who will use their own cultural orientation to determine a student's admissibility to college. A reminder that one's achievements reflect favorably on the family may also help motivate Mexican American students to be more open about discussing their special accomplishments.

Recruiters seldom let students present a transcript during a school visit, to informally evaluate the students' chances of acceptance to college. Generally, students are not required to present all documents, including transcripts, until the time that they apply to college. Then, after the documents have been reviewed by members of an admissions committee, a decision is made about whether to admit or reject the applicants. Considering the sociocultural background of a Mexican American student, it is highly practical and productive for a college admissions office to be able to evaluate a transcript on an informal basis beforehand. The *personalismo* demonstrated by this action makes it much more likely that the student will choose to attend if accepted. We found several instances where this practice led to certain commitment to a college even though school officials recommended that a student attend a community college prior to application to the four-year institution.

To be effective, an admissions officer must be aware of and sensitive to the social and cultural factors that influence the lives of many Mexican Americans. This awareness of a unique culture often requires that admissions officers assume unusual responsibilities to ensure that qualified Mexican American students are not lost to other institutions. We have had many experiences with prospective students that demonstrate this point. For example, the socialization of females in the Mexican American community is usually different from the socialization of females in the rest of the population. In line with this socialization, females are usually required to remain under the protection of the family until marriage, which means that females are not generally encouraged by their parents to enter a residential college away from home. Moreover, to leave without parental consent is a *falta de respeto* or *falta de educación,* each a violation of proscribed behavior and a potential injury to the *honor* of the *familia.* The admissions counselor must be prepared to speak effectively to convince the female's parents that it is a good decision to let her go away to college. By arranging an argument according to the parents' language and customs, we have been convincing. In some instances, we pointed out that the college was relatively close to home or that a sibling, relative, or trusted friend attended the same institution. At other times, a counselor, dean, or professor assured parents that they would *encargarse de su hija*—that is, assume personal responsibility for their daughter's well-being. The counselor, dean, or faculty member thus becomes a link between the student and her parents and adds to the *personalismo* of the recruitment and admissions process. Also, if a high school counselor has good rapport with a female's family, the counselor's suggestion that she attend a particular residential college will be given considerable weight in the parent's decision due to the counselor's status as a family friend and educator.

Would time be better spent concentrating efforts on

Mexican American females who are less traditional and therefore easier to work with? The obstacles posed in recruiting
traditional Mexican American females are not as formidable as
they at first appear. Research (Buriel and Saenz, 1980) indicates
that college-bound Mexican American females more often come
from traditional backgrounds than non-college-bound females
of this group, who tend to be from less traditional families.

One must also understand the role of a male in the Mexican American community. The eldest male has an important
role in the Mexican American family because his responsibilities
include looking out for the emotional and physical well-being of
the family in the event of the father's absence or disability. Failure to accept this responsibility may result in a loss of face or
dishonor in the Mexican American community and therefore is
a problem for a potential male college applicant with aged or in-
firm parents at home. Assuming parents are able to sustain
themselves at least temporarily without depending on their
eldest son, an admissions counselor may successfully persuade a
male in this situation to attend college by noting that a college
education will put him in a better position to provide for his
parents' and family's welfare. The counselor could also note
that by entering college he could serve as an educational role
model for his younger brothers and sisters.

We are familiar with many male students who have great
responsibilities to the family. One student, for example, solved
his dilemma by selecting a residential college close to his aged
and disabled parents' home. He visits the home on weekends to
drive his mother to the grocery store and arranges medical appointments for his parents around his class schedule (not surprisingly, Mexican American students, on the average, attend
college closer to home than Anglo American students). Another
male student, responsible for his younger siblings, solved his
problem by encouraging them to pursue a liberal arts education
and arranged for them to join him at the college where he was
enrolled as an undergraduate.

The rising cost of educational institutions, combined with
the socioeconomic situation of minority students, is a large factor influencing the decision of these students to attend college.

This is especially true for Mexican American students, since a full 33 percent of these students fall at or below the poverty income level, while 67 percent fall in the lowest middle-income category (U.S. Department of Health, Education and Welfare, 1974). Keeping this in mind, recruiters must discuss costs and the availability of financial aid with prospective Mexican American college applicants. Mexican American students and their parents must understand details of the financial aid process before the students will apply to any college. It must be made clear that financial aid will be offered according to need and that a student's main concern must be admittance to the institution of his or her choice, not cost.

Because Mexican Americans often fear that disclosing their family's financial status may make them the object of ridicule, they may purposely refrain from asking vital financial aid questions. Therefore, counselors and recruiters should routinely take the initiative by pointing out financial aid opportunities without waiting for students to ask. Also, the need for appropriate clothing, transportation, books, and special equipment such as a typewriter can be a drawback for a prospective student who is poor. It is important therefore that early in the recruitment process recruiters thoroughly explain to students how they can help themselves acquire these necessary items through summer earnings, college work-study programs, and special stipends and scholarships for qualified students.

Recruiters and counselors should also bear in mind that Mexican American culture embodies a philosophy of cultural pluralism. Socialization and religious practices of Mexican Americans work together to assure a structure of solidarity within the family and community. Moreover, while the culture strongly maintains the concept of honor for the family, it does so through mechanisms nurturing respect and dignity of the individual. The culture validates the individual. It grants each individual the right to be unique within the social structure.

In this same way, Mexican Americans expect to be able to maintain their unique cultural character while participating in mainstream education. Mexican Americans seeking college information recognize that they are validated as individuals

when college recruiters state that they are seeking cultural
diversity for their colleges and therefore want Mexican American students to apply. One way this statement is made is
by the physical presence of the college representative on the
high school campus. But this physical presence can be felt only
if the recruiter goes to the schools where Mexican American students can be found in significant numbers. Because the schools
attended by most Mexican Americans are generally segregated
and located in low-income neighborhoods, this is also a non-
orthodox recruitment technique, since it departs from the philosophy that middle-class, white students are most suited for institutions of higher learning. Once on campus, the recruiter
must be able to relate to the world view and orientation of
prospective Mexican American applicants, and the prospective
student must also be able to make a clear cultural identification
with the recruiter. This cultural identification must be felt as a
result of the content of the recruiter's presentation. In addition,
an admissions officer might find it very useful to train "peer
recruiters," undergraduate students who make high school visits
and carry out other recruitment-related activities, often at their
former high schools or at schools with large concentrations of
students of their same ethnic group. Since Mexican Americans
have a cultural inclination to link their identity with others of
their own community and ethnic group, utilizing peer recruiters
from the same high school and neighborhood as the prospective student group has an assuredly positive impact on recruitment.

A college also states that it is seeking cultural diversity via
the content of the recruiting officer's brochures and literature.
Use of the Spanish language in the literature that goes home to
parents can be a very effective tool in the recruitment process.
Spanish monolingual parents seldom have an opportunity to
read anything written in Spanish and therefore eagerly read any
Spanish language materials sent home. Consequently, since parents usually have considerable influence on the student's decision to attend college, such literature can have a potentially significant impact on recruitment.

In their presentation to prospective Mexican American

students, recruiters should also point out any aspects of the college curriculum relating to the student's cultural background. Mentioning faculty and support staff who are either Mexican American or Latino can also be helpful. Over the years, as support staff and faculty at independent colleges, we have discussed with students their concerns about a curriculum and faculty that relates to them and validates their presence not only in the college they attend but also in relation to the society of which they are a part. The students, as members of the largest minority in the Southwest, are justifiably concerned that more is not done in college curricula and faculty appointments to reflect a Mexican American perspective. They are concerned because they are aware of the pluralist nature of our society and are skeptical that both minority and nonminority students will be prepared to face the realities of that society upon entering the job market.

Recently, we conducted a survey of Mexican American alumni of the Claremont Colleges to determine the impact of the Chicano Studies Center on their education. Questionnaires were distributed to Mexican American alumni of Pitzer College, Pomona College, Scripps College, Harvey Mudd College, and Claremont McKenna College. Mexican American students overwhelmingly responded that they were very appreciative that their respective colleges had provided them with a Chicano Studies Center and repeatedly stated that the curricula and support services of the center had been an invaluable aid. Answering the question pertaining to recruitment, Mexican American alumni stated that they were drawn to the college because of the presence of the Chicano Studies Center. They also mentioned that they use the Chicano Studies Center as a selling point to encourage other Mexican Americans to attend the Claremont Colleges. In connection with these findings, we have noted that members of the same family are often found at these campuses. The results of our survey demonstrate the significant impact that special educational and support services can have for recruiting and retaining Mexican American students in college. The results also demonstrate the significant influence that Mexican American alumni can have in the recruitment process, since college graduates are usually viewed as success models in the community.

Efforts to recruit Mexican American students can also be enhanced by consulting with community-based institutions that can help identify qualified minority students. Such organizations or agencies include churches and church groups, the League of United Latin American Citizens (LULAC), community action groups (CAG), barrio-based counseling agencies, Comisión Feminil Mexicana Nacional, the American GI Forum, and other professional Hispanic associations. Establishing contacts with any of these organizations should yield some immediate responses, but surely an extended network will have long-range results.

Admissions officers, working both as individuals and collectively under such professional organizations as the National Association of College Admissions Counselors, should strive for a strong college advising unit in every high school. The single-purpose high school counselor is a very effective tool (refer to Chapter Sixteen, by Jack Wright) but one that is lacking in most high schools, especially in lower-income areas where large concentrations of Mexican Americans are present. Such action would have a positive long-range impact on Mexican American recruitment.

Another way in which admissions officers can positively affect the recruitment of Mexican Americans is by sponsoring workshops and seminars designed to train high school counselors in recruiting Mexican American students. Very often high school counselors are not trained to work with non-Anglo students and need to be made aware of cultural and social variables that affect the recruitment of nonmajority students. After one such workshop on our campuses, a high school counselor remarked, "Some very different points of view have been presented here. I'm going to try some of these new techniques with my students." Subsequently, this counselor told a campus recruiter that he had successfully encouraged two Mexican American females to apply to a private college. He stated that he had not been aware of their desire to attend college until he took the initiative to apply his "powers as their respected counselor." These workshops can also show counselors that the college's commitment to recruit Mexican American students is sincere and, in addition, open up new networks for admissions people and high school counselors.

We have found that career workshops and college fairs that bring minority students onto the college campus can be very important aids in recruiting these students. These fairs and workshops should include information about college programs, describe the benefits of a liberal arts education and the careers that can be attained through such educational programs, and provide information about the application process and the availability of financial aid. Whenever possible, minority professionals should be used to maximize the impact of career workshops and college fairs that involve Mexican American or other minority youths. Events such as these introduce a student to a particular college campus and therefore strongly increase the probability that a student will apply to that institution at a later date.

Many of the suggestions presented here require that a college employ at least one Mexican American male or female whose full-time responsibility it is to coordinate activities geared toward maximizing minority recruitment efforts. In situations where an individual admissions counselor has only part-time responsibilities in this effort, and where no single person is responsible for the outcome, there is a very high likelihood of failure in recruiting Mexican American and other minority students. The person responsible must not only relate well with Mexican American students but must also be able to design and carry out recruitment strategies predicated on the cultural background of these students.

Finally, census data projections are that colleges and universities will experience a shrinking population of potential applicants within the next decade (1980 to 1990). This shrinkage is expected because demographers and educators still base their projections on age trends for Anglo Americans, the typical college-bound group in society. However, age trends for Mexican Americans indicate that, with a median age of nineteen years, this group is ripe for college. All indications are that college-age Mexican Americans (and other Hispanic groups as well) will exist in larger proportions than college-age Anglo Americans for at least the next fifteen years. Consequently, this difference in age trends has important implications for relieving the anticipated admissions crunch arising from a shrinking population of "traditional" Anglo American college applicants.

Conclusion

It is our firm conviction, based on both empirical research and personal experiences, that, if given an equal opportunity, Mexican Americans can be recruited to colleges and universities and succeed in these institutions in numbers proportional to their size in the population. One reason for discussing the topics covered in this chapter is to engender a greater understanding and appreciation of the fact that Mexican Americans are not "just like" other minorities (each of which has its own unique history) or Anglo Americans; therefore, the criteria of what constitutes "equal opportunity" for this group must be tempered by a recognition of the diverse historical, social, and psychological forces that have shaped the Mexican American. Thus, by "equal opportunity" we do not mean being treated "just like" a typical Anglo American college candidate, being subjected to the same recruitment efforts and admissions criteria developed for use with Anglo Americans. Such efforts and criteria ignore the Mexican American experience; as a result, Mexican Americans are admitted to colleges and universities in disproportionately low numbers.

By "equal opportunity" we mean that college recruiters and admissions officers have to familiarize themselves with the Mexican American experience, to uncover those culturally unique aspects of behavior that can be used to increase the enrollment of qualified Mexican Americans in institutions of higher education. We do not advocate a "separate but equal" educational policy toward Mexican Americans. Instead, we advocate *broadening* standardized college recruitment and admissions procedures to encompass the Mexican American experience. If we sincerely hope to attract Mexican Americans to our institutions of higher education, we must make the Mexican American experience a part of the institutional process. We must continue to intensify our efforts to recruit and admit Mexican American and other minority students into institutions of higher education, not because they are minorities but because they are a part of our pluralistic society.

10

Providing Special Services
for Adult Students

Eileen M. Rose

Irene Kovala Campanaro

Midlife does not necessarily mean "middle age," as Webster defines it. The search for and exploration of job-occupational-personal "fit" often leads an individual to several vocational choices along life's path, whether the individual is twenty or eighty.

Increasingly, employers are realizing that job fit often can mean advancement or an entirely new vocational selection. Where do colleges fit in? Education and training often allow an individual to explore these possibilities.

Midlife crisis must be differentiated from midlife awareness. Awareness concerns an anticipated internal event, such as the arrival of the "empty nest" or one's reentry into the labor market (Levinson, and others, 1976, p. 22) or an anticipated external event, such as promotion or planned retirement. Forty million Americans regard themselves, at any one moment, as undergoing some form of career transition (Bonham, 1979, p. 4). The adult returning to college and the individual undergoing midlife career change often share similar problems as well as a variety of unexplored potentials. Institutions must be ready and indeed should prepare services geared to the needs of this coming "new student."

The Population

The adult student in midlife who walks on to a college campus has many fears. Even though there are 31 million older people looking for the counseling and admissions offices on our campuses, each individual feels intimidated and overwhelmed at the thought of trying to reenter the world of football games and library cards that many remember from two decades ago or have experienced recently through their children's college attendance. In many cases, the attempt to reenter means the tacit confession of inadequacy, loss, and failure. That failure is often of an intense and personal nature that threatens the individual's sense of self-worth and self-perception. Even those who decide in midlife that changes in career and life-style are the only roads to fulfillment and success and who embark on those changes with energy and positive attitudes, are uncertain about how to achieve their ends. Those of us who deal as professionals in admissions counseling with the midlife adult student and retrainee need to remember the threatening nature of change and the terror that ambiguity can induce in the individual.

Adult reentry students may be as young as twenty-five or as old as fifty-five. Many factors cause them to seek retraining; one factor is change, which has affected a number of different groups:

1. *Those unemployed and seeking employment.* Up to 20 million adults a year are going to work for the first time or are trying to reenter the job market after quitting, being fired, or taking time out—to raise a family, for example.

2. *Those trying to keep pace with advances in technology.* The nation's 7,500 largest employers estimate that at least one eighth of their 32 million employees engage in on-the-job training annually, and this population is appearing on our campuses in increasing numbers as individuals try to maintain and improve their grasp of skills and jobs that are constantly changing as technology invades the market.

3. *Those trying for self-improvement.* Self-improvement means trying to change jobs or careers because of dissatisfac-

tion or desire to obtain more interesting work, better working conditions, higher salaries, greater status. More than 25 million adults—a quarter of the work force—find themselves in this category at the present time.

4. *Those trying to finish a previously initiated bachelor's degree.* Often individuals making up this reentry population began the pursuit of a degree several years ago, but because of some interruption (marriage, job, children, divorce), they were not able to complete the process. Now, with interruptions over, they are back seeking a campus to fulfill these needs.

5. *Those attending for pure leisure or recreational or intellectual stimulus.* The sixty-two-year-old woman who is finally enrolling in the art history class and the forty-five-year-old businessman taking racquetball belong to this segment, who use the institution's services for their own personal use and satisfaction. These part-time, one-class people are an important part of the reentry population.

Employers are often interested in retraining their employees, whether to realize potential in an advancing employee or to allow more appropriate job placement of another; education is synonymous with assisting each employee to a new goal.

The Delivery System

The changes that these millions face are somewhat similar to the developmental cycles of adult life (Bolles, 1979, p. 42). The parallel of work-cycle change with life-cycle change is not exact; the latter tends to be closely age-related, whereas the former tends to be related more to the external work environment. Nevertheless, self-perception and the perception of self as worker are inextricably linked.

For this returning group of students, available information often seems to describe a confusing conglomeration of mysterious schools and programs, confusing accrediting bodies, and fast-selling recruitment to "get them in" to a program. The last thing they want or need is a major that "doesn't fit," "doesn't lead to employment," or "isn't interesting." The fact that a wealth of information exists "out there" for their review often adds to their fear and notion that school may not be for them. The critical variable is not simply the creation of sophisticated information and counseling systems but the means by which nontraditional students are put in touch with these systems (Peterson and Associates, 1979, p. 223).

The need for educational brokering for the returning adult student was identified as early as the 1970s. Brokering involves not only making potential learners aware of existing opportunities but also establishing two-way communication in which providers of services can become aware of and respond to learners' needs (Peterson and Associates, 1979, p. 101). Campus-centered brokering services include admissions offices, counseling centers, and information and referral hot lines.

Nationwide networks of various types and strengths have emerged to aid the cause of Older Student Information Systems (OSIS). The concept of brokering seems to be spreading, and a National Center for Educational Brokering (NCEB) was established in 1976. NCEB describes advocacy as placing learners' interests and needs above those of institutions. It can take two forms: intercession on behalf of individual students or efforts to change institutional policies that hamper adult learners' progress (Peterson and Associates, 1979, p. 186). In this mode, the student discovers quickly the advocacy role an organization like NCEB can play on behalf of the student gathering information.

Another encouraging development in brokering is the potentially highly useful computer-based educational and occupational information system (CIS). The U.S. Department of Labor, which funded the initial program in Oregon, also supported development of computer-based information in eight states (Peterson and Associates, 1979, p. 222). The CIS can give up-to-date information about program availability in institutions within a particular state, job opportunities as a result of the program of study, and current salary ranges.

What, therefore, do these millions of potential learning, changing, and developing students expect from us in the educational delivery system? However emotionally the requests may be couched, they may be distilled into requests for information. Sometimes it is a quest for qualification or certification stated as quickly and as simply as possible: "I don't care what it is—I must have a degree by next March or not be promoted," or "be fired," or "lose my raise." "Tell me how I can finance completion of my education begun twenty years ago, now that I am in the throes of divorce." In the urban setting in which many of us work, the information needed is often of the most basic kind: "What is a credit hour?" "What is a distribution or a residency requirement?" If those seeking retraining are given direct, explicit answers, they will be able to help themselves solve their problems.

This adult in transition has now found the way, more by chance than purpose, to the admissions office on your campus and is asking for answers in establishing a new direction. Admitting this student must take a slightly different tone than admitting an eighteen-year-old freshman. With this student, emphasis must be placed on the value and potential value of the past experience. The woman who has "done nothing" for the past twenty years has probably organized a household, expended resources, kept the family afloat, and provided the center around which the lives of others revolved. The question now is which of these experiences can be used as a foundation for future achievements. The man who "went to school because my friends did" fifteen years ago and flunked out is now a husband, father, property owner, voter, taxpayer, and has twenty-four quarter hours of undergraduate credit that can be a springboard for the acquisition of more. In all cases, the past should be interpreted as a positive basis for the change and the new path the student hopes to take.

The Admissions Process

The admissions process for retraining students is not entirely different from admissions procedures for other students. The key is to *make the process as simple as possible*. These potential students do not want any more paperwork than is absolutely necessary.

Some institutions have established a part-time, non-matriculated category that simply allows the student to register for courses without being admitted per se. For many students, this fits the bill because it allows testing the waters without demanding all the admissions paperwork.

For the student who needs to be admitted formally, accessibility to forms, admissions counseling, and retrieving the paperwork (previous records) are often barriers to completing the process. Offices necessary for these procedures must be accessible during the lunch hour and after 5:00 P.M. if the institution is going to attract this market. It is also important that an appropriate role model—that is, an older person who may have gone through some career transitions or at least look as if she or he has—be available during the initial admissions counseling process.

The task of the admissions counselor is to facilitate entry into the world of higher education.

Assessment of the previous academic record can be critically important at this stage. The evaluation of the credits earned at other institutions is vital to individuals who do not want to spend any more time than necessary. This is where a tentative, on-the-spot (although unofficial) evaluation by a trained admissions person can be invaluable in making the path look easier.

Then there is the question of credit for previous learning experience. At some institutions, the College Board's College-Level Examination Program (CLEP) or Advanced Placement (AP) program is a way to earn credit in general or specific subject areas. Also, some institutions sponsor some type of challenge-by-exam program for their own courses. And some colleges and universities give credit for prior learning. Under this type of program, a student usually presents a portfolio of work in a given subject area or general area; has the portfolio evaluated by a faculty member, department, or committee; and receives credit on the basis of that previous life experience. Council for the Advancement of Experiential Learning (CAEL) is one organization that assists in developing this type of evaluation process on campuses. Whichever methods are available, they should be articulated clearly so that the student knows what options are open.

On-Campus Services

Once the value of a student's past has been established, it is necessary to help take stock of the student's present condition. Should this student be referred for extended personal counseling so that she or he can deal with the emotional stresses of the present? Few admissions counselors are competent to deal with, or want to deal with, the problems attendant on divorce, death, alcoholism, or mental disturbance. The legal aspects of firings, alleged discrimination on whatever basis, the problems surrounding bankruptcy—all are laid on the doorsteps of admissions personnel by students in transition, and it behooves those counselors to know their own limitations and to be aware of available community services.

Counseling Services. Beyond the admissions counseling needed to assist midlife retraining students to the campus, other types of counseling services are necessary and should be made available through a counseling center. *Personal* counseling is a key to evaluating aspects of life that may involve family members, friends, and, certainly, personal change. These services must help the reentry student clarify goals. The most pressing problem may be solved by the acquisition of a job, just a job. The most immediate emotional problem may be a disintegrating marriage, but when immediate emotional problems are resolved, what are the individual's long-term emotional goals? Self-motivation, independence, integrity, the ability to live alone may all be a part of a total long-term solution to emotional pressures. *Social-psychological* counseling is often a necessity as a person contemplates a new work setting and a new life-style. *Vocational* counseling, often the key to midlife retraining, requires examination of all aspects of the prospective occupational or professional change. On most campuses, vocational testing and counseling is not the purview of the admissions office. The unit dealing with testing and psychological services, or with career planning and placement, should be approached and a program developed that has this group as its focus. *Academic* counseling must help to plan the curriculum and schedule best suited to the individual's needs and to determine the skill level the individual will achieve through the program.

Goal Clarification. For the potential retraining student, a critical step toward a new interest or career goal is goal clarification.

Job-related goal clarification touches on such areas as better job satisfaction, more job-related challenge, promotional opportunities, better wages, and the like. Career assessment may also be linked to company stability, reputation, and happiness. At this stage, the individual needs information. Clear direction to college libraries and the Career Planning and Placement Office can help the individual find a solution.

Personal considerations in job reassessment include the financial burden that both career change and education for retraining will impose, home schedules, and classtime accessibility. To these ends, institutions must examine the accessibility of evening offerings and determine what courses best meet the needs of this group. Not to be overlooked are courses in job-related goal assessment, life-mapping, job-finding skills, and the like. All these can be taught by qualified counseling or placement personnel.

Employers may play an important role in the goal-clarifying process by (1) having professional staff available to provide assistance and (2) subsidizing courses necessary for advancement or job change.

College placement offices help the retraining in several ways. First, the placement office has access to vocational information. Second, counselors are available to discuss vocational and occupational outlooks. Third, new job listings are posted, often for part-time as well as full-time students; during the summer months, some placement offices have a "free" or "open" period when no class registration is required to examine the services offered by the office. Fourth, placement offices help develop interview, résumé-writing, and job-research skills. (The reentry student's need is different from that of the twenty-two-year-old senior; often the reentry student is simply updating what was learned twenty years ago.)

Once job-search skills are established, they must be supported by job-analysis skills. The acquisition of a job, any job, may solve the problem of the moment, but long-term job goals, the development of a career plan, the conceptualization of a career ladder are essential if long-term job satisfaction is to evolve from the change process. A placement office is a pivotal resource for this retraining student.

Support Services

Many of the support services needed by the traditional student become almost twice as important with an older student. Such elements as library services, access to cafeterias, use of recreational facilities, and an adviser available after 5:00 P.M. are important in students' accessibility to campus. The accessibility to financial aid is crucially important as the reentry student prepares to attend college. Another key element is the availability of childcare because women and men working 8:00 to 5:00 need classes in the evening and childcare for the children. The availability of recreational facilities for the part-time student is also a factor. Each institution must examine the accessibility of these student services.

Educating the Academic Community

One of the most fundamental yet most difficult tasks is to change a faculty "mind set" about what type of student should come to the college or university. Beginning with the examination of course offerings and how they might fit with the needs of the retraining student, the faculty should be asked to explore offering courses beyond 5:00 P.M., expanding their advising appointments over the noon hour, accompanying admissions personnel as they make "business contacts," exploring job placement opportunities for their students through cooperative education (work experience), and generally becoming more knowledgeable and adaptable to the pressing needs of the retraining student.

Only disaster can ensue if these students are encouraged to enroll and find that there is no accommodation to their presence on campus. Late afternoon classes, Saturday classes, brown bag groups for working mothers, childcare—all need to be developed. The means to utilize prior learning in a present program must also be in place before these students arrive; academe does not adapt swiftly, and these students do not have years to wait while the academic community adjusts to their presence. Above all, the teaching faculty need to be prepared to encounter re-entry students whose appearance may be similar to the professor's mother, whose attitudes may be unaccepting of the teacher's requirements and dictums, and whose stance may be one of total nonconformity to the norm of a traditional student.

Outreach

That these reentry and midlife retraining students exist in large numbers in our communities is easy to establish; that they can be an important segment of a school's enrollment is clearer. How then can they be reached and encouraged to become a part of the academic community? As in all things, there are degrees of difficulty. The urban, largely commuter, school will have comparatively little difficulty finding these students because the location and nature of the institution will almost ensure that the reentry, retraining student will seek it out. Contact with the business world, where the majority of the retraining student population is located, is essential to market the link between educational opportunities and successful job transition. This contact may begin with the institution labeling one person or one office as the resource for the off-campus clientele. This staff must contact the businesses where the potential market exists. Companies and agencies will help contact potential student groups. Liaison with local business and industry probably already exists, and outreach to women's groups, Y's, churches and temples, social groups, mental health groups is quite easily developed—provided that funds and personnel are available. Within each agency, usually in the personnel office, there is an educational coordinator with whom the contact should be made. Access to company in-house newsletters and bulletin boards is another vehicle for information and attention to the institution.

On the other hand, the four-year institution whose history and experience has been entirely with entering eighteen-year-olds must make a much more extensive effort to position itself in relation to these populations. The office of admissions should be positive that the willingness to commit to the accommodation of these students exists on the traditional campus before embarking on an outreach and inclusionary campaign. This kind of repositioning means expenditures on different kinds of publications, longer office hours, different travel schedules, different role models in admissions personnel.

Publications must be developed to respond to the needs of this group. Brochures, viewbooks, flyers—these must deal with these students' goals, outline the admissions process, stress the institution's interest in this type of student, explain resources and academic options, and address costs and payment procedures.

Conclusion

The advent of the returning adult student and the midlife career change student is upon us. For the returning adult, the incentive and motivation to go to school, stay in school, and achieve satisfactory progress are high. The social benefits of midlife change include a vision of a more flexible, adaptive society in which the individual can allocate personal time among several life phases (Lenz and Hansen-Shaevitz, 1977, p. 16).

The biggest challenge for institutions of higher learning is to put into motion the services required to meet the needs of this student population. Once able to respond to these needs, an institution may acquire the sense of a new dimension that the adult student population brings to a college.

11

Advising Students About Two-Year Colleges and Transfers

Karl L. Wolf

Students who elect to attend two-year community or junior colleges and then transfer to four-year institutions may face several problems during the transfer process. Professionals working with these students must be aware of the problems and possible solutions to them. Four major problems are presented here, with suggestions for making the student's transition from the two- to the four-year college easier.

The first and most frustrating problem is the failure of courses from the two-year institution to transfer to the four-year college. Because two-year colleges attempt to provide all types of services for all types of students, they may not exercise as much control over their academic programs as do four-year institutions, and some courses may be weak academically; even if this is not actually true, it may be so perceived by the faculties of the four-year institutions. If the academic standards of two-year colleges are questioned and truly weak programs are identified at certain colleges, the four-year institutions may refuse to grant credit for these courses and instead require students either to repeat the courses or to take challenge examinations in order to receive credit for them. Students lose whenever they are exposed to weak courses because they may not acquire adequate knowledge about the subject to be able to complete more advanced courses.

Another part of this problem is that some colleges will not grant credit for courses in a student's major field that they believe should be taken at the senior college. Since four-year colleges will eventually be granting the student's bachelor's degree, four-year faculties believe that they must maintain an academic level commensurate with the institution's reputation and that the acceptance of other than introductory courses in a major may adversely affect the integrity of the senior college's degree. The academic preparation and teaching effectiveness of community and junior college faculties and past performance by other students transferring from the same two-year colleges tend to dictate the credit transfer policies of major courses.

Professional accrediting agencies may place special limitations on senior colleges. Bachelor's-degree-granting institutions put much time, effort, and money into meeting the requirements of these agencies, such as the National League for Nursing, the Council on Social Work Education, the National Council for Accreditation of Teacher Education, and the American Assembly of Collegiate Schools of Business, so that their graduates have open to them more extensive employment opportunities as well as advantages in graduate programs. These accrediting agencies therefore place certain restrictions on their member institutions to guarantee students, graduate schools, and employers that graduates of these programs have the best preparation. For example, accredited institutions will not permit two-year-college students to transfer credits in their major field if the courses involved would traditionally be taken during the junior or senior year at the four-year college. If two-year-college students want to enter these professionally accredited programs, they must abide by more stringent credit-transfer policies than are found at colleges without professional accreditation.

Because the first two years of work are preparatory for students in a transfer program, many institutions believe that advising and counseling such students are not as important as for students enrolled in senior institutions. This is a fallacy. In fact, students wishing to transfer to senior institutions usually need more assistance to make sure that they are not wasting their time, energies, and money on unnecessary courses. Most two-year colleges view academic advisement differently than do the four-year colleges. At most four-year colleges, freshmen are assigned for advisement to faculty members in the student's major field of study. These faculty members are considered the best prepared to advise students, since they are working and teaching in the student's discipline area. Faculty advisers should know the proper sequence of courses, prerequisite requirements, and vocational and job requirements for students in their disciplines. On the other hand, two-year colleges usually assign their students to general counseling personnel for advisement. These counselors usually do not have expertise in all the disciplines in which their students are enrolled; their knowledge of a particular field of study may be only what they have read in the college's catalogue. Since they do not usually have contact with employers in all fields, they do not know the expectations many firms or agencies have for their personnel.

Many students advised by general counseling personnel have problems at the time of transfer. They may have had some courses considered required at the senior institution, but many of the courses may be used only as fillers, to meet graduation-hour requirements; some four-year colleges permit these courses to be used as electives if they are upper-level courses.

Another restriction involves the transfer of grades and quality points. Some colleges permit only the transfer of credit, not the student's grade point average. Students may therefore not be eligible for membership in senior college honor societies and may have only two years in which to earn a grade point average that will qualify them for graduation with honors from the four-year institution. Some colleges do not permit the transfer of the grade of D; other colleges do accept this grade. Statewide systems of higher education sometimes discriminate against two-year college transfers by dictating the credit-transfer policies to be used by their members and placing more restrictive policies on students transferring from outside the system to a system institution.

Credit-transfer problems may exist in meeting four-year-college graduation requirements. Senior institutions usually have a credit-hour residency requirement that must be completed for a degree to be awarded. Grade point averages for the cumulative college career, the major, and the minor are usually computed separately and must meet specified graduation requirements. Most senior colleges have a core or general studies grouping of liberal arts courses that are required for all degrees; these courses usually are taken during the student's freshman or sophomore years. Many of these core requirements are rigid and do not permit flexibility. Students who have not taken these courses at the two-year colleges may have sequencing and scheduling problems with upper-level courses and therefore may not be able to complete their degree as soon as they had expected to.

The second major problem facing the two-year-college transfer student is improper or incorrect academic advisement at the two-year institution. Incorrect advice is not limited to counseling personnel at two-year colleges; faculty members are also guilty of misleading students. Community colleges hire large numbers of part-time faculty, and full-time faculty are expected to work with large numbers of students; consequently, faculty members do not always have the time to become familiar with course requirements of four-year institutions. Students should be encouraged to contact four-year colleges directly for information and advice and not follow the advice of "Someone told me . . ." or "I heard . . ."

The third major problem facing two-year transfer students is changing a major field of study or not having selected a major at the time of the transfer to the four-year college. If a student has completed two years at an institution in a transfer program, it can be assumed that she has taken courses from the liberal arts or general studies area, but she has probably also taken introductory courses in a major field. Students who have followed correct schedules and taken two or three introductory major courses can usually complete baccalaureate degree requirements in two years.

However, the student who after two years of college work decides to change his major or who has not yet selected a major should not expect to graduate in just two years; the blame for his predicament should not be placed on either the two- or four-year institution. Students should realize that major and minor programs usually require about sixty semester hours of course work and that they must meet specific course requirements for graduation in addition to having the required number of semester hours. This problem is not limited to two-year-college students—many students at four-year institutions also change majors—but, unless these students transfer elsewhere, they do not have to worry about the loss of credits in the transfer process.

Besides meeting specific course and hour requirements for the new majors, transfer students must also meet specific grade point average requirements for graduation. Many colleges require a 2.00 or C cumulative average for graduation, but they may also require a higher average, such as 2.50 or C+, in the student's major and minor fields. Some transfer students enter senior colleges with very close to the minimum 2.00 and must exert extra effort to raise their major and minor average; often these students must take more than the minimum number of required courses in a field to be able to meet graduation requirements.

The completion of prerequisite courses in some disciplines may also delay a student's graduation. Because senior colleges expect students to follow a formal pattern of course work, some upper-level courses may have two or three lower or mid-level courses as prerequisites. And because students are at a disadvantage if they did not complete these prerequisites first, most departments do not waive these course requirements for transfer students. Therefore, the students must either attend a summer session to make up the needed prerequisite or attend college for an additional semester or year.

The fourth major problem facing the two-year-college transfer student may be the most important: The student waited too long to begin the transfer process. Each fall and spring, four-year colleges send hundreds of admissions representatives to visit two-year-college campuses, to talk with prospective transfer students and to encourage them to begin the transfer process six to eight months before their planned entry date. But each year these same four-year institutions find that many of their transfer applicants have waited until three or four months before the term begins to file an application. By this time, students have probably taken courses that will not transfer or are not needed; they have discovered that evaluations cannot be prepared in less than six weeks during summer months, that financial aid and on-campus housing opportunities have been exhausted, and that they have missed the special orientation and registration program held for transfer students in the early summer.

These same students are likely to be the ones who want the senior colleges to tell them which major they should select, to ask them to waive prerequisite course requirements, and to hedge on their major average requirements at graduation time. These students are probably the first to complain about colleges' policies and always fail to get the "message" that they do have some responsibilities as adults for their actions and future in college.

In some cases, the community or junior college must share some of the student's responsibility because many two-year colleges are geared to working with students enrolled in terminal degree programs rather than college transfer programs. Specific transfer counselors have not been designated, and other counseling personnel do not have the time or expertise to work with transfer students.

The solutions to these four problems facing two-year-college transfer students are simple, but they require a commitment from both the two-year institutions and the four-year colleges to which these students are most likely to transfer. Formal transfer articulation agreements should be developed between the community or junior college and each four-year institution to which students traditionally transfer. The agreements should state the transfer admissions requirements of the four-year colleges, the expectations for the students, and the suggested liberal arts core or general studies courses to be taken at the two-year colleges to fulfill the four-year colleges' requirements. They should list the introductory courses in majors that will transfer, and they should explain how the four-year institution will accept in transfer each course offered by the two-year college.

Specifically, the agreement should indicate that a particular course is directly transferable as a senior college course, or is transferable as an elective course, or will not transfer in any way. Special grade point requirements for graduation should be listed, so that students can know what requirements face them before they transfer.

These agreements should be updated or revised yearly to reflect new courses that either the two- or four-year colleges might add to their curricula and any changes in course content or direction. Also, when revisions are made, allowances should be made for students following older editions of the agreements, so that they do not lose credit for a course that was previously accepted but will not be accepted for transfer in the future. Enough copies of the articulation agreement should be made available at both the two-year and senior institution so students can obtain personal copies for their use. Advisement and counseling personnel as well as faculty at the two-year institutions should have access to copies of the agreement, so that they can work with students in schedule planning and course registration.

If students and advisement personnel follow the articulation agreements, fewer students will receive incorrect information as to the courses they should take, and they will know how these courses will be accepted by the four-year institutions. Students can also use these agreements to compare their opportunities at various four-year colleges; this information helps them in the application process.

Two-year colleges should designate specific counselors as "transfer counselors" to work closely with four-year institutions and the students planning to transfer. Transfer counselors should regularly visit the most popular four-year institutions and meet with senior college admissions personnel and faculty to discuss how their students are doing academically after they transfer and to note any revisions of the formal agreement. Also, two-year college faculty should be encouraged to accompany the transfer counselors so that they can meet with their academic counterparts teaching in their disciplines. When four-year-college admissions personnel visit the community or junior colleges to talk with prospective students, they should spend time with the transfer counselor, discussing problems and solutions. Four-year-college faculty should visit the community or junior colleges to talk with faculty.

The transfer counselors should develop career-vocational-college materials with a variety of college catalogues and guidance information services and conduct transfer planning programs to introduce students to the use of the transfer services. These programs should be conducted regularly to help students make the transfer transition from two- to four-year college. And sessions should be held to assist students with vocational planning, enabling students to become better informed about major fields of study and the vocational opportunities of the majors.

Admissions counselors from four-year institutions should be invited to visit the two-year campuses regularly to talk with prospective transfer students and to assist them in schedule planning. Since the two-year-college student will someday be a student at the senior college, the four-year institution should want to help the student as soon as possible after a decision to transfer has been made. In fact, many four-year colleges work with transfer students before they enroll for the first time at the community or junior colleges, mapping out one or two years of course work for an easy transfer at a later date. From a public relations viewpoint, the more that both the community-junior college and senior college can do to help students in the transfer process, the more students will avail themselves of the opportunity to attend a two-year college first and then transfer to the four-year college, boosting enrollment figures at both institutions.

While students are enrolled in the two-year colleges, they should be encouraged to select the major field they will pursue after transfer to the senior college. The transfer counselor can offer various vocational-career planning programs, to alert students to career opportunities; administer vocational inventories; and help students select a major. The sooner a student selects his intended major field, the easier his transfer will be and the sooner he will be able to begin meeting graduation requirements for the major field.

The problem of most students waiting too long to begin the transfer process can be avoided if community and junior college counseling personnel begin working with students when they first enroll. By having both individual and group sessions, counselors can impress on students the need for planning in their career and college programs. An outline of suggested dates for two-year-college planning and the transfer process should be developed and distributed to students, together with the college calendar and schedule of classes. Students can then see the time frame they should be following for both their community-junior college days as well as when to begin the transfer application process. Students should be encouraged to visit four-year colleges to talk with admissions personnel and faculty and to tour the campuses, just as high school students do when they are first thinking about attending college. Students need to learn what the four-year colleges expect of them and to see the differences between colleges and their programs.

In summary, there are four problems for students planning to transfer from two-year to four-year colleges: failure of courses to transfer, improper counseling and advisement at the two-year college, changing or late selection of a major field of study, and student procrastination in beginning the transfer process.

For the most part, the responsibility for not beginning the transfer process soon enough and for waiting too long to decide what major field to follow upon transfer lies with the student, but the responsibility for counseling and advisement lies with the community or junior college. If formal articulation agreements are developed and made available to students and counselors and followed, students should have fewer complaints about the failure of credits to transfer. And if community and junior colleges appoint specific transfer counselors and give them the materials and time needed to work with potential transfer students, advisement and counseling problems should decrease. No system can totally eliminate transfer problems for students, but the two- and four-year colleges must work together to make the transition as easy as possible for most of the students.

12

Introduction to Components of the Financial Aid System

Leonard M. Wenc

Helping students make informed choices as to what type of educational experience best meets their needs, abilities, and interests is the collective and individual responsibility of educational guidance counselors, parents, and the students themselves. All too often, families and students choose an institution out of an abysmal ignorance, particularly when the primary concern is availability of funds. It is of the utmost importance that this unwitting tunnel vision be eliminated by proper financial counseling, which would then permit students and their families to concentrate on making educational decisions rather than financial ones.

For a large segment of today's student population, paying for a college education means becoming familiar with the extensive sources of financial aid available—largely from the federal government, from various state programs, and, to a smaller extent, from educational institutions themselves. The federal role in helping finance the education of a substantial number of citizens began after World War II with the enactment of the Serviceman's Readjustment Act of 1944, better known as the GI Bill. In the years following, a number of education acts were passed, creating an ever-increasing government commitment to educational funding that culminated in the Higher Education Act of 1965. This act includes "campus-based" programs (those aid programs currently administered directly by institutions) as well as various student aid programs that give funds directly to students rather than being administered through the institution. For better or worse, this approach has characterized the major legislative positions in respect to today's overall funding patterns.

The federal role in student financial aid has grown from one of modest proportions to one of significant impact on taxpayers, students, and institutions. The growth in both the number of programs and available dollars has created a complex mechanism of rules and regulations that affect administrators and beneficiaries alike. Confusion frequently reigns as the myriad forms, notifications, and communications from various agencies exacerbate the anxiety of the very people whom such programs were originally meant to serve.

But for whom are these postsecondary education funds meant? Specifically, the national objective has been to give all those who can benefit from postsecondary education the opportunity to attend, regardless of their family situation. In reality, however, the situation is somewhat clouded because authorized legislation does not always mean that appropriations are adequate to meet the established need for funds in each of the various programs.

The College Work-Study Program gives grants to institutions as partial reimbursement of wages paid to students working on or off campus in public or nonprofit organizations. The purpose of the program is to stimulate part-time employment opportunities for needy students.

The National Direct Student Loan Program allocates funds to postsecondary institutions for the purpose of making long-term, low-interest loans to students with financial need.

The Guaranteed Student Loan Program authorizes low-interest loans made available from commercial lenders and from some educational institutions and state agencies or directly by the federal government. Such guarantees are a substitute for collateral, which is generally unavailable from students. This permits the lender to make loans directly to students, without the students having to establish credit ratings.

The Social Security Student Benefits Program provides monthly Social Security checks to students because of the death, disability, or retirement of a parent who worked long enough to qualify for Social Security.*

Other student financial aid programs that serve a more limited constituency include the Nursing Student Loan Program, the Nursing Scholarship Program, the Indian Higher Education Grant Program, the Veterans' Educational Benefits Program, and the Vocational Rehabilitation Program.

One major source of federal financial assistance is the Basic Educational Opportunity Grant Program, now known as the Pell Grant Program. This program gives grants to help qualified undergraduate students finance their postsecondary education. This is the biggest government student aid program and the starting point for most students seeking federal financial aid. The Supplemental Educational Opportunity Grant Program provides financial assistance to students of exceptional need who are attending postsecondary institutions. Federal grants are made to the institutions, which then select students for the awards.

Although the major federal student aid programs, when added to the veterans' benefits and Social Security benefits, account for the majority of available funds, the institutions themselves are also a significant source of student aid resources. Such institutional funds are often in the form of endowed scholarships that have been the product of philanthropic activity over the lifetime of the institutions. Many institutions allocate a portion of their current operating budget to fund scholarships and grants to a large number of students. Where eligibility requirements for federal student aid programs are generally restricted, the administration of institutional funds allows for a more flexible approach. This flexibility accounts for the popularity of awards for special skills and accomplishments, such as athletic grants, music awards, and academic scholarships. In addition to having a significant amount of grant dollars to administer, indi-

*This program is now limited to those who were already receiving Social Security benefits in August 1981, and who were in full-time attendance at an approved postsecondary school before May 1982. It will be phased out entirely by 1985.

vidual institutions also use their own funds to support student employment and loan opportunities.

Another source of financial assistance for students is the recent establishment and growth of state scholarship and grant programs. Most states administer modest programs, but some states, such as Illinois, Pennsylvania, and New York, have established programs that are a significant resource for students who are residents of those particular states.

A common concept associated with all the available student aid programs is awarding student aid on the basis of demonstrated financial need. This is where the student assistance programs become more complicated. Commonly, students are awarded a package of financial aid, which typically includes some grant funds, a work opportunity, and quite possibly a loan. This means that students could find themselves recipients of funds from as many as six sources. For example, a student choosing to attend a high-cost institution might receive a financial aid package consisting of a state scholarship, a Supplemental Opportunity Grant, a National Direct Student Loan, a National Merit Scholarship, a Basic Educational Opportunity Grant (the Pell Grant), an institutional grant, a local scholarship, and a work-study job.

As the number of financial aid sources increases, so does confusion. This is especially true at high-cost institutions that enroll a sizable number of students unable to meet the cost of attendance. (In many such institutions, the large number of student aid recipients reflects not so much the low family incomes of the student body as it does the high cost of attending such an institution.) This does not mean that attending a low-cost institution, in and of itself, eliminates students from financial aid consideration. Student aid is available at all types of institutions and is generally set to meet the difference between what the family can reasonably be expected to contribute and the actual cost of attendance. This difference is called "financial need."

It is the primary responsibility of student financial aid programs to fill the gap between the family's resources and the costs of education. Significant changes in the concept of fair and equitable treatment of family resources have been taking place over the past ten years. There have been recent attempts to instill a sense of reasonableness into the formula used to determine family-contribution levels. Of special note is the trend toward expecting smaller and smaller family contributions over the years, which has had the effect of increasing the need for student financial resources at all types of institutions.

If families of prospective students are ignorant about available financial aid, that ignorance has undoubtedly been compounded by a popular myth concerning just who can "afford" any kind of continuing education. That myth—that one must be either extremely affluent or destitute to consider all but the lowest-cost institution—simply is not true. There is growing evidence that the bulk of student aid funds are utilized in support of the "financially overlooked" middle class. There is also evidence that students from modest economic circumstances are not properly using the available financial aid resources to their best advantage. Expanding the educational horizons of our neediest students in light of available financial resources should be a major goal of all secondary schools. Many of the limitations perceived by these students are self-imposed because of the limited advantages afforded them by their families and their environment. Experience indicates that the best counseling and guidance is practiced in those institutions whose constituency already has other reinforcing mechanisms, such as college-educated parents, which assures a student of at least a minimum amount of timely and accurate information regarding types of educational opportunities and sources of student financial aid.

Deadlines, forms, and other items in the process of securing financial aid easily intimidate those students who need the most help and who are the least sophisticated about the application process. This is particularly true for students who are the first in their families to continue their education. Such students find it difficult to differentiate between the myriad types of institutions and educational options available to them. Early identification of those students who need the services of a trained counselor should be encouraged.

It is not sufficient to make access to postsecondary education the only objective, however. Adequate financial aid resources are now generally available to enable most qualified students to choose the type of postsecondary education that best meets their needs. Students who possess particular skills and abilities will find themselves pursued by those institutions most interested in enrolling them. Although minimizing the burden of financing postsecondary education seems to be an honorable objective, thoughtful consideration of the educational experience itself cannot be ignored. What may initially appear as a financial bargain may in the long run prove to be an educational disaster. It is becoming clear that our nation cannot afford to squander its intellectual capital. Guidance and counseling activities should ensure that every student has an opportunity to make an informed *educational* choice.

In a consumer-oriented society, the role of the well-informed consumer must not be taken lightly. With access to postsecondary education of some type virtually assured, it behooves the student to consider the wide spectrum of choices available. Careful evaluation of institutional financial aid awards must be coupled with consideration of the educational institution's offerings. This will be increasingly important as the competition for students increases during the next decade.

For most students, this should be a family decision because, in reality, the parents provide the major portion of the financial resources the student will be using. Parents should be aware that institutions assume that the cost of education will be the family's major "discretionary purchase" and so expect a reasonable amount of family financial sacrifice toward this end. Viewing educational decisions as value judgments is an issue that needs more attention by those individuals dealing directly with students and parents. As facilitator in the decision-making process, every counselor and adviser has a responsibility to address this important issue with both the student and the parents.

Along with the concept of demonstrated financial need, individuals working with students considering postsecondary education should be aware of the concept of "net cost," which is best defined as the out-of-pocket amount paid directly by the family toward their children's cost of education. The net cost or family contribution, plus available financial aid, should enable any qualified student to attend the type of postsecondary educational institution that meets his or her educational needs.

Although the cost of attendance at a high-cost institution

may initially appear an insurmountable barrier to a family of moderately low income, such an education becomes accessible if the student applies to the various aid programs available. As mentioned, the student in question could be eligible for the following resources:

- Basic Educational Opportunity Grant Program (Pell Grant Program)
- Supplemental Educational Opportunity Grant Program
- National Direct Student Loan Program
- College Work-Study Program
- Guaranteed Student Loan Program
- Institutional aid
- Social Security Benefits Program
- Veterans' Educational Benefits Program
- Vocational Rehabilitation Program
- Miscellaneous resources: National Merit Scholarships, Elks scholarships, PTA scholarships, Church scholarships, Citizens Scholarship Foundation

The responsibility for presenting informed choices needs to be addressed by both school and family. School officials, especially counselors, have an obligation to make adequate sources of consumer information easily accessible, thus making the process of informed choice a reality. Guidance and counseling personnel need to help students effectively evaluate financial aid awards and understand how such awards relate to the students' educational objectives.

Special awards are difficult to interpret because unsophisticated students are vulnerable to the awards' enticement and glamour. For instance, awards such as those given on the basis of high test scores in most cases represent an attempt to meet the institution's need rather than the student's need and may not be in the student's best long-term interest.

Another area of increasing concern is athletic scholarships, which entice students who do not meet the academic standards of an institution but who are looked at only as enhancing the athletic program of an overzealous coach. Institutions must provide prospective students with accurate information on costs of attendance in addition to the content of their educational program. All financial aid awards should clearly delineate the terms under which the student accepts or rejects any portion of the financial aid package. For example: Is there a need to maintain a certain level of scholastic performance to keep the award? Is renewal of the award contingent on participation in some sport or extracurricular activity? Must a student major in some special field to maintain the scholarship? Educational institutional policies on award renewal should be read carefully and discussed directly with the institution if necessary.

When a student employment opportunity is offered, additional questions arise. Is it clear how many hours a week a student is expected to work in order to earn the amount specified? What is the institutional philosophy regarding student employment? Although many parents prefer that their children not work, at least during the first year, they should be aware there is strong evidence that a reasonable work commitment actually enhances both a student's educational and social adjustment. In most cases the acceptance of a modest employment opportunity adds a positive dimension to the student's development.

In the case of student loans, it is especially appropriate to discuss with the student and parents the philosophy of borrowing. The general availability of student loans should make such a discussion routine, especially as it relates to institutional choice.

Most high-cost institutions incorporate a "self-help" component in each financial aid package. This self-help component is essentially a work-loan combination that allows institutions to meet the need of more students by prudently offering grant assistance only after some degree of self-help is applied to each student's need.

Student loans are exactly what they appear to be. Specifically, they obligate students to repay that part of their educational cost represented by their loan, plus interest. Students who use educational loans in effect make value judgments about financing a significant experience in the early years of their lifetime. If students need to borrow during the first academic year, most likely they will need to borrow in successive years. What may be an initial loan commitment of one thousand dollars could increase to at least four thousand dollars by the time the student completes a standard four-year course of study. For many students, it will be the first experience with the lending process, and such loans should be taken as a serious obligation.

Clearly, our nation has come a long way in achieving the goal of offering postsecondary education to all who can qualify for it, regardless of family financial circumstances. Student aid programs have now reached a level where some combination of federal, state, and institutional aid will be available to those students who are able to demonstrate a need for such assistance. These circumstances, coupled with the declining number of students in traditional postsecondary schools, may present educational opportunities that will prove unprecedented in the history of our nation.

At the same time, there is every evidence that current budget realities at both the state and federal levels will curtail any further expansion of student aid funds in the immediate future. Recent congressional action has indeed resulted in a decline in almost every federal student aid program. Under siege is the long-established federal role in assuring equal access to postsecondary education for all who might qualify for such an experience.

Although current economic realities dictate a closer scrutiny for all expenditures, one should remain optimistic that adequate funds for the truly needy will continue to be made available through a realignment of current commitments by institutions, federal and state programs, and private sources. What will need to be reemphasized is the rightful expectation that both students and parents have the primary responsibility for financing postsecondary education. It is clear that massive increases in the past ten years in student aid resources evolved in ways that did not encourage the proper role of the family and student in financing postsecondary education.

Students must be advised of the responsibilities that will be placed on them; that is, they will be expected to work and borrow for a much larger share of their educational expenses. Parents will need to reassess their own values and reaffirm their willingness to undertake reasonable sacrifices to meet the costs of their children's education.

Educational institutions must also reassess their own priorities. One hopes they will redirect more of their own resources to student financial aid. Private philanthropy will also need to assert an influence in helping to meet federal and state student aid shortfalls. Need-based student aid must be made the priority of all concerned if we as a nation are to assure ourselves that we do not squander one of our most precious resources—namely, the intellectual development of our youth. Our values must be rethought, reaffirmed, and, most important, communicated to those individuals (such as legislators) who are entrusted with the future vitality of our educational system.

Recognizing the need to restructure and strengthen all student aid programs, I remain confident that such programs will continue to serve us well, but in a more limited fashion. True, such programs will be leaner and more restrictive, but perhaps that is the way they should have been from their inception. Postsecondary educational opportunities can no longer be taken for granted. However, the continued enrollment of qualified students, irrespective of family financial circumstances, will and must remain one of our most important national and professional priorities.

Part Four

✒ ✒ ✒ ✒ ✒

Service to
School and Community

✒   To virtually all members of the admissions counseling profession, first allegiance is to the student. It is their second allegiance that determines differences in function among admissions counselors. The largest number of counselors serve as their "second masters" secondary public and private schools and the communities whose children fill those schools. Most often, the community is an extended neighborhood, but in the case of boarding schools, the community can be nearly the whole nation or at least that portion of the nation deeply concerned about educational processes. All these professionals have a common concern for the process by which students take what they have learned in secondary school, demonstrate to some adjudicators that what they have learned is a basis on which further education can be constructed, and then build on that foundation the edifice in which the future will be lived. This process demands that the student make an astute choice, but to do so demands understanding, of self, of family, of traditional and challenging values and beliefs, of cultural and economic patterns, and of possible futures—a set of demands that would cow the wisest and most mature adult. That students make such decisions at all testifies to the toughness of human beings; that

251

they make them well so often demonstrates that the American educational system, despite all its faults, allows many students to edge into understanding.

Students make their choices best with good advice. When effectively providing that advice, admissions counselors serve their schools well. The chapters in Part Four delineate various ways effective counselors can serve their "masters."

In Chapter Thirteen, Steven C. Munger and R. Fred Zuker present pertinent caveats and guidelines. They remind counselors (and, by implication, college admissions officers who listen to the persuasions of their charges) what their duties are. First they discuss the ethical and personal responsibilities of college guidance counselors. They then provide specific guidelines that counselors should follow in difficult times: ways to ask questions that will penetrate the foggy verbiage colleges can spew forth in their attempts to woo students and their parents. All members of the profession will be interested in the formulations of these practiced professionals.

Chapters Fourteen to Nineteen record the experiences of several college guidance officers in different types of public and private secondary schools. Their situations differ, but each counselor has learned what will be valuable to others in all types of schools. Moreover, their experience is worthwhile counsel for college personnel. Each pattern of strength for a school or outside counseling program implies exclusion, given the limitations on both the professional and the student's time, and college admissions officers should always bear in mind that in the best of circumstances students come to them with fragmentary understanding. No matter how much college admissions officers believe in their colleges and in their ability to serve well the potential applicants with whom they come in contact, a necessary teaching function always remains. The admissions officer, like the school counselor, exists first to allow the student to make an intelligent, informed choice.

Philip Martin describes college guidance as part of a process that enables students to develop and grow by making intelligent choices. The value of the advice the counselor gives to further the process will depend on the credibility the counselor has established and therefore on the moral depth he or she displays. Martin stresses the importance of understanding and developing relationships among all the interlocking constituencies that may affect the choice a student makes; for instance, to function well, the counselor must develop strong alliances with other staff members, teachers, parents, former students, and college admissions officers. His advice is aimed especially at the single-function counselor, but others will find most of what he says applicable to a large degree.

Margaret Elizabeth Tracy, on the other hand, addresses the counselor for whom college guidance is only part of the job. She describes how college counseling can be seen lodged within a theoretical framework designed to support all-purpose counseling for students. She describes the various functions of the generalist counselor—a description sure to quiet the admissions officer who expects generalist counselors to respond quickly to all queries and requests—and differentiates between generalist and specialist counseling approaches. She speaks of the preparation to become a college guidance counselor, the training materials available, and the ways to adapt other theoretical frameworks. Tracy finds especially useful Super's "theory that the process of vocational development is essentially that of developing and implementing the self-concept." Before summarizing her argument, she presents a schematic analysis of the program employed in one public high school in Clayton, Missouri.

Also writing from a vantage point within a public high school, Jack L. Wright serves a different clientele. Tracy's charges are mostly the children of professional men and women and executives; Wright's students are mostly minority children whose parents have not gone to college. Both authors have provided useful guidance for their clientele. Tracy's counseling framework can be adapted to work in inner-city schools that serve students representing the first generation to consider college; the techniques of communication Wright has contrived will be useful in affluent majority public schools and private schools.

Wright is especially concerned that the school itself be strong enough to prepare students to enter college. Therefore, he has worked to build support networks among parents, students, school officials, teachers, and the school board—not to mention colleges and admissions personnel professionals. Wright has sought to make all sectors take pride in students' accomplishments and has increased their willingness to participate in the counseling process. He especially emphasizes working with ninth graders before they enter high school and informing parents early of the importance of the choices students must make. He provides a complete calendar of events from the ninth grade on, with monthly suggestions for the senior year. Wright concludes with a description of the support system necessary for success.

Betty Schneider has been both specialist and generalist counselor, in both public and private secondary schools, and in each type of school she became aware that counselors have too little time, suffer from monotonous repetition, and are unable to complete all they seek to finish. She has therefore developed programs that try to alleviate those problems by utilizing group approaches. Schneider describes what different groups of students do during different stages of the process by which they choose colleges and careers. Her program starts midway through the junior year and incorporates various questionnaires. She also uses computer-generated assessment processes; two forms she has found useful are included at the end of her chapter.

Unlike Martin and Tracy, who see college guidance as an opportunity to strengthen and educate the student as an individual, Helene Reynolds reminds us that the decisions students make affect others besides themselves and that parents and siblings need to be considered and even brought into the process of making the college choice. The decision of where to go to college will affect family finances (even retirement plans), siblings' educational plans, student health, and family value patterns. Therefore, parent education must be part of the process, both because parents most often pay all or most of college costs and because college admissions has changed since parents were themselves applicants. Counselors must define their professional goal as counseling, not college placement. "College guidance . . . [is] a process in which a professional counselor supports all members of the family." It is therefore important to recognize that students and their parents are at quite different stages of life and need sympathetic handling. Reynolds uses "family counseling" as the paradigm for admission counseling.

Whereas Reynolds considers the counseling world as a microcosm, Barbara B. Reinhold views the macrocosm. She is aware of the difficulty of making the *whole* community aware of the radically different arena of choices confronting students today and yet knows the necessity of doing so. Unless choices are real within the community, they do not viably exist for the student who chooses. Counselors must first educate themselves and then their school colleagues; then they must create an information center for others to use. They must then use that information center, whatever its practical dimensions, to market to the community the different available ideas concerning educational choice. Reinhold provides a thorough discussion of specific techniques useful for reaching different segments of the community, showing the skill of the professional public relations practitioner cum counselor.

The vast majority of school systems provide college counseling much attenuated from the models described by the authors of this section, and even the best counseling systems cannot serve all clients equally well. How, then, shall students whose needs cannot be met within their schools find counsel? One answer is the independent educational counselor. In Chapter Twenty, Marilyn J. Blum and Phyllis S. Steinbrecher view the functions that independent counselors provide and the clients they serve, showing by implication and description the wide range of special and unusual problems with which school-connected counselors cannot be expected to deal. They demonstrate by example a possible resource for those professionals for whom the range of programs mandated by Martin and others is clearly impossible. Steinbrecher and Blum illustrate how potential clients should be advised to choose and use such independent professionals and what services they have a right to expect. They also point out that the independent professional can focus on special needs outside the range of usual school counseling—for example, choosing independent elementary and secondary schools and choosing a college to which to transfer after an unsatisfactory initial experience.

When working with students who have barely begun to choose, with their parents, and with their schools, college guidance officers are both counselors and guardians. Along with college admissions officers, they share the responsibility for seeing that future generations are educated as well and as sensitively as possible, to contrive social benefit and individual satisfaction. They also have the unique responsibility of guarding against the excesses of a process that is regulated neither by state nor by uniform institutional expectation. Like Janus, counselors must look both ways.

13

Discerning the Basis for College Counseling in the Eighties

Steven C. Munger
R. Fred Zuker

Credibility is the goal. Anyone who hopes to be effective as a college guidance counselor must establish credibility with the four basic constituencies of the profession: students, parents, fellow faculty and administrators, and college admissions officers. In most cases, professional and personal credibility are synonymous, since it is virtually impossible to separate a personality, an adviser's personal qualities, likes, dislikes, and values, from the profession of college advising. The establishment of credibility with the various constituencies differs in individual method but not in principle.

The exemplary principles the college adviser should follow are honesty, consistency, firmness, and sensitivity. These traits highlight the principles of college advising:

1. Provide honest communication.
2. Be consistent with all constituencies.
3. Project firm values.
4. Be sensitive to the individuals in the process.

(Adhering to the principles should produce desired results, but maintaining a keen sense of humor may be the only means of preserving sanity while doing so!)

Preparation

No formal training ever prepares a person for *all* aspects of college advising, but three areas should be emphasized. First, a college adviser should be able to communicate clearly. Second, the adviser should have some classroom teaching experience. Third, the adviser must actively develop a knowledge and understanding of the broad spectrum of higher education. Ideally, an adviser's background should include a period of work in a college admissions office, but, practically, the opportunity to order one's career that way is not always possible.

Well-developed communicative skills and the perspective on education that comes only through the classroom experience are the basic ingredients for the development of a college adviser's credibility; beyond these basics, experience is the principal source of instruction.

A few words of caution, however, are appropriate for the new college adviser. En route to establishing one's credibility, remember the principles: Be honest, be consistent, stand for something, be understanding, and keep smiling. If you are unsure about anything, seek advice from a more experienced counselor.

Constituencies of the College Adviser

Students are obviously the most important constituency with which a college adviser deals. In some schools, the college admissions process is the focus of the attention of the entire school community. Not surprisingly, student attitude toward the process has a major effect on the college advising program.

A college adviser maintains two levels of involvement with students: in groups and individually. When the adviser is dealing with groups, consistency must be the watchword. The adviser should take care not to make statements that are unclear or easily misinterpreted. What is dealt with at the group level must be easily adaptable to individual circumstances. The establishment of a good individual counseling relationship is of course the main emphasis of the college adviser, and it is on the individual level that the college counseling process must focus.

Before the initial counseling session with an individual, the college adviser should be familiar with the student's record, teacher comments, family background, and other pertinent information. Students are usually anxious about the first meeting with the adviser to discuss the future, and an adviser sets the stage for establishing credibility by being well prepared for the first encounter with an individual student.

Throughout the process, be conservative in predicting the chances for admission at individual colleges. The adviser's responsibility to the student is to give honest, accurate information, which should include an assessment of the student's chances for admission; the tact with which an adviser gradually deflates a student's bubble or introduces reality to temper unrealistic aspirations is often the key to establishing credibility with a student.

Since parental expectations and aspirations for a child are usually stronger and less in touch with reality than the child's, the parents frequently need as much good advice in bringing the future into focus as does the student. But parents have tended to be a neglected constituency in the college admissions process.

Parents of children in secondary schools are the consumers of the school's services. Certainly schools must be sensitive to parents as consumers, but institutional integrity cannot be compromised. The college adviser is a person who can be extraordinarily influential in helping parents blend expectation and reality without offense by involving the parents in the college admissions process as much as possible.

The essential step in involving parents and establishing credibility with the parental constituency is to introduce parents to the process by providing them with comprehensive and accurate information. Specific application of various aspects of the process to individual students and the parents is much more easily managed if everyone has a good understanding of the admissions process, its terminology and its procedures.

Group information sessions, distribution of booklets or guides, coffee hours, speakers from the admissions community, and private conferences with the adviser are a few proven methods of involving parents in the process. The college adviser soon learns that parental support and approval are critical to the success of the counseling program.

Parents and students are important constituencies, but they are transient in the sense that they pass through an institution and partake of its services en route. Fellow faculty and administrators are permanent residents; consequently, they are influential in supporting annually a college adviser's credibility with the students and parents. As it is with parents, the adviser's key to successful relations with fellow faculty is to provide information about and, hence, understanding of the admissions process.

College admissions counseling is an unusual profession that deals with the transition of the product (student) of one process (secondary school) to another process (college). Since the process of college admissions is an entity itself, it is rarely understood by those concerned with the other processes: the faculty of the school or college. The college adviser must work to ensure that the faculty members receive information about the entire admissions process, not merely about individual students within the process.

The relationship between the college adviser and the college admissions officer is somewhat strange. The nature of the admissions process is such that college admissions officers and college advisers work together to create the process and focus their attention on the student in the transition between educational levels, but the student and parents often view them as adversaries. The student sees the college adviser as the advocate, the admissions officer as the judge.

To establish credibility with the college admissions community, the college adviser must concentrate on three areas: (1) improving the general understanding of students, parents, and fellow faculty about the admissions process and the role of college admissions officers; (2) developing a consistent pattern of communication through honest dialogue with college admissions officers; and (3) actively supporting professionalism in all aspects of the college admissions process.

A college adviser should become involved in professional associations, attend workshops, keep abreast of important issues that affect the admissions process, and remember that the first obligation of both the admissions officer and the college adviser must be to the student in the process, not to their own institutions.

Future Trends

Decisions made by educational administrators for institutional survival in the 1980s will affect the lives of our students. Parents and students should be aware of the factors that will affect them and should understand the best ways to enter the world of higher education and take advantage of the available opportunities. As helping professionals in education, it is counselors' responsibility to prepare students and their parents for the college admissions process in a difficult time of widespread institutional retrenchment and change.

Counselors of college-bound students must understand the dynamics of the higher education environment in the 1980s. Many institutions have already been forced to close; others are in jeopardy. All these reactions to the looming crisis of reduced enrollments and ever tighter budgets contribute to a mood of uneasiness that pervades all parts of the education establishment. Uncertainty over the economy and recent federal spending cuts in higher education have intensified the misgivings of educational administrators.

This era in higher education has bred rumors and misconceptions in the wake of the bad news about projected applicant declines and unreached enrollment goals. For example, several assumptions about college admissions are now being made and discussed:

1. Colleges will have to work harder to fill the classrooms and dormitories.
2. Students will have more choices because admissions standards will be lowered.
3. Getting into college will be easier in the 1980s and 1990s than ever before.

All these statements contain some element of truth, but they may be misleading to prospective students.

Colleges were hard at work recruiting the best students long before the decline in the number of college-going students was predicted. The efforts to fill available spaces will intensify, and the pressures on prospective students to choose one institution instead of another will increase proportionately.

Very few colleges and universities are truly selective in their admissions policies. The relatively small number of the most prestigious institutions will remain highly selective. Other schools, however, may have to lower standards to maintain enrollment. Some schools will follow the difficult course of reducing the number of students to maintain academic quality.

Counselors should prepare college-bound students for the following possibilities:

- Admissions officers may make promises to students that cannot be kept.
- Students who have little chance for academic success may be admitted.
- Standards may be lowered to the extent that quality of education for everyone is reduced.
- Students who are not contributing members of the community may be allowed to continue.
- Course offerings may be reduced and academic departments weakened to the point that they do not offer the education promised in the catalogues.

The following are potential danger signals to which students and parents should be sensitive. These signals might indicate an institution that is moving in the direction of the possibilities just listed. The counselor should also become familiar with these signs so as to provide the guidance students and parents will need now and later.

Admissions/Retention

1. How does the college rate its level of selectivity?
2. How many students apply for admission?
3. How many spaces are available?
4. How many students are accepted? How many attend?

5. How strong are applicants and admitted students academically?
6. What is the rate of attrition between first and second year?
7. What percentage of students graduate within four or five years of matriculation?
8. What do students do after graduation?

Levels of selectivity range from "most selective" to "open admissions." These levels are based on many factors, including the ratio of applications to acceptances, academic preparation of candidates, and nonacademic factors such as geographical distribution and extracurricular activities. If a college rates itself as highly selective or most selective, only a relatively small percentage of students applying for admission are admitted. If the percentage of applicants accepted is very high—say, over 75 percent—the college may be experiencing difficulty in attracting good candidates. Students and parents should be reminded that many fine schools have highly "self-selected" applicant pools, which means that even though there is a high applicant-to-accepted-student ratio, the quality of all the applicants is very high and admission may still be highly selective. This may be particularly true at specialized colleges, such as institutes of technology. Selectivity ratings of schools are often subjective and not simply a matter of scores and grade point averages. Students and parents should be encouraged to pay close attention to how selective a college is, to determine whether the school is academically viable and able to attract well-qualified candidates.

A college's success in retaining students is an excellent measure of a school's quality. Colleges able to retain a large percentage of students are providing the educational experience that was represented to the students in the admissions process. Parents and students should be reminded that the national average of students graduating from the same college at which they began their careers is between 40 and 50 percent. Some attrition is inevitable for reasons beyond the control of the college, such as changed family financial circumstances or altered academic goals no longer appropriate for the first college. Retention between first and second year is also an important measure of the school's success in providing a supportive environment for new students. It is difficult to say what a good rate of retention should be between first and second year; however, if a school is losing more than 15 or 20 percent between first and second year, students and parents should find out why such a high number of students choose to leave.

Postgraduation plans of graduates and their success in achieving their goals for postgraduate training and employment are important indications of how the college is perceived by the outside world. If a large number of undergraduates who apply to graduate schools successfully gain admission to top-quality graduate programs, it is a good indication that the school is highly regarded by graduate and professional schools around the country. A warning about the manner in which some schools calculate these percentages: The counselor should tell parents and students to ask how many students apply to graduate schools and how many of these are included in the percentage of accepted students. Some colleges carefully screen those students who will be recommended for admission to graduate school, excluding from their figures those who do not receive the school's recommendation.

It is also important to know how the college advises students applying for graduate and professional school and how students are recommended. Is there a committee that helps students seek admission to training in medical science? If so, how is this committee structured, and how are recommendations composed? Are they written by one person, or are they compilations of teacher and other recommendations? Do faculty actively work with students to choose the best graduate schools for the individual, or are the students left to their own devices?

Finances

1. Is the college operating with a balanced budget?
2. What percentage of operating costs are derived from tuition?
3. What are the school's financial priorities? Is the school raising funds for new buildings, or to increase financial aid for students, or to recruit the finest faculty?

Financial health is very important in these days of sky-rocketing costs and limited resources. If an institution is able to operate on a balanced budget, this speaks highly of the administration of the school's fiscal affairs.

The size of endowments may be misleading. However, an institution should have an endowment comparable to institutions of similar caliber and type. The endowment should be large enough to allow sustained growth in the critical areas of student financial aid, faculty and staff salaries, and physical plant maintenance. If an institution is heavily dependent on tuition to meet operating costs, more than 70 percent, it could mean that the institution must continue to enlarge entering classes to stay solvent in the face of increasing inflation or must cut programs dramatically to offset rising costs. There is no magic formula by which the fiscal integrity of an institution can be measured, but admissions counselors should give parents and students the financial picture of an institution being considered. If this information is not provided, the parents and students should raise the questions just outlined.

Faculty

1. Is the university or college reducing the number of departments and decreasing the number of faculty?
2. Is the school hiring any new faculty? If so, in what departments?

Financial Aid

1. Are the college's financial aid resources adequate to meet the demonstrated need of students admitted to the college?
2. What percentage of students receive financial aid?
3. Does financial aid status influence the admissions decision?
4. In addition to regular financial aid, what programs does the school offer to help students and parents finance higher education?

Admissions professionals must become aware of parents' and students' need to plan for the financial requirements of higher education. In the current climate, parents are increasingly apprehensive that certain kinds of higher education are beyond their financial reach. It is important that the admissions counselor encourage parents to investigate before making decisions.

Federal funding for assistance to students is being reduced, but many colleges are tempering the effect of these cutbacks with their own programs, such as parent loan programs, increased opportunities for work on campus, and other programs designed to help parents meet the costs of higher education. The percentage of students who receive financial aid is an indication of the school's commitment to ensuring diversity and meeting the need of all those students who qualify for financial assistance. The percentage of students receiving financial aid will vary widely; some of the most expensive private schools will have as many as 60 to 70 percent of students receiving some form of financial assistance. Parents should be told to distinguish institutional financial aid from outside sources, such as ROTC scholarships and grants from employers. The amount of money coming from the institution or managed by the institution, such as College Work-Study Program funds and National Direct Student Loans, is a better indicator of the institution's commitment to meeting financial need.

Financial aid application status should have no effect on an applicant's admissibility. Many admissions applications ask if the student is applying for financial aid, but this information is for the purpose of processing the application, not to give the admissions officers any clues about the applicant's need.

Increasing numbers of colleges have set up special loan programs and guaranteed tuition plans that help students and parents meet the costs of higher education. Admissions officers and counselors should encourage parents and students to begin planning for higher education financing early in the student's high school career. The senior year of high school is late in the process for beginning to take steps to improve the family's financial posture. Many financial aid offices provide financial planning services and are more than willing to help families plan for higher education. The offices can explain all the available programs and how the family can best prepare for the high cost of higher education.

Admissions Practices

1. Does the college subscribe to the Statement of Principles of Good Practice of the National Association of College Admissions Counselors?
2. Does the college adhere to the Candidate's Reply Date of May 1?
3. What is the college's policy regarding the waiting list?

As admissions professionals, counselors encourage counselees who encounter any unethical admissions practices to report them as quickly as possible to a member of the NACAC. For example, in recent years, there have been abuses of the requirement for students to notify admissions offices of their decision about attending. Many students have been required to pay large, nonrefundable deposits to ensure their place in the class or a space in the dormitory. This restricts the candidate from being able to consider all the options, some of which will not be known until the first or fifteenth of April. Other students have been placed on waiting lists for inordinately long periods of time, some until the middle or end of August, with no knowledge of the possibility of their eventual admission. If students encounter any of these practices, they should be encouraged to inform their counselor. The counselor should then inform the appropriate NACAC regional or national officer for any action deemed necessary. This way, those of us in the profession of college admissions counseling can protect our own interests from the less scrupulous as well as protect the students, who are our first concern.

Students and their parents can best investigate all these areas in person on the campus, talking face to face with faculty and students. Only the on-campus visit will give prospective students and parents a feel for the place and the best sense of the kind of experience the college provides. They should be encouraged to visit campuses when possible, armed with the questions they will need answered to understand the conditions of the schools under consideration.

The coming years will be exciting and challenging for students. However, those preparing for college during these uncertain times must approach the admissions process with greater caution than did their predecessors. It is our responsibility as college admissions counselors to give students and parents the tools they will need to face the major decisions of college selection and the difficulty of financing higher education in a time of tight money and budget cutbacks. The days ahead may be difficult in many ways, but if we do our jobs as concerned, well-informed professionals, the college admissions process can be made a bridge, not a barrier.

14

Developing Links
Among Constituencies

Philip Martin

The best counselor is time. The professional in counseling is that individual who recognizes the self-worth of each student and provides the warm, caring, supportive environment in which the student is able to arrive at a decision. The counselee's time frame, not the counselor's, is important. The counselor must make time available to the student to provide the environment in which the decision may best be made.

The counseling process began long before the counselee arrived in the guidance office. With each decision students make —or have made for them by their parents—they learn about a process that will continue long after we have worked out the choice of a college with them. As professionals, we hope that the decision-making process will be improved as a result of our attempts to guide. Our goal is to help students become strong, self-sustaining, efficient, contributing members of society.

Recognizing that students bring established patterns to the counseling session, we should be aware of their needs at this time in their development. During the late teens, students are going through physical changes beyond their control and thus must learn to deal with a new set of emotional signals. All these changes affect their relations with peers of both sexes and demand energy as they try to understand what is happening. Those who live and work with the students—especially parents and counselors—must show grace as they too try to cope with the changes.

As teenagers cope with these problems, they are besieged with questions about college, career, and the life ahead. Little wonder that they seem to be on a roller coaster half the time. These years require a positive, supportive, humane environment if adolescents are to emerge with moral fiber and the proper techniques for facing the future complexities of society. The least we can do as counselors is be aware of students' problems, accept them, work patiently with them in a concerned fashion, give them strong role models, and develop with them decision-making techniques.

Concern

College guidance must be viewed as a concern—a warm, supportive, objective perception of the decision-making process through which the seniors are going. If you remember that goal, it will show in your actions.

Concern is further conveyed by not yielding to the temptation to rush in and make decisions for the student, a temptation difficult to resist. Sifting through resources leads students to deeper commitments as they implement their decision: They will be more committed to make certain their choice is right, they will work harder to prove they are right, and they will display greater staying power.

Letting students decide is hard. They want answers; their parents expect you to provide answers; the administration is happier if strong direction is exercised in the guidance office. But the student gains by working through the decision. Because transfers, changes of major, and changes of goals all impede smooth progress in higher education, careful analysis and thoughtful questioning will save time, money, and effort. Students may avoid hasty decisions; they may eschew answers that are merely socially accepted or based on the misguided advice of those who will not have to live with the consequences of the decision.

All involved persons must understand, therefore, that you will demonstrate your concern about the fate of those in your hands by asking them to make up their own minds. You will keep the worth of the individual first in your attention, and you will not rush to embrace answers that are merely expedient.

Communication

Effective, open communications are crucial to this understanding and concerned model of counseling. The counselor must make resources available and may need to expose the student to varied constituencies: parents, college officials, alumni, and other experts. There are several such relationships from which students will learn as they make their decisions.

Student-Counselor. There is constant interchange between the counselor and the students. Some of this work has to be done in *large group settings*—establishing the functions of the guidance program and the role of the counselor, parceling out information, registering students for tests, and so forth. Group meetings with freshmen and sophomores are quite appropriate and set the stage for a stronger attitude and better counseling work in later years. Establish a time for such groups, be consistent in the time, be clear in presentations, and follow up when necessary.

In addition, plan to break down into *smaller groups,* to discuss pertinent topics and allow a closer interchange of ideas. Small groups are especially effective during the junior year and give the counselor immediate feedback and clarification of ideas. An excellent source of materials for use in small groups is the College Board publication *Decisions and Outcomes* (Gelatt and others, 1979). For instance, it contains a schematic approach (shown in Figure 1) that has immediate appeal: a rectangle containing twelve circles. Six circles represent the student's grades in school, three represent standard test results, and three represent other factors (activities, athletics, recommendations). This diagram depicts the factors that comprise the basis for the college's decision about the student. It is a simple yet readily grasped approach to the topic. The amount of time and staff available to utilize the small group technique are the only constraints.

There is no more effective way to counsel than an *indi-*

Figure 1. Basis of a College's Decisions About an Individual Student.

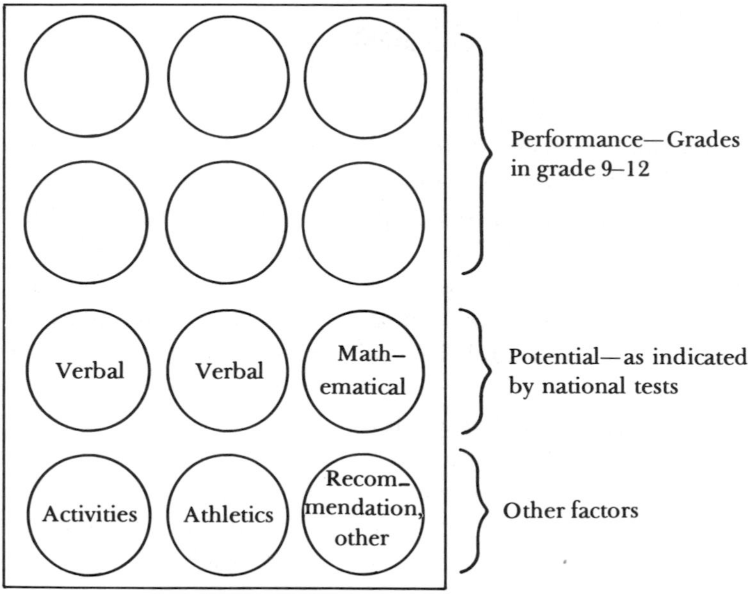

Source: Adapted from Gelatt and others, 1979.

vidual conference. However, the time required for such a conference is seldom available in the school setting. Still, every effort should be made to pursue that end, and counselors should strive continually to improve their skills. Not only will counselors have to provide time for such conferences, they will have to provide the impetus for their occurrence. Beginning in January of the junior year, set up appointments for individual conferences with each student. The time spent at that stage will save time later in the process.

A *scattergram* (shown in Figure 2) is an effective device for the individual conference. The student's achievement in academics is related to potential on a 4 × 4 matrix. Specific dots on the grid may be used, or sectors of the grid can represent the relationship between potential and performance. A student's rank in class on tests and grades, either specifically or by quarter, can then be readily related to the selectivity of certain col-

Figure 2. Scattergram for Class of 1982.

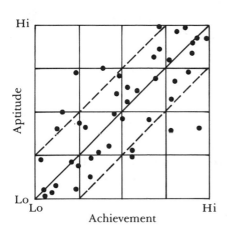

Explanation: Each dot on this 4 × 4 matrix represents an individual student. The dot reflects the student's aptitude and achievement. The vertical direction is a rough measure of your child's potential for academic matters, based on your child's relative ranking of four measures of aptitude taken during the junior year. The horizontal direction indicates your child's rank in class on the basis of averages in grades 9 to 11. Aptitude runs from *Hi* at the top to *Lo* at the bottom. Achievement runs from *Hi* at the right to *Lo* at the left. A dot on the diagonal line is an ideal relationship. Dots above the dotted line in the upper left indicate underachievers, dots below the line in the lower right represent overachievers. Dots between the lines represent students producing in relation to their capabilities.

leges. The device immediately focuses on these complex factors. It can serve as a motivation for some; for others it provides greater likelihood to their selections.

Another procedure of value in the individual conference is to use an eight-column by forty-row *flowchart*. Across the top of the column student lists her priorities for a college: size, majors, location, cost, and so forth. Then she is challenged to fill in each row with a college that interests her. The student proceeds with the use of a college guide to check off those items on her list which are met by that particular college. When the flowchart is completed, a follow-up conference is held and an active interchange occurs. This method can result in startling jumps in knowledge about college and self for both the counselee and the counselor.

The *initial conferences* may be somewhat constrained. This is often the first such conference in which the student has participated. A simple question sets the student at ease—for example, "What would you like to be doing fifteen years from now?" This global question does not require the specificity of "What college would you like to be in next fall?" or "What major will you pursue?" It focuses on the steps that will be a course for the student to follow, from the present to fifteen years down the road. Meanwhile, the student will be able to keep options open or pursue alternative goals.

Well-planned and executed individual conferences are the springboard for the student's success with similar one-on-one experiences later. The interview at college, the interview by an alumnus, the conference with a major adviser, the job interview, the business conference—all will go better for the individual as a consequence of the initial conference between the student and the counselor.

An important ingredient of the communication network supplied by the counselor is the *calendar of visits* by college admissions officers. The calendar may be on a bulletin board in a spot specifically reserved for it; the times and locations may be published in the daily bulletin or the school newspaper; visits may be announced in the lunchroom, homeroom, or other appropriate place and time in the school. In any case, constant, repetitive practices need to be pursued to ensure the widest and most effective notification. As in advertising, the student may not realize the need for the product, so the statement must be clear, forceful, and repeated.

Students need to develop the habit of consulting the calendar weekly to stay up with the changes, especially in the fall. A similar calendar or location can be used for posting college information meetings in the local area, special visiting days on college campuses, summer academic opportunities, and the myriad scholarship opportunities that inundate the counseling office.

An additional, extremely useful medium is a *weekly bulletin* of information pertinent to the college decision-making process. This bulletin is produced during the fall, tailored especially to the seniors. Monthly bulletins are appropriate for seniors later in the year or for the other classes throughout the year. Any press the counselor can use (for instance, the school or local newspaper) to highlight activities, awards, or achievements of the students and the counseling office should be solicited.

The multitude of *forms* needed by the student during the process must be readily available. A thirty-drawer file cabinet is ideal for their storage and dissemination. The counselor must ensure that the forms are current and sufficient in quantity.

Articles in both the public media and professional journals are a rich source of material. It is the counselor's responsibility to stay current with these sources, to extract appropriate material, and to maintain a file of topical viewpoints. The important step in this area is ensuring that both students and faculty use these articles. All sources of information are vital to the student as he sifts through the many resources available. Certainly the press should be scanned and made available to all students. Noteworthy articles should be posted on bulletin boards.

Because counselors are responsible for maintaining individual *activity sheets,* they must establish for each student the importance of being involved in the school, the community, and life. The counselor must be alert for that student who overextends as well as for the nonparticipating student. Therefore, the counselor must state that quality is more important than quantity where activities are concerned. Depth of involvement, breadth of responsibility—these are what colleges look for.

Outside-school activities as well as summer ones should be duly noted as valuable to the student's personal growth. In any case, all participation should be recorded in or through the counseling office, perhaps in a term-by-term (or season-by-season) accountability session once the student has begun grade 9. This practice diminishes the reliance on recollection that most students exercise when it is time to fill out college applications. It is an opportunity to remind students of the proper weighting of grades, test results, and activities accumulating on their transcript.

The guides that contain *ratings* of the various colleges will be an active area of the college counseling office. *Barron's Profiles of American Colleges, Peterson's Annual Guide to Undergraduate Study, Lovejoy's College Guide,* the *Gourman Report: A Rating of American and International Universities*—there will be heavy use of all these materials because students and parents alike find them easy to use and place a lot of stock in someone else's work. But, as with Roget's *Thesaurus,* these books are valuable only when *intelligently* used. Students who are reluctant to enter a state university because of its size think twice about the school when they see it highly rated in a number of disciplines.

A rating system that has proved worthwhile in my experience is based on the individual school's alumni. It is basically a chart showing what colleges have accepted students from that particular school, in combination with what quarter in their class the applicant ranked. The track record in college acceptances reflects only the most recent five classes of the school. It is not widely disseminated but, rather, is used during individual conferences. The intent is to stimulate thought about a variety of alternatives for the student and to bring reality into the decision when a student is unrealistic.

A similar chart based on SAT-Verbal averages can be a useful tool. If the chart is divided into twenty-five-point columns, the student's attention can be focused on a limited number of appropriate colleges. He can look within a fifty- or a hundred-point band and realize that those colleges with averages below his own score are valid choices if they also have programs that appeal to him. Wisdom in the use of ratings, either national or local, is important: Use them to stimulate thought in the conference.

The advent of the *computer,* particularly the microcomputer, has greatly changed information storage and retrieval. The College Board Search Service, NACACtion Line, revision of college admissions offices' practices—all reflect the impact of the computer on the field of education.

The microcomputer makes available to the small school the same power that once was reserved for only the large school. The counselor's expertise and creativity are the only factors restricting the adaptation of the computer's power to the counseling office. The individualized rating charts, whether by rank in class or SAT-Verbal averages, could be written as a program for local use. The tailoring to the individual school's experience will more closely reflect that population than would the acceptance of a national program.

In either case, the counselor and student need to be alert to the effect of priorities on the output derived from the computer's information. For example, a student with both biology interests and a desire to play intercollegiate football will receive appreciably different outputs depending on the order of his priorities. Biology placed first will result in keeping more options open; football first will narrow the options dramatically.

The monitoring of the *testing program* is a sizable portion of the counselor's responsibility. Since tests are crucial to the next steps for the student, the testing program is important. The counselor oversees registration for tests, proctors tests, and interprets test results (the latter can be done in an individual conference or in a group session). In any case, the counselor should be aware of the emotional impact of test results.

Registration materials needed by students have to be readily accessible to them. The testing program throughout the high school years has to be spelled out, in writing and in a group presentation. Record keeping has to be done thoroughly, and test information has to be shared and interpreted to the students, the parents, and the faculty. An appropriate test-preparation program has to be developed and supported. For example, a strong reading program will be reflected in the verbal results. The math results will often reflect involvement in mathematics courses. Therefore, a program geared to those students not pursuing a math course at the time of the test will keep their skills current. The results will reflect their attitude and participation in such a program. To serve this role adequately, the counselor must be soundly based in statistics and measurement.

Student-Parents. The student and the parents may have had many conversations concerning college. They may have shared their hopes as well as their aspirations. They will have established limitations on cost, location, and type of college. If these discussions have been pursued openly and frankly, the counselor's role is merely to be objective and provide the answers to questions that arise in the family talks. On the other hand, if the parents and students have become antagonists, the role of the counselor becomes harder to establish and carry out. The counselor serves the student best by being objective, answering questions, directing the student to the proper sources of information, and so forth. This way the counselor can decrease the pressure on the student, let the student mature in the decision-making process, serve as an ally in the environment in which the student must live, and yet not alienate the people involved or close down the lines of communication. In any case, the counselor must operate sensitively when working with the family unit. If the student is the first member of a family to enter this process, the counselor has to provide much more information about the process. Counselors' credibility is enhanced if their own children have gone through the process or if they have helped many students in the decision; the counselors can thus rely on experience and a thorough knowledge of the factors and dynamics involved.

Student-College. The counselor should assume that the student does not know much about visiting colleges. The counselor can give suggestions about what to expect, provide lists, suggest books and articles. Any of these actions will relieve the nervousness of the first-time visitor and increase the benefit the student derives; the student will then be able to return to school with his visits placed by priority and be less likely to have the different experiences blur.

Sometimes the student does not know how to begin the process. A rough draft of a *letter requesting information* (shown in Figure 3) initiates the process. The student can adapt it to her own purposes. Similarly, a draft of a *letter requesting an interview* (Figure 4) helps decrease student anxiety. The letter is adapted by the student, and action follows.

Finally, a draft of a *letter for the acceptance-decline* stage of the process (Figure 5) maintains amicable relations between the high school and the college. The key ingredients are to begin the process through such aids and to maintain open communication throughout.

The student is a novice in this process. The counselor, like a good coach, must begin with practice in the basics. The student has probably never been involved in an interview. Therefore, the conferences with the counselor serve as training for the interviews at college. An outline sheet presenting *helpful hints for interviews* can ease some of the student's nervousness. A similar outline of the recommendation phase clarifies that phase and helps the student maintain good relations with the faculty. The *application phase* also benefits from an outline sheet. The key is to help the student through the first applica-

Figure 3. Sample Request for Information Letter.

```
                              Your Street Address
                              Your City, State   (Zip Code)
                              Date


Director of Admissions
Name of College
City, State   (Zip Code)

Dear Sir:

I am a junior at _____ High School
and am interested in knowing more about _____
College (University).   I would appreciate your sending
me:

      (1)   A general bulletin explaining entrance re-
            quirements, college costs, course offerings,
            and facilities available

      (2)   Financial aid information

      (3)   Special information related to (your special
            interests).

                              Sincerely,

                              (Your Signature)

                              Your Name
                              (typed or printed in full,
                              with middle initial)
```

tion. Once one has been done, the student has correlated the necessary ingredients for any application and is over the doubting stage. One scheme that has proved helpful is to have the student as a junior fill in a college application that then may be reviewed for clarity and presentation.

Next to the actual decision in the spring, the hardest step in the process for the student is the *personal statement*. This step requires that the student take a long hard look at himself, assessing where he has been so far in his life and setting goals for his life. The student has to state who he is and why he is proceeding to college. The student has to correlate potential, performance, and projection of goals—not an easy task. Personal revelation is threatening, and in these few paragraphs the student may for the first time have to be honest and open about him-

Figure 4. Sample Interview Request Letter.

                                      125 State Street
                                      St. Louis, MO 63000
                                      May 19, 1977

Director of Admissions
Winnetka College
North Avenue
Winnetka, Illinois 19372

Dear Sir:

    I am a junior at St. Louis Priory School and am
planning to visit Winnetka, Illinois, between July 11 and
13. Because I am interested in applying for your 3/2 liberal
arts/engineering program for the fall of 1977, I would
appreciate having an interview and tour of the campus on
either July 12 or 13, if possible. I will also be applying
for financial aid and would appreciate an opportunity to
have an interview with a representative of the financial
aid office on the same day.

    If these dates are inconvenient, I would be able to
visit on any other Monday or Tuesday in July. I shall
look forward to hearing from you.

    Thank you.

                              Sincerely,

                              Lloyd Jackson
                              Lloyd Jackson

ALL LETTERS SHOULD BE NEATLY TYPED OR HANDWRITTEN.
YOUR LETTERS ARE THE FIRST IMPRESSION THAT THE COL-
LEGE WILL RECEIVE ABOUT YOU, AND YOU WILL WANT TO BE
CERTAIN THAT THEY ARE NEAT AND LEGIBLE.

self; he will greatly appreciate his counselor's warm and supportive help.

    Wide dissemination of information about *college fairs* is a
must for the counselor. The earlier a student becomes involved
in searching out information, the better prepared he will be for
each stage that follows. Those schools located in many large
metropolitan areas have access to the NACAC College Fairs and
should utilize that asset. Regional fairs, such as the Chesterfield
Mall Metro Fair in St. Louis, should also be pushed. College associations often provide informational services and should be used.

Figure 5. Sample Acceptance-Decline Letter.

```
                              Your Street Address
                              Your City, State   (Zip Code)
                              Date


Director of Admissions
Name of College
Street Address
City, State   (Zip Code)

Dear Sir:

I have been accepted by _____
in the Class of 198_.   Your time and consideration in
processing my application is greatly appreciated.   Thank
you for your confidence in my capabilities.   However,
I must decline your acceptance and ask that you withdraw
my name from your rolls.

I will be attending _____ in September
198_.   I hope that this prompt action will open up a place
for another candidate from your waiting list.

                              Sincerely,



                              Your Name
```

Another option is for the counselor to establish a college night or day at the school. These devices help develop a large fund of information upon which the student may build the eventual decision.

Student-Faculty. The faculty can give the student much impromptu, incidental counseling. The teachers usually represent a wide spectrum of institutions of higher education. The advice they offer will be as sound as that which any adult can provide, because they are role models, the teachers' advice is often better received. Therefore, it is important that the counselor communicate with the staff to ensure that the faculty work complements that of the counselor.

The staff has a decided advantage in answering questions related to academic disciplines. They are closest to the local, regional, and national subject-matter associations. They are most knowledgeable about the material appearing in the professional journals. The wise counselor defers to the teacher of a subject for the answers to discipline-related questions. In return, the teacher defers the more general questions of process to the counselor; each person is an adjunct to the other.

Student-School. The relative importance of a student's *activities* has to be established early in the high school years. If he focuses his energies early, his record when he graduates will reflect responsibility, leadership, and perseverance.

Students who have *traveled* or been involved in *foreign study* should duly note that. However, a grocery list of places proves little. The student must be alert to the different cultures, the regionalism, and the value of language. The student's perceptions should have been broadened and deepened as a result of the travel.

A student may show the *importance of education* in his life by pursuing college-level classes evenings, Saturdays, or during the summer. The record of such participation needs to be duly recorded, documented, and noted in the student's recommendation.

Many students are involved in *service-oriented pursuits,* which may be self-initiated or school-inspired. In either case, the activity should display growth, leadership, and responsibility. The project can be career, research, or volunteer oriented. But the individual needs to project development as a result of the experience. The counselor can serve the student by focusing her efforts in that direction.

Since the personal statement on a college application has such an impact on the student, any aid the counselor can offer will be greatly appreciated. One device that has proved worthwhile is the *autobiography.* A student in the junior year is asked to give the counselor an autobiography by the end of the school year. The format is left open, so that the student is free to include any facts or experiences which in his view are important. To motivate the counselees, the counselor promises to include pertinent facts in the school recommendation, which will then be read to the student. The counselor also should ensure that no sensitive material will be revealed.

The autobiography helps the student over the hurdle posed by the need for a personal statement. In addition, it gives the counselor an opportunity to provide suggestions about how to improve the statement yet lets the student maintain the pride of authorship.

Student-School-College. The myriad forms and formats for college *applications* are enough to confuse anybody, especially a student starting the application process. A worthwhile device is to have the student fill in an old application as a junior; it can then be reviewed with the student. Another suggestion is to have the student make a Xerox copy of the application to practice on before the final version is typed. Still another approach is to utilize the Common Application Form. This form is then used by the student for colleges that accept it or as a basis for gathering the data which are most commonly needed on applications. The key is that once the necessary information has been collected and one application has been completed, the student is ready to complete one, two, or ten more applications relatively easily by merely adapting the material to the form being used.

The student and parents are naturally concerned about the information the school will be providing in support of the application. Sharing the *school's transcript* helps decrease that concern. An overhead transparency of the transcript can be shown to students and parents alike. Any questions about the content can be readily resolved by this method. The grading method needs to be explicit, the course titles must be straightforward, the quality of a student's program must stand out, and the method of ranking must be clear. The description of courses the school will send can be similarly displayed by a transparency. These methods can erase any doubts about the school's role in the application process. (The high turnover of personnel in colleges' admissions offices increases the need for clarity and conciseness. The volume of material which must be read by the personnel adds to that need. Underlining advanced or accelerated courses will make the work at the college easier and at the same time highlight the quality of the record.)

The *statistical profile* used to convey to the colleges the educational environment represented by the school can be similarly shared. The counselor's responsibility is to keep the profile current and clear.

The emphasis on rank in class, especially by the larger

colleges, increases the need for the counselor to express clearly the quality represented by the student body of the school as well as that of the individual student. The percentage of students from a given school who have pursued higher education is a concise way of presenting that fact. A decided asset on any profile is a list of colleges attended in recent years by graduates of the school. This list is beneficial to the colleges that are included as well as for the school itself.

One responsibility for counselors who have used the autobiographical approach with applications and recommendations is feedback. This can be done by reading the *school recommendation* to the student. Any omissions or errors of fact can be corrected before the recommendation is sent from the school. The counselor's responsibility is to do a thorough job in writing the school recommendation. A team of faculty who help produce the student recommendations is a decided asset. The final responsibility, however, resides with the counselor who coordinates the work.

Student-Faculty-College. The teacher who has had the most recent and closest contact is often solicited by the student to write a *teacher recommendation,* and as a counselor you should agree with the student's inclination to ask a teacher who makes her feel positive and supported. The counselor can aid the teacher in this work by providing pertinent information, interpreting test results, and offering suggestions.

The counselor can further help the student maintain or improve both mathematical and verbal skills by providing materials and supporting programs, some with the faculty. Parents particularly appreciate such support.

Counselor-Parent. Faculty, parents, and students must be told of your desire to have *individual conferences.* Although family conferences are hard to schedule, they are valuable. *Parent-teacher meetings* should be capitalized on by the counseling office because they are an opportunity to be visible and to present the basic framework. Many of the topics mentioned earlier in this chapter can be the bases for such presentations.

Face-to-face contact with parents has the greatest impact, whether it occurs in individual conferences or in parent meetings. These contacts have greater value if they are preceded and followed by *mailings* that outline various aspects of the counseling process.

Counselor-College. College admissions staff *visitors* can place an added burden on the counselor's time, especially in the fall. That time can be well spent, however, if it allows some professional interchange. The college needs to keep abreast of changes at the high school level, and the counselor needs to be apprised of the particular college's new or continuing strong programs.

The personal contact keeps the visibility of the counselor, the school, and the applicants firmly established in the visitors' minds. The constant turnover among college representatives makes it imperative that the counselor take the time necessary for these fellow professionals.

Monitoring these visitors lets you know what the student hears about a particular college. A list of those college meetings that a student attends will let you see what most attracts him and will hint at changes in his priorities.

The *regional alumni representatives* for colleges are an added source of information and support for the counselor. These people often work closely with the colleges to arrange visits, provide information, ferret out answers to questions—in essence, to serve as the branch of the admissions office on the local scene. These alumni host informal get-togethers on behalf of the college and sponsor informational meetings. The counselor should get to know the representatives and how they function.

The counselor can reenforce contacts with fellow educators through *professional participation* in local, regional, and national organizations like NACAC. The benefits derived from this participation is directly proportional to the amount of time and the priority the counselor establishes for this activity.

Counselors promote visits for their students. If visits are valuable for the students, then so are *visits by the counselor.* They are a chance for professional growth and let you see any strengths and weaknesses that a school's bulletins or alumni fail to depict. The counselor changes and so do colleges, so the counselor who aims at professional growth should frequently visit compuses.

Counselor-Faculty. A school's faculty is a valued adjunct to the counseling office, and the counselor who supports the faculty will gain a strong ally for the program. This environment can be fostered further by presentations at faculty meetings. Any topics in the process can generate faculty discussion. For example, the topic of writing recommendations triggered a responsive chord at one faculty meeting. Other topics that spark faculty interest are test results, the guidance program, and follow-up studies. The important point is to keep open the lines of communication with your colleagues by responding to their stated needs.

Record keeping is an integral function of the counseling office. You should not submerge yourself in paper, but keep up with testing changes and your students' educational statistics so that you can present students' progress knowledgeably to faculty (and parents).

The faculty, the parents, and the students are all vitally interested in *follow-up studies* of the school's alumni. The faculty want to know where the alumni attend college, what kind of college, what area of study is pursued, how many higher degrees are earned, and so forth. The faculty need that feedback to assess the impact of their teaching and the curriculum. Parents perceive the image of the school through the data reported; current students compare their perceptions of colleges they may choose with the recorded experiences of their older peers. Each group interprets the data for their own purposes. Trends over time are of particular interest to the counselor. The knowledge about the alumni gives the counselor a fountain of information in conversations with faculty, parents, students, and college admissions visitors.

The usual *reporting of test results to the faculty* sparks interest among colleagues. This test reporting is improved if the test results are filed by test, by class, and by year. The longitudinal trend can then be readily ascertained, or the potential of a class or an individual student can be readily determined.

The faculty often question the amount of time devoted

to testing. The counselor needs to be in a position to answer such questions as the following: What value have Advanced Placement tests been to our students? Are ACT or SAT tests preferred, or should students take both? How can the results of testing early in the high school years be used in working with the students? What relationship if any exists between the SAT-Verbal score and the English Achievement Test? These and many more questions can be answered more readily and more clearly if the counselor initiates studies to answer just such questions.

Counselor-School. Follow-up studies are of little value unless they are shared. The quickest way to reach the largest audience is the school newspaper, especially if that publication is sent to the alumni and parents. *Articles* reporting the results are welcomed by student editors, who have trouble getting student writers to follow through on assignments. The counselor can interpret the results clearly and control the contents by writing the article, while sharing important facts and providing visibility for the counselor and the office.

An *annual report* to the head of the school summarizing the functioning of the counseling office for the year is valuable to both the reader and the writer. The report establishes the accountability for the counselor; because many counselors operate alone, the report is an objective framework within which to view the functioning of the office.

Faculty-School. The faculty are a distinct asset to the counselor and should be relied on to provide input about students. Student description forms or checklists that can be readily completed or translated to the various college formats are necessary. The teacher will then accept the added paperwork, and the counselor will find the added input invaluable when writing recommendations. Recognition of this faculty contribution needs to be built into the system. In addition, the faculty reports on academics, athletics, and activities, along with anecdotal reports, are a reservoir of information for the counselor. All these sources should be relied on for pertinent data that can be used by the counselor when writing student recommendations.

Faculty-Colleges. The faculty is called on to write letters to the academic departments of colleges. Sometimes the letter is to solicit information, sometimes on behalf of a student. This work should be viewed as an extension of the counseling office, not an assumption of the counselor's work. Colleges' recruiting work, often done through the coaches, should be similarly viewed. The counselor should be alert to operate in the wings as an objective participant to these endeavors.

School-Parent. The many mailings previously mentioned inform parents about the counseling process. Various mailings directed at specific parent groups will focus on the needs of these people. An August mailing to upcoming seniors and their parents reinforces the overview of the process. A November mailing to juniors and their parents spreads the information about the PSAT/NMSQT. A December mailing to the parents of seniors apprises them about the applications processed by the office. The intent is to ensure that all parties in the process are working in concert. All methods of communication need to be used by the counselor and the school to make this an orderly, smooth, and efficient process.

Parent-Student-College. The main way the counselor can serve this group of people is by maintaining open communications among them. Sometimes it will be information, sometimes it will be clearing up misunderstandings between them. Often it involves establishing an itinerary for visits to a number of colleges by students and their parents. Since the counselor is more familiar with the campuses and their locations, this work is a natural extension of the counselor's work.

Alumni-Student. The student is solicited by colleges' alumni to attend many informational meetings. The counselor serves this relationship best by publicizing these meetings and attending as many as possible. The counselor should establish a forum in the school wherein these communications can proceed. A meeting of alumni and current students in December or January is most valuable, especially for sophomores and juniors, and often initiates the process for these students.

Cooperation

There is no greater disappointment than failure to communicate. Think of the smile, the laughter, the love that have been sent your way. The rewards, the satisfactions, the affirmations, the smiles—all will be returned in full measure. It is in the giving that we receive.

With this attitude, cooperation will be forthcoming from students, parents, faculty, alumni, and administration. Each group will cooperate in any way it can; cooperation throughout the process is necessary for the success of counseling. If all who are involved produce up to their capabilities, they will produce a vital counseling program. The whole will be more than the sum of its parts. You will achieve your goal of producing effective, responsible, contributing, functioning adults.

15

Viewing College Counseling as Part of General Student Counseling: A Developmental Approach

Margaret Elizabeth Tracy

Most counselors in schools today are generalists. The school counseling profession began around the turn of the twentieth century as a specialty in vocational guidance, but the role of the school counselor has expanded to serve today's myriad student needs. Career and college counseling is only one important aspect of the total guidance program. Counselors today find themselves dealing with social, psychological, developmental, and educational issues and problems. More often than not, they are assigned to several grade levels which include diverse populations and age groups.

Whereas the role of the counselor may vary from school to school and even from counselor to counselor within a school, the generalist may be engaged in any of the following functions. This incomplete list gives an idea of the great diversity and complexity of the generalist counselor's role in today's secondary schools.

Counselor Functions

1. *Conflict resolution*—problem solving or mediating within the school community between such "adversaries" as student and teacher, parent and student, parent and teacher.

2. *Long- and short-term academic planning*—including scheduling, study-skills development, peer-tutoring programs, "coping with school" programs.

3. *Affective education*—classroom or small group counseling sessions dealing with such issues as values clarification, moral development, and stress management.

4. *Personal problem solving*—individual counseling sessions initiated by the student or counselor.

5. *Management of grief and loss*—dealing with issues of death and divorce.

6. *Assessment*—testing students' aptitude, skills, interests, and intelligence.

7. *College choice and career development*—developing decision-making skills, providing occupational and college information, providing opportunities for work experience, job placement, and so forth.

8. *Sex-related counseling*—dealing with pregnancy and abortion, birth control information and referral, understanding sexual feelings and sexual development.

9. *Problems of juvenile delinquency*—dealing with drug use and abuse, school dropouts, runaways.

10. *Counseling special children*—working with minority students, learning- and behavior-disordered students, students with hearing, vision, or other physical losses.

11. *Parental contact*—of all kinds, including group informational programs, parenting classes, family counseling.

12. *Administrative duties*—record keeping, changing schedules, admitting new students, research, program planning, follow-up studies.

In contrast to these functions, the college specialist primarily works with students in their last two years of high school and deals solely with the issue of college selection. These counselors are experts armed with a large body of data regarding college admissions and financial aid, and they are also familiar with a large group of colleagues and contacts in the field. How can the generalist with such a large number of job functions compete with such expertise?

The answer is good organizational skills, ready access to

information, sufficient volunteer help, and knowledge of students and their families. The last is the *crucial* variable that usually distinguishes the generalist from the specialist. After all, if the counselor has dealt previously with the student on any of the twelve job functions, then the counselor has a head start on a relationship with that student. This is an important edge because college choice is a *personal* decision involving values, self-understanding, financial planning, and family decision making. A counselor who has established rapport with both students and parents has a definite advantage.

The generalist counselor's overall role is to encourage personal growth and awareness in each client. Armed with self-knowledge, the student can make sound vocational, educational, and personal decisions. In this context, counseling for college and career choice is no longer just an isolated function but an integral part of the process of identity formation and adolescent development. One might call this a "holistic" approach to counseling, in which the student is viewed as a totality. Following the traditions of such famous psychological theorists as Alfred Adler and Erik Erikson, the individual is viewed as more than the components of the whole. The emotions, intellect, physical skills, and psychological and even spiritual makeup are considered an inextricably intertwined set that defines each person as unique. In this sense, we are each "one singular sensation." In keeping with this outlook, the counselor with a holistic viewpoint might be concerned as much with the client's general health and diet (Miller, 1980) as with academic progress. Particularly, as we come to understand better the enormous impact of organizations, institutions, and sociodemographic characteristics on the behavior of specific groups, especially women and minorities, we must become increasingly concerned with the effects of these variables on each individual client (Stulac and Stanwyck, 1980). The counselor who accepts a holistic orientation brings a qualitatively different perspective to what was once the "simple" process of college guidance.

Professional Preparation in College Guidance

"Counseling the college-bound student . . . has barely reached early adolescence" (Herr and Cramer, 1968). Although this estimation of the state of the art was written fourteen years ago, it still appears true if one can judge by the relative scarcity of recent research and printed literature in the field. Papers presented at the 1966 invitational conference on the preparation of school counselors, sponsored by the College Entrance Examination Board, called for research in several important areas related to college choice. Benson (1967) asked, "What can be done in the training of school counselors to enable them to assist students in planning their education? I am not aware of any research that specifically measures the performance of counselors in the area of educational planning." Super (1967) called for an application of vocational development theory to the college choice process. Gelatt (1967) advocated applying decision theory in the area of college planning. These ideas and others were incorporated into a collection titled *Preparing School Counselors in Educational Guidance* (Newman and Newman, 1967). Although research has developed along the lines of furthering career development and decision theory, little has been done to incorporate these ideas into an applied program for college counseling.

The two books typically referred to when discussing the relative merits of the generalist versus the specialist roles are *Guiding the Future College Student* (Reiss and Fox, 1968) and *Guidance of the College Bound* (Herr and Cramer, 1968). Unfortunately, nothing as definitive or as comprehensive has been published since these two works. This chapter, because it deals with the function of the generalist, concerns itself only with the viewpoint advocated by the Herr and Cramer book.

This viewpoint "does not involve guidance techniques different from those appropriate for other students" (Herr and Cramer, 1968). Generalists might, then, consider themselves eclectics, behaviorists, or humanists. Regarding training, one could say that everything and yet nothing has prepared the school counselor for the role of college adviser. "Everything" refers to intense preparation in counseling technique, educational and counseling theory, career-development theory, and other subjects in which the school counselor has been immersed. "Nothing" refers to the widespread absence of training among most counselors, specifically regarding the high school-to-college articulation process. Learning what amounts to a vast set of data about financial aid, college selection, and the admissions process has been relegated to on-the-job training. Benson (1967), while also advocating the generalist orientation, decried this lack of counselor preparation.

According to the data-people-things schema of the *Dictionary of Occupational Titles,* counseling is defined as a high-people, high-data profession. The college advisory role in particular must maximize the use of both data and people. There must be a balance between the image of the specialist (one who does college guidance work only and who is best known as a data specialist) and the generalist, whose reputation has been built on counseling people skills. "It seems feasible that the school counselor who enacts both roles in varying degrees ... could be most influential" (Herr and Cramer, 1968). Also, while the specialist role fragments the total guidance program by dealing primarily with grades 11 and 12, the generalist deals with an articulated, developmental program usually spanning grades 9 through 12. Such a program is described later.

College Choice as an Intermediate Career Decision

Since college choice implies a decision, knowledge of decision-making theory should be a focal point of the generalist college counselor's expertise, partly because vocational-choice theory has validity in educational guidance (Herr and Cramer, 1968). The college decision can actually be viewed as an intermediate career choice. "The ultimate outcome of the decision is the individual's choice, maintenance, and progression in an occupation" (Herr and Cramer, p. 132). Super's (1967) developmental self-concept theory is just one of several theoretical models that can be applied to the college-choice process. According to Super, the principles involved in making decisions are the same regardless of age or stage of life. He defines five stages, progressing from growth, exploration, establishment, and maintenance through decline. As he defines the stages, most adolescents would be in the exploration phase. The five most important factors in effective decision making are stated as (1) planfulness or time perspective, (2) exploration, (3) information, (4) decision making, and (5) reality orientation. Super's paradigm could be used effectively as a framework in which to develop a sequential, coordinated program of career-college guidance.

This chapter presents one such program, based on Super's theory that the vocational-development process is essentially that of developing and implementing the self-concept. Research indicates that the same can be said of the choice of a college, wherein the student is choosing a perceived image, a group of peers, a curriculum, an environment, a particular philosophy of life and learning, an intellectual orientation, and more (Newman and Newman, 1978). If one believes, then, that "college choice is a means of self-actualization, a place in which one hopes to be able to become that which one is capable of becoming" (Super, 1967), the role of the generalist as it pertains to college choice is to provide a systematic set of experiences over time designed to maximize the student's knowledge of the self and such components as psychological needs, interests, skills, values, and abilities.

Relating this perceived self-identity to various college identities is the ultimate goal of and decision to be made by each student. The counselor becomes primarily an educator, adviser, and motivator, whose duty is to provide a structured, developmental program with accessible, well-organized, up-to-date information available for student, parent, and community use. Clients in this model are viewed as active agents working toward goals and having the capability and power to influence and create their futures.

Developmental Programming

The following presentation outlines an integrated, developmental career-college program drawn principally from the program currently in use at Clayton High School in Clayton, near St. Louis, Missouri. The school is a relatively small, public institution serving approximately 700 students in grades 9 through 12. The Clayton School District is bordered by Washington University, and educational influences are strong. The community is a predominantly white, middle- to upper-middle-class socioeconomic group, with most parents involved in either business or the professions. Traditionally, approximately 90 percent of the students attend postsecondary educational institutions.

The program is based on the assumption that (1) career and college choice are interrelated; (2) career and college choice involve training in decision-making skills; (3) information-seeking behavior needs to be systematically taught; (4) counselors encourage the individual's search for greater self-awareness and identity development; (5) the career-college developmental process is sequential, with intermediate steps laying the group work for later choices; and (6) a holistic approach to career-college counseling carried out by the generalist can most effectively serve the needs of individual students.

The outline of grade-level program activities is only a descriptive example of the role that generalists can play in college guidance. It is not definitive, nor is it a step-by-step guide to college guidance.

Key to Reading the Program

1. A global or comprehensive task is assigned for each of the four high school years and listed in the heading for that particular year under the exploration stage designated by Super's model. See Super (1967) for fuller details about those stages.

2. Each program activity is keyed in the left-hand column to its predominant decision-making function according to the five-factor model outlined by Super:

P = Planfulness
R = Reality orientation
I = Information
D = Decision making
E = Exploration

3. As every generalist knows, there is a need for efficient and effective time-saving methods to accomplish the multitude of tasks involved in such a comprehensive program. Thus, each

program activity is also keyed in the right-hand column according to the method to be used:

G = Group counseling indicated
I = Informational systems used (computer systems, career center)
V = Volunteer use appropriate
E = Exclusively the function of a trained counselor

(Volunteers used in this program at CHS include trained teacher-advisers, career center paraprofessionals, alumni, parents, citizens, and other students and teachers. The teacher-advisers are from the general teaching staff and trained in communication skills and supervised by counselors. Each one works with fifteen to twenty students and is assigned to follow the same group for the first two years of high school.)

A Developmental Career-College Program
Grades 9-12

Grade 9
Exploration Stage—Substage Tentative
Task: Establishment in High School

P-R-I-D-E	*Program Activities*	*G-I-V-E*
P	1. Each student develops a four-year course outline: Students learn and discuss probable outcomes as they relate to different choices; learn what choices leave most options open; relate their personal interests to specific curriculum options; learn how choices fit into life planning.	V/G
D	2. Students participate in decision-making exercises to build proficiency in the choice process. These can be small, classroom groups facilitated by the teacher in conjunction with the coun-	V/G

P-R-I-D-E	*Program Activities*	*G-I-V-E*
	seling department. The *Deciding* materials published by the College Board are used.	
I/E	3. Students begin to learn a repertoire of information-seeking behavior through assignments involving the use of resources in the library and the career-college center. The classroom teachers assign mini-exercises in which students research information on careers as it relates to specific academic and vocational subjects.	G/I/V
R	4. Students learn school-coping skills, including study skills, effective classroom behavior, assertive behavior, and organizational skills. Students participate in small groups taken out of study hall.	G/E

Overview

P/R/I/D/E	5. Each student participates in an individual session that takes place in the career-college center, tentatively focusing on personal choices. Check on the student's ability to access career-college information from the center. Review choices made on the Four-Year Course Outline in view of changes that may have occurred through maturation or learning. This session is conducted by the student's teacher-adviser.	I/V

Grade 10
Exploration Stage—Substage Tentative
Task: Exploring Options for the Future

P-R-I-D-E	*Program Activities*	*G-I-V-E*
P	1. Students participate in groups, using a value-clarification approach to begin	G/V

P-R-I-D-E	*Program Activities*	*G-I-V-E*

	to develop a conscious awareness of a value system. Students learn through discussion how values are related to subsequent life and career choices.	
D	2. Students continue to learn about and practice decision-making skills through classroom or teacher- or counselor-led groups using the College Board *Decisions and Outcomes* program.	G/V
E	3. Students can further explore their personal interests as they relate to careers through use of the Holland Self-Directed Search, the Strong-Campbell, the Kuder revised, and so forth. Tests are readily available to students in the career center, administered by the center's paraprofessional and interpreted by the counselor when appropriate.	I/V
I	4. Large informational group session(s) give an overview of the post-high school options available. A panel of past graduates and/or college representatives presents each option (four-year colleges, vocational-technical schools, two-year colleges, immediate employment, and so forth). Students are given a statistical and descriptive breakdown of the choices of recent graduates, CEEB and ACT test information and dates, and other locally developed materials.	G/V
R	5. Students can participate in trial work experiences for high school credit through Community Service Volunteer Projects coordinated by a high school counselor.	V

P-R-I-D-E	*Program Activities*	*G-I-V-E*
Overview		
P/R/I/D/E	6. Each student participates in an individual counseling session to synthesize the information acquired so far. Tentative directions are set. Again the conference takes place in the career-college center; the four-year plan is reviewed and updated. Students meet in this session with their teacher-advisers. After this session, there will be a transition from teacher-adviser to exclusive use of a counselor for the remaining two years.	I/V

Grade 11
Exploration Stage—Substage Tentative
Task: Exploring College Preferences

P-R-I-D-E	*Program Activities*	*G-I-V-E*
I	1. Students acquire more information about various colleges from the following outside activities: visits with college representatives who come to the school; attendance at local college fairs; college visits; discussions with alumni, parents, other students; and so forth.	V
P	2. Students attend large informational group session(s), where they receive an overview of the tasks to be accomplished in grade 11. The tasks and a proposed timetable, including college entrance tests and dates, should be given in handout form to each student (see Barre, n.d.).	G
P	3. Students participate by choice in group	G/E

P-R-I-D-E	*Program Activities*	*G-I-V-E*
	preparation sessions for the PSAT. A four-session mini-course led by the counselor and using math and English teachers covers how to take a standardized test, directions and scoring, practice tests, and specific question types used on the verbal and math sections. Materials used are predominantly those readily available through the ETS and ACT testing companies.	
P/R/I/D/E	4. Each student participates in a family conference midyear, bringing together the student's parents, counselor, and teachers or teacher/adviser (if appropriate). The counselor provides an agenda and guidelines for the conference, although the student actually takes the lead in explaining what phase she or he is in in regard to the college-career-choice process. Parents give input as to limitations, financial considerations, and so forth.	E
E	5. Students are encouraged to use, through school news articles and other advertising, the resources of the career-college center, college catalogues, college handbooks, specific school brochures, and books such as *Playing the Private College Admissions Game* (Moll, 1979), *Insider's Guide* (Yale Daily News, 1978), and *I Can Be Anything* (Mitchell, 1978). All books should be available in the center for overnight checkout.	I
R	6. Interested students can participate in a work-experience program, including volunteer work, paid employment,	V

P-R-I-D-E	*Program Activities*	*G-I-V-E*
	and "shadow" experience. Students are encouraged to follow and "try out" a specific career or subject-matter interest. Most of such a program is coordinated by an experiential education teacher, although the counselor may plan the shadow experience.	
I/E	7. Each junior has an individual conference with the counselor, utilizing the college-career computer search system (Guidance Information Service or some similar program). Students tentatively select location, college major, costs, college size, and so forth, and receive a computerized printout of specific colleges that meet their requirements.	I/E

Grade 12
Exploration Stage—Substage Tentative
Task: Crystallizing a College Choice

P-R-I-D-E	*Program Activities*	*G-I-V-E*
P/R/I/D/E	1. Students are encouraged to choose four other students with whom they can work in a group (a buddy system approach) to crystallize and specify college choice. Discussion groups are sometimes counselor led, sometimes student led, and are a continuation of self-assessment of values, interests, and needs. Labor market, occupational trends, and the economic perspective are important discussion topics.	G/E
E	2. Students continue to visit college campuses, meet with representatives and alumni, read brochures, send for applications, and share their findings in their small groups.	G

P-R-I-D-E	*Program Activities*	*G-I-V-E*
I	3. Small groups can also be used by the counselor to convey information regarding testing, the application process and timetables, financial aid, and so on.	G/E
D	4. Students begin filling out applications with group support. (Group members do not necessarily proceed on the same timetable.)	G
R	5. Students practice job and/or college interviewing in the small groups. The counselor can provide videotape equipment, modeling, and the sources of information on good interviewing technique.	G
P/R/I/D/E	6. Students are encouraged to explore the relationship between sex roles and the occupational structure, how the social structure supports certain kinds of decisions by certain classes of people, and how the socialization process affects college and career choices for women and minorities. A ten-session counselor-led discussion group is offered at CHS to explore nontraditional career options for women. Materials are available from the Math and Science Education Program for Women, c/o Nancy Kreinberg, Lawrence Hall of Science, Berkeley, Calif., 94720.	G/E
R	7. Students are encouraged to participate in trial work experiences.	V
R	8. Provide placement services for those students not choosing a postsecondary educational experience. A school youth employment service run by parents may be useful for fulfilling this goal.	V

Summary

The model presented here presupposes that the counselor has access to a variety of ancillary personnel, including paid staff professionals and paraprofessionals and nonpaid individuals, including parents. In this respect, the model's very functioning and eventual effectiveness depend on the counselor's ability to go beyond personal resources and organize a team of support staff, with the counselor serving as coordinator. In a comprehensive, developmental model such as this one, the number of tasks is simply too great to be effectively discharged by any one person. Without the use of teacher-advisers, parents, paraprofessional career center workers, and other classroom teachers, such a program is impossible. The counselor must be willing to accept the idea that many people within the system possess "advising-counseling" skills aside from the professionally trained counselor and then must be willing to use such talent creatively.

Counselors who consider using this program should take into account both the student population upon which the program was developed and for whom it is geared and the community as a whole. Methods of facilitating college and career choice vary a great deal from community to community and from one geographical region to the next. For instance, because the majority of California college-bound students choose to remain in that state because of its comprehensive system of public and private colleges, college choice there may involve a less intense procedure, given the drastically reduced number of options to be considered.

This program was developed for students whose range of options is nationwide and whose choices are not drastically narrowed by financial limitations. Thus, the student from a less fortunate economic group than the middle- to upper-middle-class group upon which the program was developed may have his choices limited to a few state institutions. However, even in these two cases, there remains *some* choice or decision to be made, although limited, that may indeed still be enhanced by limited use of a program such as the one presented here. Indeed, in a career/work-oriented community, one can simply replace the word "college" where it appears in the text with the word "career." Thus, visits to college campuses could be replaced by visits to various work sites under consideration by the student.

Another consideration pertains to the "political" aspects of such a program, including parental and community pressure to make certain kinds of choices and decisions. Would such a program emphasizing college choice escalate the already present pressure among upper-middle-class children to choose the socially "correct" alternative, often eliminating the choice of immediate employment or pushing the New England Ivies and their equivalents as the only suitable measure of success? On the contrary, the counselor who is aware of such pressures can be an active modifying force in such a situation. Parents often need to be reminded that the student must take responsibility for the college choice and that any attempt to coerce or pressure the student in a certain direction frequently leads to unhappiness. Parents can often be persuaded to back off, but the student has a difficult time becoming untangled from family background and values that have been assimilated over time. Helping the student define personal values, preferences, and individual interests and developing a strong sense of personal identity is the key to modifying such pressures and crucial to the program's effectiveness.

Counselors must model genuine acceptance and approval for all types of career and college choices and actively encourage students to investigate a range of alternatives. Adolescents face intense pressure to make career and college choices. This program lessens the ambivalence, ignorance, and misinformation that leads to poor decision making and increases good and appropriate decisions by emphasizing direct teaching of decision-making skills. Furthermore, counselors in this model can help students face pressures that exist, analyze them, and become consciously aware of them. For example, women as a group have traditionally been politically pressured to accept certain career choices. In this model, women are encouraged to participate in a group-counseling situation that analyzes the antecedents and results of such narrowly defined choice and to look at nontraditional options.

In short, this model is part of a proactive, preventive

mental health program that encourages intelligent and thoughtful life choices. It uses as a framework Super's theoretical model of decision making and career development as a means of ordering, organizing, categorizing, and choosing appropriate tasks to fit various stages of development in students in grades 9 through 12. The program's greatest shortcoming may be its comprehensiveness, which some might find overwhelming. A counselor must possess both excellent organizational and communication skills to make the program work effectively.

16

Building Support
for Specific Student
Populations

Jack L. Wright

Regardless of the number of students sent on to postsecondary institutions, an injustice occurs if the academic standards at the secondary school do not equip those students with survival skills. Inner-city high schools are often beset by grade inflation, an ineffective faculty, and students who mark time. In many instances the curriculum has been diluted, and advanced college-preparation subjects have been curtailed as a result of faculty frustration and feelings of academic despair. What is the professional counselor to do in this situation?

I have been a member of the faculty of Franklin High School, part of the Los Angeles School District, for the past fourteen years, and I have witnessed the evolution of the student population from predominantly Anglo American to 84 percent minority, of which 70 percent are of Hispanic origin, primarily Mexican American. Throughout this period, conscious efforts have been made to prevent loss of academic credibility. Much of the credit for these efforts goes to the faculty and administration, who have kept avenues of communication open, thus curtailing the loss of academic status and enriching the curriculum with advanced college preparation. As a result, a much larger percentage of students today are going on to advanced education than when the school was predominantly Anglo American.

My full-time college and financial aid position is unusual in the counseling profession. Yet it is clearly justifiable in terms of the tangible results produced each year. Other schools can create an effective program that will act as a bridge for every student who leaves high school and chooses a goal in life that demands continued education.

Prerequisites for Counseling

The key to maintaining the academic standards in an enriched curriculum is, of course, set by the principal and the department chairpersons. In addition, a stable and supportive faculty is necessary to maintain the continuity of a curriculum as faculty attitudes toward teaching their particular subjects change. Franklin High School today continues to have a very stable faculty of nearly 100 persons, to which only four or five new members are added each year. Furthermore, the counseling and pupil personnel services at Franklin are far more extensive than the minimum standards set by the Los Angeles Board of Education. For a school enrollment of 2,300, there are six full-time grade counselors, one head counselor, one dean in charge of attendance, and two deans in charge of discipline and pupil-related concerns. These positions are further supported by a half-time work-experience coordinator, a part-time English as a Second Language (ESL) counselor, a full-time career adviser, and myself, a full-time college counselor. Nonclassroom teaching personnel also work hard to ensure that the academically able students are programmed correctly into key prerequisite subjects, so that advanced courses, such as calculus, advanced placement biology, physics, and advanced languages, maintain adequate enrollments to justify the assignment of teachers to classes.

In addition to skilled personnel, maintaining academic standards requires a variety of approaches that will sensitize the community and the student body to the importance of prolonged academic study and, in turn, allow individual students access to a variety of colleges and universities. For the past ten years, I have devoted my energies to the processes of college admissions and financial aid. As a result, today 79 percent of Franklin graduates are attending postsecondary institutions. Of this number, approximately 50 percent are in four-year institutions, including Ivy League schools, and the other 50 percent are attending community colleges or proprietary schools.

The image an inner-city school presents to its community is of foremost importance. Gang violence, graffiti, and student futility degrade the image of the low-income, minority-neighborhood school. Having a positive college advisement program can, in large part, turn around this image and create a high degree of optimism and pride within the community. The college advisement program can produce a continuum of events that, when made known through the media to the community, foster a positive attitude which encourages academic enhancement and individual student success. Heightened student expectation leads to greater effort to achieve a satisfactory background in preparation for going to college.

The college advisement program requires expenditures for supplies, physical facilities, and released time. First, there must be budget allocation for nonconsumable supplies, such as references relating to college admissions and financial aid and handbooks on such subjects as SAT preparation. The onslaught of material received from postsecondary institutions, including pamphlets, catalogues, brochures, and numerous miscellany from departments, has to be uniformly and intelligently filed or stored for students to be able to use them. This demands finances for appropriate storage facilities. (Bookcases are not suited for filing or storage; I have found that all the miscellaneous material for one college or system fits nicely into a four-inch tote tray, which allows students to sit down with all the collected material at their disposal.) Other budget items might include cassette recorders, typewriter(s), video cassette players, and an adequate paper supply for the counselor to produce newsletters throughout the school year.

Released time for college advisers is of prime importance to allow them to comprehend current developments in college admissions, financial aid, and the transition to postsecondary education. Little in college or graduate school prepares people to become college advisers, so learning must be done on the job. Unless the advisers have the opportunity to attend a variety of workshops and sessions throughout the school year, their advisement programs will inadequately inform fellow faculty and the student bodies of current developments and forthcoming concerns. If college advisers are functioning full time, no substitute personnel are required in their absence, and it is much easier for them to attend conferences throughout the year. Some of these conferences require an extensive budget to pay for transportation, board, and room. For college advisers to be effective, they must be encouraged and supported in their pursuit of knowledge and information.

Creating Motivation

Junior High School Articulation (Grade 9). It is vitally important that students and parents at the junior high school level be made aware of the postsecondary requirements for admission and financial aid. The requirements for admission to universities, both public and private, are sometimes very confusing. Thus, an effort must be made to enlighten not only the students and parents in the feeder junior high schools, but also their counseling staff, who have the initial responsibility of guiding the student toward college preparation in high school.

For several years, I have had the opportunity to present an evening workshop for ninth-grade students from Franklin's feeder junior high campuses. I strongly encourage parents and students to attend this session together, since they both stand to benefit from the information I present regarding the work load ahead and the need for providing adequate time and facilities for homework. The presentation precedes the time when the Franklin counselors sit down with the students to select their tenth-grade programs. During these evening presentations, my information is divided into two portions: college admissions and financial aid. To communicate with parents, I have found it necessary to have the presentation translated into several different languages. A special grant pays translators who are present, and the receptive parents are given audio devices.

At the presentation, I hand out a form to each parent and student, depicting the requirements for a high school diploma. The form permits the student to list the subjects that he hopes to complete each semester for the next three years. Next I define the details of the admissions requirements of the four California postsecondary segments. I pass out individual information for each segment, explaining the GPA, admissions test, and curriculum requirements unique to each segment. (These four segments are the community colleges, California state universities and colleges, the University of California, and independent colleges in California as well as selected eastern colleges.) This occasion gives me an opportunity to explain that students should carry a minimum of four academic solids each semester when possible and that they can continue their education in a variety of summer school programs at neighboring colleges and universities, as well as in special summer programs at eastern prep schools such as Phillips Academy. Because earlier Franklin graduates have done well, it is now rather easy to excite and motivate the ninth-grade students. Also, this program lets parents know that summer vacations need to be planned around their son's or daughter's summer school experience so as not to curtail their opportunity for enrichment programs. The fact that competitive universities seek out students with unique experiences is vividly portrayed. Thus, the underlying importance of students' taking advantage of special opportunities in the summer is widely accepted in the community around Franklin.

The second portion of the evening program at the junior high school level is directed toward providing the parents with knowledge of financial aid. Typically, minority inner-city low-income parents fear the expense involved in sending their children to college. For years the idea of the student's immediately going to work after high school to help support the family has been a traditional pattern. Thus, it is necessary to overcome parental anxiety regarding the expense of a college education. Detailed information must be presented to both the parent and the student about the various financial programs available from federal, state, and institutional resources. The College Scholarship Service publication *Meeting College Costs* enables parents to calculate their net worth and annual income, thereby arriving at the parental contribution figure, which often is under $500 per year. At this point, I stress that it is perhaps cheaper to let the student leave home and go to college than to maintain her residence within the family. I give several examples of the packaging philosophy of various colleges, and the parent and student may for the first time begin to see the opportunity to acquire an education at even an expensive private university.

The presenter must project an attitude of sincerity. To convince her audience, she must believe what she says. This workshop provides the opportunity for the college adviser to be observed, evaluated, and known by her future constituency. She must create an open and friendly atmosphere to welcome parent participation.

Grade 10 Guidance. Franklin High School provides a ten-week guidance course, which every tenth grader is required to take. The program includes a number of guest speakers from various departments and specialized counselors. I use this opportunity to remind students of requirements for the high school diploma by having each student fill out a detailed form that lists all his subjects to be completed in high school. I repeat the unique requirements of each postsecondary segment in detail. Additionally, I describe the financial aid opportunities for which there are specific requirements, to guide the students toward their individual financial aid opportunities.

Franklin High School has a diverse student body; immigrants from seventy countries are represented. English is often their second language. I have attempted to capitalize on their aptitudes by administering language-proficiency tests in twelve languages, sometimes through a cooperative college or university that will either administer the test to my students or ask me to administer the test and return it to the campus for evaluation. Also, I use the language achievement tests of the College Entrance Examination Board when appropriate, and our Spanish department gives students a proficiency test, by which two years of a foreign language can be evaluated. If the student proves his competency, the language is entered on the cumulative record with a grade and credit to allow the college or university to assess this proficiency when determining admission status. A student's demonstrated proficiency in a foreign language gives him more time to take the additional English electives so vitally important for his college success.

Grade 11 Counseling. The junior year is very important. Students crystallize their direction and embrace goals that entail postsecondary education. Students know how much effort they must expend and how much homework they must do to succeed in a vigorous college-preparatory program, and within this program some students demonstrate abilities which pronounce that for them supportive counseling can be most productive.

I view the Preliminary Scholastic Aptitude Test (PSAT) as a crucial experience in the grooming process for college admission. Thus, I take the time to visit each United States history class, in which all eleventh graders are enrolled, to explain the experience and benefits to be derived. (Franklin High School is a PSAT test center; thus, the anxiety level experienced by students is somewhat less than if they were forced to go to an unfamiliar test center. Additionally, I fortunately have a sufficient number of fee waivers to cover the cost for students from low-income families.)

The 150 PSAT test takers receive much attention as they plan for their senior year. Their grade point averages are calculated at the end of the fifth semester, and two lists are prepared, alphabetical and by rank. Each student is summoned for a conference during the school day. During the conference, a series of events occur. On the basis of the student's cumulative record, the likelihood of his being admitted to various colleges is evaluated, and the need to maintain or exert a greater effort to improve the GPA is emphasized. This conference is also an opportunity to find an appropriate summer school experience that will enable students to continue their educational journey. Often this involves going to selective preparatory schools or to special programs offered by colleges and universities throughout the state. The conference is also an excellent opportunity to encourage students to raise their level of aspiration in setting goals and choosing among colleges. As a general principle, I encourage students to attend the most selective university they can be admitted to.

In April I again visit all United States history classes, to hand out the applications for the June SAT or ACT examinations. Franklin High School is a test center for the SAT in the month of June, and students are strongly encouraged to participate. Without students' SAT scores, the counselor is handicapped in recommending to students which colleges and universities are appropriate for application. Also, if the student is disappointed with her scores, she has the opportunity to repeat the entrance examination in the fall of the senior year. Although there are approximately 150 juniors who take the PSAT, in excess of 250 will have taken the SAT before the senior year ends. Again, I have an adequate number of fee waivers to defray the cost of the examination. Each student is provided one fee waiver during the high school experience, provided he meets the financial criteria established by the College Board. Repetition of a test is at the student's expense.

Grade 12 Counseling. The senior year is very intensive if the student is to attend the college of his choice and have sufficient financial aid to provide freedom to choose it. Prior to the opening of school, the grade point averages are hand-calculated, and alphabetical and rank lists are created. On the first day of school, when students receive their schedule of classes, they also receive their first college newsletter, with her or his name and GPA attached on a label. This newsletter sets the tone for the opening months of school by explaining dates, deadlines, and applications procedures. During the course of the year, there will be an additional ten to twelve newsletters. These newsletters keep the student informed of important dates and deadlines of various programs and report a schedule of the college representatives visiting Franklin High School. Frequent public address announcements are made to highlight the events of each day and any impending deadlines. This communication not only helps the seniors in promoting timeliness but also serves as an indoctrination process for the tenth and eleventh graders, who become fully aware of the scope of the college advisement program.

Attached to the first college newsletter is a "family and activity information sheet," which is used for the initial conferences for seniors between a 4.0 and 3.0 GPA. As these forms are returned to my office, students are summoned out of class to plan their college selections. At that meeting, I recommend repeating a college entrance examination if I deem that useful, and I further analyze the student's cumulative record to suggest colleges or universities at which enrollment might become a possibility. About the third or fourth week, these information sheets are also delivered to seniors with GPAs of 2.99 to 2.50. Those below 2.50 also receive them on request. The process that leads to college enrollment continues month by month thereafter.

October. The month of October is a continuation of individual conferences regarding college selection. Also, the college representative visiting schedule is well under way; during the course of the year, about eighty colleges and universities will have been presented. Prior to the November application period, the English department cooperates by asking each senior to write a personal essay as a classroom assignment. This task is taken seriously because the essays are returned to the student for corrections, together with suggestions for more comprehensiveness.

Ideally, October is a good month to arrange college tours. A number of colleges in the San Francisco area have provided a charter bus every other year; I have taken forty-two students on a three-night, four-day tour of six to eight universities. The admissions personnel most generously provide meals and lodging accommodations. Also, my former students are very anxious to share their experiences of a particular college with my visiting seniors. In many instances, this experience bridges the gap between the high school and the vague image of a particular college or university. The students selected for this tour are those who have exhibited a strong college-preparation background and expressed an interest in one or more of the colleges included on the tour.

November. November of the senior year is traditionally the college application month. On the average, each college-

bound senior will apply to 1.7 colleges. Thus, my students greatly appreciate the College Board application fee-waiver program.
Since the average income for parents in my community is below
$10,000, many of my students qualify for applying to a college
or university for only the price of a postage stamp.

Because of the dwindling number of college-age applicants as compared to a few years ago, it is not as crucial to file
an application in the month of November, except for impacted
programs. However, I urge students to complete the application
process then, because December and January will be devoted
primarily to financial aid applications.

College recommendation letter writing is a key element
to the success of placing inner-city, low-income minority students in colleges and universities. More often than not, the students have been faced with a variety of obstacles throughout
their lives that have prevented them from achieving their full
potential. My students are given appointments for after 3:00
P.M., when an in-depth interview can proceed without interruption. This interview enables students to express themselves
fully: family experiences, aspirations, hobbies, and general
goals. This information is written up in an extensive descriptive
letter sent to admissions officers, giving them the opportunity
to understand the total educational experience of applicants
within the framework of their family, school, and community.

December. December is devoted to the financial aid process, for which workshops are set up to accommodate a maximum of forty students per day. Students are released from
classes for a 2½-hour workshop. As the financial aid application
is explained, a flowchart is used to clarify the various steps of
the analysis process and the packaging philosophy used to meet
the student's financial need. The Financial Aid Form (SAAC in
California) is explained item by item, so that the students will
be able to fill out the form with minimal parental assistance. In
addition, the grant supplements for the California Student Aid
Commission are completed, collected, and *sent by registered
mail.* (This ensures that each senior who has any possibility of
receiving a California grant has applied and completed the process.) Those students who have not appeared in a workshop are

identified and summoned individually and given intensive assistance in filling out the forms. I find this technique necessary because often students are much stronger candidates than they believe themselves to be. As a result of this positive reinforcement, these students also qualify for financial assistance.

January. January is the ideal time to focus on the students who should repeat college admissions tests or take the achievement tests. The college visiting program continues on daily.

A crucial service provided by Franklin High School is a financial aid workshop for parents. Each year a Saturday is devoted to a morning and afternoon workshop in the school library. This workshop includes an explanation of the financial aid process and the underlying importance of parents' completing the FAF on time and accurately. Since the parents bring with them their W-2 forms and a current 1040 (or last year's form), I am able, with the assistance of volunteer staff from neighboring colleges, to give individual attention to each parent in completing the financial aid form accurately. After the form has been checked for completeness, a Xerox copy is given to each parent, as a referral source in succeeding years when the process must be repeated.

February. At the end of the fall semester, the GPA and class rank list must be recomputed, to provide colleges with supplementary and seventh-semester transcripts. I find it crucial that this exercise be completed promptly because it allows my students to be admitted earlier. Also, the students will receive attention earlier from the financial aid office, which may be able to provide a financial aid package with more generous proportions of grant money. This will enable the student to make a college selection after receiving fully comparable information about financial aid packages by the May 1 Candidates' Reply Date. Unfortunately, the U.S. Department of Education has complicated this procedure for many colleges and universities, and as a result they are often late in sending their award letters. I must often intervene to urge a college to provide a financial aid offer in advance of their normal announcement process.

March. March offers flexibility; a variety of activities can be implemented. Time and opportunity allow visiting many college campuses. Students are strongly encouraged to investigate their college choices before they reach their final decision to accept the offer of admission.

March also allows time for searching out the senior class for "late bloomers" and shy, retiring students who have not applied for admission to any college. In many cases, such students are most anxious to prepare for their postsecondary experience but have not felt secure enough to decide.

April. Community college representatives are present on various days to explain their programs and hand out applications. There are four major community colleges in which my students who will not be going to a traditional university show primary interest. These students are later followed up by a college peer counselor to choose curriculum and arrange scheduling and to make plans for a successful experience. Often students who choose to go to a community college are less capable academically and therefore need much additional support and direction.

April is also the month for the big decision process of choosing the appropriate college. This involves comparing the opportunities colleges provide as well as financial aid packages.

May. May involves the responsibility of pacifying anxious seniors who have not received a decision from a particular college; this month is also dominated by the arrival of college financial aid letters and grants from the California Student Aid Commission. Consultation with each individual student about the awards is necessary. Often the students win multiple grants, only one of which can be retained. The counselor must consult with both the college and the student to secure the student's four-year financial future.

May is also the time when most community-based service groups present their applications for scholarships. Appropriate procedures and schedules are presented in the college newsletter to ensure that I receive applications and recommendation letters on time.

June. June is the month to show the year's results. For the last ten years, I have conducted an awards program, divided into two portions. The first part recognizes students who have made outstanding achievements in various departments, not only seniors but also outstanding tenth and eleventh graders. The second portion of the program recognizes students who have won competitive grants and scholarships or who have received financial award letters from the college they plan to attend. (Students who merely receive Pell Grants are not included in this program because the large number of recipients would extend the awards program beyond the point of the audience's endurance; see Chapter Twelve.) Usually, two thirds of the graduating seniors will have accumulated grants and scholarships exceeding $1.5 million when renewed over a four-year period. This awards program is enhanced by many leaders from the community, who present awards from their service groups. A photographer takes pictures of each recipient who receives an award; the pictures are then published in the local community newspaper.

The other essential activity for June is the collection of a survey card that indicates the institution to which the final transcripts are to be sent for the college-bound students. The non-college-bound students are also able to indicate their career interest, such as military service or employment. When the results of this survey are compared each succeeding year, the school can evaluate the trends and effectiveness of the college advisement program.

Program Support

The college advisement program at Franklin High School could not succeed without the cooperative efforts of many institutions and personnel. My program is provided with a secretary three hours per day; her primary responsibilities are to transcribe correspondence and type recommendation letters. About eighty hours per week of counselor support time come from peer counselors, selected seniors with an interest in the counseling profession. These peer counselors help students fill out routine forms and unravel the complexities of finding information in college catalogues. A parent volunteer works approxi-

mately twenty hours per week, typing bulletins and helping
students complete a variety of forms. Several colleges provide
me with help from students receiving funds through the College
Work-Study Program; these students work from fifteen to thirty
hours per week under my direction. They are given direct responsibilities for following up students who apply to popular
universities, and they often hand-deliver applications and transcripts to the admissions office. In addition, I have created a
relationship with a neighboring college, whose staff suggest that
upper-division students seek me out for independent study to
explore their desires to enter the counseling profession. The students are very eager to understand every area of the college advisement program, and in turn they become very effective in
working with prospective college applicants.

The support program is an essential ingredient in the successful delivery of a college advisement program. If the college
adviser is to be able to go to conferences and meet with representatives from various institutions, the office must be staffed
by competent personnel who can continue to meet the students' needs. Additionally, I have found that peer counselors
are important role models; their age and bilingual and bicultural
backgrounds are definite assets in fulfilling the needs of a variety of minority students.

A successful college advisement program involves work
and the ability to coordinate many facets. The needs of students cannot be met between eight and three o'clock. Only an
extended effort to meet the multiple needs of an inner-city minority population will create a positive environment for the
academic enhancement that leads to future success.

ᔥ *17*

Utilizing a Group Approach to Help Students Plan for College or Career

Betty Schneider

ᔥ　　　In the variety of schools in which I have worked, a group approach to giving college and career information has theoretically seemed the best method. In actuality, I have often found it difficult to implement. In the inner-city school, finding time to meet with each senior once during the final year was often a very hard-to-reach goal. In the comprehensive high school, with a large percentage of students going on to college, helping highly motivated students and their parents and others whose needs were often greater seemed to eat up most of the counseling time. In the private, college preparatory school in which I now work, organizing a plan that reaches all students, many of whom have a time commitment to credit classes and prefer individual attention, is not easy, necessary as it may be.

　　　Consequently, we have developed a flexible, simple plan, gleaned from experience, many fellow counselors, and a number of more elaborate readymade programs. Knowing the frustrations a counselor faces with lack of time, the monotony of one-to-one repetition, and the uneasiness of a job not fully completed, I present the plan with hopes that you can gain a few ideas, cut them to size, and use them in the interest of your students. In our particular organizational configuration of three counselors—one for freshmen and juniors, another for sophomores and seniors, and a college counselor—responsibilities for groups lie with the class counselor and the college counselor. This adds ideas to the planning, greater ease in implementing the ideas, and opportunities for dividing a group when student interests seem to indicate such a need.

Preliminaries

The first hurdle is finding a time for groups of students to meet and making what is offered relevant enough for their use. We moved toward a solution by programming each junior and senior into a weekly workshop during a free period or a period at the beginning or end of the day—juniors winter quarter and seniors fall quarter. For the few students who could not arrange this, we offered a lunchtime workshop late in the week, giving students who might have missed any earlier session an opportunity to attend also. It is usually a relief to juniors, who have little free time, when they find that sessions are only for six weeks at the beginning of the winter quarter. Seniors, usually full of questions as they return to school in September, accept the sessions more easily when they find that the place for answers is the workshop held during the first weeks of school.

Junior meetings are announced and well advertised in a letter sent by the parent group to juniors and their parents during the Christmas holiday. The letter invites them to an evening meeting early in January to explain the school's part in career and college planning. With the letter, we send a succinct digest of facts to be presented. This past year, we used the NACAC *Guide to College Admissions* in preference to a homemade one because it was better and cheaper. To it we added our own personalized insert, giving test dates and bibliography. Our aim is to give a skeleton of necessary information to be discussed at the parents' meeting and then flesh out the material in the workshops. Moll's (1979) *Playing the Private College Admissions Game* and Sacks's (1978) "Bloody Monday: The Crisis of the High School Senior" are excellent sources of ideas for parent discussion.

Six Junior Workshop Meetings

With the structure set, sessions begin with students introducing themselves and noting where they are at this point in their post-high school planning. Then we begin a thorough discussion of college tests as one element of the student's profile, far from the most important element but given first because we have PSAT returns. In our school, all students take the PSAT, and students are encouraged to attend workshops because that is where they receive their scores. In other school situations, taking the PSAT may be the identifying criterion for the group's membership. An individual test plan for each student is encouraged, with the SAT, the ACT, Achievement Tests, and Advanced Placement Tests described and differentiated. The career-interest inventory is explained, and students are offered an opportunity to take the Kuder Occupational Interest Survey at a convenient time during the six-week period. That inventory has been particularly apt because it offers both college majors and occupational choices related to students' interests. This coming year, we intend to try the Strong-Campbell Interest Inventory as well. If there is time, the first session concludes with a buzz group session, whereby groups list the three most important questions they want answered during the five remaining sessions.

A Questionnaire. Session 2 is devoted to the student profile as perceived through school and community activities. It concentrates on filling out what we call the Junior Questionnaire (see sample at end of the chapter). In addition, we stress the need for an individual interview with the college counselor at some time before June. Questionnaires are collected and placed in the student file, to be completed at the time of the interview. Volunteers are then chosen for a mock interview between a "college admissions counselor" and a student that will occur at the third meeting. An excerpt from an old but very good book, *Choosing a College* (Hoy, 1970, pp. 135-137), which lists questions collected from a group of admissions counselors, is given to the volunteers to help them in their presentation. This reprint is often sought by seniors as they are going to college interviews.

The role-playing interview takes up the third session. Students learn how the interview applies to the school conferences, college days, visits to colleges, and any other college contacts. There have been times when a willing college admissions counselor visiting our school has been encouraged to join one of the groups, much to our benefit.

Making college choices is the theme of sessions 4 and 5. First a brainstorming technique is defined (Gelatt and others, 1979, p. 30); the technique is then used to list on a blackboard all the things the students might want to know about a college. This is followed by having each student make a forced choice of his first priority. Then we devote time to directories, major guides, catalogues, parents, teachers, and other students as sources for finding this information. We stress the student as consumer and the kinds of information students need to gain, and we discuss access, process, and result as outlined by Hoy (1976, p. 9) in "A Question of Balance."

Personalized sources we developed that have become particularly useful are:

- A college conference book, with forms completed at the time a representative visits our school.
- A college-choice book, listing colleges and the students who have attended them in past years.
- A college questionnaire book, compiled from questionnaires sent to graduates at the end of their freshman year of college. (A sample is included at the end of the chapter.)

Individual computer programs using the National Association of College Admissions Counselors NACACtion Service are prepared at the fifth meeting. Each student is given *Time Share: The Guidance Information System Guide* (1979) and a program sheet and helped to select qualities desired in the colleges being applied to. The College 4, College 2, or Occupational Information computer bank can be used, depending on the student's preference. Programs are placed in the student's file, and students are told that they will be processed at the time of the individual interview. This gives opportunities for later changes and makes the plan workable, since thirty-five programs can be processed through the NACAC computer per month. Student participation is encouraged because the junior questionnaire must be prepared before a student is interviewed, and participation is increased as printouts are returned and students display them to classmates.

A wrap-up session concludes the meetings. Career inventories are returned, briefly discussed, and related to career materials available at the college and career center. Questions on financial aid are answered briefly, and students are told that this matter will be dealt with thoroughly in senior meetings. We teach students to pace themselves through the process of decision and application.

Nothing is dealt with in depth, and many questions remain unanswered, but students gain cursory knowledge of where and how to get help from counselors, reference sources, parents, teachers, and, more importantly, other students.

The Senior Workshop Plan

Senior sessions, which usually begin the first week of school, are even more task-oriented. At the first meeting, students are given copies of their three-year transcript with their grade point average. Students must check their transcripts by correcting errors, counting credits, and reviewing requirements. Buzz group sessions to list the three most important concerns to be dealt with in following meetings conclude the first meeting.

Session 2 concentrates on the actual application process. We project three types of applications: a state university form, the Common Application, and an application to a most competitive college. We emphasize timing, the etiquette of asking for teacher recommendations, what the counseling offices send to colleges, and what the student must take responsibility for. We tell how to get information on auditions, portfolios, and other materials. Each student is given a copy of the NACAC

Statement of Students' Rights and Responsibilities in the College Admissions Process (National Association of College Admissions Counselors, 1978).

The personal statement is the main topic of session 3. Samples of different types of statements are read (again, we find Hoy very useful), and self-descriptions of National Merit and National Achievement Scholars of previous years, copied with their permission, are analyzed. A bulletin board with sample statements draws much attention. The final week brings questions about financial aid and no-need scholarships as well as the unanswered questions students have listed early in the sessions. An evaluative questionnaire filled out at the end of the period has helped us revise plans year by year. Our students generally prefer discussion to any audiovisual materials we have used; they have disliked quizzes we have given them on, for example, the college admissions alphabet. They constantly seek more help in choosing colleges and timing themselves in the process.

Concluding Notes

While we pursue this plan, I take time away from my desk each week all through the year to write student descriptions. One morning a week is my aim; the time sometimes comes in two-period sections. In early February, as junior interviews begin, I start rough drafts of descriptions and place them in the student file. From September through January, I concentrate on seniors.

The plan does not work perfectly. Students do cut workshop sessions, but their participation is encouraged by the fact that the tasks of the workshop and involvement in them relate to profile materials that are later sent to colleges. Not all parents attend evening meetings, but they do receive pertinent information on the whole planning process, their cooperation is solicited, and they are invited to come in for advice and help if they want it. What happens in the workshops percolates through a class and helps even when participation is not 100 percent.

We will still have anxious times come April 15, and we will still have the stresses of taking tests and meeting deadlines, but their effects are often lessened because dialogue regarding them has been encouraged. Generally, our students seem to be making easier and better choices.

Junior Questionnaire

This questionnaire has two purposes. It attempts to give an idea of questions you might encounter on a college application; it also aims at getting information—confidential to counselors—that can be useful in writing good recommendations for colleges. We suggest a follow-up interview with the college counselor sometime during this spring.

Social Security # _____

1. Name _____ Age _____ Birthdate _____
    Name of years at Lab Schools _____ Place of birth _____
    Father's occupation _____
    School attended and degree _____
    Mother's occupation _____
    School attended and degree _____
    Name and grade levels or occupations of brothers and sisters:

    _____

    _____

    _____

    _____

    College entrance examinations you have taken so far: _____

    _____

    Do you plan to apply for financial aid? Yes ___ No ___
    Do you see yourself best suited by a college that is (circle those that apply):

    liberal arts   a university   a school of technology   other
    coeducational   men only   women only   urban   rural
    large (10,000 and over)   medium-sized (2,000-10,000)
    small (up to 2,000)   eastern   midwestern   southern   western
    in the Chicago area   in Illinois   far away from Chicago

If you are considering specific colleges, please name them.

2. At this time, what are your educational plans?
   What type of work do you eventually hope to do?

3. *In-school Activities*
   List school activities in which you have been involved, the years in which you have participated, and special responsibilities you have had. Comment on the honors that you have received through this activity or the activities most significant to you.

4. *Outside Activities*
   List the out-of-school activities you have had, including work experience, travel, lessons, clubs, hobbies, or anything else you feel would tend to get overlooked in the day-to-day life of school itself. Again, please mention any honors you have received because of your participation in these activities.

The following questions are *optional*. We think they will help you in your general plans for application to colleges. Also, they may give you a head start to answering similar questions on actual college application forms.

5. What are your favorite areas of study?
   Which do you like least?

6. If you have to decide to take a year off before attending college, how do you think you might like to spend the year?

7. Many college applications include some kind of "personal statement," whose aim is to enable the college to get to know you as well as possible through your application. To help you in your thinking about such a statement and to help us further personalize your applications to colleges, use the space below to write something you would like a college to know about you. Your description should emphasize how you think and feel and help distinguish you among a large group of applicants.

Questionnaire for College Student Graduates of U High*

Name of college _____

Your name _____

Address where you can be reached by students or counselor
    during the next school year _____

1. *Academic Information*
    Please list additional education you have had since leaving
    U High.
        Name of school _____
        Major field of interest _____
    How does the academic work compare to that at U High?
    More demanding ____ About the same ____
    Less demanding ____
    How has your academic record at college compared to your
    record at U High?
    Higher ____ Same ____ Lower ____
    Are there required courses for graduation? Yes ____ No ____
    Comment:
    Are you able to plan your own curriculum? Yes ____ No ____
    In order to obtain credit in the majority of your courses,
    do you take a final exam ____ write a paper ____ use other
    methods (explain) _____

    _____

    Do you have an option of pass-fail or grades? _____
    Are most of your classes conducted as lectures ____
    or discussions ____ ?
    Are most of your classes large (over 100) ____ small (25 or
    less) ____ or balanced between large and small ____ ?
    Would you say that the faculty is close to ____ removed from
    ____ the students?

*Adapted from a questionnaire used at Francis Parker School, Chicago.

Do you feel that the students are competitive academically?
Yes ___ No ___
How do you feel about competition? _____

_____

Are you getting needed help in major choice and career
planning? _____

2. *Housing Information*
Do you live in a dorm ___ apartment ___ fraternity or so-
rority house ___ ? Is your residence satisfactory?
Yes ___ No ___
Comment: _____

3. *Information on Campus Life*
What are the things about your life at college that you like
most? Social ___ Creative opportunities ___
Cultural ___ Academic ___ Personal ___ Other ___
Please explain: _____

_____

What are the things about your life at school that you like
least? Social ___ Creative opportunities ___
Cultural ___ Academic ___ Personal ___ Other ___
Please explain: _____

_____

Is there a sufficient variety of cultural events available on
the campus (theater, films, music, dance)? Yes ___
No ___
Are there creative activities available for participation (e.g.,
poetry workshops, free theater, dance troupe)?
Yes ___ No ___ Name a few: _____

_____

In your opinion, does the study body seem politically involved ___ or apathetic ___ ?
Are there political organizations on campus? _____

Do you get the impression that students are more concerned with internal campus affairs ___ or issues concerning the outside world ___ ?

4. *Pertinent Notes*

Are you considering transferring? Yes ___ No ___ . If yes, where and why? _____

Are you considering taking or have you taken a year off?

_____

In what areas would you suggest students seek more help while in high school?

_____ Academic preparation

_____ Career information and planning

_____ Specific information about college programs

_____ Specific information about college life

If you were choosing a college now, is this the type of college you would pick? Yes ___ No ___

Is this the college you would choose? Yes ___ No ___

What advice would you give to a Lab School student thinking about attending your school?

✍ *18*

Involving Families in College Selection

Helene Reynolds

✍   When college choice is seen as a process carried out in the larger context of family dynamics, it is surprising that high school counselors have given parents so little attention. They have done so for a number of reasons. Counselors want to keep the student in focus and to ensure that the process provides opportunity for fostering independence, responsibility, and maturity. Many counselors feel that including parents in the process implies that the student is not adult and thus invites the more experienced decision makers, the parents, to take over the responsibility of carrying out the task. Many counselors themselves are task oriented and see their main responsibility as getting a youngster into school; they do not focus on the journey to acceptance and on how a student learns the skills of decision making, which are essential to education and guidance. Counselors must also contend with the realities of too many students and too few hours to redefine the college guidance function in a broader context that stresses processes and individual growth.

But the college-choice process needs to move away from the view that it is simply goal oriented and student centered. Independence, responsibility, and maturity can best be encouraged by focusing on the process of choice and including the parents in the decision. It must be recognized that college choice is ultimately the student's but that the choice must be made within the context of family values, interests, limits, aspirations, and goals. Of what value is a student's decision if the "ideal college" eats into a parent's retirement or does not allow sufficient funds for a younger sister's or brother's education? How mature is the decision if it is made without considering the family's overall financial resources or the parents' concern that a college's demanding academic environment may jeopardize the student's poor health? How realistic is the decision if the student does not consider geographical limits set by the parents and will ultimately have the choice vetoed?

For many students, college choice is the first major activity recognized by the larger community as both adult and significant. For many parents, seeing a youngster through the college years is the accepted way of discharging the last parental obligation. A child's going off to college, leaving the comfortable surroundings of home and high school, relinquishing the security and advantages of dependence, trying on new and sophisticated attitudes among strangers in strange places are exciting, but awesome, experiences for both youngsters and parents to contemplate during the last years of high school.

For the traditional college-age population, college choice, then, is as much a rite of passage as it is finding a place to continue formal education. Like any transition, it offers expectation, excitement, and possibly anxiety. It highlights unfamiliar and ambivalent responses to new situations and represents a transformation of the family as a functioning unit. The college-choice process demands that parents and students respond to each other in new ways. When the process begins, the balance of family relationships and the traditional roles of parent and child are irrevocably altered. Every person in the family, not just the student, is involved in the choice and affected by it. Everyone seeks a new equilibrium in the family constellation, becomes preoccupied with the ways the decision will affect their personal lives, and feels somewhat at sea until a new pattern of family dynamics is established.

Mother may have to recognize that she is no longer essential as chief cook and bottle washer. Father will never again be able to set down all the rules. The fledgling freshman will never again be able to hide behind a facade of dependency in quite the same innocent manner. Even younger brothers and sisters are forced into viewing themselves differently and taking on new roles in the family when overnight they become the eldest or the only child. The absence of one member of the family may mean a scramble for different bedrooms, assignment of new chores, or more opportunity to use the telephone.

Reasons for Involving Parents

Even if we set aside the educational ideal that college guidance is an opportunity which can be directed toward easing a major family transition, there are other basic, more pragmatic reasons why parents need to be part of the decision-making process. Parents cannot be ignored even by those counselors who are more comfortable viewing college choice as goal oriented and student centered. Parents are part of the process, whether they are viewed as welcome participants or unnecessary roadblocks to sensible choices. The more a counselor can include the parents in the college search, the easier the student's job and the more realistic the basis for choice. There are three main reasons why parents should be involved.

First, and most obvious, is the reality that the bill for college education is usually paid by the parents, not the student. As wise consumers, parents must have the information and perspective they need to make this expensive purchase. Since virtually every aspect of financing higher education has changed in the last twenty years, including the acceptability to middle-class families of applying for financial aid, parents must be brought up to date regarding costs, procedures, government funding, and the responsibilities the youngster will incur in the financing process. The guidance office is the most logical place for parents' education to occur. Not only do counselors owe it to their schools and their clients to make financial counseling part of the regular program of college guidance, they owe it to the bill payer to provide the basis of a wise consumer investment—full information and an open forum to become familiar with it.

Second, in the generation schooled since the parents of today's college-bound students were in high school, the college admissions scene (and the college scene) have undergone radical changes. The procedures that today's students must follow to gain admission to college, the possibilities open to them in higher education, and even the new terminology (rolling admissions, mini-mester, "CLEP-ed credit") are significantly different from or foreign to the ones their parents experienced. Everyone concerned will suffer if families begin a college search while parents are guided principally by nostalgic memories and outdated information. Although in one respect the parents' personal experience may be a powerful and necessary lens through which the student can reflect and evaluate new information, in another respect parents must not be overly prejudiced by their limited perspectives. They must learn to look at admissions and college opportunity in the 1980s with information that is current, broad in scope, and often new. Again, the guidance office is the best place for this parent education to occur; it will ultimately save time and create a better learning environment for the student if the parents are educated along with the youngster.

Third, a number of studies confirm the parent as the single most important influence on a youngster's choice of higher education opportunity. Research by the College Entrance Examination Board places parents' influence ahead of that of peers, viewbooks, advertising gimmicks, former classmates, recent graduates, and certainly college counselors. If parents ultimately make the decision—tacitly or overtly—it is naive to keep them outside the counseling office. For the student's best interest, they must be part of a counseling dialogue from the start. Although the prospect of including parents may be less than pleasant because it does pose extra work for the counselor, there is no doubt that, for both educational concerns and pragmatic reasons, they should be included in the college-choice process.

Altering the present student-centered guidance procedures is a major challenge for the burdened counselor, who will look askance at the additional demand that the parents, indeed, the whole family, be served. But ultimately the student can best be served and the problems of choice resolved in the most straightforward manner if the context of family decision making is established from the start.

Principles for Counselors

High school counselors need to feel committed to a number of principles before they attempt a family-centered approach that will not sacrifice the student's autonomy and growing independence in the process.

First, they must define their major professional goal as counseling, not college placement. A counseling orientation allows the professional to concentrate on processes of growth, decision-making skills, and conflict resolutions, for example. It allows counselors to define their role as helping others make choices instead of creating lists of possible acceptances to the best schools. If high school counselors view their main function as college placement, the goal—selecting a school—is the focus rather than the journey toward that goal. The placement function as focus may steer counselors toward viewing their jobs as administrative and informational. Certainly, all college guidance counselors must balance the counseling and administrative functions, but the professional orientation must rest with the former.

Second, counselors must feel committed to developing their counseling skills, to allow for a wider range of opportunity for problem solving and conflict resolutions. College guidance is a unique profession because it demands that the counselor have ready a vast store of information on programs, financial aid, testing, and careers. For students to use information wisely and appropriately, counselors must be able to recognize both when a student is ready for the facts and figures and how new information will affect the decision-making process. Counselors need to be familiar with group counseling processes and the variety of therapeutic models that were developed by experts such as Virginia Satir (1967; Satir and others, 1976) for work with families in crises and that have been adopted for use in nontherapeutic situations.

Third, counselors need to feel committed to articulating

their philosophy to the school community. Most likely, students, faculty, and administrators will accept a broader definition of college guidance if the definition is stated in no uncertain terms. The counselor must thus be assertive and take the initiative in redefining priorities, office procedure, and focus if necessary. A family-centered approach works only if others know what this means.

College guidance in its broadest context can be defined as a process in which a professional counselor supports all members of the family toward a new equilibrium during the student's transition from high school to college. The process encourages students toward independence, responsibility, and mature action. It encourages the parents to accept a less central role and to define the areas in which they can actively take part in the student's decision. The guidance office should be a place that helps all concerned recognize the appropriateness of new roles and responsibilities. Families need to recognize which spheres of interest in this complex process are appropriately the parents' and which the student's; they need to learn to negotiate openly when there is a difference of opinion. College guidance takes into account the necessary and essential presence of the parents to make the student's transition from home to the larger world a positive affirmation of self, not a rejection of home. Through the college-choice process, students and parents should learn to cope with a family transition as well as find a new place to study.

Addressing Parents' Concerns

Typically, parents, like students, approach the senior year of high school with general concern about the future and specific anxieties regarding a definition of their role in the college-choice process. It is harder for the counselor to work with the anxious parent, however, than it is to work with the concerned or apprehensive student: Students are in school regularly, and counselors have many opportunities to give them information and build rapport and trust before the senior year or college considerations loom portentously.

On the other hand, parents may appear at the counseling office or present an irate voice or strident demand on the phone only when there is a critical reason to do so. The discussion of low standardized test scores or a forgotten application deadline is not a situation to ensure calm tempers or easy conversation between parent and counselor. In crises parents, unlike their children, cannot rely on the familiarity of the counselor relationship—the personal trust developed over time—as support and a basis for direction and problem solving.

The crisis-oriented counselor-parent working relationship can tax the counselor's good will, the parents' respect for counseling services, and everyone's good humor. It has certainly encouraged many counselors to avoid parents when possible rather than to prepare for them as part of their professional agenda. Understanding parental anxiety and troubleshooting crises are necessary steps to building a family-oriented college guidance program. Dismissing the cause of parental anxiety to the realm of "fear of the unknown" is neither sufficient nor satisfying to the professional counselor. Other reasons need to be considered.

My own favorite basis for parental anxiety can be summarized metaphorically. It is one not often discussed openly in association with high school counseling, because it highlights the generation gap and unpleasant middle-aged sentiments; but it certainly is current in popular psychological literature that focuses on life stages and the passages through which we all can expect to advance.

I sometimes think of the transition from high school to college as a nursery rhyme. The students, Jack and Jill, head up the hill, pail in hand, excited, exuberant, and carefree. They are somewhat self-indulgent and unmindful of the cost their excursion will entail. They are beginning a life climb, free of responsibility; Jack and Jill are headed for fun, headed for success, and headed for the top. Mom and Dad are at the top, or part way up the hill with little energy to go any farther. Some of the popular rhetoric might say that they were ready to go "over the hill."

College choice for Jack and Jill usually comes at a time when Mom and Dad are questioning the value of their own climb. "Did I succeed? Was it worth it? What might I have done

differently?" Jack and Jill might not have the faintest notion
that they will ever in their lifetimes ask these questions, but you
can be sure that during the year of college choice, while Mom
and Dad are musing retrospectively, these questions will be
brought to bear on their children's deliberations and choices.
Parents' concern about their own lives, opportunities missed or
achieved, will be played out in terms of their children's prospects; they will be played out in the guidance office or on the
phone, overtly or as hidden agenda items. One reason for parental anxiety, then, is that the prospect of a child's high school
graduation and departure for college is a transition for the parents that is as significant to them as it is for their children.

Let me suggest a number of other reasons for parental
anxiety. Parents recognize the college guidance process as the
first time they are not overtly directing their children's actions.
The parent is not the center of college-related activity but remains uncertain about how well the youngster can carry the
responsibility. Counselors emphasize the critical adult nature of
college choice but show parents little evidence to indicate a
youngster's readiness to carry out choice-related, consequential
tasks. Indeed, the students may not be ready, and parents know
all too well that they will be left to clean up the mess if the
youngster does not behave as an adult.

A third reason for anxiety is that parents often lack information or access to information to help them help their children and to encourage their participation in college choice in a
reasonable manner. "I would love to help, to ask questions, but
I don't know what to do or what to ask" is often a way parents
begin a counseling session. Parents are unsure of their roles and
what they are expected to do in this process. Do they act directly? Do they take a back seat? Do they wait for the counselor's cue to act, or do they make arrangements on their own
and hope that the youngster will follow along? Because parents
proceed with their own child's college choice in isolation from
other parents, it is often difficult for them to define a clear individual role.

For parents to be less apprehensive, they must realize
that there is not a strict guideline for parent participation. Par-

ents must be supported and encouraged in their search for their own individual and appropriate balance of direction and salutary neglect. They need to be encouraged to seek and establish a comfortable role within the context of their family's and their child's ability to take the reins of responsibility.

Last, the issue of college choice has been presented as so complex and complicated that parents often feel overwhelmed and impotent. Interpreting test scores, litigation and controversy about testing, the virtues of liberal arts education versus career education, the value of choosing status and reputation over substance in a college, the ratio of cost to the days on campus—all are areas of expertise that counselors encourage parents to master in order to guide their children wisely.

Parents of graduating high school students will always be anxious. They are likely to display their anxiety in the college guidance office by attempting to influence college choice. Counselors have a professional responsibility first to understand the causes of parental anxiety and then to overcome it by developing counseling techniques and educational programs that meet the needs of the family.

Techniques for Working with Parents

The specialty of family counseling includes a variety of concepts, terminology, and models that guidance counselors can apply successfully to the task of including parents in the process of college choice. For example, the entire family, not the student in isolation, can be viewed as the counselor's client, and the *process* of choice can become the focus of counseling activity. Recognition and acceptance of the changing status of each family member involved in the college planning for one family member can become goals as important as the goal of appropriate college placement. The dynamics of interpersonal relationships can be brought to bear on reaching decisions, and the counselor can become the objective "other" who intercedes in conflict resolution, teaches active listening skills, or defines the necessary tasks that will help the family agree about appropriate placement. The following counseling situations familiar to all professionals who work in high school illustrate how family counseling can be brought to bear on the college-choice process.

> A shy, reticent junior who has recently gained the confidence to present a point of view or an assignment in class discussion, but who is still unable to express himself in the presence of a strong and goal-directed father, will find that the guidance office, with its supportive atmosphere, provides a forum that enables him to speak. By encouraging each member of the family in the basic skills of active listening, the counselor not only helps the family reach a decision about appropriate college placement but teaches them the skills needed to interact with one another in a new mode.

Even in situations where youngsters feel comfortable discussing important considerations with their parents, and the parents are adept at active listening, the forum of the guidance office and the objective presence of the counselor enable each family member to articulate and state in a more clearly defined manner what is of value. Open discussion and opportunity to explore ideas or convictions in a situation where being heard is guaranteed also assure that there will be no misunderstanding among parents, child, and counselor regarding acceptable choices, possible college acceptances, or the limits in the college search.

> A petulant, independent sophomore who years ago gave up talking with her parents about matters relating to her personal life has decided to apply as an early admissions candidate to a college 2,000 miles from home. Her recently divorced mother feels that her daughter is too immature for this step, but the mother has no energy left to argue. Her only trump card—the power of the purse— became inoperative with the divorce. The sophomore is used to doing things on her own; in this case, however, she knows she must reestablish a re-

lationship with her mother but does not know how to do so. Tempers may be hot and crises may loom, but if the counseling office can be used as a forum to negotiate contracts between each parent and the student, the counselor might open lines of communication within the family and help people who heretofore had not been talking with each other toward an ultimate group decision appropriate for all concerned.

For parents uneasy about the student's ability to act responsibly and independently, the counseling office becomes a place where they can express concerns and find the encouragement and support needed to make difficult decisions or plan an appropriate course of action. Counselors can assure them that it is both acceptable and well within the range of "normal" to be concerned about a child's faltering attitude of responsibility or to feel alienated or angry because of the child's actions. In the situation just described, the guidance office could provide a forum for negotiation, suggest colleges that would offer supportive guidance services, and educate student and parent that it is inappropriate to use money as a weapon in interpersonal relations.

Establishing the college guidance process as a family counseling process demands a major counseling effort. It means reorienting and retraining for the counselor and time to create working relationships with client families. It works best if the family can meet at regular intervals with the counselor over a period of a year. Within the counseling session, parents and counselor can observe the student and measure the maturity of response. Parents can recognize the growing independence and responsibility of the youngster (if this is occurring) without feeling compromised and unneeded. All the adults can foresee problems that might occur when a youngster is not mature or capable of carrying out the tasks involved in college placement, and they can plan accordingly to encourage independence in certain areas while shoring up when necessary with directed action in others. Each person in the group—parent, student, and counselor—can divide the tasks of research, defining goals, and making decisions, so that each is involved in the process, with the counselor balancing how much responsible action is expected of the student and how much independent activity is possible within the limits of the family.

The family focus is also an opportunity to educate the student to a concept foreign to most high school students: An individual's action is not carried on in isolation. To make a mature and responsible choice, a youngster must see how his or her plans mesh with the needs, resources, and values of the whole family. Establishing the limits of financial resources for one youngster's education, the effect that a child's leaving home will have on the other members of the family, the importance of work and study in combination to meet educational goals—all are topics that might be reviewed within the context of college counseling. The discussion of these topics can be an opportunity for parents and students to express agreements and differences; both parents and students will have a chance to learn that their ideas for the future and their goals in education may have to be modified for the welfare of the whole family.

Family counseling, then, is an active process in which each party can express a point of view and learn to modify it by considering the limits and expectations of all other family members. It is a process in which differences can be negotiated and a hierarchy of family needs established. It is not ironic that, after good counseling and plenty of opportunity for discussion of the broader philosophical concerns, the question of appropriate college possibilities resolves itself. When the process of college choice is made the focus, the placement—which is the important end result—happens in a more natural, relaxed manner. Names of specific colleges are offered as examples and possibilities, not for a critical review during which the parents and students wait for the counselor to give approval or disapproval.

Of course, family counseling works best when parents and students are for the most part in concert with one another, know each other's strengths, and are willing to recognize and support each other's frailties. However, family members often do not act in each other's best interests or do not have the skills to help each other through this family transition. When this occurs, the counselor can still look to the specialty of family counseling for help. The counselor can act as a negotiator between two parties who see the choice process and the end result of placement very differently.

The counselor as negotiator can create a counseling format in which the parents' and the student's roles are separate but equal: The parent becomes the client and the student becomes the client, the counselor working with each somewhat in isolation of the other. When the counselor meets with the parent, the focus is on parental concerns; when the counselor meets with the student, the focus is on student concerns. Within this format, the parents and the student pursue their own agenda of issues, their own research: When working with each of them, the counselor tries to help each person become more flexible and aware of the other's point of view.

When it is appropriate, the counselor might suggest moving into a family counseling model, using as a premise the knowledge that each has developed a sufficient informational base and a more objective perspective to entertain the other's point of view. Often, with more information and time to develop sensitivity, each side can be more accommodating and able to develop the listening skills necessary to reach resolutions.

Whether the family works well as a unit or brings its inability to resolve problems to the guidance office, the counselor should keep this goal in mind: to create a sufficient balance within the family relationship, to allow the student to express as much independence and responsibility as is possible within the context of the family. Wherever a student may be on a spectrum of total dependency to total independence, within the context of family counseling a counselor can create situations in which the youngster can move along the scale, gaining some independence in the process. If all the individuals in the process —parents and students—feel that they have been potent decision makers, important researchers, and, ultimately, wise regarding the choice of the college for the student, the counselor will have done a greater job than just choosing a placement at which the youngster could continue education.

College counselors must keep a number of things in mind

when they embark on this new mode of counseling. It is not possible to change techniques or professional perspectives overnight; adding skills to the counseling repertoire and experimenting with new methods must be done cautiously, reasonably, and with a strong sense of humility. Counselors must also remember that the counseling process, the journey toward a goal, can be more valuable to those walking the road than the goal itself. There is importance in discussion, substance in time spent getting to know a family, and value spending college counseling time supporting parents through a traumatic event that only tangentially affects the student in question.

Counselors must also recognize their own limits of responsibility; guidance personnel are not trained to work with people in severe crisis or who have malfunctioning personalities or severe social-adjustment problems. It is the professional college counselor's first responsibility to recognize the limit of experience and training and refer problems that go beyond the scope of the guidance office to other professionals.

College guidance is a genuine opportunity to combine in one professional life work the skills of teacher, adviser, arbitrator, research specialist, and counselor. Using these skills within the context of a family decision allows the college guidance counselor a realm in which to be even more effective.

19

Educating the Community About Student Options

Barbara B. Reinhold

In this world, ever hurtling toward new forms, where nothing is certain except the inevitability of change, an area that has been transformed in the past decade is the arena of choice for people at various points in their lives. The steps we once took for granted are vestiges of a more predictable era. The boundaries of sex, race, social class, and physical handicaps are no longer delineators of appropriateness of particular educational or career choices. That women should become physicians while men train to become nurses is the merest of changes.

It is the duty of guidance personnel to collect information about changing realities and master skills that will enable them to function as bias-free as possible when guiding students and parents around key choice points. In reality, however, the research of the 1960s and 1970s has corroborated our fears that guidance personnel and teachers have not been free of option-limiting stereotypes about the choices their clients and students were making. The young woman in a construction career, the learning-disabled student in college, the inner-city student being tutored independently to improve SAT scores for college admission as a premed student, the wheelchair student assessing which colleges will enable him to pursue team sports: These phenomena exist today as laudable exceptions to an old rule, but in the next decade they will be accepted as variations on the theme of individual destiny. Guidance personnel must ask themselves candidly how prepared they are to help facilitate this evolution.

346

Ideally, all those institutions and individuals who affect students at critical choice points can be educated as to the proliferation of possible choices for all students in the last decade. The "how to" of that difficult task is the primary focus of this chapter.

The first steps toward educating the community beyond the school involve getting one's own house in order. It is imperative first that guidance staffs keep abreast of the newest information on educational and career options by whatever means possible: trips to colleges, visits from college admissions officers, college fairs, use of the computer terminal, visits to career-training institutions, in-service instruction for staff, dissemination and discussion of printed information from colleges and career schools. The second layer of the informational ripple effect must occur in the school staff. This step requires that the school administration support the broader educative functions of the guidance or pupil support services. The guidance department must have not only permission but also encouragement to share information and expertise in educational planning with teachers. Faculty meetings given over to a discussion of the college admissions timetable, sharing printed college materials with teachers, in-service workshops on alternatives to four-year colleges—these are some techniques a counseling department might use to ensure that the information students will inevitably solicit from their teachers will be timely and correct.

After educating themselves and other staff, counselors must tend to the third component of updating: creating a particular location where educational and career planning information is accessible in an appealing way. In some secondary schools, the waiting area of the guidance counselors' offices serves that function, but diverse materials and equipment are difficult to house in that setting. Similarly, some schools have designated a part of the school library as educational resource territory, but this plan also has limitations. The most obvious difficulty with a library setting is that those students most in need of career information will not find it a comfortable place to be. The approach that seems to engender the widest use of materials by a broad spectrum of students is the creation of a career center. This model interrelates career and educational planning and generally provides a wider assortment of materials: filmstrips about various careers and training programs, a career-college search computer terminal, interest- and skill-assessment instruments.

Having provided for the availability of current and engaging materials and the presence of informed personnel within the school setting, college admissions–career planning counselors must then make it their concern to educate parents and the community, the other segments who influence student decisions.

One body of information not available prior to the 1970s has tremendous potential for affecting the field of college admissions information. This is the literature of adult development, which declares, contrary to the belief of most adolescents, that there is life after thirty; in fact, the very information and decision-making skills fifteen- to eighteen-year-olds require to make sound postsecondary school plans are relevant to their parents' concurrent choices. It is not unusual in this time of midlife stresses and reevaluating to see both men and women changing career directions and women returning to the work force after raising a family or experiencing divorce or death of a spouse. In a certain number of families, therefore, there is a two-generation choice in progress, with both adolescent and parent facing decisions about careers and training. Whether the changes occur simultaneously or sequentially, U.S. Labor Department figures show that adults will make serious career changes at least five times during their working years. Thus, the imperative for the community to be educated about informed choice making is stronger than ever. Because students' choices are likely to be more satisfactory if they are made with input from parents and significant others both in and out of school, and because parents of adolescents themselves are often embroiled in major life choices, schools will be remiss in their duties to the communities they serve if they continue to operate as isolated sanctuaries of learning, with their wealth of information kept largely separate from parents and other community members.

The "how to" of this chapter concerns ways the school can reach out and inform its community of parents and citizens about the ever-widening range of choices facing adolescents, their parents, their neighbors, and indeed even their grandparents. The task of reeducation in a nonthreatening way is in many communities the companion to information sharing. For instance, in many middle-class communities, the axiom that "a college education is a lifelong guarantee of social status and financial comfort" hangs heavy in the mentality of parents, employers, teachers, and others who advise young people. That citizenry must be informed about unemployed Ph.D.s and RIF'ed teachers in crisis, as well as about crafts and trade persons who are finding secure outlets for their talents. Similarly, in some staunchly provincial communities, citizens must somehow be urged to examine their vocational biases about sex, race, and social class.

For the new school's superintendent, principal, or guidance director, who idealistically takes on this challenge of community education, an important initial step is assessing the existing links to the community. What formal and informal networks are already operational and ready to be utilized? Among the "connectors" an administrator might want to call on for dissemination of information are the following:

1. *Media.* Town, city, regional newspaper; town radio station; community art center.
2. *State and town government subgroups.* Police, fire, recreation, DPW, welfare, CETA.
3. *Private agencies and organizations.* Town mental health unit, Scouts, church or temple groups, Kiwanis, Rotary, women's club, Chamber of Commerce.
4. *Private sector businesses.*

The connectors can be used both directly and indirectly. Directly, connectors can be used to publish information about events (college fair, career days, scholarship programs). With media, the school would very likely prepare its own materials for publication but expect other agencies and organizations to use this information in a way appropriate to their constituency or clientele. Indirectly, organizations can connect by backing scholarship projects, serving as a "shadowing" site for students exploring careers, providing a community representative for a resource committee on choosing careers, or encouraging their own employees to use the facilities of the school's career center for their own career searches. Whether the thrust is direct or indirect, the essential goal is visibility—keeping high the public's awareness of the multiplicity of choices facing people in every age range.

Once an assessment of the connector network has been completed, the administrator can plot which "market segments" warrant more attention. This term is especially apt because the school system's outreach to the community is essentially an exercise in marketing, calling on many of the same insights, skills, and tactics. Although this chapter is written primarily for counselors, a guidance person attempting to implement its suggestions would need early in the campaign to secure the backing of the highest available administrator—to lend the marketing campaign force and legitimacy.

Once the connector network is in place, the next step is to ascertain the total program offered to the community: what currently goes on—in classes, in the guidance office, in the library, in the career center, in student organizations—to inform and train students in making career and educational choices? It is important to spend a few extra hours or days collecting data to evaluate current information sources before spinning off into any new outreach programs. An accountability check to apply to the programs/methods on the list is the following:

1. Is information available about all types of career preparation—four-year college, two-year college, career-training schools, apprenticeships, armed services, on-the-job training?
2. Is information free of sex-role, cultural, racial biases?
3. Is information presented in formats and times appropriate to the intended audience? (A discussion of automotive career training held after school will not be well attended because those students interested usually work.)
4. Are experiences in addition to information in traditional

"packaging" made available to students—in the form of a shadowing program, class trips to colleges or college fairs, or use of an interactive computer system?

5. *Where* is the information available? For instance, does the school legitimize the dissemination of choice-making information by providing class time for presentations?

When the thoroughness of the total information program has been ascertained, the administrator then asks: Are we lacking in any area? Do we need to augment the program before we pump energies into its "unveiling" for the community? A wise administrative strategy that prepares for the leap into marketing is to call in a community advisory committee of parents, public agents, and merchants to advise the school of any lapses in its program. Usually, community involvement at the level of problem identification vastly increases the likelihood of participation of those individuals and the organizations they represent and leads to the ultimate solutions to the problems identified.

When the product has been perfected and the packaging decided on, it is time for marketing. At this point, the school program marketeer must ask two more questions:

6. For each of my programs, what is the likelihood that the community could become interested in it?

7. Of those approaches that seem to be good prospects for a marketing push, which one seems to have the best likelihood of success: sending printed materials, involving community members in planning, utilizing organization members themselves in programs?

A school's choice-assistance program can be as intensive and extensive as the organization has the resources and funding to make it. To stimulate the reader's imagination, a thorough and far-reaching listing of the kinds of events, activities, and curricula that might comprise a total career and educational choice program follows. Not even the wealthiest and most creative high school could expect to have more than 75 percent of these offerings included in its programs, but the presence of any less than 40 percent of these components available to students and the community very likely indicates that serious program updating (product improvement) is necessary.

A schema for envisioning a diverse marketing plan is a three-layered approach to sharing data with students, parents, and the community: (1) information disseminated through media, (2) information disseminated through events, (3) information disseminated through experiences. A way to use this chapter as an accountability checklist is to note which specific suggestions under each outreach layer are actually in place in one's own school setting.

Methods for Disseminating Information

1. *Media*
   - Community newspaper—ongoing columns
   - Community newspaper—seasonal coverage of events
   - School-community radio or TV
   - Videotaped programs for classroom use
   - Guidance department publications
2. *Events*
   - College fair
   - College admissions visits
   - Career days/fairs
3. *Experiences*
   - College admissions workshops
   - Classroom or group units on career choice
   - Shadowing
   - Counseling groups
   - Parent-student-counselor sessions

Information Disseminated Through Media

Community Newspaper Column. A weekly column centered on the high school in general or career and educational planning in particular ensures constant visibility. The largest problem is convincing an editor who has only a few pages to work with that your focus has significant reader interest to warrant using six to ten inches of valuable space weekly or biweekly.

Ironically, the link to a wide readership implicit in gearing information to all age levels probably makes the career planning thrust a more marketable one than a column dedicated to high school events alone. "Legitimacy" of the writer is another issue for community paper editors generally, so it is wise to approach the paper via the school system's publicity director, if there is one, or, if not, via the highest-ranking administrator whose attention can be turned toward that task.

Timely Newspaper Articles Publicizing College and Career-Related Events. Editors are generally more receptive to sporadic articles than to an ongoing allocation of column inches. Visibility is of course decreased in this less constant approach, but it might be the best one can hope for. Tricks of the trade for garnering good coverage include such strategies as sending a photograph with the copy as often as possible and including community members in the photographs and articles. A photograph of a parent and teenager together using the career search computer, for instance, is good fare.

School or Community Radio. Coverage of events and issue-oriented interviews with students, staff, and, when appropriate, community members generally touches a very limited audience but can effectively motivate those who do hear the broadcast.

Videotape Programs. A school with a course in film making or TV broadcasting or with a resourceful English teacher interested in media can turn a learning experience for a group of students into a marketing project. Audiences for a short videotape program on some aspect of college planning, financial aid, or career choices could include the parent-teacher organization, other classes within the school, a group of school volunteers, local business people, Kiwanis Club, or various others.

Guidance Notes, Career Planning Newsletter, College News. Publication by guidance or administrative staff of information about career and educational planning can disseminate data about testing, schools, and financial aid. Whenever possible, these outreach documents should be bulk-mailed to parents rather than handed out to students, lest they go the way of other school handouts. Mailing or distributing these newsletters to clubs, businesses, and other town agencies can increase visibility immeasurably and plant in townspeople's minds the expectations that information about education and careers belongs to citizens at large as well as to the students.

Information Disseminated Through Events

College Fair. The college fair sponsored by an individual high school or regional school is an unusual opportunity for students, parents, and community members to gather for a festive information-gathering event on the home turf. Extensive publicity through media both within and outside the school is essential to attract a community crowd.

Preparation for the college fair is important also—publishing instructions about what questions students should ask, how to apply "admissions profile" information to one's own credentials, and such. It is wise to invite a wide range of colleges in terms of selectivity and to include career schools and training institutes. Even though colleges understandably prefer citywide or regional fairs to sending representatives to various local fairs, there is nonetheless an advantage to the local fair if a primary goal is to make it accessible to adults in one's community. Parents surveyed in the Brookline, Massachusetts, community indicated a much greater willingness to attend such an event in their own school district than to journey to a central college fair, even though larger fairs inevitably offer more diverse information in more quantity.

College Admissions Representative Visits. These sessions, where college representatives are able to talk informally to small groups of students interested in a particular college, are seldom utilized as well as they might be for sharing information with the community. To maximize availability of the sessions to adults, the school needs to schedule the visits at a standard time, in a central, stable place, and to publicize the schedule of visits in both school and local newspapers.

Publicity should stress that parents and community members are urged to attend the sessions to gather information and ask questions for their children and/or themselves. Typically, these sessions are held in a guidance suite or library, but a better location for those schools that have one is the career center, where community members who attend can stay on to browse through a collection of materials related to career and educational choices. A high school that hosts three to four colleges one afternoon each week and programs a variety of selectivity into each week's visiting colleges—not four Ivy League colleges on one day, say—gives the student body and adults in the community a rare chance to "shop" each week for the most important investment any of them will ever make.

Career Days/Career Fairs. There are infinite variations on this theme, and each high school seems to have a different way of organizing the presentation of career information to students. Some have speakers on various careers each week; others have a monthly career-exploration series; still others boast an annual extravaganza, where many outside speakers come to the school for a one-day potpourri of career-information presentations. Each school must choose the vehicle appropriate to the size and tempo of its student body and community.

The variable important to the purposes of this chapter, however, is the accessibility of the speakers to adults outside the school. When choosing a format, school planners should include in their selection criteria maximum potential attendance by adults—both parents and townspeople, who may well, as noted earlier, be making the same choices about career selection and training as are the eighteen-year-olds in the community. Taking care to include a large number of parents and citizens as presenters about various careers also engenders a spirit of community sharing. Again, publicity is essential, as is faculty enthusiasm for the project, and all staff members must be encouraged to urge their students and students' parents to attend the career presentations with an open and inquisitive frame of mind. Given the current reduction in force paralyzing many school systems, faculty members might do well to attend some career redirection presentations on their own behalf.

Information Disseminated Through Experiences

College Admissions Workshops. Training in the self-awareness and self-advocacy skills necessary for applying to college can be offered inexpensively and effectively to groups of students. Curricula for these workshops, which can be taught by guidance counselors or classroom teachers, cover issues such as (1) assessing student's strengths and weaknesses, (2) ascertaining the prevailing "image" the student wishes to present, (3) learning how to document that generalization with both hard and soft data, (4) choosing a range of schools along the spectrum of selectivity.

Providing at least one series of workshops for students and parents together in the evening is a worthy six- to ten-hour investment of time for a staff person. The public relations effect is almost incalculable—in my experience, parents are always overwhelmed at the teaching of both skills and information. In evaluation statements collected at the end of the workshops, parents usually admitted that they listened with one ear for their children and with the other ear for themselves. Holding these evening sessions in a location such as the career center, where college and career information reside as companions, makes an important statement about the interrelationship of the two and at the same time encourages parents to take in data about career possibilities that did not exist when they were experiencing adolescence for the first time.

Even for community members who do not elect to attend the workshops, just offering the workshops to parents makes the point that adults can use the school as a resource for themselves. Newspaper coverage of the workshops, preferably with a photograph of a workshop in session, is a necessary and lucrative strategy to ensure the visibility of information-generating experiences sponsored by the department.

Classroom or Group Units on Career Choice. Given their history of escaping teaching duties to have time for "real counseling," guidance staff are sometimes loathe to reenter the world of the classroom. That classroom, however, is "where the action is," and a wise guidance staff fights its way back to reclaiming some classroom time—not to teach history or math, of course, but to have time to teach certain skills and impart information that students need in order to make sound career choices. Just how to capture that time depends on the complexity of the school. In an informal setting, counselors can negotiate to teach a unit on career choices in one academic discipline or another at some point during each of the three or four years —with the specificity of the information increasing each year from the freshman to the senior experience.

In a more complex high school, the guidance staff will very likely have to schedule its own "course"—perhaps a freshman guidance curriculum for a term, or an elective course for seniors on choosing a career. The possibilities are infinite. The important point is that guidance staff must not forget at least to consider utilizing classroom time, either through a course they offer themselves or through informal arrangements to use several class hours borrowed from an academic discipline that is "friendly" to guidance. The potential for outreach to the community in classroom time is maximal, for parents uniformly value whatever is sanctioned by inclusion in the curriculum more than they value activities planned for after hours. One way a school can go on record as valuing decision-making skills and updated educational and career information is to teach them within the curriculum, for whatever brief period possible. A single-class lesson plan, for instance, that addresses the similarity between adolescent and midlife career examination, with a "parent interview" for homework, could have far-reaching implications for raising the consciousness of that set of parents and their associates.

Shadowing. A very time-consuming managerial enterprise, shadowing nonetheless continues to be one of the most dramatic and effective modalities of career exploration. In a shadowing program, students visit a career site for a period of time—usually between half a day and one week, with one-day experiences the most common—where their primary tasks are to observe what an individual worker does in a day and to ascertain the appropriateness of that job for themselves. Shadowing is an effective link to the community because students inevitably talk about the experience enthusiastically and community members and parents are most often used as resource people for students to visit. Community newspapers are usually eager for coverage of this kind of program, so the publicity potential is high.

Because educating the community about a wide range of educational and career choices is a priority goal, the shadowing coordinator should carefully seek out placements which demonstrate that life choices need not be limited by racism, sexism, or other traditional biases. A shadowing placement, which must be carefully discussed both before and after the experience, is essentially a powerful counseling tool. The combination of experiencing some horizon-expanding event—the young woman with math-science skills who spends a day observing and identifying with a female neurosurgeon—with debriefing that experience in terms of the biases it assails can be very dramatic. In my ten years as a high school guidance counselor, my greatest turnabouts in career and educational decisions have involved the use of shadowing as a generator of new data for a student stagnating somewhere in the maelstrom of a decision.

Counseling Groups. A short-term counseling group, usually convened to discuss a particular issue, effectively reaches students, parents, and adult community members. Publicizing the groups, finding an appropriate time and place to meet, and reaching the people who most need the group are among the many problems a school or counseling department faces when launching an effective group counseling program. Once groups are conscripted, however, a skilled leader can make visible inroads into the fear, rigidity, and ignorance that inhibit people's openness to new possibilities.

Groups open to parents are particularly effective because they give parents an opportunity to challenge misinformation or prejudices and to share uncertainties in a supportive atmosphere. Groups that have proven successful in forging across the frontier in some small way are a mothers and daughters discussion group on nontraditional careers for women; a support group for minority women in business careers; a financial aid exploration group for single parents; an alternative life-styles discussion group; a law enforcement careers seminar; a career-change discussion group for parents and other adults. The college admissions workshops, for instance, were most successful when offered for students and parents jointly, for several reasons. First, parents were genuinely involved and appreciative of being officially included by the school. Second, the two-generation discussions ensured that the students had double encouragement to test the concepts and techniques taught in the workshops. Finally, teaching the skills to both parents and the current crop of juniors or seniors gave the parents a sense of their own "self-advocacy" skills and prepared them to help younger children who were not yet ready to apply to college but were about to market their skills to a prospective employer, club, or other activity.

Parent-Student-Counselor Conferences. An expectation about choosing colleges, career training, and, over a longer period of time, even a career direction is that adolescents need to process input from the two most significant types of adults in their lives—that is, from parents and from school mentors and authorities. Clearly, it is in the best interest of the adolescents embroiled in a critical choice to experience a face-to-face discussion among themselves, their parents, and their school advisers. In many cases, the adults will be in essential agreement as to an appraisal of the young people's talents and appropriate outlets for those skills. At any rate, the degree of agreement or disagreement among the adults is apparent after such a planning conference and is therefore able to be worked with. Discrepancies between a family's educational or career expectations about a child and the realities of the hard data to which the school staff has access is a frequent problem that is best dealt with early in the deciding process.

A second most frequent source of potential problems is the family that brings to the decision process outdated, inaccurate, or culturally biased information about the choices a child is making. In a face-to-face conference (or conferences if a continuation seems desirable) lies the possibility for confronting fears and ignorance of facts that cloud decisions for some students. Examples of students caught in school-home values clashes are young men with lower science aptitude but clear human service skills who are urged to consider nursing by a school counselor but pushed toward medical school by parents; a young man skilled in crafts but feeling pressure to go to business school to take over the family corporation; a talented Chicano student whose family fears that leaving home to go to college will be her undoing; a young woman whose twin brother is told to go to college while she goes to work because boys need an education more. A well-trained counselor, backed up by a well-stocked career center, has the capability to reeducate parents and students as to the constantly changing realities of career and educational choices.

Limitations of sex, race, religion, and social class need not apply for the high school class of 1980 as they did in 1940, 1950, or 1960. A college education is no longer a guarantee of a status-filled, financially successful life. A female no longer anticipates working many fewer years than a male. Financial aid is no longer a concern of only the lower and lower-middle classes. The majority of students attending college no longer go through nonstop in four years from high school to a bachelor's degree. The world just is not the same as it was when most parents of today's adolescents were at the same choice point. And it is the responsibility of schools to gently, but clearly and forcefully, make the public aware that, while some facts of life never change, those related to education and work have been dramatically and irrevocably altered.

Conclusion

Just how those changes and their impact on the adolescents of each school community will be made known to the community at large is an exercise in advertising, marketing, and public information services. The techniques suggested in this chapter run the gamut from purely informational (printed material) to experiential—shadowing, college fairs, group experiences, and counseling. The issue is not which techniques a school administrator or counselor chooses to employ but what use they make of that technique—that is, is the question of changing data/changing expectations/changing choices addressed squarely, or is it merely hinted at? The fact that a = a (as Mom and Dad knew it) only part of the time is not a popular notion. It takes courage to accept that fact; to know where one's community really stands in its acceptance of changed realities; to find funding and staff expertise to address those pockets of misinformation; and to take your programs to the families and citizens who need them most.

20

Contributions of Independent Educational Counselors

Marilyn J. Blum
Phyllis S. Steinbrecher

Where to go to college is probably the first major decision for many young adults. At this critical juncture, many families retain the professional expertise of an independent educational counselor—a private counselor who specializes in educational planning. The counselor assesses a student's many needs, provides a list of recommended schools, trains the student to evaluate schools, oversees the application process, and carefully monitors admissions decisions. During the decade ahead, the independent educational counselor will play an increasingly important role as professional assistance in educational planning becomes a necessary ingredient for individual success.

The wide range of problems an independent educational counselor confronts demonstrates that a real need for personal services to families and students in making school and college choices not only exists but is growing. Families are encouraged to seek professional advice beyond that available in public schools because of the prospect of personal help from someone who can take the time necessary to understand special problems fully and help seek their solutions.

Other than through organizations of independent schools, there are few places where a family can find out about preparatory schools or special educational programs. As the cost of higher education escalates and selective colleges and universities become even more selective, families with college-age sons and daughters face critical decisions that public school personnel simply do not have the time to explore with them, no matter how conscientious they are or how much they may want to. Only a few of the nation's more than 20,000 public secondary schools have the staff to effectively counsel students who must make a well-considered choice. How can school counselors with a student load of more than 400 deal with the many special concerns brought to them? Only briefly, at best. The independent educational counselor can help provide advice, solutions, and answers in all these situations.

Need for Independent Educational Counselors

Annually, public high schools face budget cuts, and the number of professional staff personnel is often reduced. Guidance counselors are assigned larger numbers of students and demands. A student reported that at his school in Texas four guidance counselors served five thousand students. "You can't blame the guidance counselor for not even knowing my name," he explained. "The only ones who got the attention were the students at the top of the class and the troublemakers. The kids in the middle were on their own."

Guidance counselors, frustrated by too little time, are unable to offer a focused, personalized approach to educational planning. "All we can do is put out the fires," remarked a guidance counselor. "We are in a crisis-reactive position—if there isn't an obvious problem, then there won't be help available." Some counselors say they cannot even react to all the problems; only the serious ones get attention. Therefore, some guidance counselors are welcoming the assistance of independent educational counselors, who have time and expertise to devote to students and their needs.

Students within a single school system often have special, individual needs. These needs can run the gamut from a very bright young person with a particular talent or strength to a very bright young person with dyslexia. Sometimes the school system cannot deal with specialized problems, and sometimes the student feels the need of neutral advice from outside the system. One such case involved a young man, a senior in high school. He had a magnificent record of high achievement. His teachers were enthusiastic supporters, and they spoke of his dedication, maturity, and seriousness of purpose. One teacher commented that he never forgot a word that was spoken in class. In anticipation of continuing his education, this young man sat for the College Boards. When he got his scores, he was seriously disappointed. The SATs were a disaster. They certainly did not correspond with his superb schoolwork. There was a real question whether he would be regarded as college material by his guidance counselor or by competitive colleges.

His parents retained the services of an independent educational counselor, who talked with him and discovered that this young man was legally blind. The boy had been afraid to tell anyone at school; he thought it would be a big strike against him, so he learned to compensate in school. He developed his auditory retention skills. He took thorough notes in class and spent long hours each night reading as much as he could at his slow speed. He discovered every shortcut he could. But all his superb skills could not compensate for the small print and stopwatch of the College Boards.

The educational counselor directed the young man to the Educational Testing Service, which gave the student a large-print copy of the SAT at the next sitting. The student's performance improved substantially. Next, the counselor helped the student evaluate colleges that were both compatible with his proven abilities and equipped to provide the necessary support for his special needs. The young man was enrolled at a fine university and began what was to be a distinguished career in higher education.

Another example of a student with a special need was a boy with a peculiar transcript. During the ninth grade, he achieved straight A's in five subjects. In the tenth grade, he got straight A's in math and science, with C's in humanities. In the eleventh grade, he received straight B's in only three subjects. This student scored a 640 on the verbal SAT and a 460 on the quantitative. During his junior year his New York Regents were

all between the 94th and 96th percentile. The transcript offered
clues, but it did not tell the whole story.

This young man had developed a serious recurring medical impairment. During the tenth grade, he suffered a stroke and
missed three months of school. Although he was able to make
up the lost work in science and math, he could not compensate
for the missed class discussions in English and history. During
the eleventh grade, this courageous young man suffered a second stroke. This time he missed all but six weeks of the school
year. Nevertheless, he managed a B average. With the help of an
independent educational counselor, who spent long hours with
this bright and ambitious student, an excellent college was
chosen for him to attend and arrangements were made for him
to maintain only three courses per semester to prevent overload.
The college and the independent educational counselor worked
closely to meet his individual needs.

Clearly, this was an unusual case. The proximity of first-
rate medical attention was paramount among the institutional
criteria for this young man. The independent educational counselor persuaded an excellent school with such facilities to consider this student.

But most families who retain an independent educational
counselor do not have dramatic problems to solve. Generally,
they want to streamline the process of selecting the right
school. To "go it alone" is very time-consuming and requires
enormous energy to pore over the reams of printed matter available. Independent educational counselors generally spend 30
percent of their professional time in research, just to stay current with trends and changes in colleges. The president of the
Independent Educational Counselors Association says, "I make
it a point to visit over 100 schools per year. There is nothing to
replace the value of an independent educational counselor visiting a school campus. And you have to keep going back. A great
deal can change in three years. Education reflects our society,
and both appear to be in a constant state of change."

Parents and students offer a number of less critical reasons
for seeking professional assistance in educational planning.
Many find a need for an objective point of view from outside

the family or school to evaluate needs, identify choices, and make decisions. Others find the security of the second opinion invaluable. For many, moving from secondary school to college is a time of developmental crisis. The independent educational counselor can coordinate the intellectual and vocational needs within the framework of a psychologically sensitive perspective. The tender egos of students and parents are very much on the line. In choosing a college, one is also choosing a life-style, and both psychological and intellectual factors come into play. The independent educational counselor can be a strong source of support in resolving some of the less apparent issues present in good college choice.

The following typical examples demonstrate the challenges that make the independent educational counselor's job not only exciting and rewarding but essential:

A father recently moved his family. During his initial phone call to an independent counseling office, he said, "We may be lifelong friends. I have four children!" He did not know where to turn for valid solutions to educational problems members of his family were having. The first appointment was with the oldest child, a young man not eligible to return to his private out-of-state college the following semester. He knew little about colleges in his new state and how he might gain admission. Ultimately, with many inquiries from the counseling office, some research, and good, honest discussion with the student, he selected a college where he improved his grades and thus was able to transfer to another college, this time in his adopted state. (Note that rarely is a counseling service available to the transfer student who must find another college for whatever reason.)

The second child, a high school junior daughter, began, through the independent counseling office, to look at colleges but soon realized that her course preparation and test results did not match the profiles of the colleges she wanted. Should she lower her sights, or could she do something to strengthen her skills to become eligible for the colleges she wanted to attend? In her senior year, after a challenging and rewarding summer program recommended by the educational counselor, she was ready for demanding preparatory courses and gained admission to a college of her choice.

Another daughter in the family, a sophomore, did not feel she was getting the personal attention she needed at her public high school and so wanted to transfer to a preparatory school where she could get remedial help. She did so and is improving her basic skills.

These three students were counseled over a period of two years. The mother also went to the office for counseling with questions about tests that could help her decide on an academic course and career choice and about which colleges in her area offered programs of interest to her. It was a gratifying experience for the counselor to help members of this family find solutions for their particular concerns.

An out-of-state family called for information about colleges in California for a college-bound son. After several lengthy phone and office consultations, appointments were arranged for visits to five colleges on the west coast and to another in Switzerland, where the son ultimately enrolled.

The office acted as more than a central information agency in this case; despite the fact of distance, the counselor was able to provide some in-depth counseling on the best course for this young man's education.

His sister, a high school freshman, decided soon after that she needed a summer school remedial program that would enable her to enroll at a strong preparatory school. Arrangements were also made for intelligence testing not available in her home area. After some discussion of various school possibilities, and with test results in hand, the daughter and her mother visited four schools and chose one where she is currently enrolled.

An anxious mother who did not attend college herself wanted to send her daughter to a fine preparatory school, where good college counseling was available. Since the mother was so uncertain about the entire college admissions process, she wanted to make absolutely sure nothing was left to chance. Although the daughter discussed ideas for her college application essays with the educational counselor, the chief role for the counselor in this situation was to reassure the mother and be that "special someone" with whom she could share her anxieties and concerns.

Other people with whom the independent counselor can and does deal include parents looking for special tutorial programs for a child who has a learning disability and a young woman student who needs only one course to earn her diploma when her preparatory school closes and who seeks for that purpose a boarding school that will combine preparatory school and the first two years of college.

A young man who is both a good student and a promising college athlete finds his mailbox filled each day with tempting offers from colleges throughout the country. He comes from a sophisticated college-educated family but simply needs to talk with someone not emotionally involved with his final decision and to "think out loud" his reasons for choosing college x over college y.

A twenty-nine-year-old woman is told by her "friends" that she is too old to go back to college for her MBA. A liberal dose of support and an armload of graduate school catalogues give her the courage to apply and be accepted in a challenging program.

An extremely talented minority senior is being deluged by mail from the College Board's Student Search Service and the National Merit Scholarship program. She is bewildered and apprehensive about what the attention means and feels strongly that she wants to be admitted for herself alone, not because she fits into a special category. The counselor is able to help her sort through the material and narrow her choices to those schools whose curricular emphasis is in harmony with her interests. "I feel better already," was her comment when she knew she could concentrate her application efforts on four colleges.

Selecting an Independent Educational Counselor

How does one find a responsible and professional independent counselor? The choice of a professional consultant or counselor, whether it be in medicine, law, or education, has to be carefully considered. The Independent Educational Counselors Association (IECA, located at 128 Great Road, Bedford, Massachusetts 01730) is an association of private independent educational counselors and one source for finding the right independent educational counselor for a family. To be a member of the IECA, each counselor has to meet professional standards and work within a stated code of ethics. The IECA has members from most sections of the country but is strongest in the northeast.

Most members of the National Association of College Admissions Counselors (NACAC) have close working relationships with independent educational counselors. The NACAC and regional ACAC directories list some independent counselors. Often a local college or university admissions office can refer a family to the reputable independent educational counselors in the area.

Some independent educational counselors advertise their services, and some even claim a free service. Let the buyer beware. Who is paying for the "free service"? Some independent educational counselors are paid by the institutions that enroll the student. These headhunters generally limit their list of recommended schools to those with whom they have a contractual arrangement. Those paying for the service are the ones being served. Ethical considerations mandate that the counselor not receive compensation from schools and colleges. Fees should be paid by only the counselees.

There is no substitute for word of mouth when choosing an independent educational counselor. Referrals and recommendations can come from other families, schools, or professional offices and organizations. Independent educational counselors are a large and varied group who work in assorted ways. A family should ask for professional credentials, cost of service, description of service, and, most important, a list of families who have retained the professional services. Each family should seek a counselor with whom they can maintain a mutually satisfying working relationship. Ultimately, it is the family's responsibility to investigate the professional qualifications and the nature of the service before deciding to enter into a contractual agreement.

Some very reputable independent educational counselors are not members of the Independent Educational Counselors Association. If a family is using a nonmember, the same guidelines for checking credibility should be applied.

What a Family Can Expect from an Independent Educational Counselor

The independent educational counselor has the opportunity to view the student with fresh eyes. A student comes to the independent educational counselor with a transcript of course work, the grades achieved in those courses, the results of mass testing, and experiences in school, the community, the job market and during summers and traveling. The student does not come as a human being who has been seen in a system for many years, often prejudged or slotted. The independent educational counselor does not have a behavioral input from others and is therefore free to see each student at the present level of development.

When the service of an independent educational counselor has been retained, the family can expect the following assistance. During the first visit, the counselor talks at length with the student and parents, both together and separately. The interview with the student alone is critical, and it is done most often in the counselor's office before the counselor looks at test scores and grades provided by the student. It is critically important that the counselor hear the student articulate personal aspirations and goals, to establish a personal rapport and foundation for an honest relationship. The student must feel that the counselor is on her or his side and is there to help.

The interview with the parents is equally important. Parents' influence on the student's decisions should never be disregarded. The counselor frequently determines that the student and parents have misconceptions about choosing a school or college or that they hold opposing views that need reconciliation.

At the end of this visit, the student usually leaves with appropriate lists and material about programs and schools, based on the counselor's evaluation of the student's needs and credentials.

Next, the counselor instructs the student in developing skills with which to evaluate schools: how to read the catalogue, what questions to ask the admissions office, and what to look for on the campus. Prospective students must assess degree requirements, work loads, honors work available, facilities, nature of the student body, and placement assistance available to graduates. This decision-making process makes the selection of colleges to which to apply more substantive.

The independent educational counselor also helps the student apply to the colleges selected. Following completion of the application process, the independent educational counselor then can monitor the admissions process. Naturally, the family's counselor is a valuable resource in making the final decision: where to go to college.

A Final Word

Sound educational planning requires a balance in its admissions input. Retaining an independent educational counselor has been found an expeditious and effective means of achieving the necessary balance between high school guidance and placement counselors and college admissions officers. During the decade ahead, it is expected that an increasing number of families will secure the professional services of an independent educational counselor to round out the team of advisers as they plan to meet the special needs of their children.

Cases that present real problems call on all the counselor's resources. The independent counselor must make the time to research individual requests and interests, exploring all possibilities and resources. This quantity and quality of caring provides continuity in the entire process and is especially valuable if more than one member of a family seeks assistance over a period of time. It allows for referral and reflection to make further suggestions and for matching of aptitude and ability with appropriate school choices. A good supply of recent printed material on as many colleges and schools as possible should be kept readily available in the counselor's office. The counselor will, as well, make judicious, knowledgeable use of guidebooks and school profiles as supplements to the literature. Unrealistic choices can be discouraged when adequate information is available and explained appropriately.

It must always be clearly understood that even though every attempt will be made to make wise and realistic school choices, the final admission decision is reached by each school or college and its admissions committee. There may be situations in the counselee's school setting unknown to the counselor, and it is helpful if a line of communication is established between the independent counselor and the counterpart in the secondary school. Unfortunately, this is rarely possible, but ideally such communication should and could exist.

To remain well informed, the independent counselor must seek out and attend all professional meetings relevant to any aspect of the counseling function of the office. The counselor must develop a working relationship with other professionals in related fields to establish mutual trust and respect because referrals are sometimes required, for example, for intelligence testing, analysis of learning disabilities, and career-assessment techniques. Such expertise is not normally found in the educational counseling/school-college placement office.

Keeping up with what is going on in the world of higher education as well as in preparatory schools is a must for the counselor. The interested and competent counselor devotes time and resources to visiting schools and colleges, meeting with personnel, and becoming familiar with curricula, unique qualities of many campuses, and a host of other details. It is their time and professional expertise devoted to each concern that makes independent educational counselors valuable options for an increasing number of students and families.

Part Five

✐ ✐ ✐ ✐ ✐

Service to the College or University

✐   The college admissions officer has responsibilities other than presenting a particular college or university to student clients so that they can decide whether to apply for admission. Even if she or he does not participate in a subjective selection process, or counsel students unsure about the link between education and career, or help administer the institution generally, the college admissions officer bears principal responsibility for ensuring that enrollment remains high enough for the institution to function according to its principles, its view of what should be taught to whom.

Marketing is a hot term among admissions officers today, and secondary school counselors may see "marketing" as a thinly disguised attempt to fool them and students. The authors in Part Five would agree, I think, that effective, ethical, and intelligent marketing—whether for students who live here or abroad—should instead be seen as the way in which an institution can make itself a real choice for a student. Students must choose; in choosing, they can also reject. In any event, whether they ultimately select or reject an institution, students must see that institution as clearly as possible, in the light that shows the institution's greatest strengths and virtues. Good marketing pro-

373

vides that light. Good office management allows admissions officers to shed that light with power for the right audience.

Chapters Twenty-One to Twenty-Four address the issue of how admissions officers can more effectively help the college or university address the public. Chapters Twenty-One to Twenty-Three discuss the large question of marketing and its place in the operation of the college admissions office. In Chapter Twenty-Four, Karen Lowe Raftus describes a segment of the college-going population about which most admissions officers have little knowledge: the international student. In Chapter Twenty-Five, B. Barbara Boerner shows how any admissions professional in charge of an office can work with the staff to make that office better serve both the institution and the students.

Quoting Phillip Kotler's description of marketing for non-profit organizations as "the effective management by an organization of its *exchange relations* with its various markets and publics," James C. Walters establishes the need for marketing intelligently in a period of severe competition for students. Walters summarizes the phases of marketing: research, planning and positioning, and promotion. He feels that marketing should be equated not with selling and manipulation but with research to identify needs and response to those needs. Unethical and desperate promotional campaigns are the result of no marketing, no research, no planning—they are mere reactions to a decline in the available pool.

Marketing is necessary for the college or university that plans to thrive for the next two decades, but what happens when everyone markets effectively? Will these well-planned efforts cancel each other out? Or will ethical marketing be replaced by unethical misrepresentation? That is the worst scenario, reports Theodore D. Kelly. But he argues that such an outcome is unnecessary. Market planning is market *creation*—creation of an awareness of the need for what the institution offers. Kelly describes various marketing stances and also demonstrates that there are alternatives to marketing besides cutthroat competition. They include fair-share concepts and regulated markets, which will work well in some states. Under the stress created by declining numbers, colleges are also likely to develop more effective recruitment and profiling techniques, so that blanket appeals to all students diminish. More careful marketing techniques will narrow the effective choices available to students, not by eliminating possibilities but by making stronger and clearer those choices that echo most precisely the notes of students' deepest interests. Those targeted through marketing are likely to become better selectors. Even so, Kelly warns, colleges must engage in ethical procedures, or they will ruin themselves with their various constituencies.

Both Walters and Kelly assume that an institution knows itself and its various markets; Jan Krukowski and Herman W. Kane discuss ways in which that knowledge can be developed or refreshed. They show how research regarding opinions and motivation has been used in other areas and might be used by colleges and universities. More important, they show how that research must be conducted if it is to be really instructive. Even universities that teach students how to perform good social science research rarely do internally relevant market research; Krukowski and Kane explain why, as they argue that the external research firm often is better qualified than the institution itself to provide useful information. They show the sources of information, what new data a research instrument ought to seek, how to get those data, and what research can reveal. Finally, they provide rather convincing arguments that the expertise necessary to conduct effective attitude and behavioral research is rarely available in admissions offices.

The approaches that Walters, Kelly, Krukowski, and Kane present are useful to the institution that hopes to provide service for the international student. There are thousands of young people outside the boundaries of the United States who wish to study here, and for them the colleges and universities must provide different information to satisfy different needs. Karen Lowe Raftus differentiates the pool she describes into three categories: foreign nationals, American students whose parents work in other countries, and American students attending Department of Defense schools.

Because foreign students are highly important to some institutions, and because other schools wish to attract foreign students, Raftus painstakingly describes precisely what information such students need to know before they embark on an

American educational journey. She also points out how different the cultural patterns of these potential students may be, and stresses that the school must be willing to tolerate or, better, embrace, these patterns. She shows how to evaluate the students' records and gives technical instruction, advice, and addresses of pertinent additional services.

Raftus concludes with a description of the different kinds of American students abroad and discusses what they need to know. As "international" students, many of them need highly sophisticated attention different from what might be appropriate for their contemporaries living in the United States, and some will also have been exposed to the intellectual rigor of the International Baccalaureate Degree, available to only a few students in the United States.

Unlike college counseling offices in secondary schools, admissions offices are rarely one-person operations. With increasing demands on them, members of admissions staffs need to have a better sense of how they can cooperate and coordinate their efforts to serve an institution—and student clients—effectively. Thus, more managerial expertise needs to be developed within each admissions office. Because no formal training systems have been developed for college admissions officers, there is a great need to provide internal training for staff members. In Chapter Twenty-Five, B. Barbara Boerner tells how to provide effective training through in-service training workshops. She shows how one can learn to delegate effectively and encourage staff growth and development, thus preventing territoriality. She stresses improving communication, evaluation, and developing and implementing a team concept. Her remarks are most useful to those who manage staffs, but all staff members will find her suggestions of how staff members can interrelate in an effective operation valuable.

Readers may also want to consult *Admissions, Academic Records, and Registrar Services: A Handbook of Policies and Procedures* (Quann and Associates, 1979); the chapter by E. Eugene Oliver, "Implementing Admissions Policy," includes a section on marketing. Those interested in developing a more effective office should read *Professional Audit for Admissions Officers* (Rowray and others, 1977).

21

Marketing Higher Education: Research, Planning, and Promotion

James C. Walters

As higher education moves from the boom times of the 1960s to the anticipated difficult decade of the 1990s, a number of factors are forcing profound changes in United States colleges and universities. The projected decline in the number of eighteen-year-olds is common knowledge; depending on the projector, the higher education enterprise is facing a 20 to 40 percent decline of high school graduates in the 1980s. Stagnant curricula, stabilization or decline of tax levels, lowering prestige of educators, and growing inflation, along with predicted enrollment declines, have transformed colleges and universities from elitist institutions to outreaching marketing organizations.

The marketing movement emerged in the early 1970s, when several writers (for instance, Wolf, 1973; Fram, 1974) discussed the use of modern business marketing principles within the context of higher education. In 1975 Kotler published an important book on the topic, and the College Entrance Examination Board sponsored a colloquium, *A Role for Marketing in College Admissions*. Since then, the number of articles, conferences, and workshops on the subject has proliferated. Today advertised descriptions of admissions positions frequently state that applicants with backgrounds in marketing are preferred. Terms such as "market research," "positioning," "market strategy," and "market penetration" are now commonly used—not only by admissions officers but also by vice-presidents, deans, and even faculty.

The development of marketing has been disconcerting to many educators. To refer to students as clients, to programs of study as products, and to academic divisions as profit centers rubs against the traditions of academe. Certainly some recruitment practices that have been carried forward under the idea of marketing have caused adverse reaction and alarm in both the general public and educators. The popular media (Fiske, 1979) have already pointed out questionable and unethical recruitment techniques, such as tuition rebates for students who recruit new students, handing out promotional Frisbees to high school students on spring break in Florida, distributing misleading brochures that resemble cigarette advertisements, and using hard-sell and cutthroat pressure techniques. The ultimate aggressive promotional technique, canceled at the last minute, involved a college that planned to release 103 balloons filled with scholarship offers.

Marketing and Marketing Research

Marketing is not the same as advertising or the generation of information for prospective students. It is not just being nice to prospective students, parents, and guidance counselors. It is more than a plan or set of strategies for student recruitment.

Kotler (1975, p. 13), probably the best-known writer in the nonprofit marketing field, provides a good working definition of marketing: "Marketing is the effective management by an organization of its *exchange relations* with its various markets and publics. All organizations depend upon exchange relations to attract resources that they need, to convert them into useful products and services, and to distribute them efficiently to target markets. Marketing is a systematic approach to planning and achieving desired relations with other groups."

Marketing characterizes a responsive organization concerned with the problems and means of effectively bringing students into contact with programs that will be beneficial and rewarding. Marketing seeks to provide services or products to people who want and need them.

Ihlanfeldt (1980) breaks the marketing concept into three phases. In the research phase, the institution analyzes the student market demand for various programs, evaluates how new programs would relate to existing programs in the institution and in competing institutions, and estimates the costs of continuing and new programs. Once such research is completed, the institution moves to the planning phase, in which program offerings are revised and staff for new programs secured. Related to the planning phase is the process of developing strategies for marketing the identified programs. Sometimes this is called positioning. The institution must decide what student market should be used for promotion and focus and how the program can be positioned or differentiated in relation to competing institutions. The third phase, communication or promotion, involves the typical problems facing the admissions staff, such as publications design, travel strategy, and the many means of communicating with prospective students and related publics.

An important aspect of the total marketing concept is marketing research. This is the point at which an institution must attempt to answer basic marketing questions. Following is a partial list of questions an institution would need to ask about itself:

1. Why do students choose or not choose our institution?
2. Why do students leave?
3. Why do students continue at our institution?
4. What are our primary and secondary markets in terms of geography, economics, aptitude, age level, and program offerings?
5. Are we ignoring possible new markets?
6. What is our public image among students, parents, alumni, faculty, and the general public?
7. What recruitment techniques are effective as perceived by prospective students?
8. What are our major strengths and weaknesses in faculty, programs, facilities, and so forth?
9. Who are our major competitor institutions?
10. What competitive benefits do we want to offer our target market?

Too few institutions can answer basic questions about themselves objectively, so the schools carry out their institutional planning and recruitment program based on subjective feelings. The marketing approach requires an orientation toward research and data analysis.

A number of survey techniques are available to an institution that seeks answers to the marketing research questions. The techniques include surveying accepted students, surveying nonapplicants, student attrition-retention studies, demographic studies, job market research, student outcome studies, and pricing-policy studies. A number of references provide guidelines, formats, and examples as to how such studies can be carried out (Larkin, 1979; Gaither, 1979; Howard, 1979; Ihlanfeldt, 1980; Litten, 1979).

Planning and Positioning

The science of marketing research must be followed by the art of interpreting the data effectively, so that management decisions can be made. Such decisions are based not on the institution's historical record but on the idea of satisfying the customers' needs. Each institution must develop its own methods of how to work through the process of planning for its future, based on the marketing research effort. Kotler (1979) suggests a number of approaches for the planning effort. A modest approach is for the president to appoint a small "blue ribbon" marketing committee, which not only supervises the research audits but also makes recommendations for institutional action. The effort may also be approached through a five-year institutional plan involving various committees. Other approaches involve engaging an outside marketing specialist firm or creating a director or vice-president of marketing; such a person is responsible for continual market research, planning, positioning, and institutional promotion and communication.

However the planning phase is organized, the result should be an institution that purposely makes decisions about what programs it should offer, how they should be priced, when and where they should be distributed, and how they should be promoted.

Related to the total marketing concept is the idea of positioning (Gettzer and Rico, 1976), which is similar to Ihlanfeldt's phase of developing alternate strategies for an institution's future. Positioning is the adoption of a specific and unique role for an institution that will set it apart from other institutions and that will have a special appeal to a segment of the population. Perceptions of market position include not only program offerings but also such factors as facilities, type of student body, nature of the faculty, location of the institution, and the ambience of the college.

A major institutional concern is that, in the years ahead, broad general promotion of a college's attributes will get lost in an overcommunicated society. Higher education will be faced with too many institutions, too few students, and too much general promotion. Colleges will be communicating, but they may be saying the same things, such as stressing a beautiful campus, an outstanding faculty, and an outstanding science program. The problem is that the consumer mind is selective and builds defenses against the volume of communications; the mind screens out general information and selects positions.

Some colleges—such as Harvard, Oberlin, Reed, and the University of North Carolina at Chapel Hill—already have well-defined positions. Some colleges have defined positions in certain areas of study, such as communications, engineering, business administration, and special two-year programs. Positioning may occur in serving certain segments of the population, such as older women, middle-management executives, prisoners, or members of labor unions.

The position strategy that a college develops, whether as a type of college or in terms of specific programs and services, should be a part of the marketing process if enrollments are to be maintained. Very few institutions will enjoy the luxury of status quo in the future, and very few will be able to attempt to be all things to all people. Kotler (1976) describes the steps involved in institutional positioning:

1. The college should know how it is perceived by its publics.
2. Various alternative positions should be examined, both in

light of competitive institutions and the requirements to adopt them.
3. A position that holds the best long-run promise should be selected, and a plan to achieve it, both financially and otherwise, should be put in place.

Following are several actual examples of institutions that have used positioning strategies to change and have experienced increased enrollments as a result:

1. A midwestern university in a rural area learned through marketing research that one of its strongest attributes was its classic residential ambience. It had been failing to stress its residential nature, beautiful setting, and outstanding student-life program. The university began to communicate very directly its strong residential program and has enjoyed enrollment increases for five straight years.
2. A small New England college, faced with a declining student body, learned through research that there was a serious shortage of physical therapy programs of study in the six-state New England area. By making significant changes in its curriculum, it now offers a physical therapy program that has resulted in an unusually large number of applicants. Clearly, the college's future will be secured by further program positioning in the allied health area.
3. A public, two-year college founded in the 1960s has taken advantage of its setting in the forests of the Appalachian foothills and stressed career programs in forestry and natural resources. This position, tied with the creative selection of other two-year programs unduplicated in other colleges, has led to twelve years of enrollment increases, with students from an unusually large geographical area seeking out the college.
4. A midwestern college learned through research that its college of communications already held an excellent reputation among prospective students and institutional publics. With the prospects of lower enrollments ahead, a purposeful decision was made to strengthen the communications areas, in order to position them with the "best" in the na-

tion. Here the positioning strategy involved improving an already strong position, to continue to identify a large market sector in the future.

Vaccaro (1979) has suggested that a good way to evaluate the relative development of marketing at an institution is to look at its product, pricing, packaging, and promotion. The institution must be in a position to introduce new products (programs) that meet the demands of student consumers. Elimination of programs must also occur when necessary. The tenured faculty system and other unique characteristics of higher education certainly limit the flexibility of institutions as compared with the typical portfolio planning of the private business world. However, many institutions have implemented faculty-development programs (Mayhew, 1979) that overcome faculty tenure and productivity problems, leading to institutions that can adapt to change. Institutions that exhibit flexibility in terms of their product stand greater chances of institutional success in the difficult years ahead.

Good pricing strategies are rarely found in colleges and universities, yet the cost of an institution and the perceived value of attendance and the potential benefits do affect college choice. Institutions need to study price in relation to market position (Ihlanfeldt, 1980, pp. 98-115) and also the effect of financial aid and no-need scholarships on recruiting and retaining students.

Packaging refers to the way in which the product is delivered: where, according to what schedule, by what mode of presentation, at what time of year. Institutions that move into the marketing mode must consider consumer needs, not what is convenient for the faculty or student service offices. Many institutions that have successfully developed new market positions have done so by packaging the product in various ways.

Promotion

When marketing is mentioned, most people first think of promotion. But promotion should be the end product of the total marketing approach, after the marketing research, institutional planning, and positioning have been done. Promotion based on consumer desires is not a hard-sell process but a planned information presentation to the identified institutional publics or markets. Effective promotion need not be associated with huge advertising budgets or questionable student-recruitment techniques. An effective marketing program will make selling less necessary than when there is no such approach.

The primary task of the admissions office is to develop an institutional promotion and communication strategy. Such a plan details approaches to recruitment travel, publications, off-campus information programs, advertising, direct-mail system, and alumni support of the promotion effort. The goal of the plan should be to make effective use of time, personnel, and budget.

Certainly, one major problem in dealing with marketing is the limited understanding of the concept and the negative connotations of the term. Marketing should be not equated with selling and manipulation but with research and response—with identifying and responding to needs. Overloading prospective students with advertising, pressuring them on the telephone or in person, and making dishonest and misleading statements are hard-sell techniques—not part of a total marketing plan but simply responses to a declining pool of high school graduates.

Honest and helpful admissions counseling must remain a cornerstone of the recruitment phase of the marketing plan. Simple recruiting for applications involves sales-oriented persuasion tactics rather than a counseling or facilitating approach. Institutions that have simply recruited for numbers of applications learn that, in the long run, such a persuasion approach does not work. Students who are "sold" on an institution typically become unhappy with their experience and become part of an attrition problem.

The current codes of conduct of professional admissions associations have effectively curbed unethical recruitment practices and must continue to be highly visible in the future. A total marketing philosophy indicates to all concerned that goals center around the real needs of students. In the long run, the college-seeking public will favor those institutions that offer meaningful education and customer satisfaction.

22

Sharing the Market: Implications of Increased Competition for Students

Theodore D. Kelly

The first example of market sharing in American higher education began, if the story is true, when Benjamin Franklin, as a fund raiser for the University of Pennsylvania, and the person raising funds for Harvard decided to share the London market. According to the story, the two men decided that, rather than compete with each other for financial support for their institutions, they would divide their combined prospect lists and at the end of the year equally share the results. They reasoned that the donors would be less confused by conflicting requests for funds; that a divided list of donors would not feel besieged for gifts; and that, by carefully selecting which prospect to call on, they would have to work less to achieve better results.

Their efforts were marked by success, and for three years they continued to raise more funds than previously. That is, they were successful until each institution discovered their marketing arrangement and promptly dismissed each despite the success of their efforts. One suspects that the dismissals came about because each institution believed more could have been done through aggressive competition rather than with so rudimentary an approach to the market.

The moral of the story is that should all institutions become marketing oriented in their admissions programs, there will instantly be those who believe the way to acquire an in-

coming class is simply to "be there first with the most." Consequently, the fear that not everyone can share the market will
push some institutions into assuming that the best market plan
is to preempt competition. In turn, this assumption will cause
the reactionary response that the only way to prevent being
forced out of the market for students is to develop covert, unethical means for beating the competition at its own game,
thereby giving rise to all sorts of abuses, with tragic consequences for the student. This will cause all institutions involved
in recognizable marketing approaches to be discredited. As a result, institutions will divide into those that appear to be non-
marketing ones, because they will continue to be demand institutions, and those highly aggressive, often abusive smaller or
struggling institutions that are desperate for students. And the
thinking student will know which is the better institution to
choose.

Now that I have stated all the worst consequences of a
marketing-oriented higher education, let me hasten to say that I
do not expect these consequences to occur. Rather, there are
many positive probable outcomes to soundly developed institutional marketing programs. If developed along proven marketing
principles, these programs will tend to integrate with the marketing plans of other institutions in a harmonious way. Not that
all will be rosy, but all will certainly not be stormy.

What industries have known for decades American higher
education will discover: Market planning is really largely market
creation. The market was *created* for deodorants, electric tooth-
brushes, life insurance, and even vacuum cleaners. A part of
every institutional marketing plan must pay attention to ways
to *create awareness for the need* for the particular brand of educational product being offered to the public.

Surprisingly, most academic institutions are unaware of
their basic marketing thrust. Because these marketing activities
have been done so long and are done by so many, they are not
really seen as marketing activities. For how many decades have
colleges produced catalogues of offerings, including terms of
sale and credit? Almost as long as Sears. And the traveling sales-
man routines are familiar to college admissions officers. One-

night stands in Peoria, Cleveland, Buffalo, and Erie are not unknown in the college recruitment circuit. One counselor for an eastern two-year college for women once told me that Holiday Inn notifies her of every new Inn that opens, so she can maintain a perfect record of having slept at least once in every Holiday Inn from Bangor, Maine, to Baltimore, Maryland.

What about that pillar of sales, direct mail? Mailboxes of college-bound prospects are filled with junk mail—produced in full color by process printing and with enamel-coated stock—courtesy of the best academic marketer in the business, College Entrance Examination Board, and its prodigy, Student Search Service. Some students measure their popularity by the number of Search letters received. Then there are those venerable "trade shows" where all the new "product lines" are "introduced to the market" to measure "consumer response" at NACAC college fairs and an infinity of college days and nights in local high schools. The question is not "Will everyone be marketing?" but "What will happen when everyone *is* marketing?"

One has only to look at the number of colleges using Student Search Service, about 900, to realize that when a productive marketing idea comes along, a high percentage of colleges will use it. Some colleges will also try to imitate the successful marketing activities of other colleges without doing their own marketing research. This is what I call the "hamburger school of marketing": If McDonald's thinks a location is good for business, another chain will open across the street. Soon there will be four in an area that can support only two. Two will quickly fold. Be certain that McDonald's will not close, just as Harvard will not. One college president who has been very successful in academic marketing practices is frequently asked to give advice about advertising in newspapers to attract high school graduates. He always recommends the practice but confides to friends, "Let them spend their money—as I did—to find out that newspaper advertising does not work."

Two basic approaches are open to institutions when everyone is marketing. One is to plagiarize the marketing activities of other institutions; the other is to conduct original research. Original research is the assumed better course and should be organized around a growth opportunity matrix (shown in Figure 1). The institution should determine from research

Figure 1. Growth Opportunity Matrix.

Product

	Old	New
Old	Market Penetration	Product Development
New	Market Development	Diversification

Market ─

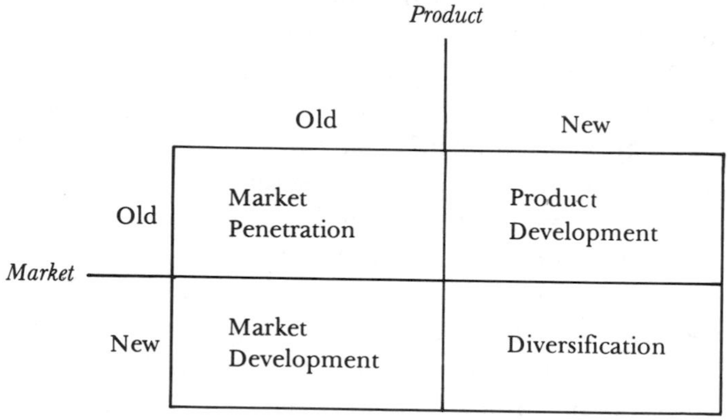

Source: From Ansoff, 1957.

whether to take existing product lines to existing markets (market penetration), or new product lines to existing markets (product development), or existing products to new markets (market development), or new products to new markets (diversification).

A challenge, therefore, for institutional market planners may be to increase the percentage of postsecondary education prospects at the same rate that the eighteen-year-old population will decline. This is market development if product lines do not change, or it is diversification if new programs are added. This will not be done by putting a better package on an existing product. General Motors, Ford, and Chrysler found out that better styling for an inefficient engine worked just so long. Instead, institutional market planners must discover the need factors of their constituent markets, respond to the needs, and demonstrate ability to meet those needs. This is product development. The creation of awareness of the consumer's need and the institution's ability to meet need will in turn create a natural leveling of demand in the marketplace.

This leveling of demand will cause the demise of marginal institutions. But in any marketing enterprise, marginally offered products go under—no matter how excellent the product or service. Do you remember the car whose manufacturer was so sure of its excellence that he said, "Ask the man who owns one"? The recent demise of superior-quality liberal arts colleges, especially among women's colleges, was caused by the marginal understanding and acceptance of the buying public for their product. Marginality can be a consequence of overextension of resources without consumer acceptance, not always of poor product quality. It is therefore axiomatic that the large or strong get bigger or stronger.

One of my clients, the business manager of a women's college, confided to me that the college's "contingency reserve funds" were such that if no students enrolled in the college for two years, it could still meet all budget obligations, including full salaries. Stretched out over five years of decline, we projected that it could outlast its competitors. And this institution is more than 90 percent tuition-dependent.

On April 15, 1980, the *Wall Street Journal* reported that "200 schools, mostly liberal arts colleges, will starve to death." This could be the cause of "will it be us" questions among administrators across the nation. Each will claim it probably will not be "us"—what college is on record with its accrediting association that it will be closing in the 1980s? What most small colleges must be assuming is that the consequences of the marketing thrust of other colleges will somehow pass them over because they are so small, so isolated, so old, and so well served by alumni who will not let them close. But some broker somewhere will call the margin, and the larger, stronger college nearby will be the winner.

A more optimistic option is that there is a fair share for every college. There are market areas where this will certainly be true. In states where the development of higher educational institutions has been in response to state needs or limited to nearby states or where the decline in the eighteen-year-old population is less severe, market penetration will easily offset minimal market declines. In South Carolina, for example, a mere 5 percent decline in high school graduates is forecast. Furthermore, a statewide cooperative effort is under way to produce at minimal cost for both public and private colleges the names of rising seniors. In the first year of this effort, 22,000 names were produced through voluntary completion of a form by students in high schools. The names were forwarded to the University of South Carolina and entered on a computer. Names were made available to South Carolina colleges that promised to use them for their institutions only. One college that used these names, Limestone College in Gaffney, South Carolina, cross-referenced the names from the tape with its in-house names and matched the desired majors of names on tape with institutional offerings, netting about 8,000 names. One mailing produced a response rate in excess of 7 percent, which was 2 percent better than response from Search names the previous year for South Carolina.

Five states are projected to have an increase in student populations in the 1980s. Among them is Vermont, where the largest industry in the state is higher education. As a result, the state of Vermont has protective legislation for higher education, and there is one cooperative association of all colleges in the state. Recently, the president of one of the smallest private colleges in Vermont was chairman of the association. In states like Vermont and South Carolina, there will be a better chance that each college will get a fair share of the market.

Conceivably, this fair-share concept could go a step further to a regulated market. Should abuses develop and state regulatory and planning agencies cooperate, a condition of regulated growth (not marketing) could occur. For example, in its early planning for the growth of state educational facilities, Illinois mandated the maximum enrollment capability of state schools, to ensure a population for private colleges that was greater than the percentage they currently served. After all, governmental agencies regulate the growth of health care facilities. Why not education?

The problems of viability will occur in states, or in less populous areas of some states, where the decline of the basic eighteen-year-old market cannot be offset by institutional change or successful appeals to new markets. In these cases, where the spaces to be filled exceed the supply, a fair-share concept cannot exist. As a result, colleges with a superior market position or marketing techniques will prevail, and other colleges will close. It should be noted that, as in any marketing condition, the true value of a product is not always the basis for successful marketing efforts. Consequently, the mere claim for academic excellence will not in itself attract sufficient students without a sound program of promotion to get the message across and an effective system of response to market interest to get the required yields.

Horror stories abound about the ability of colleges to attract students either through extracurricular possibilities or the persuasiveness of the admissions counselor. In instances where the two factors exist together, students will choose a college without real regard for academic offerings. My favorite example is the student who was aggressively recruited to a private college in Arkansas, where she could bring her boat for sailing. She arrived with a twenty-two-foot sailboat for the college's three-acre pond. She was a quick attrition statistic!

A consequence of a condition whereby all, or nearly all, colleges are marketing is the probability of more efficient recruitment programs. In the colleges that have done even simple demographic studies, the once popular "hit every high school in seven states" approach has yielded to the establishment of primary, secondary, and tertiary markets. In such cases, all high schools in the primary market are visited, only the best ones in the secondary, and none in the tertiary. Travel budgets drop considerably, staffing requirements change, and support services reflect increased activity with higher mail and telephone costs. The total budget may not change, but enrollments frequently rise.

Further efficiencies result from careful use of data on enrollment patterns. One institution discovered that the majority of students came from high schools within twenty-five miles either side of the two major interstate highways that crossed within its city. Profiling techniques will lead to a pattern of not working areas that produce nonacceptable students and intense concentration on areas producing students meeting entrance requirements. The use of profiles with the College Board's Student Search Service or the American College Testing's Educational Opportunity Service will "target" prospects, determine market size and distribution, and predicate travel patterns. All these activities will reduce the role of "prospecting" and increase the direct, one-to-one contact pattern. The net effect of this approach is to leave some students untouched by one college and available for others, or at least to reduce the multiplicity of contact that is ultimately very frustrating or confusing to many college-bound students.

Evidence supports my statement that profiling techniques reduce multiple applications. Institutions should attempt to verify this for their own satisfaction, but two recent college surveys of incoming freshmen revealed a surprisingly high percentage of students applying only to the college they attended. These results are causing the two colleges to identify prospects by profile earlier, so as to be able to approach likely responders more effectively. The result may well be a quicker response by the prospects, eliminating or reducing later competition. What will happen when the prime prospects get 100 Search or E.O.S. letters in the same week is anybody's guess.

Travel patterns will most certainly change in the near future because of energy costs or better market research. Assuming that better profiling will tell colleges where *not* to travel, there certainly will be fewer colleges *or* a narrower range of colleges to choose from or to see during the traditional college day or night or the private high school visit. The marginal institutions will not be at Crannybrook Country Day, nor will Excellence U. be at P.S. 461. Less competition in the market will narrow choice options for students.

Once the majority of colleges are marketing, the resulting pressure of colleges successful in their marketing (recruitment) efforts will cause more colleges to depend on market response and become more aware of and sensitive to what the purchaser/consumer (parent/student) wants. Public institutions that operate in a controlled market, with restrictions on recruitment areas, will be forced to sustain growth through market penetration.

These public institutions may also be forced to go beyond their market areas, usually defined by county or state
lines, to get numbers to keep state funding levels at a desired
total. In Wisconsin the 1980-81 recruitment budgets for state
institutions were cut by state mandate. The director of admissions of one branch of the University of Wisconsin reported a
high degree of wall climbing and resignations from an office-
bound staff. They could not function well with telephone calling, increased campus interviews, and on-campus "sales events"
such as visiting day. When market development is cut off, market penetration is the best recourse.

Private colleges will explore means for market development and market penetration (cover larger territories or old territories better) before they exercise the product development
and diversification concepts. These concepts require alternatives
and continuing education opportunities that are harder to
achieve in a typical liberal arts environment.

The real danger to all colleges in an all-out market effort
by a majority of the colleges is the possibility of a heightened
purchaser/consumer sophistication. It is conceivable that, to protect themselves from a barrage of marketing colleges, prospective students with professional help (in the high school or from
other advisory services) will develop a reverse Search—that is, a
profile of the colleges they will not consider. Using this filter,
students can lock out colleges not worth considering. This approach could be encouraged by the consumer movement, which
is trying to create a generation of educated consumers. Consequently, the best-articulated approach to the market could gain
a response in enrollments based on truer market understanding
and not necessarily on institutional quality.

What happens when all colleges are marketing is not,
as some would have it, an automatic souring of attitude by prospective purchasers and consumers of academic services. The response from students, parents, and guidance counselors will not
necessarily be "If it's a good college, they don't need to sell it."
Rather, a carefully planned and implemented marketing effort
will increase the *quality* of enrolled students because it allows
the institution to maintain desired quantity. To do this, all colleges will need to market (not merely "sell") better now than in

the past. A reasonable outcome is the student who will say "I'm glad I found out about Obscure College because that's my kind of college and I never would have known it if it hadn't found me."

Marketing activities that seek consumer satisfaction and not producer goals will distinguish academic marketing only if enough institutions force on the marketplace correct processes instead of trying to ignore the changes in academe that a declining traditional market will inevitably bring.

✐ 23

Using Marketing Research to Develop an Admissions Plan

Jan Krukowski
Herman W. Kane

✐   In recent years, university administrators have come to recognize the contributions that behavioral and attitudinal research can offer the admissions process. Unhappily, some reasons for this recognition are negative. Schools and colleges have turned to such research only after experiencing an appreciable lowering of entering-class academic quality, dwindling applications and enrollments, failure to make continuing education profitable, or fear of the consequences of the downturn of the birthrate in the late 1960s. It is never too late for an institution to benefit from research, but the best moment for a university to undertake a research effort that will redefine its admissions market is during prosperous times. Research peers into the future. With the foresight it provides, an institution can meet changing quantitative conditions as well as variations in demand, so that problems do not evolve into crises.

What Is Behavioral and Attitudinal Research For?

Despite their repeated assertions that they are not prognosticators, political polltakers have recently received the most severe criticism since the surprise ending to the 1948 Truman-Dewey presidential contest. The occasion was a Reagan landslide not publicly forecast by anyone. Whatever the merits of the case against the pollsters, presidential elections force us to note the increasing influence of survey research on the political process. Throughout major political campaigns, we are besieged by results of newspaper and television polls. Most polls do little more than describe a dynamic condition in static terms. Often these polls are devised more to stimulate interest in the news medium than in the electoral count.

In contrast, most serious surveys, including political surveys, are privately commissioned and have as their major purposes the solution or at least the alleviation of one or more problems and the development of tactical or strategic plans to achieve a desired outcome. When a candidate for public office commissions a poll, he should—and, if he has retained a qualified consultant, typically does—intend the survey to generate a set of indicators. These will pinpoint geographical or demographic subgroup targets, suggest likely campaign themes, weigh the relative merit of a campaign based on candidates' own positive attributes versus one based on opponents' negative characteristics, and in general help make the best use of campaign funds and energies.

When using these techniques, politicians are simply borrowing practices developed years ago by commerce and industry. Every major corporation has at least one market research division (some have three or four), either to undertake research activities or to commission research from outsiders. Most of this research is withheld from public view, unless the sponsoring organization finds publication in its best interest. But few major marketing decisions—whether the introduction of new products, the development of advertising campaigns, the entrance into new markets, or changes in packaging and merchandising—are made today without research guidance.

In addition to commercial and political research, government research is of major importance. The opinion survey is a primary tool of the many research projects government agencies sponsor each year. Some of these government outlays are distributed contractually to academic and nonprofit umbrella-research organizations. Assignments handled in this fashion deal with problems and issues in such areas as defense, commerce, health, education, and housing.

Sometimes the federal government awards grants to individuals or organizations (usually university affiliated) for testing intellectually interesting hypotheses. Such grants tend to be made for projects that need time; two or three years is not uncommon. The findings, often reported in academic journals, are rarely concerned with pragmatic problem solving and are seldom of interest to those outside relatively small academic circles. Thus, universities know how to do research, do a lot of it, and earn money from it. Yet, oddly, not until recently have they wanted to turn market research to their own use, for several reasons. Some academics fear that research into student and parental course preference will undercut traditional liberal arts curricula and turn colleges and universities into vocational schools. Some social science or business school faculties reject the use of outside research consultants on the ground that they themselves can do better, less costly research. And some institutions thrust research aside entirely, convinced that market data cannot shed any light on academe.

It hardly needs repeating that the ethical, professional research firm has as its purpose the collection and appraisal of attitudinal, behavioral, and descriptive data, not the transformation of a client institution into something it does not wish to be. Nor is it a rejection of the skills of faculty research specialists to point out that the outside research firm dealing in attitudinal-behavioral research can almost always perform more effectively. After all, the consulting firm specializing in admissions work has a ready frame of reference for evaluating a particular institution's performance. Its skills in identifying the groups to be studied, designing the study, drawing the sample, designing the instrument, and supervising field interviews are sharply honed. And its professional distance from its client institutions helps assure total objectivity. (The reputable consultant welcomes help from knowledgeable faculty members, even though their teaching and research commitments generally tie up most of their time.) For the final argument, it would seem that research, done properly, could uncover meaningful truths about any human social institution, whether commercial, academic, cultural, or governmental.

Many universities, recognizing the need, now maintain institutional research offices. Although most of these offices are not administered by experienced research professionals, they can perform a valuable service. For example, a university research office can follow yearly the geographical and demographic characteristics of each entering and graduating class and of all transfers and dropouts. Properly organized, such offices can reveal *what* is happening. But they do not often possess the requisite skill, or in most cases the funds, to go further and probe descriptive information for the reasons that explain student behavior. Nor do they have the expertise necessary to target selected subgroups or develop promotional themes that improve a college or university's competitive position.

But an equipped, organized, and funded institutional research office can be an important source of crucial data. These data should include, for each entering or departing student, academic performance (secondary and higher education), location of residence, type of secondary school attended, intended and actual major, preentering and subsequent career objectives, postgraduation plans, application history (undergraduate and graduate), and financial characteristics. In addition, the research office should keep records of the destination of no-shows (students who decline offers of admission) and dropouts. (This list is not inclusive and should be modified as needed to record the background and behavior of continuing education and other evening or part-time students.)

Some useful information is available from the College Board and the American College Testing Program, which extensively monitor their examinees. To College Board and ACT data should be added broader trend data, available from such sources as the Bureau of the Census, the National Center for Education Statistics, the Educational Testing Service, the Consortium on Financing Higher Education, and state education departments. From these sources, one can follow population statistics, projections of high school graduates, occupational forecasts, GRE and other test performances, and trends in continuing education.

Direction of the Primary Research Design

Survey research, in the context we discuss it, is the collection of original attitudinal, behavioral, and descriptive data from constituencies of significance to a university, whether in student recruitment, financial development, alumni relations, or public relations. This chapter focuses on student recruitment and is concerned with research findings and conclusions that become the major component of a marketing plan.

Depending on the university's priorities, information can be sought from any or all of the following groups, each of which may affect or be affected by recruiting. No one study is likely to approach all these groups, but two or more can be compared to provide increased perspective.

- Present students.
- No-shows.
- Dropouts.
- Alumni.
- Prospective students (broadly or narrowly defined).
- Parents of prospective students.
- Inquirers who did not apply.
- Present or prospective continuing education students.
- College-university faculty and administration.
- Guidance counselors and other secondary school officials.
- Prospective employers.
- Other leaders.

How to Design a Research Project

The first and most important lesson in design is: Do not waste time gathering irrelevant information. In a recruiting study, questionnaires should focus on recruiting issues and generate findings that suggest specific courses of action. For example, if a single-sex institution has emphatically stated its intention to remain single sex, the researcher should not explore the potential for a coeducational program. Broadly stated, recruitment research should bring in enough accurate data to let the

recruiting staff identify and approach the right prospects as readily and inexpensively as possible and avoid the wrong prospects.
To do this, many of the following questions must be asked and
answered:

- To what extent are we known and how are we perceived in
  relation to our competition?
- What characteristics (size, type, affiliation, quality, location,
  curriculum, and so on) are associated with us; on what bases
  have these judgments been formed; what are the consequences of these perceptions for us?
- What are the purposes of higher education, and what is the
  relative importance of specific career and educational objectives?
- What specific academic preparation and personal characteristics are employers and graduate schools seeking? To what extent are we meeting their needs?
- What is the relative importance of selection criteria in determining applications as well as final choice?
- How do students learn about colleges; whom do they rely on
  for counseling at the various decision-making stages?
- What factors influence students to select or reject particular
  colleges? To what extent are their judgments based on
  stereotypes?
- What link does the group detect between education and life
  after graduation?
- How do those who attend a particular institution assess its
  conditions and programs?
- What is the impact of financial aid on the college-selection
  process and the educational experience?

Research Technology: Sampling, Questionnaire
Construction, and Data Collection

Determination of the populations to be sampled and the
subjects to be covered in the interview should emerge from discussions with the client. But the method of selecting the sample
and the language and order of the questions are the responsibility

of the consultant, subject to client approval. The objective of the research assignment is what primarily determines the sampling universe. Other considerations—such as geography, accessibility, academic potential or performance, sex, intended or actual major, year in school or college, and type of high school —also may affect the choice of a sample.

The number of respondents to be interviewed can vary considerably. For example, if the number of freshman no-shows at a small liberal arts college is 200 to 250, the sample will probably be not much larger than 100. But if the idea is to cover a large urban university's market for continuing education, the sample could be as large as 1,000. Although no rules govern sample size, we suggest three key questions:

1. Will the sample yield enough interviews to allow the consultant to project trends (in the absence of high statistical accuracy?
2. What degree of analytical flexibility is desired? That is, what is the maximum number of subgroups to be compared across any single variable?
3. What is the budget?

Questionnaire construction is perhaps the most underrated and least appreciated skill of the researcher. It requires a blending of general expertise with the specific knowledge that only the faculty and staff of the institution can supply. Balancing the blend can be difficult. Often, research consultants must deal with a committee representing the university. Its members, who represent differing administrative divisions or academic disciplines, may be at odds with one another. Each may want the questionnaire to stress a particular subject or issue. The consultant must balance the divergent views, always keeping in perspective the allotted interviewing time. Most important, the questionnaire must be limited to important issues.

A sound procedure is for the consultant to hold a meeting with the client representative to clarify the research objectives, set forth a sampling plan, and discuss the issues that should be covered in the survey instrument. After this working session, a draft questionnaire (or questionnaires if more than one group is to be studied) should be submitted for review. Further discussion will generate revised drafts until both parties agree that the survey instrument will achieve its objectives. The questionnaire should then be pretested for timing, wording, and flow. After completion of pretesting and any further revisions, the study is ready for its field stage.

There are three major ways to collect survey data: in person or face to face (by appointment or at random), by telephone, and by mail. We feel, as do most other research consultants, that the merits of the face-to-face and the telephone interview far outweigh those of the mail survey, except in cost. Both personal and telephone interviews allow a flexibility in sampling design to stratify, to impose quotas, or to assure random distributions under tight control. They also offer the opportunity to probe responses that are initially unclear or incomplete. In its turn, the in-person interview has several advantages over the telephone interview. The length of time a respondent is willing to devote to an interview is greater and the attention span longer if the interview is conducted in person. Personal interviews often last an hour, or even longer; in contrast, telephone interviews rarely extend beyond thirty minutes. The face-to-face interview also allows the interviewer to use visual aids. Relatively long, complex questions can thus be asked without worry that the respondent will miss or forget part of the question.

The one great advantage of the telephone interview over the face-to-face interview is its lower cost. Because most subjects can be handled within the thirty-minute limit, and it is a rare college or university that is not cost conscious, the telephone has increasingly become the primary tool for information gathering. However, sometimes accessibility helps shape methodology. For example, if the population to be studied is composed of high school juniors or seniors and the sampling unit is the school, it is far easier to secure permission to interview at the school than to screen households by telephone.

Too often, however, in an effort to minimize costs, institutions turn to the mails. Some consultants condone this procedure and apply its findings, using the dubious argument that any research is better than none. Research by mail has many weaknesses. Some of them:

- One cannot control the *distribution* of respondents whatever the response rate. Self-selection makes impossible any judgment about the behavioral and attitudinal "representativeness" of those who respond.
- The opportunity to read through the entire questionnaire destroys the subtleties of sequencing that are part of personal and telephone interviews. There is also a potential bias, in that those with strongest opinions may be the most likely respondents.
- Absence of the interviewer eliminates probing and renders open-ended questions nearly useless.
- There is no guarantee that the questionnaire is completed by the respondent for whom it was intended.

For these reasons and others, whenever attitudinal, perceptual, and behavioral data are required, we strongly oppose the use of mail questionnaires.

Respondents like to answer questions with what they judge to be the legitimate response; that is, what the interviewer expects to hear. The designer must be ingenious to counter this tendency. Some techniques are using hypothetical situations, which alleviate the sometimes tedious routine of question and answer, and framing questions in the third person, so that respondents can more freely express a controversial or sensitive position without its seeming to reflect on themselves.

Processing and Analyzing the Data: The Computer

Before data can be interpreted, they must be coded, keypunched, and programmed, after which the computer generates a complete set of data. The most significant items that differentiate respondents from one another are treated as independent variables and become column headings. Virtually all questions are then designated as dependent variables and cross-tabulated against the column headings. The column headings typically include geographical breaks, socioeconomic divisions, academic discipline, occupational-professional categories, and standard demographic classifications, to which are often added type of college or high school. It is important to remember that the computer is only as good as the researcher who uses it. It will generate what it is programmed to produce.

In addition to the relatively straightforward cross-tabulations just discussed, the computer can perform more complex multivariate statistical operations, such as multiple regression and factor analysis. Given the timing and budgeting constraints of marketing projects, such procedures are rarely employed. However, magnetic tapes of the complete data set can be provided, and to these any number of advanced procedures can be applied later. The research report that accompanies the raw output analyzes and interprets the findings within the context of the study's objectives and sets the stage for the final step in the process: the development of an institutional marketing plan.

Application of the Findings: The Marketing Plan

A good marketing plan evaluates an institution in relation to its competition, determines which promotional activities should be added or improved or dropped, and suggests better ways of reaching prospects. These recommendations are partly based on cost-benefit analyses. The plan differentiates the areas that require change from those that are improperly understood or relatively unknown and that therefore require promotional and informational attention. A recruitment marketing plan should:

1. Define the institution's most promising markets and suggest the priorities that should be assigned to each.
2. Recommend the practical steps that should be taken to strengthen market position.
3. Suggest the methods that will explain and communicate to prospects faculty, departmental, and other curricular strengths.

4. Name some ways to contact and convince prospects and applicants, to raise the conversion rate of inquiries into applications and applicants into enrolled students.
5. Target the likeliest student subgroups by geographical, demographic, and educational characteristics.
6. Spell out ways to reach guidance counselors and parents.
7. Devise programs to involve students and alumni in recruiting.
8. Explain how to use the written word as part of the recruiting program.

The best safeguard against future recruiting crises is an understanding of one's present situation. Research can play a major role in clarifying one's competitive position and suggesting actions that will improve it. We suggested that the independent outside firm specializing in attitudinal and behavioral research is the appropriate resource to use because its expertise and objectivity are the best guarantees of efficient and useful research results. But before retaining a specific consultant, be sure to ask these questions:

1. Is the consultant a true professional, with verifiable credentials?
2. Does the consultant understand the complexities of institutional marketing?
3. Is the consultant prepared to work with your institution's own staff, using its expertise as a complement to his skills?
4. Does the consultant grasp your institution's problem?
5. Is the consultant concerned with your long-term advantage rather than with a "quick cure" that may not be permanent?
6. Is the consultant's approach tied to action rather than to philosophizing?
7. Does the consultant appear to understand that you operate within a budget and that your program has a deadline?

Conversely, some pitfalls and danger signals:

1. An inadequate budget. (Poor research is worse than one's intuition and judgment.)

2. The promise that a sure and quick solution will automatically emerge from the research.
3. Suggestions that the research team can get along without the participation of administrators and faculty.
4. The mail survey, especially if directed at amorphous populations.
5. A research team with no marketing expertise or experience in strategic planning.

✍ 24

Recruiting and Enrolling Students from Abroad

Karen Lowe Raftus

✍   Let me define the term "international student" as it is used in my office. The applicants we refer to as international students are comprised of three subgroups:

1. Foreign nationals applying from outside the United States, who will be studying here on student visas.
2. Permanent residents who have emigrated to the United States but have not obtained citizenship.
3. Overseas American students, who are the children of American citizens living abroad.

Any applicant who is not a United States citizen is classified as a foreign student, regardless of visa status. The term "international students" includes in its larger group the overseas American students.

        This chapter deals with a variety of issues, including credential evaluation and admission of foreign students; the abuses and guidelines in foreign student recruitment; the nature of international and American schools overseas; and the concerns of American high school students living abroad.

Foreign Student Admissions

        For some institutions, foreign student admissions may be a minor or even nonexistent element of the total admissions picture. But according to the 1979-80 *Open Doors,* published by

the Institute of International Education, there are more than
285,000 foreign students currently studying at the tertiary level
in the United States. That number is an 8.5 percent increase
since the 1978-79 edition of *Open Doors* and a 738 percent increase since the first edition of *Open Doors* was published in
1954-55, when there were just over 34,000 foreign students
studying at colleges and universities in the United States.

Although the majority of foreign students are concentrated on the campuses of a few major universities, the significant increase in recent years indicates that a larger number of
colleges and universities, both private and publicly supported,
are now enrolling foreign students. Furthermore, since it is predicted that there will be a 15 to 20 percent decline in the number of American high school graduates by the mid-1980s, it
seems likely that the number of foreign students studying in the
United States will continue to increase in the future, as colleges
and universities look beyond our shores for the answer to their
enrollment problems.

Graduate and undergraduate programs alike are and will
continue to be affected. In 1979 foreign students earned 15
percent of all Ph.D. degrees awarded in the United States. According to the National Association of Graduate Schools, they
received 30 percent of all graduate degrees in engineering alone.
Although presently only about 2 percent of the nation's 11.4
million college students are foreign, they may easily represent
10 percent of the total college population by 1990.

Not only is the number of foreign students increasing; the
global representation is also changing. In the past, the largest
number of foreign students came from Southeast Asia. Currently, according to *Open Doors,* 35 percent come from the thirteen
OPEC nations, with Iran (51,310 students) and Nigeria (16,360
students) representing 67 percent of the OPEC total.

Students from other countries come to the United States
to study for a variety of reasons. Paramount is the need to acquire technological knowledge not available in their countries
and the inability of universities in their home countries to accommodate the numbers of qualified candidates. For example,
last year in Hong Kong, there were over 100,000 candidates

qualified for university entrance but only 25,000 places. Table 1 (from the 1979-80 *Open Doors*) gives a percentage breakdown by major fields of study for foreign students currently enrolled in American colleges and universities.

Table 1. Major Fields of Study.

Field	Percentage
Engineering	26.9
Business and management	16.4
Social sciences	7.9
Natural and life sciences	7.6
Undeclared	7.0
Math and computer science	5.4
Fine and applied arts	5.0
Other	4.4
Education	4.3
Intensive English language	4.2
Humanities	4.0
Health professions	3.8
Agriculture	3.1

Given the number of foreign students currently studying in the United States, and realizing that an increasing number will seek admission in the future, it is very important that colleges and universities enrolling foreign students continuously evaluate their admissions process and the support services provided for them. This pertains to both large and small universities.

It is a difficult task for foreign students from so far away to choose the most appropriate American university. In some countries, agencies such as the International Communications Agency of the United States Department of State, the Fulbright Commission, Amideast, and the Institute of International Education have offices that try to help foreign students in their college search. It should be the responsibility of the foreign admissions officer at each American institution to send up-to-date catalogues and university information to reputable counseling services overseas. This information should not only answer general questions about the university but respond to the specific needs of the foreign student. Following is a list of pertinent information that prospective foreign students should be provided with:

University Information

1. Type of school. Public, private, church affiliated, community college, undergraduate, graduate, competitive, and so forth.
2. Exact location and size.
3. Accreditation.
4. Academic majors and degrees (separate graduate and undergraduate).
5. Number of years to complete each degree.
6. Facilities.
7. Faculty. Qualifications, ratio to students, availability to students, average class size.
8. Residence halls. How housing is arranged; whether or not it is guaranteed and for how many years; whether there is special housing for foreign students; off-campus housing possibilities and costs; housing for married couples.
9. Student body. Number of men and women, graduate and undergraduate students, geographical distribution of students, and so forth.
10. Orientation and registration (when they take place and what is involved).

Foreign Student Specifics

1. Number and diversity of foreign students on campus and information about campus foreign student organizations.
2. Admissions procedures. Be specific—list every document that must be submitted. Be especially specific about which tests are required and expected minimum scores, and explain how they are evaluated and used in the admissions process.
3. Foreign student adviser (FSA). Make sure the foreign candidate has the name, address, and telephone number for the FSA and/or the International Students Office. Explain the role of the FSA.
4. Costs. Be specific and realistic: Explain the difference be-

tween in-state and out-of-state tuition; enumerate fees for tuition, room and board, health insurance; give realistic estimates for books, supplies, clothing, off-campus housing, utilities, groceries, transportation, and maintenance expenses when school is not in session.

5. Financial aid. Is financial aid available to foreign students? If so, to what extent and in what form: grant, loan, job? What financial documentation must the student supply?

6. Calendar. Type of calendar, when classes begin, length of vacations, housing and campus job possibilities during vacation periods. Are classes offered during the summer (when using seasonal terms, be sure the student knows what months constitute a particular season)?

7. English as a second language. Is there an ESL program? If so, what does it cost? Can a student attend the university and the ESL program at the same time? Can a student enter the university directly from the ESL program? If the student plans to attend the university after completion of the ESL program, what academic credentials are needed? Where do students attending the ESL program live; and so forth?

8. Married students. Programs available for spouses and children, local elementary and secondary schools, community activities available, and so forth.

9. Arrival. Nearest airport, transportation from airport to campus; if a student has to arrive early, what should he or she do; area hotels and addresses.

10. Community. Describe the town: population; characteristics like "industrial" or "agricultural"; shopping possibilities, with some idea of prices; local banking possibilities; regional customs and "personality"; climate and temperature range in centigrade; college community relationship; host family program; "home stay"; and so forth.

Although some students will be able to take advantage of counseling centers overseas, many will write for information directly to the institutions in which they are interested. It is advisable, if you are dealing with a significant number of foreign inquiries, to develop special informational brochures and application forms. (*Note:* Because all materials going overseas should be sent air mail, it is best to print them on lightweight paper.)

All foreign academic credentials should be evaluated by someone knowledgeable about the foreign educational system, certificates, and degrees involved. The National Liaison Committee on Foreign Student Admissions (NLC) has four regional Credential Evaluation Projects. Degree-granting colleges, graduate and undergraduate, enrolling fewer than 100 foreign students may use their services free of charge. This can be particularly helpful to many of the smaller colleges. Further information, materials, instructions, and forms may be obtained from: Credential Evaluation Projects, c/o NAFSA, 1860 19th Street N.W., Washington, D.C. 20009.

Schools that enroll more than 100 foreign students should have someone on their admissions staff who is qualified to evaluate foreign credentials. Even the most experienced person, however, cannot know all foreign educational systems. Therefore, foreign admissions officers should keep a well-stocked library of references for credential evaluation:

The National Association of Foreign Student Advisors (NAFSA) has written many workshop reports that cover the educational systems of most areas of the world and include admissions and placement recommendations. Write to: NAFSA, 1860 19th St. N.W., Washington, D.C. 20009.

The American Association of Collegiate Registrars and Admissions Officers (AACRAO) publishes the World Education Series, describing more than fifty educational systems around the world and offering placement recommendations. Write to: AACRAO, 1 DuPont Circle N.W., Washington, D.C. 20036.

The Institute of International Education (IIE) provides periodic profiles and reports on schools in Southeast Asia, Mexico, and Central and South America. Write to: IIE, 809 United Nations Plaza, New York, N.Y. 10017.

The Country Index, written by Theodore Sharp, Inez Sepmeyer, and Martena Sasnett, does not go into detail on educational systems but does offer a "quick glance" review of most systems in the world, with placement recommendations for more experienced credential evaluators. Write to: The Country Index, International Educational Research Foundation, Inc., P.O. Box 24679, Los Angeles, Calif. 90024.

Besides the actual evaluation of the foreign academic credentials, at least two more items—English-language ability and financial status—should be documented before determining whether to admit a foreign candidate and issuing the Immigration and Naturalization Service's (INS) Certificate of Eligibility, more commonly referred to as the I-20 form.

It is very important to determine the foreign candidates' English-language ability. If your institution does not offer courses in English as a second language, it is obviously necessary that the foreign students enrolled be able to understand, speak, and write English without difficulty. Even the best students cannot be expected to do well if they cannot understand the lectures, answer questions, or write assignments. Furthermore, language problems can slow down lectures and disrupt classes, thus affecting native English-speaking students in a class.

There are a variety of ways to determine a student's English-language ability. The most commonly used standardized test is the Test of English as a Foreign Language (TOEFL), written and distributed by the Educational Testing Service (ETS). TOEFL is administered at test centers all over the world on dates specified annually by ETS. For further information, write to: Test of English as a Foreign Language, Box 899, Princeton, N.J. 08540.

Two other commonly used tests of English-language ability are the Michigan Test of English Language Proficiency (MTELP) and the test from the American Language Institute of Georgetown University (ALIGU). These tests are administered on an individual basis overseas. Further information about MTELP and ALIGU can be obtained from: Teaching English as a Foreign Language Section, NAFSA, 1860 19th Street N.W., Washington, D.C. 20009.

Keep in mind that these tests of English-language ability are not measures of academic ability. In July 1979 a symposium sponsored by the Institute of International Education and the Educational Testing Service discussed the appropriateness of the major aptitude tests for foreign students. The College Board tests, the Graduate Record Examinations (GRE), and the Graduate Management Admission Test (GMAT) were all reviewed. TOEFL was also discussed in relationship to the verbal ability needed for these aptitude exams and scores received on them. The symposium's foremost recommendation was that testing alone should never be the sole criterion for determining a student's admissibility. A copy of the report from the symposium, "Testing and the Foreign Student," is available from the Educational Testing Service in Princeton, N.J.

Whether or not your college or university offers financial assistance to foreign students, it is essential to have some sort of documentation of the financial resources available to the foreign candidate. According to the 1979-80 *Open Doors,* 81.4 percent of the foreign students studying in the United States are receiving their financial support either from family members or a private sponsor. Financial verification is a legal responsibility of the university, and an I-20 form should never be issued without having the verification on file. There are various ways to verify financial support. The College Scholarship Service (CSS) provides a special financial form for foreign candidates: the Declaration and Certification of Finances. Attached to the same form is the Foreign Financial Aid Application, which is useful for schools that do offer financial assistance to foreign students. (*Note:* The Financial Aid Form used by American students should *not* be sent to foreign students.) Besides the foreign form from CSS, the INS Affidavit of Support (form I-134) can be obtained from the nearest Immigration Office. Also, many institutions have developed their own financial forms. In addition to these basic forms, you may wish to request official statements from the individual sponsor's bank.

Admissions procedures for foreign students are quite different from those for Americans, as are the legal responsibilities of the university. If they are not already in your admissions library, two publications from NAFSA that are most useful are *A Guide to the Admission of Foreign Students* and *Selection and Admission of Foreign Students, Guideline Series 2.* Both can be obtained by writing to the NAFSA central office in Washington, D.C.

Foreign Student Recruiting

There are many ways foreign students choose a university in which to study. Many decide on the basis of what they hear from family, friends, and teachers. For the most part, the guidance counselor system as we know it in the United States does not exist overseas in non-American-based schools. As I mentioned earlier, reputable counseling agencies and centers such as ICA, IIE, Amideast, and the Fulbright Commission do exist in some countries, but in many cases the sheer number of students needing their assistance is overwhelming.

Because of the lack of adequate counseling services abroad for foreign students, "counseling agencies" masquerading in various guises have formed in many countries to fill the need. Unfortunately, not all are reputable, and it is often difficult to tell the difference between bona fide ones and those that are not. Before an institution becomes involved with unfamiliar overseas counseling agencies, it should investigate the background and credentials of those agencies as thoroughly as possible. Are they providing a counseling service or just headhunting? It is important to know how they counsel students; how much they know about American colleges and universities; if they have had any educational experience themselves in the United States; who makes the final admissions decision—the overseas agent or the American university; whether they are requesting I-20 forms be issued; what types of fees are charged and from whom—the student, the university, or both.

Many of the third-party agencies charge exorbitant fees for placement in American universities. Many have no credentials to qualify them for college counseling, and they have no regard for the proper placement of their counselees. They may invent programs at a university that do not exist; encourage students to study something that will be of no value to them when they return home; misrepresent the location, size, and costs of a university; and so on.

In some countries, students have come to believe that for the right price they can buy their way into an American university. Misled by ill-informed and unscrupulous recruiters, many students are disappointed and discouraged when they arrive at their American university and discover that it is not what they were promised.

Colleges and universities that get involved with these less reputable agencies, viewing them as a good source of students, may later find themselves in a difficult situation. Campuses and communities not prepared to handle foreign students are bound to have problems, particularly if the foreign students themselves are disappointed in their placement. Schools should avoid agencies that request application forms in bulk and should never send blank signed I-20 forms overseas. The best policy is to avoid third-party agents who charge the university a per capita fee for enrollment or charge students exorbitant prices for college placement.

Some colleges and universities are already actively recruiting overseas, and, given current demographics, it seems likely that more schools will do so in the future. Recruitment is a legitimate and viable part of most college and university admissions programs. It takes many forms, and even the most highly competitive colleges recruit. There is nothing wrong with recruiting, but it must be done ethically, with a clear understanding of the institution's commitment and the student's interests.

The reasons for recruiting are as varied as the techniques employed. Some are highly respectable; others are plainly unethical. Articles on abuses in foreign student recruitment have appeared in national magazines and newspapers. In 1979 ABC News presented a three-part special report on the topic. In March 1980, concerned with the increasing abuses in foreign student recruitment, the National Liaison Committee on Foreign Student Admissions, in cooperation with the Johnson Foundation and with the assistance of the United States International Communications Agency, held a colloquium at Wingspread in Racine, Wisconsin, to discuss the issue. Member organizations of the National Liaison Committee are the American Association of Collegiate Registrars and Admissions Officers, the College Entrance Examination Board, the Council of Graduate Schools, the Institute of International Education, and the National Association of Foreign Student Advisors.

The following statement on abuses in foreign student recruitment and the criteria for ethical recruitment was approved by the members of the Wingspread Colloquium. It has since appeared in various news articles, including one in the *Chronicle of Higher Education.*

Noting that this colloquium has brought together a wide representation which includes college presidents, university administrators, institutional and associational representatives and members of government agencies, we believe it important to identify those abuses in the recruitment of foreign students which are of common concern. We consider them to be detrimental to the welfare of foreign students and the reputation of higher education in the United States.

They are as follows:

1.   The use of placement agencies which charge institutions a per capita fee
2.   The recruitment of foreign students without prior consideration of and commitment to providing necessary campus services
3.   Failure to represent properly the institution in advertising, publications, informative materials, personal interviews, etc.
4.   The use of inadequately trained foreign admissions officers
5.   The improper delegation of admissions authority
6.   The misuse of immigration forms with regard to a student's academic qualifications, English-language proficiency, and financial resources
7.   The practice of granting admission to English-language programs to foreign students who are college bound, without regard to their academic qualifications
8.   The practice of granting admission to foreign students to English-language programs that do not qualify as full-time intensive programs and are therefore not in compliance with Immigration and Naturalization Service regulations
9.   The practice of promising and/or implying that admission to intensive English-language programs constitutes admission to an academic degree program

Criteria for Ethical Recruitment

To eliminate the abuses cited, institutions that recruit foreign students should:

1. Provide enough candid and pertinent information in order that a foreign student who is unfamiliar with United States practices in higher education may make informed academic judgments
2. Avoid contractual arrangements with agents which require fee-for-enrollment payments
3. Develop an admission policy for foreign students which:
   Requires that admission judgments be made by institutional personnel who rule on other admissions
   Is based on a system of written criteria
   Is applied in competition with other applicants
4. Seek a match between the needs and aspirations of the prospective student and the educational opportunities the institution affords
5. Accept the commitment to provide effective educational opportunity for foreign students and establish appropriate institutional policies governing foreign student recruitment, admission, support activities, specialized programs and curricula
6. Provide realistic estimates of costs for tuition, educational expenses, subsistence, related fees, and the extent to which financial aid or scholarships are available to foreign students
7. Clearly state to students admitted to English-language programs the extent of commitment made for their further education in the United States.

It was also proposed that a clearinghouse be established which would help centralize information on foreign student recruiting practices, agencies, overseas recruiting agents, and so forth. Such a clearinghouse could help distinguish between reputable and nonreputable practices and agencies. The National Liaison Committee is currently undertaking the organization of such a clearinghouse.

A report on the colloquium, edited by Hugh Jenkins, retired executive vice-president of the National Association of Foreign Student Advisors. The report was published in 1980 by the College Board and can be obtained from Department of Publications, College Entrance Examination Board, 888 Seventh Avenue, New York, N.Y. 10019.

Foreign student recruiting demands a *total institutional commitment*! Administrators, admissions officers, faculty, trustees, students, staff, and community representatives should be involved in the discussions of whether to increase the number of foreign students on campus. The reasons for recruiting should be faced realistically and should be part of a well-planned total international perspective, not just an immediate means of stabilizing enrollment.

Following are several factors to consider when making an institutional commitment to the recruitment of foreign students:

1. There should be a realistic evaluation of the expenses involved. Estimates should be drawn up for an admissions staff position, a foreign student adviser, printing of special publications, mailing by airmail post, membership in pertinent national organizations, and possible travel expenses.

2. There has to be an admissions staff member who is qualified to evaluate foreign credentials and English-language ability and who has a feeling for the foreign cultures involved.

3. Preadmissions materials, such as special application forms and brochures that speak specifically to the needs of international students, have to be developed.

4. Membership in organizations such as NAFSA and AACRAO help keep everyone at the university up to date on immigration regulations, credential evaluation, English-language programs, study-abroad opportunities, community programs, and cross-cultural counseling.

5. Proper support services have to be provided. There should be a foreign student adviser who is knowledgeable about U.S. Immigration and Naturalization (INS) regulations and trained in cross-cultural programming, orientation, and personal counseling.

6. Faculty need special training to be sensitive to the background and needs of foreign students for more effective academic counseling.

7. If an ESL program does not exist on campus, some con-

sideration has to be given to establishing a tutorial program for foreign students who still need to improve their
English-language skills. Even a fairly high score on TOEFL
does not mean that a student's English ability is perfect.

8. Input from community representatives is important to determine the extent of community support for an increase
of foreign students in the community. Are they willing to
help establish a host family program or help locate housing for married students and assist with the community
orientation of spouses and children?

9. The institution needs to determine the number and geographical representation of the foreign students it wants
on campus. Whether financial assistance is going to be
made available and to what extent may have a definite effect on where they recruit.

10. The academic strengths and weaknesses of the university
have to be evaluated. The programs most appropriate for
foreign students should be identified and evaluated. Faculty members from these departments should be involved
in the preliminary discussions.

11. Finally, the institution has to evaluate the effectiveness of
its existing support programs and facilities; determine
what changes and additions need to be made; and decide
whether it is willing to make the immediate financial commitment when it may not see any benefits for several
years, if ever.

Once an institution has discussed the aforementioned
concerns and obligations and made a commitment to increase
its foreign student enrollment, it has to decide how the recruitment will be done. Adequate personnel and facilities must be
provided to ensure the greatest degree of success.

How an institution is presented and who makes the admissions decisions are perhaps the two most important criteria
in international recruiting. The best representative is a regular
member of the campus-based admissions staff. Sending a staff
member overseas means that the institution will be represented by someone thoroughly familiar with the school, its poli-

cies, programs, and academic standards. This person should also be familiar with the educational systems and local customs of the countries to be visited.

The College Board has published a pamphlet titled *Guidelines for the Recruitment of Foreign Students,* which outlines the steps to be taken in establishing an effective and professional foreign student recruitment program and offers guidelines for conducting a recruitment tour overseas. It also gives the names and addresses of many associations and agencies in the United States and overseas that are invaluable to the foreign admissions officer planning to recruit abroad. Copies of this pamphlet can be obtained from College Entrance Examination Board, International Education Office, 1717 Massachusetts Avenue N.W., Washington, D.C. 20036.

Obviously, not all schools can afford to send a representative overseas; however, there are many other professional ways to approach increasing your foreign student enrollment. Students' names and addresses can be requested from the Student Search Service of the College Board. These could include students with APO/FPO addresses, foreign addresses, or both. Catalogues and information can be sent to reputable counseling agencies and centers overseas, such as offices of the International Communications Agency, Fulbright Commission, the Institute of International Education centers, and Amideast. Overseas alumni, students studying abroad, and faculty members on overseas sabbaticals can also be excellent sources of assistance.

Although there are many students overseas who are eager to study in the United States, and although more and more institutions may consider recruiting foreign students in the future, it must be kept in mind that bringing foreign students to campus is not appropriate for every school. Each institution must evaluate the effectiveness of adding more foreign students to its campus and ask whether foreign students can truly benefit from its academic programs. Of paramount importance is that all dealings with foreign students be handled in a professional manner.

To further assist colleges and universities in the area of ethics in foreign student recruitment, the National Liaison Committee on Foreign Student Admissions is currently working on a statement on foreign student recruitment standards, similar to the *Joint Statement on Principles of Good Practice in College Admissions and Recruitment,* written by the American Association of Collegiate Registrars and Admissions Officers, the College Entrance Examination Board, the National Association of College Admissions Counselors, and the National Association of Secondary School Principals and endorsed by the American Council on Education.

Overseas American Students

Currently, thousands of American families are living overseas, for various reasons. Some are involved in international business; others in foreign service, military service, or missionary work. Their reasons for being overseas may affect how frequently they move, where their children go to school, how many languages they speak, how they view the foreign culture, and the ultimate adjustment of their children when they return to the United States for college studies. It seems likely that, with our increasingly mobile society and internationally interdependent economy, more American families will be living overseas in the future.

The two key factors that seem to affect the experience and attitudes of American families living overseas are the nature of their sponsorship group and how frequently they move. Actually, these two are interrelated because the number of moves directly correlates to the type of sponsorship. There are four main sponsorship groups: missionary, Department of State, international business, and Department of Defense.

Missionary families tend to be overseas for long periods of time but are usually located in one country or region of the world. They live and work directly and regularly with the host country nationals and tend to identify with them socially and culturally more than do families from other sponsorship groups. Because of their stability in location and close rapport with the local culture for many years, missionary families frequently consider that country "home" regardless of their citizenship.

Department of State families and those in international business also tend to spend long periods of time overseas. However, in contrast to missionary families, they rarely spend more than two to five years in a given place. This disruptive life-style and tenuous feeling of security leads to different cultural and adjustment attitudes. Families in these two groups also live and work with the host country nationals. However, because of the nature of their work, the status ascribed to them places them in higher social echelons. Although they may live in local communities, they tend to be in the wealthier sections populated by other Americans, foreign businessmen and diplomats from other countries, and the host country upper class. Although they work and socialize with the host country nationals, they usually have a more superficial experience than do the missionary families because it is difficult to develop and maintain close relationships outside the family when frequent moves are part of the life-style. Therefore, immediate family relationships become closer and more important.

Families in the fourth sponsorship group, Department of Defense, generally have an overseas experience quite different from that of the other groups. These families usually live on military bases, where the ambience and facilities are fairly "American." The PX or commissary supplies them with American food products, clothing, and appliances. Recreational facilities, sports programs, and entertainment are very similar to those found in the United States. It is not really necessary to speak the local language or to go off base for much of anything. Only those families who really want to learn about the host country people, culture, and language do so.

Many parents, regardless of sponsorship group, worry that their children may be at a disadvantage when applying to American colleges because they are living overseas. They are concerned that admissions personnel may not know as much about the overseas schools, or that their children may not be as well prepared for college as those graduating from stateside high schools. Most of these concerns are needless, but some are justified.

American students overseas attend two main types of

schools: Department of Defense (DOD) schools and American/International Schools. They differ in degree of academic competitiveness, availability of college counseling, types of extracurricular programs, and intercultural relations with the local country.

DOD schools are located on American military bases overseas and are like large comprehensive public high schools in the United States. Course offerings range from college preparatory to vocational. Therefore, although some graduates of DOD schools will be prepared to enter competitive colleges, others will not. If a school profile is not included with a student's transcript, it should be requested. Guidance counselors in the DOD schools are fully certified; but, because of the high student-counselor ratio, the amount of time given to college counseling may be limited.

There are advantages and disadvantages to the American environment of the DOD schools. Students from these schools have the opportunity to participate in the same wide range of extracurricular activities as their stateside peers and tend to maintain their American identity. In this respect, they will have little difficulty identifying with classmates and participating in activities when they go to college. On the other hand, because they tend to become isolated on these bases, they do not benefit as much from the cultural enrichment of the foreign country.

The American/International schools overseas include schools established by the Department of State, various missionary groups, and international businesses. Although each school is unique, generally they can be compared to college-preparatory schools in the United States. Some are boarding schools. In all cases, students pay tuition to attend. Although the ratio of American, foreign, and host country national students may vary from school to school, there is a much stronger sense of "internationalism" in these schools than in the DOD schools.

Most American/International schools offer quite demanding college-preparatory programs, including Advanced Placement courses. It is not uncommon for students to take from six to eight major subjects per year. For the most part, these schools are small, and students receive a great deal of personal attention and counseling. They are encouraged to be creative and learn how to do independent research, thus developing good study habits. Students are usually required to study the local language and culture. Field trips are conducted, and travel is encouraged. Depending on how many countries a student has studied in, she or he may speak from two to five foreign languages. Students from American/International schools tend to be more mature and have a broader perspective than most high school graduates.

Besides the usual college-preparatory program, some of the international schools now offer the International Baccalaureate Degree (I.B.). The International Baccalaureate Office was established in Geneva, Switzerland, in 1965, with the goal of developing a degree that would meet the needs of the growing number of international students throughout the world. It has since received the approval of most major countries of the world, which recognize the I.B. as satisfying their university entrance requirement. It is a very demanding program, and a student who completes the full I.B. program normally qualifies for one year of college credit in the United States. Information on the International Baccalaureate Degree can be obtained by writing to International Baccalaureate Office, Palais Wilson, Ch-1211 Geneva, Switzerland.

As mentioned, a few concerns of overseas American families are legitimate. Some families move frequently, causing their children to change and readjust to new school systems. This can affect grades as well as curricular progression. Performance on standardized tests such as the SAT may be another problem. Statistics from the International Division of the College Board show that the mean SAT verbal and math scores are higher for most regional groups overseas than the national mean scores. Nevertheless, many American students overseas believe they are at a disadvantage in taking the SAT because of their lack of experience in taking standardized tests and because of the multiplicity of languages they speak. This seems to be particularly true for students studying in schools where more than one language is commonly spoken, as is the case in Central and South America.

Admissions officers should take into account multiple moves and languages when evaluating the academic credentials of overseas American students. In spite of the aforementioned concerns, the vast majority of overseas American students feel that they have been well prepared for college, and I concur. Regardless of their sponsorship group, these unique individuals have a great deal to offer American colleges and universities.

A nonacademic problem is the ability to meet application deadlines because of the frequently slow international mail. To complicate the problem further, students often are sent the wrong application forms. Just because a letter comes from overseas does not necessarily mean it was written by a foreign student! Admissions officers should try to identify inquiries from Americans overseas and should always send all forms and correspondence airmail. It is also a good idea whenever possible to personalize correspondence. The overseas American feels isolated enough without receiving form letters.

Colleges enrolling Americans from abroad should try to be sensitive to their needs. Many overseas Americans entering college for the first time face different adjustment problems than United States high school graduates. Because of the nature of the overseas American community, the students tend to come from a closely knit family structure. Some, particularly those with no relatives in the United States, may feel a greater degree of isolation and loneliness.

There is also a type of culture shock involved. These students may not know the latest football hero, the current songs and singing rage, the most popular television shows, or the current slang. Many are, however, used to discussing current events and world issues and to being part of a fairly sophisticated adult world. It is frustrating for them when their college peers do not seem to be interested in what is happening in a given country, may not even know where it is located, and give the impression that they do not care. If a student's family has moved from one country to another, the adjustment to each new country is likely to be easier than returning to the "true" American environment.

The search for identity is perhaps one of the most important concerns of the adolescent. From a survey of overseas American students on our campus, I found that the majority of those who had spent a significant portion of their lives overseas felt more like "world citizens" than simply Americans. In keeping with that identity, all the students questioned indicated that they intended to pursue some sort of international career.

The following list of school associations can provide valuable information for those desiring to learn more about international and American schools overseas:

State Department-Assisted Schools

> Office of Overseas Schools
> Room 234-SA6
> Department of State
> Washington, D.C. 20520

Associations of American Overseas Schools

> *Africa*

> Association of International Schools
> c/o Clifford Strommen, President
> International School of Lusaka
> P.O. Box 50121
> Lusaka, Zambia

> Maghreb Association of International Schools (MAIS)
> c/o Michael J. Arndt, President
> Rabat American School
> c/o American Embassy Rabat
> Department of State
> Washington, D.C. 20520

> *American Republics*

> Association of American Schools in the Republic of
>   Mexico
> c/o Kenneth Crowl, Director
> American School of Guadalajara
> Colomos 2100
> Guadalajara, Jalisco, Mexico

Association of American Schools of Central America
Donald Kingsbury, President
Lincoln School
P.O. Box 1919
San José, Costa Rica

Association of Colombian and Caribbean American
    Schools
c/o Curtis C. Harvey, Director
Colegio Bolivar
Avenida Diez de Mayo
Apartado Aereo 4875
Cali, Colombia

Association of American Schools of South America
    (AASSA)
c/o Jack Schliemann, Executive Director
AASSA Regional Development Center
Florida International University
Bay Vista Campus
Biscayne Blvd. at 151st St.
North Miami Beach, Fla. 33181

East Asia

East Asia Regional Council of Overseas Schools
    (EARCOS)
Mark Crouch, Executive Secretary
c/o International School
P.O. Box 323, MCC, Makati
Metro Manila, Philippines 3117

Europe

European Council of International Schools
    (ECIS)
W. G. Mattern, Executive Secretary
18 Lavant St.
Petersfield
Hampshire GU32 3EW, England

Near East and South Asia

Near East and South Asia Council of International
    Schools
Stanley Haas, Executive Secretary
NESA, Deree College
P.O. Box 15, Aghia
Parashevi, Athens, Greece

U.S. Department of Defense

Office of Dependents Schools
Room 152, Hoffman Building #1
2461 Eisenhower Ave.
Alexandria, Va. 22331

25

Staff Development and Training in the Admissions Office

B. Barbara Boerner

Managing an extensive recruitment-marketing-admissions effort requires extensive planning and the plotting of objectives. These objectives must be aligned with and supportive of the public objective—or mission—of the institution. Furthermore, they must be coordinated with the objectives of the public relations and development efforts. Clearly, we have many markets, and our future depends on our share of those markets. Setting goals and attaining them defines our operations. But because of the democratic character of an educational organization, authority is diffuse, so successful completion of objectives depends on everyone's investment in the formulation and carrying out of the goals.

Once the operation has been identified, staffing needs can be determined. This area is perhaps one of the most haphazard in any organization, so staffs generally just grow without any apparent overall plan. Much like the old farmhouse onto which rooms are added here and there as the family grows, the original structure gets obliterated and the whole becomes less efficient. In admissions offices, it is very easy for a top-heavy staff to develop, with several professional positions and relatively few support positions. This not only is expensive but also is a situation where people without requisite expertise are attempting tasks for which they are not suited. In short, their jobs lose all definition and are difficult to describe. Lack of description means lack of parameters and consequently lack of benchmarks to measure performance against.

It is indeed a rarity to conceive of a staffless office. How, then, does one go about determining needs with a staff already in place? The job description is a logical starting place. However, it is disastrous to attempt any job description without specific input from the one person doing the job. We must differentiate between the *expectations* of the manager and the *description* of worker by the employee in the job; often these are shockingly diverse.

The Personnel Office

On file in the personnel office should be job descriptions of each position. If there are none, making them is the first step in analyzing and subsequently organizing the work. Even if descriptions do exist, all too often they are laughable, at least according to the person in the job. That individual should review and then list what he or she does; the manager in turn reviews and lists expectations and needs. Once this has been done, people can effectively communicate with the personnel office. This office is invaluable for advertising, recruiting, preliminary screening, and salary-level negotiations. Of course, the manager should have additional standards by which to screen and finally choose a person. However, like a physician, the personnel officer cannot be much help unless the manager can effectively communicate staff needs.

Training: In-Service Workshop

Training staff is never completed and always beginning. However, it is important to create moments that focus on specific problems and opportunities and create highlights in each person's development. One of the most common frustrations of admissions offices is the "fear of closing," a kind of guilt over not being accessible to the public at all times. This creates problems for planning staff development and generally limits training to a time when the office is not busy. However, for most institutions, the recruiting-admissions cycle extends twelve to fifteen months, with comparatively little slack time. There must be times for reflection and analysis throughout the cycle. Scheduling such occasions creates time as well as expectations. Obviously, the timing and tenor of staff workshops will differ for each organization; however, the following model was successfully implemented in an office where there had been no previous in-service training.

In August 1978, we held our first workshop, which necessarily focused on information and operations. Our personnel office gave us a substitute to cover the reception desk and telephones, and we retreated to another area of the college to discuss recruitment, admissions considerations, the college, and professional development. The main purpose of this workshop was to educate each of us about all aspects of our operations and to introduce a team concept. Discussions were most productive because each of us gained insight into others' jobs and pressure points.

Focusing on interpersonal relationships and the role of discipline, we turned to the question of how to improve information flow among ourselves, within the college community, and to the public we served. This initial effort was reinforced by weekly staff meetings, held whether or not the director was on campus. The most exciting result of our first workshop was that everyone wished to have another, and at this point we decided to hold workshops each quarter.

The second workshop grew out of planning into which every staff member had input. We began by reviewing where we had been, by giving each staff member a specific reporting responsibility, and followed with a preview of the next quarter and long-range considerations. We then broke into two subgroups—one planning, the other operational—to discuss how the projections might be facilitated. At the end of the first day, the subgroups reconvened to report and inform. A similar pattern was followed the second day. By this time, the staff workshops had become an integral part of our work, and people began to initiate suggestions for future workshops. They also began to volunteer their homes as future workshop sites.

The third meeting, in spring 1979, centered around "individual tasks and how they fit into the whole." This workshop produced a charting of all our tasks, time allocations, correlation of tasks and assignments, and a charting of the recruitment-admissions year. It was a great revelation for each of us to see the peaks and valleys of our individual tasks and to note that there were truly appropriate times for individuals to schedule their major vacation and travel plans. In this workshop, we developed our first flowchart, which indicated how the various tasks could be carried out and coordinated. The second day, we returned to campus for planning sessions, focusing particularly on the management of our massive student search program.

The fourth and final workshop of our first year focused on evaluation and sorting out future responsibilities. At this point, we were able to discuss the practicing of economies, and every staff member had positive suggestions to make in regard to her particular area.

Appropriately, the first workshop of the second year had as its central theme "looking forward," and each staff member was energized by anticipation. As in the previous year, we invited key people—the president and other senior staff members—to preview the planning in their respective areas. We then retreated and together digested and synthesized what we had heard into our own planning and organizing of tasks.

The second workshop, held in December, focused on "dynamics of team work in the 1980s." This workshop planning was indeed a group effort, since the dynamics of the group had changed appreciably as a result of staff turnover and numerous promotions from within, involving staff members moving from support staff to professional positions.

The two days spent in each workshop required substantial planning and some degree of risk, because we had to close up shop sometimes during our busiest times. However, the long-range benefits far outweighed the short-range inconveniences.

The main benefit was hygienic. Each person's job was enriched by the opportunity to educate her colleagues about her responsibilities and to sensitize all about each individual's job pressure points. The director found the workshop an invaluable vehicle for effecting evaluation and upward feedback. A local norm developed that every staff member had a need to know and had the opportunity for input into the decision-making process. Consequently, the normal tendency to resist change was reduced. Leadership, both formal and informal, was encouraged and divergent opinions elicited.

As a staff we matured, even though the composition of the staff changed. Productivity increased, absenteeism decreased, and dysfunction all but disappeared. The team became capable of coping with uncertainty of outcomes because there was a feeling of confidence in the planning. In short, each person—no matter what the job, authority, span of control, and responsibility—had a vested interest in the efforts. And each person learned how to anticipate when there was a need for help and how to ask for help.

Effective Communication

To prevent the development of a top-heavy staff, those who hold the professional positions require specific training in delegation. Delegation is a skill and an art; it requires tolerance of, patience with, and confidence in the person(s) to whom a task is delegated. One can delegate authority, or control, but not responsibility. Consequently, upward communication is essential. Herein lies the art: How much direction does one give to the person to whom a task is delegated? The degree depends on the experience and expertise of both people. One of the best teaching devices in this situation is the model provided by the director, who should delegate areas of decision making to the professional staff. This requires organized follow-up with the staff member. The least experienced member should be given an area in which he or she is most familiar, even if that particular area is the pet of another staff member. Too often delegation gets terribly firm and rigid and results in strong feelings of territoriality. Greater strength results from flexibility, when tasks are rotated each cycle. Ideally, each person should perceive the potential for growth and the opportunity to accrue expertise in more than one area. This kind of flexibility not only combats boredom and stagnation but also enables staff members to be consultants for one another.

The main thing is to provide opportunity for each professional to manage, no matter how minimal the authority. This means that the individual should be expected to plan, make decisions, solve problems, evaluate, and report fully on each operation managed. To make decisions and be accountable for them requires thorough knowledge of and constant focusing on the objectives. To teach these skills, the project manager must have an opportunity to present the plan, receive and respond to questions and criticism, and direct the actual project. This can be done in regularly held planning meetings, where the plans of each manager, including the director, are reviewed.

It is often difficult, however, for the junior member to be assertive when confronted with a peer who previously had been assigned to lead the task. In this case, it is imperative that the director maintain strict discipline, which allows each person to be heard completely. Assertiveness training works well, but it is essential to have an outsider direct such training and for *all* levels of staff to participate. There are excellent resources within most institutions, particularly in the continuing education, psychology, management, and education departments. However, the top must be committed to, and encourage, assertiveness in the staff or the result is inevitably disastrous dysfunction, wherein an assertive staffer is perceived by the superior as insubordinate.

Intraoffice communication is most easily accomplished by constant reinforcement through regularly scheduled meetings of the entire staff. In offices where traveling is extensive, it is a temptation to skip a staff meeting. In my opinion, such an omission is a mistake because it reinforces a perception that some staff members are more essential than others. (If this is truly the case, then most likely the office is overstaffed.) Usually the director is responsible for conducting the meetings, which should be well organized, with a set meeting time and place, an agenda, and opportunity to hear from each staff member. It is difficult to hold a meeting without telephone interruptions. One way to resolve this problem is to assign a student worker to cover the reception desk during the staff meeting.

The group meeting is important because it "routinizes" getting together to discuss work in progress and reduces anxiety about problems. If, upon being summoned to a meeting, an employee wonders what is wrong, then that staff does not meet often enough. The same applies to individual conferences. The director hires and evaluates and promotes or fires. However, these should not be the sole occasions for conferences. Individual conferences should be held regularly with both operations and planning personnel. A model that seems to work well uses short daily meetings with the operations lead person (office manager or equivalent), twice-weekly hourly meetings with the second-in-charge, weekly meetings with each of the other professionals, and monthly meetings with each support staff. Even though they report to someone else, the director is still *responsible* for them and should be a resource for discussing promotion opportunities and career paths. Too frequently this is done haphazardly, if at all, and staff members either stultify or grow by leaving.

Evaluation: A Positive, Ongoing Experience

Evaluation, particularly at the professional level, should be an ongoing process, with the result that the individuals themselves are evaluating rather than just doing the job. Usually there is some sort of annual review, but if it is the only opportunity for employees to discuss the job, they are anxious to get a good rating and a raise and at best are cautious about discussing any problem areas. Turnover is a problem in many admissions offices because people often use the job opportunity as a stepping-stone. Also, the pressures of recruitment, travel, and simultaneously dealing with many publics result in burnout. Evaluation should include review of the work *always* in relation to the tactic and objective. It should be a reciprocal process, wherein the director and the subordinate freely exchange assessments, questions, criticisms, and formulating of goals, both personal and professional.

Opportunities to evaluate positions during the whole-staff workshops are foundations on which to build the individual evaluative process. Being a mentor for staff is one of the most rewarding aspects of the director's work. Creating opportunities for growth requires flexibility and is challenging to a director because new problems—and the need for new solutions—arise. However, it is this very freshness that is required for successful marketing and accurate analysis and projection of trends.

Job Enrichment

Realistically, enrichment does not just happen; it requires constant encouragement. "Enrichment" refers to all those aspects of work that are not the tasks themselves. In most cases, nonprofit organizations do not pay as high a salary as profit-making organizations. Why, then, would anyone work in the lower-paying job? The answer is complex but lies in factors that meet needs of a higher order than basic survival. Most educational institutions are perceived as a "nice" place to work because the individual is considered important, and the organization is more democratic than autocratic in nature. Furthermore, unique benefits are available. Tuition remission for oneself is an obvious one but may present problems to the office, since the employee has to be out of the office to take advantage of the benefit. Tuition remission for spouses and/or dependents is another and extremely valuable benefit—so much so that, with shrinking revenues, many colleges are taking a second look at it. Free lunches, free parking, and reduced ticket prices are other benefits. The important thing is to take an active role in your institution to develop benefits or to protect those already in place.

Another factor that is often overlooked but a central theme of this chapter is the potential for participation. Each staff member can have a vested interest in the task and perceive the task as essential to the success of the entire effort, which requires careful selection of staff, training, and confidence that each person will deal maturely with sensitive information. This leads to the building of a strong team. Each person shares successes and failures. "Fault" does not enter into the analyses because there is a collective perception as to responsibility for meeting recruitment-admissions goals. As the team members change, the integrity of the team is preserved, thus providing continuity. Each person strives to evaluate his or her own work and to continually develop higher standards of performance.

The team concept—increased professionalism of the admissions staff—is the key to successful market positioning, recruitment, admissions, and enrollment. However, the team cannot be developed as a fixed entity. Development is a daily, time-consuming, crucial part of the activities; time and priorities should be budgeted accordingly. With all staff having a stake in the effort, people begin to grow more comfortable with taking risks, so essential to creative thinking. Subsequently, opportunities for growth are created because people learn more about others' tasks and can aspire to sharing or doing those tasks. Growth need not always result in "advancement," but it always reduces or eliminates tedium. Thus, the admissions director's executive function requires sensitive cajoling, encouragement, motivation, discipline, and leadership of people.

Part Six

✐ ✐ ✐ ✐ ✐

Service to Members of the Profession

✐   To perform their functions well, regardless of their allegiance to high school, college, university, or student, professional college admissions officers must share some of what they have learned with each other. In Part Six, professionals of long standing, writing from several vantage points, present information useful to others within the profession, regardless of their institutional affiliation.

In Chapter Twenty-Six, Mary Anne Schwalbe, who has been both an admissions officer and a college guidance counselor, assumes that at some scale, even reduced, colleges will continue to visit secondary schools. What can make the one point of contact—the school visit—more mutually beneficial for the college and the high school? Schwalbe explains the necessity of planning ahead, of knowing one's material, of being ready to adapt to the situation in different schools. She says that admissions officers should be informative to schools in advance of visits. She instructs readers in the technicalities of setting up appointments and managing the visit. She advocates meeting on other ground, through professional organizations, and she describes ways for schools to unite to present programs for the joint benefit of students and parents. Finally, she stresses the

439

importance of honesty and thoroughness in communications between the high school and college.

In Chapter Twenty-Seven, Ina Miller writes of the college guidance counselor in isolation, subject to a variety of pressures that make it difficult to perform well as a professional. To provide effective counseling to students, the professional must deal with pressure from parents, student peers, school boards (at both public and private schools), the armed services, religions (either from groups or within families), and colleges. Miller shows that there are ways these pressures can be dealt with and, in some cases, even turned into positive experiences. Several forces may make it difficult to write honest letters of reference or recommendation in light of the Buckley Amendments; Miller describes one way of dealing with that situation. She also shows how to use the *Statement of Principles of Good Practice* and the *Statement of Student Rights and Responsibilities in the College Admissions Process.*

Like Miller, Pamela K. Fay concerns herself with the reference letter. In Chapter Twenty-Eight, focusing on the importance of the transmission of unique information about the individual, Fay assumes a different kind of admissions process than may be obtained in a large public university: where either open admissions or admissions largely by formulas may be legally mandated. She begins with basic principles, because both the admissions officer and the counselor are primarily concerned with the student as an individual: "The primary tool that the secondary school counselor possesses to communicate the essence of an individual student as a human being with dignity to the college admissions officer is the reference letter." She further states what the reference letter should be, what impact it will have in the admissions process, and how it should be written to serve most effectively the needs of both the student and the college. She describes the Buckley Amendments and their impact at great length and evaluates the legal stipulations within the Amendments. Fay also assesses different professional organizations' stands regarding the Amendments, and she ultimately reaches a different conclusion than Miller regarding confidentiality and the reference letter. She shows how to involve others in the reference process and advocates open sharing of the reference letter with the student subject. Finally, she describes the best use of the reference letter: as a basis for counseling students once they arrive on campus.

Although many secondary school members of the National Association of College Admissions Counselors are familiar with the admissions process at the highly selective college, most high school counselors never deal with the application process described by Douglas C. Thompson in Chapter Twenty-Nine. As the profession expands, or as the number of persons responsible for whatever college counseling schools provide increases, it is important that a wider range of people become familiar with the nature of the truly selective admissions process. Thompson first describes how selectivity might be defined, using the ratio of applicants to places or the yield among those admitted or the percentage admitted. He shows how selectivity arrived with the baby boom after World War II and with it the advent of widescale recruiting; he describes recruiting activity at selective colleges, evaluation of applications, and selection. Thompson also discusses candidly the admission of special groups of candidates, such as alumni children, minorities, and athletes. After presenting the mechanics of the process, he argues that its impact is ultimately fair and equable, asking that readers remember that virtually all the applicants to a highly selective college are academically capable of surviving in those institutions.

Probably no single element of the college admissions process has caught the attention of the lay public more than admissions testing. Yet few lay people and a surprisingly small number of admissions professionals have much technical information about the tests and the degree they should be relied on. To repair that gap, both Stephen Lovette (Chapter Thirty) and Jane W. Loeb (Chapter Thirty-One) discuss admissions testing as provided by the College Entrance Examination Board and the American College Testing Program.

Lovette presents the nature of national college admissions tests and discusses the relationship between tests and high school curricula. He discusses the decline in the last two decades of scores on nationally administered tests, its significance, and its causes—which include possible changes in the SAT itself, societal factors, changes in schools, and the changing student pool. He writes about the possibility of changing an individual student's test scores, the impact of coaching, and the counselor's function in raising scores. The chapter includes statistical information about the reliability and validity of tests and guidelines for both counselors and admissions officers. Lovette speculates on the future of admissions testing, in light of investigations sponsored by Ralph Nader, and other controversies. Finally, he argues that eliminating tests would be returning to the state we had before tests were widely used, a "pecking order of high schools. . . . Under such a system, students with high grades from elite schools would be in a more preferential situation than they are today."

Loeb replicates to a small degree Lovette's evidence regarding tests, but her thrust is different, focusing on denial. She feels that denial is a key question in framing and evaluating admissions policy. Like Lovette, she discusses the range of tests and their predictive validity. She illustrates her points with a far-ranging discussion of the effects of admitting students to the Urbana-Champaign campus of the University of Illinois without using tests, indicating that tests provide socially beneficial results. She correlates high school records and various measures of college success at her institution and then correlates the same measures with test results. Using her experience at the University of Illinois as a guide, Loeb describes public reaction to denial based on random selection and then discusses other ways to select students, besides using tests, and the likely results of such methods. Because the University of Illinois once experimented with random selection, she knows what the effect on a given pool would have been if tests together with grades had been relied on to make selections, and she can demonstrate that the use of tests would have provided fairer results. After discussing a number of other statistical variations in the selection process, Loeb points out that the high school record alone is not equitable, nor is reliance on chance. Thus, admissions tests are useful as selection devices and should continue to be used.

In the concluding chapter, Marilyn Kimball and James E.

Cavalier show ways in which the professional—either experienced or beginning—can benefit from the accumulated knowledge of others. Ranging from formal conferences to casual colloquy, the methods are based on universally shared goals. Because both college personnel and secondary school employees believe so firmly that what they do is of great benefit to the student, and because they know that generally they can trust the ethical commitment of other professionals, Kimball and Cavalier believe that significant learning can always take place through sharing information, principles, practices, and anecdotes. It is a truism that admissions people—on both sides of the liaison process—always talk business when together. Their profession is never far from the surface of their minds, and the ardent professional therefore is always learning from peers.

26

Preparing for Visits from College Personnel

Mary Anne Schwalbe

What does the college admissions officer expect from the high school counselor? And what should the high school counselor expect from the college admissions officer? As a college admissions officer for fourteen years and a high school guidance counselor for two, I have culled from my experience suggestions for communication between the two professionals and their separate responsibilities.

We begin with the college admissions officer's visit to the high school. What preparation is necessary for that first visit? My first visit to a high school was done with an "old pro," so I was spared many time-consuming mistakes. Having no clear plan in mind makes visiting more difficult than it needs to be. The first visit, and even some later ones, may be confusing and induce nervousness. It is not easy within a short time to present the total institution to a diverse group of students, some of whom may know a great deal about the institution but some of whom may not. Planning is therefore very important.

If driving to a school, find out if there is visitor parking. Ask in advance what door to enter—a huge public school in the suburbs has many doors; an inner-city school may have three of its four doors locked. The American flag is the first clue; wherever that is displayed, the main entrance and a bulletin board, map, or information office is close by. Determine if you should ask for a counselor by name or for the counseling office. And is it called the career center or the college counseling office or the guidance office?

Each high school visit is a kind of performance, and the stage is partly set by what is going on at the school when you arrive. Early in the morning are the loudspeaker announcements about the day's or week's activities. Sometimes you have to compete with these announcements during a presentation. Later in the day or during class time, a school may feel deserted, even though you know that there are numerous students somewhere. The school may have an "open campus," with students coming and going as they choose, or there may be guards at entrances. These are things a college visitor gets to know about a school after several visits, but quite often the first impression stays and the admissions officer bases the presentation according to that impression. It is essential therefore that the presenter be prepared.

Being comfortable with the material also helps you adjust to the wide range of environments. The same speech may come out differently if you are visiting a school in New England on a grim winter day than a California school with the sun shining, flowers in bloom, and everyone smiling.

To help the high school counselor prepare for the visit, the college visitor can have the college write ahead to make the appointment and let the school know if the person coming to visit is an admissions officer, an alumnus, a member of the faculty, an area representative, or a student. The visitor should know if any students from the school are presently at the college. The visitor should also know if students applied but none were admitted—the school may wonder why you are visiting again.

The counselors should stagger visits; some weeks as many as fifty colleges will try to visit a high school, but other weeks only one or two will be in town. It is better to schedule a visit at a mutually convenient time, and it is essential to know if the admissions officer wants to see students, talk with the counselor, or do both.

The admissions officer must be prepared to handle a large group of students or see only one or two. On a first visit, unless the college office has kept good records, it is hard to know what the numbers will be. You know that you must be prepared to talk all day, but you usually do not know if you will be seeing one student, a counselor, or a group. Although it is sometimes possible to guess from the previous year's number of applicants to your school, you can never really know what to expect until you get to the office or classroom.

As a new high school counselor, I listened to almost every presentation by admissions officers visiting my school. It was easy to tell when a representative was a good advocate for an institution and also interested in students and their questions. Sometimes the speech was rehearsed; sometimes it was improvised. It did not matter which if the person could adapt according to the interests of the students in the group and to how much they knew about an institution. A first question might be about whether any students have visited your college. If all have done so, there is no reason to describe how to get there and what it looks like. Given limited time, other subjects might be more engaging.

Often college representatives, especially when they are traveling a distance from their home base, are asked about other colleges in their area. Last fall, one admissions officer from the South very helpfully answered questions about differences between going to college in New York and New England and in the South, differences that related to many southern institutions, not just his own. It is good practice for a college representative to be both fair and knowledgeable about other colleges. However, the representatives should not bring in the world of competition and distortion. Praising one's own institution and criticizing, by name, similar places, not only makes the audience suspicious but also often harms one's own image. Written material sent out by a college admissions office does not compare that particular college to others; an oral presentation should not do so either.

What are the best times for visiting schools, and how should the appointments be set up? It is hard to lay down specific guidelines because so much depends on the college and high school. Some college admissions officers plan their visits months ahead. Counselors often receive cards during the summer with dates and times far in the future and a return postcard asking whether that date and time would be convenient. Some schools allow visits only on certain days and during certain periods; some do not let students leave classes to meet with college visitors. If possible, something in writing should come from the college to the school about an appointment. A phone call can set up a time and date and confirm the arrangement. The letter from the college should give the name of the person visiting; the school should write back confirming the appointment and naming the person and office to ask for.

Neither the high school nor the college should rush appointments. Students are unhappy if they are kept waiting for half an hour, and they are angry if their questions go unanswered because the admissions officer has only a few minutes to spend with them and they have left a class or an activity to meet with the officer. When I was working in an admissions office, I was fortunate because local alumni of that college set up appointments for me. They knew how long it would take me to get from one school to the next and which schools would need one hour, which only thirty minutes. I never felt a visit was wasted if I learned anything at all or if I could share any information. It was disappointing not to see students, but as long as I was expected and had someone to talk to, I felt my time was well spent. College admissions officers have tight schedules, and school guidance counselors have many things to do in a day other than to meet with college representatives. The relationships one can establish are important and so are the visits, but only if both counselor and admissions officer are ready for each other.

Managing the Visit

On a first visit to any school, the college visitor should have a quick tour of the school, be able to see the facilities, and perhaps meet with a faculty member or another administrator along with the particular guidance counselor to be seen that day. It is important for the counselor and the admissions officer to spend a few minutes together without students so that each can be updated on the past year. With students, fifteen minutes is usually long enough for any admissions officer to talk about the institution; another fifteen or twenty minutes should be spent answering questions from the group or from individual students. After the general meeting, if a large group has been present, one or two students may desperately want to talk with the representative alone.

At my high school, we try to schedule college visitors at least one hour apart. We do not have many rooms available for our visitors, and I do not like to have people think they are being pushed out to make way for others. It is a good idea for the counselor and admissions officer to agree on a period of time for the visit.

How many colleges should be scheduled at a school on a particular day? One day in October, six colleges asked to visit my school, and, because I was new, I said "yes" to them all. That was a mistake. Many of our students wanted to hear three or four representatives and ended the day not having gone to classes and feeling confused. Clearly, when there are that many visits in a given day, comparisons are going to be made, and often not made from the best perspective. It is too easy to compare visitors' personalities rather than listening to what is being said about the institution; the visit thus becomes a small popularity contest. Just as colleges should not criticize each other, a school should not put a college into a competitive situation. Students should not miss several classes on any one day. (In an ideal world, two colleges would visit every day all fall and a few more would come by in the spring to talk with juniors, but of course that is not the way travel schedules work.)

How many visits can the admissions officer make and still effectively represent the institution? This is also a hard question to answer because some people give a brilliant presentation to start and never reach that peak again; others get better and better as the day progresses. A college admissions officer has to allow at least 1½ hours for both a visit and travel; if the officer starts at 8:30 A.M., there is probably time for only four visits in a day. Some schools let visitors come in the afternoon, when students are often more relaxed, rather than in the morning. Inasmuch as each visit to a school is not complete until notes have been made on it, and because admissions officers often push themselves too hard over a long period of time, schools should not make extra demands on the visitor's time unless some notice has been given.

What kind of space in a school works best for the college counselor alone and works equally well when college admissions people come to visit? Where should the office be located in a school, how much room should it have, and what should it hold? Answers to these questions depend on the school's size and nature and on what goes on in the office other than college counseling. Location is important: The office should be centrally located, easy to find from the outside, and easy for both faculty and students from all parts of the school to reach. A private room should be available to the counselor. It is hard for an admissions officer to be straightforward privately with high school seniors and parents, but it is even harder when other people may be listening. Space in which the college representative can talk with three or thirty students without interruption and with a degree of peace should also be available. I can remember every minute of a visit to a small school in California. Six young women wanted to hear about my college, and we were in a room where there was space for only three of us to sit. One teacher was using a desk and a phone and someone else was using another desk and a typewriter. Needless to say, it was not a successful visit. If the message was that the school did not want me to come, they should have refused the appointment.

Designing Materials

A main area of communication between college and student is the school's publications, and the high school counselor may be the link in this part of the process. Thus, there should be shelf space available for large catalogues, file space for small, special ones, and space on the walls for all the glorious posters and schedules sent by colleges and associations. The School Code Number should be displayed, as should a calendar with important dates, deadlines, and names of colleges coming to visit.

For the counseling office's record system, a variety of

notebooks and forms for the students to use should be available, and the counselor can refer to these when talking with the admissions officers, sharing information about a particular student or group of students. A workbook with a page for each senior should be set up to let the counseling office know when applications have been sent and transcript deadlines occur. Reference books should be easily available to students, parents, and visitors. I prefer student artwork in my office, but posters announcing sports events, plays, concerts, or other activities are equally welcome and give the students and the college visitor something to look at while waiting. They are also another way of judging the school. The school newspaper and literary magazine should also be available to the college visitor.

A well-stocked counseling office makes the job of deciding what the college admissions officer has to bring considerably easier. After the first visit, the representative from the college knows how well prepared to be. As a counselor, I appreciate material that comes to the office with the college admissions visitor. It may be a special pamphlet not usually sent to the high school, or a course catalogue the college finds too expensive to mail to all the schools on its mailing list; it may be a set of updated booklets and admissions information. A college representative coming from a distance probably will prefer to not load the already overweight suitcases with enough material for everyone, so the visitor may be carrying cards for students and counselors, to fill out requests for various kinds of information to be sent. These cards are also useful for remembering students seen during a session in a high school. After a general session, the college and high school counselor may often talk about some of the students, and impressions can be shared directly after the meeting with students.

Colleges have so much material, and schools have students with such diverse interests, that even if a college visitor comes with a full supply of material from the school, often just what one needs is missing. Many times I had too few of a particular pamphlet; when I remembered and brought it with me the following year, the students I saw were no longer interested in athletics but wanted material on the performing arts. One year I would run out of financial aid information and the next out of

"Preparing for a Career in Medicine." Some colleges have tried supplying students with cards with several labels that they could peel off, but too often the handwriting was not legible, the zip code was left off, or the labels were not needed. If the counselor has a list of the students present for the session, and the college has a list, then all other information can be sent later.

Although I never carried a viewbook containing large, glossy photographs of the college, I find now that it helps when I have not seen a college campus; furthermore, I can learn a great deal about a college or university by listening to the representative and noting what has been put into those views and what has been left out. The country surrounding the New England institution may be beautiful in the spring, but what about during the mud season? The athletic facilities may be extraordinary, but why are there no pictures of the library? So many spectacular views of buildings have no students around them at all. Having been responsible for publications when I was an admissions officer, I was used to receiving questions and criticisms, some of the best of which came from high school counselors. The counselor knows when a college is really getting a message across and whether the image is the one it wants to project. A counselor can be helpful by telling the admissions office if the officer is doing a good job for the college and if the publications and material are as strong as they should be.

Joining Professional Organizations

So far, our discussion of communication between college and school has been involved with the college admissions officer visiting a particular high school, but there are other ways of "bringing in the world" for both counselor and admissions officer. Other than in college office and high school, my growth as a professional has come from sharing experiences and ideas through national and local meetings of professional organizations. The first and most important to me has been the National Association of College Admissions Counselors (NACAC) because it represents both sides equally, the college and the school; so its publications, programs, conferences, and panels are planned accordingly. The College Board is the other organization I have been involved with as an admissions officer and a high school counselor. These organizations are vital; because they are both membership organizations, it is necessary to support them.

Many policies and procedures mentioned earlier in this chapter result from panels and discussions with schools and colleges at local and national meetings of these two organizations. Institutional representation in these organizations should be included in every school and college budget so individuals can have the opportunity to attend meetings and read the publications, thus supplementing their professional lives. Because both jobs carry professional status, it is essential to have forums for developing skills and planning for the future. And growth in a vacuum is not easy. The admissions officer travels a large part of the year. The high school counselor, unless there is a large counseling staff, has no one to share particular problems with and no one in the school to learn from. Some schools have large counseling staffs with senior counselors, but these large offices with people doing only college counseling are hard to find. Professional meetings provide more than a time for getting to know each other; both college and high school learn and share at these sessions. Each time, I come away with new ideas for publications, more information on difficult counseling situations, what is new in financial aid for the coming year, or information about bills affecting education being considered in Washington. Most of all, these meetings illustrate that high school and college cannot survive alone and that by communicating with each other, procedures can be changed. When an individual college visits a single school, there is sharing, but with hundreds of school and college representatives meeting together, specific changes can occur much faster because information has been exchanged and programs developed in conferences and meetings. Many ideas for college programs within a school have come from professional meetings.

Guiding the Selection Process

When should students be exposed to the general process of applying to colleges, and how can the colleges help high schools prepare students properly for the learning experience the college process should provide? Schools differ in size, location, and diversity of the student body, so programs for students vary in focus and design.

Some contact with college admissions officers may begin for students before their junior year, but it is essential that during the junior year students and their parents become exposed to parts of the college admissions process and hear about it from someone other than their own guidance counselor. An example of several schools working together on a program is having a small version of a college fair in the fall, shared by the schools and hosted by a different one each year. Representatives from postsecondary institutions are invited to come with descriptive material, assigned separate space in classrooms for sharing their material, making presentations, and answering questions. Time should be planned so that each student can hear a number of presentations during the morning or afternoon. Later in the year, a representative from one college or university can be invited to speak to the junior class and parents at a particular school about the process of applying to colleges. The fall program should be shared because it is difficult to get a number of colleges to visit one school, but admissions officers are happy to come when there will be a larger population present that might include seniors who are still looking as well as juniors who are starting the process.

The second part of the program—having an admissions officer come to speak to one's own students and parents—is equally important for the counselor. Although the high school counselor may have all the information and know exactly what kind of advice to give to a junior class, it is not nearly so effective to hear from someone in the high school as it is to hear from someone "in the business."

If it is not feasible to have a number of schools share a program in the fall, the introduction to the process can be in the form of a panel of admissions officers, who speak to the junior class, parents, and faculty immediately after the start of the winter term. The panel should be balanced; both different parts of the country and different kinds of institutions should be represented. One format is to have one admissions officer speak about the process of choosing a college, another about the application and how to write it, and a third about the college visit and the interview. An alternate plan is to have six or seven admissions officers representing all parts of the country and all kinds of institutions talk about specific programs instead of process. Still another idea is to have the college counselor prepare a list of the questions most students asked during the year; the panel can then respond individually to those questions. What is most important is that the panel not turn into a competition, with each college pushing its own location and program, doing such a hard sell that the others feel they have to respond in kind. This sort of program is meant to be for information only; if juniors and their parents can sense that college admissions officers themselves work as a team with the school counselor, the whole process will look less threatening from the start.

Another way of bringing the college world into the high school is to ask a faculty member from a local college or university to speak about a subject, an activity, or anything at all other than the admissions process. It may be naive to say so here, but college is more than the admissions process, and few high school students know much about it other than what they have heard from family and friends. Presenting a faculty member or a member of the administration who deals with something like residential life in the college may not only help interest a student in the college experience but also focus some aspects of study in the junior and senior years.

So far, the programs mentioned have concentrated on college cooperation in the educational process of the high school student and on the looking and choosing. Another option is to ask a group of college admissions officers to go over case studies with groups of parents and students so that they see the process from the other side. These cases can be made up by the high school counselor, based on students from that school, or they can be prepared by the college admissions office. Students and parents should be split into small groups, given cases to read, and then asked to present them as if they were an actual admissions committee. This has proved helpful for giving students and parents a clearer picture of what the college considers important and for reassuring students that there are strong points to every application. Only the college admissions officer can tell the students, so they believe the officer who says that the essay is carefully read and all parts of the application are important. Even if the conversation is about a fictitious student, real communication may occur, and the student may come away feeling that admissions officers are people and that the work is not done by computer.

After years of visiting as a college admissions officer and spending time at regional and national professional meetings, and after having many college visitors come to my school this year, I have been fortunate in getting to know a number of college admissions officers around the country. It is easier to write or call when I can put a face to the name than it is to call college admissions offices without even knowing a name.

How much can one communicate with a college admissions office at application-reading or decision-making time? Some colleges welcome phone calls from counselors; some do not. New high school counselors should be told not to take it personally if a call is not returned by a college admissions officer within a matter of hours: Sometimes committee meetings last all day, officers are not able to get to a telephone, or the folders have not been read, so there is nothing to comment on on that day or week.

It is helpful to keep a notebook in the counseling office, with each college listed together with the contacts which exist within that particular college. Is the person visiting your school the one who will be reading the applications? Is the visitor able to suggest a time to call about early decision and early action applicants or about the regular applicants after the first of the year? Or would the visitor prefer to call you after all the applications from students at your school have been read? It is frustrating for the counselor to make a number of calls and be told each time that the admissions office is not ready to receive them. It is even more frustrating to be told that the call has come too late and the decision has already been made. Some college admissions offices want to discuss applicants with counselors; others want only to discuss extraordinary cases.

In this part of the communication process that occurs among school, college, and student, honesty is, as always, the best quality one can bring. If students have been honest with the counselor, then they have the right to expect that school and college will be honest with each other. If a college thinks that a school is not doing an adequate job for its applicants, the school should be told so. If a school thinks it is sending strong applicants to a college and they are all being rejected, then the school ought to be able to question the decision. As a college admissions officer, I wanted to be able to present applications to our committee with all the information I could gather, and I often called high school counselors for extra material. As a high school counselor, I want to be able to answer any questions that come up along the way.

My favorite philosopher, Charlie Brown, said to one of his friends when under stress, "There is no heavier burden than having a great potential." He sums up my feelings about the subject of this chapter. The potential for effective contact and cooperation between school and college is enormous. It can be a rewarding process of sharing and growth for all concerned.

27

Job-Related Pressures Affecting Secondary School Counselors

Ina Miller

The high school counselor responsible for helping students choose among thousands of postsecondary options has to deal with a variety of concerns: the students' needs and goals, pressures from outside sources, and professional responsibilities and ethics. Students have vaguely formed ideas of career interests and goals, many of which have been influenced by people or institutions with biased interests. The counselor, who in ideal situations can make a sound, well-documented evaluation of the student, is frequently pressured to respond to more subjective and often self-serving concerns of others who wish to influence the decision-making process. How can one maintain a balance and effect an outcome beneficial to students?

First, it is important to consider the problems facing students and parents in the admissions process. Students with little education about making career decisions come to the counselor for the first planning session uneasy and confused. They assume they are supposed to have their life work planned and a group of potential colleges selected. Even students with practice in career exploration feel the pressure of family, peers, and community, which have asked them since they were six, "What do you want to be when you grow up?"

Students and their families are also generally unaware of the various kinds of colleges or vocational training available.

They know little or nothing about financial aid; they know college is expensive, but they are ignorant of the constantly changing financial aid opportunities that will help them pay for it. They are usually unaware of the free vocational aptitude and interest tests available from many schools and state agencies. They are confronted with a bewildering assortment of acronyms —SAT, ACT, BEOG, NDSL, and so forth—which may confuse even professionals. They face deadlines and fees for applications for college entrance tests, admissions, and financial aid. They cannot realistically judge the chances of one particular student to be admitted and, more important, to be successful in any given school or program. At the beginning of this critical process, students (and often the parents) lack precise information about their strengths and weaknesses, the postsecondary programs and financial aid available, and the steps necessary for formulating a basis on which to make this all-important decision.

Parental Pressures

The counselor's job is complex, with enormous pressures. Obviously, students with good grades and test scores and some extracurricular involvement are going to have a number of choices. When the counselor's suggestions, students' self-perceptions, and parents' expectations are aligned, the selection is usually a fairly smooth process. However, many parents may exert certain pressures on their children, which in turn creates difficulties for the counselor.

For example, some parents want their child to attend the same college they did, even though the student may not be qualified or eager to go there. Sometimes the college may not have the courses that the students want or that are suitable to their needs or goals. Sometimes parents force on children a career choice they do not want to pursue because the parents feel it provides more social status or financial security than the ones the children are interested in. Sometimes sexual biases are involved; for example, a girl may choose to attend a college because of its strong premed program, whereas her parents want her to go somewhere else and become a nurse. I have dealt with several fine, sensitive boys who love young children, but their parents were horrified at my suggestion that they consider kindergarten or preschool education as a career. Parents who have sent their children to independent secondary schools are particularly averse to junior colleges and vocational schools. Their feeling is that, since they have paid all that money for tuition, it is the counselor's responsibility to make sure their child goes to a four-year college.

Parents of minority children who are having academic difficulties pose a particular problem. If John is having trouble in math and science and his parents want him to be an engineer, what does the counselor do? If the counselor discourages John, the parents may charge discrimination. On the other hand, if the counselor says nothing about John's potential problems in college or suggests no other career alternatives or exploration, a great disservice to that student, his family, and even the counselor is being committed. John will probably have access to engineering programs at a home state college or university, even if he would not be accepted elsewhere, so the counselor can easily slip out of a confrontation on this issue. However, the question is whether the counselor is discharging his professional obligation by doing so.

One way to prevent some of these problems is to hold an information night for juniors and their parents late in January, early enough for the counselor to encourage students to sign up for the March SAT. The main speaker is an admissions director of a nearby college or university, who urges the audience to explore, to keep options open, and to utilize the expertise of the counseling office. The director urges the parents not to push their needs and desires on their children and suggests that they influence and guide their children but not pressure them. I explain the philosophy of the guidance department and its procedures for college counseling, and I encourage the parents to see me during the spring of the junior year. I tell them that I will be honest about their child's strengths and chances for success in a particular school or program but that the final decision about making an application is theirs. I also explain very carefully our policy on writing recommendations. Essentially, I try to inform parents about the operation of our office, their responsibilities in the process, and our willingness to help them explore choices with their children. But the message is also clear that the student and the student's needs are our primary concern.

We also hand out a selection of written materials: copies of newspaper articles pertaining to the college experience, admissions, financial aid, and so forth; specific instructions for the college application procedures used by our office; information about SAT, ACT, and other tests. In 1980 we also started handing out the NACAC booklet on college admissions. Since we ask everyone to sign in, we know which students' families are not represented at the meeting. We call in those students later and give them the materials, which we ask them to take home to their parents.

By using these procedures, particularly written materials like the NACAC booklet on college admissions, the counselor can spell out the general college admissions process without singling out one student or one group of students. The counselor can clarify the financial aid process and can make parents aware of their numerous options. The meeting is a point of reference when the parents have a conference.

Peer Group Pressures

The peer group is another source of pressure on the counselor. Often a student's friends will be attending one school, perhaps the state school near home, and they try to influence other students to enroll at that institution with them. So secure a move is tempting, but friends' choices are inadequate bases on which to make decisions. The counselor must explain to students how important it is for them to make decisions based on their own goals and that going to a place where there will be many new faces and experiences may be a valuable part of their education. This is particularly tricky if there is a disparity between a student's academic ability or social effectiveness and that of his friends, who plan to attend a school which would be a poor choice for him. The counselor must be sensitive and tactful to ensure that none of the group feels he is being advised into accepting a less desirable situation than that of his friends.

The counselor can encourage counselees to investigate a range of colleges and universities by arranging to have currently enrolled college students call the prospective candidate during vacation. College admissions offices can help make these arrangements.

If the secondary school sends students to a variety of colleges, there may be someone from the home school on a campus to reassure her about the school's academic and social life. It is therefore very helpful for the guidance office to keep a record of the current location of recent graduates. High school alumni still attending college are usually eager to return to the home school to do a presentation for the current juniors and seniors, and they are excellent sources of information for the counselors as well.

School Board Pressures

The school board may be another source of pressure, in both public and independent schools. In some independent schools, the value of the education received by the children is measured by admission to "prestigious" colleges. Parents of prospective applicants frequently ask for the admissions statistics of previous graduates to various colleges. In one unforgettable case, at a meeting for parents of applicants to an independent school, one man wanted complete statistics on admissions to certain highly competitive colleges. He became more and more insistent as the college counselor explained the school's low-key counseling philosophy—that students were not pushed into one certain kind of school. We discovered at the end of this meeting that the child of the man so concerned about admission to prestige colleges was nine years old!

Some boards of trustees have the same attitude as that father. The counselor therefore feels pressured to steer students to certain schools, regardless of the students' suitability. This can be disastrous. (Generally, the weaker student will not be admitted. If he is, he may be so defeated and frustrated that he may not finish his studies there or anywhere else.) It is essential to educate board members about the goal of the school and the guidance office, to promote happiness and successful performance of graduates in whatever college they attend.

Public school boards, especially in small communities, exert a form of pressure that may cause a great dilemma for a counselor. Sometimes a school board member assumes that the counselor will take unusual steps to help gain admission to a competitive college for a young person in whom the school board member has a strong interest. Sometimes the board member is a graduate of old Siwash and wants students from the local school to go there. Sometimes his business partner's son, an average student, is encouraged to try for admission to Prestige U.—the idea being that the school board member will "encourage" the high school counselor to write an "extra-special" recommendation. The counselor in a small community is both visible and vulnerable, and the job may depend on the good will of the principal and the school board. If this school board exerts pressure to get Susan or Tom into certain colleges for which they are not qualified (and which they may not want to attend), what is the counselor to do? Writing a "stretched" recommendation not only hurts that student but puts the counselor's own credibility in jeopardy. If the counselor tells the truth, it is highly unlikely that Susan or Tom will be admitted, which may lead to ugly confrontations and further pressures from the school board and the community in general.

The situation is further complicated for all counselors by the provisions of the Family Educational Rights and Privacy Act of 1974 (the Buckley Amendments). A student enrolled in an institution has right of access to personal permanent records, unless the student specifically waives the right. In a period of declining enrollment, it will become more prevalent for colleges to accept students with lesser credentials and less favorable recommendations than they have accepted in the past. Therefore, the counselor's recommendation, regardless of its content, may be open to scrutiny after the student is enrolled, causing the counselor to be even more cautious.

There are various ways high school counselors and college

admissions officers have dealt with the problem. Some high schools, ours being one, ask the parents and student to sign a general waiver of access. We explain very clearly our policy on recommendation writing: We interview all students individually, ask them to tell us what they feel they would like the college to know about them, and speak with teachers who know them well. We explain that we will not lie or stretch the truth. If students and families accept those ground rules (practically all our families do), they sign our waiver. The reputation of the college counselor in the school community, the school's college admissions statistics, and the presentation of this philosophy can enormously affect the success of this procedure. For example, fewer than five families have refused to sign our waiver in the past three years.

If the family refuses to sign the waiver, the matter can be handled various ways. Sometimes families who refuse to sign a blanket waiver at first will do so later when they see that a number of colleges also provide for a waiver on their own blanks. Sometimes an explanation of the advantages of confidentiality to the credibility of the recommendation is sufficient to convince the parents. Sometimes nothing will convince them, in which case the counselor has to make some choices.

Many counselors will write a very objective, noncommittal, and rather uninformative recommendation that is basically a summary of the student's grades and activities. If they have further information they would like the college to have, they call the college. Most college admissions offices will accept a collect call; they are all most understanding and receptive to any information counselors wish to give them.

In other cases, particularly when a counselor has had a long-term relationship with a certain college, the admissions officers will know from the style of the recommendation that it is incomplete, and they will call themselves to check on the candidate. Some counselors attach an additional note to the recommendation asking that someone call. The message is clear to an alert college admissions office that there is more involved than is written in the recommendation. The counselor who faces this problem should first consult other counselors in the school or the principal to learn the school's policy. It is important to do this before recommendation-writing season begins. If the policy is not already clearly defined, it is essential to have it done. The difficult situation may not arise very frequently, but it is very unsettling for the counselor who has to devise a spontaneous way of dealing with it.

Opportunities These Pressures Create

Depending on the delicacy of the situation, pressures from parents, school boards, and so forth may actually give the counselor opportunities for more fruitful sessions with a student than would ordinarily occur. A student pressured into applying to colleges or programs that may be inappropriate or damaging to his emotional and professional growth may very well be searching for alternatives, and an alert counselor can work with the student to find the choices. This is particularly true in the traditionally college-preparatory high school for the small percentage who choose not to go to a four-year college and perhaps not to go on for further training at all. These students' self-images frequently suffer because all their friends are discussing applications, financial aid, and housing. The counselor has an obligation to clarify her or his position concerning the dignity and value of all productive work and to help the student and parents deal more positively with a wider range of career and educational alternatives.

Many counselors have stories such as the following. Several years ago, a seventeen-year-old boy at our school was failing most of his courses. When I called him in, I found that he was having a terrible time convincing his parents to let him leave high school. He wanted to attend beauty college to become a hairdresser, and they were adamantly opposed to his decision. Therefore, he had stopped working at school, to force his parents into permitting him to leave. He was going to be eighteen fairly soon, at which point he was going to leave school regardless of their feelings, but then he would have neither their financial nor moral support. Since our school is highly college oriented and many parents are sacrificing to pay the tuition, this kind of decision by a student almost inevitably evokes negative response from a parent. In this particular case, it was complicated by the student's choice of profession, which the parents considered inappropriate. I called the mother in, and, after several sessions with her and the boy, she reluctantly allowed him to leave school, take the GED, and enroll in beauty college. Several months later, the lady reappeared in my office, radiant about her happy, successful son who was doing such fine work at the beauty school. Her pride in her son was evident, and she remarked how much she had gained through the experience. Obviously, not all cases of this kind will turn out so well, but I believe it is an essential part of the counselor's job to help each student through such difficulties.

Pressure from Armed Services

An outside organization that frequently pressures counselors is the military. Counselors receive all kinds of promotional materials, magazines, desk calendars, and so forth. They also receive invitations to visit military bases, to encourage them to make their counselees aware of the armed services as a possible postsecondary option. Military recruiters are eager to visit classes on career or to come to career days and will pressure counselors to permit them to give the Armed Services Vocational Aptitude Battery. Most schools have an established policy about visits, which applies to military visitors as well as to college representatives, but counselors may wish to discuss the administration of ASVAB with their principals. Although it is an aptitude test, ASVAB is also a means of recruiting and needs to be presented as such to the students.

In our city, a group of alumni from the military academies host annual luncheons to which the local high schools send five of their outstanding juniors. One of the five as the result of an interview after the luncheon, will have his or her name engraved on a plaque that hangs in a prominent place in each school. This military academy leadership award is presented publicly at the schools' annual Honors Convocations and carries great prestige among students and parents. The sponsors of the luncheons openly admit that this procedure is a recruiting device to interest top students in attending the service academies or applying for ROTC scholarships.

It may be necessary for counselors planning career programs and college days or nights to apply some restraints on military recruiters, who have all kinds of audiovisual materials. Not only do they bring movies or slide shows, they may have other more realistic props. One of the favorite stories of college admissions representatives is that of the career night in a high school in which the Marines set up a machine-gun display in the front hall!

There are a number of ways counselors can work with the military to the mutual satisfaction of both groups. Some schools have a corner of the guidance office set aside for military information. In larger communities, the recruiters periodically update or replenish the supply of materials. In smaller ones, it is necessary for the counselors to request replacements of needed materials.

Some schools have a week or two during the year when recruiters from all military branches are invited to visit during regular school hours or right after school for individual presentations. Interested students, parents, and faculty are welcome to attend. After that, it is up to the student to contact the recruiters on an individual basis.

Religious Pressures

In some families, parochial schools, and communities with a strong religious commitment, the counselor is pressured to steer students to schools with the same religious heritage. The counselor needs to be very sensitive to this issue, particularly if the student wants to go to a secular institution. Some students have been in parochial schools all their lives and wish to try something new. In these cases, it is better to have a parent-student-counselor conference about the college admissions process to ascertain the guidelines within which the counselor must operate.

It may be necessary to alert parents and students to the

opportunities for members of all the major religious groups to find spiritual guidance on most campuses today. If there is no group on the campus, there is generally a church or synagogue nearby that works closely with the office of student affairs. When the family is in doubt, a call to the admissions office usually brings quick information about the support group available to the student's religious denomination.

Also in some cases, students attending one college may have the privilege of taking theology or religion classes at another college nearby. By mentioning these possibilities, or by calling the admissions office to get the address of the local religious center, whether on the campus or in the community, the counselor can usually effect a compromise between parents and student.

Pressures from Colleges

In a period of declining enrollments and inflation, counselors and students are going to be pressured by private and public colleges, which compete for the reduced number of seniors graduating from high schools. "Marketing" is a key term used by admissions directors; in fact, this year, for the first time, I received a copy of an admissions letter sent to one of my students signed by the vice-president for marketing instead of the director of admissions.

The most selective and prestigious private colleges will always have an abundance of applicants to choose from; the rest will not be so fortunate and thus will have to devise new methods of attracting traditional students and develop new programs to appeal to other segments of the population. Many private colleges are offering extensive programs of no-need scholarships to make their campuses more attractive to more desirable candidates who might not qualify for financial aid. (This has recently become a controversial issue within NACAC and will probably remain so as long as the pressure of declining enrollments continues.) Some schools are developing special honors programs, independent study, concurrent enrollment for high school students, and campus visits for prospective students.

Although the high school counselor may sympathize with the problems the college admissions officer faces, the counselor must also remember that the first priority is the students. The counselor must explain to the students why they will receive mountains of promotional material and numerous telephone calls from alumni, faculty, and currently enrolled students of various institutions. Just as students learn in class to be educated consumers of tangible goods, so they must also learn to be educated consumers in our current admissions system. They must learn to sift through the various educational opportunities available in institutions that frequently are unknown or indistinguishable to them. Therefore, the counselor's experience and expertise are invaluable because many students and parents are bewildered (and often flattered) by all the attention they receive. The counselor needs to help students acquire a proper educational and economic perspective—namely, by pointing out that these are additional options to be explored in the light of the students' own perceived objectives. Counselors should also point out to students that the fact that they have had frequent or infrequent contact with a particular school does not necessarily reflect the value of that institution's programs or its interest in them as candidates for admission; it may simply reflect that school's decisions about its chosen course in the admissions process.

Counselors are starting to receive a special kind of pressure from their in-state colleges and universities. Because these institutions have fixed overhead and costs are constantly rising, they must have an abundance of students, so that they can receive adequate funding from the state legislatures to maintain their financial stability. This is particularly true when funding is based on the total number of credit hours in progress. The more students, whether full or part time, traditional or nontraditional, the higher the allocation of state money. Thus, in some states there is pressure, some subtle and some overt, some "patriotic," to encourage students to stay within the state. The argument is that if we keep students at home, our money goes into the local economy and there is a higher body count for funding. The student gets educated, the local economy is supported, and the universities get their funding.

The professional counselor has a serious problem with this type of reasoning. First, the counselor is asked to limit the options presented to the student rather than broaden them. Also, the emphasis is on the state's financial concerns, not on the student's needs. This requires that the counselor question his philosophy of counseling and his perception of his professional responsibilities. If the counselor believes that students should investigate a variety of schools that may suit their needs, regardless of location, such beliefs will preclude his following this line of thinking. If the counselor is in a school located in the same community as a state institution, strong arguments for his point of view may have to be presented when parents, peers, and that state institution are applying pressure to keep that student at home. In a public school, the pressures are most severe because there is a sort of "gentleman's agreement" (and in some cases actual financial involvement) between the local state-funded university or college and the school system. The public high schools are viewed as funnels that pour into the public universities, and the counselor who encourages students to do a thorough search (which may end by their enrollment in an institution in another state) is considered suspect. In many cases, the high school counselors themselves are graduates of the local university and have had little exposure to other institutions. They may have numerous other responsibilities that prevent them from becoming knowledgeable about college opportunities in other areas. They may also agree with the philosophy of encouraging students to explore only local opportunities.

Counselors need to examine their own biases. If they feel they lack information, they should try to stock their offices with a broad selection of reference materials and catalogues. They should hold college day or college night programs for their students or join with other schools to present them. They should encourage students to attend a college fair if there is one in the area, and they should attend it themselves. They should try to attend meetings of their regional Association of College Admissions Counselors and, if possible, the National Association of College Admissions Counselors. They should encourage students to visit colleges during summer vacation and should visit colleges themselves. They should also invite representatives of post-secondary institutions and programs to visit the school. Counselors should use the computerized information that is becoming more and more available, either through terminals placed directly in the schools or through the NACACtion Center service. If the counselor opens avenues of information to students, the eventual choices the students make will occur as the result of a conscious decision-making process, not through lack of knowledge. If the student decides to remain in the hometown area, that should also be a positive choice.

Another current pressure being applied to students—a pressure that the NACAC's Admissions Practices Committee may have to deal with in the near future—is offering a scholarship to a student who has not applied to that school. More and more, we are finding that colleges are identifying students through computer searches and offering "enticement" money. This is very bewildering to students who may know nothing about that institution or who may have no interest whatsoever in attending it. Recently one of my students was offered a "leadership" scholarship from an institution whose only contact with him was through an interest card filled out at a college fair. The boy had subsequently decided to attend a different college that has an engineering course and was already enrolled. The college offering the "leadership" scholarship tried to persuade him to enroll there by telling him it offered "preengineering" courses! The student was very puzzled by the admissions officer's behavior, which he reported to me. I expressed my own confusion and dismay to this admissions officer, who seemed to think my point of view was unusual. I found, however, that when I mentioned the NACAC *Statement of Principles of Good Practice,* the tone of the conversation changed quickly. Other counselors in the area have reported similar experiences with other colleges, and we need to alert our students and parents to this practice. Our school gives parents and students the NACAC *Statement of Principles of Good Practice* as well as its *Statement of Students' Rights and Responsibilities in the College Admissions Process.* This is an excellent way to set up the ground rules for ethical behavior by all interested parties.

The Counselor's Responsibility

Pressures will come from many sources. The most important pressure comes from within the counselor: to discharge responsibilities honestly and competently, always with the welfare of the students as the paramount concern. This implies first that the counselor must have a well-defined philosophy of counseling on which to base professional procedures. To deal with the pressures discussed, the counselor must be aware of the policies and philosophy of the school system (or board of trustees), the principal, and the guidance department. In fact, it is much easier for an individual counselor to deal with a number of problems if they are already addressed in published policy statements. For example, a number of educational institutions and programs request lists of seniors, to mail them recruitment materials. Many school systems refuse to give out lists for any purposes, and the NACAC *Statement of Principles of Good Practice* has a clear statement on that type of request. A decision already made on that issue takes away the burden of deciding which requests to honor and which not to.

I have made several references to the NACAC *Statement of Principles of Good Practice.* This is an excellent source of information on all kinds of admissions and financial policies. Because all members of the organization promise to comply with them, this relieves some pressure on the counselor to monitor a number of practices. Clearly, therefore, it is to the counselor's advantage to be familiar with the statement and to publicize it to parents, students, and school officials. Even if the school is not a member of NACAC, the counselor can obtain copies of that statement as well as the *Statement of Students' Rights and Responsibilities.* Most colleges are members of NACAC; even those that are not are generally familiar with the provisions of these statements and will respect a high school's decision to abide by them.

The counselor stands as the main interpreter of information on postsecondary institutions and financial aid to students, their families, the school, and the community. Frequent changes in society force the counselor to adapt to differing professional and ethical standards. The pressure that results from such adaptation makes his job more difficult but also more important. It is the counselor's obligation, therefore, to be aware of the pressures placed on him and his students and to know how to deal with them, so that the vital decisions about his students' futures can be made under the most favorable conditions.

✍ 28

Communicating Individuality When Writing Reference Letters

Pamela K. Fay

✍   Concern for the student as an individual, with unique abilities, interests, values, needs, goals, and desires—this concern is paramount for responsible admissions officers and secondary school counselors involved in the college admissions process. The profession recognizes this fact in the opening of the *Statement of Principles of Good Practice for Members of the National Association of College Admissions Counselors* (1976): "High schools, colleges, and universities, and other institutions and organizations dedicated to the promotion of formal education believe in the dignity, the worth, and the potentialities of every human being."

The primary tool of the secondary school counselor for communicating the essence of an individual student as a human being with dignity to the college admissions officer is the reference letter. Its importance cannot be overemphasized, for it can make an applicant come alive and be the most persuasive element of the application. It can explain school standards, the competition within a class, and the student's respective standing within that class; it can describe outside pressures or internal situations that have affected the student's performance; it can relate the manner in which the student has handled challenges; it can present qualities of the student's personality that are pertinent to academic performance; it can reflect the impact of nonacademic contributions made by the student; in general, it can present the student as an individual human being instead of a number resulting from a predictive analysis plugged into a computer.

With the plethora of numbers available on each applicant and the pressure to stress objective data, the reference letter is frequently the only verbal item that becomes a part of the admissions process. For colleges and universities that do not require an essay by the student, the reference letter is likely to be the only written communication in the student's folder.

Communication between the secondary school counselor and the college admissions officer is of the utmost importance if appropriate care and attention is to be given to each applicant. Numerous influences are beginning to erode that communication, many of which have been described by Ripple (1979, p. 5): budget cuts at secondary schools, resulting in increased loads for counselors and an inability or lack of interest by the counselors in attending professional conferences and workshops; a changing emphasis on career rather than college planning by secondary school counselors; and a diminishing number of visits to secondary schools by college admissions officers.

In evaluating the results of the College Admissions Questionnaire and the High School Counselor Questionnaire distributed during the spring of 1979 by the National Association of College Admissions Counselors, Dominick and his colleagues (1980, p. 7) describe a "shift away from travel" by college admissions officers and project that such a shift will result in less direct communication between those involved in the college admissions process. Seeing this as detrimental in the process, they state (p. 6) that "cooperation between the admissions officer and the high school counselor is widely considered to be an essential element of good recruiting." Because of the potential diminution of communication between secondary school counselors and college admissions officers, it is therefore vital that the reference letter continue to be submitted by counselors and requested by admissions officers as part of the college admissions process.

According to the report of the Task Force on Confidentiality (Hersey and others, 1978, p. 8), institutions that request or require letters of reference do so "to increase their sensitivity to the special human qualities of the individual. . . . During the process they argue for individuals who otherwise might be discarded by a strictly objective formula." In the NACAC *Statement of Principles of Good Practice,* secondary school members agree that they will "provide accurate descriptions of the candidates' personal qualities that are relevant to the admissions process." Writing an "accurate description" demands objectivity and an accepting rather than a judgmental attitude on the part of the secondary school counselor. "Clear, intelligent, informative letters of support" (Potier, 1980, p. 16), as desired by college admissions officers, are ones that describe the student honestly, interestingly, and impartially, yet without detachment.

Should the reference letter be an analytical essay? Should it be an outstanding piece of creative writing? Or should it be a marketing pitch? An argument could be posed for or against each approach, but it is preferable to produce a letter that reflects a balanced approach, making appropriate use of each style.

As an analytical essay, the reference letter must dissect the student's actions, to provide a comprehensive description of academic, nonacademic, and personal qualities. However, it is not the purpose of the reference letter to analyze the internal order of the student or to examine each quirk the student may exhibit. The responsible writer focuses only on those elements that are relevant to college admission, maintaining the attitude of an observer describing actions that will help the admissions staff understand the student as a complex, unique human being and so make as enlightened a decision as possible.

Creativity in the reference letter is in style, not content. The use of uniquely worded phrases, anecdotes to illustrate actions, fresh adjectives, humor, and even poetry can give a lift to the admissions reader who has to face a grueling load of meaningless, dull, and repetitive phrases that typify the hundreds of reference letters submitted.

Although counselors should not bow to the marketing trend current in recruitment by writing a sales pitch for each student, they should adopt a positive and helpful posture that will aid both the student and the college.

Even though objectivity is required, it is unrealistic for a counselor to expect to be able to maintain a totally detached stance while writing a reference letter. The secondary school counselor typically—and justifiably—becomes involved with students in a caring way and will reflect that care in the letter. Even while attempting to be objective, counselors may unwittingly choose adjectives, anecdotes, and phrases that reflect their basic attitude toward the students. It is important that both counselors, in writing, and admissions officers, in reading, be aware of this inherent bias in the letter.

College admissions personnel admit that a well-written reference letter will aid the applicant in the admissions process. In *Playing the Private College Admissions Game,* Moll (1979, p. 189), writes, "the college Admissions Office is grateful for them [recommendations] —and clearly the candidate who comes alive in the folder has an advantage over others."

Potier (1980, p. 16) praises secondary school counselors who write reference letters: "For some of our larger colleges and universities, these letters are perhaps extraneous; however, for many of us, they are extremely important and underscore important personal and extracurricular attributes about the students."

Those counselors who do not write reference letters, or who write them so poorly that they are meaningless, are potentially hurting their students in the admissions process by forcing the admissions office to make a decision based on whatever unexplained numerical data are made available. In such an instance, the counselor rejects the role prescribed by the NACAC *Statement of Principles of Good Practice* and fails to be a student advocate in the college admissions process.

Legal and Ethical Influences

Since the enactment of the Family Educational Rights and Privacy Act of 1974 (the Buckley Amendments), secondary school counselors have borne conflicting pressures regarding the college application process, the maintenance of records, and the reference letter. The two primary results of the conflict are a dramatic reduction in the number of counselors who submit reference letters to colleges and a change from providing detailed letters to submitting general, meaningless ones—not because authors comply with the Buckley Amendments but because they misunderstand what the law requires. Many agencies, organizations, and institutions were panicked by the Buckley Amendments and, before carefully examining the requirements of the law, hastily sought to destroy records and change policies regarding the release of information about students.

The first sentence of Section 438(a)(1)(A) of the Amendments was of particular concern to institutions and prompted immediate reaction. It states that "no funds shall be made available under any applicable program to any educational agency or institution which has a policy of denying, or which effectively prevents, the parents of students who are or have been in attendance at a school of such agency or at such institution, as the case may be, the right to inspect and review the education records of their children." Part (B) of Section 438, however, exempts "confidential letters of recommendation respecting admission to any educational agency or institution" if the student has signed a waiver of right of access. Therefore, a counselor clearly may write a reference letter in confidence if the student has signed a waiver of right of access; or the counselor may write a reference letter and allow the parents or the eligible student (eighteen or over) to review it.

No legal provision in the Buckley Amendments restricts the submission of a reference letter as part of the college admissions process, even though some secondary schools refuse to provide one. These schools state that the provision of such information is against the policy of their professional organization. Regarding this point, let us examine the ethical codes and policies of the various professional organizations to which secondary school administrators, counselors, and teachers belong.

The NACAC *Statement of Principles of Good Practice for Members* has also been endorsed by the American Association of Collegiate Registrars and Admission Officers, the College

Board, and the National Association of Secondary School Principals. A revised statement of *Ethical Standards,* published by the American Personnel and Guidance Association in 1974, states that "the counseling relationship and information resulting therefrom must be kept confidential, consistent with the obligations of the member as a professional person." A later statement adds that "revelation to others of counseling material should occur only upon the express consent of the counselee." But a further qualification states that "should the member be engaged in a work setting that calls for any variation from the above statements, the member is obligated to consult with other professionals whenever possible to consider justifiable alternatives." Therefore, when a student who wants to apply to a college does give a release, the counselor is in compliance with APGA policy when writing a confidential letter of reference to that college.

The American School Counselor Association's (1972) *Code of Ethics* makes several statements pertinent to the reference letter. One of the six basic tenets of the code is: "The school counselor may share information gained in the counseling process for essential consultation with those appropriate persons specifically concerned with the counselee. Confidential information may be released only with consent of the individual except when required by court order." A principal responsibility of the school counselor, according to the ASCA *Code of Ethics,* is to "supply accurate information according to his professional judgment to community agencies, places of employment, and institutions of higher learning."

Although the American Federation of Teachers has not published a code of ethics, the National Education Association (1975) does have a statement regarding confidentiality in its *Code of Ethics for the Education Profession.* The association endorses the concept of confidentiality unless there is a "compelling professional purpose" or a "legal requirement."

A summation of the ethical policies and the legal requirements of the Buckley Amendments reveals three basic guidelines for secondary school counselors: (1) that secondary school counselors provide "accurate descriptions" (NACAC, 1976) of each student applying to colleges and universities; (2) that secondary school counselors obtain from students written permission to release such information; (3) that secondary school counselors allow parents or eligible students the opportunity to review the reference letter, except when the student has signed a waiver of right of access, in which case the review can be optional.

Making reference letters available for inspection to parents or eligible students undoubtedly is threatening to some administrators and counselors because of the openness of past and present communication implied in such an action. If the reference letter accurately describes the student's actions and attitude at school, as NACAC principles demand, then it should not reveal information unknown to the parent. If the parent is not aware of the information, then the school must examine its communication policy between parents and teachers, administrators, and counselors.

The *Guidelines for the Collection, Maintenance, and Dissemination of Pupil Records* established by the Russell Sage Foundation (1970, p. 6) make clear the reason for increased communication: "The promise of the human resource represented by the pupils in our schools is compelling in its importance; the plastic nature of the growing young personality underlines the delicacy of the issues; and the commitment of our society to the development of every child's full potential establishes the paramount social objective within which the human dimension must be preserved."

Counselors and admissions officers must constantly be aware that they are dealing with delicate human beings in their final development stage before adulthood. Open communication, with sensitivity and respect for the student, must be practiced by all persons involved in the college admissions process.

Conflicting Pressures for Accountability

In writing the reference letter, the counselor faces conflicting responsibilities. The primary responsibility of the secondary school counselor, as indicated by the several codes of

ethics quoted previously, is to the counselee—the student. However, legally, until a student reaches the age of eighteen, the
school is responsible to the parent. Educational institutions,
with their own ethical standards, needs, and priorities, frequently demand the counselors adhere to responsibilities determined
by the institutions. Two years after the Buckley Amendments
were passed, a study commission, formed to examine how the
act was functioning, found that educational institutions were
still assuming "that information they receive is their property
. . . that a student or parent has no right to know the information
exists, to see it, correct it, etc." (Goldwater, 1980, p. 11). A
counselor paid by, employed by, and supervised by such an educational institution is placed in a position of direct conflict with
legal and professional ethical standards.

Even when educational institutions comply with the law
and professional ethics, they can still pressure the counselor to
withhold relevant information from the reference letter, to facilitate a student's chances of obtaining admission at a certain
college or university. There is also the covert pressure to refer
students on the basis of their academic performance, as a representative of the secondary school.

At times the community may pressure the counselor to
promote students at certain colleges in order to bring prestige
to the community; to conform with the mode of the community; to break racial patterns; to help alumni for financial, business, or athletic reasons; or for a variety of other reasons. When
the counselor is asked—or feels pressured—to promote a student
to a particular institution that represents an impossible academic challenge for the student or that the student, for other
reasons, is hesitant to attend, the counselor is faced with a conflict of professional ethical standards, responsibility to the student, and, possibly, future employment. Needless to say, writing
the reference letter in such a situation is a delicate undertaking,
but counselors must bear in mind that their primary responsibility is to the student.

The counselor must be truthful, candid, and fair when
writing the reference letter, to ensure that students who are
truly capable of satisfactory academic work are understood to

be so. The academic capabilities of the student must be completely described so that the admissions office can make a well-informed decision. It is not in a student's best interest to be placed in a college that presents too rigorous an academic challenge. The long-term relationship between the secondary school and the college depends on candid and honest communication between the counselor and the admissions officer.

Ultimately, the counselor must produce a reference letter that ethically describes the student, taking into consideration the appropriateness of the student's attendance at a particular college or university, and must be prepared to respond to those who may disagree with the approach. This does not mean that the counselor is obliged to promote the student at any given college or university to which the student has chosen to apply. It does mean that the counselor is obligated to present the student's aptitudes realistically and must be prepared to discuss candidly those aptitudes with the student.

Techniques of Writing

A good reference letter should include any information that is relevant to the student's past or present academic or non-academic performance. Herr and Cramer (1968, pp. 203-204) propose seven don'ts to keep in mind when writing reference letters:

1. Don't write generalizations; use specific illustrations.
2. Don't write information that is available from other sections of the application.
3. Don't use strings of adjectives.
4. Don't present solely the positive.
5. Don't neglect important factors.
6. Don't use "educationese."
7. Don't neglect to explain distortions (of grades, tests, rank, interview, personality record).

Instead of citing each grade made in each class (available on the school transcript), the reference letter should explain which grades are particularly important and why they have been given special attention. Reasons range from the particular student's problems to the competition within a class, which helps compare the student's performance with that of other members of the class. For example: "Beth's grade in English for the first trimester, 3.0, is lower than her other grades, but it is the second highest grade in that class, which is an Honors section. Ms. Doe insists on grammatically perfect papers from her seniors and counts every misplaced comma on each paper."

A student's academic interests can be illustrated by citing strengths in particular departments or courses or by showing balance: "Although John has found special satisfaction and interest in the theater, he is firmly committed to the pursuit of an enriched and balanced liberal arts education. His solid grade point average becomes all the more impressive in light of the voluminous number of credits he accrued in an effort to make up for lost time. He has done his best work in English and social science" (Moll, 1979, p. 187).

Only nonacademic pursuits of relevance to the secondary school or community or of special interest to the student need be included in the letter. A list of the student's activities has no place in the reference letter because it is included elsewhere in most applications. Specific examples illustrating the depth and quality of the student's interest should be used in the description: "In football and lacrosse, he was without a doubt the best competitor, pound for pound, in school. His football coach recently referred to him as the most fearless carrier he had ever coached" (Vasquez, 1976, p. 19).

Traumas that have affected the student's performance in school, such as the long illness or death of a parent, unusual home responsibilities, or student illness, should be mentioned with sensitivity: "Because she was sick with mononucleosis last winter and missed virtually all the third trimester—thirty-six school days—junior year scholastic work is not indicative of what she can accomplish."

Personal characteristics are specifically requested by most colleges. The charts provided are a nuisance—rating a student among the top 1 percent in sense of humor appears to label a clown. However, in the written letter, counselors can explain important qualities that characterize the student as an individual. The Common Application Form, used by an increasing number of colleges in the United States, asks the following from counselors on the Secondary School Advisor Evaluation form: "Please feel free to write whatever you think is important about the applicant, including a description of academic and personal characteristics. We are particularly interested in evidence about the candidate's intellectual promise, motivation, relative maturity, integrity, independence, originality, initiative, leadership potential, capacity for growth, special talents, and enthusiasm. We welcome information that will help us to differentiate this student from others."

When describing personal qualities, the writer should illustrate each quality with incidents or anecdotes, rather than adjectives that may be misinterpreted and that carry less impact than an anecdote: "Roxanne could be described as a 'low-keyed bohemian—or a moderate individualist.' This I gather from her gypsy jaunty dress and her description of clashes she has had with the journalism staff, who, she says, fail to give her articles bylines. She's not afraid to be herself nor to speak her mind freely, though she's not a full-fledged maverick" (Moll, 1979, p. 174).

Counselors must be careful to use excellent grammar, a wide variety of precise adjectives, and fresh phrases. College admissions officers have long lists of overused, meaningless clichés that appear regularly in reference letters and are regularly dismissed as irrelevant: "a late bloomer"; "well liked by faculty and peers"; "shows great potential for success"; "one of the finest students ever to graduate"; "family has been respected and loved by the community"; "cooperative, responsible, reliable"; "test scores are not truly indicative of ability"; "has taken a very good solid academic program all four years"; "recommend John highly as a person and as a student"; "would be an asset to the University of Excelsior"; "is highly motivated."

The use of quotations from others knowledgeable about the student, such as teachers, coaches, advisers, and sponsors of organizations, can be very effective if they are directly related to a point being made; such comments should not be used if they appear elsewhere in a separately written letter of reference. "Susan's exceptional creativity is influential in her work, but so is her interest in the world. Mrs. Smith commented on Susan's contributions to Junior English class discussions of local news events and global problems with the following: 'I have never taught a student who had read and retained so many facts ... always able to put this information into proper perspective and see the many results of a single action ... demonstrates wise knowledge of and sophisticated ability to interpret news events and trends.' "

Quotations must be copied directly from written evaluations previously released by the quoted person to the parent or eligible student, or written permission from the person to use the quotation must be obtained.

On occasion, delicate situations that are difficult to handle arise. A sample case was discussed at a professional workshop held recently; it involved a varsity football player with the potential for playing under scholarship at several competitive colleges. Contrary to his father's wishes, he wanted to take a year off from school and was questioning whether he wanted to play football at any time during college. During the discussion of this case, it was generally believed that the reference letter should not include any mention of the potential conflict or the possibility of collegiate football but should be confined to a description of the candidate's football ability and performance on the secondary school team.

Suspension from secondary school for either social or honor breaches is another type of concern. Some secondary school counselors feel that the student has already been punished for the act and therefore should not be punished again by having that included in a letter of reference. Some college admissions officers, however, ask on the application whether the candidate has been suspended and why; and others feel they have the right to know even if it is not requested in writing because it attests to the student's integrity. Public school counselors generally prefer to withhold such sensitive information from colleges; private school counselors usually consider the release of such information part of their responsibility.

Involving Others in the Reference Process

Most secondary school counselors do not have daily contact with all the students for whom they write reference letters, so they cannot provide independent knowledge of the diversity and complexity of each of their students. Although it is imperative that counselors create situations in which a better firsthand knowledge of the student can be developed, such as through personal interviews, small group gatherings, attendance at school functions, and casual conversation, the counselor must seek input from others directly associated with the student, to ascertain the student's behavior in a variety of settings and with a variety of people. Often interests and abilities that the student overlooks or is too modest to discuss are revealed by others.

Such resource persons are present or past teachers, advisers, coaches, sponsors of clubs or activities on and off campus, supervisors of volunteer or paid work outside the school, and peers who have worked closely with the student on projects, trips, or other activities. The student should ask some of the resource persons to write separate letters of reference, discussing in detail the student's qualities.

As a guide to such resource persons, the counselor can design and distribute a sheet of instructions to those writing, who typically are not accustomed to the college admissions process. The following rules should be incorporated into the guidelines: (1) the letter must be typewritten and can be copied; (2) the student's complete (first, middle, and last) name should be in the first sentence or at the top of the letter; (3) the first paragraph should clearly state the relationship of the person writing to the student; (4) the student's specific personal characteristics and qualities should be discussed as they have been observed by the writer and illustrative examples or anecdotes included; (5) the writer should not attempt to discuss anything that he or she is not qualified to mention (for instance, the student's academic performance, since the secondary school counselor and teachers are in the best position to discuss it and the resource person has no direct knowledge of the student in a different situation); (6) the writer should make sure that her or his complete name, address, and title are included.

Only resource persons who have something specific and meaningful to say about the student should be asked to write reference letters. Alumni of colleges to which the student is applying who are social or business acquaintances of the student's parents but who have no direct relationship with the student should not, as a rule, be asked to write reference letters because they have nothing to add about the applicant that will be meaningful to the college admissions office. An exception is the alumni interviewer who is part of the college's admissions process. Sheer volume prohibits the student from asking every resource person to write a letter of reference, and there is some truth to the adage "thick folder—thick child," making it best to avoid sending to the college admissions office a letter from every acquaintance.

Those persons not requested to write reference letters can be asked for input orally or in writing. It is helpful to have all school personnel involved with all juniors complete an evaluation or description at the end of the junior year. This may be a checklist including items most often requested by colleges, such as academic abilities, qualities, and potential. If the resource persons are encouraged to write comments on students in whom they have a particular interest, their notes may provide helpful insights.

The most important resource person to involve in the composition of the reference letter is the student. There are many ways to involve the student: by obtaining an autobiographical sketch; interviewing the student (the counselor should discuss what will be included in the reference letter and get specific input about strengths, weaknesses, needs, goals, interests, abilities, and qualities); and asking the student to complete a personal evaluation form. Finally, it is recommended that every student read the rough draft of the reference letter and have the opportunity to make changes, to discuss its contents, and to evaluate it. This beneficial practice is a vehicle for open communication and makes the student aware, ideally not for the first time, of his or her contributions, abilities, and qualities as seen by others. It also generates a positive feeling between the student and the school, which typically is trying to help, not hurt, the student in the college admissions process, and it ensures that the information included is correct. Finally, it helps ensure compliance with the Buckley Amendments.

Etiquette

The reference letter should be only a reference letter; it need not include a recommendation in words such as "I highly recommend Henry Jones to Superior College" in one letter and "I recommend Henry Jones with reservation to Excelsior University" in another letter. If a college wants such a recommendation, it will provide the necessary request form. Therefore, it is suggested that one letter be written for each student and that it be copied, after being typed, and sent to each college or university to which the student is applying. If the budget allows an original letter to each school, that certainly is an elegant touch, but it is not necessary.

The student—not the college or university—is being described in the reference letter and will be the same person, regardless of the college or university chosen. The student's academic performance will be different at a school with rigorous academic standards than at a college with less competition. If the counselor feels that the information provided by the school is not sufficient to reveal that prediction, then she or he may want to write a separate note to the individual colleges or elaborate on the secondary school report form.

School stationery, with the school address, including zip code, and the school telephone number, with area code, should always be included in the reference letter. At the top of the letter or in the first sentence, the student's complete name (first, middle, last) must be given so the filing staff at the college can easily find the right student.

The letter should clearly indicate that it is an official one written by the secondary school counselor, whose complete name and title must be included. The letter should be dated, so that the admissions office will know what portion of the year is omitted. If necessary, an updated reference may be requested

by the college admissions officer or volunteered by the secondary school counselor when new, pertinent information (such as
the end of the first semester of the senior year, or the end of
an athletic season) is available.

The counselor should automatically review those letters
written before the midyear senior term is finished and should
provide updated information, if relevant, with the midterm report.

Efficient handling of the reference letter in the secondary
school counseling office, particularly careful record keeping,
copying, and filing, ensures easy access when subsequent applications are made.

A succinct, interesting, and relevant letter with no grammatical or spelling errors is essential. It helps to have a secretary
with a B.A. in English from Vassar.

Recommendations for Using the Reference Letter

The reference letter is a valuable source of information
concerning a student when it has meaningful, descriptive, and
detailed passages. It is generally very carefully considered, with
hours of time spent by the secondary school counselor making
it appropriate. However, currently most colleges and universities
destroy it after the admissions process is finished, which seems a
tragic waste.

Beals (1979, p. 4), in examining "The Changing Role of
the Admissions Officer," suggests that admissions officers consider themselves educators: "The admissions officer must take
the initiative in this effort (as an educator) by proving to the
faculty and administration that he or she has invaluable information about students, college-going conditions, and other aspects of the institution's well-being. This must be accomplished
in a professional manner and with a spirit of concern and cooperation."

Research undertaken by Henton and her colleagues (1980)
adds another element to the consideration of students in the
college admissions process. They found that those college freshmen who experienced the highest amount of crisis, as measured

on Halpern's Crisis Scale, had the fewest "number of relatives in the community" and were the greatest "distance from home" (p. 509). In their summary, the researchers write: "Not only do students desire and seek validation of their existence from friends, they also need and seek validation of their existence from adults in their new community" (p. 510).

"Adults in their new community" can be those counselors at the college who are sensitive to adjustment problems of their freshmen—such as the admissions officers, the faculty advisers, or the college counseling staff—and who have access to the reference letter as a source of help in understanding the entering student. A sense of background and continuity is necessary for adjustment; the reference letter can be an important vehicle for the transmission of such information.

To facilitate this transferral of information, some colleges so indicate on the secondary school report form that the information provided will be retained to help the matriculating student. For example, Harvard-Radcliffe includes the following statement, which is recommended: "The purpose of this recommendation is to assist in making the admission decision and, if the applicant is admitted and enrolls, to aid in making rooming assignments and in advising and counseling and otherwise assisting the student. Under the provisions of this Act, you [the student] have the right, if you enroll at Harvard or Radcliffe, to review your educational records. The Act further provides that you may waive your right to see recommendations for admission. Please indicate below by circling the appropriate phrase and signing your name whether or not you wish to waive this right."

Also recommended is the statement of confidentiality on the Secondary School Advisor Evaluation form of the Common Application: "We value your comments highly and ask that you complete this form in the knowledge that it may be retained in the student file should the applicant matriculate at a member college. In accordance with the Family Educational Rights and Privacy Act of 1974, matriculating students do have access to their permanent files, which may include forms such as this one. Colleges do not provide access to admissions records to applicants, those students who are rejected, or those students who decline an offer of admission."

The reference letter is an important document that respectfully depicts the student as an individual human being to the admissions officer when it is written honestly, carefully, meaningfully, and descriptively, with attention to legal regulations. To help the student adjust to college life, it is essential that the reference letter be retained by the college and used by those involved in supportive roles.

29

Understanding Admissions Procedures at Highly Selective Colleges

Douglas C. Thompson

A very few of the hundreds of colleges and universities in the United States are fortunate enough to receive applications each year from many more highly qualified candidates than they can possibly admit. Hence, the admissions function at these selective institutions can be markedly different from those at nonselective ones. These selective institutions use different procedures and methods, but there are some remarkable similarities among them.

Definition of a "Selective College"

What does the term "selective" mean? Many institutions use this word to describe their admissions situation because they feel it is more prestigious to be considered selective. In reality, the vast majority of colleges and universities are not, or are only slightly, selective; generally, they admit those applicants who appear able to succeed academically and deny those who do not. There are many ways to quantify selectivity; one is to use the ratio of applicants to the available places in the freshman class. For example, in 1980 Princeton University and Brown University led the Ivy League, with almost ten applicants

491

for each place. This ratio has two inherent flaws that make it a less-than-perfect definition of selectivity. First, it ignores the academic quality of the applicant pool. If most of Princeton's applicants were not qualified academically, the use of this ratio would make Princeton seem more selective than it actually was.

Second, the ratio ignores the yield of admitted applicants. (Yield is the percentage of admitted applicants who ultimately matriculate.) If Princeton's yield were only 10 percent, it would have to admit everyone in the applicant pool to fill the freshman class and could hardly be called selective. Yield has often been used as an indication of selectivity. For example, Harvard currently has the highest yield of those institutions we shall call selective, with about 75 percent of its admittees enrolling. Most highly selective schools have yields of 45 percent or higher. However, yield is not a good index of selectivity. Many nonselective institutions with exclusively commuting students have very high yields because their applicants apply to only one school. Yield at selective institutions is often misleading as a gauge of selectivity because most of these schools offer first-choice early decision plans: An applicant specifies that the school being applied to is his or her first choice and agrees that he or she will matriculate there if admitted. Hence, an institution may fill up to half of its freshman class with applicants who will matriculate at close to a 100 percent yield. These applicants may or may not be as well qualified as those in the regular admissions pool, but they want to attend their first-choice college and presumably will be happy members of the freshman class. If a college filled half of its freshman class with early decision candidates (and they all came) but enrolled only 40 percent of those candidates admitted in its regular pool, it would have a yield of 57 percent, which is considered a very good yield. Actually, the yield on those candidates for whom it was competing with other schools was only fair at 40 percent.

Probably the best way to quantify selectivity is simply by the percentage of applicants admitted. In the 1978-79 admission year, Harvard admitted only 17 percent of its applicants. About nine schools admitted fewer than one quarter of their applicants, and about another twenty-five admitted from one half to one quarter of their pools. Although the use of this figure ignores the academic quality of the applicant pool, all those institutions admitting fewer than 50 percent of their candidates happen to have extremely strong applicant pools, with very few unqualified people to reject.

Some specialized colleges of art, music, and engineering are extremely selective in their admissions, but their applicant pools are generally limited to those with very particular talents or abilities. Because the admissions function at these institutions is generally limited to judging those particular talents, they are arbitrarily excluded from the following discussion. Probably the most selective admissions situation in the United States today is the competition for entrance to one of the six- or seven-year accelerated undergraduate medical school programs. In 1979-80 Brown received 1,437 applications and admitted only 54 students to its seven-year Medical Education Program. Because of the specialized nature of the programs, their admissions process varies a great deal from program to program, and such schools are not considered here. Some public institutions are very selective with regard to out-of-state residents, but because their regular admissions procedures are usually fairly rigid and prescribed, and because out-of-state residents constitute only a fraction of their total pool, they too are not considered here.

This chapter restricts itself to considering admission at those few institutions that admit 50 percent or fewer of their applicants and whose applicants are almost all academically qualified for admission. The schools qualifying under these criteria are all private liberal arts institutions with national reputations and applicant pools. Colleges qualifying under these rigid and arbitrary criteria vary with time as their popularity waxes and wanes or as their visibility becomes greater or smaller. In the late 1960s, Swarthmore College's applicant pool grew more than 50 percent following publication of a highly laudatory article in *Time Magazine*. Bowdoin College's applications more than doubled after it went coeducational, changed the image presented in its published materials, and received much favorable publicity following its faculty's decision to make the submission of SAT scores an optional part of the admissions procedure.

Selectivity as discussed here is a fairly recent phenomenon in higher education. Prior to 1900, selection for higher education occurred principally at the secondary school level. Few students finished high school, and only a few of those took the necessary courses to meet the rigid entrance requirements for admission to the best universities. Between 1900 and 1945, there was a gradual relaxation of entrance requirements, the SAT was introduced as a common entrance examination for a number of academic institutions, and there was a gradual expansion of the land-grant universities. But it was during the post-World War II era that the greatest changes in college admissions occurred. First came the wave of veterans attending college on the GI Bill. Then came the 1950s and a period of relative affluence following the privations of the war years and the Depression. The suburbs grew, and with them grew good public high schools. A higher percentage of high school graduates decided to go to college each year, and more and more of these students began to seek admission at the best colleges and universities. On top of this came the postwar baby boom, and selectivity of a very high order became an established fact at about forty colleges and universities.

The Recruitment Function

How does the selective admissions office operate? The three basic functions of any admissions office are recruitment, evaluation, and selection. At most private and some public institutions, recruitment is the most important function, for without students a school cannot survive. As the number of high school graduates plummets throughout the 1980s, recruitment will play an even larger and more important role in most admissions offices. But what of the highly selective institutions? One might assume that these schools, flooded as they are with highly qualified applicants, would recruit very little or not at all. Such is not the case; these colleges recruit as widely and heavily as any institution.

There are three basic reasons for this recruitment. First, these schools have a real commitment to social, economic and racial diversity in their student bodies. Such diversity does not come easily because students with unusual backgrounds have not traditionally thought of attending college, much less highly selective, expensive, private ones. Finding these students and convincing them to apply means recruitment of a high order, and selective colleges spend much of their recruiting time, money, and effort in this direction. They visit inner-city and rural schools, travel to Indian reservations, and publish special brochures to attract these candidates.

Second is the honest desire to find better candidates. In some areas of the country, students rarely think of attending an out-of-state college, no matter how good they may be academically. Many people are prejudiced against private colleges, considering them elitist and only for the wealthy. To combat all this, admissions officers visit far-flung cities and schools to talk about their institutions. But admissions officers do not just visit distant schools with diverse student bodies. They spend much of their time in the private and suburban schools from which they attract most of their applicants. Why visit these schools? The third basic reason that a selective institution recruits is because all the other selective institutions do. The pool of highly qualified applicants is fairly small. In 1978-79, only 21,069 high school seniors scored 650 or higher on the verbal portion of the SAT. The competition to enroll these students is intense, and personal contact through high school visits and group meetings is considered an effective method of convincing them to apply and ultimately to matriculate if admitted. Indeed, an old admissions office fact of life is that the major reason you recruit in New Jersey and Long Island, where many, many students already apply to the most selective colleges, is to ensure a decent yield in April, when most decisions go out.

The selective colleges recruit in basically the same ways as do most nonselective ones, but they do so nationally and internationally. They visit high schools and conduct meetings for prospective applicants and parents in virtually every major urban area in the country. The larger universities like Stanford and Yale may visit more than one thousand high schools each year, and smaller places visit almost that many. For a number of years, Amherst, Bowdoin, Bryn Mawr, Haverford, Swarthmore, Wesleyan, and Williams have traveled cooperatively to encourage students to consider the advantages of a small liberal arts college for their postsecondary education. While few institutions can afford to have five admissions officers recruiting simultaneously in San Francisco, as one eastern school did recently, or to have one person spend two weeks visiting Indian reservations, as did another, the selective schools spread their nets very far indeed. A number of them even recruit internationally, sending admissions officers to Europe, Asia, and South America in search of the best students.

The selective institutions also make extensive use of the College Board Student Search Service to reach those qualified candidates who may not attend a school or live in an area that will be visited by an admissions officer. Minorities are intensely recruited this way. A key to attracting candidates through the mails is excellent publications, and so the selective colleges invest much money and effort each year to ensure the quality of their brochures. As the competition for good students becomes more intense, selective institutions are turning more and more to professional designers, writers, and outside suppliers to produce their brochures and keep them ahead of the competition.

The area of recruitment in which the selective colleges are most distinctive is their extensive use of alumni. Virtually every one of these schools has a well-developed network of dedicated alumni working hard to identify prospective students and convince them to apply, to interview them, and then to urge them to matriculate if admitted. Loyal alumni have always recruited for Old Siwash, but until about twenty years ago their efforts were largely restricted to athletes. Since then, alumni have been organized to visit high schools and attend college nights—to recruit geniuses as well as those with broad shoulders and minority students as well as WASPs, and to help the evaluation process by interviewing applicants. At many of the larger institutions, fewer than half of the candidates can be interviewed in the admissions office each year because of the limited size of the office staff and facilities. Far more candidates are interviewed by alumni; at Harvard, for example, an application is not considered complete until an alumni interview is in the folder. At Brown, more than 2,500 alumni yearly conduct interviews around the world. Without these armies of dedicated volunteers, the battle for many attractive candidates would be lost and the selective admissions offices would have to be much larger to continue to attract and enroll the kind of student body their colleges now enjoy.

The Evaluation Function

The admissions year is a cyclical one, and as the admissions officers return from travel and recruiting at the end of the fall, the admissions office begins to work on its second task of the year: evaluating the applicants. This evaluation is the heart of the admissions process at a highly selective institution and is something that takes an extraordinary amount of time and effort. Evaluation is the point at which an institution's admissions policy interacts with the applicant pool and initial judgments are drawn about a candidate's place in the spectrum of abilities, talents, and strengths present in the pool.

The process of evaluating is called "reading a folder." This procedure varies little from place to place. Admissions officers (and sometimes faculty) pore over all the material they have about a given candidate. They carefully examine and read every word in the folder and try to place what they find in the larger context of what they know of the pool as a whole. At most places it is expected that a reader working full time will read about forty to fifty folders a day. This will take about ten hours, or roughly ten to fifteen minutes a folder. During this short time, biographical information is noted, the school report perused, the transcript and scores absorbed, the essay critiqued, the activities analyzed, the teachers' recommendations read, and the interview report compared to everything else. The reader then usually makes some sort of summary judgment or rating and writes a paragraph or two characterizing the salient points. Then it is on to the next folder. Starting in early December and on through the long winter nights, many tubs or bins of folders cross the admissions officer's desk. The evaluation of candidates continues on into late February, when it becomes commingled with the selection process, which is discussed later.

Academic Evaluation. In general, the evaluation process

tries to answer two questions about the candidate. The first and most important is: What kind of a student will this applicant be at our institution? The reader wonders if this is an applicant with a truly superior mind who will excite the faculty and fellow students and provide the kind of academic leadership that all colleges need. If not, perhaps this is someone in the middle of the pool who can do all the work and has some areas of academic expertise where excellent work can be expected. If the candidate is neither of these types, the reader must decide whether he or she is capable of surviving academically at all. The answer to the question of what kind of a student the applicant will be is found primarily in the high school record: grades, courses taken, and rank in class if available. Recommendations from the school and teachers are scrutinized and weighed heavily. An applicant with a guidance counselor who writes well and knows the candidate personally has an advantage over one without such an ally. The candidate who selects teachers with similar skills and knowledge to write recommendations also has an advantage.

Standardized tests like the SAT play much less of a role in this academic evaluation than most people believe. Scores are generally viewed as a supplement to the high school record and seldom are a key factor in a decision. There is a correlation between scores and acceptance, but it is a relatively flat one. This means that people with 700 scores get in more frequently than those with 500s, but the acceptance rate may only be 35 percent of the former and 20 percent of the latter. Most experienced admissions officers have a full repertoire of stories about candidates with high scores who did poorly in college and ones with low scores who graduated with superb academic records. Faculty at highly selective colleges want students who can develop, understand, and communicate ideas to the faculty and fellow students. They generally feel that these abilities are not really tested on the multiple-choice examination but *are* tested in the secondary school classroom. There is some institutional variation in regard to the importance of test scores, and there are some groups of applicants for whom scores are viewed as being more important. For example, when an applicant who wants to pursue a career in the sciences is being evaluated, more emphasis is placed on scores—especially the mathematical part of the SAT—because research has often shown a good correlation between these scores and success in such an academic curriculum.

Like their counterparts at less selective colleges, faculty at the highly selective colleges have become increasingly concerned about the writing ability of high school graduates, and this ability is now considered carefully during the evaluation of an applicant. More emphasis is now placed on the essay or essays a candidate is asked to write, although the relative importance of the essay does vary somewhat from institution to institution. The essay takes many different forms. Some schools ask for an explication of a specific topic; others ask very open-ended questions that allow a student great freedom in the response. A student is well advised to write the essay as carefully as possible because it is often a key part of the application and can, like a good recommendation, greatly enhance an application folder. Some colleges, like Hamilton, now request that a student submit a sample of his or her writing for a school assignment, to judge better the candidate's writing ability.

Nonacademic Evaluation. The second question the reader is trying to answer while evaluating a folder is much more complex and difficult than the first, namely: What will the impact of a candidate be on the college? More specifically, the reader is wondering what qualities or talents the applicant will bring and contribute to the community while taking an education from it, and whether the candidate has the personal energy to make a contribution despite the pressures of academic work. The selective colleges should be populated not just by extremely bright students but also by busy, energetic, diverse, and interesting people who get involved in an extremely wide array of activities and enrich one another's lives. It would be easy to fill a campus with hard-working bookworms who will get straight A's and rarely be seen outside the classroom, library, and laboratory. The selective admissions office will admit some applicants of this sort, but it will deny many more of them. Because students learn much from their peers during college and often learn the most from those who are most different from themselves, the selective admissions office tries to include applicants of all types and with as many different backgrounds as possible in the freshman class. It also must consider how well the candidate will fit in with others in a close residential living situation.

Judging a candidate's potential impact on the college is not easy. The admissions officer reads the applicant's list of activities carefully. The colleges want students who have participated in depth as well as breadth, and the candidate who has explored an interest in great detail is preferred over one with a long shopping list of clubs briefly belonged to and activities pursued once. Evidence of leadership is a positive factor, as is evidence of activities in the service of others. If the student writes an essay on personal activities, as many do, it is read as a corollary to the list. The school report and teacher recommendations often refer to the student's involvement with in- and out-of-school activities; those statements are considered too. Many applicants submit evidence of their accomplishments, and most colleges welcome such evidence. Generally, art portfolios, musical tapes, abstruse scientific treatises, and the like, are reviewed by the appropriate academic department, although literary and culinary efforts are usually reviewed "in house." The candidate who has had much work experience is rated just as positively as one who has had the time to do other things out of school. Indeed, the applicant who has worked to earn money to help the family is usually viewed very sympathetically by the selective admissions office.

Judgments about a candidate's personality are rendered very carefully, and only when there is a consensus in the evidence. Virtually everything in a folder can be a factor in this sensitive area, and most admissions offices do their best to avoid jumping to an incorrect conclusion. A single negative comment by a teacher, the author of the official school reference, or the interviewer is generally ignored, or it may be checked out by an admissions officer. Similarly, an extremely positive report by one individual is usually ignored or checked out further. Occasionally, a singular viewpoint will turn out to be valid and helpful, and an applicant will be denied or accepted as a result. One quality that is viewed as a danger signal is "brittleness." The candidate who seems rigid, inflexible, or driven may have problems in an environment where everyone is as smart as he is, and where a grade of C occasionally befalls even a dedicated student. A well-balanced candidate, or one who has encountered some adversity and persevered, is generally viewed more favorably than the candidate who appears one-sided or sheltered.

The interview might be expected to play a major role in the evaluation of a candidate's potential impact on the college, and it sometimes does. However, the importance of the interview varies greatly from institution to institution; there is no consensus regarding its value. Some colleges require a personal interview, whereas others make it totally optional. Some feel strongly that applicants should have on-campus interviews with an admissions officer, staff member, or student intern; others believe that alumni interviews are just as valuable. Generally, the interview has declined in importance since the 1950s. This may be partly attributed to the fact that most admissions offices cannot interview all their applicants, so they feel that the lack of an interview should not be held against a candidate because of the office's lack of ability to conduct one. Even the best alumni network may not be able to match an alumnus with the candidate applying from a rural high school in the Ozarks or a mud hut in Ethiopia, and poor applicants may find it impossible to travel to their college choices (although some colleges will help them financially to do so). Some parents feel that the only interview that "counts" is one held in the admissions office with a senior officer, preferably the dean or director. They think that the report of a student, newly graduated admissions officer, or alumnus will not be weighed as heavily in the admissions process. This is not true, as often the additional experience of the older staff member is offset by the ability of a younger interviewer to relate to the applicant or by the community knowledge possessed by an alumni interviewer, which permits a better judgment of the candidate's performance in that community.

As with any personal judgment based on limited contact with an individual, the interview is regarded cautiously in the selective admissions office. Even the best admissions officer or most conscientious alumnus or alumna can misjudge an applicant in what can be a tense and trying situation for a nervous high school senior. Many institutions feel that the interview should be viewed primarily as an information session for the applicant and that the evaluative component should be held to a minimum. Others disagree and feel that valid impressions of an individual's maturity, personality, and sense of humor and self can be gleaned from the interview. Whether the interview is viewed as important or not, the information gathered from it is weighed against everything else in the folder. If this information is found to be at odds with the preponderance of other evidence, then it is checked further or disregarded. In most cases where the interview plays an important role in the decision, it is a positive factor, contributing color and vitality to what can occasionally be a dry assemblage of numbers and verbiage.

Occasionally, an applicant will feel that the route to admission lies in obtaining as many references as possible. But such submissions often serve to prove the truth in an old admissions office saw, "the thicker the folder—the thicker the kid." Such references, solicited or unsolicited, are of value only when they provide additional insight into an applicant's character, personality, or abilities through the writer's personal knowledge of same. References intended mainly to impress by the prestige of the writer are disregarded and occasionally may harm a candidate whose judgment in soliciting them may be questioned.

The Selection Function

Selection of those to be admitted is the final stage of the admissions process and a logical extension of evaluation. All colleges and universities have statements of admissions policy that attempt to delineate what they want in a freshman class. (An example of one of the best is the eloquent *amicus curiae* brief filed with the Supreme Court by Harvard University in the celebrated *Bakke* case.) Basically, the selective admissions office seeks to create a well-balanced and well-rounded freshman class.

Such a class will contain some of the best students who apply but not all, some of the best musicians and artists who apply but not all, and some of the best athletes but not all. To create the well-rounded class requires the admission of some odd-shaped souls, and sometimes these admissions may seem anomalous to an observer. However, when viewed within the total context of the applicant pool and the admitted class, those admissions usually make sense.

Meeting Institutional Needs. The major constraint on the admissions office as it strives to admit what it will probably term "the best class ever" is institutional need. While the best interests of the applicants are always a concern, the admissions office must also consider the necessities of the college. In a sense, up to one half of the available places in the freshman class are given away before the first decision is ever made. These places have been given not to individuals but to various groups the institution has decided it must have in the class. To accept members of these groups, admissions offices "give away" some of the academic and personal excellence they expect from other members of the pool. How much is given away is determined by the desirability of the individual and the group to the college, but in general there is a limit. The limit is simply that no one is admitted who is judged incapable of succeeding academically, no matter how desirable the applicant may be. That limit is exceeded only under very rare circumstances, and often such an admission is accompanied by a letter warning the student that doubts exist about her or his academic survivability. Students who enroll despite these warnings have occasionally done quite well, perhaps because they arrived knowing they needed to work much harder than their peers and were prepared to do so, or perhaps because they arrived determined to prove that the judgment about their academic ability was wrong.

Colleges and universities like to think of themselves as extended families. Faculty, alumni, and friends are some components of these families, and every institution tries to keep its family a happy one. Unfortunately, the desire of children of faculty and alumni to join the family often tends to promote a form of internecine warfare with the admissions office. In an age when faculty salaries tend to lag farther and farther behind the cost of living, many faculty seem to feel that admission of their children is a fringe benefit like the tuition rebates they frequently get. Unfortunately, the admissions office may have a different idea when it reviews Junior's high school record, but generally, most admissions offices try hard to admit as many faculty children as possible, to keep the immediate family as happy as can be. Colleges depend on their alumni for financial and personal support, and alumni giving often provides the cushion between a tide of red ink and a balanced budget. Some alumni seem to feel that admission of their children is a just reward for their efforts and support. Again, the admissions office may have a different opinion, but it will make a concerted effort to be as nice to these members of the family as possible. A general rule of thumb that seems to work year after year is that alumni children are admitted at a rate twice that of the pool as a whole. This may sound fair and even generous, but at the most selective institutions it means that more than half of the alumni children are rejected. To soften the blow, special letters are often sent to these candidates and their parents.

A related small group of applicants who meet another institutional need are those who may be called "development cases." These are usually applicants with parents or close alumni friends who are in a position to aid an institution substantially, either politically, economically, or in a public relations way. The number of such candidates each year is very small, and, as with alumni children, an extra effort is made to include these applicants in the list of those admitted.

Athletes are another group of applicants whose admission will fill an institutional need. Much publicity and alumni support depend on the success or failure that Old Siwash encounters on the fields of play. The blame for failure is often laid at the door of the admissions office. The larger the university and the higher the level of athletic competition at which it aspires to compete, the higher the pressure the admissions office will encounter. Smaller colleges generally feel less pressure, but it is still there. If an applicant is identified by the coaches as someone who can contribute to the athletic program, then the admissions office gives special attention to that person's folder. As stated, the greater the candidate's contribution is expected to be, the greater the favor given the person in the selection process. Five years ago, little favor would have been shown the female athlete, but now the recruitment and admission of these applicants are just as important as they are with male athletes. Athletic activity of any sort is a plus for any applicant, but unless the coaches feel the student will be able to make the team, athletics is viewed from the same perspective as any other extracurricular activity, such as music, art, or journalism. (Incidentally, activities like music, art, or journalism may also be raised to the status of an institutional need—as, for example, when the orchestra needs a cellist or when the drama program finds itself with no technical people.) In all these areas, the selective admissions office makes the final decision about who is admitted. Coaches may rant and rave and remonstrate, but some applicants they dearly want will be denied each year.

A final group whose admission is an institutional need is minorities. In the 1960s, the selective college began to realize the necessity of including these people as part of their student bodies. Because minorities generally attend poor high schools, it is very difficult to find minority candidates with the preparation that will enable them to succeed in a rigorous academic program. Hence, the competition for a good minority student can be as intense as the competition for a good quarterback. There is a great deal of overlap in minority applications among the top colleges, and many candidates will receive multiple acceptances. Multiple acceptances bring about lower yields of matriculated students at the accepting institutions, which means that a school must admit a particularly high percentage of minorities if it is to achieve the minority population it desires. Although minority applicants are admitted at a higher rate than average for the entire pool, many are also denied admission. The scores of those admitted may not be as high as those of other applicants, but generally their high school records are just as impressive. The selective admissions office works hard to admit as many minorities as it can, just as it works hard with alumni children and athletes.

Mechanics of the Process. The mechanics of the selection process vary widely from school to school due to differences in the way institutional admissions procedures have developed over the years. Decisions may be made by individuals, committees, or by some mixture of these. One extreme method—in which the dean or director, after reading the evaluations made by others about the candidates, makes all the decisions—is called the "gatekeeper" model. At the other extreme, all decisions are made by a committee. Most selection procedures fall somewhere between these extremes, and varying proportions of decisions are made one way or the other. Often committees are composed of admissions officers only; sometimes they have one or two faculty members; and at some schools they have a majority of faculty members.

The way in which committees operate also varies a great deal from place to place. Some operate by consensus judgment and continue to discuss a candidate until a decision can be agreed on. Some reach decisions by conducting strict votes, and at one institution such votes are taken secretly, with committee members operating hidden buttons to indicate their choices. Over the last two decades, there has been a general movement toward more admissions office responsibility in the selection process and less involvement by faculty. Some faculty are willing to invest the great amount of time required to be a part of the evaluation and selection process, but it seems harder and harder each year to find such individuals. Nearly all colleges and universities have committees charged with overseeing the entire admissions process and setting admissions policy. Gradually, these committees' deliberations have supplanted the active participation of faculty in the evaluation and selection process itself.

After a folder has been evaluated randomly or alphabetically one or more times by readers, it enters the selection phase and is sent to the admissions officer who has the responsibility for that applicant. Most admissions offices are organized geographically, with each officer handling all applicants from a given area. Generally, all decisions on applicants from one high school are made at the same time, whether they are made by an individual or a committee. The area admissions officer compares all the candidates from a given school with each other and then, within the context of the pool as a whole, makes recommendations as to what the decisions for that school should be. Every attempt is made to keep the decisions within a given high school as logical and understandable as possible, but occasionally a candidate meeting a university need is admitted with lesser overall qualifications than others who are rejected. In such cases, the admissions officer in charge often calls the school to explain the reasons behind the action being taken.

Fairness and Equity in Selective Admissions

Many outsiders have reviewed the admissions process at various selective institutions. Almost all reported that they found the process as fair and even-handed as possible. They might have faulted an occasional decision, but these observers felt that any group of intelligent and conscientious people would make the vast majority of decisions in the same way, given the same applicant pool. A few people try to tamper with the process each year by attempting to pressure the admissions office and influence decisions. Letters and calls from the powerful and wealthy are a fact of life in the selective admissions office, and they are politely but firmly shunted aside. Only in exceptionally rare cases does an admissions office heed such pleas. Few processes in our flawed world are as inviolable as the admissions process at the selective colleges and universities.

The admissions process at the selective institution may be as fair and equitable as human beings can make it, but what matters to the individual applicant is whether he or she is admitted. Each institution tries to select the best people possible while still meeting its own particular needs. Since these needs vary somewhat from year to year and the composition of the applicant pool also varies each year, the decisions reached will also vary. This variation makes prediction a risky business, and a guidance counselor can never be sure who will get in and who will not. It does not follow, for example, that everyone admitted to Harvard will be admitted everywhere else they apply, and, in fact, they usually are not. An individual who seems very desirable in the applicant pool at Dartmouth may look very ordinary in the pool at Stanford or Amherst, or vice versa. As with many things in life, the more unpredictable something is, the more interesting it will seem, and the admissions process at the highly selective college or university is both unpredictable and interesting. As long as these schools continue to attract a plethora of well-qualified applicants, the decisions they make will generate great suspense for our best high school students.

✍ *30*

Standardized Testing in Admissions Counseling

Stephen Lovette

✍   Since the 1920s, the Scholastic Aptitude Test (SAT) of the College Board has been used by many colleges to help assess academic aptitude of undergraduate applicants. Today, along with the Assessment Program of the American College Testing Program (ACT), the SAT is widely used as one factor in evaluating academic abilities related to successful performance in college. Although a 1980 survey conducted by the College Board and the American Association of Collegiate Registrars and Admissions Officers (AACRAO) found that the importance of test scores in admissions may be declining, it is quite evident from the same survey that admissions test scores remain a very important factor in deciding who is admitted to the majority of selective colleges nationwide. Therefore, it is imperative that those who serve college-bound students be informed about the nature of the admissions tests, factors related to declining scores, the appropriate use of admissions tests, and issues related to the future of admissions testing, given the current swell of antitesting legislation.

The Tests Themselves

Aptitude tests, such as the SAT, are designed to measure verbal and mathematical abilities that develop over years of study. The verbal portion of the SAT contains four types of questions: (1) antonyms—looking for a word opposite in mean-

ing to a word given, (2) analogies—identifying a word relationship equivalent to the relationship given, (3) sentence comple-
tions—completing a sentence by selecting a word or words that
best fit its meaning, and (4) reading passages—answering questions referring to a reading passage of about 400 words. The
questions are designed to assess a number of verbal abilities. Antonyms, for example, are a most efficient means of testing
vocabulary. Students may answer two to three antonym questions per minute, each containing six words whose meaning
they must know to answer the question correctly. Analogy
questions assess developed vocabulary along with the ability to
identify precisely the logic underlying a particular word relationship, such as an object and its function, a word and its syn-
onym, or an action and its effect. Sentence-completion questions ask students to select the most appropriate words to
complete a sentence by using the grammatical cues and meaning of other words in the sentence. They require a good vocabulary as well as familiarity with conventional sentence construction. Reading passages test reading rate, reading comprehension,
and the student's ability to analyze and critically review a given
passage.

The verbal skills assessed by the ACT are similar, but the
format of the test differs considerably. The English Usage Test
of the ACT consists of several prose passages, with certain portions underlined. Given a number of alternative choices, a student must decide which choice is most appropriate according to
the context of the passage. The choices include items related to
conventional English usage, expository writing, grammar, punctuation, style, and organization. In addition, there are two other
reading tests, one in social science and one in natural science.
Each test assesses reading rate and comprehension as well as
analytical and problem-solving skills relevant to that particular
academic area. Unlike the SAT, a student taking the ACT is expected to have general background information in both social
studies and natural sciences to score well on the informational
questions in each particular area.

The math portion of the SAT contains standard multiple-
choice questions and questions requiring students to make

quantitative comparisons of the value of two given quantities. The mathematical concepts that are assessed are (1) arithmetic —including the four functions, properties of integers, decimals, and percents; (2) algebra—including negative numbers, simplifying algebraic expressions, linear equations, factoring, inequalities, quadratic equations, exponents, and roots; and (3) geometry— including the determination of area, perimeter, circumference, and volume, properties of triangles, parallel and perpendicular lines, transversals and intersecting lines, and the location of points as coordinates. In addition, quantitative comparison questions test the ability to recognize equalities and inequalities and to estimate the value of given variables. The Mathematics Usage Test of the ACT assesses quite similar concepts but uses only the standard multiple-choice format.

Those familiar with high school curricula realize that the skills and concepts outlined thus far are usually found in a group of core subjects. English classes that develop grammar, punctuation, and expository writing are prerequisite. Also, literature classes that require independent reading of serious literature are vital for vocabulary development and familiarity with conventional written English. The National Association of Secondary School Principals recommends that college-bound students enroll in an English class during each year of secondary school attendance. Furthermore, the Association issues specific guidelines for college-preparatory English classes: "Reading should be extensive as well as intensive. Writing should grow from the single paragraph to the five-paragraph theme as students improve their composition skills. Every paper should be evaluated by a teacher and returned with appropriate comments. Opportunities to write should be frequent and the papers relatively short. Long and infrequent tomes are of dubious value. Writing is a craft, and attaining craftmanship in any field requires constant practice" (National Association of Secondary School Principals, 1978).

In mathematics, at least three year-long courses in advanced arithmetic, algebra, and geometry are vital preparation for the SAT and ACT. Whereas verbal ability can be enhanced by beneficial experience in the home and community, the development of mathematical ability is highly specialized and usually almost exclusively school-based learning. Therefore, there is little likelihood that students who do not enroll in core mathematical subjects will develop these abilities through experience outside the classroom.

Beyond core course work in English and mathematics, course work in social and natural sciences is particularly helpful for students planning to take the ACT, which presumes some understanding of content and method in these fields. The College Board suggests that the study of foreign language complements English course work in developing verbal abilities. In summary, then, a program of study most likely to develop academic abilities typically assessed by admissions tests should include English composition and literature, algebra, geometry, social studies, natural science, and foreign language.

Since aptitude tests are designed primarily to measure developed ability in *general* areas, they do not give adequate information about what a student knows and is able to do in a particular *subject* area. Achievement tests, unlike aptitude tests, are designed to measure knowledge in a specific subject area. The most widely used achievement tests are offered by the College Board and include fifteen different tests in the fields of English, history, mathematics, foreign languages, and sciences. Many selective colleges use achievement tests along with the SAT or ACT for admissions, course placement, or both. For example, because a certain level of writing ability is prerequisite for successful completion of most college majors, it may be desirable to screen students whose composition skills are poor despite generally high verbal aptitude and a favorable high school record. Such students can be admitted to college but enrolled in remedial work prior to beginning regular core courses in English. The eight undergraduate campuses of the University of California use the English composition achievement test in this way. Students who score below 600 in the achievement test can be admitted to the university, but they must pass a college-readiness English course or equivalent before enrolling in freshman English courses.

Declining Scores

For the past sixteen years, national average SAT scores have declined steadily. Even though the high school record persists as the single best predictor of college-related skills, declining aptitude and achievement tests scores have perplexed students, parents, and educators. In 1964 the average verbal score was 475 and the average math score was 498, for a combined average of 973 out of a possible 1,600 points. In 1981 the average verbal score was 424 and the average math score was 466, for a combined average of 890. Scores on College Board achievement tests and the ACT assessment have also declined. In 1976 the average achievement test score was 538; in 1981 the average score was 532. In 1967 the average California student scored 20.1 on the ACT; in 1979 the average student scored 18.7. Concerned by the persistent and significant SAT decline, the trustees of the College Board appointed a panel in 1977 to identify factors contributing to the score decline. The panel commissioned twenty-seven studies focusing on a number of central topics, including (1) the SAT itself, (2) societal factors, (3) changes in the schools, and (4) the changing student pool.

The SAT Itself. In essence, the panel concluded that there has been no significant change in the construction or scoring of the SAT that would contribute to the decline in test scores. Using the extensive data available from Project TALENT and the National Longitudinal Study, Beaton, Hilton, and Schrader (1977) concluded that the SAT administered to the 1960 Project TALENT students was actually slightly more difficult than the SAT administered to the 1972 National Longitudinal Study students. If, in fact, the 1972 SAT was slightly easier, one can infer that the decline in test scores is larger than mere numbers indicate. Modu and Stern (1977) corroborated Beaton's findings. Using the 1963 and 1973 forms of the SAT, they found that matched samples scored an average of eight to ten points higher on the 1973 form of the SAT than on the 1963 form.

Questioning whether the exam had strayed from its original purpose of predicting college-level performance, Ford and Campos (1977) studied the predictive validity of the SAT since 1969. Predictive validity, discussed later in more detail, is defined by the College Board as the correlation between SAT scores and grade point average in the freshman year of college. Ford and Campos reported that, even though high school grades endure as the best predictor of college grades (although not as effective as in 1969), the predictive validity of the SAT has, in fact, risen slightly. Maxey's (1980) ACT research data show that the predictive validity of the ACT has also risen over the last ten years.

Societal Factors. Schramm (1977) reviewed research studying the effect of television viewing on academic performance. He found that there is an inverse relationship between above-average rates of TV viewing and academic performance for students beyond the age of nine. Up to that point, television viewing tends to give a student a "fast start on vocabulary and general knowledge," but soon the intellectual value of television diminishes and the entertainment and relaxation value increases. Schramm also cited a number of studies which indicated that students do less general reading, comparatively less homework, and stay up later in homes where television is freely accessible. Inferentially, Schramm concluded that television is one of a group of strong interacting variables that negatively affect school performance.

A number of other societal factors that may have contributed to declining test scores are discussed by Glover (1977). Among the variables cited by Glover as likely to influence academic performance are declining confidence in government, open admissions, alternative schools, new math, decline of liberal arts, flexible class scheduling, and Watergate. Again, only by the broadest inference can one draw any relationships between such a set of variables and declining test scores.

Changes in the School. Harnischfeger and Wiley (1975) found that the number of basic or core courses in high schools has declined since the late 1960s and the number of electives has risen substantially. This is particularly true of English classes, in which enrollments in the schools studied declined 50 percent in upper-division college-preparatory courses. And in schools requiring advanced English, the range of courses that fulfilled the requirement had broadened considerably. Weinman (1977), in a study of forty-three Massachusetts high schools, found a 50 percent increase in English/language arts electives and that science fiction and radio-television-film were the two most commonly added electives. When enrollments in these two courses were matched with SAT summary reports, those schools that showed the greatest increase in such elective enrollments also showed the greatest declines in SAT scores.

In mathematics a decline in SAT subscores has also been evident, but not nearly as marked as the decline in English subscores. It is interesting to note that Weinman's study also reported no proliferation of electives in mathematics compared to the proliferation in English.

Regarding reading aptitude, Chall (1977) analyzed the level of reading difficulty on the SAT and samples of textbooks for six cohorts of SAT takers from 1947 to 1975. She concluded that the level of difficulty had remained rather constant for the SAT but that reading passages had become progressively easier in the textbooks analyzed.

Besides the curriculum, the panel proposed that a number of other factors may be related to declining test scores. Citing the National Association of Secondary School Principals (1975), the panel reported that national absenteeism has increased to an average range of 15 to 20 percent of the students enrolled in the school districts polled. Grade inflation has also driven up students' expectations about their relative ability and their technical eligibility for colleges with grade-based admissions requirements. The American College Testing Program (1977) found that the proportion of A's and B's in high school English courses increased 25 percent in the last ten years.

Changing Student Pool. The initial decline in SAT test scores in the early 1960s coincided with major policy decisions to increase access to postsecondary education. The National Center for Education Statistics (1975) reported that about one third of the traditional college-age youth were going on to college in 1964. By 1970 the proportion increased to nearly 50 percent. Beaton, Hilton, and Schrader (1977) reported that the greatest percentage of new students had comparatively lower high school grade point averages and standardized test scores than traditional students. The students who scored lower on the SAT came from at least three overlapping subsets of students who historically have scored lower on similar standardized exams: students from low-income families, minority students, and female students. The latest data on family income level and SAT scores replicate the findings that, on the average, students from low-income families score approximately 100 points lower on the SAT than do students from the highest income category (Educational Testing Service, 1980a). (Yet being from a low-income family does not doom a student to low scores. Nearly one third of students whose family income is below $6,000 earn scores that rank them in the top half of all SAT takers.) Nelson (1977) studied the family income distribution of freshmen entering college from 1967 to 1977. According to his data, there was a 6 percent decrease in students falling in the highest quartile. After 1972, enrollment rates had stabilized across all four family-income quartiles. Even though the early data on the number of minorities sitting for the SAT are sparse, the Wertz panel estimated that less than 2 percent of the 1963 cohort were black. By 1972 the percentage of blacks had risen to 8 percent and has remained rather constant since. As far back as the Coleman report (1966), the relatively lower level of achievement of minorities along with the history of inequality of educational opportunity has been well documented.

Jackson (1976) compared SAT subscores for men and women from 1960 to 1976. He showed that women and men have averaged about the same scores on the verbal portion of the SAT, but women have averaged almost fifty points lower than men on the mathematical portion. Also, the proportion of women taking the SAT has continued to rise. Women comprised 43 percent of the test takers in 1960, 48 percent in 1970, and 51 percent in 1977.

In summary, the declines in SAT scores are no doubt attributable to an array of interacting variables. Societal factors, nontraditional students, and student motivation have all in some way contributed to the persistent drop in admissions test scores. Schools also appear to have a role in the decline, particularly those schools with (1) expanding elective programs, particularly in English, and declining core course enrollment; (2) high absenteeism and low achievement motivation; (3) inflated grades and automatic promotions; and (4) textbooks with reading levels substantially below the actual grade level in which the books are used. Summarizing score changes in a variety of educational tests, Cleary and McCandless (1976) concluded that score declines have been observed in so many different groups and so many tested areas that serious attention must be devoted to them. If decreasing test scores signal decreasing motivation to learn, it is worth speculating that perhaps the era of increased access to postsecondary education has decreased incentives for traditional students. The classic market concepts of supply and demand, inflation and evaluation, have equal application in education as they do in other goods or services. Historians may interpret this time as a period of overabundant education, and, if this is truly so, education is much less likely to have retained its historical value. Some in education interpret score declines as evidence that modern youth are generally a lethargic and uninspired lot. However, the case may be just the opposite. What many may construe as a motivational malaise may simply be a tactical shift to bypass formal education and target directly on the incentives that have been natural outcomes of college going, such as economic achievement, power, status, mobility, and self-awareness. Contrary to Howard Bowen's hopeful study (1977), a college degree simply does not hold the same economic or intrinsic value for the general public as it did twenty years ago.

Improving Test Scores

The effectiveness of special coaching courses for improving SAT scores is an issue presently causing a great deal of controversy. If coaching, usually provided by proprietary schools, does in fact raise SAT scores significantly, then those students who can afford to pay for coaching will have a privileged position in admissions to selective colleges. The College Board presents a repertoire of research supporting the position that short-term coaching has no substantial effect on test scores and reserves judgment about the effectiveness of longer-term preparation, given the modest increases in test scores of students in a number of special preparation programs.

Recent research by the College Board (Alderman and Powers, 1979) studied eight coaching programs and found an average increase of eight points over the control group in the verbal section of the SAT. Other studies by the College Board showed slightly larger gains in the mathematical section of the SAT, especially for students not presently enrolled in a math course. However, a number of other studies claim that the effects of coaching on test-score improvements is a little more dramatic than the College Board has found to date. The Federal Trade Commission (1979) studied two commercial coaching schools and found that one had higher gains than the College Board studies—about forty points higher than normal increases of students who take the test a second time. The College Board claims that the FTC report failed to match coached and non-coached students on all important characteristics. In an attempt to resolve the controversy, Slack and Porter (1980) compiled a number of studies about the effects of coaching, including College Board and FTC studies, and report average gains of approximately sixty points on the SAT verbal and math sections combined. The Educational Testing Service has rebutted some of Slack and Porter's interpretations (Jackson, 1980; Messick and others, 1981).

At this point, there seems to be less need for further research than for digestion of what already exists. First, coaching must be defined carefully. If coaching means a relatively short-term review of verbal and math concepts and familiarity with the test prior to taking the SAT, then there appears to be little controversy about its value. The College Board (1982, p. 13) itself states: "It is especially important for all students to be familiar with the various types of questions in advance of the test. Students should know what the test is about and how it is structured, how to make the most efficient use of time limits, how to 'attack' the different kinds of questions, and when an 'educated' guess using partial knowledge is sensible. Students with such skills and knowledge about test taking are able to perform to the best of their ability." The College Board provides preparation material for this purpose and encourages schools to help students via group meetings and discussion sessions conducted by knowledgeable staff. This sort of preparation assumes students have taken a college-preparatory curriculum, including courses in English composition, literature, algebra, and geometry.

If coaching means intensive coverage over an adequate time of concepts normally covered in high school and relevant to admissions tests, the chances are that scores will improve significantly. Some military academy prep schools are designed along this line, and they regularly post dramatic gains in their students' College Board scores. Marron (1965) studied over 700 high school graduates who spent seven months in post-high school preparatory schools trying to improve their SAT scores. The average gain was 137 points, which is over 100 points higher than the College Board studies would predict. In other words, if coaching replicates rigorous college-preparatory course work, it is likely to have the same dramatic effect on admissions test scores as on subsequent college performance.

However, if coaching means the attempt to compress three or four years of college preparation into a short-term series of cram sessions, it is unlikely to improve significantly either students' academic abilities or their admissions test scores. For students who have not chosen appropriate courses in high school or have performed poorly in them, the only value such a cram course has is what one College Board official called a "neurotic payoff." Such students—and the parents who pay for the coaching—at least have the satisfaction of knowing that in the eleventh hour they gave it the old college try.

If cram courses alone are unlikely to improve test scores, what factors are related to test-score improvement? The research indicates that there are several. First, repeating the SAT can have some positive effect on the average student's score. The College Board states that juniors who score 400 on either the math or verbal sections of the SAT are likely to score 419 in their senior year. This could mean a thirty-eight-point gain by retaking the test after an additional year of high school. Second, because of regression effects, students who score lowest on the SAT are more likely to score higher on a second administration of the test. Students who average 300 on the math or verbal sections in their junior year should average 336 on the same sections in their senior year. Obviously, regression can have a negative effect on students who post particularly high initial scores. For example, juniors with a math or verbal score of 700 should average 694 on senior-year tests. However, most colleges count a student's highest score, not the most recent, so negative regression is unlikely to have any significant effect on a student's eligibility. Finally, College Board studies show that a review of math concepts for motivated students presently not enrolled in math course work should have a beneficial effect on the math section of the SAT.

Beyond the improvement of test scores for any one single student is the challenge to raise test scores in the aggregate. More precisely, what can a school district or site administrator do to improve the average scores of their college-bound students? The key figure in the process is the high school counselor, who collaborates with students to determine their course of study. Those who counsel college-bound students should make every effort to keep students in solid subjects, including math and English, for the duration of their high school career. The primary effect of such counseling will be more adequate development of those abilities related to successful performance in college. Also, admissions test scores reflecting the same developed abilities should also improve.

Using and Misusing Admissions Tests

Admissions tests, like any other type of measurement, have statistical limitations that must be understood by those who use them. Test reliability indicates the extent to which an individual could achieve the same score on repetition of an equivalent form of the test. A reliability coefficient of zero indicates that there is no relationship between a student's relative performance on two forms of the same test; a coefficient of 1.0 indicates a perfect relationship. The reliability estimates for students taking equivalent forms of the SAT typically average .91 to .92. ACT reliability levels are equally high (American College Testing Program, 1978). A more meaningful measure of reliability is the standard error of measurement. If a test were perfectly reliable, it would yield exactly the same results for a person who repeated the same or alternate forms of the test—provided there were no changes in the type or amount of the trait measured. However, since no test is perfectly reliable, the scores students obtain differ from their "true score" by a certain amount. The standard error of measurement is a measure of that difference or error between the student's "true score" and his obtained score. For the SAT, the standard error of measurement is thirty points on the scale from 200 to 800. This means that two thirds of all students taking the test will obtain verbal and math scores within thirty points of their true scores. Therefore, any SAT score should be interpreted as falling within a range, which for most test takers is thirty points on both the verbal and math sections of the SAT. Likewise, on the ACT composite scale of 1 to 35, the standard error is approximately 1.5, and any composite score should be interpreted accordingly.

A second characteristic of the test is validity: how well a test measures what it is supposed to measure. College admissions tests are supposed to measure abilities related to successful academic performance in college. One generally available measure of academic performance is the college grade point average. Therefore, the correlation between college admissions test scores and freshmen's college grades is one index of an admissions test validity for predicting college achievement. A number of available studies give differing figures for the predictive validity of college admissions tests. In its most recent publication, the College Entrance Examination Board (1980) cites a thirteen-year study of the nineteen colleges of the University of Georgia system (Fincher, 1974), which found that SAT scores alone correlated .49 with college grades in the first year. The high school record correlated .54 with college performance, and the combination of high school record and SAT correlated .65, an increase of .11 over the high school record alone. Slack and Porter prefer to quote an ETS study (Ford and Campos, 1977), which claims that the SAT adds only .08 to the predictive validity of the high school record. (For the record, Slack and Porter recomputed Ford and Campos's figure and claim that the correct figure is .06.) American College Testing Program studies claim that the ACT adds .09 to the predictive validity of the high school record. Even though incremental, such a gain is statistically significant.

For the practitioner, the actual figures are not as important as the relative value of admissions tests in assessing college readiness. Most studies show that the high school record consistently ranks first as the best single academic predictor. Admissions and achievement tests generally rank second. Does this mean that admissions testing should be abolished? Doubtful. When SAT scores and the high school record are combined, the resultant predicts college performance better than any single factor. Furthermore, Schrader (1971) provides evidence that a combination of achievement tests may be a better predictor of college performance than the SAT. In any event, researchers study students in large groups, where individual differences tend to cancel out; admissions offices at selective colleges admit students one at a time, where individual differences are quite important. In one case, test scores may add little to what is already known about an applicant; in another case, they may be vital in admitting a student who otherwise would have been overlooked.

However, because test scores are quantifiable and easily compared, an overreliance on their relative merit is always possible. Those who counsel college-bound students provide a service by explaining to their counselees the range of test scores for admitted students at colleges under consideration, and they provide a disservice to their counselees when they advise against application to a particular college solely on the basis of low scores.

Guidelines for Using Admissions Tests

Because of the importance of college admissions tests, the statistical limitations of the tests, and the legal rights of students regarding confidentiality, the high school guidance counselor should consider the following guidelines when setting office practices:

1. Current registration materials for all forms of admissions tests should be readily available for student consumption.
2. Group meetings should be held regularly to instruct students on registration procedures, the reporting of scores, and the nature and limitations of test scores when predicting college performance.
3. Individual students should be counseled regarding test requirements and the distribution of scores of matriculants for the colleges under consideration.
4. School staff should take every precaution to safeguard the confidentiality of individual students' scores and release individual data only with the consent of the students or their legal guardians.
5. The availability of fee waivers should be explained, and eligible students should be encouraged to use them.
6. Interested students should have the opportunity to attend school-endorsed, extracurricular review sessions aimed at reviewing appropriate concepts and familiarizing students with test items and relevant testing procedures.

College admissions officers also have a responsibility for appropriately using test scores. According to College Board guidelines, admissions officers should:

1. Use test scores as one of a number of factors in determining the admissibility of an applicant.
2. Use test scores as approximate, not exact, indicators of student's ability or achievement.
3. Weight admissions test scores in a way that reflects validity studies for various subgroups within the applicant pool at their college.
4. Ensure the protection of the confidentiality of all admissions data, including test scores.

Furthermore, admissions officers should provide adequate training for their staff, to ensure that each staff member:

1. Is sufficiently knowledgeable about test data to use test
    scores properly and be able to explain their use to poten-
    tial applicants.
2. Understands limitations in using test scores to predict col-
    lege performance.
3. Is aware of the results of regularly updated predictive valid-
    ity studies for students at their institution.

Although most of these guidelines have been followed by
guidance and admissions offices for a number of years, there has
been a groundswell of controversy regarding standardized admissions tests. This controversy has been generated in part by
recent New York legislation, the National Education Association, and Ralph Nader. The debate is only in its early stages,
but, in closing, some remarks are warranted.

Speculations on the Future of Admissions Testing

At least three levels of attack have been discharged against
standardized admissions testing. The first level would keep tests
as they are but require greater disclosure to students about their
results. For example, starting May 1980, the New York State
legislature required admissions testing agencies to return answer
sheets and actual test copies to students who requested them.
The College Board contends that such disclosure requires the
costly elimination of all disclosed test items from further use.
Consequently, the board has increased student fees and reduced
the number of dates on which the tests are given in New York.
The legislature assumes that the demand for greater disclosure
warrants increased cost and decreased test availability for all
students. It is difficult in the long run to predict how many students will request their tests, considering that sample copies of
the test are already free to any student planning to take the
SAT. So far, only 7 percent of the students who took the March
1980 SAT—the first SAT to be disclosed—have requested a copy
of their answer sheet and test questions. Requests for disclosure
for the second SAT appear to be even less. Because of increasing
consumer concerns, the College Board has changed a number of

practices in order to provide more information to students; for example, it now disseminates practice tests to PSAT and SAT applicants, gives students the opportunity to verify the machine scoring of their answer sheets, and has increased external review procedures.

The second level of attack would replace norm-referenced tests like the SAT with criterion-referenced tests. Norm-referenced tests measure students relative to each other. In other words, individual scores are related to the overall performance of the group. The National Education Association, a teachers' professional organization, contends that such ranking is inevitably going to label some students as less able. In place of norm-referenced tests, the NEA advocates criterion-referenced tests, which are based on a precisely defined set of performance objectives and spell out in great detail what a student must know and be able to do. Such tests are appropriately used within individual schools to assess how well students meet the curricular objectives established by that particular high school. The objectives usually vary from school to school; some have very modest objectives, and others have much more rigorous ones. One cannot help but speculate on the consequences of such a change. Certainly teachers and school groups have not been immune to criticism because of declining scores. One way to stem the declines would be to modify the tests. But there is equal probability of a "boomerang effect"; that is, rather than school curricula shaping the tests, the test would begin to shape school curricula.

The final and most aggressive level of attack has been spearheaded by Ralph Nader. He calls ETS admissions tests a "respectable fraud" and leads one to believe that they should be done away with entirely. Nairn (1980), the author of *The Reign of ETS: The Corporation That Makes Up Minds,* sponsored by Nader, claims that ETS aptitude tests predict college success little better than a roll of dice, that they discriminate against minority and low-income students, and that ETS holds a monopoly on admissions testing. William Turnbull, former president of ETS, in a press conference (January 14, 1980) presented convincing evidence that Nairn's interpretation of predictive value of the SAT was based on serious statistical errors. In Turnbull's view, Nairn's report wrongly blamed tests for showing that minority and low-income students are less well prepared than majority students. The tests, Turnbull said, "do not create the difference; they reveal it." Society should do something about differences in educational opportunity besides simply doing away from the evidence. Finally, Turnbull expressed that the pervasiveness of ETS in testing is less a question of monopoly than of quality. "ETS does not set policy on how tests are to be used but develops them at the request of associated schools and colleges, which determine their use," according to Turnbull.

Despite the rebuttals (see Educational Testing Service, 1980b) against Nairn's report, public confidence in standardized testing has been shaken. It is interesting to speculate on what consequences the elimination of standardized testing would have on college admissions. Clearly, the portion of the admissions decision traditionally assigned to test scores would have to go somewhere. Perhaps selective colleges that wish to use an admissions test would continue to do so by developing their own. However, the logistical problems for both students and colleges practically precludes such an alternative. It is more probable that the weight presently assigned to standardized tests would simply go in with other existing factors, especially the high school record. To improve the validity of the high school record, colleges could differentiate among high schools and make more refined assessments of the qualitative differences among them. The net effect would be a return to what existed before the College Board was constituted—namely, a pecking order of high schools and an increased determination of students' academic capabilities based on their school of origin. Under such a system, students with high grades from elite schools would be in a more preferential position than they are today.

In the long run, the decreasing numbers of college-age youth are bound to diminish the importance of admissions tests. Simply stated, more colleges will be less selective until supply and demand stabilizes the market for postsecondary education. The question practitioners in college admissions must answer is whether standardized tests, carefully developed and conscientiously interpreted, are useful in helping make decisions of considerable importance to the clients they serve. The campaign against admissions testing is well organized and well financed. Its passionate advertising shows children who were bright and happy yesterday but are now branded and scarred for life because of the results of a standardized test. Certainly, poorly trained practitioners have made unwarranted assumptions about students based on their test scores. The results of malpractice in education are likely to be as consequential and long-lasting as malpractice in any other profession. But the treatment indicated is improved testing and better training for the practitioners who use the tests, not the elimination of the tests themselves.

✎ *31*

Evaluating the Validity and Equity of Standardized Tests

Jane W. Loeb

✎   A voluminous literature documents and supports the widespread use of objective test scores in combination with a student's high school record in college admissions and denials. This chapter examines the use of admissions tests, their validity in predicting college performance, equity questions associated with their use, and the results to be expected from alternate criteria that could be used for admitting and denying prospective college students. A central thesis is that clear thinking about admissions policy requires a focus on denial as well as admission decisions. Practiced admissions and high school guidance personnel will quickly recognize that admissions actions require no defense, except in relation to denial actions. It is the student denied admission, and the student's family, who will try to show that the portfolio presented is in some sense more deserving than those of admitted applicants. Thus, denial is a key question in framing and evaluating admissions policy.

Use of Tests

In 1978-79 the College Board and the American Association of Collegiate Registrars and Admissions Officers (AACRAO) jointly surveyed colleges and universities concerning their admissions policies and practices. As a result of the survey, it is possible to make informed statements about the use of tests and other criteria in the selection of college students. All institutions of higher education listed in the *Education Directory* were surveyed. With the exception of private two-year colleges, response rates were greater than 50 percent. Thus, this survey provides solid evidence on current admissions practices.

Not surprisingly, selectivity was found to vary and, along with selectivity, the use of tests in admissions. Institutions indicating that they would "admit any individual wishing to attend" were classified as "open door." On the average, open-door institutions admitted 97 percent of their applicants, compared to an average of 76 percent for more selective institutions. Of the open-door institutions, 29 percent required a test score from all applicants; 61 percent required a complete high school transcript. Of the more selective institutions, 71 percent required a test score from all applicants and 89 percent a high school transcript. Thus, test scores are not as widely required as high school transcripts.

About 2 percent of selective and 1 percent of open-door institutions stated that test scores were the single most important factor in admissions; about 57 percent of the selective schools and 15 percent of the open-door schools rated them a very important factor. At about 33 percent of the selective and 16 percent of the open-door institutions, tests were considered one of several factors. At 5 percent of the selective and 7 percent of the open-door institutions, tests were considered a minor factor in admissions. Clearly, tests are rarely of overwhelming significance in admissions, but at selective institutions they are often very important. Because selectivity varies, with about 91 percent of the public two-year and 20 percent of the public four-year institutions being open door, it appears that in many states access to public higher education is not heavily affected by admissions tests. Rather, tests contribute, along with the high school record and other factors, to a sorting function that places students within the system of higher education.

The two widely used college admissions tests are the Scholastic Aptitude Test (SAT) of the College Entrance Examination Board and the American College Test (ACT) of the

American College Testing Program. The SAT is generally described as an aptitude test; the ACT is generally referred to as an achievement test. As Cleary and others (1975, p. 19) point out, achievement and aptitude tests do not differ in kind but in the repertoires of "acquired skills, knowledge, learning sets, and generalization tendencies" they sample. These authors list four dimensions along which tests vary: breadth of coverage, the extent to which a test is tied to a specific educational program, the recency of the learning that the test samples, and the use to which the test is put. In general, aptitude tests are broader in coverage than achievement tests, are less tied to a specific educational program, sample older learning, and are used for predicting future performance rather than evaluating past accomplishment. Looked at against these four dimensions, the SAT and ACT appear to be similar tests. They attempt breadth of coverage, the educational programs to which they are applicable are general rather than specific, and both are used to predict future educational performance. If both function as aptitude tests, then it is important to reiterate that "tests measure current status" (Cleary and others, 1975, p. 22) rather than a forever-fixed capacity. Since admissions tests do not define once and for all an individual's capacity for higher learning, the question of how they can be appropriately used hinges on their validity in predicting college performance.

Predictive Validity of Admissions Tests

Predictive validity of college admissions tests and other selection devices is usually evaluated by using first-semester or first-year grades as the criterion. Without knowledge of an individual's past academic record and current intellectual status, one could only guess that, if admitted, the student would earn the mean grade point, have a chance of graduation equal to the institution's overall graduation rate, and have a probability of facing academic drop action equal to the institution's current rate of drop actions. To the extent that factors such as high school record and test scores are related to grade point average, graduation rate, and academic drop rate, however, one can use an individual's past record and test scores to predict with better than chance success his or her accomplishments if admitted. Perfect prediction is neither possible nor to be expected. The purpose of validity studies is, then, to gauge the improvement in prediction that can be gained by the use of preadmission variables in the selection process. If first-year grades are the criterion and test scores and high school record are either unknown, unused, or unrelated to first-year grades, then each applicant is predicted to earn the institution's mean grade point average. The variance of the errors of prediction—that is, actual minus predicted grades—then equals the variance of the grades earned. If test scores and high school record are available, used, and related to first-year grades, the variance of the errors of prediction is smaller to the extent that the preadmission variables are related to the criterion. Elimination of error is not possible. The goal, then, is reduction of error.

Generally, the best single predictor of college grades is a high school performance measure, either grade point average or high school percentile rank (HSPR) (Lavin, 1965; Loeb, 1972; Ford and Campos, 1977). Recent data from ACT suggest that high school grades and ACT scores are about equally valid in predicting freshman college grades (Sawyer and Maxey, 1980). Typically, however, a correlation coefficient of about .50 is expected between a high school performance measure and college freshman grades. If an admissions test score is added to it as an additional predictor, a multiple correlation in the high 50s to 60s is expected. The 1974 median validity coefficient for the high school record alone and for the record plus SAT-V and SAT-M—arrived at by Ford and Campos (1977) in their review of 70 collegiate validity studies—indicates a combined R of .58 compared to an r for the high school record of .50. This means that the variance of the errors is reduced by 25 percent (r^2) when high school record alone is used. The variance of the errors is reduced by 33.6 percent (R^2) when test score and high school record are used together. Thus, an additional 8.6 percent reduction in error variance is accomplished, on the average, when test information is added to high school record data. This reduction in error variance, although it does not provide a full evaluation of the contribution of test scores to the selection process, does indicate that tests add valid information to the decision process.

Nairn (1980) argues that the predictive validity of admissions tests is not strong enough to warrant their use in admissions decisions. The statistical basis for some of Nairn's arguments is questionable (see Educational Testing Service, 1980b). However, his arguments reflect a growing public concern, which must be addressed. To evaluate the usefulness of admissions tests in selection, let us examine the practical effects of their use and contrast them with the effects of alternative models not involving admissions tests. The University of Illinois at Urbana-Champaign (UIUC) admissions policy and applicant pool will serve as an example.

Admissions at UIUC

UIUC, a state institution, includes among its freshman admissions policy the following goals:

1. Objectivity.
2. Empirical validity.
3. Selection of those students best qualified for study at the campus.
4. Provision of access to a broad segment of the Illinois populace.

As a state institution, the school is properly held accountable for the decisions it makes, especially in defending the denial of Illinois residents. Objectivity and empirical validity of the factors used in the decision are thus quite important.

By policy, minimum qualifications include a specified set of high school courses completed and a combination of high school percentile rank (HSPR) and ACT composite or SAT total score that predicts at least a 3.0 (A = 5.0) grade point average (GPA) at the end of the first term. If more qualified students apply to an academic program than there are spaces, those best qualified on the basis of predicted GPA (PGPA) are admitted.

To provide broader access than might otherwise be the case and to meet institutional needs, such as the admission of athletes, up to 10 percent of the previous year's freshman class spaces may be held for students who will be judged by different criteria. The result of this policy applied to UIUC's applicant pool is a freshman class that typically has a mean ACT of about 26; a mean HSPR of about 86; black and Spanish-surnamed enrollment of about 300 to 350, or roughly 5 percent; and Illinois-resident enrollment of about 97 percent.

Langston and Chang (1980) examined the cross-validity of the predictive equations used for selecting UIUC freshmen for the 1974 to 1978 fall terms. For the eight colleges that admit freshmen, the median correlations of PGPA and actual first-semester GPA ranged from .364 to .478. The UIUC colleges range from moderately to highly selective; thus, all these correlations are less than they would be in an unselected population. That is, the ranges of both predictor variables are restricted by selectivity. As a result, the correlations of PGPA and actual GPA are reduced. Loeb (1969) investigated the estimated correlations of PGPA and actual GPA for the 1968 UIUC class and found that the median difference between the coefficient estimated for the entire applicant pool and the actual correlation was .169.

This example shows that in a situation of selective admissions, both the validity coefficients and the ranges of the variables used in selection are reduced. In fact, the estimated unrestricted variation is reduced by a number of factors. Some students drop out of high school, others do not go on to college; of those who go on to college, not all appear in the UIUC applicant pool, which is limited by applicant self-selection: The range of variation in the applicant pool is reduced by information given to applicants about minimum and expected standards.

One way to provide an unbiased test of the validity of the selection criteria would be to study the validity of the predictors for an entirely unselected pool of students, a pool not restricted by institutional or self-selection. Such a test is obviously not possible. However, early validity studies at UIUC, before the institution became progressively more selective, allow an investigation of the validity of the admissions criteria in a pool considerably less restricted in range than is currently the case. Among fall 1963 liberal arts and sciences students, Bowers (1964) found that the mean HSPR was 77 and standard deviation was 20; mean ACT was 24.7, with a standard deviation of 3.4; mean GPA was 3.24, with standard deviation of .78. The multiple correlation of HSPR and ACT with GPA was .56. In comparison, the 1979 data for the same college indicate mean HSPR of 87.7 with standard deviation of 9.59; mean ACT of 25.9 with standard deviation of 3.22; mean GPA of 3.88 with standard deviation of .67. The multiple correlation had declined to .42.

Given that HSPR and test scores provide valid information concerning a student's predicted first-term grades, the next question is whether these variables are useful in predicting more important performance criteria, such as academic survival and graduation. Once again, selectivity by applicants and the institution lessens the apparent validity of the predictors. However, a comparison of academic drop and graduation rates for the freshman classes of 1962 and 1968, the period when the institution became increasingly more selective, provides evidence bearing on the question. In 1962 mean ACT was 24 and HSPR 74. By 1968 these means had increased to 26 and 86, respectively. The first-semester drop rate simultaneously fell from 6 to 3 percent; the second-semester drop rate went from 17 to 5 percent. At the same time, the percent of the freshman class graduating within eight semesters increased from 28.3 to 46.1 percent; the percent graduating within ten semesters went from 40.8 to 60.7. These data are correlational rather than experimental and do not indicate causation. However, they do suggest that increasing selectivity has the expected effect of raising graduation rate while lowering the academic drop rate. Furthermore, within the group selected for any given year, both HSPR and test score are positively related to graduation rate. For example, among students entering in 1972 the College of Commerce and Business Administration and the related curricula of restaurant management, business education, and economics and finance in other colleges, the graduation rate within ten semesters was 63 percent. Those with ACT above 30 had a graduation rate of 78 percent; those with ACT of 25 to 30 had a graduation rate of 68 percent; those with ACT of 22 to 24 had a graduation rate of 58 percent; 40 percent of those with ACT below 22 graduated. Those graduating in the top 10 percent of their high school class graduated from the university at a rate of 72 percent; those in the second 10 percent had a graduation rate of 68 percent. For those with HSPR in the 70s, 61 percent graduated from the university. With HSPR below 70, the university graduation rate was 52 percent. These data indicate that both high school record and test score are related to a student's probability of graduation.

Equity in Admissions

One important way to evaluate the perceived validity and equity of an admissions program is to examine the public's reaction to it. The admissions office regularly deals with the public about questions of admissibility, but the most heated public questions are raised over the point of denial. There are no available statistical data about the types of questions raised concerning the denial of students. However, the experienced admissions officer builds up a sense of what reaction to expect once the denial letters are mailed out. In recent years, typical complaints at UIUC are the following:

1. The rank is based on an unusually solid high school program and/or was earned at an unusually competitive high school and therefore should not be considered on a par with other HSPRs.
2. The test was taken on a bad day and therefore is not valid, or the student is one who generally and spuriously scores poorly.
3. Surely there must be back doors to the university.
4. Too many out-of-state students are admitted, leading to denial of state residents.
5. Admissions cutoffs were higher than those the public was led to expect.

The first complaint is probably the most common and, in fact, is a major reason that admissions tests are valid and used. Loeb and Mueller (1970), with data from the Chicago Circle campus of the University of Illinois (UICC), investigated the use of a scale of high schools to predict college grades. For each high school supplying at least ten freshmen to UICC during the 1966 and 1967 fall terms, the mean difference between actual and predicted first-term grades was used as an index of the school's "quality." The PGPA was a linear combination of HSPR and ACT score. First-term GPA was then predicted from HSPR, ACT, and high school index for the 1968 entering class. HSPR alone correlated .39 with GPA. HSPR plus the high school index had a multiple correlation of .47 with GPA. HSPR plus ACT had an R of .50. Finally, all three predictors had an R of .53 with GPA. The results suggest that a scale of high schools adds little to HSPR and test score in predicting GPA. In fact, test score accounts for about the same variance in GPA as does the high school scale value. Admissions tests correct for curricular and grading differences among high schools.

To defend denial, UIUC staff point out that a solid high school preparation should build the test score. Thus, a lower rank because of heavy competition is somewhat compensated for by the higher test score. Furthermore, the use of high school rank tends to distribute access to the institution evenly throughout the state's high schools, whereas the use of test scores tends to compensate for the considerable high school variation within the state.

That programs for the disadvantaged limit opportunities for the advantaged is frequently a corollary concern to that about the use of HSPR. Again, reasonable access to the institution is cited as a goal of the admissions program. The use of HSPR nonetheless remains the most controversial component of the admissions program.

As Cleary and others (1975) points out, rigorous accreditation of high schools could conceivably control variation in high school standards. Alternatively, a scale of high school quality could be used to substitute for an individual admissions test score. The first alternative appears unfeasible and the second inequitable. The excellent student at a poor school would have little hope of being admitted to a selective institution that used a high school scale in place of an admissions test.

The use of test scores, when challenged, is typically easier to deal with. Occasionally a strong case is made that a particular student spuriously and typically receives scores which underestimate that student's ability to do collegiate work. UIUC practices a nonpunitive policy of ignoring all but the highest test score received, and an ACT administration is regularly available on campus. Thus, students who believe that their test scores underestimate their current readiness to do collegiate work can retake the test several times. Time constraints exist, as programs fill, but these constraints are well publicized. Furthermore, students who believe that their circumstances require special review are urged to submit petitions with documentation of those circumstances with the application form. Thus, with the bulk of our applicants, test score use is a relatively noncontroversial question in comparison to HSPR.

The belief that unpublished rules for admissions exist, and that one can get admitted if only one can figure out the real rules, tends to persist even though it is simply not true. Exceptions are made, to a maximum of 10 percent of the size of the previous freshman class, but these exceptions are based on preestablished criteria. Open discussion of these criteria typically convinces inquirers that they understand the rules of the game.

Out-of-state applicants are frequently pictured as taking large numbers of spaces deserved by Illinois taxpayers' sons and daughters. As referenced, this is not the case. Sometimes the argument is made that all Illinois students should have the opportunity to study at UIUC. Although this is clearly not possible, and publicly supported opportunities do exist within the state for virtually all students seeking higher education, this argument suggests the alternate admissions strategy of randomly admitting and denying students from the population of Illinois high school graduates. A variation of that alternative is discussed in a later section.

Experience with denial defense clearly points out the

need to warn the public about admissions requirements. For example, on the few occasions when published estimates of admissions requirements have turned out to be too low, the level of disappointment and anger has been particularly high, even though publications emphasize that the printed cutoffs are only estimates. Clear information is quite definitely seen as a necessary attribute of an equitable admissions program.

Equity must be judged both from the point of view of the individual applicant and from the point of view of groups of applicants presenting different qualifications. The typical experience is that denied applicants feel fairly treated, although unhappy, if it can be demonstrated that those admitted are objectively better qualified for admission than the rejected students. Group differences in educational background, competitiveness of high school, and test scores raise equity problems, however. In a system of secondary education that tends to be segregated racially and variable in intensity, for example, differences in high school programs are seen as correlated with ethnicity. The use of HSPR may thus appear unfair to the parents of the suburban denial; the use of test score may be seen as a biased criterion by the parents of the inner-city applicant.

In the past decade, there has been considerable literature about evaluating bias in selection. No clear consensus has emerged, but it does appear clear that no one model of selection—given test score and educational differences, which are related to race and socioeconomic status (SES)—will seem fair to all reviewing it. That the administrator must make basic value judgments without the aid of an agreed-on statistical model of equity is indeed apparent. Nor will values ever remain static, allowing an admissions policy to remain static over the course of many years. As long as merit, reward for achievement, and equal access to higher education are simultaneously valued and as long as past record and test scores show differences related to race and SES, any admissions policy will remain a compromise. Although not presented as ideal, the UIUC policy appears presently workable. That is, the admission of most students on a "best qualified" basis, and the remainder based on special individual circumstances and institutional priorities, such as the need to provide access to a broad group of individuals within the state, appears currently palatable to most residents of the state. Specifically, the use of a combination of HSPR and test score as an objective index of a student's qualifications for admission appears to provide a generally acceptable basis for decisions.

Alternatives to Using Admissions Tests

Alternatives to the use of tests include sole reliance on the high school record, the development of other measures to replace objective academic admissions tests, and various forms of random selection. Interviews, biographical data forms, personality measures, indexes of strengths in other than traditional academic areas, and letters of recommendation are but some of the measures suggested as potentially useful in predicting college performance. Aside from obvious problems of reliability, validity, fakeability, and cost (especially for interviews, where both individuals and institutions bear sizable costs), it appears unlikely that noncognitive measures, even if reliable, can replace the existing cognitive measures in predicting academic achievement. The existing admissions tests are similar in format, timing, and content to the objective final examinations on which some course grades hinge. Even factors considered by some to have a spurious effect on admissions test scores—for example, test wiseness and test anxiety—are probably also related to course grades earned. Thus, it seems likely that objective academic tests could not be entirely replaced by other individual measures.

The high school record alone could probably be an adequate basis for admissions if the high schools from which a college admits students had homogeneous curricula and standards. Lacking homogeneity, a scale of high school quality could, it appears, replace admissions test scores in predicting college performance. This approach would, however, substitute a group-membership variable, high school of graduation, for an individual measure, the test score. This seems generally inequitable; but, in addition, the use of a high school scale would tend to advantage those who can afford private school tuition or housing in an excellent school district over those who cannot, with no regard for the individual's current readiness for collegiate study.

Use of the high school record alone, with no regard for differences among high schools, would have other equity problems connected with it. To illustrate the effects of such a strategy, fall 1980 applications to the UIUC College of Liberal Arts and Sciences (LAS) were analyzed. It must be emphasized that the characteristics of an existing applicant pool are partially determined by the information available concerning admissibility. UIUC publicizes its expected admissions cutoffs throughout the state. Students slightly below these estimated cutoffs may well gamble the $20 application fee, hoping the estimates are high. However, not many students who are far below the expected cutoffs apply. If test scores were eliminated as an admissions criterion, many more students with high HSPR and modest test score would undoubtedly apply. Thus, any analysis of the existing applicant pool undoubtedly underestimates the effect of a change in admissions policy. Nonetheless, the use of HSPR alone would have had fairly striking effects if applied to the fall 1980 LAS applicant pool.

The pool of 5,832 applicants to LAS who presented HSPR and an ACT score represents 91 percent of the total pool of LAS applicants. A few students not in the sample would have presented transcripts from high schools that do not rank; most presented SAT but no ACT score. Admissions decision, HSPR, ACT, and PGPA were examined for these students. If the class had been filled on HSPR alone, without regard to test score so long as campus minimum requirements were met, it is estimated that an HSPR of 73 or higher would have been required for admission. As a result, 122 students who were admitted with HSPR below 73 but ACT high enough that they met the cutoff of a 3.5 PGPA would have been denied. In their place, 129 students who did not meet the PGPA cutoff but whose percentile ranks were at least 73 would have been admitted. (These numbers are not identical because applications are usually received from multiple students with very similar qualifications. For this and other reasons, targets are never precisely met.)

The students falling just above and just below the HSPR cutoff of 73 were compared, to investigate the effects of this strategy on individuals with very similar high school ranks. In all, 61 denied students with percentile rank of 73 to 75 would have been admitted, whereas 83 admitted students with percentile rank of 70 to 72 would have been denied under a rank-only strategy. The 61 new admits would have had slightly higher ranks than the 83 students actually admitted who would have been denied. The means are 73.9 and 71.2. Similarly, a small difference in the opposite direction was noted on PGPA: Those to be denied on HSPR had a mean of 3.5; those to be admitted had a mean of 3.3. The large difference observed was, of course, the mean ACT of the two groups. Those actually admitted, who would have been denied, had a mean ACT of 27.2; those actually denied, who would have been admitted in their stead, had a mean ACT of 20.2. This is a large difference—in fact, larger than a standard deviation among college-bound high school students taking the test in 1974-1977 (American College Testing Program, 1978). In addition, it is instructive to compare the individual students in the two groups. For example, 11 students with ACT of 18 or less would have been admitted based on an HSPR of 73 to 75. At the same time, 37 students with HSPR of 72 would have been denied, even though their test scores ranged from 25 to 30. To admit a student with HSPR of 73 and ACT of 12 while denying a student with HSPR of 72 and ACT of 30—as would have been done—places an incredible reliance on the high school record as a reliable measure of past performance and a valid, sole predictor of future achievement. The use of a rank-only strategy under these circumstances would indeed be difficult to defend, given variability in high school programs.

The *Digest of Education Statistics* (National Center for Education Statistics, 1979) indicates that, in 1977, 142,040 students graduated from public high schools in Illinois. This source estimates that an additional 24,000 graduated from nonpublic high schools, for a total of 166,040. UIUC typically would admit a total of about 8,900 students to its undergraduate colleges to fill a target of 5,800 freshmen. It is not known what the UIUC applicant pool would be like if a rank-only criterion were put into effect. However, if more than 36 percent of students graduating in the top 15 percent of their class had applied to UIUC, a cutoff higher than the 85th percentile rank would have had to be instituted for this group under a rank-only policy. Again, given high school differences, the rigid exclusion of students bearing lower high school ranks would be difficult to defend. In all likelihood, some additional variable, such as a ranking of high schools, or some different selection method, such as random selection above a reasonable rank minimum, would have to be put into effect.

Random selection of students for admissions and denial, often suggested as an equitable strategy for providing access to an institution, is certainly one alternative to the use of admissions tests. Random decisions can be made on the entire unscreened applicant pool, providing a form of open admissions. Alternatively, random decision might be applied to only those applicants who meet minimum requirements for admission, determined on the basis of qualifications, allowing a reasonable chance for academic success at the institution. Finally, random decisions might be applied to a smaller group of applicants who meet minimum requirements but are not superlatively well qualified, allowing the extremely well-qualified student to be admitted without facing the possibility of random rejection. For the fall of 1970, UIUC chose to admit and deny students who met minimum requirements by selecting them in or out on a random basis. The institution's experiences are instructive for considering the effects of a random admissions and denial model.

In the late 1960s, UIUC experienced growing concern, both on and off campus, that the institution was becoming too "elitist." In particular, fairly strong faculty sentiment supported the belief that the distribution of socioeconomic status in the student body was too narrow and that academic selectivity was responsible for this. Some believed that the relationship between family income and other SES variables, on the one hand, and the academic achievement variables used in selection, on the other, was sufficiently strong that a modest decrease in selectivity could produce a significant increase in the range of SES represented in the student body. Thus, in the spring of 1969, the University Committee on Admissions and the campus senates passed a revised freshman admissions policy that was approved by the Board of Trustees the following fall, for implementation in 1971. The policy set a one-in-two chance of a C average as the minimum admissions requirement and stated that if, on the first day for action on applications, more applicants meeting these requirements had applied than could be accommodated, qualified students would be randomly selected to fill available space. It was anticipated that random selection would need to be put into effect for the UIUC College of Liberal Arts and Sciences, then the most popular college at the campus among beginning freshman applicants. Faced with the probability of too many qualified LAS applicants for fall 1970, the campus administration decided to implement the plan a year early. In August the admissions office advised Illinois high school principals, counselors, and directors of guidance that random selection would be used if needed. Representative high school counselors and principals were consulted and endorsed the plan, although with some reservations. In October a standard newsletter to schools and colleges again described the plan. Early in November, a news release, with copies sent to each high school, referred again to random selection. On November 26, another press release indicated that random selection had led to the denial of 847 qualified applicants, who would learn of the decision on December 1.

Consultation a decade later with ten administrators and staff members involved at the time elicited vivid recall of massive public outcry, described by one as "a roar." Early in December, extremely negative newspaper articles and editorials appeared, and complaints and inquiries from the public arrived in large quantity. On December 8, Jack W. Peltason, then chancellor of the Urbana campus, issued a press release designed to clarify the policy and correct the fairly common misinterpretation that completely unqualified students had been admitted. On December 12, Chancellor Peltason issued a press release indicating that the 839 randomly rejected Illinois residents would be admitted. On April 15, 1970, the Board of Trustees adopted a policy requiring the admission of those best qualified when qualified applicants exceeded space available.

Before evaluating the short life of random selection—really, random denial—at the Urbana-Champaign campus, I must state that the public had not been adequately warned of its impending implementation. A single sentence in a long policy proposal led to 847 random rejections; press releases mentioned but did not focus on random selection; counselors were told that selection would be by chance, but individual applicants were not informed of that fact. Furthermore, public reaction was also compounded by other factors having to do with the timing of the implementation of random selection: A $15 application fee was put into effect at the same time, allowing one *Chicago Tribune* caption to read "Lottery—$15 a ticket" (*Chicago Tribune*, December 14, 1969, p. V-16); a year earlier, the special educational opportunities program for disadvantaged students had been implemented, causing some complaints that disadvantaged students were being served better than super scholars; nationwide campus dissent at the same time suggested to some that universities' admissions procedures, of all kinds, were designed to admit the "wrong" students. Nonetheless, of the ten administrators interviewed after the fact, only one believed that the campus could have or would have stuck with random selection beyond at most that first year. Several volunteered their opinion that no amount of advance notice would have made the policy palatable to the public.

Here is a typical public complaint about the procedure, from a *Chicago Tribune* editorial of December 5, 1969: "We do condemn random selection. We resist, as well as deplore, the practice of telling high school valedictorians and high test scorers that there is no room for them, while less well-qualified freshmen are being admitted. We resist and deplore telling applicants that they have lost out in a game of chance, rather than under the presumably informed and judicious scrutiny of the admissions office" (p. I-24).

Denial by chance disturbed many people, for two reasons: It signaled a loss of control over the environment, and it did not reward effort. The former problem was well stated in a

December 12, 1969, letter to the editor of the *Chicago Daily News*: "When we voluntarily accept determination by chance, we surrender control over our environment. We admit defeat, not to what is beyond our influence but to affairs of our own creation" (p. 8). The theme of helplessness and loss of control certainly runs through many of the protest letters received from parents of students denied. The expectation that reward should follow hard work is another constant theme in these letters. For example, here are excerpts from one typical letter from the mother of a randomly denied student:

> Even though it is possible that our son will never attend your university, this great learning institution has already been most effective in teaching him several lessons.
>
> He has learned that personal efforts toward excellence do not count. . . .
>
> By using the lottery to select next year's freshman class—so everyone will be equal regardless of ability or effort—you have negated our years of trying to build the belief that if one has a measure of intelligence, tries to do his best on each educational task, and follows the rules of society, he can expect to receive further chances to develop as he chooses.
>
> Perhaps our son would not have been accepted at your school on the usual basis of high test scores and grades, although he is in the top fifth of his class. He would have taken rejection on this basis as a judgment that he was not good enough, and, while he probably would have been disappointed, he would have gone on to find another, less demanding school, and continued to work hard. No doubt he will still go someplace else. I am not so sure he will overcome the suspicion that it doesn't make much difference how hard one tries.

Reward for work and merit is clearly a deeply ingrained expectation. In the files from the time and in recent retrospective interviews with those involved, there were multiple references to how hard it was to explain to the denied student and the family why the student had been denied. An admissions officer who was then a receptionist stated that people are able to accept a decision explained in terms of objective evidence of merit, but not a decision based on chance. Public acceptance of random decision making seems unlikely to occur, especially when students who are very well qualified are denied.

There were in fact significant differences in the qualifications of some students who were admitted and some who were denied. Minimum requirements were set at a first-term PGPA of a 3.0, requiring, for example, an ACT of 30 (SAT total of 1332 to 1381) for an HSPR of 51 or an ACT of 13 (SAT total of 655 to 679) for an HSPR of 86. A student with ACT of 32 (SAT total of 1438 to 1509) and a HSPR of 86 would have had PGPA of 3.9. Such a student would clearly be better qualified than the student with much lower rank (51) and slightly lower ACT (30) or the student with the same rank and substantially lower ACT (13). Yet 20 percent were denied across the board, and 353 of the random denials had a PGPA of 3.9 or higher.

Public outcry killed random selection. Once the public attitude became clear, however, some degree of rethinking occurred at UIUC and some issues became clearer. The goal of the admissions policy had been more variation on socioeconomic status with little change in academic qualifications. Yet a correlation of about .4 between academic qualifications and SES in an unselected pool of students is about as high as one might expect, based on the literature. This moderate correlation means that the expected change in average SES status would have been substantially less than any given change in average academic qualifications. To have had a major impact on the SES distribution, substantial change would have had to been made in the qualifications of the students admitted.

Ironically, a major change in the SES distribution would also have required a major change in the applicant pool. Loeb (1970) correlated twelve indexes of SES with HSPR, ACT, and PGPA for fall 1967 LAS freshmen. Of the twelve variables, six correlated significantly with PGPA. All significant correlations were negative. The six variables were anticipated college expenditures, percent of high school class college-bound, hours worked during high school senior year, estimated family income, and mother's and father's cultural activities.

In all cases except work during high school, the significant negative correlations indicated that broadening the range of acceptable PGPAs would slightly increase the frequency of well-off students accepted. The variance of PGPA was larger in this group of admitted students than it was for the 1970 qualified applicant pool. Hence, restriction of range by selection does not appear to account for these results. Furthermore, of the six SES variables that correlated significantly with PGPA, five also correlated significantly with HSPR, whereas none displayed a significant linear relationship with ACT. Thus, the negative correlations were probably a result of upper-SES students' tendency to experience greater academic competition in high school and hence to emerge with slightly lower HSPRs than lower-SES students. The applicant pool would have had to change before a broadening of acceptable qualifications could have broadened the SES distribution of the student body.

A change in the applicant pool might have resulted in some broadening of the SES distribution on the campus, but most likely it would have reduced the qualifications of the group admitted. This was seen, after the fact, as a likely but undesirable outcome. That is, it was expected that students who were exceptionally well qualified and who might have planned to enroll at UIUC would have had to look elsewhere because of the uncertainties involved in random selection-denial. On the other hand, students of more average qualifications who would not be admissible without random selection were expected to apply in greater numbers. In the long run, such changes in the applicant pool would probably have widened somewhat the SES spread on campus. They would also, however, have required some reduction in the entering level of course work in some curricula. Without a publicly supported campus geared to serve the well-prepared student, well-prepared students from low- and middle-income families would have faced reduced opportunity. As one couple wrote to the Board of Trustees, "The charge that the University of Illinois with its present admissions policy may be catering to an economic elite strikes us as phony. The affluent are not likely as a large group to select Illinois for their children. On the other hand, those parents with limited means but bright children clearly have no other choice but Illinois."

Conclusion

A review of the literature indicates that high school performance measures and admissions test scores combined are the most valid predictive measures of college performance. Test scores add to the predictive power of the high school record. Although the use of test scores or, for that matter, any imperfect predictors of college performance, has been questioned by many, the failure to use these measures is also subject to criticism. The use of the high school record alone raises significant questions of equity, as does reliance on chance in college admissions. Thus, admissions tests continue to be useful as college selection devices and should continue to be used.

32

Learning from Members of the Profession

Marilyn Kimball
James E. Cavalier

For new admissions counselors, what can be passed on from one professional to another is of special importance. Books such as this one and articles such as those appearing in recent numbers of *The Journal of College Admissions* codify some of the ephemera, but oral transmission is still important. For seasoned professionals, this chapter has two functions. First, it will remind you of the ways in which we have learned and spark you to revive old learning practices. More important, it urges you to remember your responsibility as a teacher to the newcomer.

Because of the many different skills required, the need to educate oneself, and the tiring work pace, there has always been considerable turnover in admissions personnel, although longevity is greater among college guidance counselors in secondary schools. We must share our experiences and work together to reduce turnover and establish admissions counseling as a true profession. The development of a strong network of secondary school and college admissions counselors is essential to provide the perspective, encouragement, and information needed in our work.

Let us first list essentials; you must frame your mind properly to proceed further.

1. Know your own values and your institution's goals. If you are to be effective and happy, these must be consistent.

2. Meet important people whom you respect at both the college and secondary levels of admissions work. Their personal qualities and their knowledge and contacts will be valuable to you.
3. Do your homework and make the best use of your time, even if it appears that no one else is working or cares. You need to know your college and your school, its strengths and problems, its past experience with the institutions that you visit or that visit you.
4. Remember that the informal yet exhausting nature of admissions work can be misleading. You need to be able to keep going and yet learn when to stop.

The keynote to your development is not learning *things,* although facts and ideas are important. Rather, you must build a *network,* a web of individuals in schools, colleges, and quasi-academic institutions (like NACAC) whom you can use endlessly as sources of information, advice, and policy and as models for ethical and professional behavior. This network is especially important because the counselor is frequently the first source of information for students and their parents. Most often they come to the counselor completely ignorant of the college admissions process; it is the counselor's advice, direction, and suggestions that are their bases for the college search. Thus, it is crucial that a college admissions office try to see that the counselors in the schools from which it traditionally recruits students are well informed and to develop in those counselors a positive feeling for the college. Because counselors not only know the people in the admissions office but also have a sense of the college's quality, they will have a comfortable relationship with that college and recommend it with greater confidence to their students.

The relationship of the college admissions office and the guidance counselor is a combination of personal and professional contact, best combined in the school visit. To be really worthwhile, the visit should be an exchange of information about school, college, and students. The counselor needs honest, direct information on which to base recommendations about the college. Therefore, the exchange between the counselor and college admissions officer must be open; they have got to give each other a true picture of their respective schools, "warts and all." Above all, counselors do not want a hard sell or a public relations pitch. They need solid information on which to base their counseling decisions, and they most appreciate the college admissions officer who gives them that information and then adds to it the personal dimension.

Counselors can also be a truly valuable source of feedback to the college. They frequently have both formal and informal methods of gathering information from their students attending a particular college or from the parents and students who visit colleges. Making allowances for individual experiences, they often begin to make judgments about a college based on the opinions of their students who have attended it over a period of years. They might use a formal means of opinion gathering, such as a questionnaire, or they might invite students to return to school during vacation and other breaks, either to talk to the guidance staff or to be part of a college-orientation program for students. Then, too, some counselors keep a record of their students' admissions patterns and use it as a guideline for counseling. However, at times such a record may be misleading, and a counselor may make a conclusion about admissions standards based on a limited number of students. He may say, for example, "You haven't taken anyone out of our third quintile for the last three years, so I just don't recommend your college to a student in that category." But the fact may be that rank alone was not the factor on which those students were rejected.

It is important, therefore, that the admissions officer try to find out what the guidance counselor's view of the college is and what the counselor's experience with that college has been. Also, the admissions officer should solicit any information the counselor can give about the students' views of the college, and the image the college has in the eyes of both the students and their parents. Given that information, the officer has a chance to correct or counteract anything negative or incorrect and, if necessary, take the information back to the college and share it with colleagues on the admissions staff and with whatever other division of the college is involved. Such feedback can be enormously valuable, but it occurs only when the relationship between the school guidance counselor and the college admissions officers is trusting and respectful.

Developing a good rapport with the high school counselor can be beneficial in learning about schools in an area or setting up travel schedules. For example, the counselor can advise an admissions office about holidays and in-service days scheduled in the district. The counselor can help the college set up more efficient travel schedules by suggesting schools that are grouped geographically. This can be particularly valuable to a college that is going into an area for the first time. Counselors can also provide information concerning meetings of the counselors' associations and provide the names of the officers. Such information is clearly of value to any visiting college.

The time spent cultivating contacts and friendships among high school counselors is well worth the effort. The coffee breaks, the social hours, the mealtimes at meetings, conferences, and workshops are particularly good times for meeting counselors and developing the casual but important exchange of ideas and information. Whether the talk is about admissions or the World Series, the personal contact is what is important, especially when it results in mutual confidence. The end result of such activities is the situation where counselor or admissions officer feels at ease in picking up the phone and making a call to discuss a student or a transcript. Such a relationship can help make the admissions process better and of greater benefit to all concerned.

Let us look now at the network an admissions professional might build. Given the more peripatetic life of college officers, we address ourselves mostly to their experiences; but professionals in secondary schools will note that when we advise attending meetings and colloquiums, we mean that *all* professionals should be there.

When you first begin your new job, it is important to investigate the history of your institution by reading. The official institutional history is a good place to start, but do not forget that for you as a professional the most revealing story may lie in files, annual reports, and memos, especially recent ones. Ask other staff members, faculty active in admissions, students, and others at the college and in neighboring institutions what you should know about developments, policies, and problems the college has faced. Besides important areas of agreement, you will find *differences* in attitude and point of view. You will discover the inconsistencies with which you will have to deal, and at the same time you will be building relationships for your institution and yourself. You should look for the positive side—you need to take that approach in your presentations, and you thus build healthier expectations in others and in yourself—but you should also listen to *all* sides. Caring enough to ask and listen may actually heal some old misunderstandings and incorrect assumptions.

Although there may not be very many faculty members around in the summer, those who are deserve your special attention. They would probably love to tell you about the excellence of their departments and of how there must be hundreds of students out there waiting to discover the glories of hieroglyphics. Other administrators are, like you, generally around during the summer, and sometimes they are more accessible then than during the school year. You should especially try to get to know the registrar, financial aid officers, and student deans or their assistants who work in curriculum and student life; you will need to turn to them for information and support as the year progresses.

Make calls to and visit admissions officers at neighboring colleges. If you can plan some coordinated travel to certain areas, you will reinforce one another's impact at school visits. You can also arrange suppers together on the road to share information. You will benefit, and in time you will also be able to help your new colleagues by comparing information on the schools from which your college attracts students. You may also be able to plan some cooperative programs, such as events for local counselors, or visits by counselors from another city.

Most colleges belong to regional associations or special-interest groups. You should learn about and at least initially participate in such groups whenever possible. Some of these groups—for example, the Women's Independent Colleges (WIC) or the Eastern Group of Admissions Directors (EGAD)—may involve comparable or competing institutions. Some—such as the Association of Black Admissions and Financial Aid Officers of the Ivy League and Seven Sisters (ABAFAOILSS) or the Consortium on Financing Higher Education (COFHE)—represent an athletic league or other special concerns. In other groups, such as the Pittsburgh Council on Higher Education (PCHE), geographical location is the common factor. You should investigate any such association to which your college belongs or which it is eligible to join. You will get to know your institution better and will be able to compare plans and developments with people who have some similar concerns. You will also get to know your competition better, which is essential in learning how your institution is perceived by others.

During your first summer, you should attend a workshop by the regional association of the National Association of College Admissions Counselors (NACAC), preferably in your own region. These workshops last about a week and deal with important issues and skills with which you should become well acquainted during your first year. Staff members are admissions officers and guidance counselors who know their business well and are good people for you to know. Your classmates can become colleagues and a source of consolation and companionship if you end up traveling the same college fair or college night circuits. Friends you make early in the business will remember and trust you, and you will be able to rely on them years later. Your professional admissions associates become your credentials as well as some of your best friends.

In your contact with the regional Association of College Admissions Counselors at the workshop, ask for a list of members and officers. You will find that it is the busiest and the most famous admissions and counseling professionals who are most willing to help you. When one of us was a new director of admissions in the Midwest, it was well-established guidance counselors and admissions officers (NACAC presidents and College Board trustees) who went out of their way to provide support.

In the fall, try to attend either the NACAC annual meet-

ing or the annual College Board National Forum. You may find
it easier to justify going to one of these meetings if you can plan
a school visiting trip in the general area just before or after. It
may be worthwhile for you to pay some of your own expenses.
A director should attend both national meetings. When you get
to the meeting, find some people you know and respect, or who
have connections, or who are lively, and spend much of your
time with them. If they have been in admissions work longer
than you, they should be able to introduce you to others. Do
not forget your name tag; it reinforces your name with people
you meet. Review the list of conference attendees for people
you know, have met, or have heard of, and look for excuses to
meet people who work at the college that a friend attended or
that is in your home region. Remember that many people at
these meetings are old friends who want to spend time with
one another, so they may appear less enthusiastic about meeting
new people than greeting old colleagues. Do not let that slow
you down; the second or third time you meet them, you may
be one of those old friends. We all want to share what we know
and whom we know, so even though old-timers may hang
around together, they will usually welcome your joining them
and listening in.

   You should especially use meeting times to get to know
high school counselors better, to reinforce your visits, and to
become familiar with schools you may never get to visit. It is
very tempting, and sometimes useful, to spend your time with
fellow admissions people you have met in your travels. It is
comfortable to be with people you know and to whom you do
not have to represent the college. But you are at these meetings
to work, and you always represent your institution; so take this
opportunity to befriend counselors, most of whom have had to
sacrifice and often pay some of their own way to attend these
conferences.

   Throughout the fall, you will be attending college days
and visiting high schools, ones you have chosen carefully to reflect your college's history of applicants and enrolling students,
current inquiries, and Student Search responses. You will get to
know the schools and counselors in your college's feeder areas.

As you talk with counselors, find out their views and experiences with your college and their suggestions about how to improve relationships with high schools. They will also be glad to share with you information about the local history, traditions, businesses, places of interest, and good restaurants. Throughout all this, you will be building contacts for your college and yourself.

After college nights, a group of counselors will often go out together for a nightcap. If you have the strength left, join them, at least for a little while, because there will be interesting and helpful shoptalk going on. Many social events with other admissions officers are really part of the job because admissions people talk business nearly all the time. It is important, however, to find your own pace; many people spend their entire first year in admissions in a state of near exhaustion. To save yourself, avoid the clearly "fun only" events, except when you can afford the time and energy.

As fall goes into winter and traveling tapers off, ask questions about how projects were handled in the past and whether it has been determined that those were the best ways to do them. Become curious about all your office practices, to make sure you contribute properly to the team you are a part of. Become familiar with the services of the College Entrance Examination Board (CEEB), especially the Summary Report and Validity Study services. Investigate free workshops on these services and others run by College Board, the American College Testing Program (ACT), and the American Council on Education (ACE), which are often particularly worthwhile. Sometimes there are free presentations by word processing or marketing outfits that want to sell their services. Even though you may not be ready to become their client, you could learn from them about what they have to offer. The telephone company, for example, does presentations on how to sell on the phone, from which you might learn some points to help you in follow-up calls.

Be sure to attend the winter regional meetings of the College Board and carefully read its mailings beforehand. If ACT is active in your region, pay attention to its activities too. New

ideas and proposals from these organizations to their membership are usually presented first at these sessions. Sit with some
old-timers who can explain to you the shortcomings and complexities of the proposals.

With winter, the selection process becomes central to
your operation. Although you are not on the road, the season is
ideal for getting further help and solidifying relationships with
others. Call your admissions colleagues for information about
schools and application trends. Follow up with the counselors
you have met and whose students have applied. Telephone them
and ask them to give further information about the students, to
clarify any inconsistencies in the students' records, and to answer questions about transcripts or their curriculum. Read their
recommendations carefully, and devise formal and informal systems to thank them for their help. Contact by phone those
counselors you have not met but whose students have applied;
they will often be most helpful and appreciative. (You may
wish that you had visited their schools.) Learn from faculty
members on the admissions committee what preparation they
have found that students need in order to succeed at your college. That experience, research by the registrar, and the results
of your College Board Validity Study are your guidelines, but
not strict cutoffs or rules, for selecting students. Personal judgment, based on careful weighting of many factors, is still the
way most admissions decisions are made. Your judgment will be
improved by the quality of your information, especially from
knowledgeable, sensitive guidance counselors, who can help you
help their students. Remember to plan for appropriate feedback
to the counselors so they will know what your committee decided, and if possible why.

You should also find out about the experience and needs
of different populations at your college: women in engineering,
minority students, older students, and so forth. Learn from
the students directly as well as from statistics about them. Entirely different factors may predict success and satisfaction for
certain subgroups of your student body; you will want to use
such factors to improve your admissions decisions.

As it becomes time to plan spring travel, investigate the

annual meetings of the National Association of Independent
Schools (NAIS), the National Association of Principals of
Schools for Girls (NAPSG), and the American Association of
Collegiate Registrars and Admissions Officers (AACRAO). The
first two meetings are good for making connections with private
schools, although often the heads rather than the counselors attend, and their programs reflect many concerns that may not be
relevant to you. But the problems that private schools face,
whether declining enrollments, handicapped students, or curriculum development, will sooner or later be your problems as
their students become your students. NAPSG is particularly interesting because it is a small intimate group of people, many of
whom know each other very well.

AACRAO includes admissions officers in its title, but the
association is primarily oriented to registrars and to admissions
officers at large public institutions. It is a serious, businesslike
group that can produce first-rate panels presenting technical discussions of computers, foreign students, and other subjects.
You should read over its detailed program when it is sent out in
advance of the meeting. If it is possible for you to attend, do so.

One major goal during your first year should be to discover areas of special interest that you can develop as you go on
in the profession. Some areas to consider are financial aid, foreign students, continuing education, minority students, computer expertise, or marketing. Depending on the areas you
choose, you may want to attend the AACRAO meeting, the
meeting of the National Association of Student Financial Aid
Administrators (NASFAA) or one of its regional meetings, or
the National Association of Foreign Student Advisors (NAFSA)
meeting.

Although your travel budget will be nearly depleted by
spring, you should attend some of the well-organized programs
for juniors in New York and New Jersey if your college draws
students from those states. Spring travel to your feeder areas is
good because counselors want to know how the year went,
what you did with their applicants, and whether you can handle
any late applicants. They have a little more time than they did
in the fall and may be able to relax briefly with you. They may

ask you to help them in their counseling of juniors by having you talk to a general group about the advantages of a liberal arts education, about how colleges make their decisions, or about the availability of financial aid. They will be helping you by letting you help them. Many counselors are very busy in the spring, however, with scheduling and advising students about course selection, so your opportunities to visit will vary widely.

In a year, the cycle is completed and begins again. But now you are able to help others as well as being helped by them. As you go into the spring season, you should definitely plan to attend your state or regional ACAC meeting. While there, continue to utilize the clues mentioned above. You also now have a new responsibility: to look for newcomers whom you can welcome and introduce to your growing network of admissions counselor colleagues. Remember also that these associations want and welcome new people on their committees, and now that you have gotten your feet wet, you might be just the person they need. We are counting on you to continue, renew, and revitalize admissions to meet the challenges of the future, including going on further in helping each other.

Resource A.
Statement of Principles of Good Practice for Members of the National Association of College Admissions Counselors

High schools, colleges, universities, and other institutions and organizations dedicated to the promotion of formal education believe in the dignity, the worth, and the potentialities of every human being. They cooperate in the development of programs and services in postsecondary counseling, admissions, and financial assistance to eliminate bias related to race, creed, sex, political affiliation, or national origin. Believing that institutions of learning are only as strong ultimately as their human resources, they look upon counseling individual students about their postsecondary plans as an important aspect of their responsibilities.

They support, therefore, the following Statement of Principles of Good Practice for members of the National Association of College Admissions Counselors:

Approved June 1976; revised October 1981.

I. **Admissions Promotion and Recruitment**
    A. College and university members agree that:
        1. Admissions counselors are professional members of their institution's staff. As professionals, their compensation shall take the form of a fixed salary, rather than commissions or bonuses based on the number of students recruited.
        2. Admissions officers who are responsible for the development of publications used for their institution's promotional and recruitment activities shall:
            a. State clearly and precisely requirements for secondary school preparation, admissions tests, and transfer-student admissions.
            b. Include a current and accurate admissions calendar.
            c. Give precise information about opportunities and requirements for financial aid.
            d. Describe in detail any special programs such as overseas study, early decision, early admission, credit by examination, or advanced placement.
            e. Include pictures and descriptions of the campus and community that are current and realistic.
            f. Indicate that the institution is a member and has subscribed to this Statement.
        3. College and university members are responsible for all people who the institution involves in admissions, promotional, and recruitment activities (including their alumni, coaches, students, and faculty) and for educating them about the principles outlined in this Statement. Colleges and universities that engage the services of admissions management firms or consulting firms shall be responsible for assuring that such firms adhere to this Statement.

4. Admissions counselors shall be forthright, accurate, and comprehensive in presenting their institutions to high school personnel and prospective students, and shall:
   a. State clearly the admissions and other requirements of their institutions.
   b. Make clear all dates concerning application, notification, and candidates' reply requirements for both admissions and financial aid.
   c. Furnish data descriptive of currently enrolled classes.
   d. Avoid invidious comparisons of secondary or postsecondary institutions.
5. Admissions counselors shall avoid unprofessional promotional tactics, such as:
   a. Contracting with high school personnel for remuneration for referred students.
   b. Contracting with placement services that require a fee from the institution for each student enrolled.
   c. Encouraging students to transfer if they have shown no interest in doing so.
6. Admissions counselors shall not recruit students enrolled, registered, or who have filed an intent to register in writing or submitted a contractual deposit with other institutions unless the students initiate inquiries themselves or unless cooperation is sought from institutions that provide transfer programs.
7. College and university members shall be aware of the nature and intent of all admission referral services utilized by their institution (including their alumni, coaches, students and faculty) and seek to insure the appropriateness of such sources.

B. Secondary school members agree that they will:
1. Provide a program of counseling that does justice to the college opportunities sought by students and available to them.

2. Encourage students and their parents to take the initiative in learning about colleges and universities.

3. Invite college and university representatives to assist in counseling candidates about college opportunities.

4. Avoid invidious comparisons of secondary or postsecondary institutions.

5. Refuse unethical or unprofessional requests (e.g., for lists of top students, lists of athletes, etc.) from college or university representatives (e.g., alumni, coaches, etc.).

6. Refuse any reward or remuneration from a college, university, or private counseling service for placement of their school's students.

7. Be responsible for all personnel who may, on their behalf, become involved in counseling students on postsecondary options available and for educating them about the principles outlined in this Statement.

8. Be responsible for compliance with state/federal regulations with respect to the students' rights to privacy.

C. Associate members and other institutions or organizations which have subscribed to this statement agree that they will:

1. Provide accurate descriptions of the services available through such associate members or other institutions or organizations and shall disseminate without discrimination such descriptions to all interested students, parents, secondary schools, colleges, and universities.

2. Provide students with up-to-date information on postsecondary institutions and processes.

3. Assist students in discovering the colleges and universities that meet their abilities, needs, and interests.

4. Counsel students on all postsecondary options:

       college, university, vocational education, and job opportunities.

    5.   Report to secondary schools on students who have been referred to them so that accurate files can be maintained in the schools.

    6.   Be responsible for all personnel who may, on their behalf, become involved in admissions, promotional recruitment, and counseling activities, and for educating them about the principles outlined in this Statement.

  D.   College fairs, clearinghouses, and matching services that provide liaison between colleges and universities and students shall be considered a positive part of the admissions process if they effectively supplement other high school guidance activities and adhere to this Statement.

II.   **Application Procedures**

  A.   College and university members agree that they will:

    1.   Accept full responsibility for admissions decisions and for proper notification of those decisions to candidates and, when possible, to their secondary schools.

    2.   Receive information about candidates in confidence and respect completely, within the confines of federal or state law, the confidential nature of such data.

    3.   Notify high school personnel when the institution's admissions selection committee includes students.

    4.   Not apply newly-revised requirements to the disadvantage of a candidate whose secondary school course has been established in accordance with earlier requirements.

    5.   Notify candidates as soon as possible if they are clearly inadmissible.

    6.   Not deny admission to a candidate on the

grounds that the institution does not have assistance funds to meet the candidate's apparent financial need, except for foreign students.

7. Not require candidates or their schools to indicate the order of candidates' college or university preferences, except under early decision plans.

8. Permit candidates to choose without financial penalty among offers of admission until they have heard from all colleges and universities to which they have applied, or until May 1, whichever is earlier.

9. Not maintain a waiting list of unreasonable length or for an unreasonable period of time.

10. State clearly the application procedures for transfer students by informing candidates of deadlines, documents required, courses accepted, and course equivalency.

11. Not apply newly-revised requirements to the disadvantage of a candidate who has met all required deadlines, deposits and commitments according to the students' original notification from their institution.

B. Secondary school members agree that they will:

1. Provide colleges and universities with accurate, legible, and complete transcripts for the school's candidates.

2. Provide colleges and universities with description of the school's marking system and method of determining rank in class.

3. Describe clearly special curricular opportunities (e.g., honors, advanced placement courses, seminars, etc.).

4. Provide accurate descriptions of the candidates' personal qualities that are relevant to the admissions process.

5. Report any significant change in candidates'

status or qualifications between the time of recommendation and graduation.

6. Urge candidates to recognize and discharge their
    responsibilities in the admissions process by:

    a. Complying with requests for additional in-
        formation in a timely manner.

    b. Responding to institutional deadlines on
        admissions and refraining from stockpiling
        acceptances.

    c. Responding to institutional deadlines on
        room reservations, financial assistance, health
        records, and prescheduling, where all or any
        of these are applicable.

7. Not, without permission of candidates, reveal
    the candidates' college or university preference.

8. Advise students not to sign any contractual agree-
    ment with an institution without examining the
    provisions of the contract.

C. Associate Members and other institutions or organi-
    zations which have subscribed to this Statement
    agree that they will:

    1. Exercise their responsibility to the entire educa-
        tional community.

    2. Reduce unnecessary multiple applications.

    3. Discourage students from stockpiling offers of
        admission.

III. Financial Assistance

Member institutions are encouraged to support the principle of distributing financial assistance funds on the basis
of financial need. Where such assistance is based on need:

A. College and university members agree that:

    1. Financial assistance may be offered to a candi-
        date in the form of scholarships, grants, loans,
        or employment, either alone or in combination.

    2. They shall strive, through their publications and
        communications, to provide schools, parents,
        and students with factual information about

their institution's assistance opportunities, programs, and practices.

3. Financial assistance from colleges, universities, and other sources shall be viewed only as supplementary to the efforts of a student's family when the student is not self-supporting.

4. In determining the financial contribution of a candidate's family, they shall use methods that assess ability to pay in a consistent and equitable manner, such as those developed by the College Scholarship Service and the American College Testing Program.

5. They shall clearly state to each candidate for admission the total yearly cost of attending the institution, and shall state to each student seeking financial assistance an estimate of the amount of assistance which can be made available to the candidate.

6. They shall permit candidates to choose, without penalty, among offers of financial assistance until they have heard from all colleges and universities to which they have applied, or until May 1, whichever is earlier.

7. They shall clearly state policies on renewals of financial assistance.

8. They shall not announce publicly the amount of financial award to an individual candidate.

9. A student's need for financial assistance shall not be a criterion for admissions selection.

10. Notices of an institution's financial assistance decisions shall go to applicants before the date by which they must reply to the institution's offers of admission.

11. The full need of students shall be met to the extent possible within the institution's capabilities.

12. Awards shall be made to students who apply for renewal of financial assistance by reviewing the student's financial circumstances and establish-

ing the amount of assistance needed with full
consideration of the student's current need.

13.   They shall not offer financial awards to students
enrolled, registered, or who have filed an intent
to register in writing or submitted a contractual
deposit with other institutions unless the students initiate inquiries themselves or unless cooperation is sought from institutions that provide transfer programs.

14.   They shall not make financial awards to students
who have not submitted an admissions application.

B.   Secondary school members agree that they will:

1.   Refrain, in public announcements, from giving
the amounts of financial assistance received by
students.

2.   Advise students who have been awarded financial assistance by sources outside colleges that it
is their responsibility to notify the colleges to
which they have applied of the type and amount
of such outside assistance.

3.   Provide adequate opportunity within the school
for all able students to receive special recognition for their accomplishments, thus making it
unnecessary for colleges and universities to provide such honorary recognition through their financial assistance programs.

IV.   Advanced Standing Students and the Awarding of Credit

A.   College and University Members agree that:

1.   Placement, credit, and exemption policies that
are designed principally to recruit students are
inimical to the best interests of students.

2.   Student competency shall be evaluated through
use of validated methods and techniques.

3.   Policies and procedures for granting credit shall
be defined and published as part of an institution's pre-admissions information.

      4.   The evaluation of previously earned credit shall be done in a manner that insures the integrity of academic standards published by the admitting college or university.

B.   Secondary School Members agree that they will:

      1.   Alert students to the full implications of college and university placement, credit, and exemption policies with regard to the students' educational planning and goals.

      2.   Make students aware of the importance of accreditation.

      3.   Make students aware of the possibilities of earning credit through nontraditional educational experiences and examinations and alternative methods of instruction.

Resource B.
Statement of Students' Rights and Responsibilities in the College Admissions Process

YOU HAVE THE RIGHT.

1. To full information from colleges and universities concerning their admission and financial aid policies.

   Prior to applying, you should be fully informed of policies and procedures concerning application fees, deposits, refunds, housing and financial aid.

2. To defer responding to an offer of admission and/or financial aid until you have heard from all colleges and universities to which you have applied, or until May 1 (whichever is earlier).*

   *Should you be denied this right: (1) immediately request the college/university to extend the reply date; (2) notify your counselor and ask him/her to notify the President of the State or Regional ACAC. For ad-

Approved by NACAC Assembly October 1978.

570

ditional assistance, send a copy of your admission notification letter and all correspondence to:

Executive Director
NACAC
9933 Lawler Avenue, Suite 500
Skokie, Illinois 60077

YOU HAVE THE RESPONSIBILITY.
1. To be aware of the policies (deadlines, restrictions, etc.) regarding admissions and financial aid of colleges and universities of your choice.
2. To complete and submit required material to colleges and universities.
3. To meet all application deadlines.
4. To follow college application procedures of your high school.
5. *To notify the colleges and universities which have offered you admission of your acceptance or rejection of their offer as soon as you have heard from all to which you have applied, or by May 1 (whichever is earlier).*

Bibliography

Abramowitz, S., and Rosenfeld, S. (Eds.). *Declining Enrollments: The Challenge of the Coming Decade.* Washington, D.C.: U.S. Government Printing Office, 1978.

Alderman, D. L., and Powers, D. E. *The Effects of Special Preparation on SAT Verbal Scores.* RDR 78–79, No. 4. Princeton, N.J.: Educational Testing Service, 1979.

American Association of Collegiate Registrars and Admissions Officers. *A Guide to Postsecondary Institutions for Implementation of the Family Educational Rights and Privacy Act of 1974 as Amended.* Washington, D.C.: American Association of Collegiate Registrars and Admissions Officers, 1976.

American Association of Collegiate Registrars and Admissions Officers, College Entrance Examination Board, and National Association of College Admissions Officers. *College Admissions: A Broadening of Perspectives.* Papers presented at Colloquium on Marketing, Student Admissions, and the Public Interest. New York: College Entrance Examination Board, 1980.

American College Testing Program. *The High School Profile Report, Years 1975–1976.* Iowa City: American College Testing Program, 1977.

American College Testing Program. *Using the ACT Assessment on Campus.* Iowa City: American College Testing Program, 1978.

573

American Council on Education. *The American Freshman: National Norms for Fall 1979.* Los Angeles: Graduate School of Education, University of California, 1979.

American Personnel and Guidance Association. *Ethical Standards.* Washington, D.C.: American Personnel and Guidance Association, 1974.

American School Counselor Association. *Code of Ethics.* Washington, D.C.: American School Counselor Association, 1972.

Ansoff, H. I. "Strategies for Diversification." *Harvard Business Review,* 1957, *35* (5), 113–127.

Astin, A. W. "Further Validation of the Environmental Assessment Technique." *Journal of Educational Psychology,* 1963, *54,* 64–71.

Astin, A. W. *The College Environment.* Washington, D.C.: American Council on Education, 1968.

Astin, A. W. *Predicting Academic Performance in College.* New York: Free Press, 1971.

Astin, A. W. "Racial Considerations in Admissions." In E. A. Epps (Ed.), *Black Students in White Schools.* Worthington, Ohio: Charles Jones, 1972.

Astin, A. W. *Preventing Students from Dropping Out.* San Francisco: Jossey-Bass, 1975.

Astin, A. W. *Four Critical Years: Effects of College on Beliefs, Attitudes, and Knowledge.* San Francisco: Jossey-Bass, 1977.

Astin, A. W., and Panos, R. "A National Research Data Bank for Higher Education." *Educational Record,* 1966, *47,* 5–17.

Astin, A. W., and Panos, R. *The Educational and Vocational Development of College Students.* Washington, D.C.: American Council on Education, 1969.

Astin, H., and others. *Higher Education and the Disadvantaged Student.* Washington, D.C.: Human Science Press, 1972.

Baird, L. L., Hartnett, R. T., and Associates. *Understanding Student and Faculty Life: Using Campus Surveys to Improve Academic Decision Making.* San Francisco: Jossey-Bass, 1980.

Barre, M. E. *Counselor's Sourcebook for College Planning.* Boston: Houghton-Mifflin, n.d.

Barron's Profiles of American Colleges. Woodbury, N.Y.: Barron's Educational Series, 1978.

Bartlett, W. E., and Oldham, D. "Career Adjustment Counseling of 'Young-Old' Women." *Vocational Guidance Quarterly*, 1978, *27* (2), 56–164.

Beals, E. W. "The Changing Role of the Admissions Officer." *College Board Review*, 1979, *112*, 2–7.

Beaton, A. E., Hilton, T. L., and Schrader, W. B. *Changes in the Verbal Abilities of High School Seniors, College Entrants, and SAT Candidates Between 1960 and 1972*. New York: College Entrance Examination Board, 1977.

Benson, L. L. "Students' Problems in Educational Planning and Their Need for Assistance." In P. Newman and B. Newman (Eds.), *Preparing School Counselors in Educational Guidance*. New York: College Entrance Examination Board, 1967.

Binstock, R. H., and Shanas, E. (Eds.). *Handbook of Aging and the Social Sciences*. New York: Van Nostrand Reinhold, 1976.

Birren, J. E., and Schaie, K. W. (Eds.). *Handbook on the Psychology of Aging*. New York: Van Nostrand Reinhold, 1977.

Bisconti, A. S., and Solmon, L. C. *College Education on the Job— The Graduate's Viewpoint*. Bethlehem, Pa.: CPC Foundation, 1976.

Bok, D. *President's Report, 1976–1977*. Cambridge, Mass.: Harvard University, 1978.

Bolles, R. N. *What Color Is Your Parachute?* Berkeley, Calif.: Ten Speed Press, 1972.

Bolles, R. N. "Training for Transition: Changing Careers." *Change*, 1979, *11* (5), 40–44.

Bonham, G. W. "Inching Toward the Learning Society." *Change*, 1979, *11* (5), 3–7.

Boorstin, D. J. *The Lost World of Thomas Jefferson*. Boston: Beacon Press, 1960.

Borup, J. S. "The Validity of American College Test for Discerning Potential Academic Achievement Levels: Ethnic and Sex Groups." *Journal of Educational Research*, 1971, *65*, 3–6.

Bowen, H. R. *Investment in Learning: The Individual and Social Value of American Higher Education*. San Francisco: Jossey-Bass, 1977.

Bowen, H. R. *The Costs of Higher Education: How Much Do Colleges and Universities Spend Per Student and How Much Should They Spend?* San Francisco: Jossey-Bass, 1980.

Bowers, J. E. "Selection of Beginning Freshmen at the University of Illinois." Mimeographed. Urbana: Office of Admissions and Records, University of Illinois, 1964.

Boyan, D. R. (Ed.). *Open Doors: 1979/1980.* New York: Institute of International Education, 1981.

Boyd, W. M., II. *Desegregating America's Colleges: A Nationwide Survey of Black Students, 1972-1973.* New York: Praeger, 1974.

Boyd, W. M., II. "The Forgotten Side of the Black Undergraduate: An Assessment of Academic Achievements and Aspirations During the 1970s." Paper presented at annual meeting of the American Educational Research Association, San Francisco, April 1979.

Brawer, F. B. *New Perspectives on Personality Development in College Students.* San Francisco: Jossey-Bass, 1973.

Breland, H. M. *Family Configuration Effects and the Decline in College Admissions Test Scores: A Review of the Zajonc Hypothesis.* New York: College Entrance Examination Board, 1977.

Breland, H. M., and Ironson, G. H. "DeFunis Reconsidered: A Comparative Analysis of Alternative Admissions Strategies." *Journal of Educational Measurement,* 1976, *13*, 89-99.

Brody, E. (Ed.). *Minority Group Adolescents in the United States.* Baltimore: Williams & Wilkins, 1968.

Broudy, H. S. *Building a Philosophy of Education.* Englewood Cliffs, N.J.: Prentice-Hall, 1961.

Brown, G. H., and others. *The Coalition of Education for Hispanic Americans.* Washington, D.C.: National Center for Education Statistics, 1980.

Brown, L. K. "Women and Business Management." *Signs,* 1979, *5* (2), 266-288.

Brown, S., and Ervin, L. "Relationship of Special Studies to Dropout Rates of Black and White College Students." *Psychological Reports,* 1979, *44*, 73-74.

Buriel, R., and Saenz, E. "Psychocultural Characteristics of College-Bound and Noncollege-Bound Chicanas." *Journal of Social Psychology,* 1980, *110*, 245-251.

Burlew, K. H. "Black Youth and Higher Education: A Longitudinal Study." *Resources in Education.* ERIC/CAPS. Ann Arbor: University of Michigan, 1980.

Carnegie Council on Policy Studies in Higher Education. *Fair Practices in Higher Education: Rights and Responsibilities of Students and Their Colleges in a Period of Intensified Competition for Enrollments.* San Francisco: Jossey-Bass, 1979.

Carp, F. M. "Housing and Living Environments of Older People." In R. H. Binstock and E. Shanas (Eds.), *Handbook of Aging and the Social Sciences.* New York: Van Nostrand Reinhold, 1976.

Carter, T. P., and Segura, R. D. *Mexican Americans in School: A Decade of Change.* New York: College Entrance Examination Board, 1979.

Carter, V. L., and Garigan, C. W. (Eds.). *A Marketing Approach to Student Recruitment: The Best of Case Currents.* Washington, D.C.: Council for the Advancement and Support of Education, 1979.

Cass, J., and Birnbaum, M. *Comparative Guide to American Colleges.* New York: Harper & Row, 1979.

Centra, J. A., and Rock, D. A. "College Environments and Student Academic Achievement." *American Educational Research Journal,* 1971, *8,* 623–634.

Chall, J. S., Conrad, S. S., and Harris, S. H. *An Analysis of Textbooks in Relation to Declining SAT Scores.* New York: College Entrance Examination Board, 1977.

Chamberlain, F. M. "A Blueprint for Student Recruitment." *Association of Governing Boards Reports,* Jan./Feb. 1977, pp. 31–37.

Chapman, D. W., and others. *College Recruiting in the Next Ten Years.* Ann Arbor: Center for Helping Organizations Improve Choice in Education, University of Michigan, 1979.

Chickering, A. W. *Education and Identity.* San Francisco: Jossey-Bass, 1969.

Chickering, A. W. *Commuting Versus Resident Students: Overcoming Educational Inequities of Living Off Campus.* San Francisco: Jossey-Bass, 1974.

Clark, B. R. *The Distinctive College: Antioch, Reed, and Swarthmore.* Hawthorne, N.Y.: Aldine, 1970.

Clark, B. R., and others. *Students and Colleges: Interaction and Change.* Berkeley: Center for Research and Development in Higher Education, University of California, 1972.

Clark, K. *Civilisation.* New York: Harper & Row, 1969.

Cleary, T. A. "Test Bias: Prediction of Grades of Negro and White Students in Integrated Colleges." *Journal of Educational Measurement,* 1968, *5,* 115–124.

Cleary, T. A., and McCandless, S. A. *Summary of Score Changes (in Other Tests).* New York: College Entrance Examination Board, 1976.

Cleary, T. A., and others. "Educational Uses of Tests with Disadvantaged Students." *American Psychologist,* 1975, *30,* 15–41.

Coffin, W. S., Jr. "Not Yet A Good Man." *New York Times,* June 19, 1973, p. 39.

Cohen, A. M., and Brawer, F. B. *The American Community College.* San Francisco: Jossey-Bass, 1982.

Cole, N. S. "Bias in Selection." *Journal of Educational Measurement,* 1973, *10,* 237–255.

Coleman, J. S. *Equality of Educational Opportunity.* Washington, D.C.: Office of Education, Department of Health, Education and Welfare, 1966.

Coles, R. "Students Who Say No: Blacks, Radicals, Hippies." *International Psychiatry Clinics,* 1970, *7,* 3–14.

College Board. *ATP Guide for Schools and Colleges.* New York: College Board, 1982.

College Board and American Association of Collegiate Registrars and Admissions Officers. *Survey of Undergraduate Admissions Policies, Practices, and Procedures.* New York: College Board, 1980.

College Entrance Examination Board. *Access to College for Mexican Americans in the Southwest.* Higher Education Surveys, Report 6. New York: College Entrance Examination Board, 1972.

College Entrance Examination Board. *A Role for Marketing in College Admissions.* New York: College Entrance Examination Board, 1976.

College Entrance Examination Board. *ATP Guide for High Schools and Colleges.* New York: College Entrance Examination Board, 1980.

Connors, E. T. *Student Discipline and the Law.* Bloomington, Ind.: Phi Delta Kappa Educational Foundation, 1979.

Cope, R. *Revolving College Doors*. New York: Wiley, 1975.

Copeland, L. L. "An Exploration of the Causes of Black Attrition at Predominantly White Institutions of Higher Education." Unpublished doctoral dissertation, University of Michigan, 1976.

Cortes, C. E. "Concepts and Strategies for Teaching the Mexican American Experience." In *New Approaches to Bilingual, Bicultural Education*. Austin, Texas: Dissemination and Assessment Center for Bilingual Education, 1977.

Cranford, B. "Defending Liberal Arts Graduates." *Chronicle of Higher Education*, Oct. 22, 1979, p. 8.

Cronbach, L. J. "Equity in Selection—Where Psychometrics and Political Philosophy Meet." *Journal of Educational Measurement*, 1976, *13*, 31–41.

Cross, K. P. *Accent on Learning: Improving Instruction and Reshaping the Curriculum*. San Francisco: Jossey-Bass, 1976.

Cucio, W. H. (Ed.). *Readings in American Education*. Chicago: Scott, Foresman, 1963.

Darlington, R. B. "A Defense of 'Rational' Personnel Selection, and Two New Methods." *Journal of Educational Measurement*, 1976, *13*, 43–52.

Davis, R. G., and Lewis, G. M. "The Demographic Background to Changing Enrollments and School Needs." In S. Abramowitz and S. Rosenfeld (Eds.), *Declining Enrollments: The Challenge of the Coming Decade*. Washington, D.C.: U.S. Government Printing Office, 1978.

Derbyshire, R., and Brody, E. "Marginality, Identity, and Behavior in the American Negro: A Functional Analysis." *International Journal of Social Psychiatry*, 1964, *10*, 7–13.

Dewey, J. *Democracy and Education*. New York: Macmillan, 1916.

Dissemination and Assessment Center for Bilingual Education. *New Approaches to Bilingual, Bicultural Education*. Austin, Texas: Dissemination and Assessment Center for Bilingual Education, 1977.

Dominick, C. A., and others. "College Recruiting in the Next Ten Years." *National Association of College Admissions Counselors Journal*, 1980, *24* (2), 2–7.

Douglass College Women's College Study Committee. *Summary of Research Literature and Working Bibliography*. New Brunswick, N.J.: Douglass College, Rutgers University, 1974.

Dressel, P. L. *Handbook of Academic Evaluation: Assessing Institutional Effectiveness, Student Progress, and Professional Perfor-*

mance for Decision Making in Higher Education. San Francisco: Jossey-Bass, 1976.

Drew, D. E., and Schuster, J. H. "Recommended Reading for College Presidents." *Change*, July–Aug. 1980, pp. 33–38.

Dubin, R., and Taveggia, T. C. *The Teaching-Learning Paradox.* Eugene: Center for Advanced Study of Educational Administration, University of Oregon, 1968.

Dunn, S. L. "The Case of the Vanishing Colleges." *Futurist*, Oct. 1979, *13*, 385–388.

Educational Testing Service. *Test Scores and Family Income.* Princeton, N.J.: Educational Testing Service, 1980a.

Educational Testing Service. *Test Use and Validity: A Response to Charges in the Nader/Nairn Report on ETS.* Princeton, N.J.: Educational Testing Service, 1980b.

Eisenberg, L. Lecture given at Renard Hospital, St. Louis, Missouri, 1980.

Epps, E. A. (Ed.). *Black Students in White Schools.* Worthington, Ohio: Charles Jones, 1972.

Erikson, E. *Identity, Youth, and Crisis.* New York: Norton, 1968.

Erikson, R. J. "Characteristics of Black College Freshmen." *College Student Journal*, 1979, *13*, 147–152.

Federal Trade Commission, Bureau of Consumer Protection. *Effects of Coaching on Standardized Admissions Examinations: Revised Statistical Analysis of Data Gathered by the Boston Regional Office of the Federal Trade Commission.* Washington, D.C.: Federal Trade Commission, Bureau of Consumer of Protection, 1979.

Feldman, K. A., and Newcomb, T. M. *The Impact of College on Students.* San Francisco: Jossey-Bass, 1969.

Fincher, C. "Is the SAT Worth Its Salt? An Evaluation of the Scholastic Aptitude Test in the University System of Georgia over a Thirteen Year Period." *Review of Educational Research*, 1974, *44*, 292–305.

Fishlow, H. "Demography and Changing Enrollments." In S. Abramowitz and S. Rosenfeld (Eds.), *Declining Enrollments: The Challenge of the Coming Decade.* Washington, D.C.: U.S. Government Printing Office, 1978.

Fiske, E. B. "The Marketing of the Colleges." *Atlantic*, 1979, *244* (4), 93–98.

Flaugher, R. L. "The Many Definitions of Test Bias." *American Psychologist,* 1978, *33,* 671–679.

Ford, D. H., and Urban, H. B. "College Dropouts: Successes or Failures." In L. A. Pervin, L. E. Reik, and W. Dalrymple (Eds.), *The College Dropout and the Utilization of Talent.* Princeton, N.J.: Princeton University Press, 1966.

Ford, S. F., and Campos, S. *Summary Validity Data from the Admissions Testing Program Validity Study Service.* New York: College Entrance Examination Board, 1977.

Fram, E. H. "Marketing Revisited." *College Board Review,* 1974, *94* (4), 7–8, 22.

Gaither, G. H. "Some Tools and Techniques of Market Research for Students." In J. A. Lucas (Ed.), *New Directions for Institutional Research: Developing a Total Marketing Plan,* no. 21. San Francisco: Jossey-Bass, 1979.

Garcia, S., and Seligsohn, H. "Undergraduate Black Student Retention Revisited." *Educational Record,* 1978, *59,* 156–165.

Geiger, R. L. "The Case of the Missing Students." *Change,* 1978–79, *10,* 64–65.

Gelatt, H. B. "Information and Decision Theories Applied to College Choice and Planning." In P. Newman and B. Newman (Eds.), *Preparing School Counselors in Educational Guidance.* New York: College Entrance Examination Board, 1967.

Gelatt, H. B., and others. *Decisions and Outcomes.* New York: College Entrance Examination Board, 1979.

Gettzer, H., and Rico, A. "The Positioning Era: A Marketing Strategy for College Admissions in the 1980s." In *A Role for Marketing in College Admissions.* New York: College Entrance Examination Board, 1976.

Gibbs, J. T. "Black Students/White University: Different Expectations." *Personnel and Guidance Journal,* 1973, *51,* 463–469.

Gibbs, J. T. "Patterns of Adaptation Among Black Students at a Predominantly White University." *American Journal of Orthopsychiatry,* 1974, *44,* 728–740.

Gibbs, J. T. "Use of Mental Health Services by Black Students at a Predominantly White University: A Three-Year Study." *American Journal of Orthopsychiatry,* 1975, *45,* 430–445.

Gibbs, J. T. "Black Students at Integrated Colleges: Problems and

Prospects." In C. V. Willie (Ed.), *Black, Brown, White Relations.* New Brunswick, N.J.: Transaction Books, 1977.

Gibbs, J. T. "The Interpersonal Orientation in Mental Health Consultation: Toward a Model of Ethnic Variations in Consultation." *Journal of Community Psychology,* 1980, *8,* 195–207.

Glover, R. H. *Major Societal Changes in U.S. (1933–1944 and 1945–1975): Contextual Mapping.* New York: College Entrance Examination Board, 1977.

Goldman, R. D., and Hewitt, B. N. "An Investigation of Test Bias for Mexican American College Students." *Journal of Educational Measurement,* 1975, *12,* 187–196.

Goldman, R. D., and Richards, R. "The SAT Prediction of Grades for Mexican-American Versus Anglo-American Students at the University of California, Riverside." *Journal of Educational Measurement,* 1974, *11,* 129–135.

Goldman, R. D., and Widawski, M. H. "An Analysis of Types of Errors in the Selection of Minority Students." *Journal of Educational Measurement,* 1976, *13,* 185–200.

Goldwater, B., Jr. "Proposed Changes in the Privacy Act." *National Association of College Admissions Counselors Journal,* 1980, *22* (3), 9–11.

Grabowski, S. M. *Marketing in Higher Education.* AAHE-ERIC/ Higher Education Research Report No. 5. Washington, D.C.: American Association for Higher Education, 1981.

The Great Core Curriculum Debate: Education as a Mirror of Culture. New Rochelle, N.Y.: Change Magazine Press, 1979.

Guildroy, J. "Counselor-Student-Parent Relationships: Ethical Quandaries and Legal Quagmires." *College Board Review,* 1979, *113,* 8–13.

Haagen, C. H. *Venturing Beyond the Campus: Students Who Leave College.* Middletown, Conn.: Wesleyan University Press, 1977.

Haettenschwiller, D. "Counseling Black Students in Special Programs." *Personnel and Guidance Journal,* 1971, *50,* 29–37.

Halstead, D. K. (Ed.). *Higher Education Planning: A Bibliographic Handbook.* Washington, D.C.: U.S. Government Printing Office, 1979.

Hammond, C. "Paranoia and Prejudice: Recognition and Management of the Student from a Deprived Background." *International Psychiatry Clinics,* 1970, 7, 35–48.

Harnischfeger, A., and Wiley, D. *Achievement Test Score Decline: Do We Need to Worry?* Chicago: CEMREL, 1975.

Haro, C. M. *Criticisms of Traditional Post Secondary School Admissions Criteria: A Search for Alternatives.* Occasional Paper No. 1. Los Angeles: Chicano Studies Center Publications, University of California, 1978.

Harper, F. D. *Black Students, White Campus.* Washington, D.C.: APGA Press, 1975.

Harvard University and Radcliffe College. *Secondary School Report.* Cambridge, Mass.: Office of Admissions and Financial Aid, Harvard University/Radcliffe College, 1980.

Haynes, L. L., III (Comp.). *A Critical Examination of the Adams Case: A Source Book.* Washington, D.C.: Institute for Services to Education, 1978.

Heath, D. H. *Growing Up in College: Liberal Education and Maturity.* San Francisco: Jossey-Bass, 1968.

Heist, P., and others. "Personality and Scholarship." *Science,* Feb. 10, 1961, pp. 362–367.

Hennig, M., and Jardim, A. *The Managerial Woman.* New York: Doubleday, 1976.

Henton, J., and others. "Crisis Reactions of College Freshmen as a Function of Family Support Systems." *Personnel and Guidance Journal,* 1980, 58 (8), 508–511.

Herr, E. L., and Cramer, S. H. *Guidance of the College Bound.* New York: Appleton-Century-Crofts, 1968.

Herr, E. L., and Cramer, S. H. *Career Guidance Through the Life Span.* Boston: Little, Brown, 1979.

Hersey, J., and others. "Task Force on Confidentiality—A Report." *National Association of College Admissions Counselors Journal,* 1978, 22 (4), 7–9.

High School Graduates: Projections for the Fifty States. Boulder, Colo.: Western Interstate Commission for Higher Education, National Institute of Independent Colleges and Universities, Teachers Insurance and Annuity Association, 1979.

Holinger, P. "Violent Deaths Among the Young: Recent Trends in Suicide, Homicide, and Accidents." *American Journal of Psychiatry,* 1979, 136, 1144–1147.

Hollingshead, A., and Redlich, F. *Social Class and Mental Illness.* New York: Wiley, 1958.

Hood, A. *What Type of College for What Type of Student?* Minneapolis: University of Minnesota Press, 1968.

Howard, W. R. "Community Transactions and the Marketing Process." In J. A. Lucas (Ed.); *New Directions for Institutional Research: Developing a Total Marketing Plan,* no. 21. San Francisco: Jossey-Bass, 1979.

Hoy, J. C. *Choosing a College.* New York: Dell, 1970.

Hoy, J. C. "A Question of Balance." *College Board Review,* Fall 1976, pp. 6–10, 29–32.

Hunter, J. E., and Schmidt, F. L. "Critical Analysis of the Statistical and Ethical Implications of Various Definitions of Test Bias." *Psychological Bulletin,* 1976, *83,* 1053–1071.

Hutchins, R. M. "Is Democracy Possible?" *Saturday Review of Literature,* February 21, 1959, p. 17.

Ihlanfeldt, W. *Achieving Optimal Enrollments and Tuition Revenues: A Guide to Modern Methods of Market Research, Student Recruitment, and Institutional Pricing.* San Francisco: Jossey-Bass, 1980.

Inhelder, B., and Piaget, J. *The Growth of Logical Thinking from Childhood to Adolescence.* New York: Basic Books, 1958.

Jackson, R. *Comparison of SAT Score Trends in Selected Schools Judged to Have Traditional or Experimental Orientations.* New York: College Entrance Examination Board, 1976.

Jackson, R. "The Scholastic Aptitude Test: A Response to Slack and Porter's 'A Critical Appraisal.'" *Harvard Educational Review,* 1980, *3,* 382–391.

Jacob, P. E. *Changing Values in College.* New York: Harper & Row, 1957.

Jacobson, R. L. "Campus Managers Shift Focus to Academic Quality." *Chronicle of Higher Education,* March 10, 1980, pp. 9–10.

Jefferson, T. "Letter to George Wythe." In I. R. Sawvel (Ed.), *Complete Annals of Thomas Jefferson.* New York: De Capo Press, 1970.

Jencks, C. "The *Wrong* Answer for Schools Is: (b) Back to Basics." *Washington Post,* Feb. 19, 1972, C1, pp. 4–5.

Jenkins, H. M. (Ed.). *Foreign Student Recruitment: Realities and Recommendations.* New York: College Entrance Examination Board, 1980.

Johnson, R. "Blacks and Higher Education—A Decade in Review." *Journal of Afro-American Issues,* 1977, *5,* 88–97.

Jones, L. G. *Black Students Enrolled in White Colleges and Universities: Their Attitudes and Perceptions.* Atlanta: Southern Regional Education Board, 1979.

Kanter, R. M. *Men and Women of the Corporation.* New York: Basic Books, 1977.

Katz, J., and Associates. *No Time for Youth: Growth and Constraint in College Students.* San Francisco: Jossey-Bass, 1968.

Kohlberg, L., and Kramer, R. "Continuities and Discontinuities in Childhood and Adult Moral Development." *Human Development,* 1969, *12,* 93–120.

Kotler, P. *Marketing for Nonprofit Organizations.* Englewood Cliffs, N.J.: Prentice-Hall, 1975.

Kotler, P. "Applying Marketing Theory to College Admissions." In *A Role for Marketing in College Admissions.* New York: College Entrance Examination Board, 1976.

Kotler, P. "Strategies for Introducing Marketing into Nonprofit Organizations." *Journal of Marketing,* 1979, *43,* 37–44.

Kuder, G. F. *Kuder DD Occupational Interest Survey.* Chicago: Science Research Associates, 1979.

Kuehn, J. K., and Kuehn, J. L. "Conspiracy of Silence: Psychiatric Counseling with Students at High Risk for Academic Failure." *American Journal of Psychiatry,* 1975, *132,* 1207–1209.

Langston, I. A., and Chang, O. H. "The Predictive Power of a Selection Index Based on Five Years Data, at the University of Illinois at Urbana-Champaign." Mimeographed, Research Memorandum 80-2. Champaign: Office of School and College Relations, University of Illinois, 1980.

Larkin, P. G. "Market Research Methods for Improving College Responsiveness." In J. A. Lucas (Ed.), *New Directions for Institutional Research: Developing a Total Marketing Plan,* no. 21. San Francisco: Jossey-Bass, 1979.

Lavin, D. E. *The Prediction of Academic Performance.* New York: Russell Sage Foundation, 1965.

Lawton, M. P. "The Impact of Environment on Aging." In J. E. Birren and K. W. Schaie (Eds.), *Handbook on the Psychology of Aging.* New York: Van Nostrand Reinhold, 1977.

Learned, W. S., and Wood, B. D. *The Student and His Knowledge.* Bulletin 29. New York: Carnegie Foundation for the Advancement of Teaching, 1938.

Lenning, O., and others. *Nonintellective Correlates of Grades, Persistence, and Academic Learning in College.* Iowa City: ACT Publications, 1974.

Lenz, E., and Hansen-Shaevitz, M. *So You Want to Go Back to School: Facing the Realities of Reentry.* New York: McGraw-Hill, 1977.

Levinson, D. J., and others. "Periods in the Adult Development of Men: Ages 18 to 45." *Counseling Psychologist,* 1976, *6*, 21–25.

Linn, R. L. "Fair Test Use in Selection." *Review of Educational Research,* 1973, *43*, 139–161.

Linn, R. L. "In Search of Fair Selection Procedures." *Journal of Educational Measurement,* 1976, *13*, 53–58.

Litten, L. "Market Structure and Institutional Position in Geographic Market Segments." *Research in Higher Education,* 1979, *11*, 59–83.

Loeb, J. W. "Validity of the Selection Index for Fall 1968 Urbana-Champaign Campus Freshmen." Champaign: Office of School and College Relations, University of Illinois, 1969.

Loeb, J. W. "The Relationship of Socioeconomic Status and Selection Index Among Urbana-Champaign Liberal Arts and Sciences Freshmen." Mimeographed, Research Memorandum 70-3. Champaign; Office of School and College Relations, University of Illinois, 1970.

Loeb, J. W. "High School Performance as Predictive of College Performance." *National Association of Secondary School Principals Bulletin,* 1972, *56*, 19–26.

Loeb, J. W., and Mueller, D. J. "The Use of a Scale of High Schools in Predicting College Grades." *Educational and Psychological Measurement,* 1970, *30*, 381–386.

Lowman, R. P., and Spuck, D. W. "Predictors of College Success for the Disadvantaged Mexican American." *Journal of College Student Personnel,* 1975, *16*, 40–48.

Lucas, J. A. (Ed.). *New Directions for Institutional Research: Developing a Total Marketing Plan,* no. 21. San Francisco: Jossey-Bass, 1979.

Lyons, J. E. "The Adjustment of Black Students to Predominantly White Colleges." *Journal of Negro Education,* 1973, *42*, 462–466.

McCurdy, J., and Speich, D. "The Decline of American Education." *Los Angeles Times,* Aug. 15, 16, 17, 1978.

Mackey, E. "Some Observations on Coping Styles of Black Students on White Campuses." *Journal of American College Health Association,* 1972, *21,* 126–130.

McLeish, A. *Education in the Nation's Service.* New York: The Woodrow Wilson Foundation, 1960.

Magarrell, J. "The 1980's: Higher Education's 'Not-Me' Decade." *Chronicle of Higher Education,* Jan. 7, 1980, p. 8.

Malone, D. (Ed.). *The Jeffersonian Heritage.* Boston: Beacon Press, 1953.

Marron, J. E. *Preparatory School Test Preparation: Special Test Preparation, Its Effect on College Board Scores, and the Relationship of Affected Scores to Subsequent College Performance.* Study No. 1-A 1 02-63-001. West Point, N.Y.: U.S. Military Academy, 1965.

Martinez, J. L. (Ed.). *Chicano Psychology.* New York: Academic Press, 1977.

Martinez, V. "Affirmative Action Being Eroded." *Bridge the Gap,* April 1978, *3,* 5, 7.

Maxey, J. Personal correspondence with Stephen Lovette from American College Testing Program. Iowa City, 1980.

Mayhew, L. B. *Surviving the Eighties: Strategies and Procedures for Solving Fiscal and Enrollment Problems.* San Francisco: Jossey-Bass, 1979.

Messick, S., and others. *The Effectiveness of Coaching for the SAT: Review and Reanalysis of Research from the Fifties to the FTC.* Princeton, N.J.: Educational Testing Service, 1981.

Miller, M. "Cantaloupes, Carrots & Counseling: Implications of Dietary Interventions for Counselors." *Personnel and Guidance Journal,* 1980, *58* (6), 421–425.

Mitchell, J. S. *I Can Be Anything.* New York: College Entrance Examination Board, 1978.

Modu, C., and Stern, J. *The Stability of the SAT-Verbal Score Scale.* New York: College Entrance Examination Board, 1977.

Moll, R. "The College Admissions Game." *Harper's Magazine,* March 1978, pp. 3, 36.

Moll, R. *Playing the Private College Admissions Game.* New York: Times Books, 1979.

Moos, R. H. *Evaluating Educational Environments: Procedures, Measures, Findings, and Policy Implications.* San Francisco: Jossey-Bass, 1979.

Munger, S. *A Guide to the College Admissions Process.* Skokie, Ill.: National Association of College Admissions Counselors, 1979.

Nahemow, L., and Lawton, M. P. "Toward an Ecological Theory of Adaptation and Aging." In. W.R.E. Preiser (Ed.), *Environmental Design Research,* Vol. 1. Stroudsberg, Pa.: Dowden, Hutchinson, and Ross, 1973.

Nairn, A. *The Reign of ETS: The Corporation That Makes Up Minds.* Washington, D.C.: Learning Research Project, 1980.

Nardone, T. "The Job Outlook in Brief." *Occupational Outlook Quarterly,* Spring 1980, *24,* 3.

National Association of College Admissions Counselors. *Statement of Principles of Good Practice for Members of the National Association of College Admissions Counselors.* Skokie, Ill.: National Association of College Admissions Counselors, 1976.

National Association of College Admissions Counselors. *Statement of Students' Rights and Responsibilities in the College Admissions Process.* Skokie, Ill.: National Association of College Admissions Counselors, 1978.

National Association of Secondary School Principals. "Student Attendance and Absenteeism." *The Practitioner,* March 1975.

National Association of Secondary School Principals. *Guidelines for Improving SAT Scores.* Reston, Va.: National Association of Secondary School Principals, 1978.

National Center for Education Statistics. *Digest of Education Statistics, 1975.* Washington, D.C.: U.S. Government Printing Office, 1975.

National Center for Education Statistics. Unpublished data from the survey of "Fall Enrollments in Institutions of Higher Education, 1978." Washington, D.C.: U.S. Department of Health, Education and Welfare, 1978.

National Center for Education Statistics. *Digest of Education Statistics, 1979.* Washington, D.C.: U.S. Government Printing Office, 1979.

National Education Association. *Code of Ethics for the Education Profession.* Washington, D.C.: National Education Association, 1975.

Nelson, J. E. *A Review of Data Available Regarding Family Income and Financial Aid Characteristics of Students.* New York: College Entrance Examination Board, 1977.

Newcomb, T. M. *Personality and Social Change: Attitude Formation in a Student Community.* New York: Holt, Rinehart and Winston, 1943.

Newman, P., and Newman, B. (Eds.). *Preparing School Counselors in Educational Guidance.* New York: College Entrance Examination Board, 1967.

Newman, P., and Newman, B. "Identity Formation and the College Experience." *Adolescence,* 1978, *13* (50), 311-326.

Nicholi, A. M., "Harvard Dropouts: Some Psychiatric Findings." In O. Lenning, and others, *Nonintellective Correlates of Grades, Persistence, and Academic Learning in College.* Iowa City: ACT Publications, 1974.

Nichols, R. C. "Effect of Various College Characteristics on Student Aptitude Test Scores." *Journal of Educational Psychology,* 1964, *55* (1), 45-54.

Noel, L. "College Student Retention—A Campus-Wide Responsibility." *National Association of College Admissions Counselors Journal,* 1976, *21* (1), 33-36.

Novick, M. R., and Ellis, D. D., Jr. "Equal Opportunity in Educational and Employment Selection." *American Psychologist,* 1977, *32,* 306-320.

Novick, M. R., and Lindley, D. V. "The Use of More Realistic Utility Functions in Educational Applications." *Journal of Educational Measurement,* 1978, *15,* 181-191.

Novick, M. R., and Petersen, N. S. "Towards Equalizing Educational and Employment Opportunity." *Journal of Educational Measurement,* 1976, *13,* 77-78.

Oates, J., and Williamson, S. "Women's Colleges and Women Achievers." *Signs,* 1978, *3,* (4), 795-806.

Ochsner, N. L., and Solmon, L. C. *College Education and Employment—The Recent Graduates.* Bethlehem, Pa.: CPC Foundation, 1979.

Oliver, E. E. "Establishing Admissions Policy." In C. J. Quann and Associates, *Admissions, Academic Records, and Registrar Services: A Handbook of Policies and Procedures.* San Francisco: Jossey-Bass, 1979.

Oliver, E. E. "Implementing Admissions Policy." In C. J. Quann and Associates, *Admissions, Academic Records, and Registrar Services: A Handbook of Policies and Procedures.* San Francisco: Jossey-Bass, 1979.

Olmedo, E. L. "Psychological Testing and the Chicano: A Reassessment." In J. L. Martinez, Jr. (Ed.), *Chicano Psychology.* New York: Academic Press, 1977.

Pace, C. R. *College and University Environment Scales: Technical Manual.* (2nd ed.) Princeton, N.J.: Educational Testing Service, 1969.

Pace, C. R. *The Demise of Diversity?* Berkeley, Calif.: Carnegie Commission on Higher Education, 1974.

Pace, C. R. *Measuring Outcomes of College: Fifty Years of Findings and Recommendations for the Future.* San Francisco: Jossey-Bass, 1979.

Pace, C. R., and Stern, G. G. "An Approach to the Measurement of Psychological Characteristics of College Environments." *Journal of Educational Psychology,* 1958, *49,* 269-277.

Panos, R., and Astin, A. W. *Attrition Among College Students.* Washington, D.C.: American Council on Education, 1967.

Peng, S., and Fetters, W. "Variables Involved in Withdrawal During the First Two Years of College: Preliminary Findings from the National Longitudinal Study of the High School Class of 1972." *American Educational Research Journal,* 1978, *15,* 361-372.

Perry, W. G. *Forms of Intellectual and Ethical Development in the College Years.* New York: Holt, Rinehart and Winston, 1970.

Pervin, L. A. "Performance and Satisfaction as a Function of Individual-Environment Fit." *Psychological Bulletin,* 1968, *69,* 56-58.

Pervin, L. A., Reik, L. E., and Dalrymple, W. (Eds.). *The College Dropout and the Utilization of Talent.* Princeton, N.J.: Princeton University Press, 1966.

Petersen, N. S., and Novick, M. R. "An Evaluation of Some Models for Culture-Fair Selection." *Journal of Educational Measurement,* 1976, *13,* 3-31.

Peterson, M. D. *Thomas Jefferson and the New Nation.* New York: Oxford University Press, 1970.

Peterson, M. W., and others. *Black Students on White Campuses:*

The Impacts of Increased Black Enrollments. Ann Arbor: Institute for Social Research, University of Michigan, 1978.

Peterson, R. E., and Associates. *Lifelong Learning in America: An Overview of Current Practices, Available Resources, and Future Prospects.* San Francisco: Jossey-Bass, 1979.

Pfeifer, C. M., Jr. "Relationship Between Scholastic Aptitude, Perception of University Climate, and College Success for Black and White Students." *Journal of Applied Psychology,* 1976, *61,* 341–347.

Pierce, C. M. "Problems of the Negro Adolescent in the Next Decade." In E. Brody (Ed.), *Minority Group Adolescents in the United States.* Baltimore: Williams & Wilkins, 1968.

Population Bulletin. Washington, D.C.: U.S. Government Printing Office, 1975.

Potier, R. "A Letter to the Editor." *National Association of College Admissions Counselors Journal,* 1980, *24* (1), 16–18.

Preiser, W.R.E. (Ed.). *Environmental Design Research,* Vol. 1. Stroudsberg, Pa.: Dowden, Hutchinson, and Ross, 1973.

Quann, C. J., and Associates. *Admissions, Academic Records, and Registrar Services: A Handbook of Policies and Procedures.* San Francisco: Jossey-Bass, 1979.

Ramirez, M., and Castañeda, A. *Cultural Democracy, Bicognitive Development, and Education.* New York: Academic Press, 1974.

Reed, H. B. "College Assessment Inventory." In O. Lenning, and others, *Nonintellective Correlates of Grades, Persistence, and Academic Learning in College.* Iowa City: ACT Publications, 1974.

Reed, R. J. "Increasing the Opportunities for Black Students in Higher Education." *Journal of Negro Education,* 1978, *47,* 143–150.

Reihling, J. "The Adult Woman: A New Challenge for Career Planning and Placement." *Journal of College Placement,* 1979, *39* (4), 36–39.

Reiss, J., and Fox, M. *Guiding the Future College Student.* Englewood Cliffs, N.J.: Prentice-Hall, 1968.

Rioux, J. W., and Sandow, S. A. *Children, Parents, and School Records.* Columbia, Md.: National Committee for Citizens in Education, 1974.

Ripple, G. G. "College Admissions: From Problems to Priorities." *College Board Review,* 1979, *112,* 4–5.

Roark, A. C. "Science in the 1980s: Breakthroughs and Troubling Trends." *Chronicle of Higher Education,* Jan. 7, 1980, p. 5.

Rock, D. A., Centra, J. A., and Linn, R. L. *The Identification and Evaluation of College Effects on Student Achievement.* Princeton, N.J.: Educational Testing Service, 1969.

Rowray, R. D., and others. *Professional Audit for Admissions Officers.* Washington, D.C.: American Association of Collegiate Registrars and Admissions Officers; Skokie, Ill.: National Association of College Admissions Counselors, 1977.

Russell Sage Foundation. *Guidelines for the Collection, Maintenance, and Dissemination of Pupil Records.* New York: Russell Sage Foundation, 1970.

Sacks, H. S. "Bloody Monday: The Crisis of the High School Senior." In H. S. Sacks and Associates, *Hurdles: The Admissions Dilemma in American Education.* New York: Atheneum, 1978.

Sanford, N. (Ed.). "Personality Development During the College Years." *Journal of Social Issues,* 1956, *12* (4), entire issue.

Sanford, N. (Ed.). *The American College.* New York: Wiley, 1962.

Sanford, N. *Where Colleges Fail: A Study of the Student as a Person.* San Francisco: Jossey-Bass, 1967.

Sanford, N., Webster, H., and Freedman, M. "Impulse Expression as a Variable of Personality." *Psychological Monographs,* 1957, *71* (11), entire issue.

Satir, V. M. *Cojoint Family Therapy.* Palo Alto, Calif.: Science and Behavior Books, 1967.

Satir, V. M., Stachowlak, J., and Taschman, H. A. *Helping Families to Change.* New York: Aronson, 1976.

Sawyer, R. L., Cole, N. S., and Cole, J.W.L. "Utilities and the Issue of Fairness in a Decision-Theoretic Model for Selection." *Journal of Educational Measurement,* 1976, *13,* 59–76.

Sawyer, R., and Maxey, J. *The Predictive Validity of the ACT Assessment.* Iowa City: American College Testing Program, 1980.

Schmidt, G. P. *The Liberal Arts College: A Chapter in American Cultural History.* New Brunswick, N.J.: Rutgers University Press, 1957.

Schrader, W. B. "The Predictive Validity of the College Board Admissions Tests." In W. H. Angoff (Ed.), *The College Board Admission Testing Program.* New York: College Entrance Examination Board, 1971.

Schramm, W. *Television and the Test Scores.* New York: College Entrance Examination Board, 1977.

Schuerger, J. *Counseling for College Choice.* Itaska, Ill.: Peacock, 1970.

Sedlacek, W. E., and Webster, D. W. *Admission and Retention of Minority Students in Large Universities.* ERIC/CAPS Research Report No. 377. Ann Arbor: University of Michigan, 1977.

Shertzer, B., and Stone, S. C. *Fundamentals of Guidance.* (3rd ed.) Boston: Houghton Mifflin, 1976.

Silberman, C. *Crisis in the Classroom: The Remaking of American Education.* New York: Random House, 1970.

Slack, W. V., and Porter, D. "The Scholastic Aptitude Test: A Critical Appraisal." *Harvard Educational Review,* 1980, 2, 154–175.

Smith, D. H. *Admissions and Retention Problems of Black Students at Predominantly White Universities.* Department of Health, Education and Welfare Research Report No. 143. Washington, D.C.: U.S. Government Printing Office, 1979.

Speer, A. *Inside The Third Reich.* New York: Macmillan, 1970.

Spielberger, C. D. "Effects of Anxiety on Complex Learning and Academic Achievement." In O. Lenning and others, *Nonintellective Correlates of Grades, Persistence, and Academic Learning in College.* Iowa City: ACT Publications, 1974.

Spurlock, L. "Still Struggling: Minorities and White Colleges in the Mid-Seventies." *Educational Record,* 1976, 57, 186–193.

Stanford University Bulletin: Courses and Degrees, 1979–1980. Stanford, Calif.: Stanford University, 1979.

Stern, G. G. *Studies of College Environments.* Syracuse, N.Y.: Syracuse University Press, 1966.

Stern, G. G. *People in Context: Measuring Person/Environment Context in Education and Industry.* New York: Wiley, 1970.

Strong, E. K., Jr., and Campbell, D. K. *Strong-Campbell Interest Inventory.* Minneapolis: National Computer Systems Inc., 1979.

Stulac, J., and Stanwyck, D. "The Revolution in Counseling: A Sociological Perspective." *Personnel and Guidance Journal,* 1980, 58 (7), 491–495.

Super, D. E. "Self-Concept and Vocational Development Theories Applied to College Choice and Planning." In P. Newman and B. Newman (Eds.), *Preparing School Counselors in Educational Guidance.* New York: College Entrance Examination Board, 1967.

Thomas, G. E. "The Influence of Ascription, Achievement and Educational Expectations on Black-White Postsecondary Enrollment." *Sociological Quarterly,* 1979, *20,* 209-222.

Thomas, L. E. "Causes of Mid-Life Change from High Status Careers." *Vocational Guidance Quarterly,* 1979, *27* (3), 202-208.

Thorndike. R. L. "Concepts of Culture Fairness." *Journal of Educational Measurement,* 1971, *8,* 63-70.

Tidball, E. M. "Perspective on Academic Women and Affirmative Action." *Educational Record,* 1973, *54,* 130-135.

Time Share: The Guidance Information System Guide. Boston: Houghton Mifflin, 1979.

Tinto, V. "Dropout from Higher Education: A Theoretical Synthesis of Recent Research." *Review of Educational Research,* 1975, *45* (1), 89-125.

U.S. Bureau of the Census. *Persons of Spanish Origin in the United States.* Series P-20, No. 310. Washington, D.C.: U.S. Government Printing Office, 1977.

U.S. Commission on Civil Rights. *Ethnic Isolation of Mexican Americans in Public Schools of the Southwest.* Mexican American Education Study, Report 1. Washington, D.C.: U.S. Government Printing Office, 1971.

U.S. Commission on Civil Rights. *Toward Quality Education for Mexican Americans.* Mexican American Education Study, Report 6. Washington, D.C.: U.S. Government Printing Office, 1974.

U.S. Department of Health, Education and Welfare. *A Study of Selected Socio-Economic Characteristics of Ethnic Minorities Based on the 1970 Census.* Vol. 1: *Americans of Spanish Origin.* Washington, D.C.: U.S. Government Printing Office, 1974.

Vaccaro, J. "Marketing on the College Campus: Underdeveloped or Oversold?" *College Board Review,* 1979, *113* (2), 18-23.

Vacher, C. J. "The Self Concept of Underachieving Freshmen and Upperclasswomen College Students." In O. Lenning and others, *Nonintellective Correlates of Grades, Persistence, and Academic Learning in College.* Iowa City: ACT Publications, 1974.

Vasquez, R. "Do Admissions Counselors Read?" *National Association of College Admissions Counselors Journal,* 1976, *20* (3), 17–19.

Walsh, W. B. *Theories of Person-Environment Interaction: Implications for the College Student.* Princeton, N.J.: American College Testing Program, 1973.

Warren, J. R. "Prediction of College-Achievement Among Mexican-American Students in California." In *College Entrance Examination Board Research and Development Reports.* Research Bulletin RB-76-22. Berkeley, Calif.: Educational Testing Service, 1976.

Washington, K. R. "Special Minority Programs: Dupe or New Deal?" *Journal of Afro-American Issues,* 1977, *5,* 60–65.

Webster, D., Sedlacek, W., and Miyares, J. "A Comparison of Problems Perceived by Minority and White University Students." *Journal of College Student Personnel,* 1979, *20,* 165–170.

Weinman, J. *Declining Test Scores: A State Report.* Massachusetts: Massachusetts Department of Education, 1977.

Willie, C. V. (Ed.). *Black, Brown, White Relations.* New Brunswick, N.J.: Transaction Books, 1970.

Willie, C. V., and McCord, A. S. *Black Students at White Colleges.* New York: Praeger, 1972.

Wing, C. W., Jr., and Wallach, A. *College Admissions and the Psychology of Talent.* New York: Holt, Rinehart and Winston, 1971.

Wohlwill, J. F., and Altman, I. *Human Behavior and Environment.* New York: Plenum, 1976.

Index

A

Abramowitz, S., 20, 21, 22, 573
Academic achievement, college impact on, 54-56, 71
Accessibility, issue of, 13-14
Accountability, and reference letters, 479-481
Accrediting agencies, and transfers, 232
Achievement Tests, 287, 323
Achievement tests, predictive validity of, 522
Activities Index (AI), 77
Adler, A., 292
Admissions: evaluating bias in, 538; on high school record alone, 539-542; for international students, 407-415; issues in, 262-263; issues of practices in, 267; marketing research for, 395-406; principles of practice in, 560-569; by random selection, 542-546. *See also* College placement
Admissions officers: autumn activities of, 554-556; calendar of visits by, 274; communication effectiveness among, 434-436; communication with, 455-456, 474;

as constituents, 260-261; counselor relationship with, 550-552, 555-556, 557, 558-559; development and training for, 430-438; essentials for, 549-550; evaluation of, 436-437; in-service workshop for, 431-434; job descriptions for, 431; job enrichment for, 437-438; and juniors programs, 558-559; and Mexican American students, 207-218; new role of, 28; panels of, 453-454; professional networks of, 549-559; and professional organizations, 451-452; school visits by, 285, 354-355, 444-456; and selection process, 452-456; spring activities of, 557-559; summer activities of, 553-554; at two-year colleges, 238; winter activities of, 556-557
Admissions tests. *See* Standardized tests
Adult students: admissions counseling for, 220-230; admissions process for, 224-225; counseling services for, 226; and credit for prior learning, 225; delivery system for, 222-224; goal clarifica-

597

tion for, 227-228; and midlife awareness, 220; outreach for, 229-230; population of, 221-222; support services for, 226-228

Advanced Placement (AP) program, 225, 287, 323, 424

Advanced standing, principles of practice for, 568-569

Affirmative action, review of, for black students, 163-166

Africa, American overseas schools in, 427

Alabama, Mexican American students in, 198

Alaska, Mexican American students in, 198

Alcohol abuse, and misplacement, 103

Alderman, D. L., 518, 573

Altman, I., 68, 69, 85, 595

Alumni: and communication, 285, 288; and counselors, 285; of high school, questionnaire for, 329-331; as selective college recruiters, 496-497

American Assembly of Collegiate Schools of Business, 232

American Association of Collegiate Registrars and Admissions Officers (AACRAO), 412, 416, 419, 422, 477, 509, 528, 558, 573, 578

American College Testing (ACT) Program, 515, 541, 573; Assessment Program of, 509; and declining scores, 441, 513-517; described, 510-512; Educational Opportunity Service (EOS) of, 392; and predictive validity, 522; professional services from, 153, 398, 460, 556-557; reliability of, 521; scores on, 91, 100, 106, 200, 201; use of, 287, 299, 301, 314, 323; and validity and equity issues, 529-530, 531-535, 536, 537, 540-541, 546-547. See also Standardized tests

American Council on Education, 169, 422, 556, 574

American Federation of Teachers, 478

American GI Forum, 216

American Language Institute of Georgetown University (ALIGU), 413

American Personnel and Guidance Association (APGA), 478, 574

American School Counselor Association, 478, 574

Amherst College, recruitment by, 495-496

Amideast, 409, 415, 421

Anger, and misplacement, 102

Ansoff, H. I., 574

Antioch University: and curricular change, 8; and experiential learning, 134, 136; and student development, 79

Anxiety states, and misplacement, 101-102

Applications: forms for, 283; phase of, 278-279; principles of practice for, 564-566; workshop session on, 325-326

April, counseling activities in, 318

Arizona, Mexican Americans in, 193, 198

Arkansas: aggressive recruitment in, 391; Mexican American students in, 198

Armed services, pressures from, 465-466

Armed Services Vocational Aptitude Battery (ASVAB), 465

Arndt, M. J., 427

Asia: schools associations in, 428, 429; students from, 408

Asian Americans, and higher education, 149

Associated Colleges of the Midwest, 130-131

Association of American Schools of Central America, 428

Association of American Schools in the Republic of Mexico, 427

Association of American Schools of South America (AASAA), 428

Association of Black Admissions

and Financial Aid Officers of the Ivy League and Seven Sisters (ABAFAOILSS), 554

Association of College Admissions Counselors (ACAC), 469, 554, 559, 570

Association of Colombian and Caribbean American Schools, 428

Association of International Schools, 427

Astin, A. W., 45, 47, 48, 49, 50, 51, 52, 53, 54, 55, 56, 57, 58, 61, 62-63, 64, 65, 70-71, 76, 77, 78, 81, 87, 88, 90, 92, 94, 95, 97, 98, 109, 131, 143, 172, 174, 574, 590

Astin, H., 164, 574

Attitudes, beliefs, and values, college impact on, 58-59

B

Baird, L. L., 78, 81, 574

Bakke case, 188, 502

Barnard College, achievers from, 142

Barre, M. E., 300, 574

Bartlett, W. E., 575

Basic Educational Opportunity Grant Program (Pell Grants), 242, 246

Bates College, and College Venture Program, 136

Baudelaire, C., 112

Beals, E. W., 488, 575

Beaton, A. E., 513, 516, 575

Bennington College: characteristics of, 113-114; and student development, 77; and test scores, 119

Benson, L. L., 293, 294, 575

Binstock, R. H., 575

Birnbaum, M., 107, 577

Birren, J. E., 575

Bisconti, A. S., 130, 575

Black students: adaptation and retention of, 177-182; admissions counseling for, 161-190; admissions input of, 174-175; and affirmative action, 163-166; background on, 161-163; characteristics of, 166-168; counseling needs and strategies for, 182-187; and demographic trends, 171, 187-188; enrollment trends of, 168-169; evaluative criteria for, 173-174; and financial aid, 172; implications of current developments for, 187-190; and incongruent expectations, 178-179; increased pool of, 176-177, 190; and institutional environment, 173, 176, 182, 190; institutional flexibility for, 183-184; issues in recruiting, 170; outreach programs for, 185; psychological problems of, 179-180; recommendations regarding, 189-190; recruitment and selection of, 169-177; support services for, 175-176

Blum, M. J., xviii, 255-256, 361-371

Boerner, B. B., 374, 376, 430-438

Bok, D., 75, 81, 575

Bolles, R. N., 222, 575

Bonham, G. W., 220, 575

Boorstin, D. J., 575

Borup, J. S., 200, 575

Bosworth, S., 39-40, 111-125

Bowdoin College: recruitment by, 495-496; as selective, 493

Bowen, H. R., 45, 46, 50, 51, 56, 57, 59, 61, 65, 78, 80, 81, 82, 517, 575-576

Bowers, J. E., 534, 576

Boyan, D. R., 576

Boyd, W. M., II, 163, 164, 166, 167, 168, 173, 175, 176, 180, 181, 576

Brawer, F. B., 77, 82, 152-153, 576, 578

Breland, H. M., 576

Brody, E., 183, 576, 579

Brokering services, for adult students, 223

Brookline, Massachusetts, college fairs in, 354

Broudy, H. S., 53, 82, 576

Brown, G. H., 197n, 199n, 209, 576

Brown, L. K., 141, 576
Brown, S., 168, 176, 181, 576
Brown University: alumni interviews for, 496-497; characteristics of, 113-114; and College Venture Program, 136; Medical Education Program of, 493; as selective, 491-492
Bryn Mawr: achievers from, 142; recruitment by, 495-496
Buckley Amendments, 440, 462-463, 476-479, 480, 487, 489-490
Buriel, R., 150-151, 191-219, 576
Burlew, K. H., 167, 577

C

Caine, C. J., 148, 154-160
California: ACT scores in, 513; admissions requirements in, 311; college choice in, 304; community colleges in, and student development, 77; Mexican Americans in, 193, 196, 198; Proposition 13 in, 187
California, University of: and English achievement tests, 512; and Mexican American students, 150, 196, 197, 200
California at Berkeley, University of: and curricular change, 8; engineering specialty at, 107; Mathematics, English, and Science Achievement Program (MESA) at, 177
California at Davis, University of, and internships, 135-136
California at Irvine, University of, Educational Opportunity Program at, 200n
California Student Aid Commission, 316, 318
Cambridge University, development of, 10
Campanaro, I. K., 151-152, 220-230
Campbell, D. K., 593
Campos, S., 514, 522, 531, 581

Career days/career fairs, and community leaders, 355
Career orientation and implementation, college impact on, 61-63
Career planning: academic learning integrated with, 126-146; background on, 126-128; and changes, 131-132; college choice as step in, 294-295; context of, 145-146; exploration for, undergraduate, 133-138; and graduate or professional training, 139-140; group counseling for, 356-357; and liberal arts or vocational-technical training, 128-132; services for, 143-144; by women, 140-143
Carnegie Commission, 23
Carnegie Council on Policy Studies in Higher Education, 15, 22, 27-28, 577
Carnegie Foundation for the Advancement of Teaching, 24
Carnegie-Mellon University, strategic planning at, 26
Carp, F. M., 68, 82, 577
Carroll, L., 118
Carter, T. P., 196n, 577
Carter, V. L., 577
Cass, J., 107, 577
Castañeda, A., 204, 591
Casteen, J. T., III, 1-2, 3, 4-16, 148
Cavalier, J. E., 442-443, 549-559
Centra, J. A., 55, 56, 82, 84, 577, 592
Chall, J. S., 515, 577
Chamberlain, F. M., 577
Chang, O. H., 533, 585
Change, and counseling, 346, 360. See also Demographic changes
Change Magazine, 9
Chapman, D. W., 18-19, 26-27, 577
Chaucer, G., 114
Chavez, C., 206
Chicago, University of, and College Venture Program, 136
Chickering, A. W., 45, 46, 49, 50, 54, 57, 59, 61, 65, 70, 76, 79, 82, 577

Citizens Scholarship Foundation, 246

Claremont Colleges, and Chicano Studies Center, 215-216

Claremont McKenna College, and Chicano Studies Center, 215

Clark, B. R., 45, 46-47, 50, 54, 57, 58, 59-60, 61, 65, 78-79, 82, 577-578

Clark, K., 158, 578

Clayton High School, developmental career-college program at, 295-304

Cleary, T. A., 517, 530, 536, 578

Coaching: concept of, 518-519; for standardized tests, 517-520

Coeducational institutions: and student development, 51-52, 56, 57, 58, 60, 62, 64, 65; and women's career patterns, 141-142

Coffin, W. S., Jr., 156, 578

Cohen, A. M., 152-153, 578

Coil, A., 37-38, 42-85

Cole, J. W. L., 592

Cole, N. S., 578, 592

Coleman, J. S., 516, 578

Coles, R., 179, 578

Colgate University, and College Venture Program, 136

College and University Environment Scales (CUES), 77-78

College Board, 118, 521, 528, 578; and coaching issue, 518-519, 520; and disclosure, 524-525; International Division of, 425; National Forum of, 30; as professional organization, 377, 416, 422, 451-452, 477-478, 554, 555; research by, 196, 293, 335; role of, 526; scores from, 118, 171, 363; services of, 271, 298, 299, 316, 398, 556; Student Search Service of, 276, 367, 387, 390, 392, 421, 496, 555; tests from, 225, 312, 414, 441, 509, 512, 513, 523, 529

College Characteristics Index, 77

College choice: computers for, 324-

325; and financial aid, 245-246; as rite of passage, 333

College Entrance Examination Board (CEEB). See College Board

College fair, and community members, 354

College Level Examination Program (CLEP), 55, 225

College placement: analysis of, 86-110; background on, 86-87; and departmental strength, 106-109; and grades, 90-91, 95, 106; negatives in, 109-110; professional planning for, 104-110; social quality matching for, 109; in specialized programs, 108; test score matching for, 106. See also Admissions; Misplacement

College Placement Council, 30

College Scholarship Service (CSS), 153, 311-312, 414

College Venture Program, and experiential learning, 136

College Work-Study Program, 137, 144, 241, 246, 266, 320

Colorado, Mexican Americans in, 193, 198

Columbia University, selective excellence at, 25

Comisión Feminil Mexicana Nacional, 216

Common Application Form, 283, 325, 483, 489

Communication: among admissions officers, 434-436; with admissions officers, 455-456, 474; alumni-student, 288; between constituencies, 271-278; counselor-college, 285-286; counselor-faculty, 286-287; counselor-parent, 284-285; counselor-school, 287; faculty-colleges, 287-288; faculty-school, 287; parent-student-college, 288; parent-student-counselor, 359-360; student-college, 278-281; student-counselor, 271-277; student-faculty, 281-282; student-faculty college, 284; student-parents, 277-278, 288; student-school, 282-283; student-school-college, 283-284

Community colleges. *See* Two-year colleges

Community counseling: analysis of, 346-360; background on, 346-352; events for, 354-355; experiences for, 355-360; groups for, 358-359; links in, 349-350; location for, 347-348; by media, 352-354; outreach in, 350-351; and parent involvement, 348, 355, 356, 358-359; workshops for, 355-356

Community Service Volunteer Projects, 299

Competition, implications of, 385-394

Computers: for college choice, 324-325; for counseling, 276-277; for data analysis, 403-404; for listing seniors statewide, 390; searches by, and enticement money, 470

Congruency: concept of, 38, 68; and student development, 68-70, 74

Connecticut, Mexican American students in, 198

Connors, E. T., 579

Conrad, S. S., 577

Consortium on Financing Higher Education (COFHE), 398-554

Constituencies, linking, 269-289

Control of institutions, and student development, 48, 56, 57, 58, 60-61

Cooperative Education Program, and career planning, 134, 136

Cooperative Institutional Research Program (CIRP), 131-132

Cope, R., 99, 104, 579

Copeland, L. L., 181, 579

Cornell University, and College Venture Program, 136

Cortes, C. E., 193, 579

Council for the Advancement of Experiential Learning (CAEL), 225

Council of Graduate Schools, 416

Council on Social Work Education, 232

Counseling: for adult students, 220-230; basis for, 257-268; for black students, 161-190; communication in, 271-288; community, 346-360; creating motivation through, 310-319; developmental approach to, 290-306; family, 332-345; financial, 240-249; forms for, 274, 283, 286; generalist, 290-306; in groups, 271, 321-331; individual attention in, 111-125; in individual conferences, 271-274; institutional marketing by, 373-438; justification for, 111-112, 124-125; for Mexican American students, 191-219; and misplacement, 100; program support for, 319-320; school and community services of, 251-371; school prerequisites for, 308-310; scope of, 1-35; social function of, 148, 154-160; and social services, 147-249; as student service, 37-146; supplies and materials for, 309; as support for students, 307-320; trends in, 261-268

Counselors: and admissions interview, 120-121; admissions officer relationship with, 550-552, 555-556, 557, 558-559; as advocates, xiii-xiv; and articles, 275, 287; and college fairs, 280-281; and communication, 271-277, 284-287, 359-360; concern by, 270-271; constituencies of, 258-261, 269-289; and cooperation, 288-289; credibility of, 257; and demographic change, 32-35; and essays, 114-118; functions of, 290-291; independent, 361-371; influence of, 27; job-related pressures on, 457-472; as negotiators, 344; newsletter from, 314-315, 353-354; opportunities for, 464-465; and placement, 86-110, 118-120; preparation of, 258,

292-294; principles for, 336-337, 344-345; professional concerns of, 439-559; and professional organizations, 451-452; and. references, 121-124; released time for, 309-310; religious pressures on, 466-467; responsibility of, 345, 471-472; role of, ix-x, xi-xii, 292; school board pressures on, 461-464; and school visits by admissions officers, 444-446; and selection process, 452-456; as travel agents, 112-114; visits to colleges by, 285-286; weekly bulletin from, 274; workshops for, on Mexican American students, 216-217

Course availability, and misplacement, 92

Course material, and misplacement, 91

Course selection, and career planning, 133-134

Cramer, S. H., 292, 293, 294, 481, 583

Cranford, B., 30-31, 579

Credit, awarding, principles of practice for, 568-569

Cronbach, L. J., 579

Cross, K. P., 53, 80, 82, 579

Crouch, M., 428

Crowl, K., 428

Cucio, W. H., 160, 579

Cundiff, M. F., 1, 2, 3, 17-35

D

Dalrymple, W., 590

Darlington, R. B., 579

Dartmouth College, "legacy" at, 119

Data collection, for market research, 402-403

Davis, R. G., 22, 579

December, counseling activities in, 316-317

Declaration and Certification of Finances, 414

Delaware, Mexican American students in, 198

Demographic changes: analysis of impact of, 17-35; background on, 17-18; and black students, 171, 187-188; and counselors, 32-35; and employment trends, 29-30; and institutions, 18-24; and Mexican American students, 193-197, 217-218; and students, 24-32

Denial actions, related to standardized tests, 528, 535-539, 544-546

Depression, and misplacement, 101

Derbyshire, R., 183, 579

Developmental career college program: analysis of, 295-306; background on, 295-296; key to, 296-297; model of, 297-303; summary of, 304-306

Developmental self-concept theory, 294-295

Dewey, J., 53, 82, 579

Dissemination and Assessment Center for Bilingual Education, 579

District of Columbia, Mexican American students in, 198

Dominick, C. A., 474, 579

Douglas College Women's College Study Committee, 52, 82, 579

Dressel, P. L., 79-80, 81, 82, 580

Drew, D. E., 75, 82, 580

Dropping out, and misplacement, 99

Drug abuse, and misplacement, 103

Dubin, R., 55, 82-83, 580

Dunn, S. L., 31, 580

E

East Asia Regional Council of Overseas Schols (EARCOS), 428

Eastern Group of Admissions Directors (EGAD), 554

Economic pressures, and misplacement, 97

Educational Testing Service (ETS), 301, 363, 398, 413, 414, 516, 518, 522, 525-526, 532, 580

Eisenberg, L., 101, 580

Eisenhower, D. D., ix

Eleventh grade: counseling for motivation in, 313-314; descriptions of, for reference letters, 486; developmental career-college planning in, 300-302; group meetings for, 322; information nights for, 459-460; questionnaire for, 323-324, 327-328; school visits for, 453-454; workshop meetings for, 323-325

Ellis, D. D., Jr., 589

Eliot, T. S., 120

Employment trends: and black students, 188; and demographic change, 29-30

English Achievement Test, 287

Enrollment trends: of black students, 168-169; and institutions, 18-22. *See also* Demographic changes

Environmental Assessment Technique (EAT), 77

Epps, E. A., 163, 173, 580

Equity: issues of, 535-539; and out-of-state applicants, 537

Erikson, E., 292, 580

Erikson, R. J., 167, 580

Ervin, L., 168, 176, 181, 576

Essays: by Mexican American students, 210; priorities in, 114-118; for selective institutions, 499; by students, 279-280, 282-283; workshop session on, 326

Ethics: in recruitment, 417-418; and reference letters, 476-479; and statement of principles, 560-571

European Council of International Schools (ECIS), 428

Evaluation, of admissions officers, 436-437

Experiential learning: and career planning, 134-137; rationale for, 134-135

Extracurriculum, and career planning, 137-138

F

Faculty: and communication, 281-282, 284, 286-288; as constitu-

ents, 260; test results reported to, 286-287

Family counseling: addressing parental concerns in, 337-340; analysis of, 332-345; background on, 332-334; concept of, 337; counselor principles in, 336-337, 344-345; reasons for, 334-336; techniques for, 340-345

Family Educational Rights and Privacy Act of 1974 (Buckley Amendments), 440, 462-463, 476-479, 480, 487, 489-490

Fay, P. K., 440-441, 473-490

February, counseling activities in, 317

Federal Summer Intern Program, 136

Federal Trade Commission (FTC), Bureau of Consumer Protection, 518, 580

Feldman, K. S., 45-46, 50, 52, 53, 54, 57, 65, 68, 78, 80, 83, 580

Fetters, W., 167, 168, 172, 182, 590

Finances, institutional, issues in, 264-265

Financial aid: analysis of components in, 240-249; and athletic scholarships, 246-247; and black students, 172; and educational choice, 245-246; and family counseling, 334; federal role in, 240-242; and financial need concept, 243-244; goal of, 243-244; institutional funds for, 242, 246-247; issues in, 265-266; and Mexican American students, 213; and motivating students, 311-312, 316-317; and net cost concept, 245; principles of practice for, 566-568; state funds for, 243; and student employment, 247; and student loans, 247-248; trends in, 248-249

Financial Aid Form (FAF), 316, 317

Fincher, C., 521, 580

Fishlow, H., 21-22, 23, 24, 32, 33, 580

Fiske, E. B., 25-26, 378, 580

Flaugher, R. L., 581
Florida: Mexican American students in, 198; promotional stunt in, 378
Flowchart, for individual conference, 273
Ford, D. H., 98, 104, 581
Ford, S. F., 514, 522, 531, 581
Foreign Financial Aid Application, 414
Foreign students. *See* International students
Fourteenth Amendment, 9, 11, 13
Fox, M., 293, 591
Fram, E. H., 377, 581
Francis Parker School, 329n
Franklin, B., 154, 155, 385
Franklin High School, college advising system at, 307-320
Freedman, M., 77, 84, 592
Friendships, and misplacement, 89-90, 94
Fulbright Commission, 409, 415, 421

G

Gaither, G. H., 380, 581
Garcia, S., 165, 581
Garigan, C. W., 577
Geiger, R. L., 29, 581
Gelatt, H. B., 271, 272n, 293, 324, 581
Georgia, Mexican American students in, 198
Georgia, University of, and SAT predictive validity, 521-522
Germany, Federal Republic of, educational efficiency in, 7
Gettzer, H., 381, 581
Gibbs, J. T., 149-150, 161-190, 581
GI Bill, 240, 494
Glover, R. H., 514, 582
Goal clarification, for adult students, 227-228
Goldman, R. D., 201, 202-203, 582
Goldwater, B., Jr., 480, 582
Government, federal: financial aid role of, 240-242; funding patterns of, 23-24

Grabowski, S. M., 582
Grades: and college placement, 90-91, 95, 106; transfer of, 233
Graduate education, and career planning, 139-140
Graduate Management Admission Test (GMAT), 139, 414
Graduate Record Examination (GRE), 55, 109, 139, 398, 414
Griswold, W., 28
Group counseling: analysis of, 321-331; background on, 321-322; for career planning, 356-357; on college choice, 324-325; for community members, 358-359; junior workshop for, 323-325; preliminaries for, 322; senior workshop for, 325-326
Guaranteed Student Loan Program, 241, 246
Guildroy, J., 582

H

Haagen, C. H., 582
Haas, S., 429
Haettenschwiller, D., 186, 582
Halpern's Crisis Scale, 489
Halstead, D. K., 582
Hamilton College, writing samples for, 499
Hammond, C., 186, 582
Hampshire College, self-discipline at, 96
Hansen-Shaevitz, M., 230, 586
Harnischfeger, A., 514-515, 583
Haro, C. M., 202, 583
Harper, F. D., 179, 583
Harris, S. H., 577
Hartnett, R. T., 81, 574
Harvard University, 583; admissions statement by, 502; alumni interviews for, 496; characteristics of, 113-114; and core curriculum, 12, 15; dropouts from, 101; early purpose of, 4, 6; and market sharing, 385; position of, 381; reference letters used by, 489; as selective, 492; and student development research, 75

Harvey, C. C., 428
Harvey Mudd College, and Chicano
  Studies Center, 216
Haverford College: recruitment by,
  495-496; and student develop-
  ment, 77
Hawaii, Mexican American students
  in, 198
Haynes, L. L., III, 13, 583
Heath, D. H., 77, 83, 583
Heist, P., 56, 83, 583
Hennig, M., 142, 583
Henton, J., 488-489, 583
Herr, E. L., 292, 293, 294, 481,
  583
Hersey, J., 475, 583
Hewitt, B. N., 201, 582
Hidalgo, M., 206
High school grade point average
  (HSGPA), and Mexican American students, 197, 200-202
High school percentile rank (HSPR),
  and validity and equity issues,
  531-532, 534-541, 546-547
Higher education: accessibility issue in, 13-14; analysis of function of, 4-16; assumptions about,
  11; career preparation related to,
  126-127, 145-146; curricular
  changes in, 7-9; and demographic
  changes, 17-35; dichotomies in,
  4-5; future of, 14-16; goals of,
  157-160; individual within system of, 10-11; marketing of,
  377-438; mission of, 16; in nation's service, 155-160; need for,
  154-160; norms in, 6; planning
  in, 32; progress in, 12-14; purposes of, 4-6, 9, 16; and student
  development, 42-85
Higher Education Act of 1965,
  240-241
Higher Education Research Institute, 131
Hilton, T. L., 513, 516, 575
Hitler, A., 156
Holinger, P., 101, 583
Holland Self-Directed Search, 299
Hollingshead, A., 90, 584

Hong Kong, students from, 408-
  409
Hood, A., 89, 90, 93, 94, 95, 584
Howard, W. R., 380, 584
Hoy, J. C., 323, 324, 326, 584
Hunter, J. E., 584
Hutchins, R. M., 31, 154, 155, 158,
  584

                    I

Idaho, Mexican American students
  in, 198
Ihlanfeldt, W., 379, 380, 381, 383,
  584
Illinois: financial aid program in,
  243; Mexican American students
  in, 198; regulated growth in,
  390
Illinois at Chicago Circle, University
  of, admissions policy at, 536
Illinois at Urbana-Champaign, University of (UIUC), admissions
  policies at, 442, 532-548
Immigration and Naturalization
  Service (INS), 417, 419; Affidavit
  of Support (I-134) from, 414;
  Certificate of Eligibility (I-20)
  from, 413, 414, 415
Independent educational counselors: analysis of, 361-371; background on, 361-362; effectiveness of, 370-371; examples of
  work of, 363-364, 365-367; expectations from, 369-370; need
  for, 362-367; selecting, 367-369
Independent Educational Counselors Association (IECA), 364,
  367-368, 369
Indian Higher Education Grant Program, 242
Indiana, Mexican American students in, 198
Inhelder, B., 68, 83, 584
Institute of International Education
  (IIE), 408, 409, 412, 413, 415,
  416, 421
Institutions: changing colleges within, and misplacement, 99; char-

acteristics of, related to student development, 44-53; coeducational, 51-52, 141-142; and communication, 278-281, 283-284, 285-286, 287-288; control of, 48, 56, 57, 58, 60-61; and demographic change, 18-24; departmental strength of, and placement, 106-109; and enrollment declines, 18-22; environment of, for black students, 173, 176, 182, 190; financial issues of, 264-265; flexibility of, for black students, 183-184; marketing of, 373-438; pressures from, 467-470; public, market penetration by, 392-393; public, pressure from, 468-469; ratings of, 275-276; recovery of, 22-24; religious affiliation of, 52-53, 56, 58, 59, 60, 65; residential nature of, 49-50, 57, 68, 71-72, 73; selective, 491-508; selectivity of, 47-48, 56, 57, 58, 59, 61, 64, 71-72; setting of, and career planning, 138; single-sex or coeducational, 51-52, 56, 57, 58, 60, 62, 64, 65; size of, 50-51, 57, 58, 63-64, 65, 70, 71-72; staff reductions in, 32-33

Intellectual, cultural, and esthetic orientation, college impact on, 56-58

International Baccalaureate Degree (I.B.), 376, 425

International Baccalaureate Office, 425

International Communications Agency (ICA), 409, 415, 416, 421

International students: academic credentials of, 412-413; admissions for, 407-415; analysis of services for, 407-429; defined, 407; English-language ability of, 413-414; financial resources of, 414; information needed by, 410-411; institutional commitment to recruiting, 419-420; ma-jor fields of, 409; number of, 408; overseas Americans as, 422-429; and overseas counseling agencies, 415; reasons for, 408-409; recruitment of, 415-422

Interviews: approach to, 120-121; role-playing, 324; for selective institutions, 501-502

Involvement: academic, 65; athletic, 65; and student development, 49, 51, 65, 68, 72-73; and student-faculty interaction, 65; and student government, 65

Iowa, Mexican American students in, 198

Iran, students from, 408

Ironson, G. H., 576

J

Jackson, R., 516, 518, 584

Jacob, P. E., 77, 83, 584

Jacobson, R. L., 26, 584

January, counseling activities in, 317

Jardim, A., 142, 583

Jefferson, T., 5, 6, 10, 13, 154, 155, 584

Jencks, C., 15, 584

Jenkins, H. M., 418, 584

Jobs, part-time and summer, and career planning, 137

Johnson, R., 168, 585

Johnson Foundation, 416

Jones, L. G., 167, 180, 585

June, counseling activities in, 318-319

Juniors. See Eleventh grade

K

Kane, H. W., 375, 395-406

Kansas, Mexican American students in, 198

Kanter, R. M., 585

Katz, J., 53, 77, 83, 585

Kelly, T. D., 374-375, 385-394

Kentucky, Mexican American students in, 198

Kimball, M., 442-443, 549-559

King, M. L., Jr., 161
Kingsbury, D., 428
Knowledge, acquisition of, 54-56
Kohlberg, L., 68, 83, 585
Kotler, P., 374, 377, 378, 380, 381-
    382, 585
Kramer, R., 68, 83, 585
Kreinberg, N., 303
Krukowski, J., 375, 395-406
Kuder, G. F., 585
Kuder Occupational Interest Sur-
    vey, 299, 323
Kuehn, J. K., 88, 100, 585
Kuehn, J. L., 88, 100, 585

                    L

Langston, I. A., 533, 585
Larkin, P. G., 380, 585
Latin America: schools associations
    in, 427-428; students from, 425
Lavin, D. E., 531, 585
Lawton, M. P., 68, 83, 585, 588
League of United Latin American
    Citizens (LULAC), 216
Learned, W. S., 76-77, 83, 585
Learning disabilities, and misplace-
    ment, 93-94
Lenning, O., 586
Lenz, E., 230, 586
Letters of recommendation. *See*
    Reference letters
Levinson, D. J., 220, 586
Lewis, G. M., 22, 579
Liberal arts: and career planning,
    128-132; rationale for, 129-130
Liberal arts colleges, preservation
    of, 30-31
Limestone College, marketing by,
    390
Lindley, D. V., 589
Linn, R. L., 55, 84, 586, 592
Litten, L., 380, 586
Living arrangements, and misplace-
    ment, 88-89. *See also* Residence
Loeb, J. W., 442, 528-548, 586
Louisiana, Mexican American stu-
    dents in, 198
Lovette, S., 441-442, 509-527

Lowery, E., xviii
Lowery, W. R., xii, xiii-xviii, 1-3,
    37-41, 147-153, 251-256, 373-
    376, 439-443
Lowman, R. P., 201, 586
LSAT, 139
Lucas, J. A., 586
Lyons, J. E., 179, 586

                    M

McCandless, S. A., 517, 578
McCord, A. S., 164, 173, 180, 595
McCurdy, J., 586
Mackey, E., 179, 587
MacLeish, A., 160, 587
Magarrell, J., 25, 587
Maghreb Association of Interna-
    tional Schools (MAIS), 427
Magruder, J., 156
Maine, Mexican American students
    in, 198
Major fields: and career planning,
    130; of international students,
    409; and transfers, 234-235, 238
Malone, D., 5, 10, 587
March, counseling activities in, 317-
    318
Market sharing, early example of,
    385
Marketing: analysis of, 377-384;
    background on, 373-376; and
    competition, 374-375, 385-394;
    concept of, 378-379; and con-
    sumer movement, 393-394; as
    creating awareness of need, 386;
    efficiencies in, 391-392; growth
    of, 377-378; growth opportunity
    matrix in, 388; implications of,
    385-394; for international stu-
    dents, 375-376, 407-429; and
    marginality, 389; need for, 374,
    377-384; phases of, 379; plan
    for, 404-406; planning and posi-
    tioning in, 380-383; and promo-
    tion, 383-384; research approach
    to, 375, 387-388, 395-406; re-
    search questions in, 379-380;
    and training, 376, 430-438

Markets, primary, secondary, and tertiary, 391
Marron, J. E., 519, 587
Marshall, C. A., ix-xii
Martin, P., 252-253, 255, 269-289
Martinez, J. L., 587
Martinez, V., 200, 587
Maryland, Mexican American students in, 198
Maryland, University of, and racism, 182
Maslow, A. H., 74
Massachusetts: education crucial in, 154; English electives in, 515; Mexican American students in, 198
Mathematics and Science Education Program for Women, 303
Mattern, W. G., 428
Maxey, J., 514, 531, 587, 592
May, counseling activities in, 318
Mayhew, L. B., 383, 587
Mazzuca, L. C., x*n*
MCAT, 139
Media, information disseminated through, 352-354
Medsker, L. L., 59
Men: development of, college impact on, 52, 56, 65; Mexican American, 212
Messick, S., 518, 587
Mexican American students: admissions counseling for, 191-219; background on, 191-192; and Catholic ideology, 206; and community-based organizations, 216; conclusions on, 218-219; and cultural pluralism, 213-215; and demographic change, 193-197, 217-218; essays by, 210; and family, community, and ethnic identification, 204-205, 208-209; and financial aid, 213; historical background of, 192-193; and interpersonal relationships, 205, 209, 210-211; and men's roles, 212; recruitment strategies for, 207-218; and standardized tests, 197-203; and status and role definitions, 205-206; terms referring to, 192; value system of, 203-206; and women's roles, 211-212, 216-217
Michigan, Mexican American students in, 198
Michigan, University of, recruitment study by, 26-27
Michigan Test of English Language Proficiency (MTELP), 413
Middlebury, characteristics of, 113-114
Miller, I., 440, 457-472
Miller, M., 292, 587
Minnesota: Mexican American students in, 198; placement study in, 89, 90, 95
Minorities: and higher education, 148-151, 161-219; and selective institutions, 505
Misplacement: causes of, 92-98; and peer groups, 89-90, 94; practical reactions to, 98-100; and preexisting problems, 97-98; proximate causes of, 88-92; scope of, 87-98; unsuccessful responses to, 100-104. See also College placement
Mississippi, Mexican American students in, 198
Missouri, Mexican American students in, 198
Missouri, University of, journalism specialty at, 107
Mitchell, J. S., 301, 587
Miyares, J., 182, 595
Modu, C., 513, 587
Moll, R., 28, 301, 322, 476, 482, 483, 587
Monson, J. C., 40-41, 126-146
Montana, Mexican American students in, 199
Moos, R. H., 88, 588
Moral Majority, 188
Motivation, creation of, through counseling, 310-319
Mount Holyoke, achievers from, 142

Movimiento Estudiantil Chicano de Aztlan (MECHA), 207-208
Mueller, D. J., 536, 586
Munger, S. C., 252, 257-268, 588

N

Nader, R., 442, 524, 525
Nahemow, L., 68, 83, 588
Nairn, A., 525-526, 532, 588
Nardone, T., 29, 588
National Achievement Scholars, 326
National Achievement Scholarship Competition for Black Students, 171
National Association for the Advancement of Colored People (NAACP), 164
National Association of College Admissions Counselors (NACAC), 588; Admissions Practices Practices Committee of, 470; College Fairs of, 280, 387; computer service of, 324-325; and independent educational counselors, 368; materials from, 322, 460; mission of, x-xi; NACACtion Centers of, 470; NACACtion Line, 276; NACACtion Service of, 324; principles of, xi, 267, 470, 471, 473, 475, 476, 477, 478, 479, 560-569; as professional organization, xii, xiv-xv, 216, 285, 422, 441, 451, 467, 469, 550; publications committee of, xviii; questionnaires from, 474; and student rights and responsibilities, 325-326, 570-571; Task Force on Confidentiality of, 474-475; workshops and meetings of, 554-555
National Association of Foreign Student Advisors (NAFSA), 412, 413, 414, 416, 418, 419, 558
National Association of Graduate Schools, 408
National Association of Independent Schools (NAIS), 558
National Association of Principals of Schools for Girls (NAPSG), 558
National Association of Secondary School Principals, 422, 478, 511, 515, 588
National Association of Student Financial Aid Administrators (NASFAA), 558
National Center for Education Statistics, 169, 398, 515, 541, 588
National Center for Educational Brokering (NCEB), 223
National Commission on Excellence in Education, xn
National Council for Accreditation of Teacher Education, 232
National Defense Education Act of 1958, ix
National Direct Student Loan Program, 241, 246, 266
National Education Association, 478, 524, 525, 588
National League for Nursing, 232
National Liaison Committee (NLC) on Foreign Student Admissions, 416, 418, 421-422; Credential Evaluation Projects of, 412
National Longitudinal Study, 513
National Merit Scholars, 93, 94, 246, 326, 367
National Merit Scholarship Qualifying Test (NMSQT), 55, 171, 288
National Urban League, 164
Near East and South Asia Council of International Schools, 429
Nebraska, Mexican American students in, 199
Needs-press/congruency model, and student development, 68-69
Nelson, J. E., 516, 589
Nevada, Mexican Americans in, 193, 199
New Hampshire, Mexican American students in, 199
New Jersey: juniors programs in, 558; Mexican American students in, 199
New Mexico, Mexican Americans in, 193, 197, 199

New York: financial aid program in, 243; juniors programs in, 558; Mexican American students in, 199; testing legislation in, 524
New York Regents tests, 363-364
Newcomb, T. M., 45-46, 50, 52, 53, 54, 57, 65, 68, 77, 78, 80, 83, 580, 589
Newman, B., 293, 295, 589
Newman, P., 293, 295, 589
Nicholi, A. M., 101, 103, 589
Nichols, R. C., 55, 83, 589
Nietzche, F., 124
Nigeria, students from, 408
Ninth grade: articulation for motivation in, 310-312; developmental career-college planning in, 297-298
Nixon, R. M., 156
Noel, L., 589
North Carolina, Mexican American students in, 199
North Carolina at Chapel Hill, University of, position of, 381
North Dakota, Mexican American students in, 199
November, counseling activities in, 315-316
Novick, M. R., 589, 590
Nursing Scholarship Program, 242
Nursing Student Loan Program, 242

O

Oates, M. J., 51-52, 83, 141, 589
Oberlin College: black and white dropouts from, 168, 181; characteristics at, 121; position of, 381; and test scores, 119
Ochsner, N. L., 589
October, counseling activities in, 315
Ohio, Mexican American students in, 199
Oklahoma, Mexican American students in, 199
Older Student Information Systems (OSIS), 223
Oldham, D., 575

Oliver, E. E., 376, 589-590
Olmedo, E. L., 200, 590
Omnibus Personality Inventory (OPI), 59, 79
OPEC nations, students from, 408
Oregon: computer-based information system in, 223; Mexican American students in, 199
Outreach: for adult students, 229-230; for black students, 185; in community counseling, 350-351
Overseas American students: adjustment problems of, 426-427; from American/International schools, 424-425; analysis of services for, 422-429; associations regarding, 427-429; from Department of Defense families, 423; from Department of Defense schools, 424; from Department of State families, 423; from international business families, 423; as international students, 422-429; from missionary families, 422
Oxford University, development of, 10

P

Pace, C. R., 47, 53, 55, 57-58, 60, 77-78, 79, 83-84, 127, 130, 131, 590
Painter, N., 39, 86-110
Painter, P., 39, 86-110
Panos, R., 55, 76, 81, 87, 88, 92, 94, 95, 97, 98, 574, 590
Parents: and communication, 277-278, 284-285, 288, 359-360; and community counseling, 348, 355, 356, 358-359; concerns of, 337-340; as constituents, 259-260; information nights for, 459-460; minority, 459; and motivating students, 310-312, 317; pressures from, 458-460; reasons for involving, 334-336; techniques for working with, 340-345
Peer counselors, role of, 319-320

Peer groups, and misplacement, 89-90, 94

Peer recruiters, for Mexican American students, 214

Pell Grant Program, 242, 246, 319

Peltason, J. W., 543

Peng, S., 167, 168, 172, 182, 590

Pennsylvania: dropouts in, 98, 104; financial aid program in, 243; Mexican American students in, 199

Pennsylvania, University of, and market sharing, 385

Pennsylvania State University, dropouts from, 98

Perry, W. G., 68, 84, 590

Persistence, and student development, 70-71

Personal development, college impact on, 59-61

Personality disorders, and misplacement, 102-103

Pervin, L. A., 68, 84, 590

Petersen, N. S., 589, 590

Peterson, M. D., 5, 590

Peterson, M. W., 163, 164, 165, 167, 169, 173, 176, 177-178, 179, 181, 184, 189, 190, 590

Peterson, R. E., 223, 591

Pfeifer, C. M., Jr., 176, 182, 591

Phillips Academy, summer program at, 311

Piaget, J., 68, 83, 584

Pierce, C. M., 183, 591

Pittsburgh Council on Higher Education (PCHE), 554

Pitzer College, and Chicano Studies Center, 215

Placement. See Admissions; College placement; Misplacement

Placement offices, and adult students, 227-228

Pomona College: characteristics at, 121; and Chicano Studies Center, 215; Liberal Arts Field Experience Program at, 136

Porter, D., 518, 522, 593

Positioning: concept of, 381; examples of, 382-383; steps in, 381-382

Potier, R., 475, 476, 591

Powers, D. E., 518, 573

Predicted grade point average (PGPA), and validity and equity issues, 532-533, 536, 540-541, 546-547

Preiser, W. R. E., 591

Preliminary Scholastic Aptitude Test (PSAT), 288, 301, 313, 314, 323, 525

Preoccupied and confusional states, and misplacement, 102

Princeton University: "legacy" at, 119; as selective, 491-492

Professional services: background on, 439-443; and pressures of job, 440, 457-472; and professional knowledge, 443, 549-559; and reference letters, 440-441, 473-489; and school visits, 439-440, 444-456; and selective admissions, 441, 491-508; and standardized testing, 441-442, 509-548

Professors: and adult students, 228-229; attitudes of, and black students, 180-181, 184-185; attitudes of, and misplacement, 91; issues of, 265; reduction of, 32-33

Project TALENT, 513

Promotion. See Marketing

Psychiatric illness, and misplacement, 103

Purdue University, aeronautical engineering specialty at, 107

Q

Quann, C. J., 376, 591

Questionnaires: for high school alumni, 329-331; for juniors, 323-324, 327-328; for market research, 401-402

Quinlan, J. E., xviii

R

Radcliffe College, 583; achievers from, 142; reference letters used

by, 489. *See also* Harvard University
Raftus, K. L., 374, 375-376, 407-429
Ramirez, M., 204, 591
Reagan, R., ix, 395
Recreational facilities, and misplacement, 92
Recruitment: of black students, 169-177; changing emphases of, 25-28; ethical, criteria for, 417-418; of foreign students, abuses in, 417; international, criteria for, 420-421; of international students, 415-422; of Mexican American students, 207-218; principles of practice in, 561-564; reasons for, 416, 494-495; by selective institutions, 494-497; Spanish-language literature for, 214; and student development, 74
Redlich, F., 90, 584
Reed, H. B., 100, 591
Reed, R. J., 167, 168, 591
Reed College: position of, 381; and student development, 79
Reference letters: and accountability, 479-481; analysis of, 473-490; as analytical essay, 475; approach to, 121-124; background on, 473-476; in communication process, 284; and confidentiality, 462-464; counselor role in, 316; creativity in, 475; etiquette of, 487-488; guidelines for, 485; involving others with, 485-487; legal and ethical influences on, 476-479; and students, 486-487; uses for, 488-490; writing techniques for, 481-484
Reihling, J., 591
Reik, L. E., 590
Reinhold, B. B., 255, 346-360
Reiss, J., 293, 591
Reliability, of standardized tests, 520-521
Religious institutions, and student development, 52-53, 56, 58, 59, 60, 65

Research, marketing: for admissions, 395-406; application of, 404-406; data analysis in, 403-404; direction of, 399; institutional offices for, 398; project design for, 399-400; purposes of, 395-398; technology for, 400-403
Research consultants: advantages of, 397-398; criteria for, 405-406
Residence: and student development, 49-50, 57, 68, 71-72, 73; types of, and placement, 88-89
Retention, issues in, 263-264
Reynolds, H., 254-255, 332-345
Rhode Island, Mexican American students in, 199
Richards, R., 201, 582
Rico, A., 381, 581
Rioux, J. W., 591
Ripple, G. G., 474, 592
Rivera, S., 150-151, 191-219
Roark, A. C., 24, 592
Rock, D. A., 55, 56, 82, 84, 577, 592
Rose, E. M., 151-152, 220-230
Rosenfeld, S., 20, 21, 22, 573
Rosovsky, H., 8, 12
Rowray, R. D., 376, 592
Russell Sage Foundation, 479, 592

S

Sacks, H. S., 322, 592
Saenz, E., 212, 576
St. Louis, Chesterfield Mall Metro Fair in, 280
Sampling, in market research, 400-401
Sandow, S. A., 591
Sanford, N., 53, 77, 78, 80, 84, 592
Sarah Lawrence College, and test scores, 119
Sasnett, M., 412-413
Satir, V. M., 336, 592
Satisfaction with college, college impact on, 63-64, 72
Sawhill, J., 30
Sawyer, R. L., 531, 592

Scattergram, for individual conference, 272-273

Schaie, K. W., 575

Schliemann, J., 428

Schmidt, F. L., 584

Schmidt, G. P., 592

Schneider, B., 254, 321-331

Scholastic Aptitude Test (SAT): and achievement, 55; coaching for, 309, 346, 517-520; and declining scores, 442, 513-517; described, 509-512; and disclosure, 524-525; predictive validity of, 521-522, 526; reliability of, 521; scores on, 91, 93, 105, 106, 119, 197, 201, 202-203, 276, 363, 425; and selectivity, 493, 494, 498-499; use of, 287, 314, 323, 459, 460; and validity and equity issues, 529-530, 531-532, 540, 546. See also Standardized tests

School and community services: background on, 251-256; for community as a whole, 255, 346-360; and constituency links, 252-253, 269-289; and counselors' responsibilities, 252, 257-268; and family approaches, 254-255, 332-345; and generalist counselors, 253, 290-306; and group approaches, 254, 321-331; by independent counselors, 255-256, 361-371; and support networks, 253-254, 307-320

School-holding power, of southwestern ethnic groups, 194-196

School visits: analysis of, 444-456; calendar of, 274; and college fairs, 453; managing, 447-449; materials for, 449-451; preparing for, 444-447; and selection process, 452-456

Schools: changes in, and standardized tests, 514-515; and communication, 282-284, 287, 288; follow-up studies of alumni from, 286; statistical profile of, 283-284. See also Eleventh grade; Ninth grade; Tenth grade; Twelfth grade

Schrader, W. B., 513, 516, 522, 575, 592

Schramm, W., 514, 593

Schuerger, J., 593

Schuster, J. H., 37-38, 42-85, 580

Schwalbe, M. A., 439-440, 444-456

Scope of counseling: background of, 1-3; and demographic impacts, 3, 17-35; and development of education system, 2, 4-16

Scripps College, and Chicano Studies Center, 215

Sedlacek, W. E., 163, 180, 181, 182, 593, 595

Segura, R. D., 196n, 577

Selective institutions: and academic evaluation, 497-499; admissions procedures at, 491-508; alumni recruiters for, 496-497; concept of, 45, 491-494; and evaluation of applicants, 497-502; fairness and equity in, 507-508; institutional needs of, 503-505; mechanics of selection at, 506-507; and nonacademic evaluation, 499-502; recruitment by, 494-497; selection function at, 502-507; and special categories of applicants, 504-505; and standardized tests, 498-499

Selectivity: concept of, 45; factors in, 263; and student development, 47-48, 56, 57, 58, 59, 61, 64, 71-72

Self-discipline, and misplacement, 96

Seligsohn, H., 165, 581

Seniors. See Twelfth grade

Sepmeyer, I., 412-413

Serviceman's Readjustment Act of 1944, 240, 494

Sexual expectations, and misplacement, 102

Shadowing, effectiveness of, 357-358

Shanas, E., 575

Sharp, T., 412-413

Shertzer, B., 593

Silberman, C., 159, 593

Single-sex institutions: and career

planning, 141-142; and student development, 51-52, 56, 57, 58, 60, 62, 64, 65

Size of institution, and student development, 50-51, 57, 58, 63-64, 65, 70, 71-72

Skidmore College, and College Venture Program, 136

Slack, W. V., 518, 522, 593

Smith, D. H., 167, 180, 593

Smith College, achievers from, 142

Social Security Student Benefits Program, 242, 246

Social services: and adult students, 151-152, 220-230; background of, 147-153; and black students, 149, 161-190; as counseling function, 148, 154-160; and financial aid, 154, 240-249; and Mexican American students, 150-151, 191-219; and two-year colleges, 152-153, 231-239

Socioeconomic matching, and misplacement, 90

Socioeconomic status (SES), and equity issues, 538, 542, 546-547

Solmon, L. C., 61, 130, 575, 589

South Carolina: market penetration in, 389-390; Mexican American students in, 199

South Carolina, University of, and marketing, 390

South Dakota, Mexican American students in, 199

Speer, A., 156, 593

Speich, D., 587

Spielberger, C. D., 101, 593

Spuck, D. W., 201, 586

Spurlock, L., 165, 593

Stachowlak, J., 592

Standardized tests: alternatives to, 539-548; analysis of, 509-527; changes in, and scores, 513-514; coaching for, 517-520; counselor monitoring of, 277; criterion-referenced, 525; declining scores on, 513-517; described, 509-512; factors in improved scores on, 519-520; future of, 524-527; guidelines for using, 522-524;

and Mexican American students, 197-203; predictive validity of, 514, 521-522, 530-532; reliability of, 520-521; reporting results of, to faculty, 286-287; and school changes, 514-515; and selective institutions, 498-499; and societal factors, 514; and student changes, 515-516; survey on use of, 528-530; use and misuse of, 520-522; validity and equity issues of, 528-548

Stanford University: black students at, 179; mission of, 128; recruitment by, 495

Stanwyck, D., 292, 593

State University of New York at Stony Brook, and curricular change, 8

Steinbrecher, P. S., 255-256, 361-371

Stern, G. G., 68, 69, 77, 84, 590, 593

Stern, J., 513, 587

Stone, S. C., 593

Strommen, C., 427

Strong, E. K., Jr., 593

Strong-Campbell Interest Inventory, 299, 323

Student development: analysis of college impact on, 42-85; background on, 42-44; categories of research on, 76-79; and congruency, 68-70, 74; implications of, 71-76; and institutional inputs, 44-53; and involvement, 49, 51, 65, 68, 72-73; literature on, 76-81; obstacles to research on, 80-81; outcomes of, 53-64; and research limitations, 79-80; and student characteristics, 45-47

Student services: and appropriate college choice, 39, 86-110; background on, 37-41; and career preparation, 40-41, 126-146; individualized, 39-40, 111-125; research on, 37-39, 42-85

Students: ability of, and misplacement, 92-93; academic achievement of, 54-56; activity sheets

for, 275, 282; attitudes, beliefs, and values of, 58-59; career orientation and implementation of, 61-63; career planning by, 126-146; changes in, and standardized tests, 515-516; characteristics of, and development, 45-47; and communication, 271-284, 288, 359-360; competition for, 385-394; as constituents, 258-259; as consumers, 468; and demographic change, 24-32; essays by, 279-280, 282-283; family background of, 46, 96-97; and family counseling, 343; financial aid to, 240-249; individual attention to, 111-125; initial conferences with, 273-274; intellectual, cultural, and esthetic orientation of, 56-58; interests of, discovering, 112-114; interview hints for, 278; letters by, 278-281; nonconforming, and misplacement, 95-96; peer group pressures on, 460-461; personal development of, 59-61; placement of, 86-110; preparation of, and misplacement, 94-95; pressures on, 305; and reference letters, 486-487; rights of, 11-12, 570-571; satisfaction with college by, 63-64, 72; support networks for, 307-320. *See also* Adult students; Black students; International students; International students; Mexican American students; Overseas American students
Stulac, J., 292, 593
Super, D. E., 253, 293, 294-295, 296, 306, 594
Supplemental Educational Opportunity Grant Program, 242, 246
Support services: for adult students, 226-228; for black students, 175-176; and misplacement, 92
Swarthmore College: recruitment by, 495-496; as selective, 493; and student development, 79

Sweden, educational efficiency in, 7

T

Taschman, H. A., 592
Taubman, P., 61
Taveggia, T. C., 55, 82-83, 580
Tennessee, Mexican American students in, 199
Tenth grade: developmental career-college planning in, 298-300; guidance for motivation in, 312-313
Test of English as a Foreign Language (TOEFL), 413, 414, 420
Test of General Education, 55
Testing program. *See* Standardized tests
Texas: counselors overworked in, 362; Mexican Americans in, 193
Thomas, G. E., 167, 594
Thomas, L. E., 594
Thompson, D. C., 441, 491-508
Thorndike, R. L., 201, 594
Tidball, E. M., 141, 594
Tinto, V., 69, 84, 594
Todd, W. G., 160
Tracy, M. E., 253, 290-306
Transcript, in communication process, 283
Transfers: advising about, from two-year colleges, 231-239; articulation agreements for, 236-237; counselors specializing in, 237-238; of courses, 231-232; of grades and quality points, 233; of graduation requirements, 233-234; and independent educational counselors, 365; late in beginning process for, 235-236, 239; and major fields, 234-235, 238; and misplacement, 99; planning for process of, 239; recommendations for, 236-239
Treaty of Guadalupe Hidalgo, 192-193
Trent, J. W., 59
Tufts University, characteristics of, 113-114

Turnbull, W., 525-526

Twelfth grade: counseling for motivation in, 314-319; developmental career-college planning in, 302-303; workshop for, 325-326

Two-year colleges: academic advisement in, 233, 234; admissions officers' visits to, 238; advising about transferring from, 231-239; black students in, 169, 172; and demographic changes, 22-23; and student development, 49-50, 57, 58-59, 61, 62, 64, 65, 70, 77; transfer counselors in, 237-238; visits to high schools by representatives of, 318

U

Undergraduate Assessment Program, 55

Union College, curricular change in, 5

Union of Soviet Socialist Republics, educational efficiency in, 7

U.S. Bureau of the Census, 23, 191, 193, 194, 398, 594

U.S. Commission on Civil Rights, 194, 209, 594

U.S. Department of Defense (DOD), 423, 424, 429

U.S. Department of Education, xn, 317

U.S. Department of Health, Education and Welfare, 193, 194, 213, 594

U.S. Department of Labor, 29, 223, 348

U.S. Department of State, 423, 424, 427

Upward Bound, 172

Urban, H. B., 98, 104, 581

Utah, Mexican Americans in, 193, 199

V

Vaccaro, J., 383, 594

Vacher, C. J., 98, 594

Validity, predictive, of standardized tests, 514, 521-522, 530-532

Vasquez, R., 482, 595

Vassar College: achievers from, 142; and student development, 77

Vermont: cooperative association in, 390; Mexican American students in, 199

Veterans' Educational Benefits Program, 242, 246

Virginia, Mexican American students in, 199

Virginia, University of, design of, 5

Visits. See School visits

Vocational Rehabilitation Program, 242, 246

Vocational-technical training, and career planning, 128-132

W

Walker, E. E., Jr., xviii

Wallach, A., 43, 85, 595

Walsh, W. B., 69, 84-85, 595

Walters, J. C., 374, 375, 377-384

Warren, J. R., 201, 595

Washington, K. R., 165, 595

Washington, Mexican American students in, 199

Washington University: and early admission to medical school, 107; influence of, 295

Webster, D. W., 163, 180, 181, 182, 593, 595

Webster, H., 77, 84, 592

Weinman, J., 515, 595

Wellesley College, achievers from, 142

Wenc, L. M., 153, 240-249

Wesleyan University: and College Venture Program, 136; recruitment by, 496; student-faculty ratio at, 25

West Virginia, Mexican American students in, 199

Western Interstate Commission for Higher Education, 8

Widawski, M. H., 202-203, 582

Wiley, D., 514-515, 583

William and Mary, College of: and

College Venture Program, 136; early purpose of, 4

Williams College: characteristics at, 121; "legacy" at, 119; recruitment by, 496

Williamson, S., 51-52, 83, 141, 589

Willie, C. V., 164, 173, 180, 595

Wilson, W., 155, 160

Wing, C. W., Jr., 43, 85, 595

Wingspread Colloquium, 416-417

Wisconsin: Mexican American students in, 199; recruitment budgets in, 393

Wisconsin, University of, and recruitment budget, 393

Wohlwill, J. F., 68, 69, 85, 595

Wolf, K. L., 152, 231-239, 377

Women: college choice and career patterns of, 140-143; development of, college impact on, 51-52, 56, 57, 58, 60, 62, 65; Mex-

ican American, 211-212, 216-217; ratio of, to men, 29, 140

Women's Independent Colleges (WIC), 553-554

Wood, B. D., 76-77, 83, 585

Working, and misplacement, 99-100

Wright, J. L., 216, 253-254, 307-320

Wyoming, Mexican American students in, 199

Y

Yale University: characteristics of, 113-114; early curriculum of, 6; recruitment by, 495; and test scores, 119

Yeats, W. B., 121

Z

Zuker, R. F., 252, 257-268